CAT

THE ONE YOU LOVE

WOMAN

VOLUME **4**

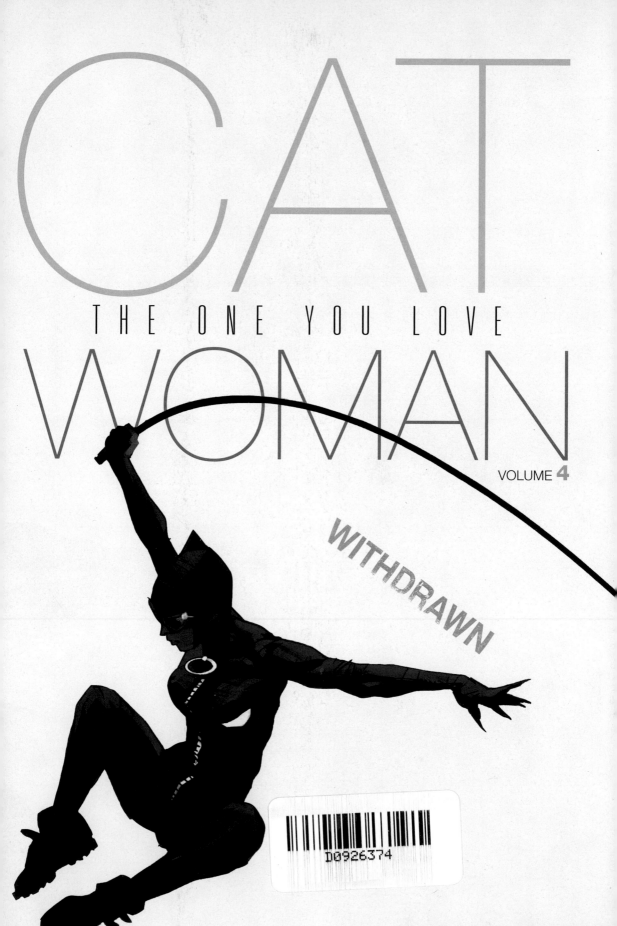

Will Pfeifer
Matteo Casali
Anderson Gabrych
Scott Morse
Writers

Pete Woods
Rick Burchett
Paul Gulacy
Diego Olmos
Brad Walker
Pencillers

Alvaro Lopez
Jimmy Palmiotti
Inkers

Brad Anderson
Giulia Brusco
Laurie Kronenberg
Colorists

Jared K. Fletcher
Rob Leigh
Ken Lopez
Clem Robins
Letterers

Adam Hughes
Collection Cover Artist

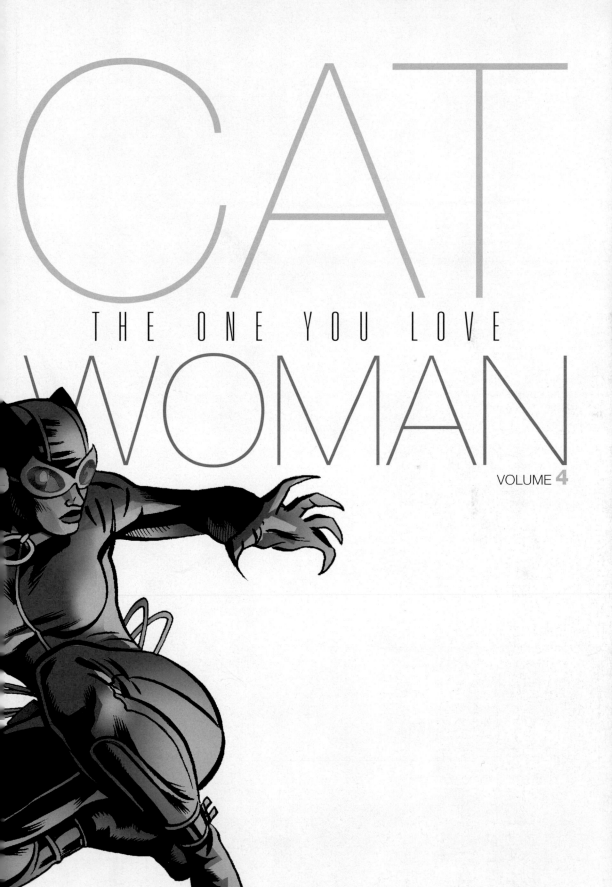

CAT

THE ONE YOU LOVE

WOMAN

VOLUME 4

Matt Idelson Editor – Original Series
Nachie Castro Michael Wright Associate Editors – Original Series
Jeb Woodard Group Editor – Collected Editions

Bob Harras Senior VP – Editor-in-Chief, DC Comics

Diane Nelson President
Dan DiDio and **Jim Lee** Co-Publishers
Geoff Johns Chief Creative Officer
Amit Desai Senior VP – Marketing & Global Franchise Management
Nairi Gardiner Senior VP – Finance
Sam Ades VP – Digital Marketing
Bobbie Chase VP – Talent Development
Mark Chiarello Senior VP – Art, Design & Collected Editions
John Cunningham VP – Content Strategy
Anne DePies VP – Strategy Planning & Reporting
Don Falletti VP – Manufacturing Operations
Lawrence Ganem VP – Editorial Administration & Talent Relations
Alison Gill Senior VP – Manufacturing & Operations
Hank Kanalz Senior VP – Editorial Strategy & Administration
Jay Kogan VP – Legal Affairs
Derek Maddalena Senior VP – Sales & Business Development
Jack Mahan VP – Business Affairs
Dan Miron VP – Sales Planning & Trade Development
Nick Napolitano VP – Manufacturing Administration
Carol Roeder VP – Marketing
Eddie Scannell VP – Mass Account & Digital Sales
Courtney Simmons Senior VP – Publicity & Communications
Jim (Ski) Sokolowski VP – Comic Book Specialty & Newsstand Sales
Sandy Yi Senior VP – Global Franchise Management

CATWOMAN VOLUME 4: THE ONE YOU LOVE

DC Comics, 4000 Warner Blvd., Burbank, CA 91522
A Warner Bros. Entertainment Company.
Printed by RR Donnelley, Salem, VA, USA. 11/13/15 First Printing.
ISBN: 978-1-4012-5832-0

Library of Congress Cataloging-in-Publication Data is Available.

PEFC Certified

Printed on paper from
sustainably managed
forests and controlled
sources

PEFC

PEFC/29-31-75   www.pefc.org

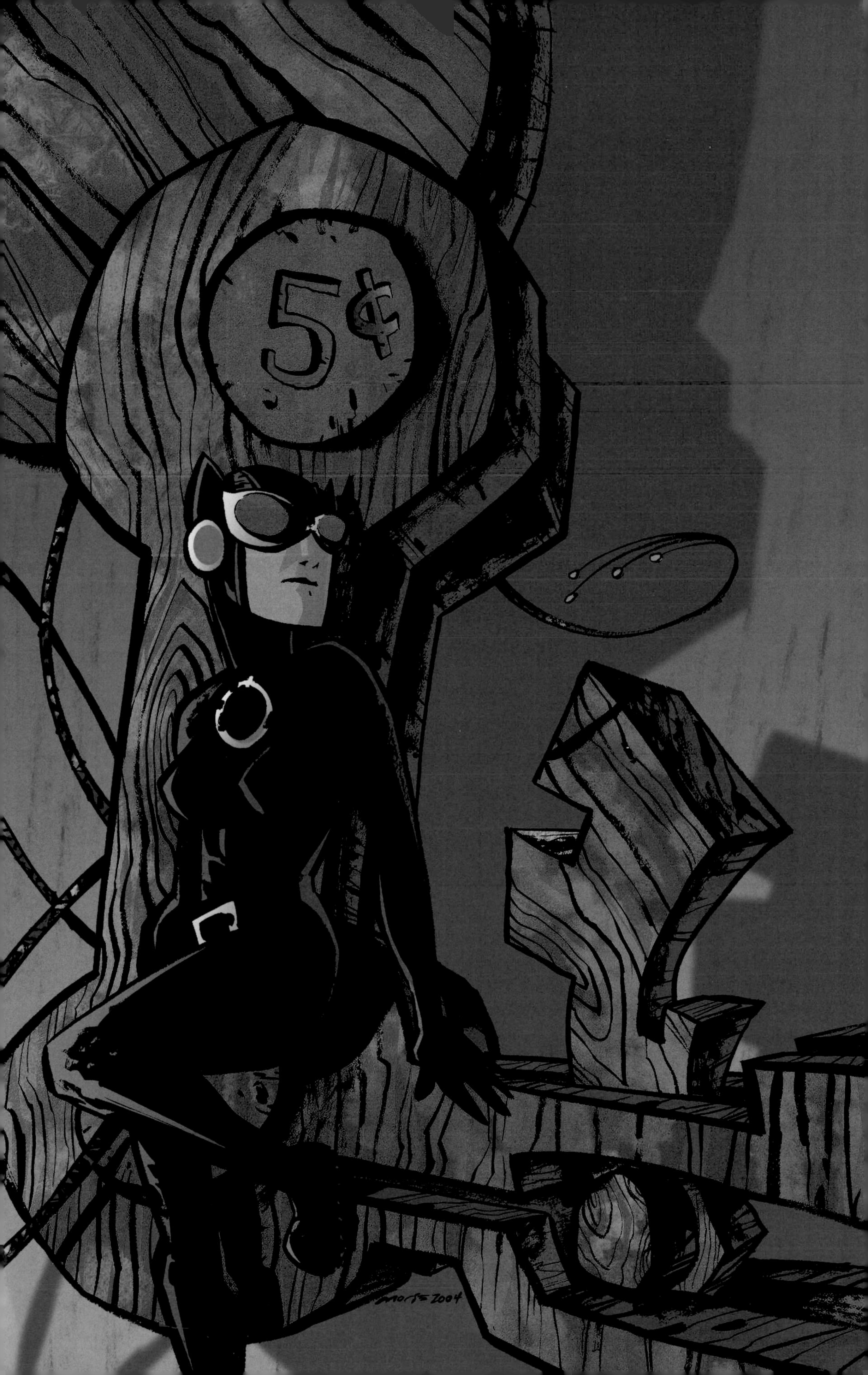
5¢
Morse 2004

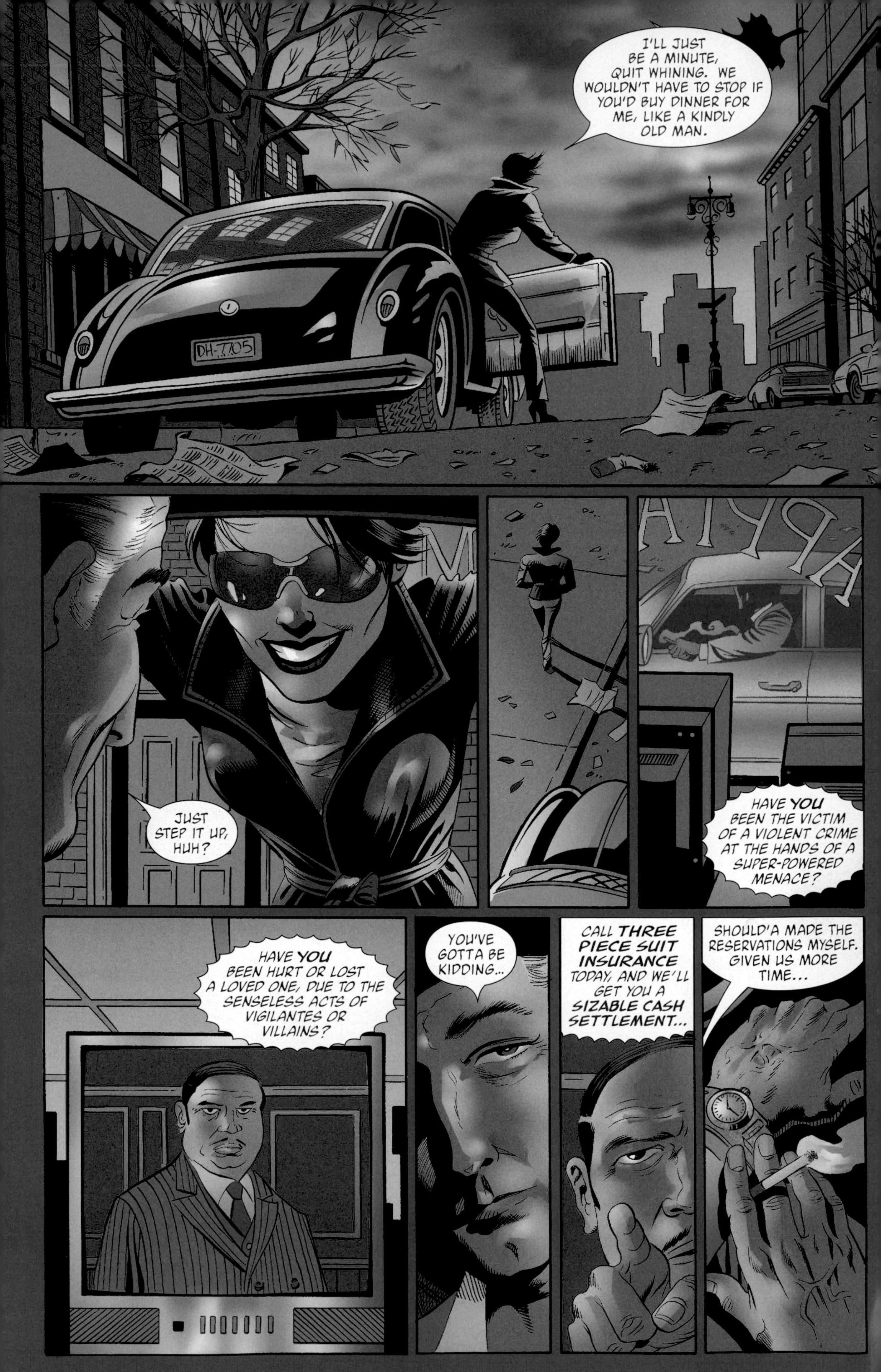
I'LL JUST BE A MINUTE, QUIT WHINING. WE WOULDN'T HAVE TO STOP IF YOU'D BUY DINNER FOR ME, LIKE A KINDLY OLD MAN.
DH-7705
JUST STEP IT UP, HUH?
HAVE YOU BEEN THE VICTIM OF A VIOLENT CRIME AT THE HANDS OF A SUPER-POWERED MENACE?
HAVE YOU BEEN HURT OR LOST A LOVED ONE, DUE TO THE SENSELESS ACTS OF VIGILANTES OR VILLAINS?
YOU'VE GOTTA BE KIDDING...
CALL THREE PIECE SUIT INSURANCE TODAY, AND WE'LL GET YOU A SIZABLE CASH SETTLEMENT...
SHOULD'A MADE THE RESERVATIONS MYSELF. GIVEN US MORE TIME...

It's amazing how oblivious a grown man can be about something simple like a dinner date.

I mean, you'd think he would have learned in **HIGH SCHOOL** that the guy pays for dinner.

Of course, being from **HIS** generation, he probably expected me to **MAKE** dinner and bring it in a picnic basket or something.

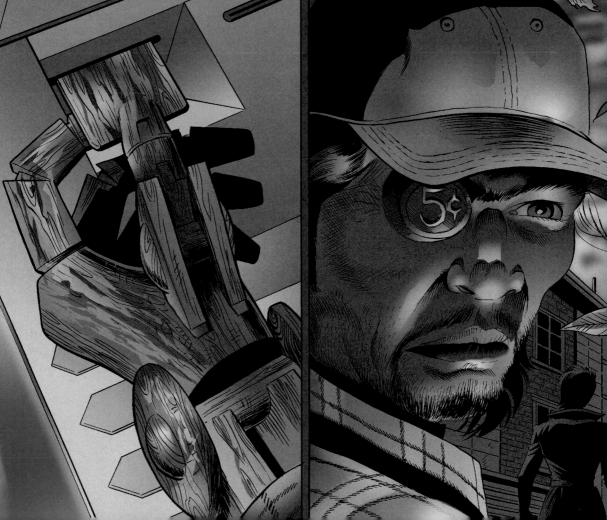

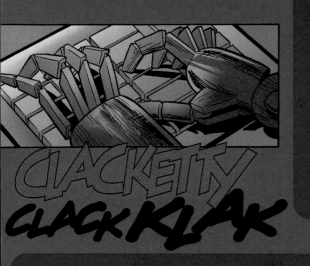

- Withdraw Cash
- Deposit
- Account Balance/Statement
- Stamps

CLACKETTY CLACK KLAK

Tech ID #369823-4
Login Time: 19:39pm
Account #558392022***
User: Catrina Dolares
Transaction: Cash Withdrawal
Account balance as of 19:38pm: $205,343.86

List last ten transactions Y N
List all transaction/user history Y N

CLACKETTY CLACK KLAK CLICK

Welcome to Gotham City Savings
Please Press 1 for English
              2 for Español

WHUP!

EH--
EXCUSE
ME...

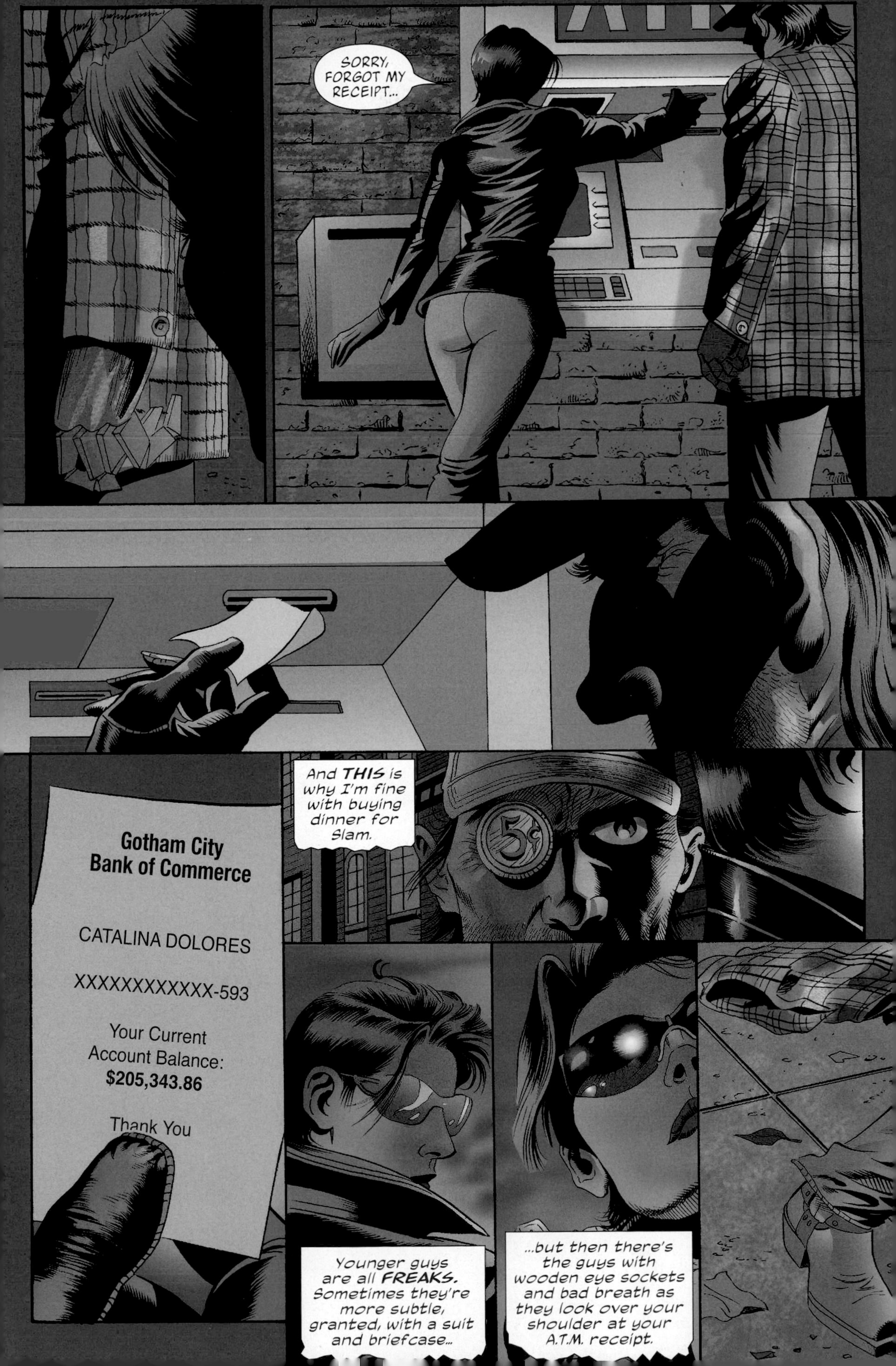
SORRY, FORGOT MY RECEIPT...
Gotham City
Bank of Commerce
CATALINA DOLORES
XXXXXXXXXXXX-593
Your Current
Account Balance:
$205,343.86
Thank You
And THIS is why I'm fine with buying dinner for Slam.
Younger guys are all FREAKS. Sometimes they're more subtle, granted, with a suit and briefcase...
...but then there's the guys with wooden eye sockets and bad breath as they look over your shoulder at your A.T.M. receipt.

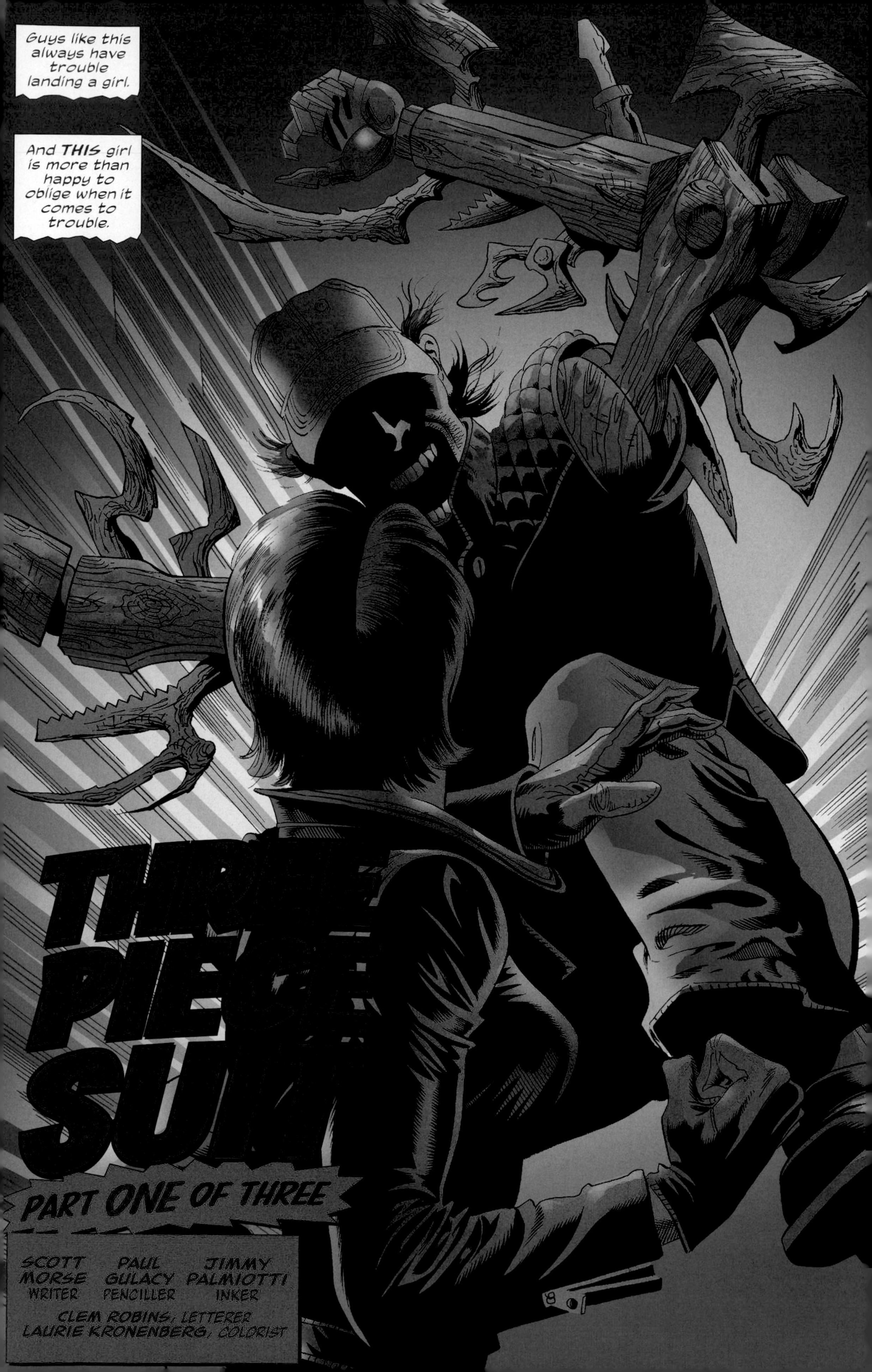
Guys like this always have trouble landing a girl.
And THIS girl is more than happy to oblige when it comes to trouble.
THREE PIECE SUIT
PART ONE OF THREE
SCOTT MORSE WRITER
PAUL GULACY PENCILLER
JIMMY PALMIOTTI INKER
CLEM ROBINS, LETTERER
LAURIE KRONENBERG, COLORIST

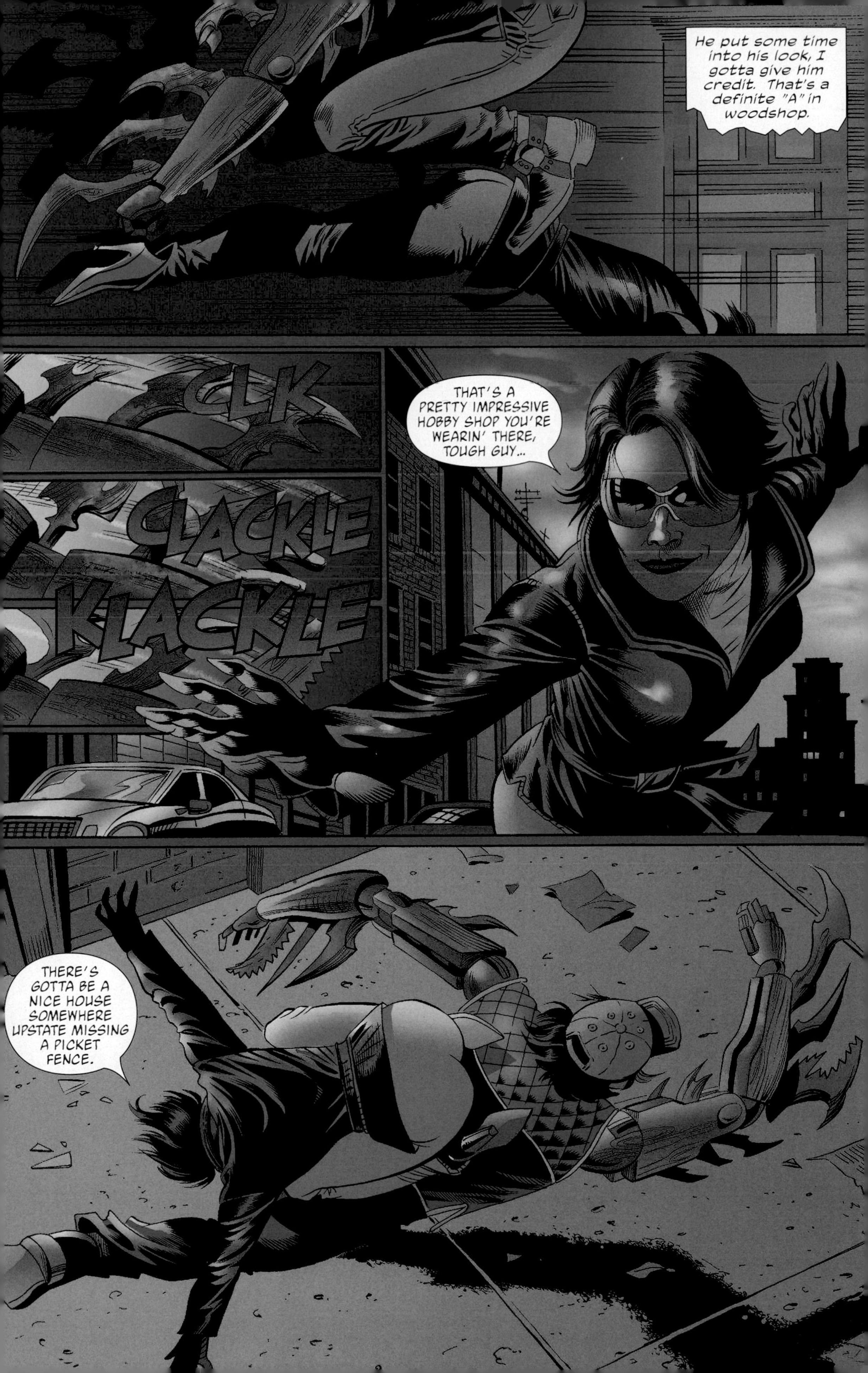

He put some time into his look, I gotta give him credit. That's a definite "A" in woodshop.
CLK
CLACKLE
KLACKLE
THAT'S A PRETTY IMPRESSIVE HOBBY SHOP YOU'RE WEARIN' THERE, TOUGH GUY...
THERE'S GOTTA BE A NICE HOUSE SOMEWHERE UPSTATE MISSING A PICKET FENCE.

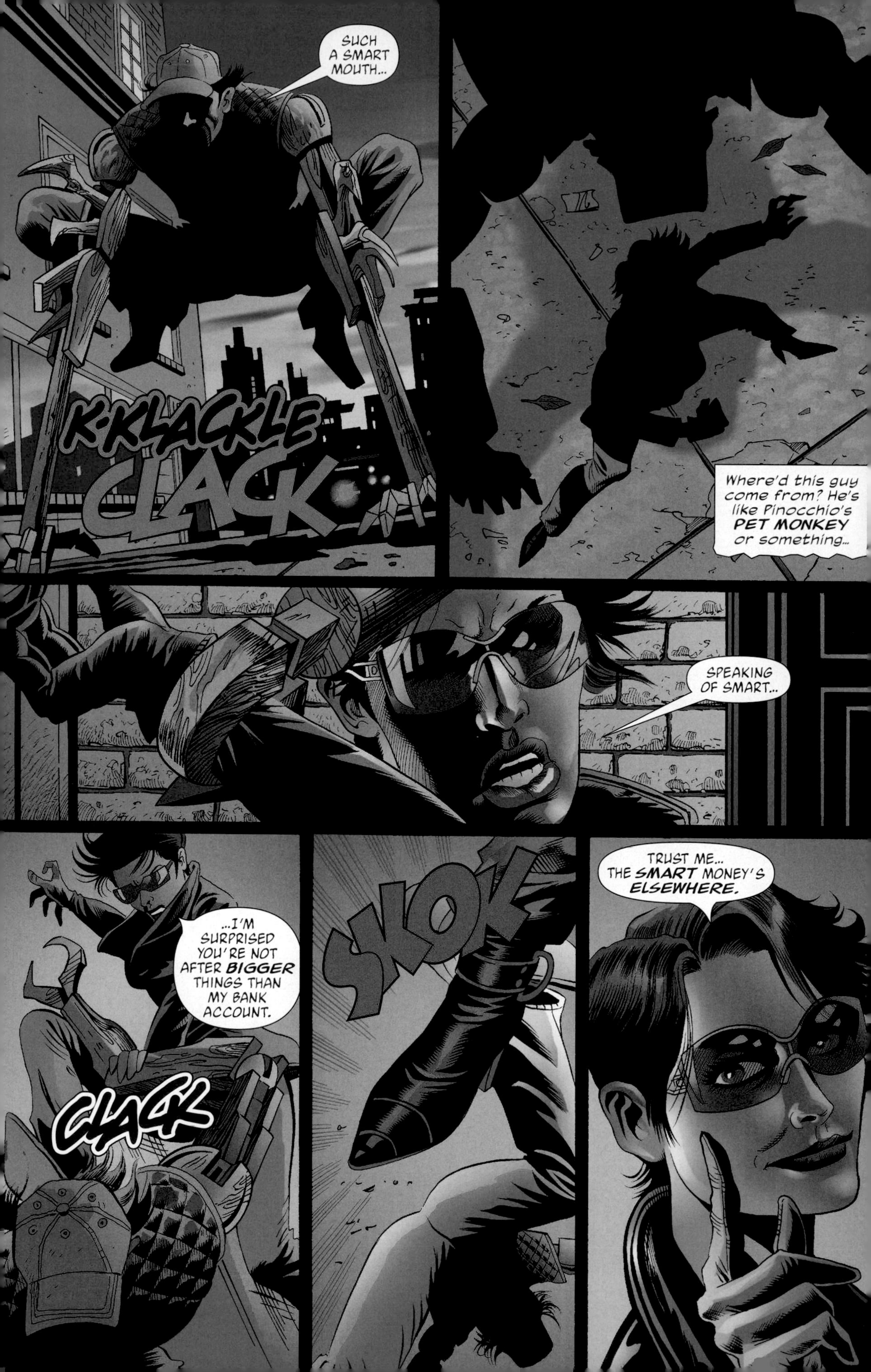
SUCH A SMART MOUTH...
K-KLACKLE
CLACK
Where'd this guy come from? He's like Pinocchio's **PET MONKEY** or something...
SPEAKING OF SMART...
...I'M SURPRISED YOU'RE NOT AFTER **BIGGER** THINGS THAN MY BANK ACCOUNT.
CLACK
SKOK
TRUST ME... THE **SMART** MONEY'S **ELSEWHERE.**

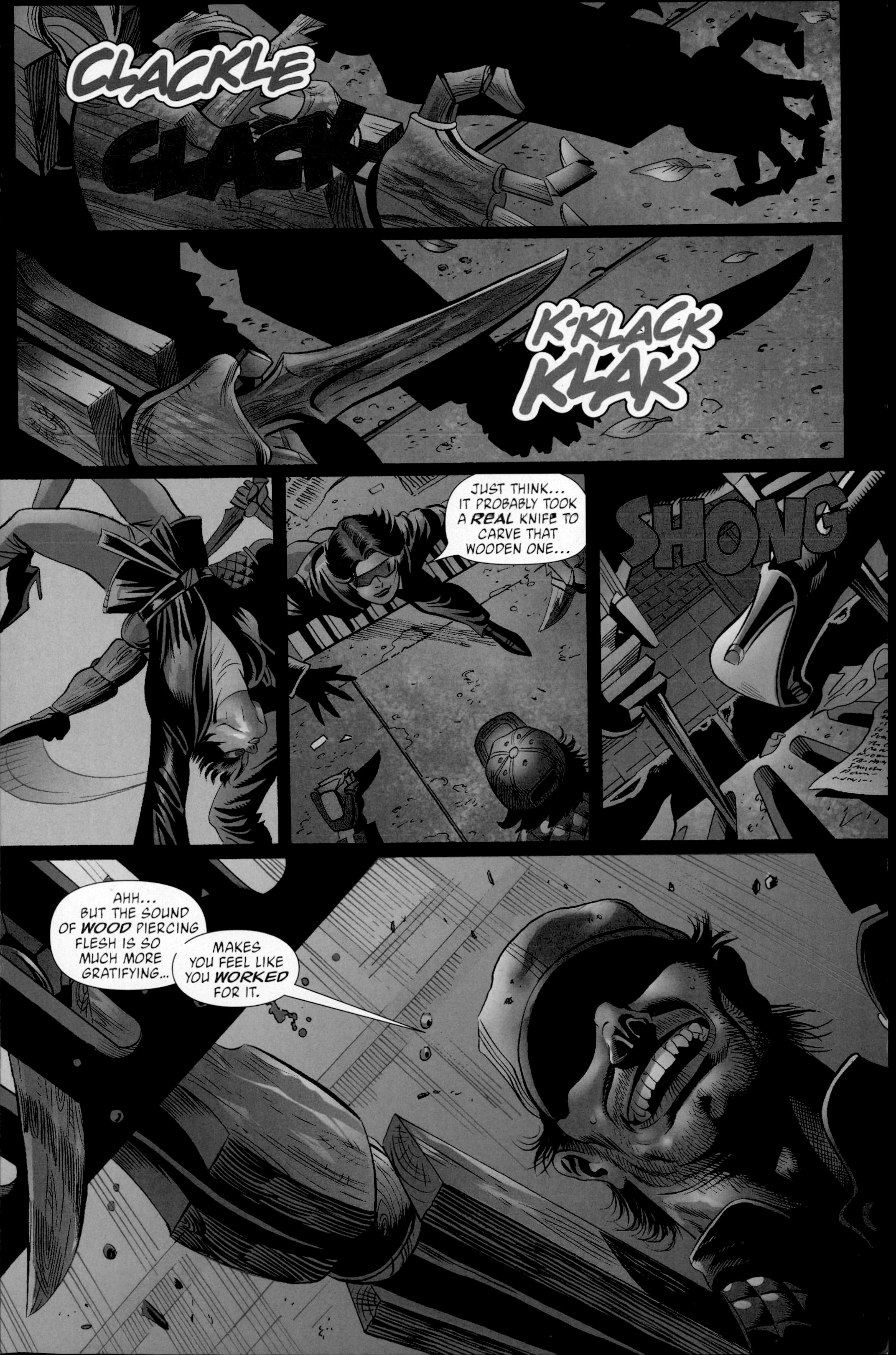
CLACKLE
CLACK
K-KLACK
KLAK
JUST THINK... IT PROBABLY TOOK A REAL KNIFE TO CARVE THAT WOODEN ONE...
SHONG
AHH... BUT THE SOUND OF WOOD PIERCING FLESH IS SO MUCH MORE GRATIFYING...
MAKES YOU FEEL LIKE YOU WORKED FOR IT.

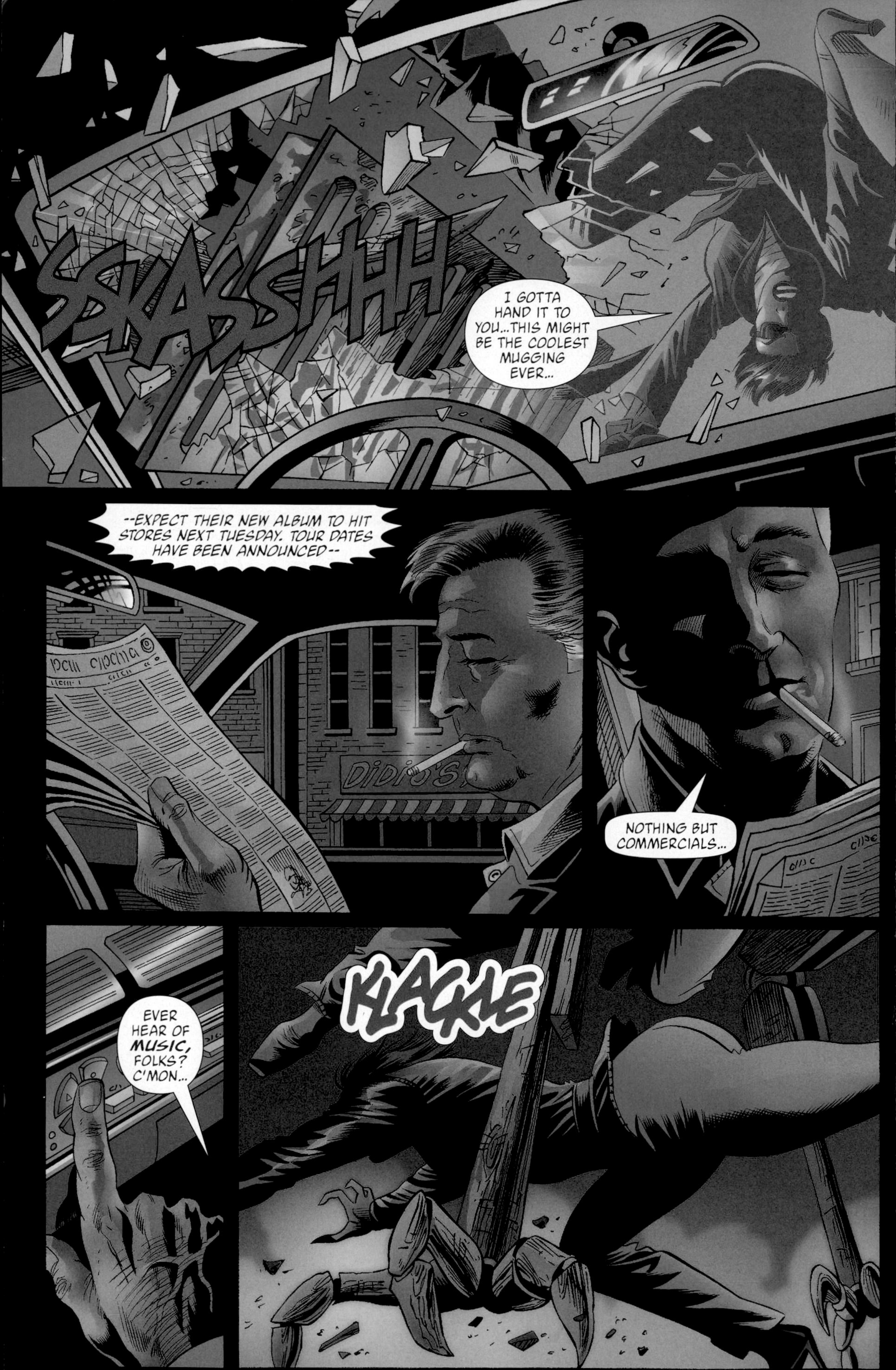
SSKASSHHH
I GOTTA HAND IT TO YOU...THIS MIGHT BE THE COOLEST MUGGING EVER...
--EXPECT THEIR NEW ALBUM TO HIT STORES NEXT TUESDAY. TOUR DATES HAVE BEEN ANNOUNCED--
NOTHING BUT COMMERCIALS...
EVER HEAR OF **MUSIC,** FOLKS? C'MON...
KLACKLE

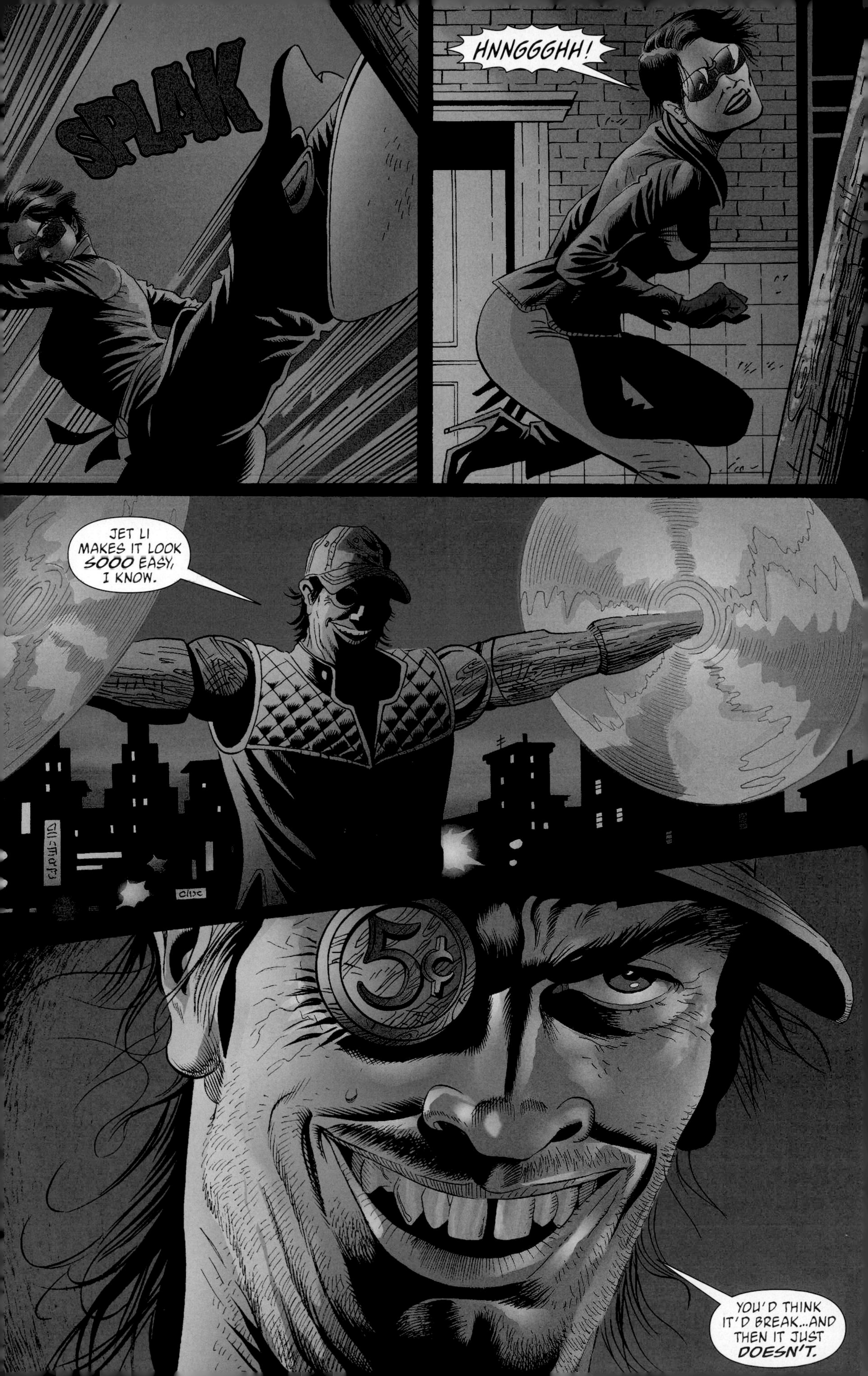
SPLAK
HNNGGGHH!
JET LI MAKES IT LOOK SOOO EASY, I KNOW.
YOU'D THINK IT'D BREAK...AND THEN IT JUST DOESN'T.

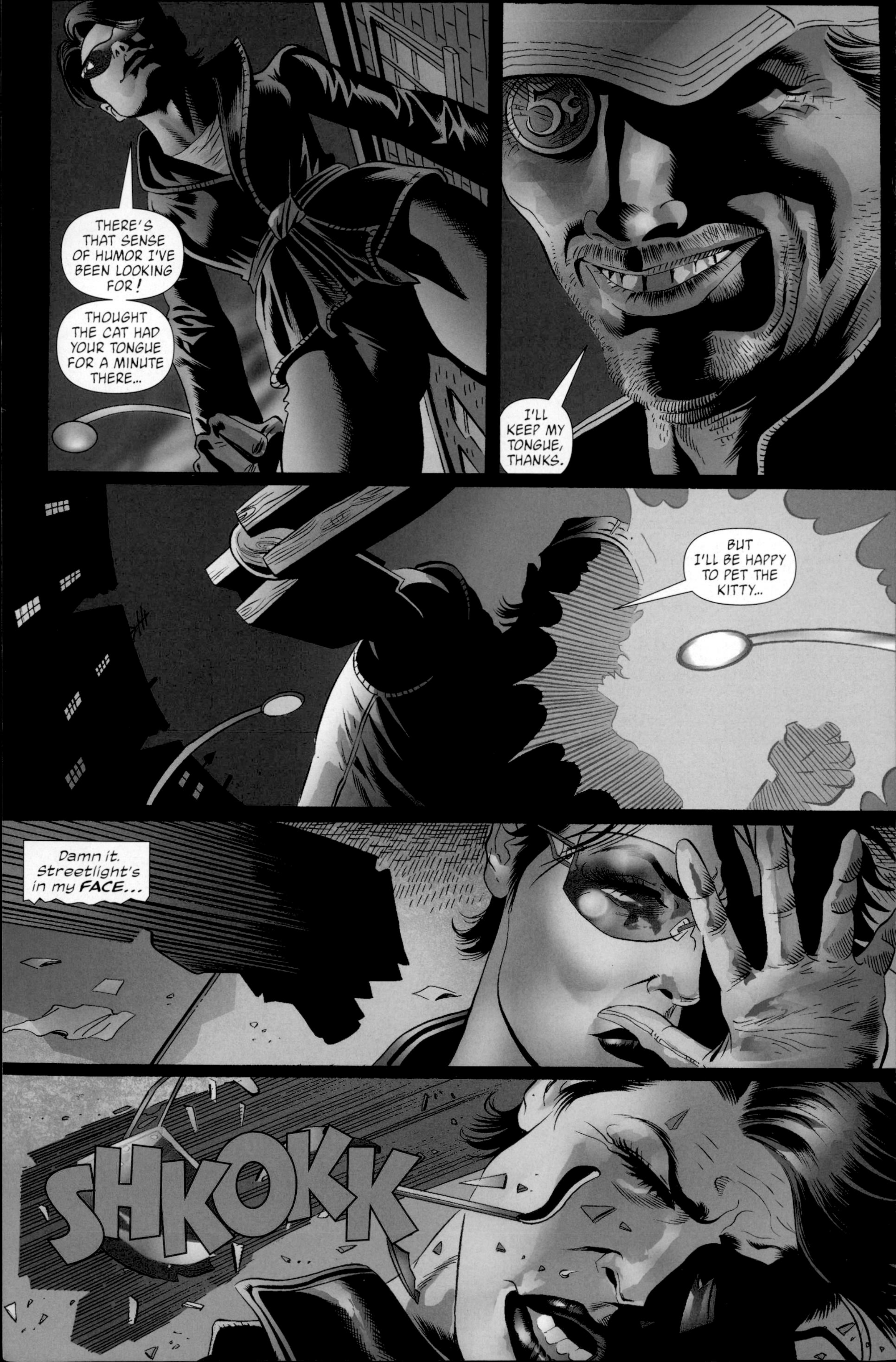
THERE'S THAT SENSE OF HUMOR I'VE BEEN LOOKING FOR!
THOUGHT THE CAT HAD YOUR TONGUE FOR A MINUTE THERE...
I'LL KEEP MY TONGUE, THANKS.
BUT I'LL BE HAPPY TO PET THE KITTY...
Damn it. Streetlight's in my FACE...
SHKOKK

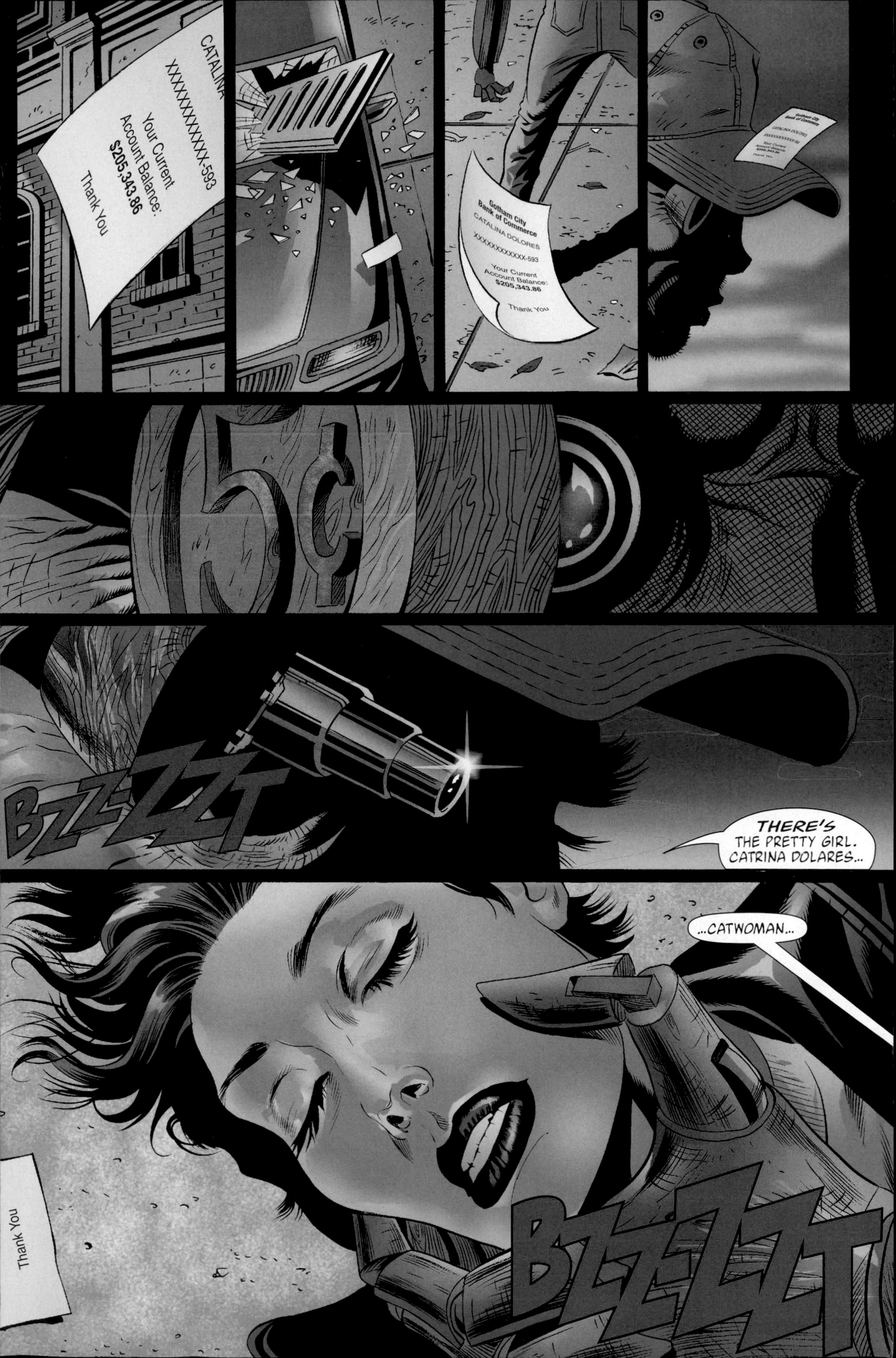
CATALINA
XXXXXXXXXXX-593
Your Current Account Balance:
$205,343.86
Thank You
Gotham City Bank of Commerce
CATALINA DOLORES
XXXXXXXXXXX-593
Your Current Account Balance:
$205,343.86
Thank You
BZZ-ZZT
THERE'S THE PRETTY GIRL. CATRINA DOLARES...
...CATWOMAN...
BZZZZT
Thank You

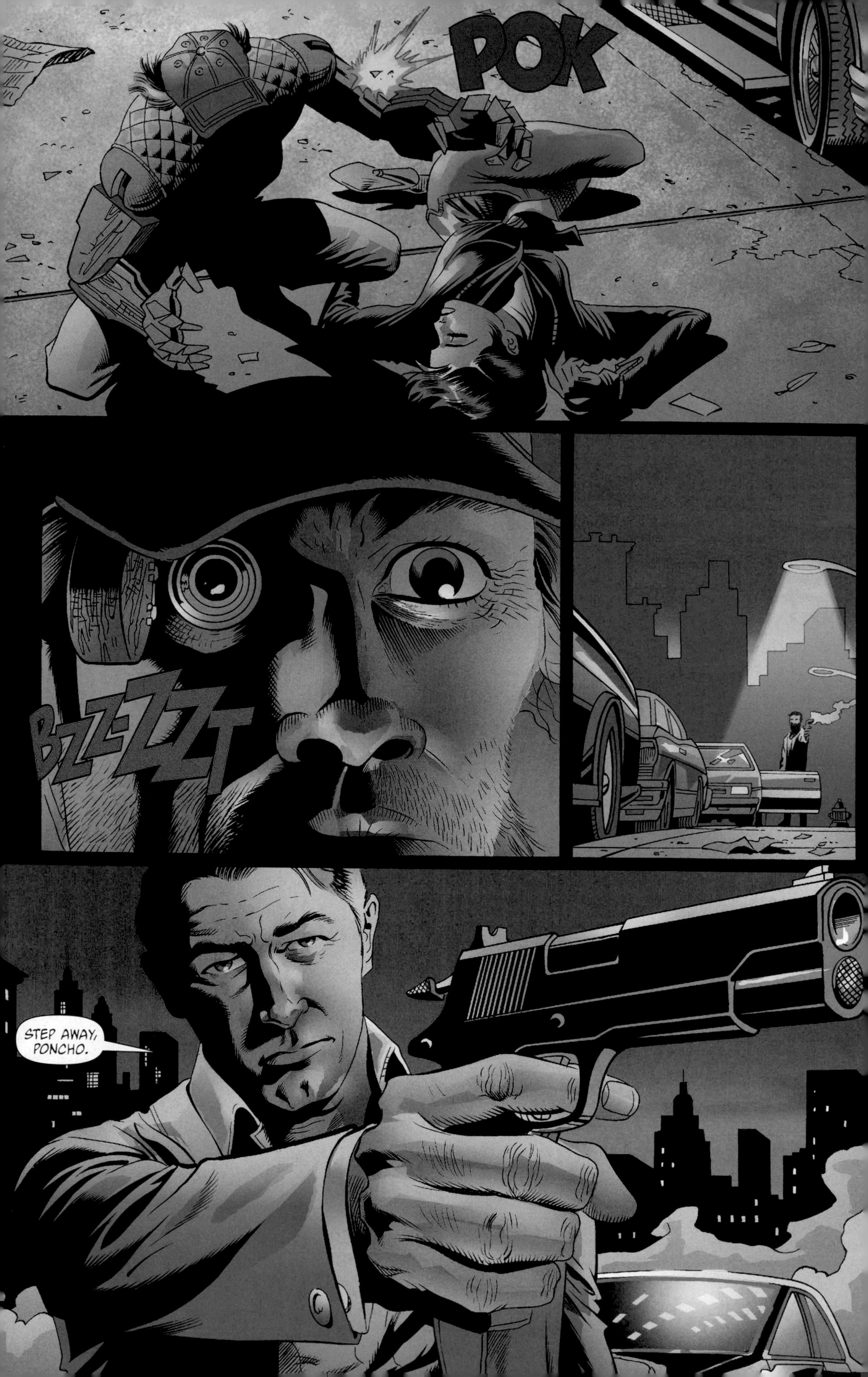
POK
BZZ-ZZZT
STEP AWAY, PONCHO.

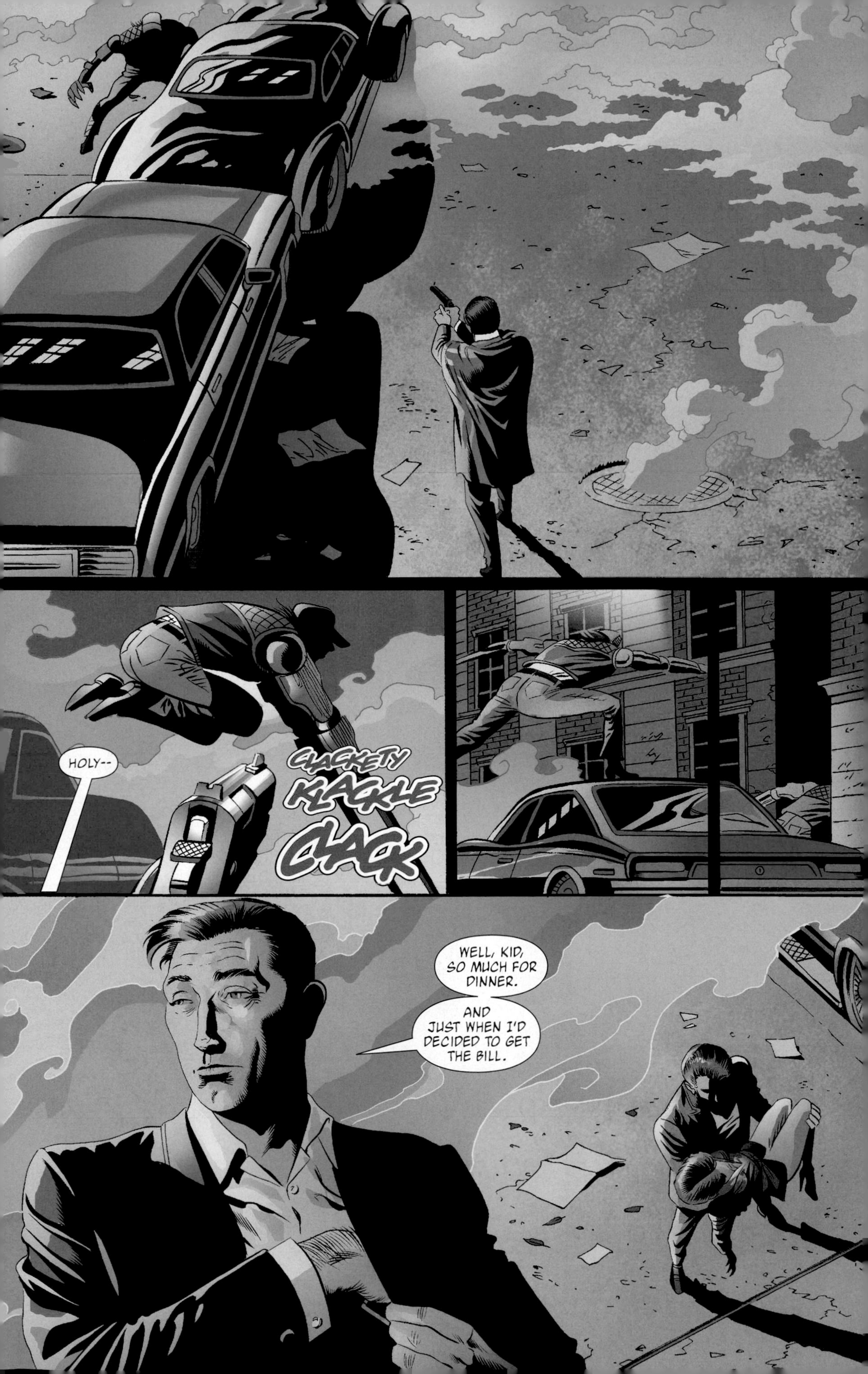
HOLY--
CLACKETY
KLACKLE
CLACK
WELL, KID, SO MUCH FOR DINNER.
AND JUST WHEN I'D DECIDED TO GET THE BILL.

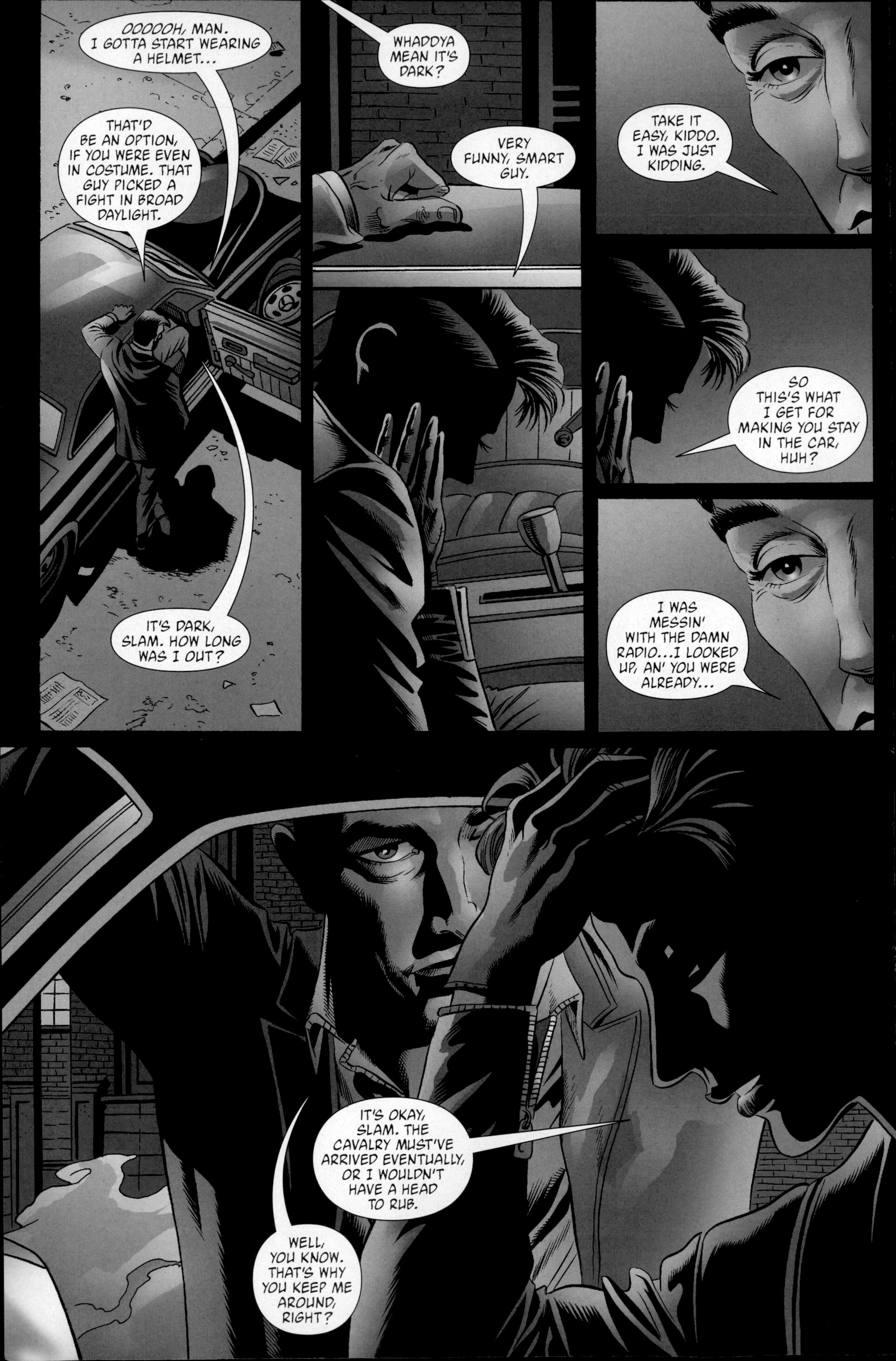

OOOOOH, MAN. I GOTTA START WEARING A HELMET...
THAT'D BE AN OPTION, IF YOU WERE EVEN IN COSTUME. THAT GUY PICKED A FIGHT IN BROAD DAYLIGHT.
IT'S DARK, SLAM. HOW LONG WAS I OUT?
WHADDYA MEAN IT'S DARK?
VERY FUNNY, SMART GUY.
TAKE IT EASY, KIDDO. I WAS JUST KIDDING.
SO THIS'S WHAT I GET FOR MAKING YOU STAY IN THE CAR, HUH?
I WAS MESSIN' WITH THE DAMN RADIO...I LOOKED UP, AN' YOU WERE ALREADY...
IT'S OKAY, SLAM. THE CAVALRY MUST'VE ARRIVED EVENTUALLY, OR I WOULDN'T HAVE A HEAD TO RUB.
WELL, YOU KNOW. THAT'S WHY YOU KEEP ME AROUND, RIGHT?

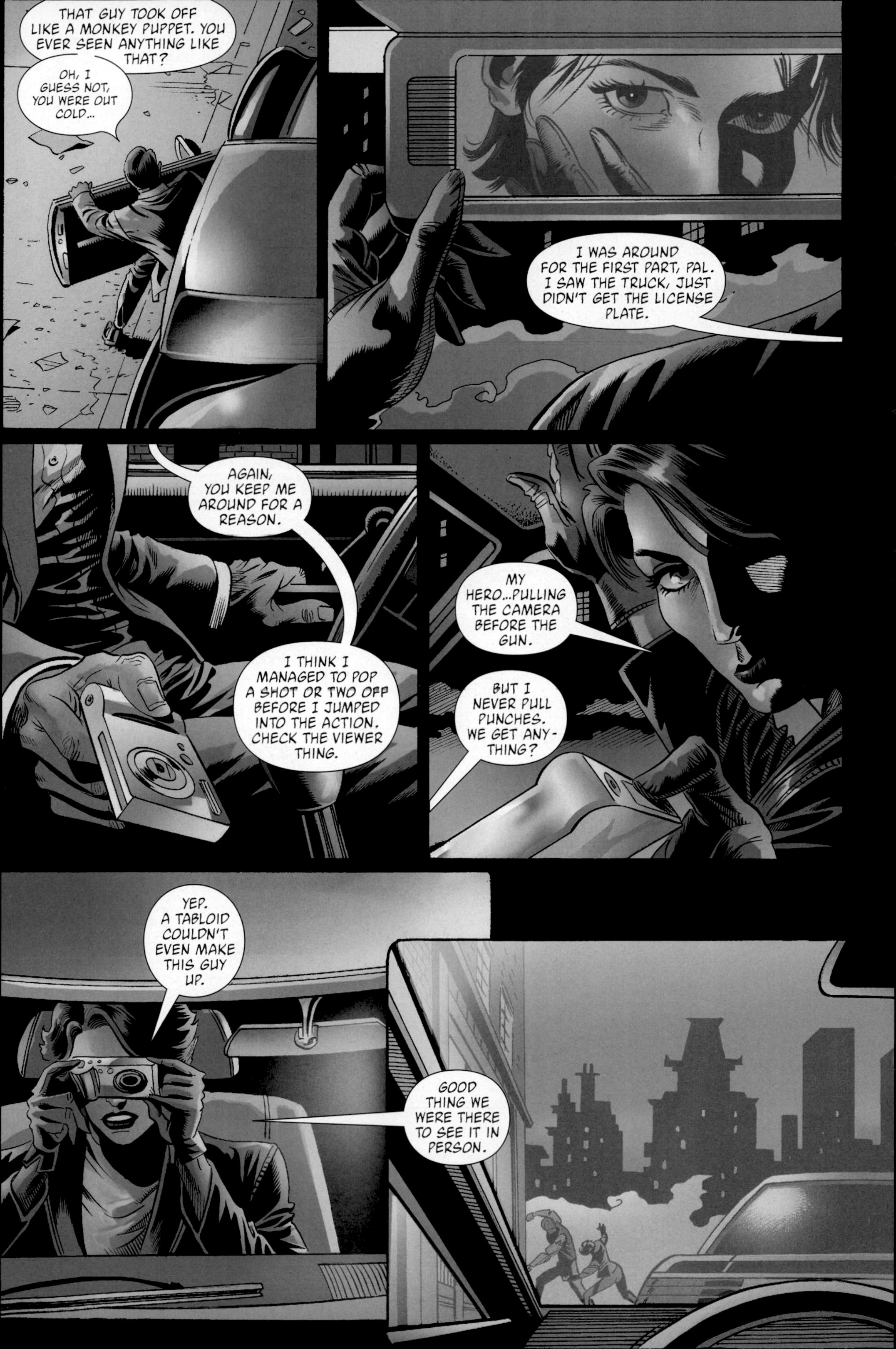

THAT GUY TOOK OFF LIKE A MONKEY PUPPET. YOU EVER SEEN ANYTHING LIKE THAT?
OH, I GUESS NOT, YOU WERE OUT COLD...
I WAS AROUND FOR THE FIRST PART, PAL. I SAW THE TRUCK, JUST DIDN'T GET THE LICENSE PLATE.
AGAIN, YOU KEEP ME AROUND FOR A REASON.
I THINK I MANAGED TO POP A SHOT OR TWO OFF BEFORE I JUMPED INTO THE ACTION. CHECK THE VIEWER THING.
MY HERO...PULLING THE CAMERA BEFORE THE GUN.
BUT I NEVER PULL PUNCHES. WE GET ANYTHING?
YEP. A TABLOID COULDN'T EVEN MAKE THIS GUY UP.
GOOD THING WE WERE THERE TO SEE IT IN PERSON.

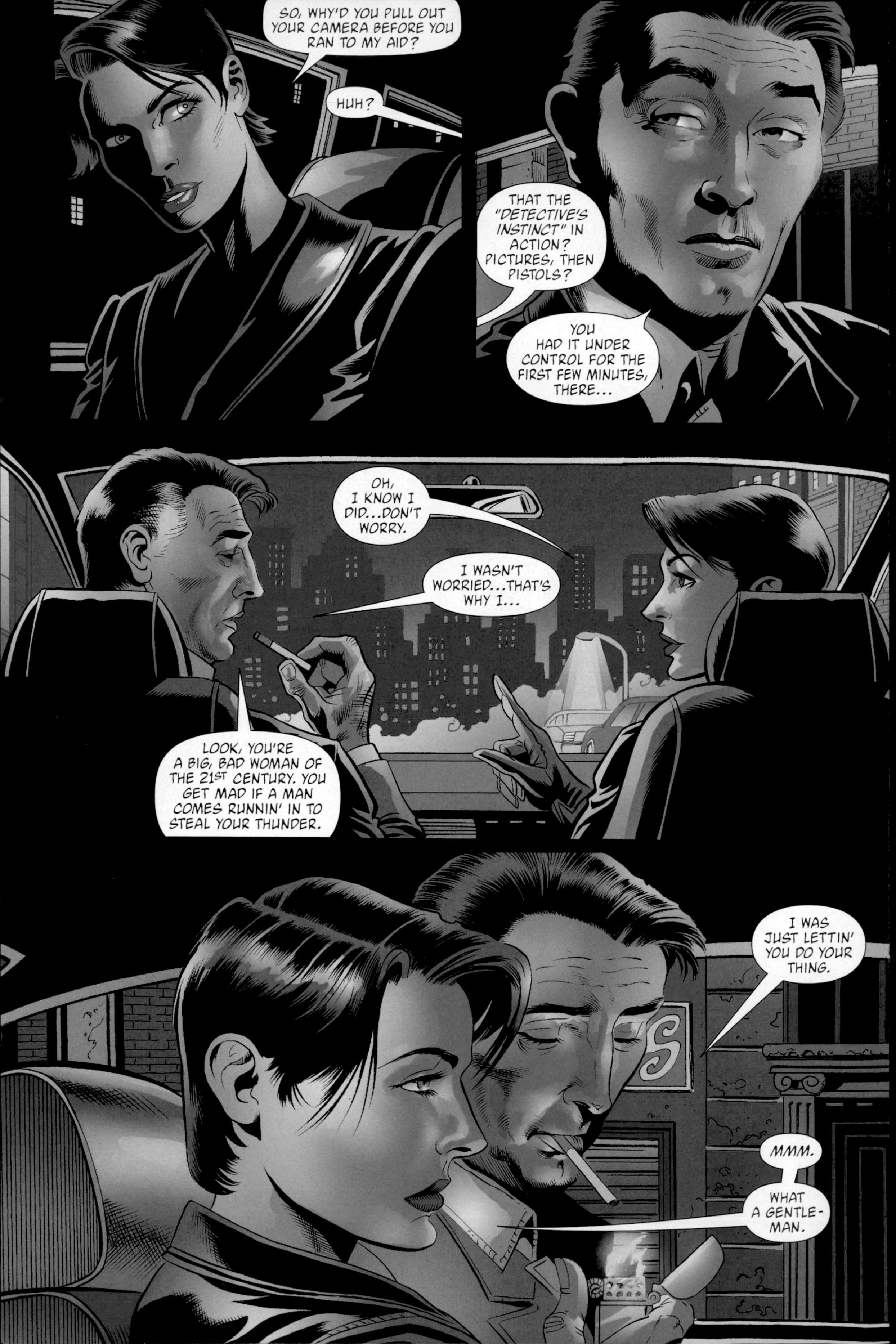
SO, WHY'D YOU PULL OUT YOUR CAMERA BEFORE YOU RAN TO MY AID?
HUH?
THAT THE "DETECTIVE'S INSTINCT" IN ACTION? PICTURES, THEN PISTOLS?
YOU HAD IT UNDER CONTROL FOR THE FIRST FEW MINUTES, THERE...
OH, I KNOW I DID...DON'T WORRY.
I WASN'T WORRIED...THAT'S WHY I...
LOOK, YOU'RE A BIG, BAD WOMAN OF THE 21ST CENTURY. YOU GET MAD IF A MAN COMES RUNNIN' IN TO STEAL YOUR THUNDER.
I WAS JUST LETTIN' YOU DO YOUR THING.
MMM.
WHAT A GENTLE-MAN.

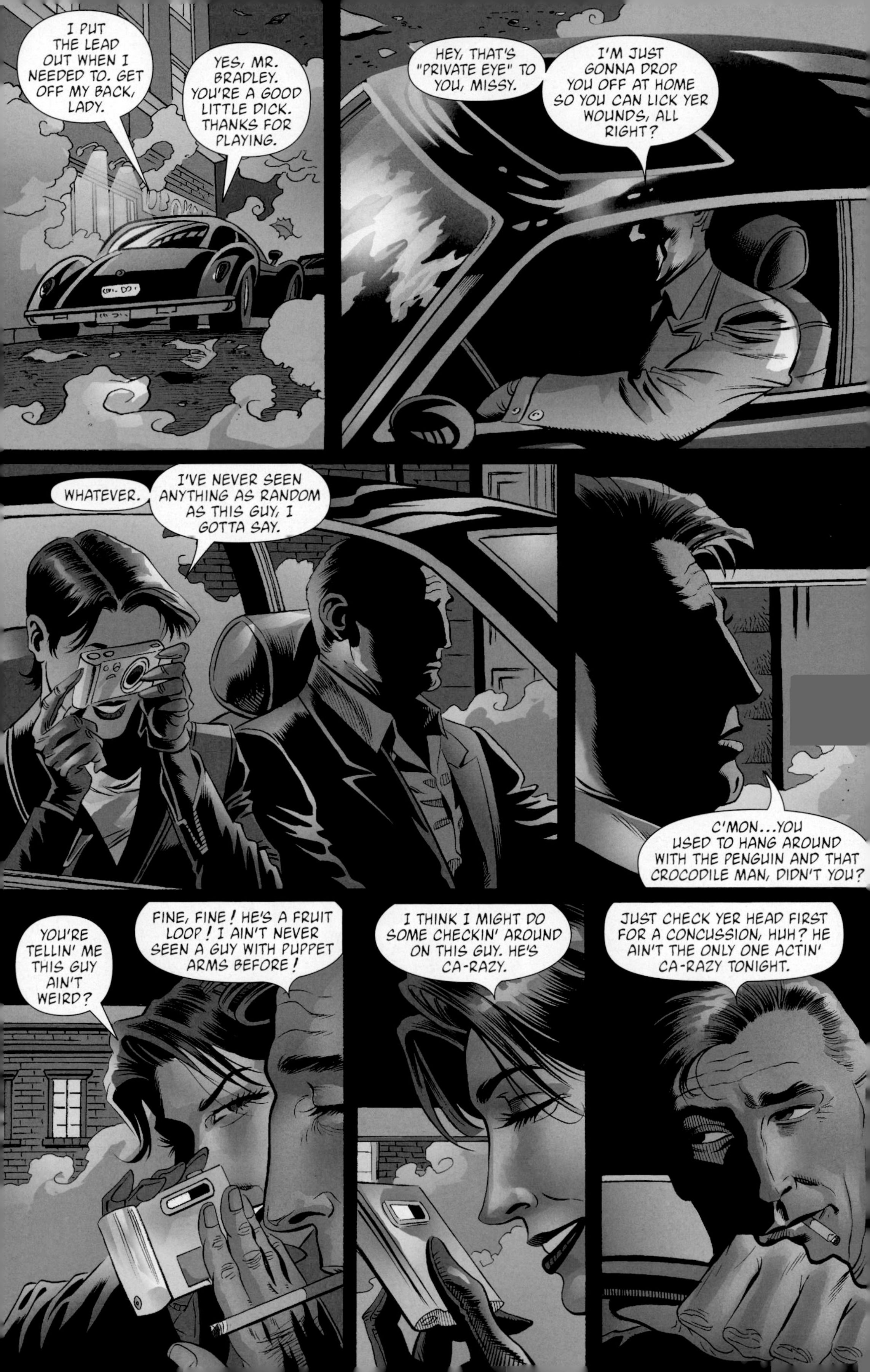
I PUT THE LEAD OUT WHEN I NEEDED TO. GET OFF MY BACK, LADY.
YES, MR. BRADLEY. YOU'RE A GOOD LITTLE DICK. THANKS FOR PLAYING.
HEY, THAT'S "PRIVATE EYE" TO YOU, MISSY.
I'M JUST GONNA DROP YOU OFF AT HOME SO YOU CAN LICK YER WOUNDS, ALL RIGHT?
WHATEVER.
I'VE NEVER SEEN ANYTHING AS RANDOM AS THIS GUY, I GOTTA SAY.
C'MON...YOU USED TO HANG AROUND WITH THE PENGUIN AND THAT CROCODILE MAN, DIDN'T YOU?
YOU'RE TELLIN' ME THIS GUY AIN'T WEIRD?
FINE, FINE! HE'S A FRUIT LOOP! I AIN'T NEVER SEEN A GUY WITH PUPPET ARMS BEFORE!
I THINK I MIGHT DO SOME CHECKIN' AROUND ON THIS GUY. HE'S CA-RAZY.
JUST CHECK YER HEAD FIRST FOR A CONCUSSION, HUH? HE AIN'T THE ONLY ONE ACTIN' CA-RAZY TONIGHT.

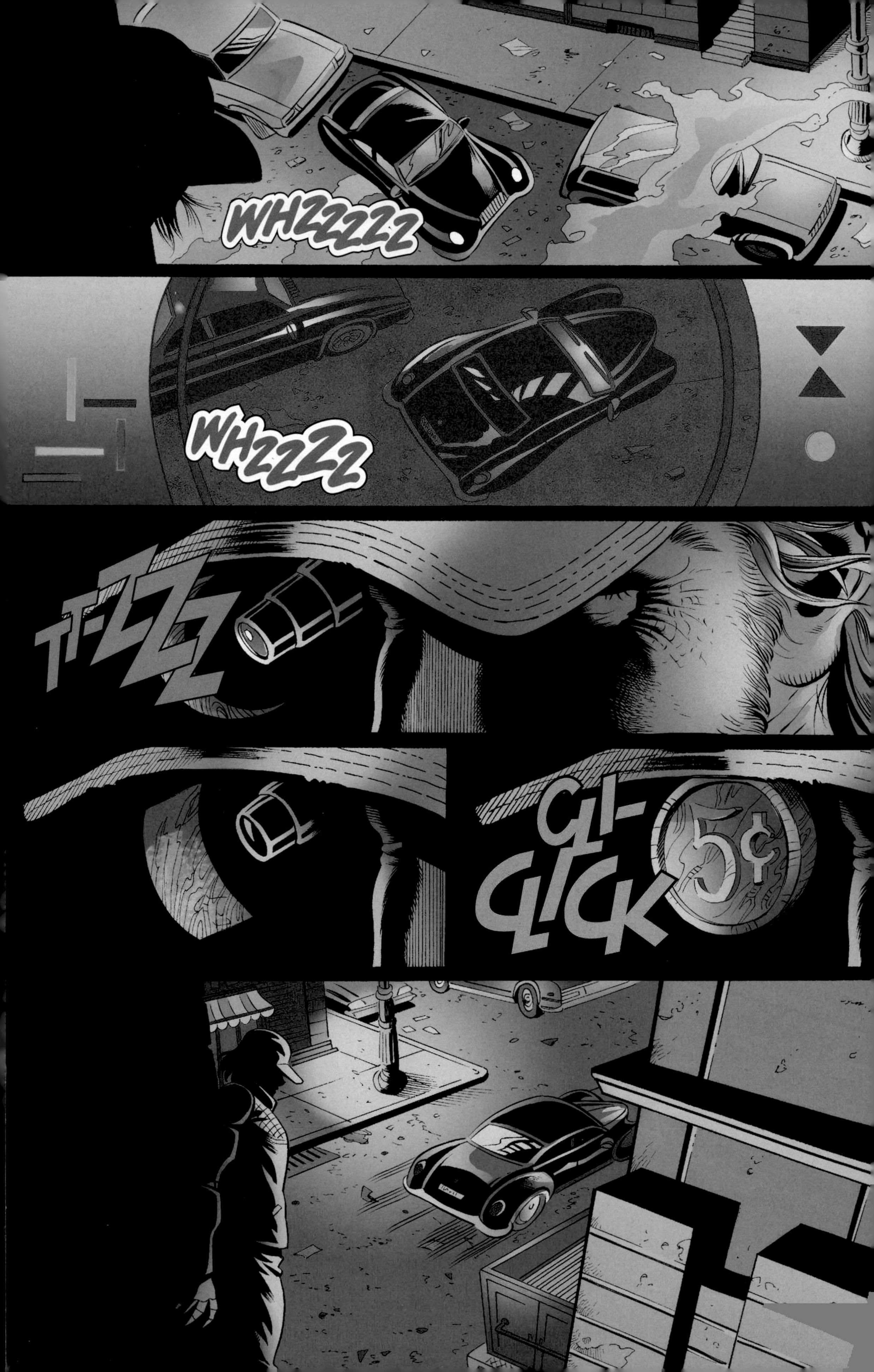
WHZZZZZ
WHZZZZ
TT-ZZZ
CL-CLICK
5¢

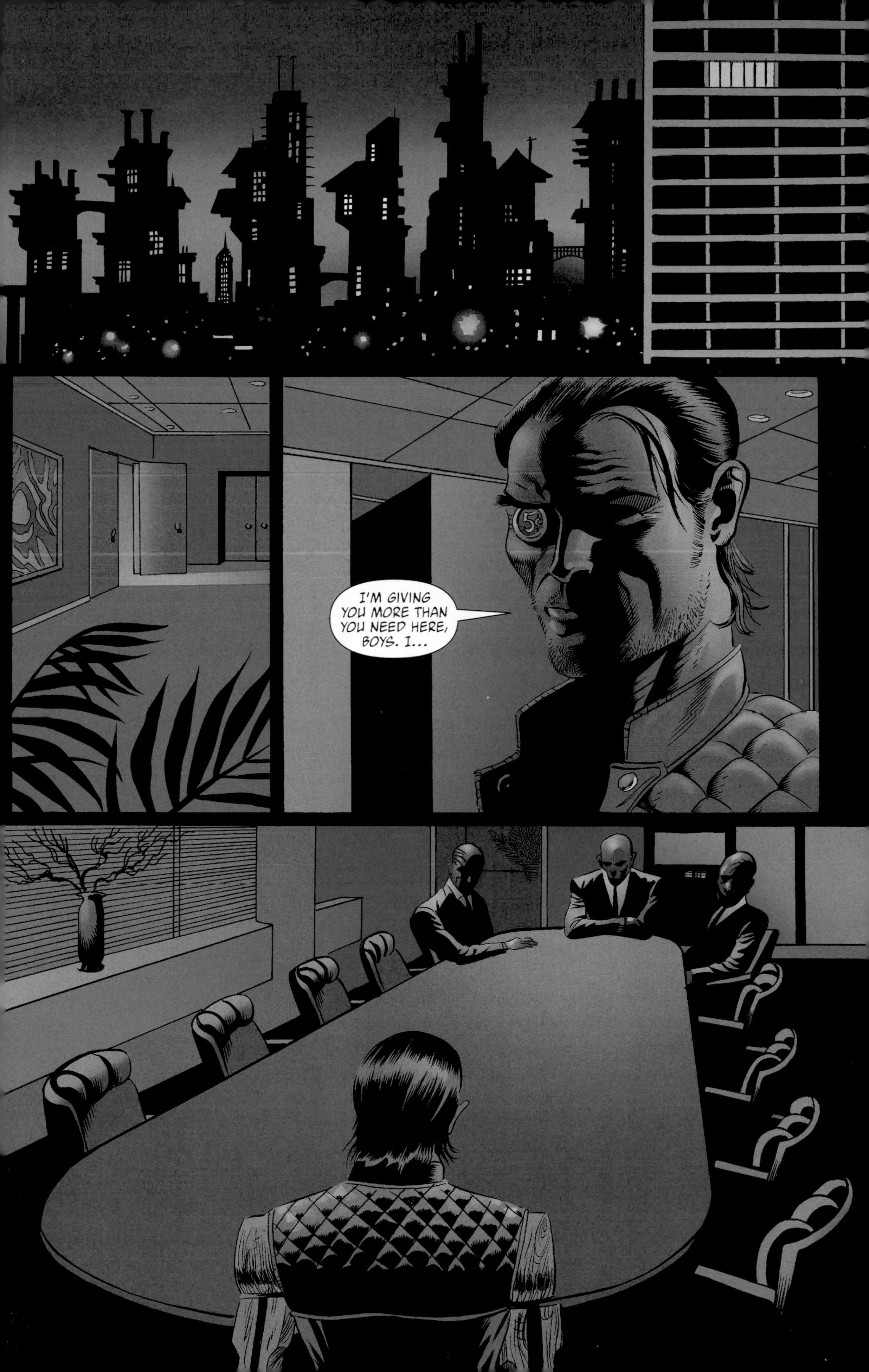
I'M GIVING YOU MORE THAN YOU NEED HERE, BOYS. I...

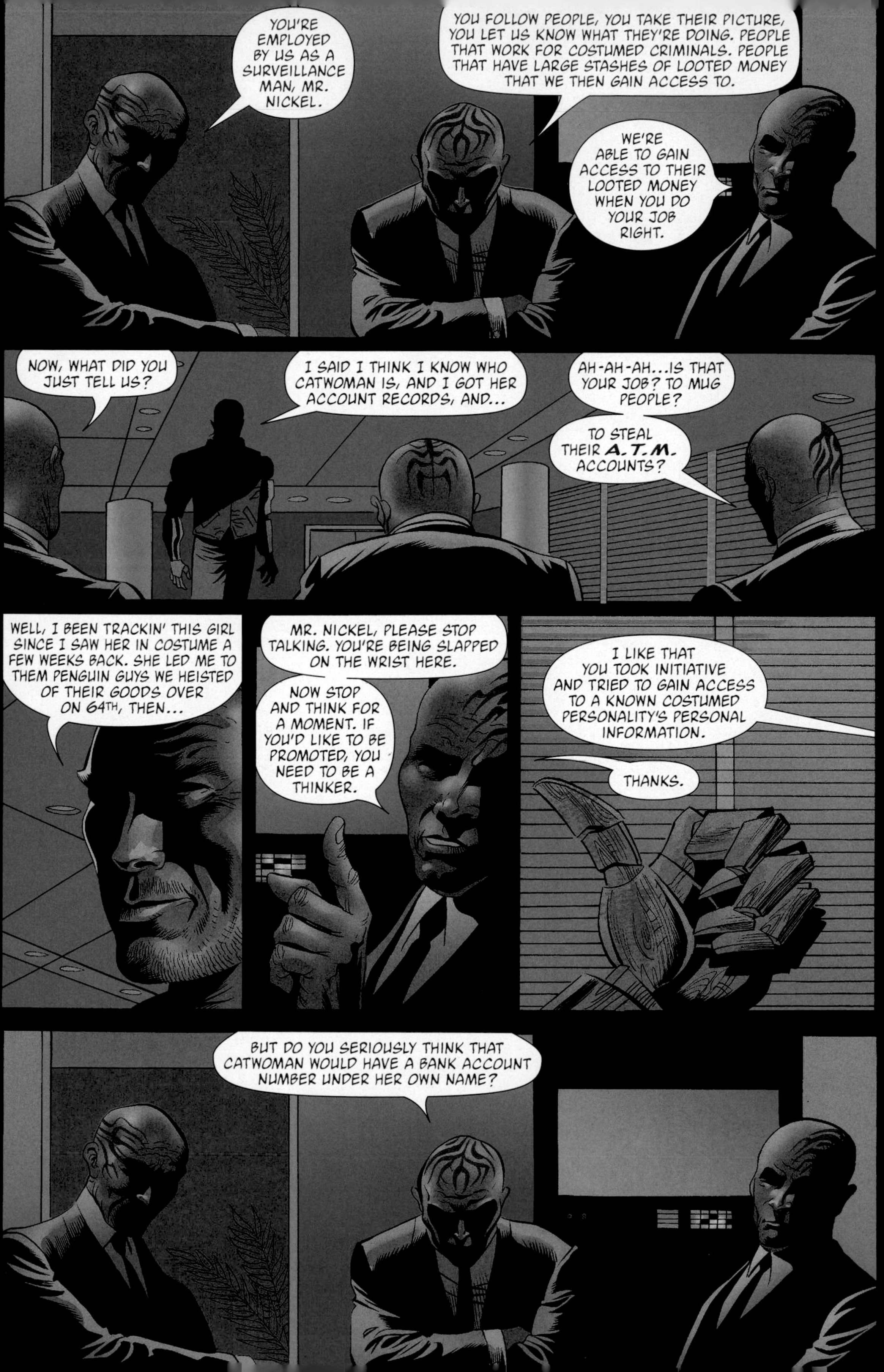

YOU'RE EMPLOYED BY US AS A SURVEILLANCE MAN, MR. NICKEL.
YOU FOLLOW PEOPLE, YOU TAKE THEIR PICTURE, YOU LET US KNOW WHAT THEY'RE DOING. PEOPLE THAT WORK FOR COSTUMED CRIMINALS. PEOPLE THAT HAVE LARGE STASHES OF LOOTED MONEY THAT WE THEN GAIN ACCESS TO.
WE'RE ABLE TO GAIN ACCESS TO THEIR LOOTED MONEY WHEN YOU DO YOUR JOB RIGHT.
NOW, WHAT DID YOU JUST TELL US?
I SAID I THINK I KNOW WHO CATWOMAN IS, AND I GOT HER ACCOUNT RECORDS, AND...
AH-AH-AH...IS THAT YOUR JOB? TO MUG PEOPLE?
TO STEAL THEIR A.T.M. ACCOUNTS?
WELL, I BEEN TRACKIN' THIS GIRL SINCE I SAW HER IN COSTUME A FEW WEEKS BACK. SHE LED ME TO THEM PENGUIN GUYS WE HEISTED OF THEIR GOODS OVER ON 64TH, THEN...
MR. NICKEL, PLEASE STOP TALKING. YOU'RE BEING SLAPPED ON THE WRIST HERE.
NOW STOP AND THINK FOR A MOMENT. IF YOU'D LIKE TO BE PROMOTED, YOU NEED TO BE A THINKER.
I LIKE THAT YOU TOOK INITIATIVE AND TRIED TO GAIN ACCESS TO A KNOWN COSTUMED PERSONALITY'S PERSONAL INFORMATION.
THANKS.
BUT DO YOU SERIOUSLY THINK THAT CATWOMAN WOULD HAVE A BANK ACCOUNT NUMBER UNDER HER OWN NAME?

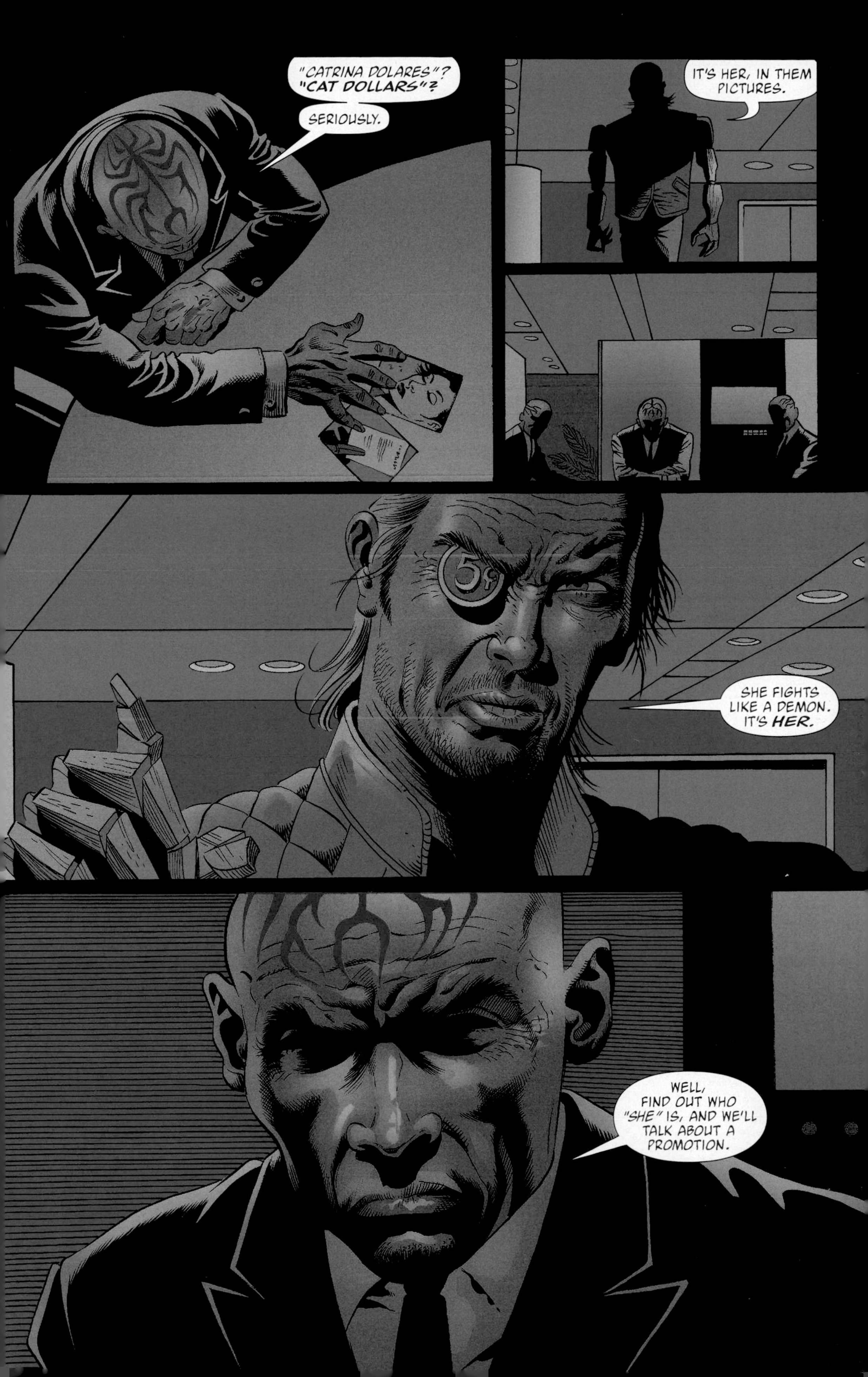
"CATRINA DOLARES"? "CAT DOLLARS"?
SERIOUSLY.
IT'S HER, IN THEM PICTURES.
SHE FIGHTS LIKE A DEMON. IT'S HER.
WELL, FIND OUT WHO "SHE" IS, AND WE'LL TALK ABOUT A PROMOTION.

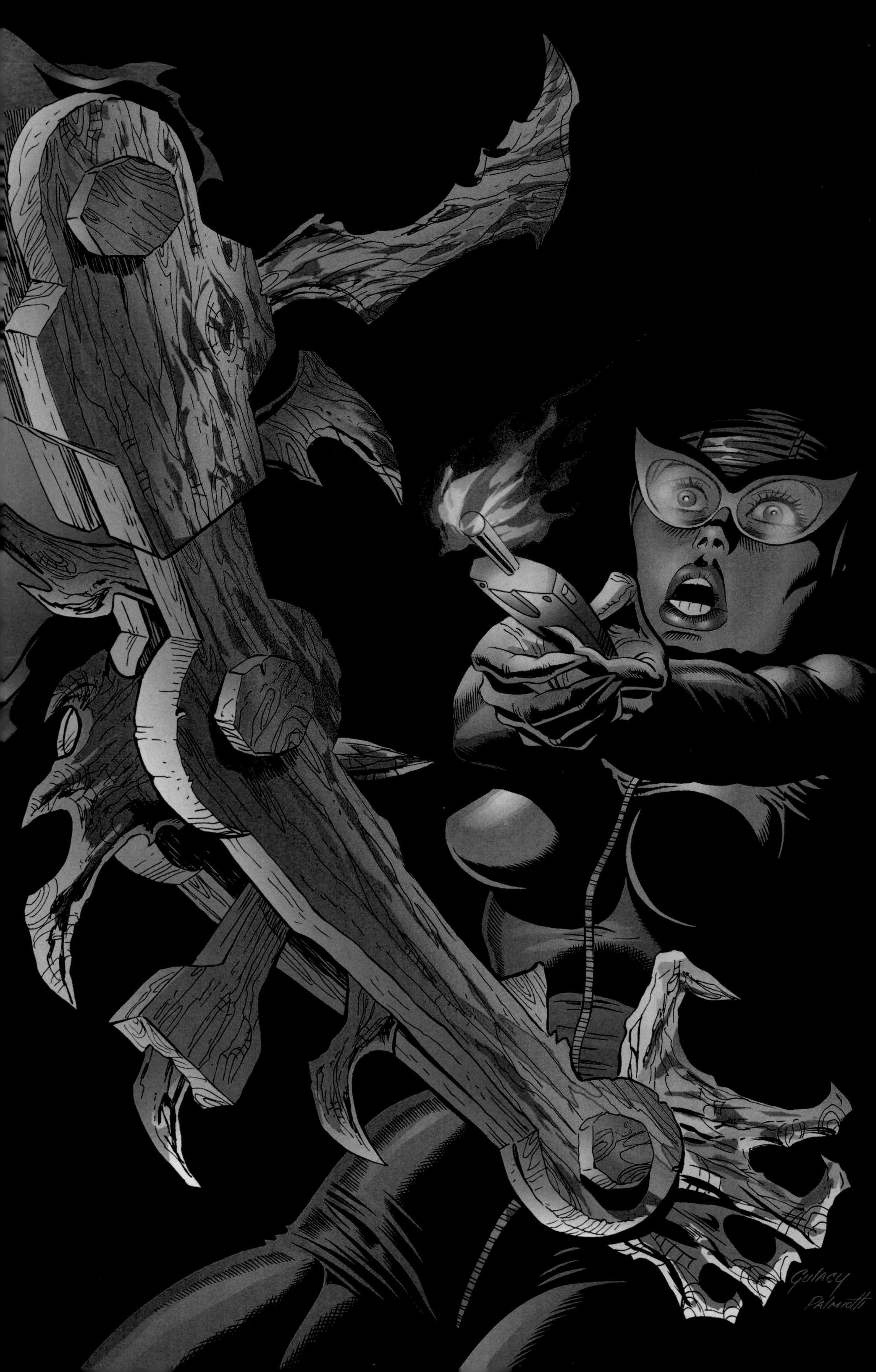
GULACY
PALMIOTTI

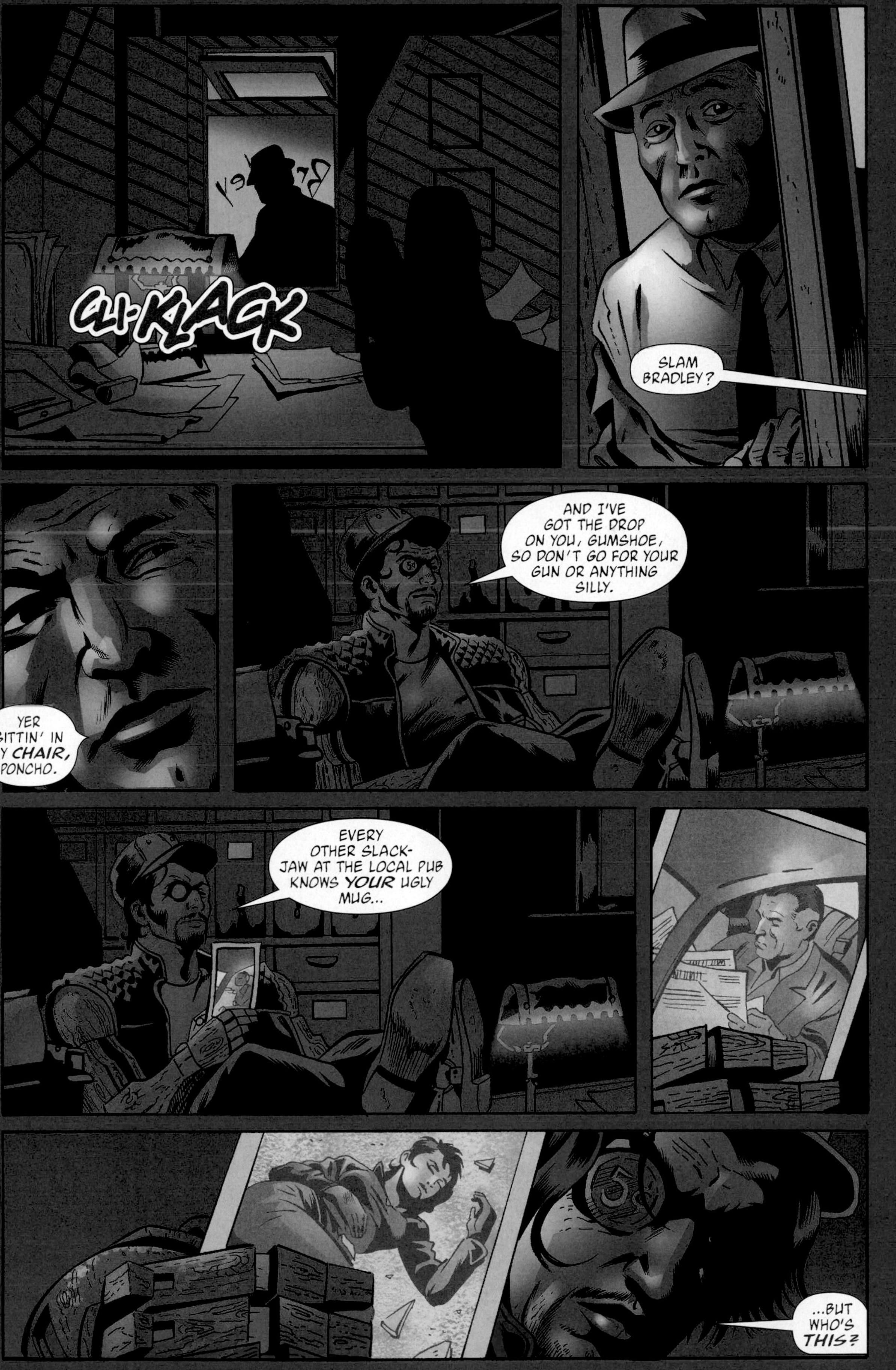
CLI-KLACK
SLAM BRADLEY?
YER SITTIN' IN MY CHAIR, PONCHO.
AND I'VE GOT THE DROP ON YOU, GUMSHOE, SO DON'T GO FOR YOUR GUN OR ANYTHING SILLY.
EVERY OTHER SLACK-JAW AT THE LOCAL PUB KNOWS YOUR UGLY MUG...
...BUT WHO'S THIS?

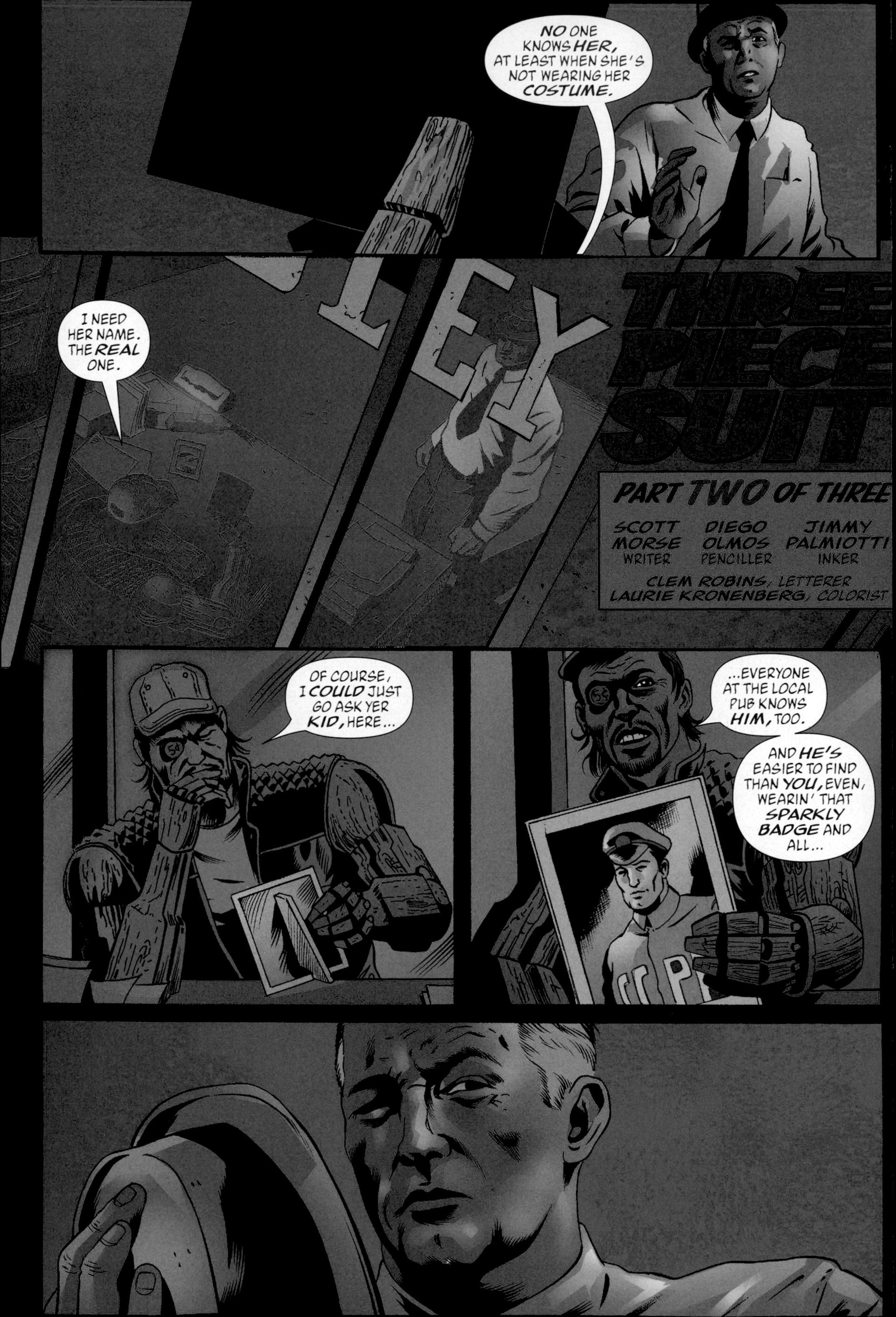
NO ONE KNOWS HER, AT LEAST WHEN SHE'S NOT WEARING HER COSTUME.
I NEED HER NAME. THE REAL ONE.
THREE PIECE SUIT
PART TWO OF THREE
SCOTT MORSE WRITER
DIEGO OLMOS PENCILLER
JIMMY PALMIOTTI INKER
CLEM ROBINS, LETTERER
LAURIE KRONENBERG, COLORIST
OF COURSE, I COULD JUST GO ASK YER KID, HERE...
...EVERYONE AT THE LOCAL PUB KNOWS HIM, TOO.
AND HE'S EASIER TO FIND THAN YOU, EVEN, WEARIN' THAT SPARKLY BADGE AND ALL...

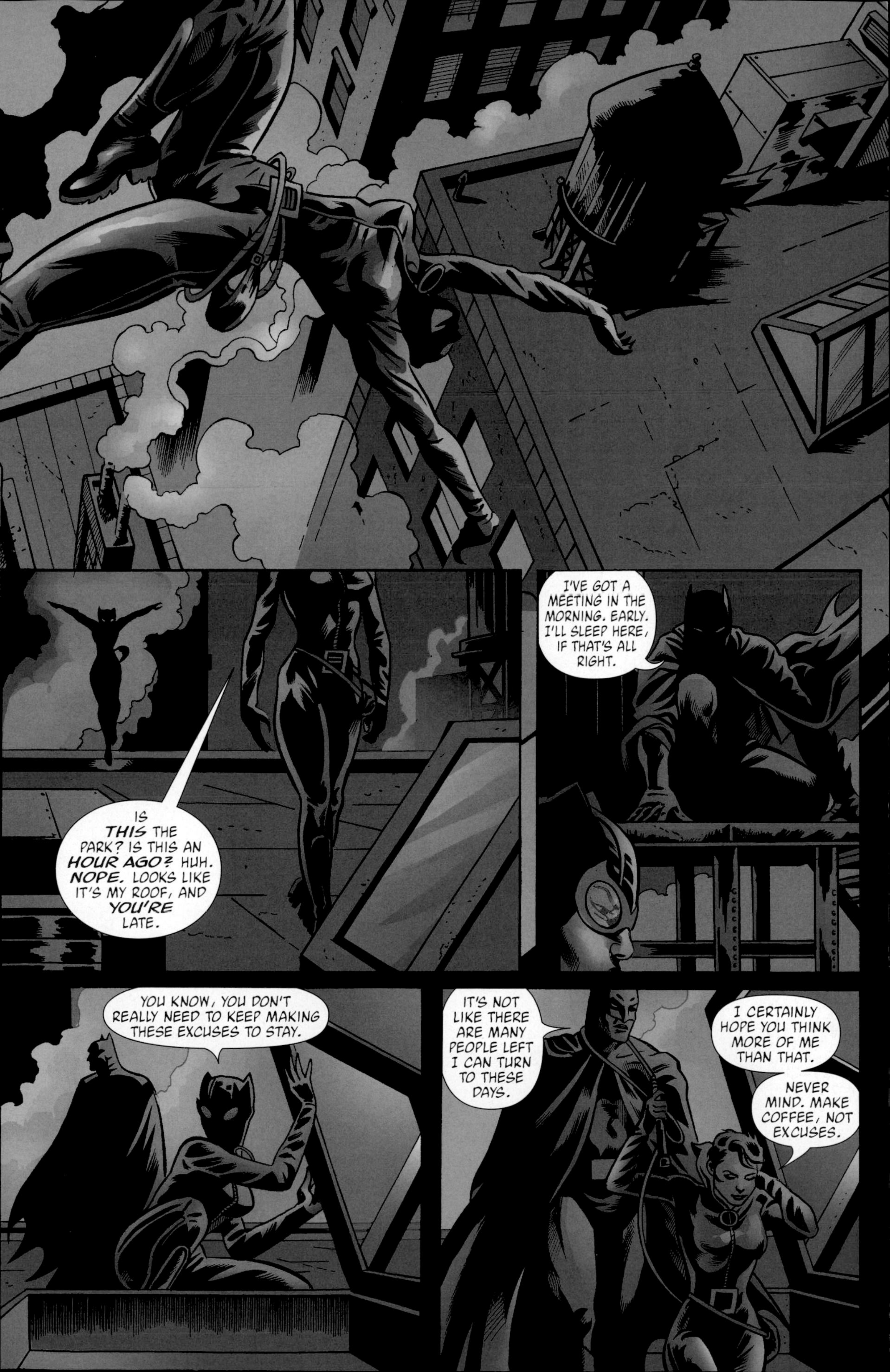
IS THIS THE PARK? IS THIS AN HOUR AGO? HUH. NOPE. LOOKS LIKE IT'S MY ROOF, AND YOU'RE LATE.
I'VE GOT A MEETING IN THE MORNING. EARLY. I'LL SLEEP HERE, IF THAT'S ALL RIGHT.
YOU KNOW, YOU DON'T REALLY NEED TO KEEP MAKING THESE EXCUSES TO STAY.
IT'S NOT LIKE THERE ARE MANY PEOPLE LEFT I CAN TURN TO THESE DAYS.
I CERTAINLY HOPE YOU THINK MORE OF ME THAN THAT.
NEVER MIND. MAKE COFFEE, NOT EXCUSES.

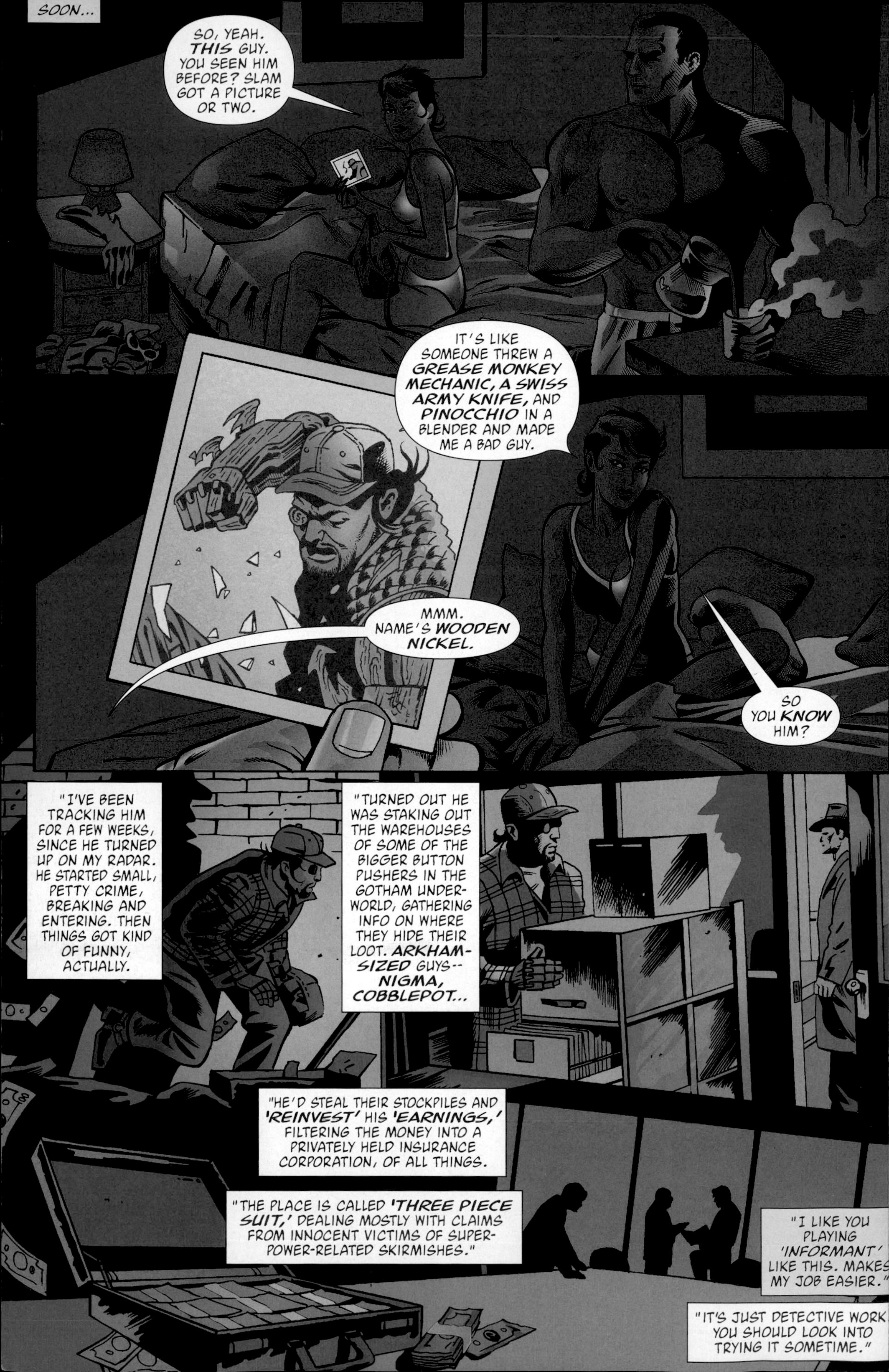

SOON...
SO, YEAH. THIS GUY. YOU SEEN HIM BEFORE? SLAM GOT A PICTURE OR TWO.
IT'S LIKE SOMEONE THREW A GREASE MONKEY MECHANIC, A SWISS ARMY KNIFE, AND PINOCCHIO IN A BLENDER AND MADE ME A BAD GUY.
MMM. NAME'S WOODEN NICKEL.
SO YOU KNOW HIM?
"I'VE BEEN TRACKING HIM FOR A FEW WEEKS, SINCE HE TURNED UP ON MY RADAR. HE STARTED SMALL, PETTY CRIME, BREAKING AND ENTERING. THEN THINGS GOT KIND OF FUNNY, ACTUALLY.
"TURNED OUT HE WAS STAKING OUT THE WAREHOUSES OF SOME OF THE BIGGER BUTTON PUSHERS IN THE GOTHAM UNDERWORLD, GATHERING INFO ON WHERE THEY HIDE THEIR LOOT. ARKHAM-SIZED GUYS-- NIGMA, COBBLEPOT...
"HE'D STEAL THEIR STOCKPILES AND 'REINVEST' HIS 'EARNINGS,' FILTERING THE MONEY INTO A PRIVATELY HELD INSURANCE CORPORATION, OF ALL THINGS.
"THE PLACE IS CALLED 'THREE PIECE SUIT,' DEALING MOSTLY WITH CLAIMS FROM INNOCENT VICTIMS OF SUPER-POWER-RELATED SKIRMISHES."
"I LIKE YOU PLAYING 'INFORMANT' LIKE THIS. MAKES MY JOB EASIER."
"IT'S JUST DETECTIVE WORK. YOU SHOULD LOOK INTO TRYING IT SOMETIME."

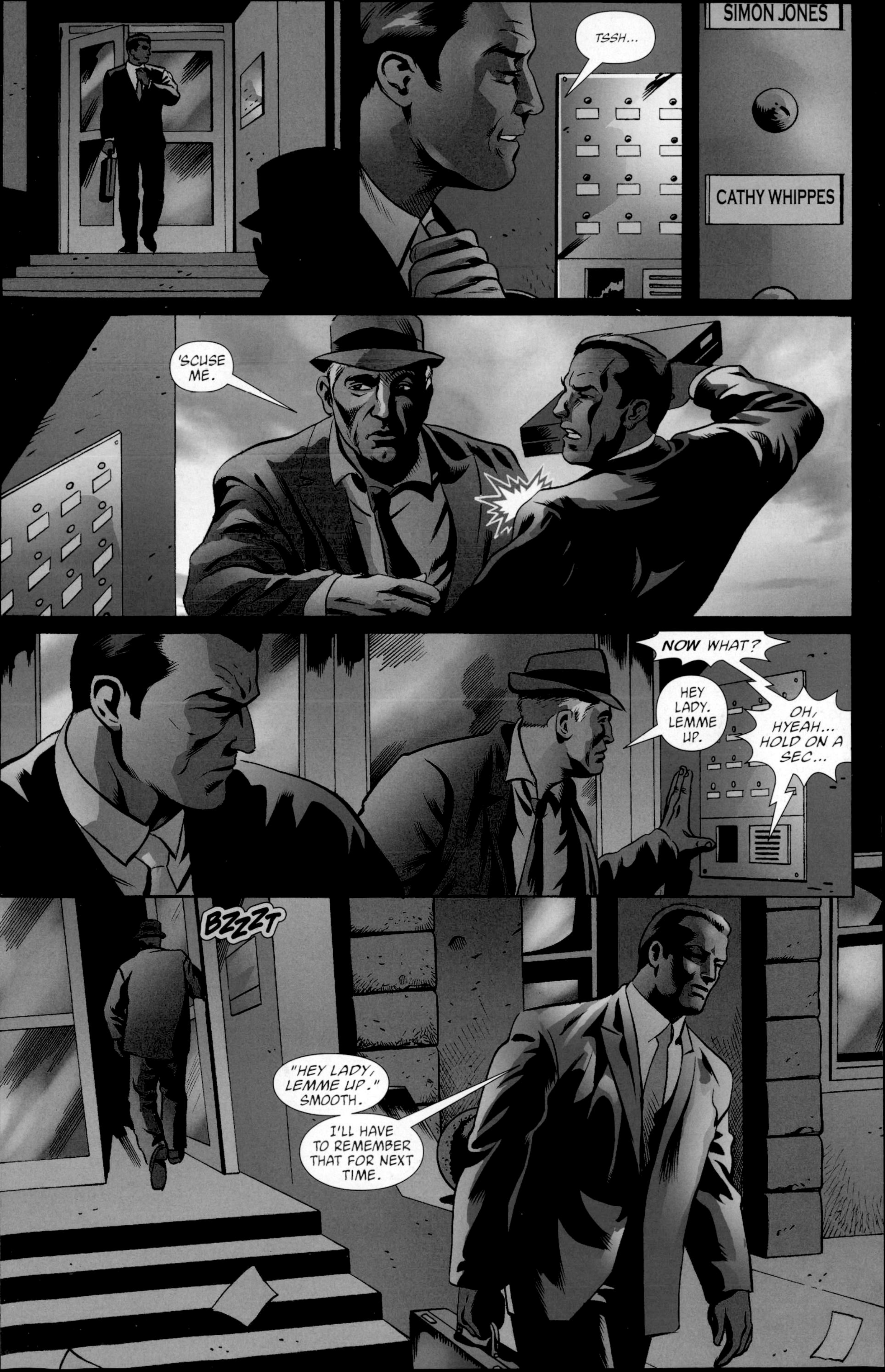
SIMON JONES
CATHY WHIPPES
TSSH...
'SCUSE ME.
NOW WHAT?
HEY LADY. LEMME UP.
OH, HYEAH... HOLD ON A SEC...
BZZZT
"HEY LADY, LEMME UP." SMOOTH.
I'LL HAVE TO REMEMBER THAT FOR NEXT TIME.

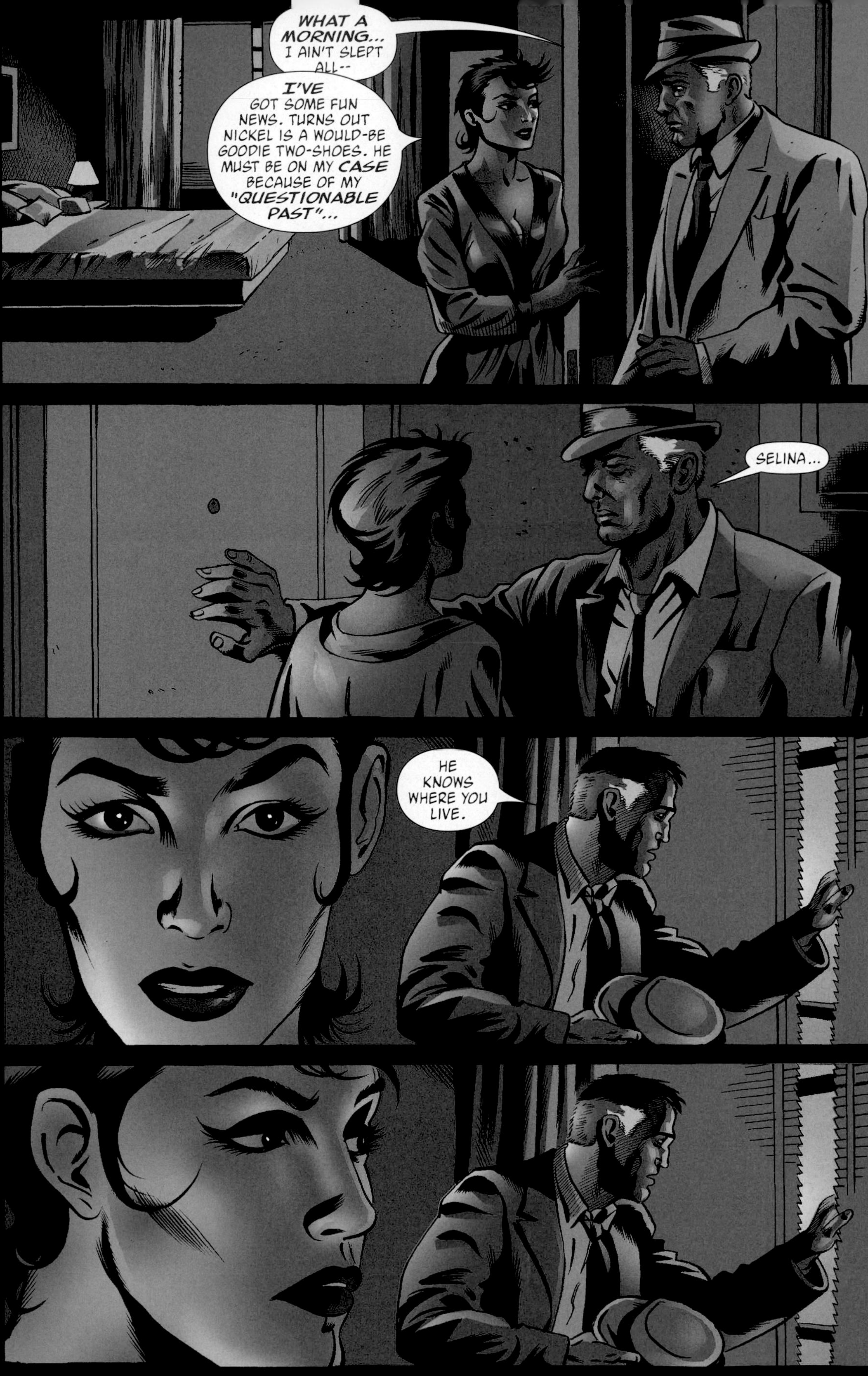
WHAT A MORNING... I AIN'T SLEPT ALL--
I'VE GOT SOME FUN NEWS. TURNS OUT NICKEL IS A WOULD-BE GOODIE TWO-SHOES. HE MUST BE ON MY CASE BECAUSE OF MY "QUESTIONABLE PAST"...
SELINA...
HE KNOWS WHERE YOU LIVE.

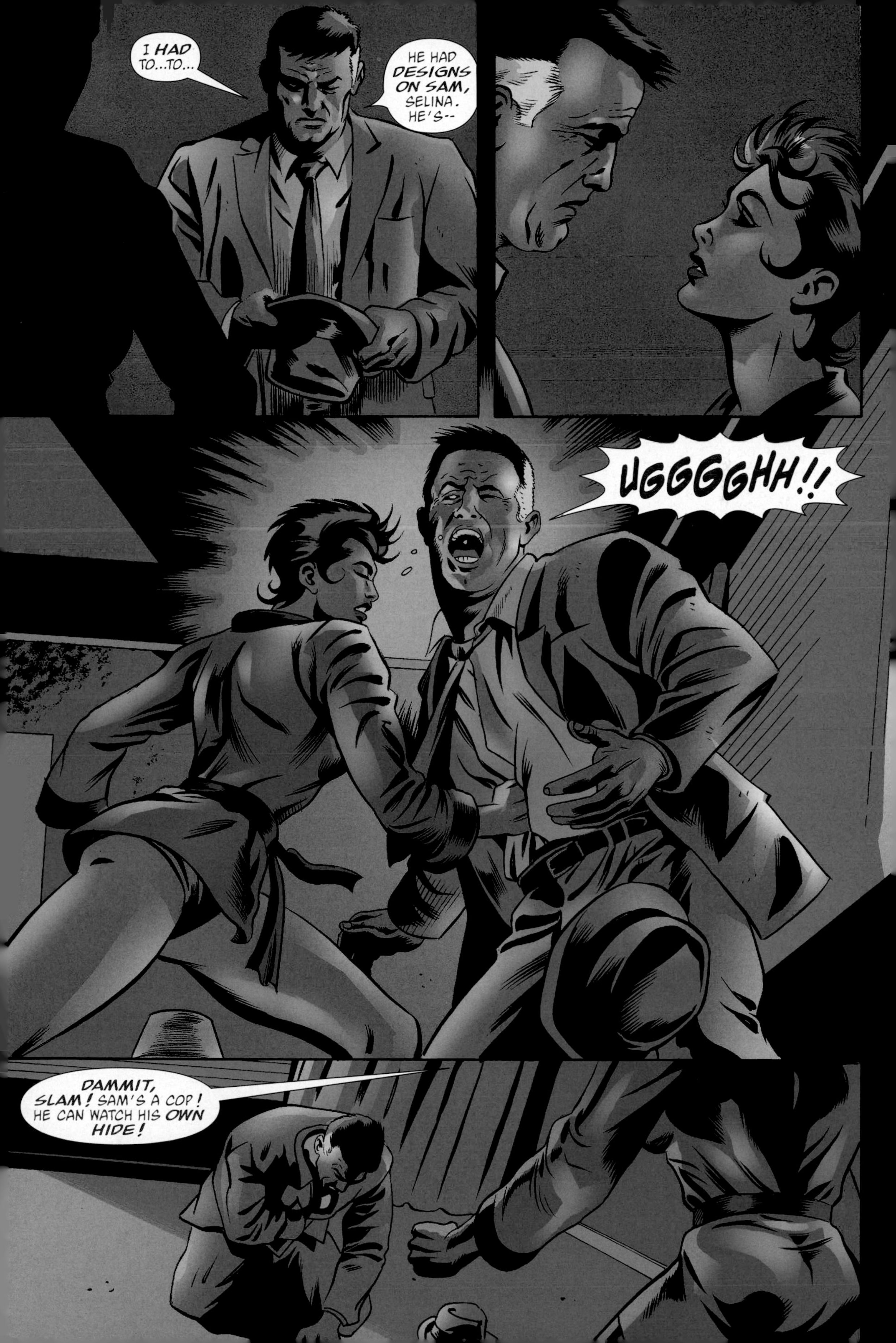
I HAD TO...TO...
HE HAD DESIGNS ON SAM, SELINA. HE'S--
UGGGGHH!!
DAMMIT, SLAM! SAM'S A COP! HE CAN WATCH HIS OWN HIDE!

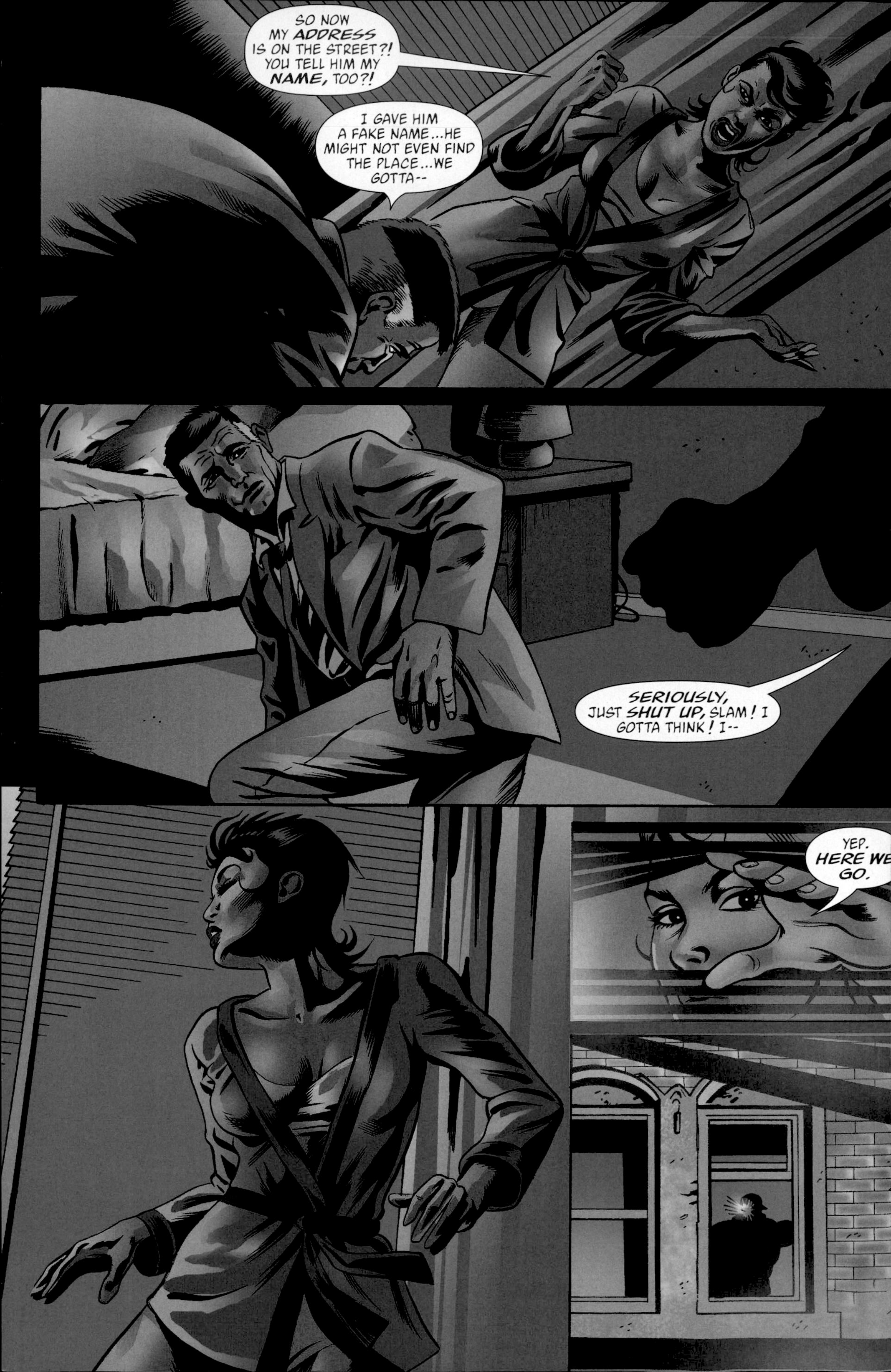
SO NOW MY ADDRESS IS ON THE STREET?! YOU TELL HIM MY NAME, TOO?!
I GAVE HIM A FAKE NAME...HE MIGHT NOT EVEN FIND THE PLACE...WE GOTTA--
SERIOUSLY, JUST SHUT UP, SLAM! I GOTTA THINK! I--
YEP. HERE WE GO.

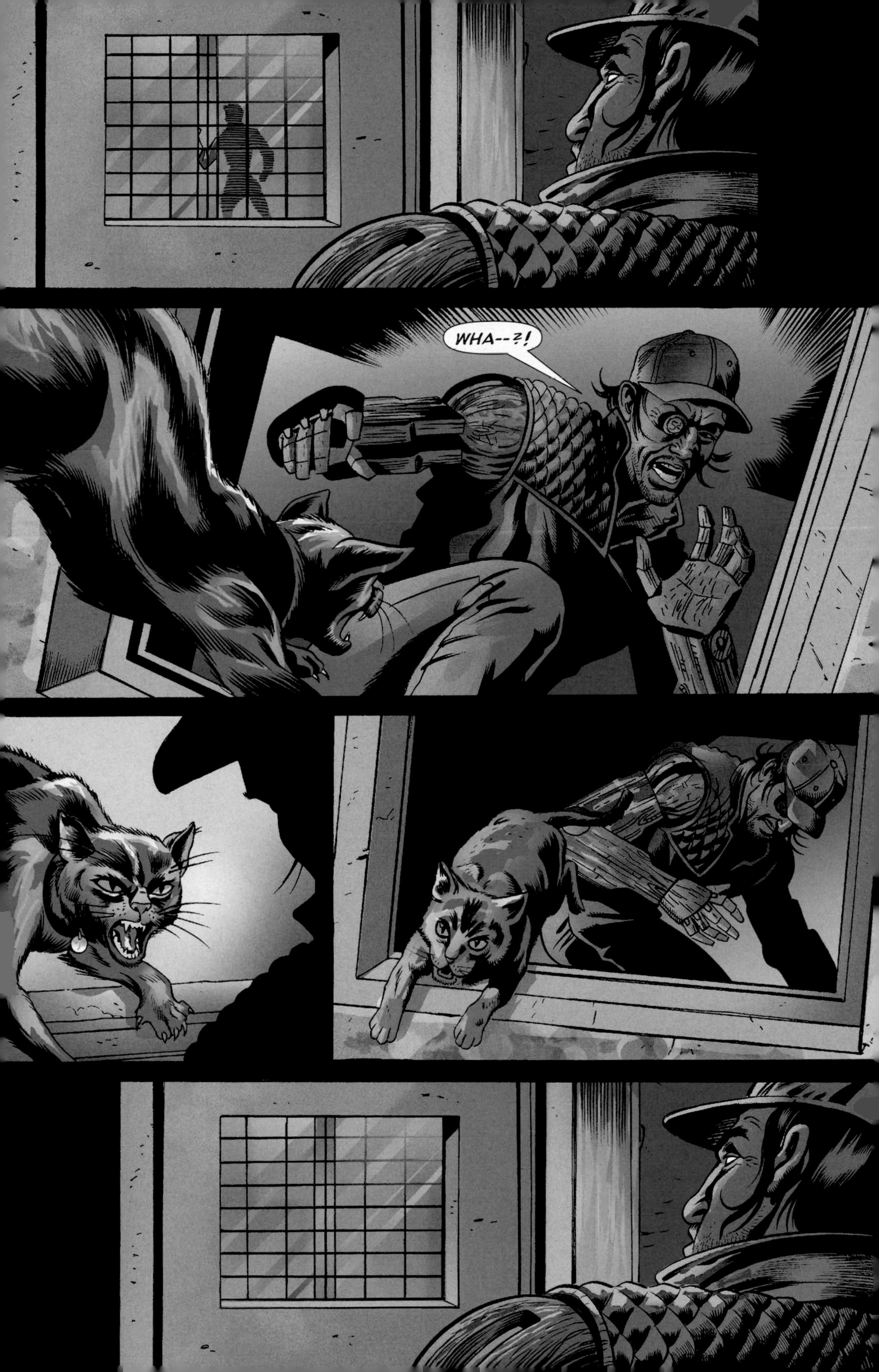
WHA--?!

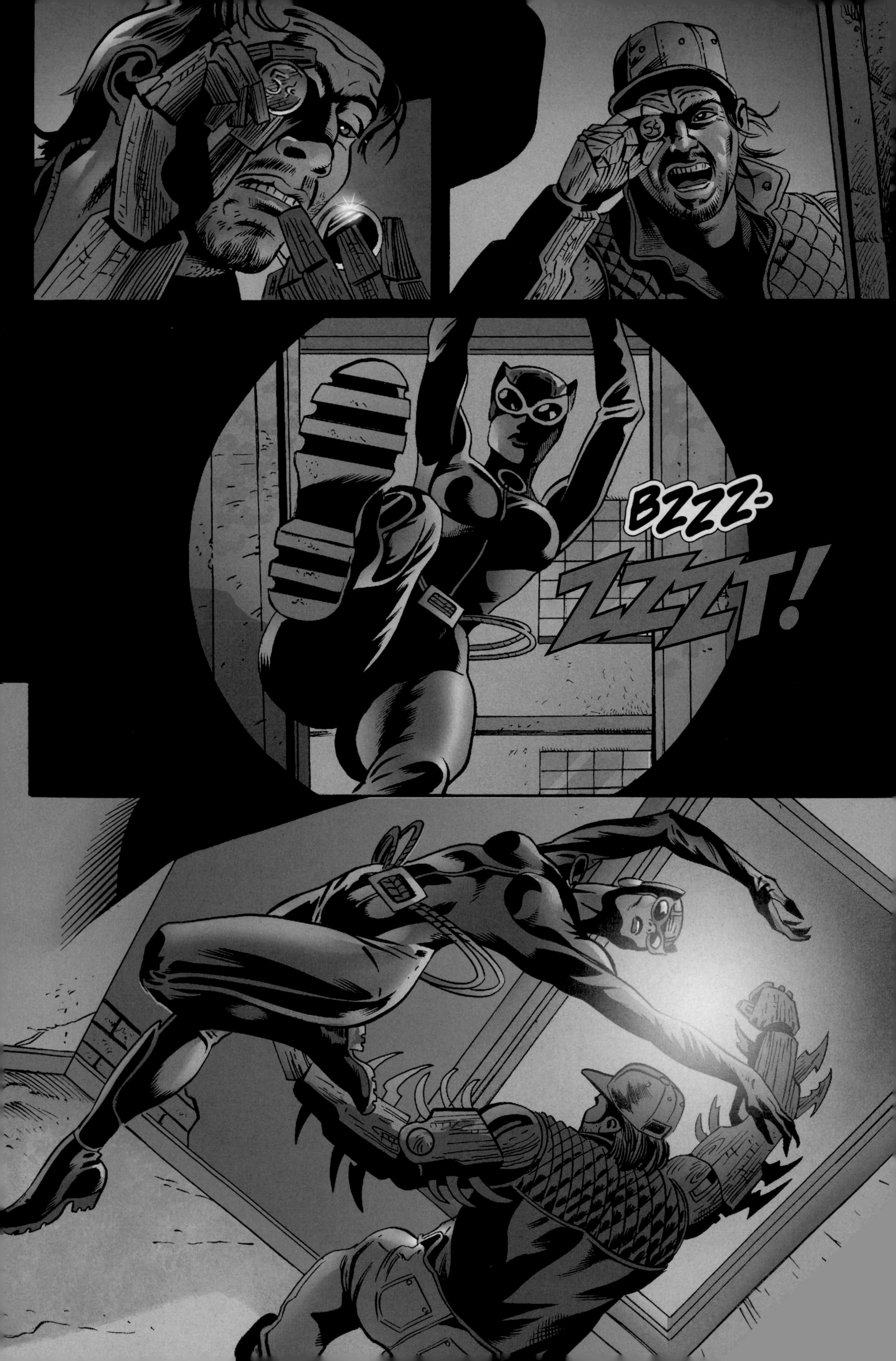
BZZZ-
ZZZZT!

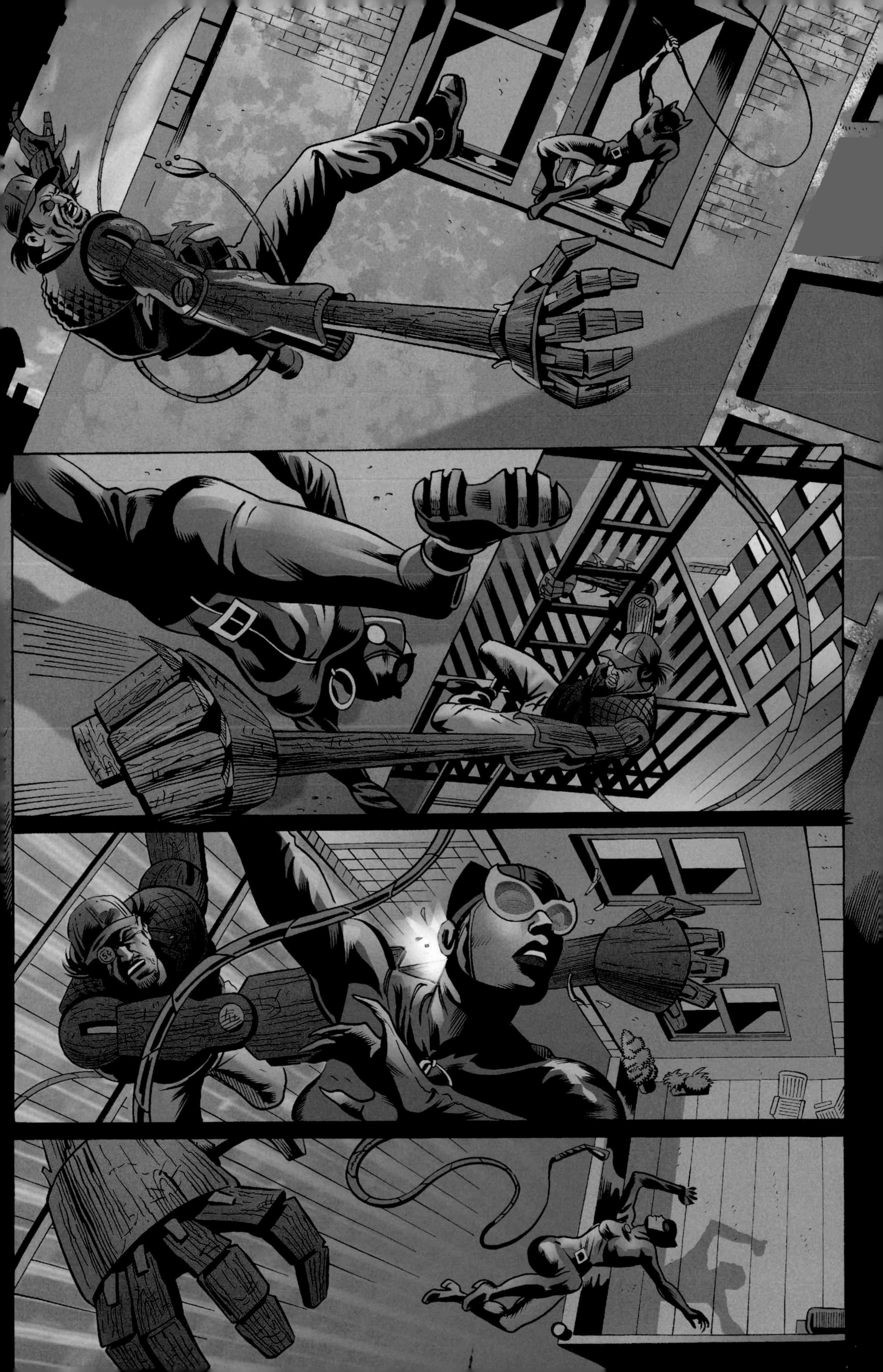

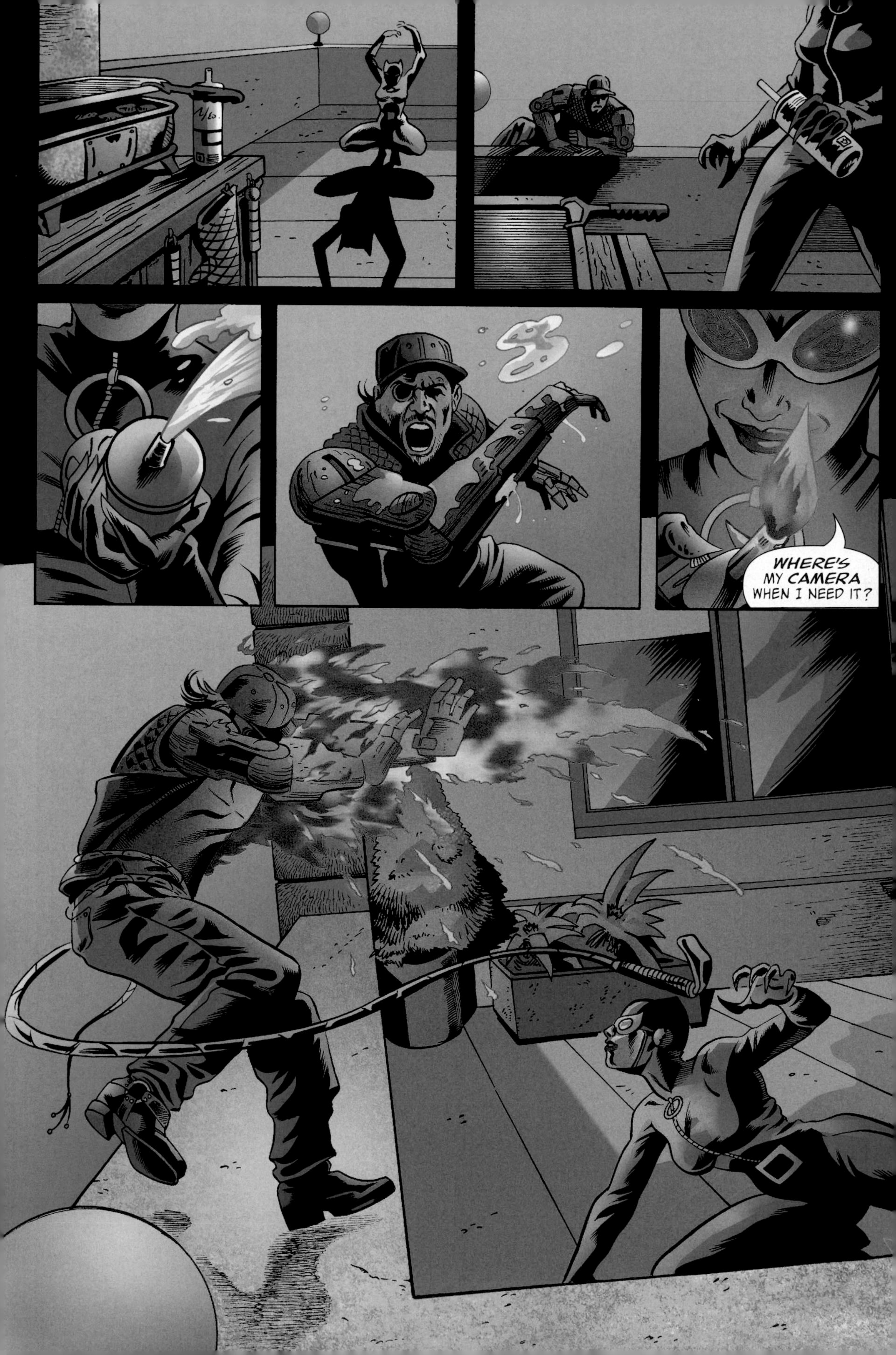
WHERE'S MY CAMERA WHEN I NEED IT?

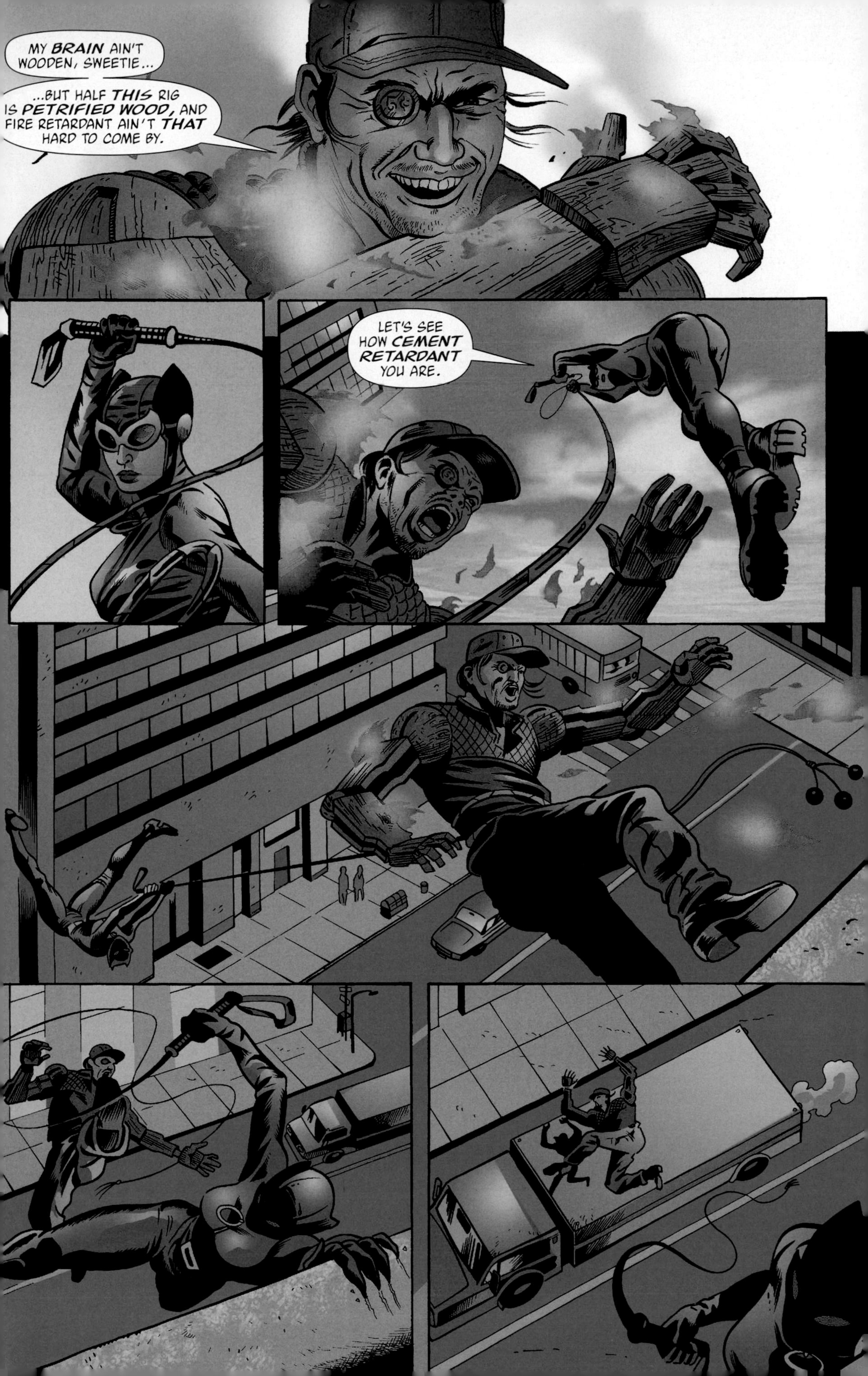
MY BRAIN AIN'T WOODEN, SWEETIE...
...BUT HALF THIS RIG IS PETRIFIED WOOD, AND FIRE RETARDANT AIN'T THAT HARD TO COME BY.
LET'S SEE HOW CEMENT RETARDANT YOU ARE.

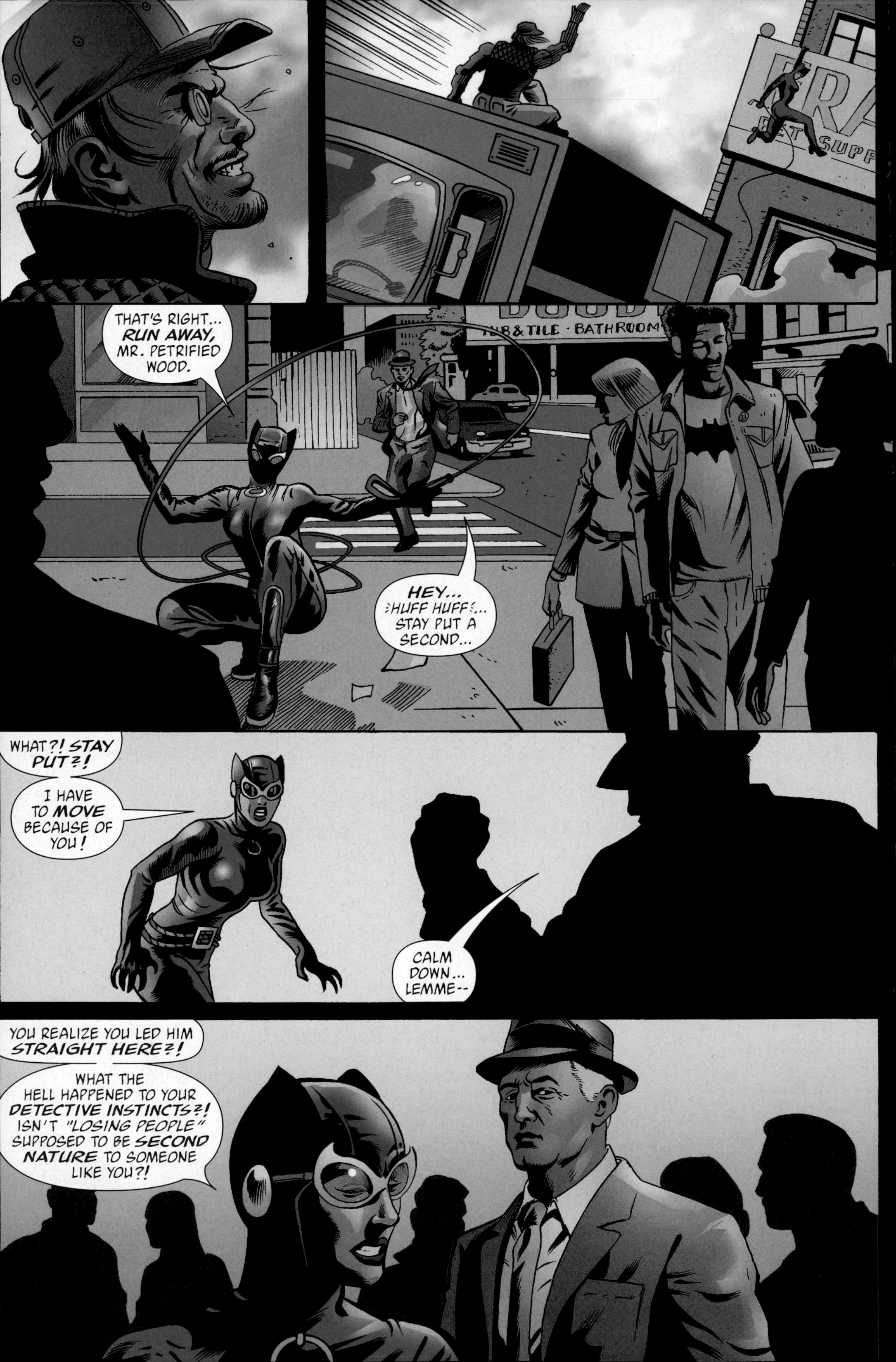
FRA... PET SUPP...
TUB & TILE - BATHROOM
THAT'S RIGHT... RUN AWAY, MR. PETRIFIED WOOD.
HEY... ≥HUFF HUFF≤... STAY PUT A SECOND...
WHAT?! STAY PUT?!
I HAVE TO MOVE BECAUSE OF YOU!
CALM DOWN... LEMME--
YOU REALIZE YOU LED HIM STRAIGHT HERE?!
WHAT THE HELL HAPPENED TO YOUR DETECTIVE INSTINCTS?! ISN'T "LOSING PEOPLE" SUPPOSED TO BE SECOND NATURE TO SOMEONE LIKE YOU?!

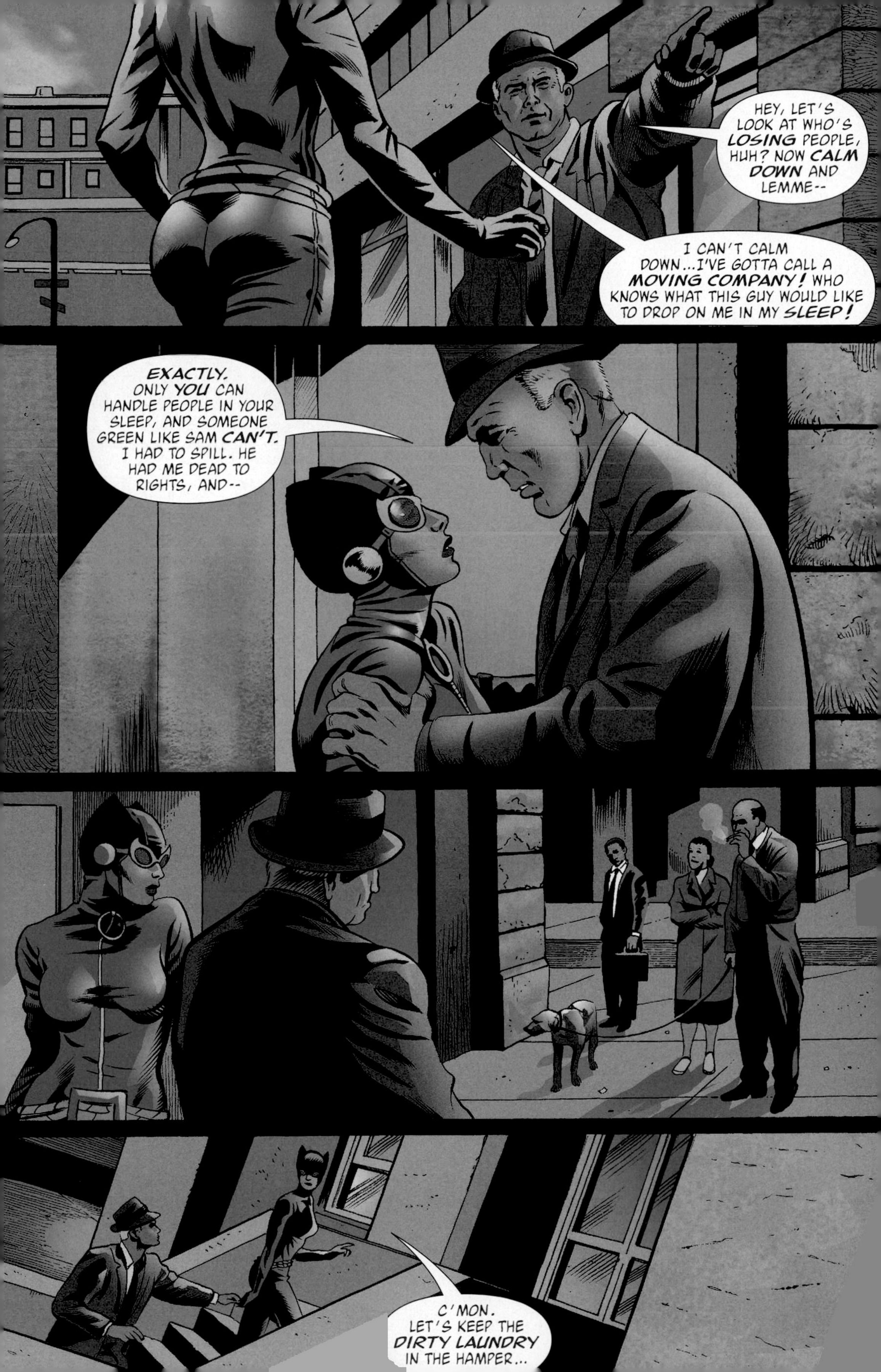

HEY, LET'S LOOK AT WHO'S LOSING PEOPLE, HUH? NOW CALM DOWN AND LEMME--
I CAN'T CALM DOWN...I'VE GOTTA CALL A MOVING COMPANY! WHO KNOWS WHAT THIS GUY WOULD LIKE TO DROP ON ME IN MY SLEEP!
EXACTLY. ONLY YOU CAN HANDLE PEOPLE IN YOUR SLEEP, AND SOMEONE GREEN LIKE SAM CAN'T. I HAD TO SPILL. HE HAD ME DEAD TO RIGHTS, AND--
C'MON. LET'S KEEP THE DIRTY LAUNDRY IN THE HAMPER...

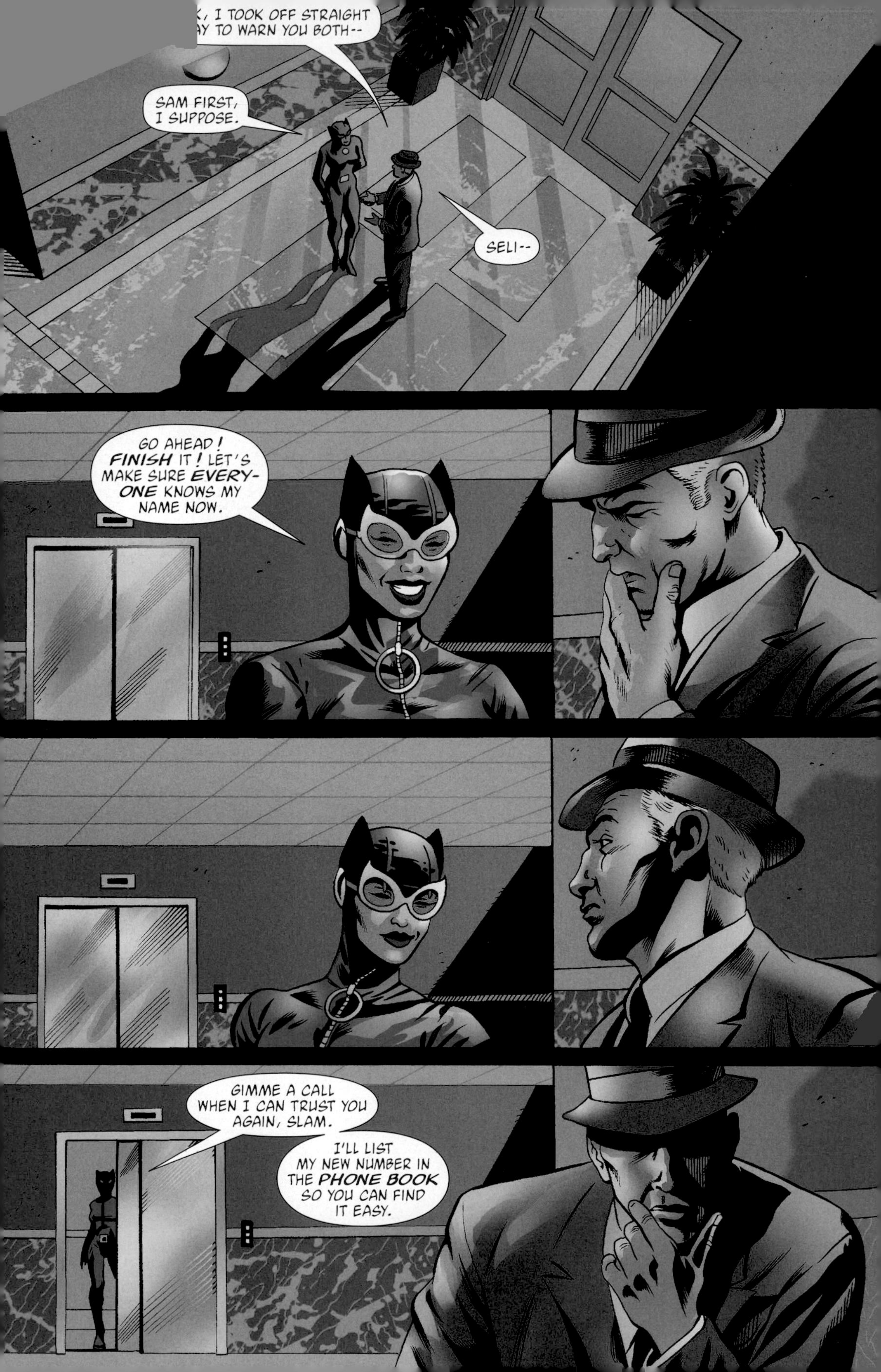

I TOOK OFF STRAIGHT TO WARN YOU BOTH--
SAM FIRST, I SUPPOSE.
SELI--
GO AHEAD! FINISH IT! LET'S MAKE SURE EVERY-ONE KNOWS MY NAME NOW.
GIMME A CALL WHEN I CAN TRUST YOU AGAIN, SLAM.
I'LL LIST MY NEW NUMBER IN THE PHONE BOOK SO YOU CAN FIND IT EASY.

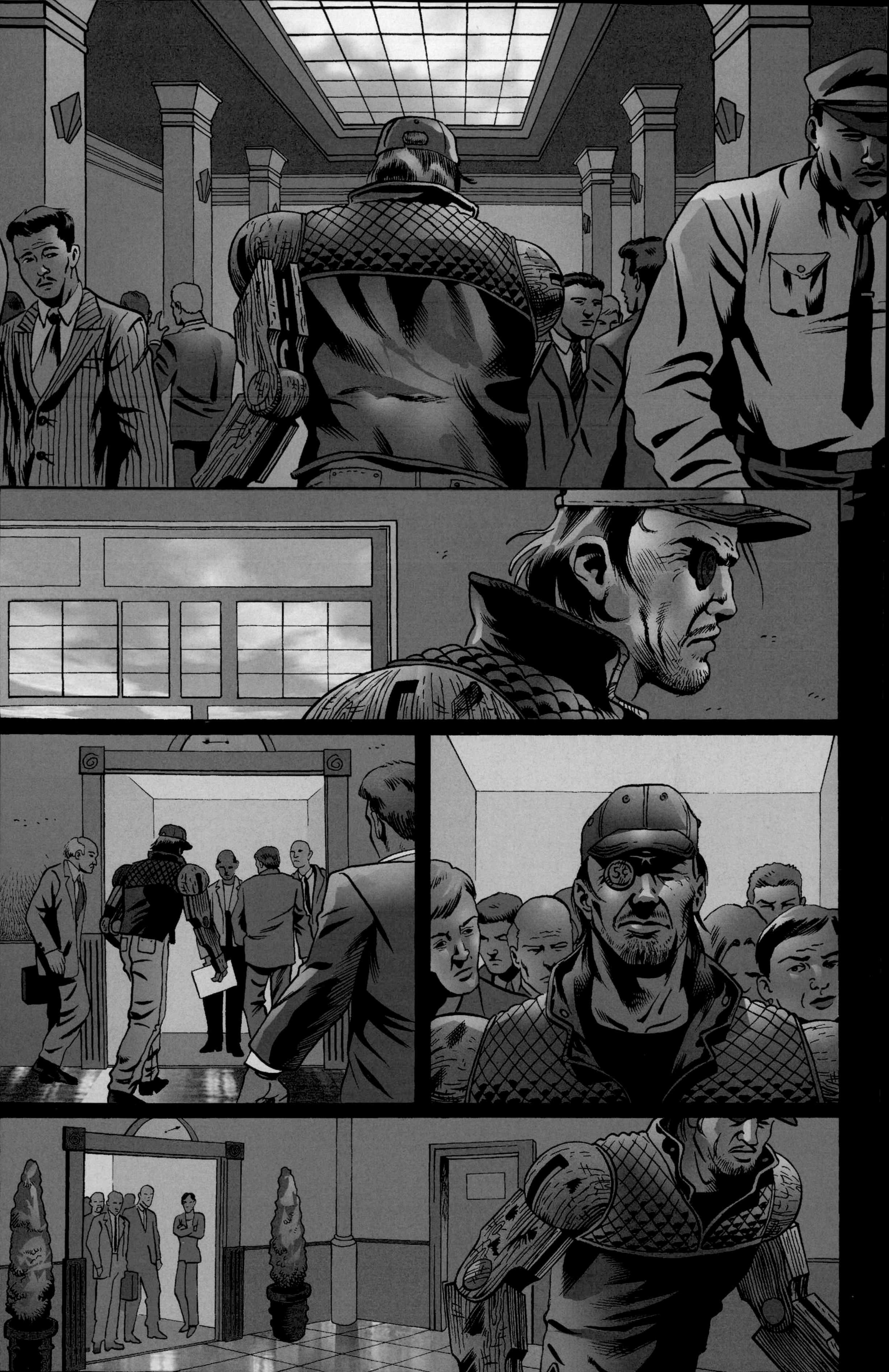

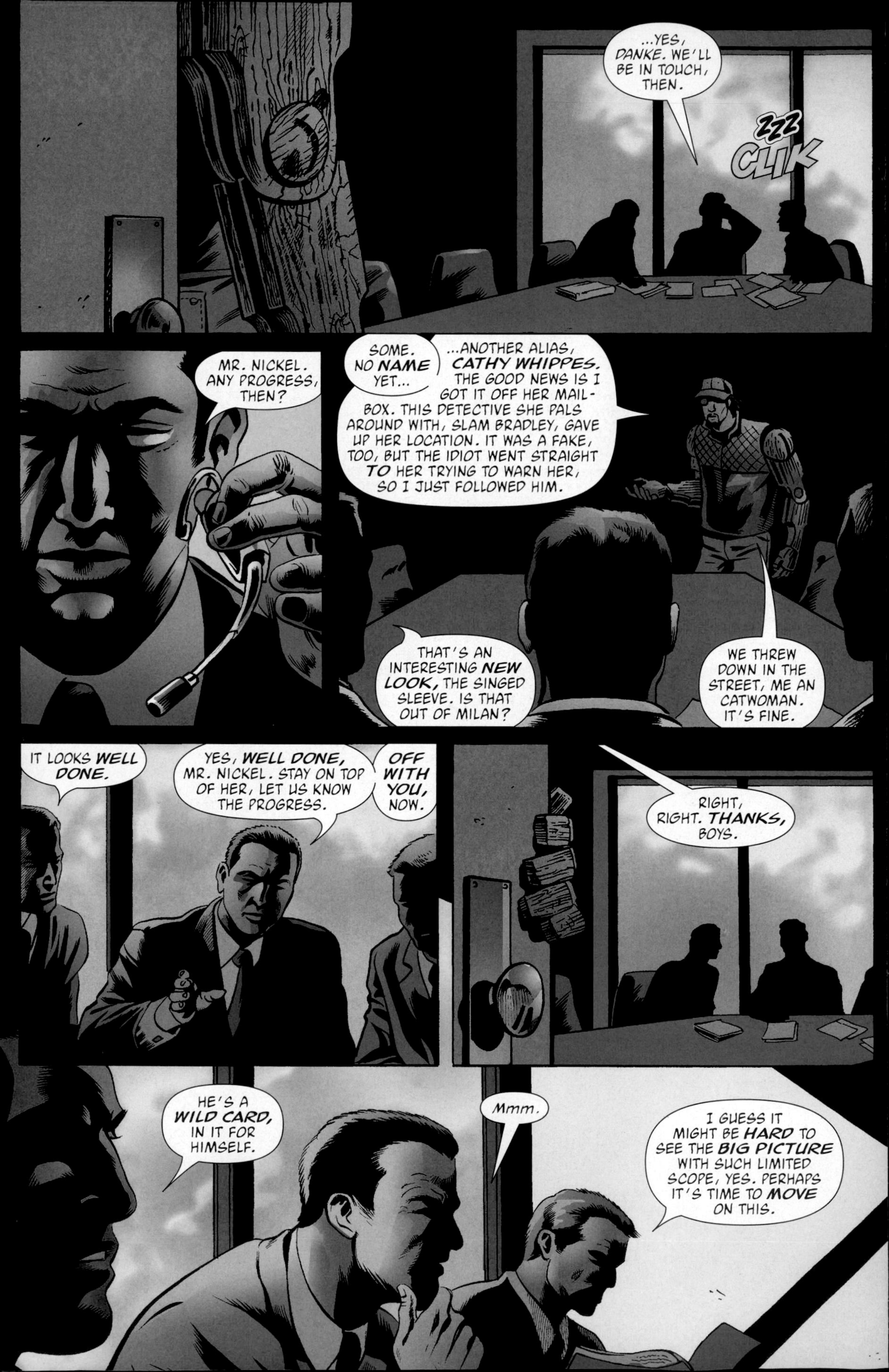
...YES, DANKE. WE'LL BE IN TOUCH, THEN.
ZZZ CLIK
MR. NICKEL. ANY PROGRESS, THEN?
SOME. NO NAME YET...
...ANOTHER ALIAS, CATHY WHIPPES. THE GOOD NEWS IS I GOT IT OFF HER MAIL-BOX. THIS DETECTIVE SHE PALS AROUND WITH, SLAM BRADLEY, GAVE UP HER LOCATION. IT WAS A FAKE, TOO, BUT THE IDIOT WENT STRAIGHT TO HER TRYING TO WARN HER, SO I JUST FOLLOWED HIM.
THAT'S AN INTERESTING NEW LOOK, THE SINGED SLEEVE. IS THAT OUT OF MILAN?
WE THREW DOWN IN THE STREET, ME AN CATWOMAN. IT'S FINE.
IT LOOKS WELL DONE.
YES, WELL DONE, MR. NICKEL. STAY ON TOP OF HER, LET US KNOW THE PROGRESS.
OFF WITH YOU, NOW.
RIGHT, RIGHT. THANKS, BOYS.
HE'S A WILD CARD, IN IT FOR HIMSELF.
Mmm.
I GUESS IT MIGHT BE HARD TO SEE THE BIG PICTURE WITH SUCH LIMITED SCOPE, YES. PERHAPS IT'S TIME TO MOVE ON THIS.

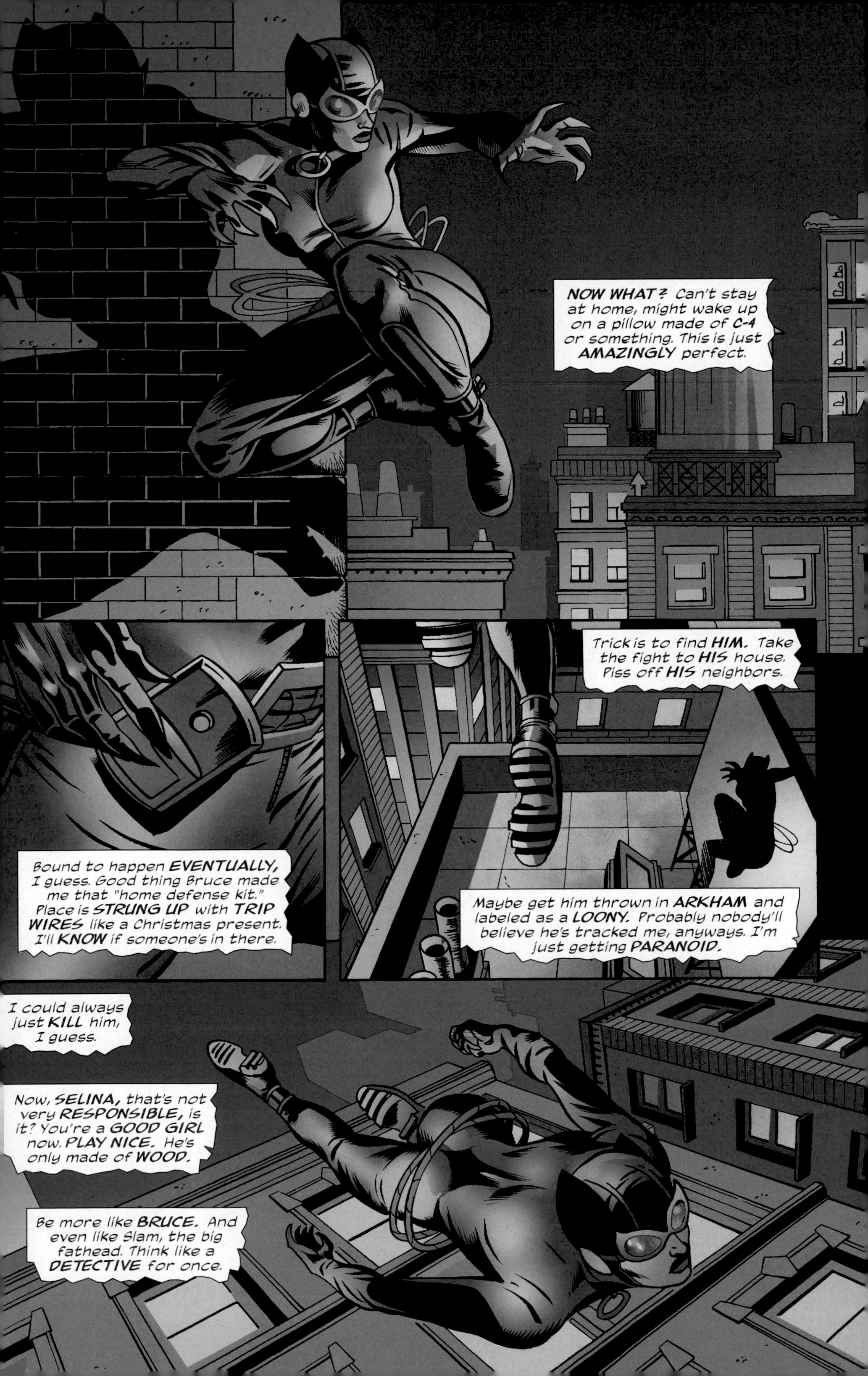
NOW WHAT? Can't stay at home, might wake up on a pillow made of C-4 or something. This is just AMAZINGLY perfect.
Bound to happen EVENTUALLY, I guess. Good thing Bruce made me that "home defense kit." Place is STRUNG UP with TRIP WIRES like a Christmas present. I'll KNOW if someone's in there.
Trick is to find HIM. Take the fight to HIS house. Piss off HIS neighbors.
Maybe get him thrown in ARKHAM and labeled as a LOONY. Probably nobody'll believe he's tracked me, anyways. I'm just getting PARANOID.
I could always just KILL him, I guess.
Now, SELINA, that's not very RESPONSIBLE, is it? You're a GOOD GIRL now. PLAY NICE. He's only made of WOOD.
Be more like BRUCE. And even like Slam, the big fathead. Think like a DETECTIVE for once.

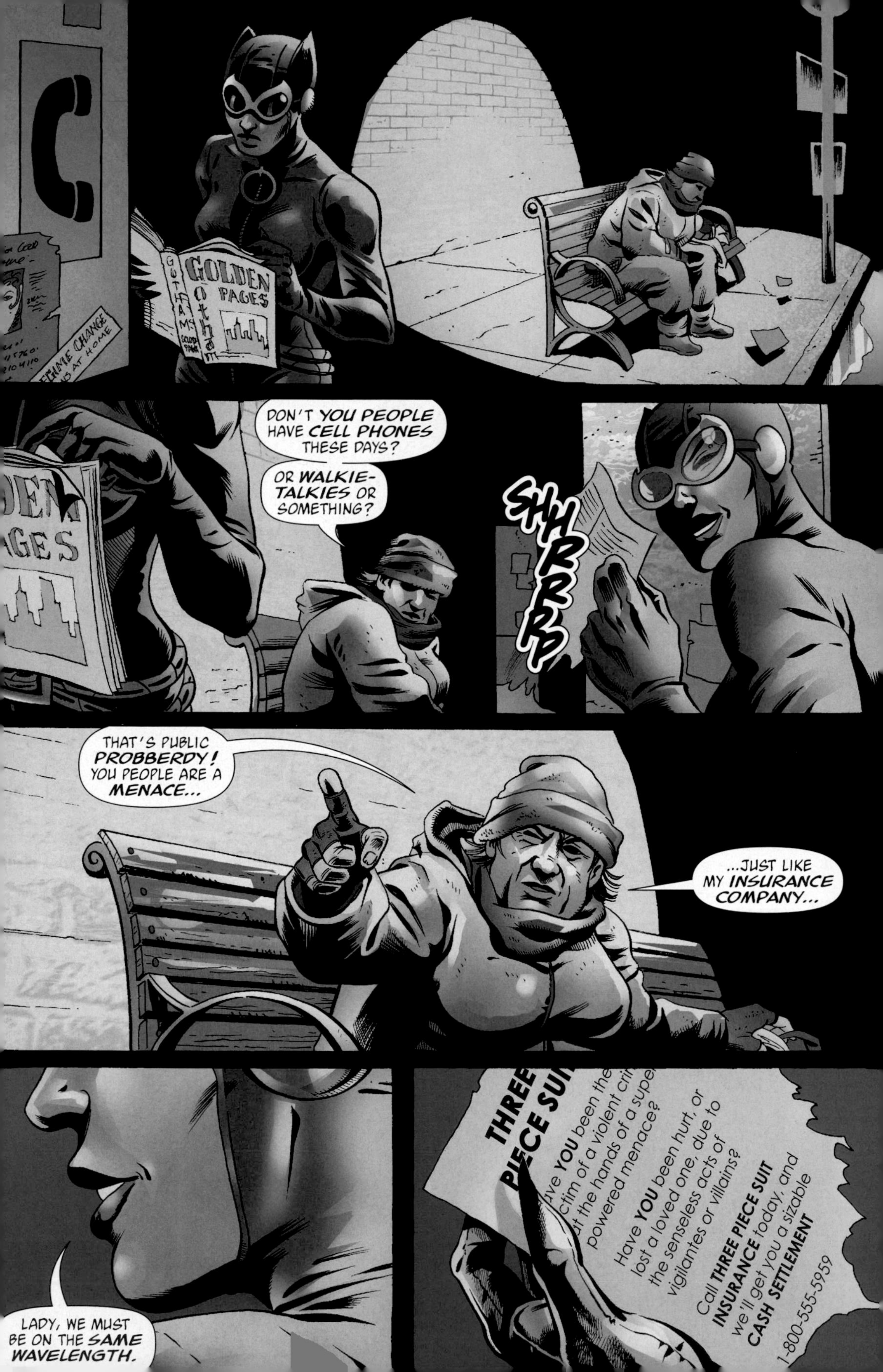

GOLDEN PAGES
DON'T YOU PEOPLE HAVE CELL PHONES THESE DAYS?
OR WALKIE-TALKIES OR SOMETHING?
SHHRRRP
THAT'S PUBLIC PROBBERDY! YOU PEOPLE ARE A MENACE...
...JUST LIKE MY INSURANCE COMPANY...
LADY, WE MUST BE ON THE SAME WAVELENGTH.
powered menace?
Have YOU been hurt, or
lost a loved one, due to
the senseless acts of
vigilantes or villains?
Call THREE PIECE SUIT
INSURANCE today, and
we'll get you a sizable
CASH SETTLEMENT
1-800-555-5959

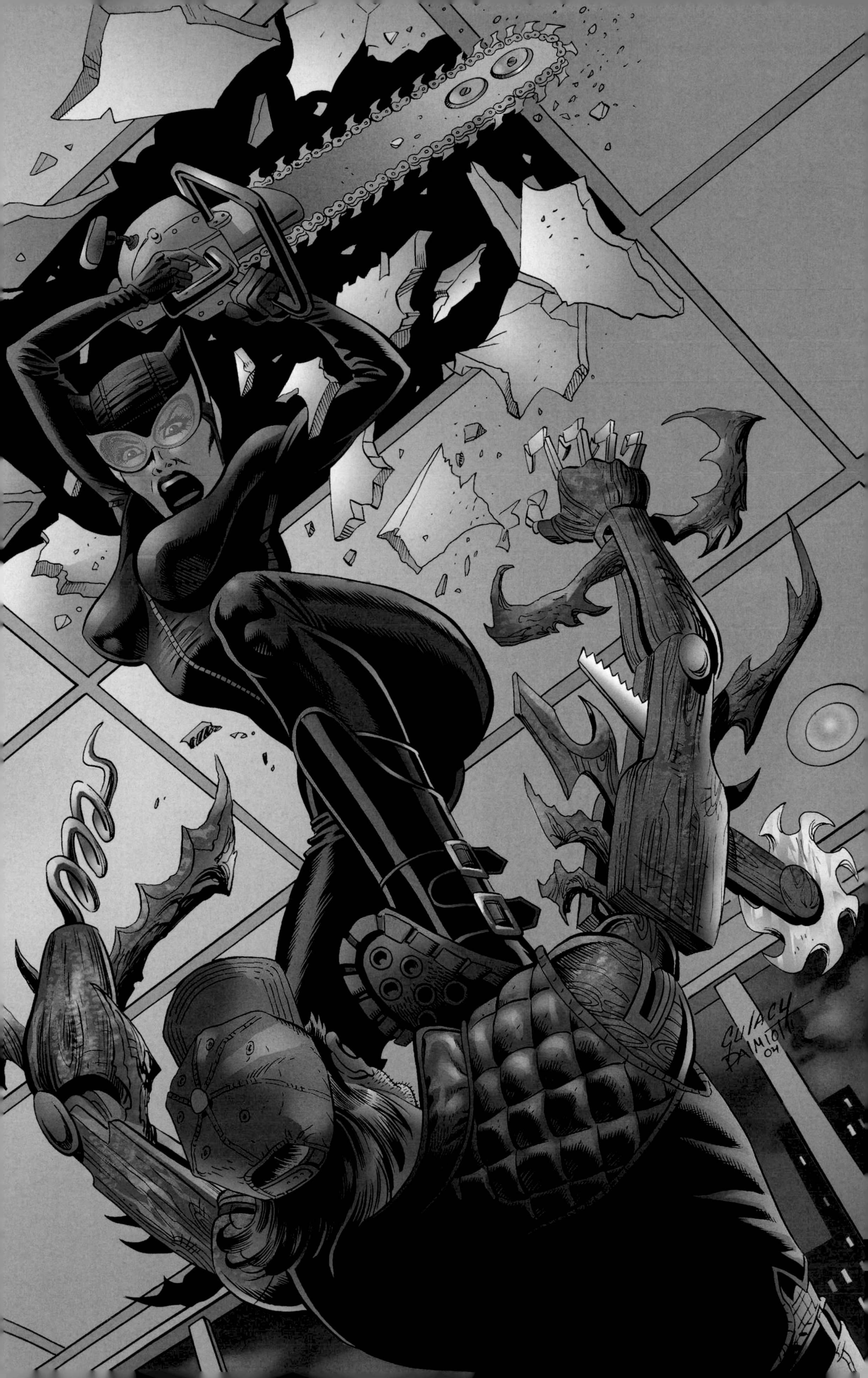
GULACY
PALMIOTTI
'04

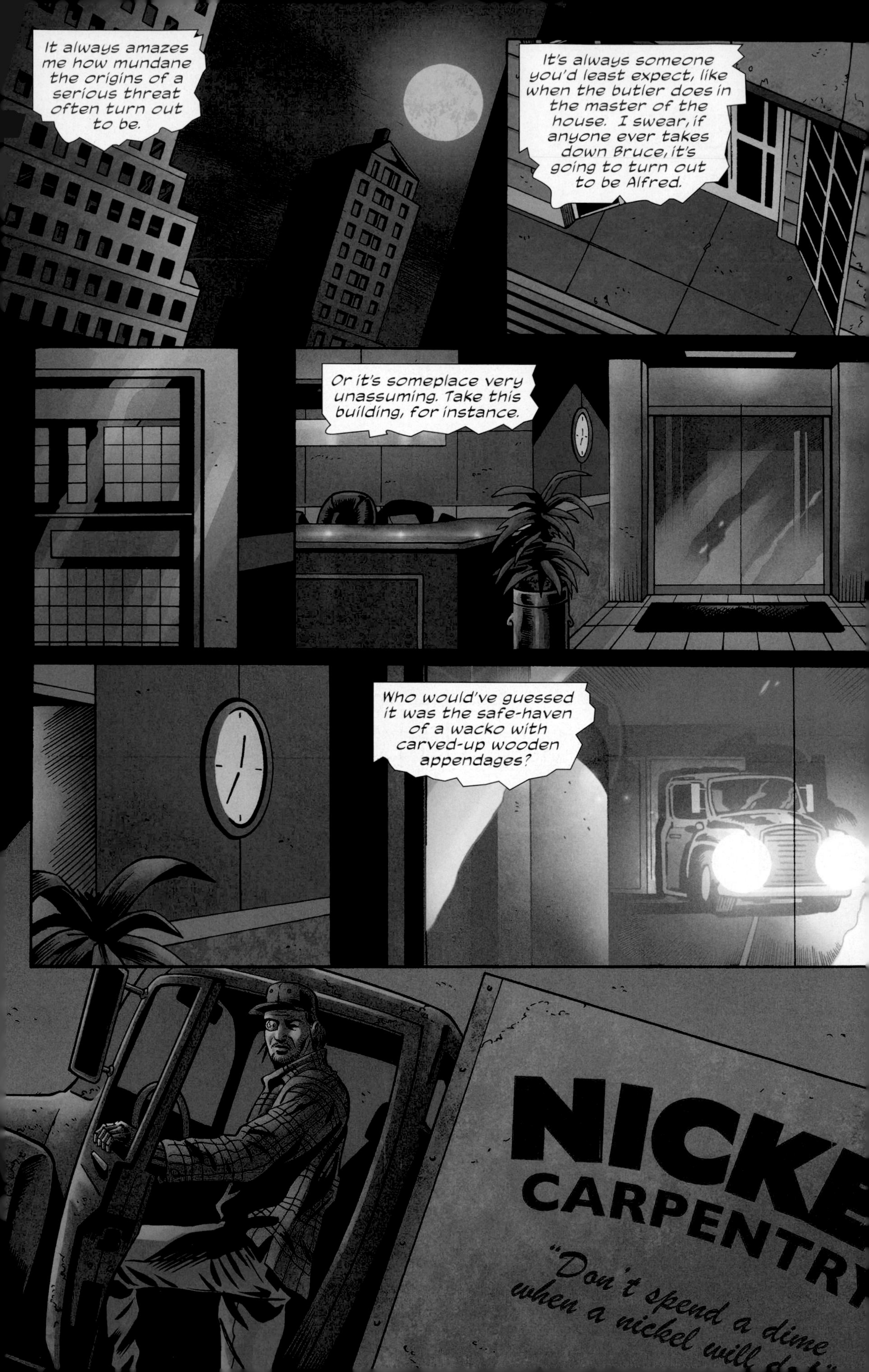
It always amazes me how mundane the origins of a serious threat often turn out to be.
It's always someone you'd least expect, like when the butler does in the master of the house. I swear, if anyone ever takes down Bruce, it's going to turn out to be Alfred.
Or it's someplace very unassuming. Take this building, for instance.
Who would've guessed it was the safe-haven of a wacko with carved-up wooden appendages?
NICKE
CARPENTRY
"Don't spend a dime
when a nickel will d

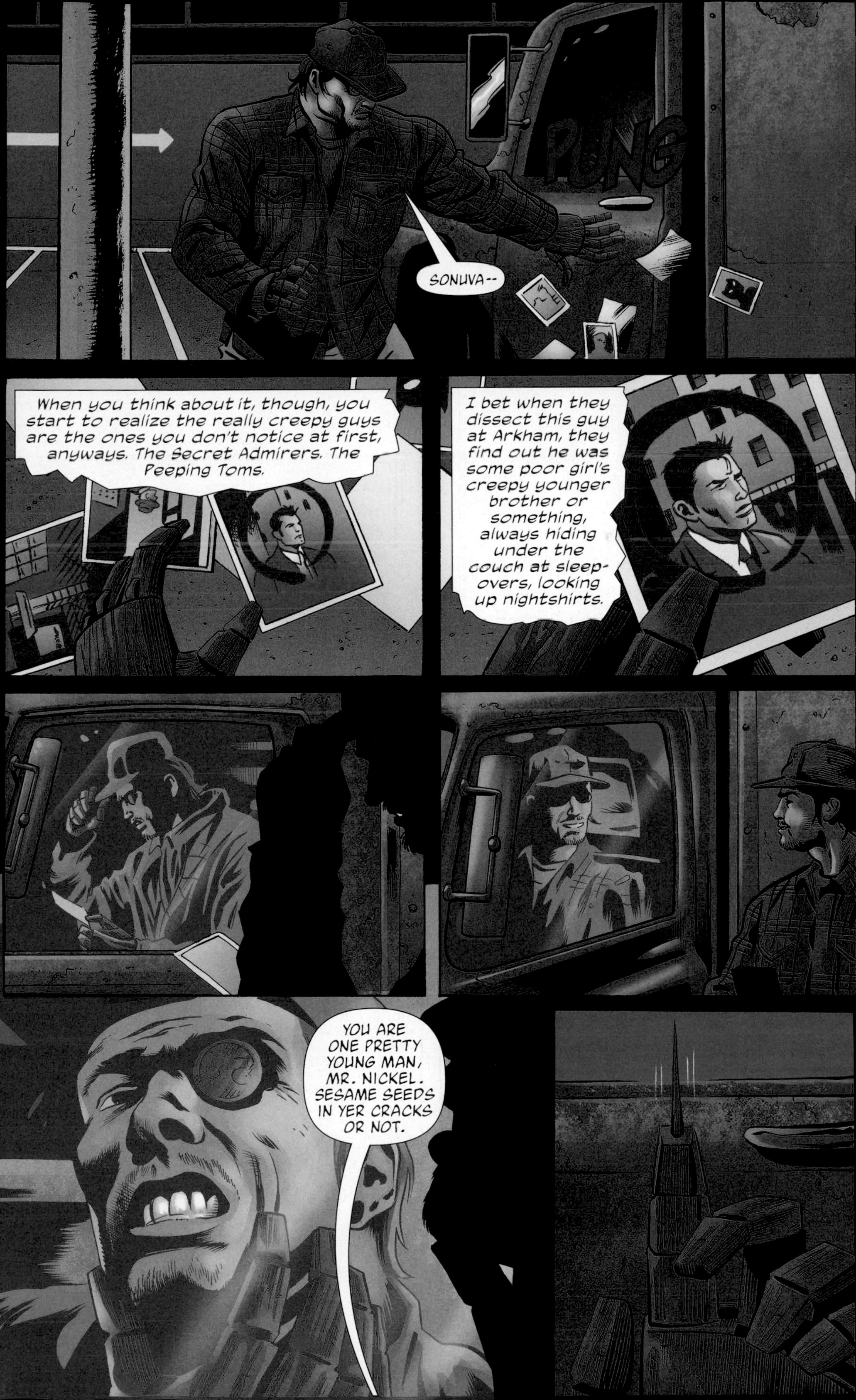
PUNG
SONUVA--
When you think about it, though, you start to realize the really creepy guys are the ones you don't notice at first, anyways. The Secret Admirers. The Peeping Toms.
I bet when they dissect this guy at Arkham, they find out he was some poor girl's creepy younger brother or something, always hiding under the couch at sleep-overs, looking up nightshirts.
YOU ARE ONE PRETTY YOUNG MAN, MR. NICKEL. SESAME SEEDS IN YER CRACKS OR NOT.

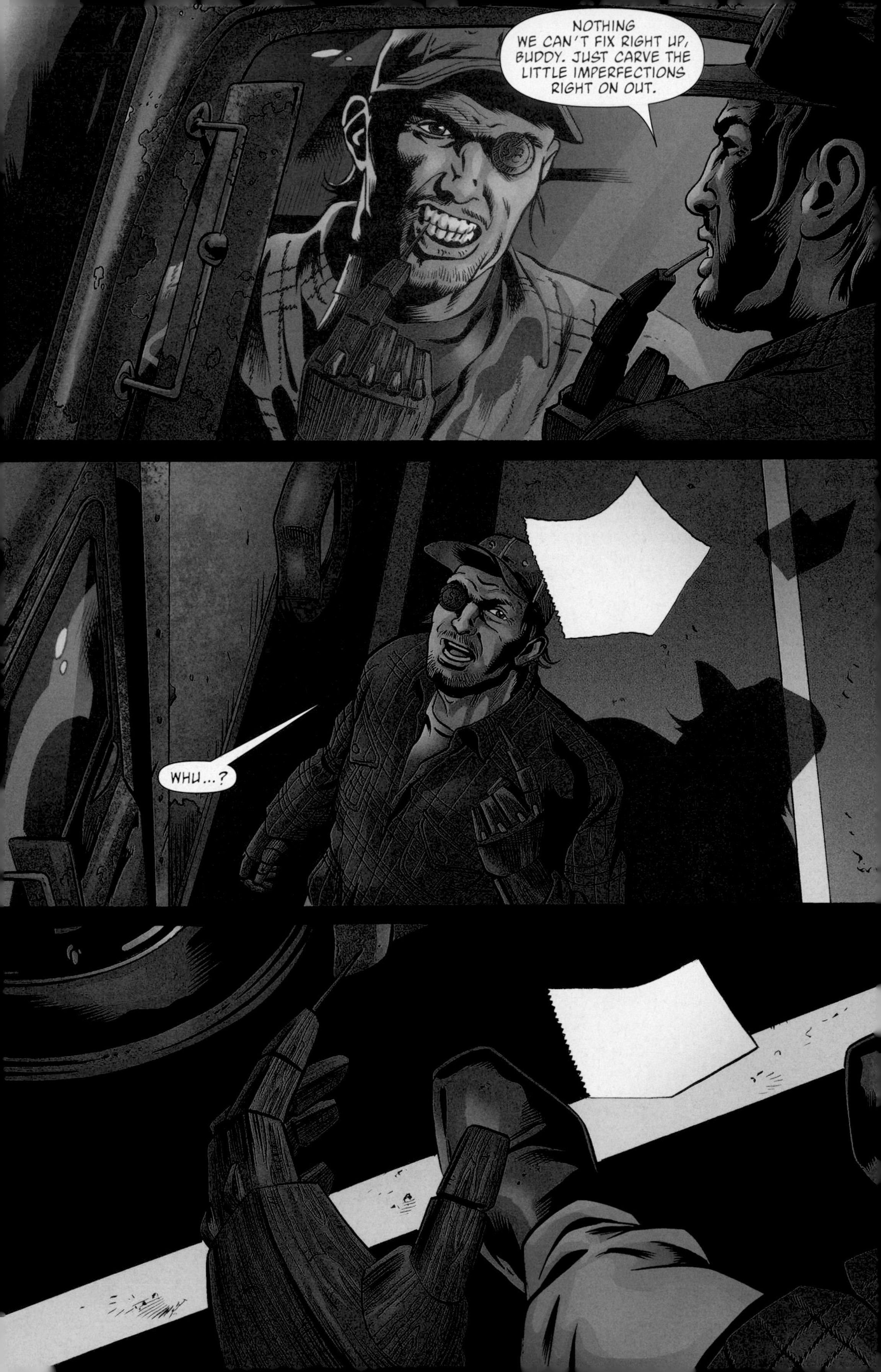
NOTHING WE CAN'T FIX RIGHT UP, BUDDY. JUST CARVE THE LITTLE IMPERFECTIONS RIGHT ON OUT.
WHU...?

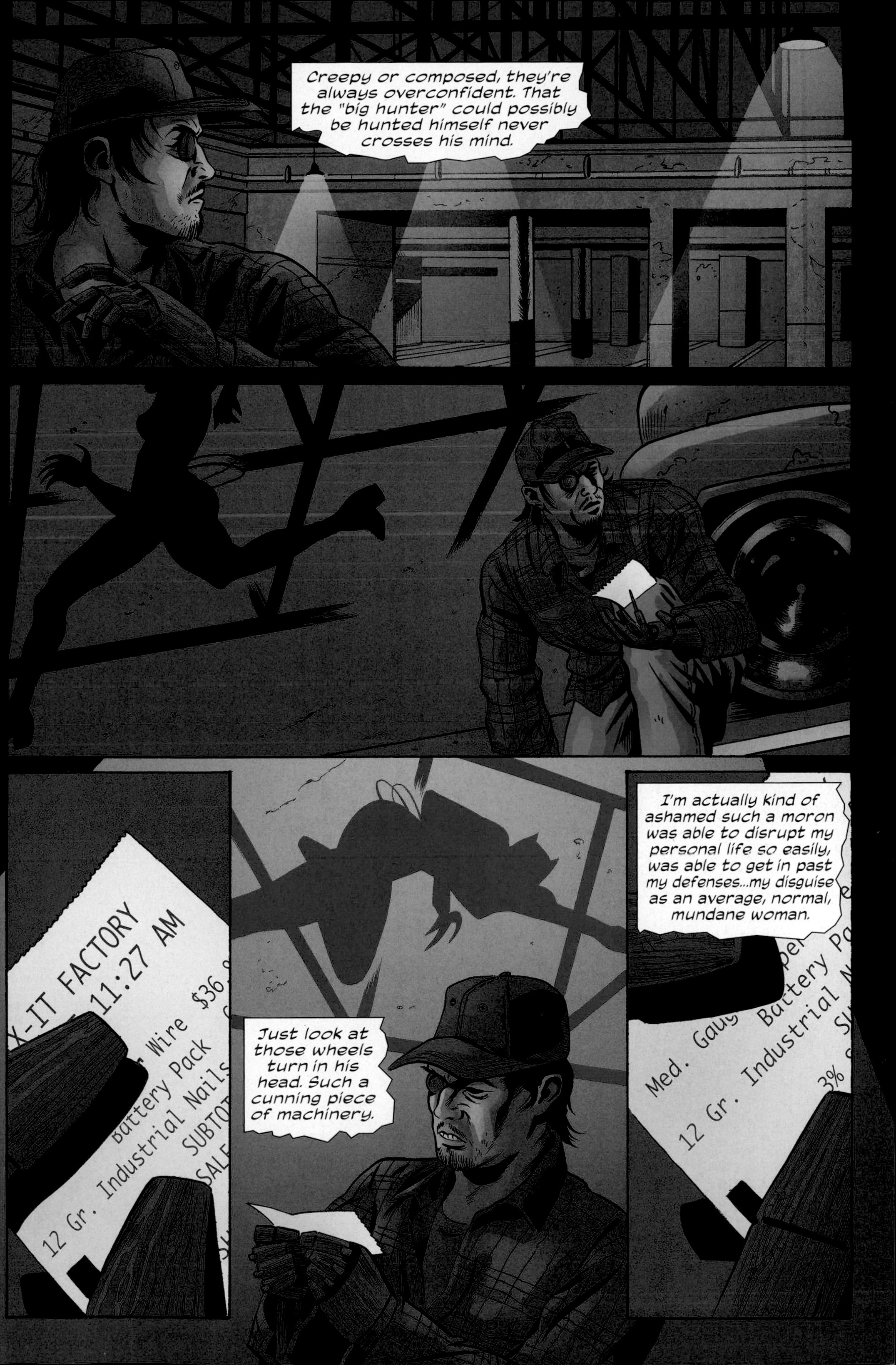
Creepy or composed, they're always overconfident. That the "big hunter" could possibly be hunted himself never crosses his mind.
X-IT FACTORY
11:27 AM
Wire $36.
Battery Pack
12 Gr. Industrial Nails
Just look at those wheels turn in his head. Such a cunning piece of machinery.
I'm actually kind of ashamed such a moron was able to disrupt my personal life so easily, was able to get in past my defenses...my disguise as an average, normal, mundane woman.
Med.
Battery
12 Gr. Industrial
3%

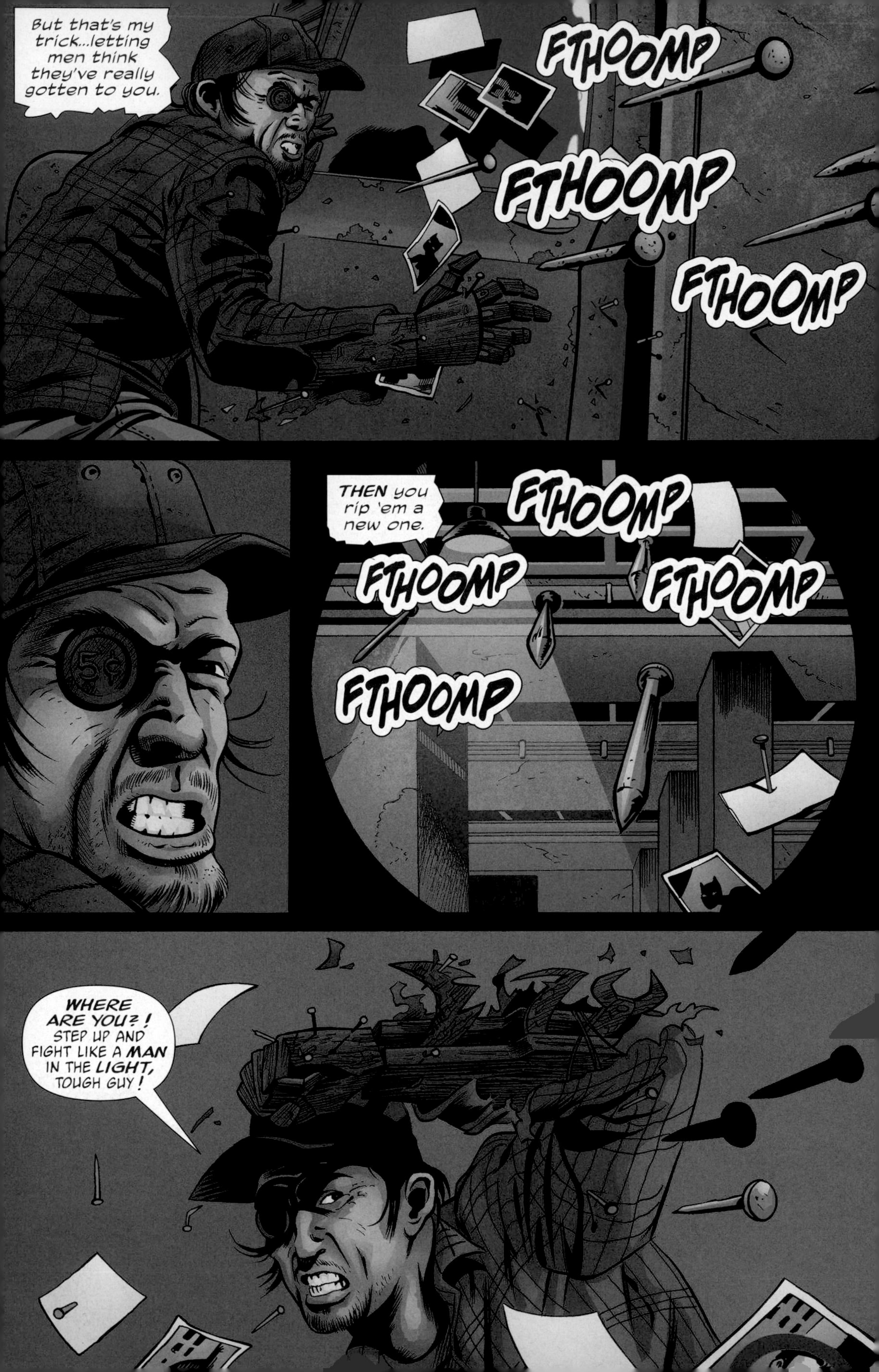
But that's my trick...letting men think they've really gotten to you.
FTHOOMP
FTHOOMP
FTHOOMP
THEN you rip 'em a new one.
FTHOOMP
FTHOOMP
FTHOOMP
FTHOOMP
WHERE ARE YOU?! STEP UP AND FIGHT LIKE A MAN IN THE LIGHT, TOUGH GUY!

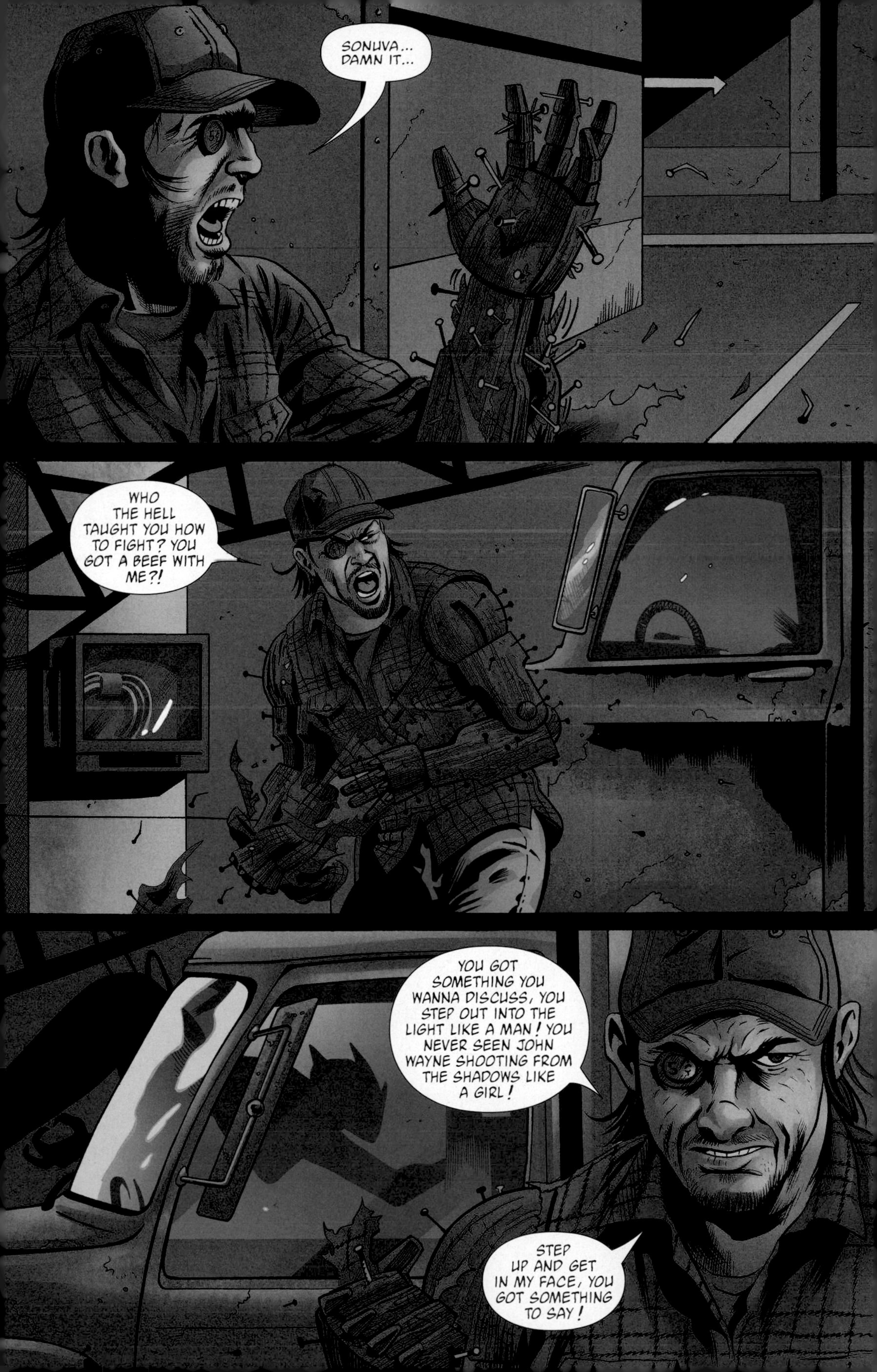
SONUVA... DAMN IT...
WHO THE HELL TAUGHT YOU HOW TO FIGHT? YOU GOT A BEEF WITH ME?!
YOU GOT SOMETHING YOU WANNA DISCUSS, YOU STEP OUT INTO THE LIGHT LIKE A MAN! YOU NEVER SEEN JOHN WAYNE SHOOTING FROM THE SHADOWS LIKE A GIRL!
STEP UP AND GET IN MY FACE, YOU GOT SOMETHING TO SAY!

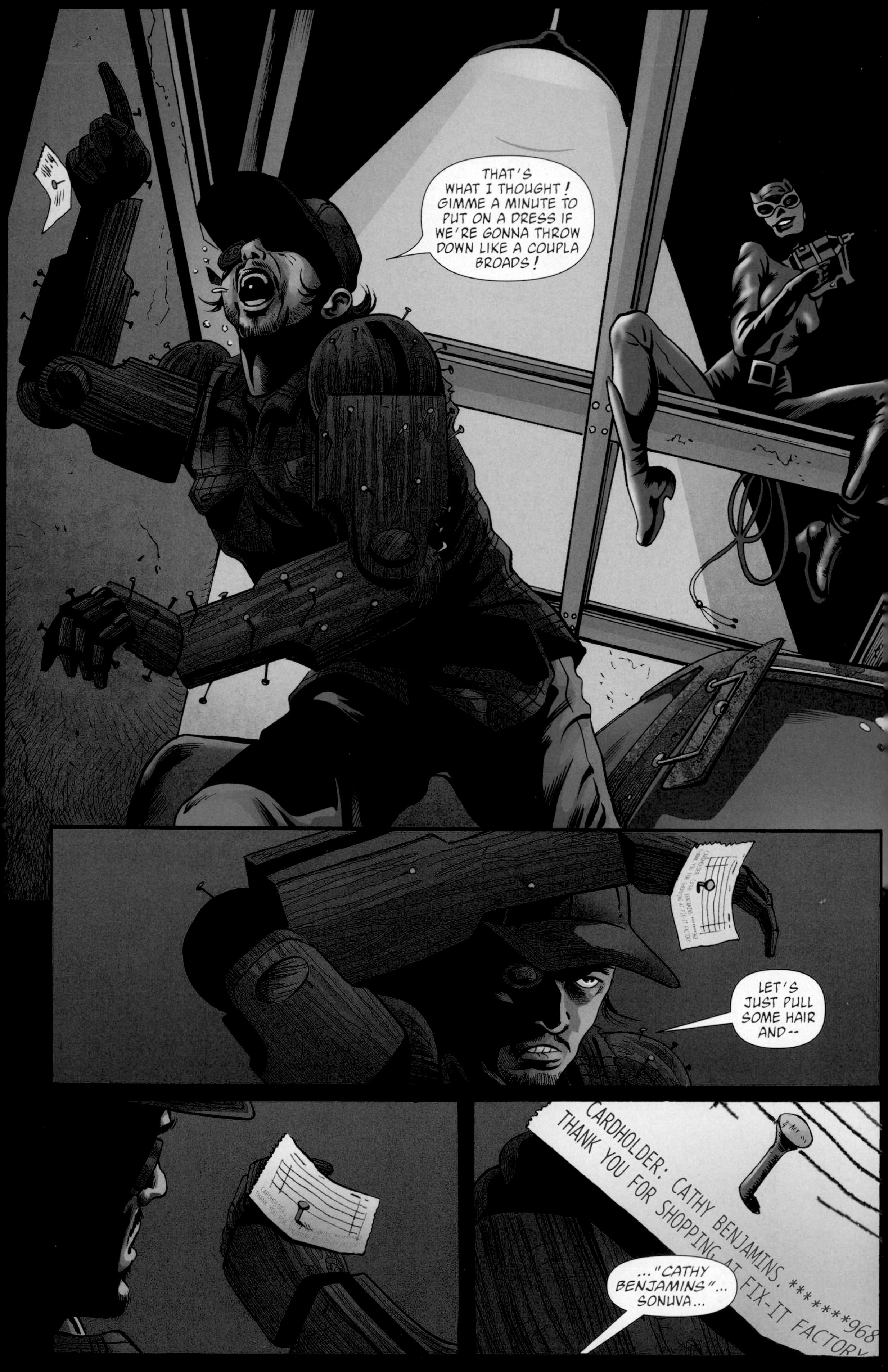
THAT'S WHAT I THOUGHT! GIMME A MINUTE TO PUT ON A DRESS IF WE'RE GONNA THROW DOWN LIKE A COUPLA BROADS!
LET'S JUST PULL SOME HAIR AND--
CARDHOLDER: CATHY BENJAMINS. ******968
THANK YOU FOR SHOPPING AT FIX-IT FACTORY
..."CATHY BENJAMINS"... SONUVA...

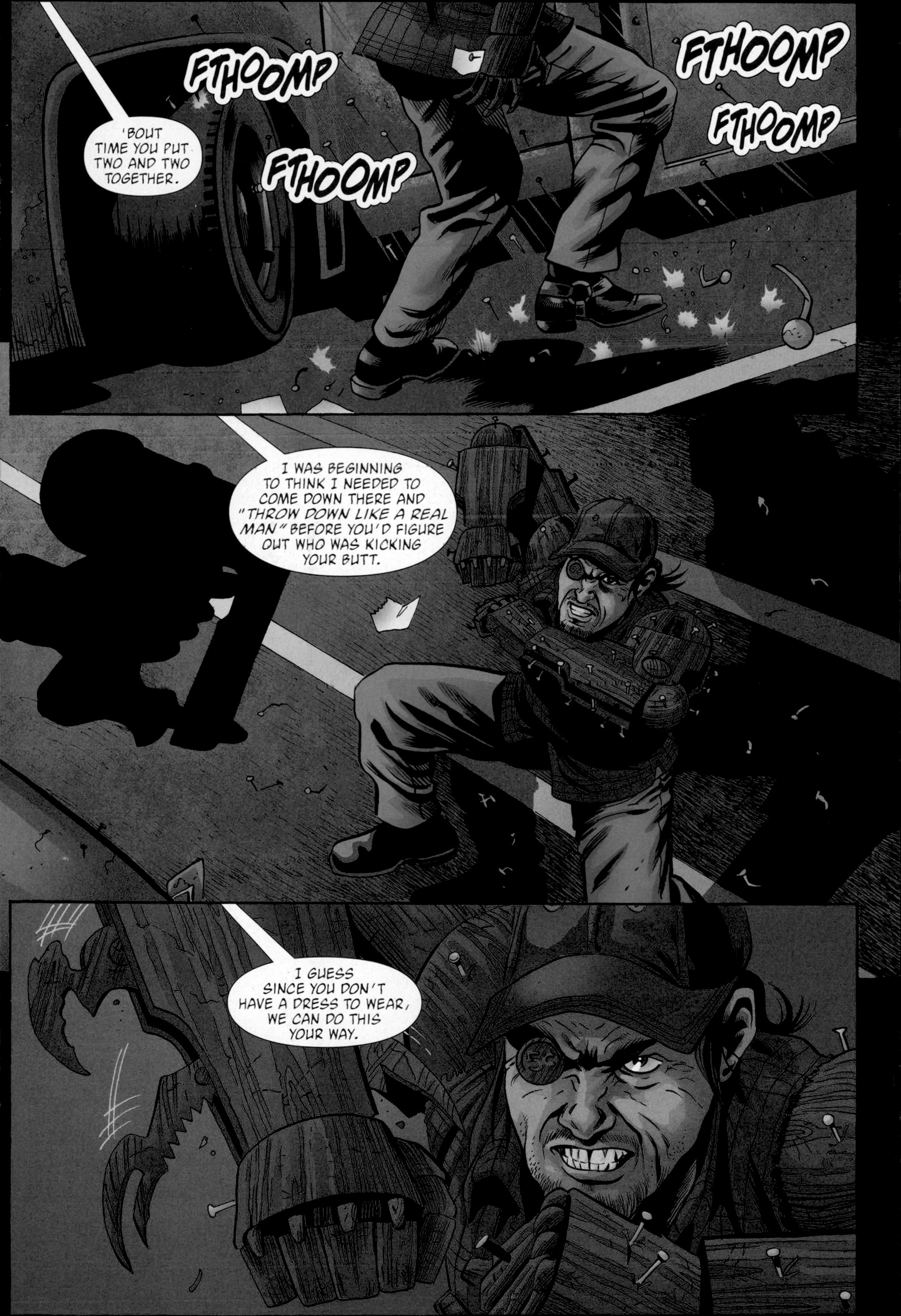
FTHOOMP
'BOUT TIME YOU PUT TWO AND TWO TOGETHER.
FTHOOMP
FTHOOMP
FTHOOMP
I WAS BEGINNING TO THINK I NEEDED TO COME DOWN THERE AND "THROW DOWN LIKE A REAL MAN" BEFORE YOU'D FIGURE OUT WHO WAS KICKING YOUR BUTT.
I GUESS SINCE YOU DON'T HAVE A DRESS TO WEAR, WE CAN DO THIS YOUR WAY.

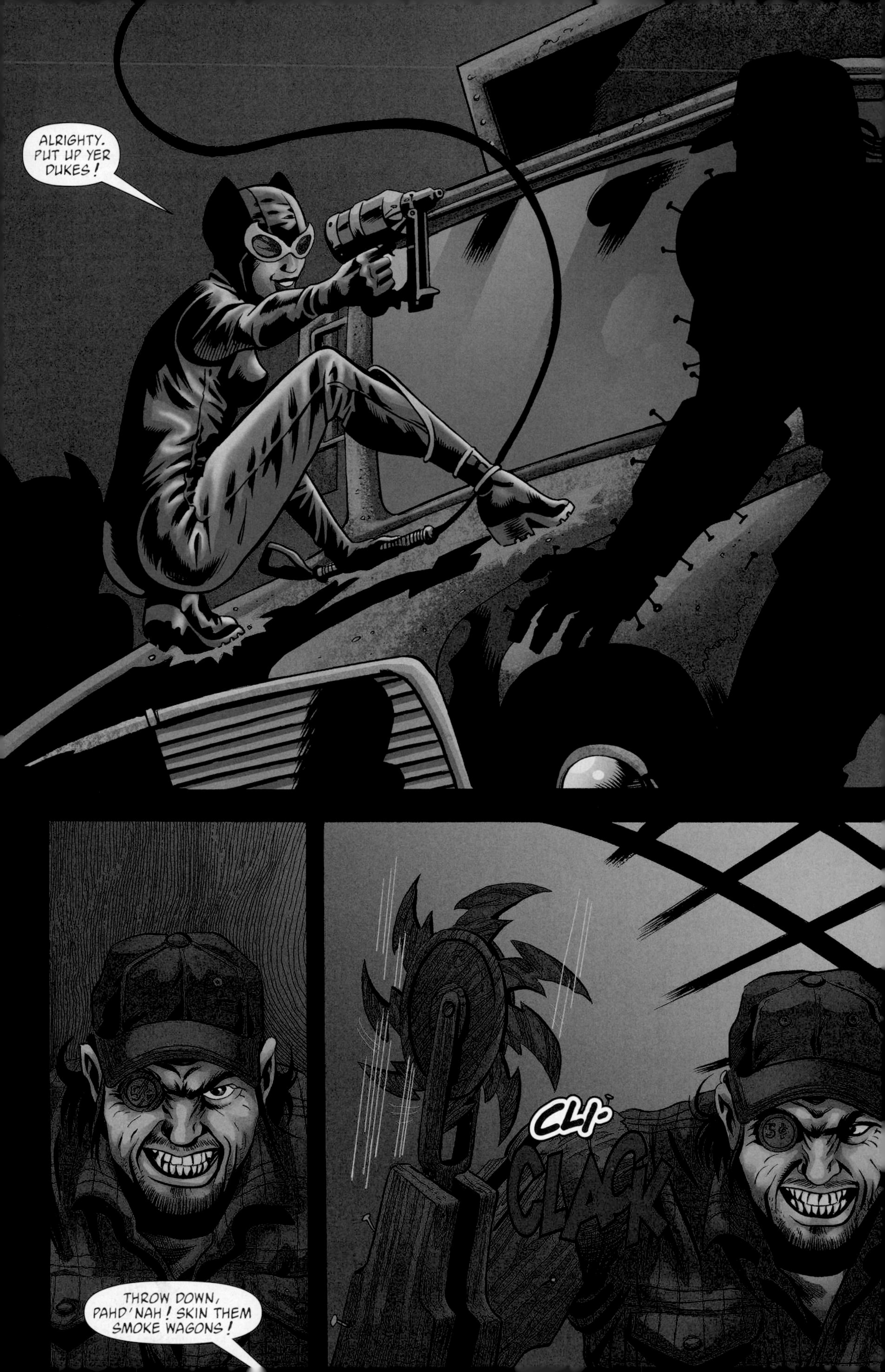
ALRIGHTY. PUT UP YER DUKES!
THROW DOWN, PAHD'NAH! SKIN THEM SMOKE WAGONS!
CLIP
CLACK

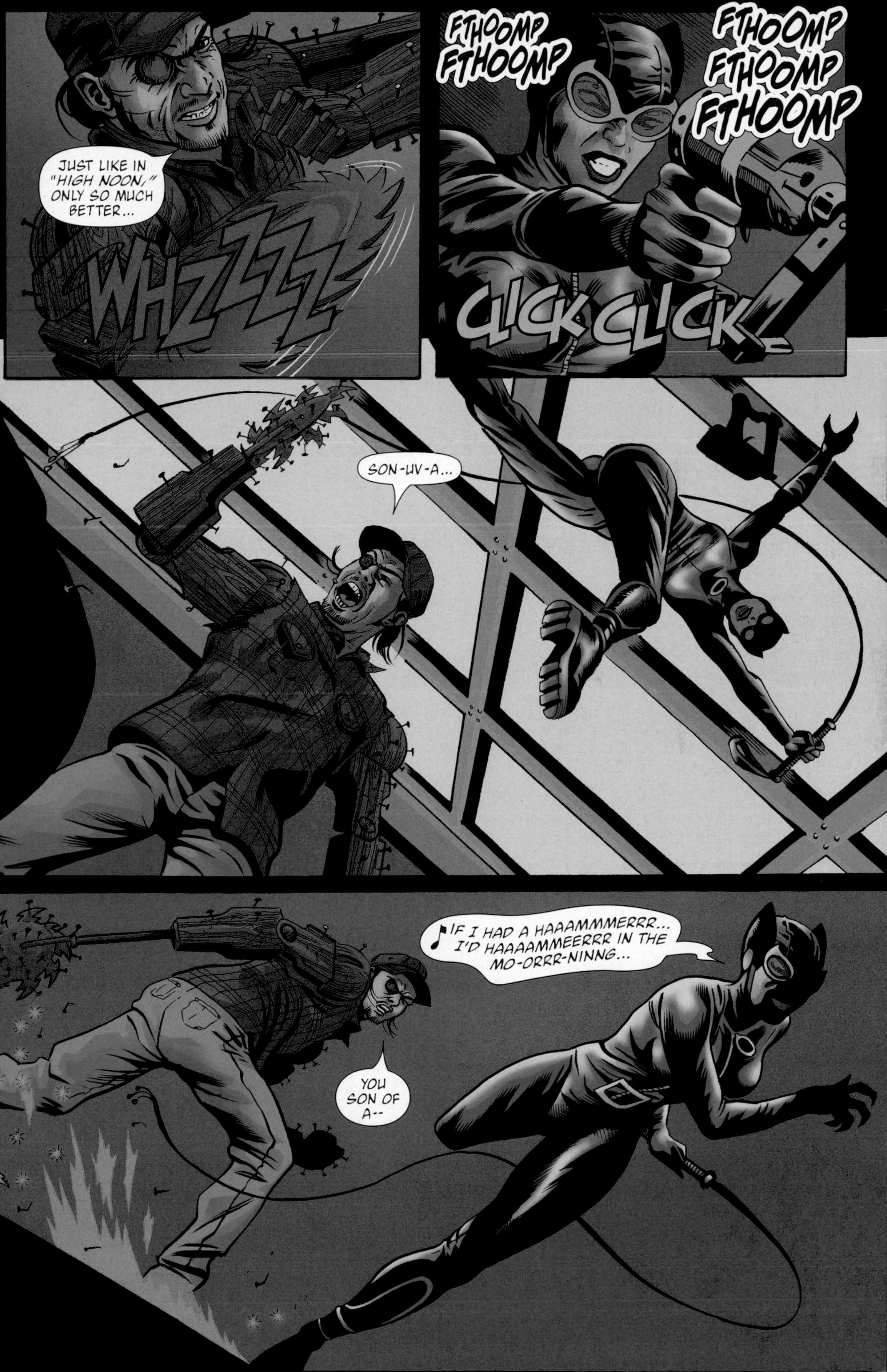
JUST LIKE IN "HIGH NOON," ONLY SO MUCH BETTER...
WHZZZZ
FTHOOMP FTHOOMP
FTHOOMP FTHOOMP FTHOOMP
CLICK CLICK
SON-UV-A...
♪ IF I HAD A HAAAMMMERRR... I'D HAAAAMMEERRR IN THE MO-ORRR-NINNG...
YOU SON OF A--

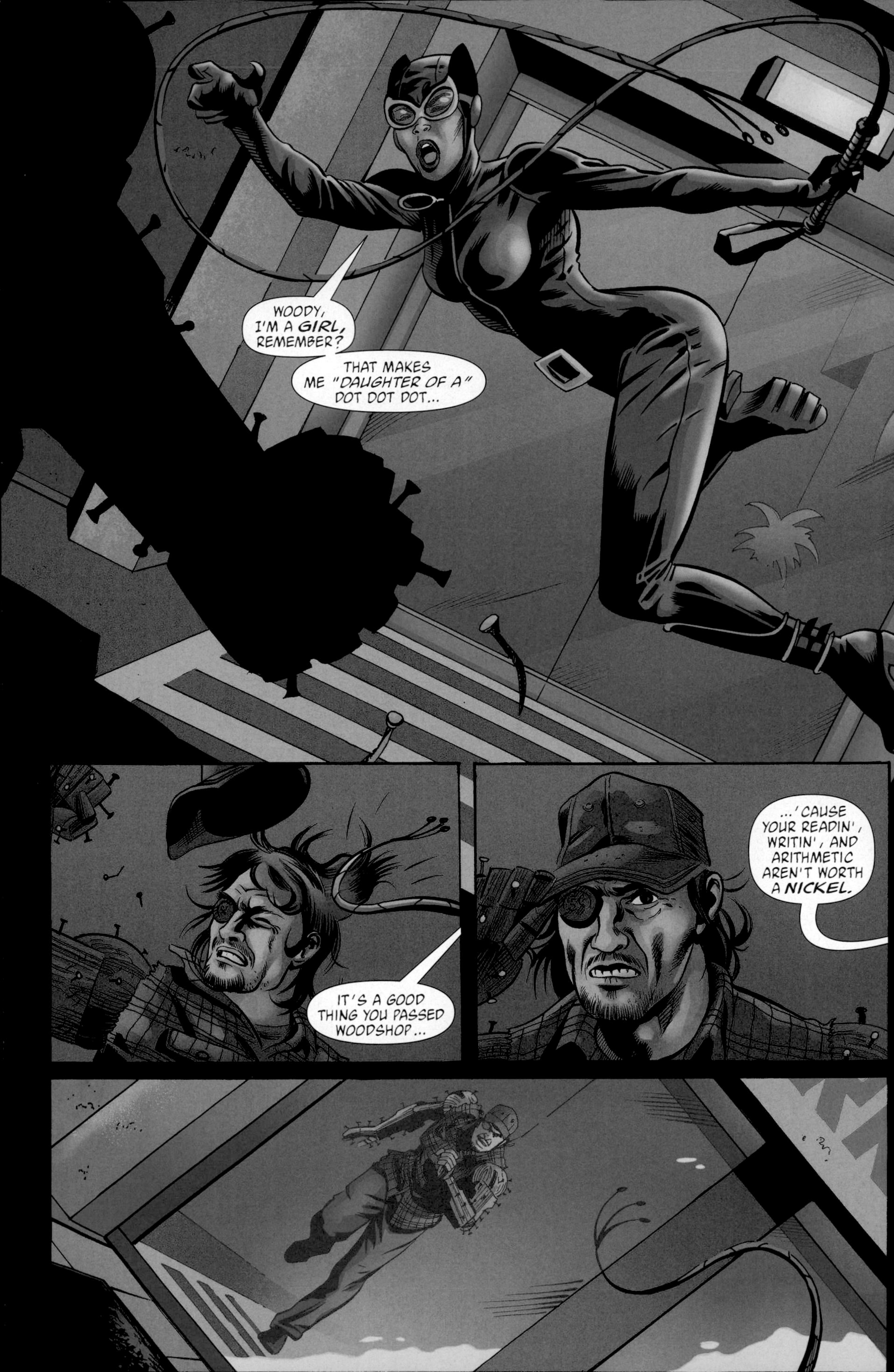
WOODY, I'M A GIRL, REMEMBER?
THAT MAKES ME "DAUGHTER OF A" DOT DOT DOT...
IT'S A GOOD THING YOU PASSED WOODSHOP...
...'CAUSE YOUR READIN', WRITIN', AND ARITHMETIC AREN'T WORTH A NICKEL.

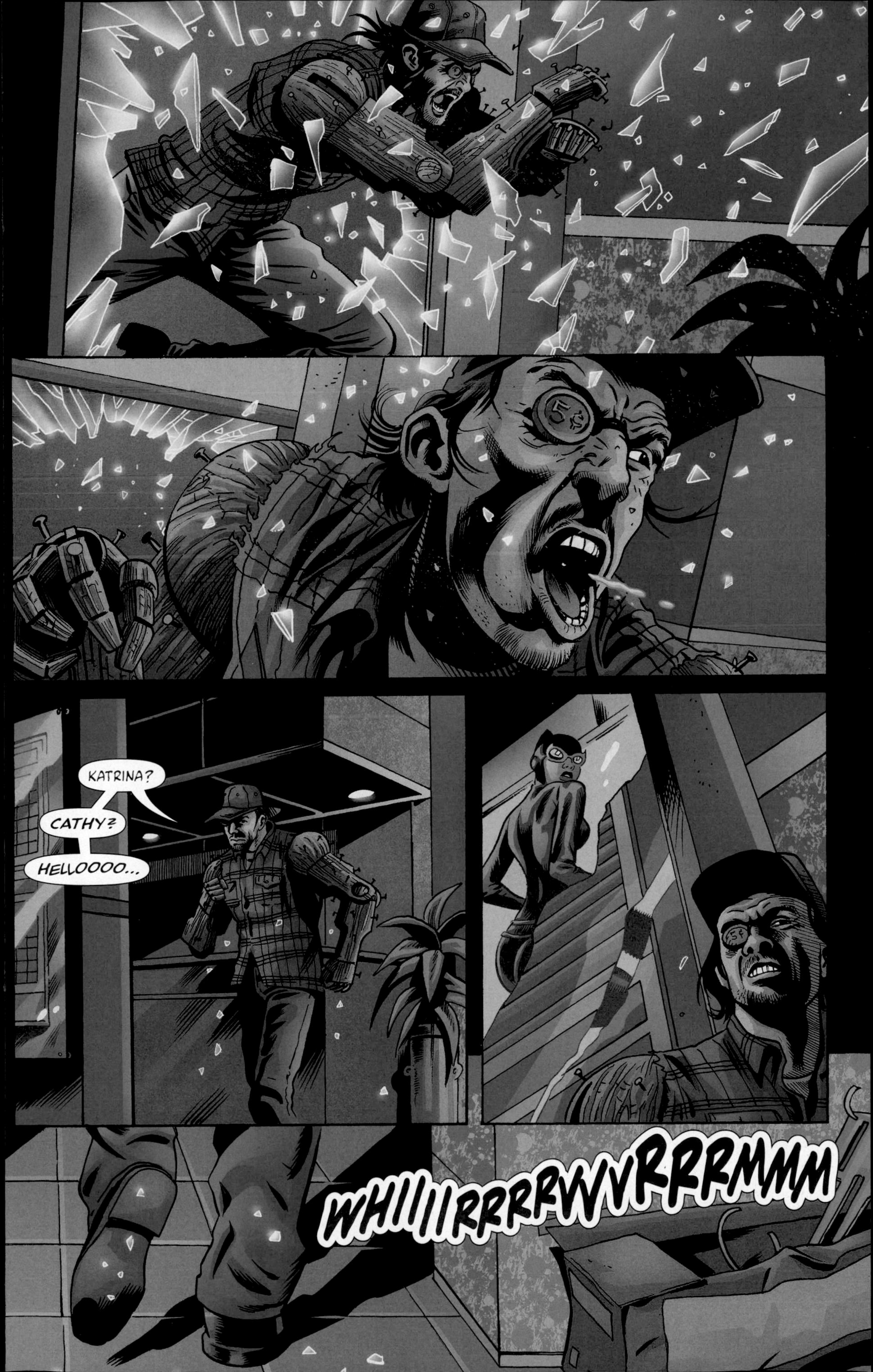
KATRINA?
CATHY?
HELLOOOO...
WHIIIIIRRRRVVVVRRRMMM

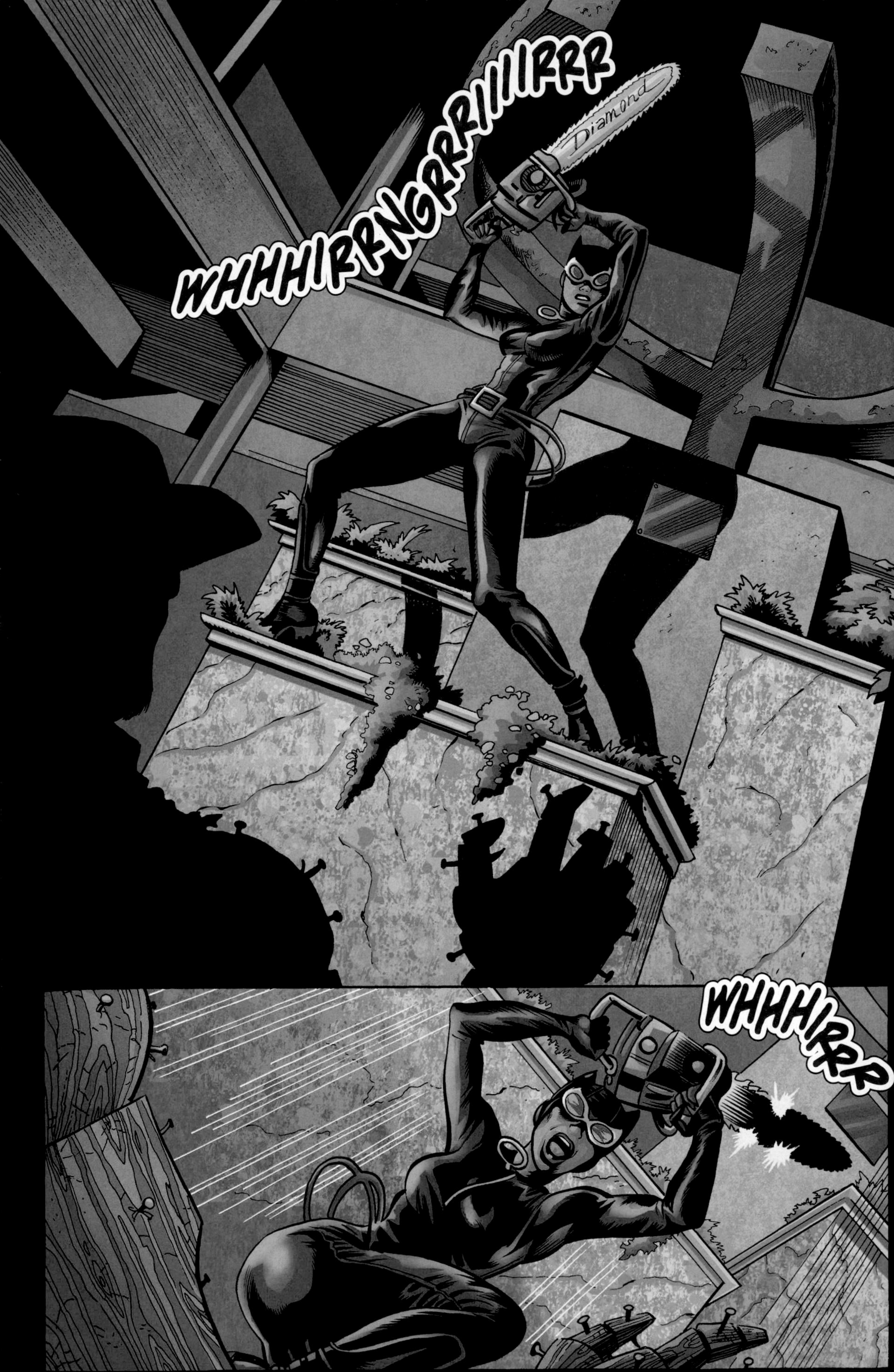
WHHHIRRNGRRIIIIRRR
Diamond
WHHHIRRR

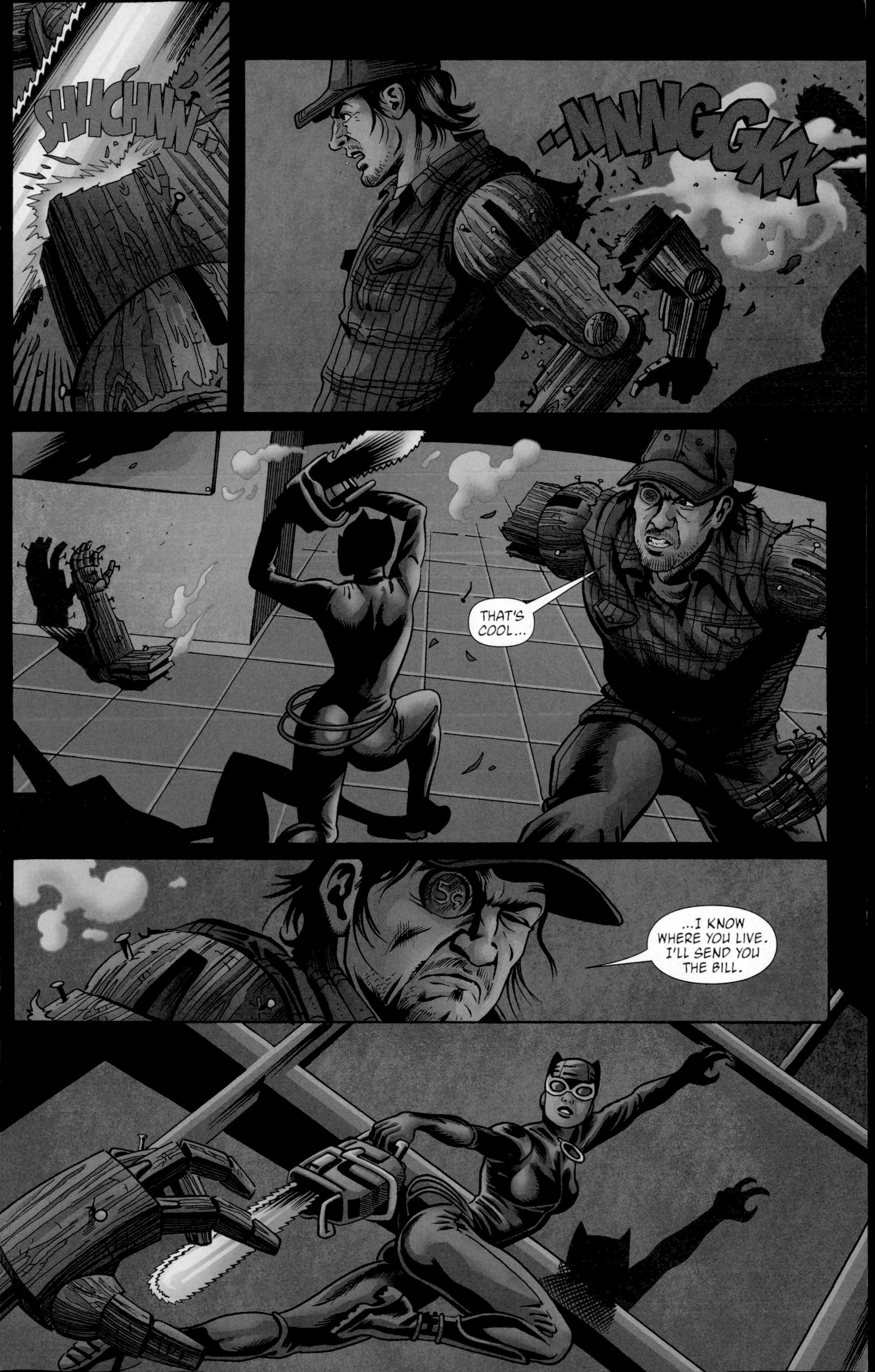
SHHCHNN..
..NNNGGKK
THAT'S COOL...
...I KNOW WHERE YOU LIVE. I'LL SEND YOU THE BILL.

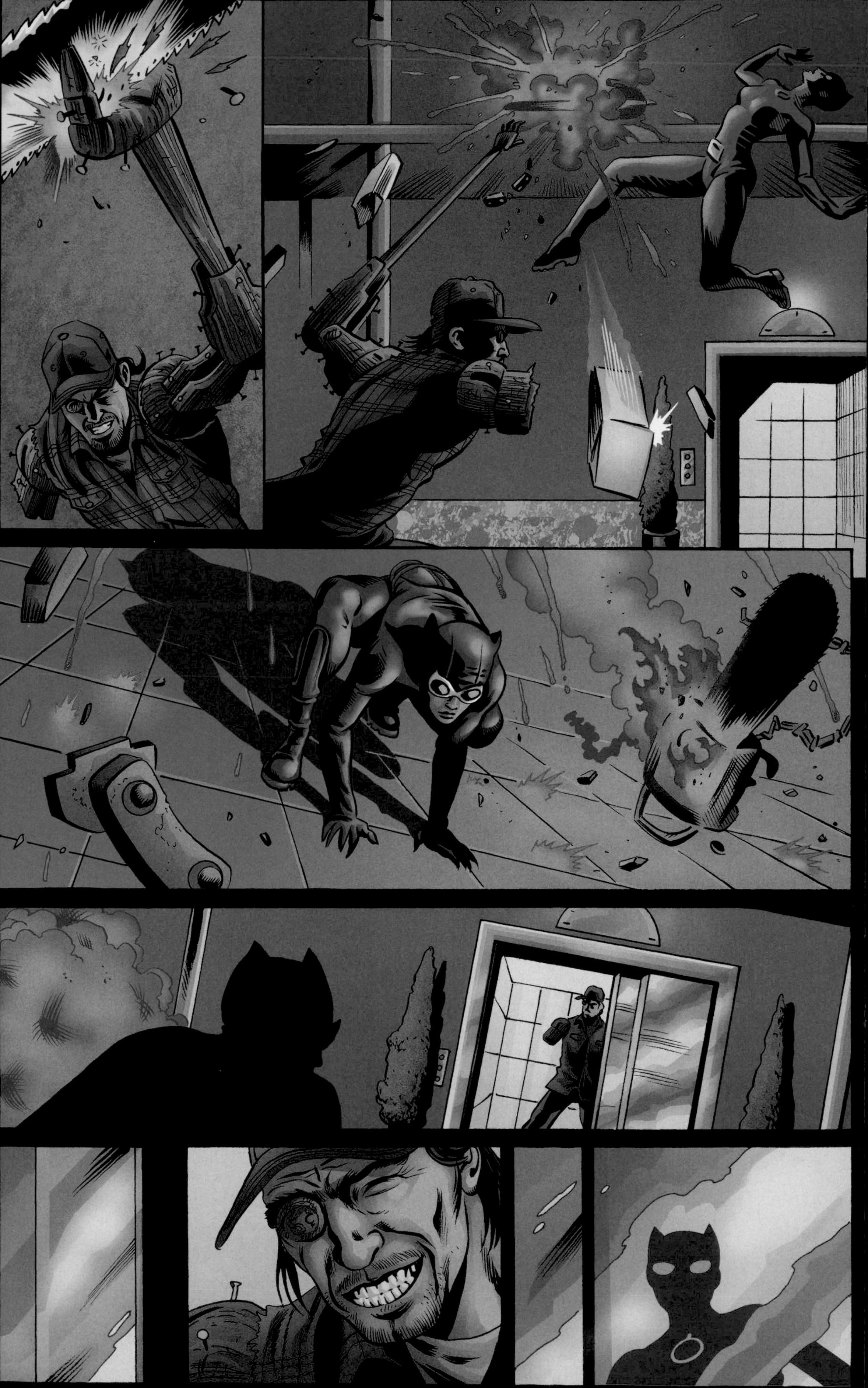

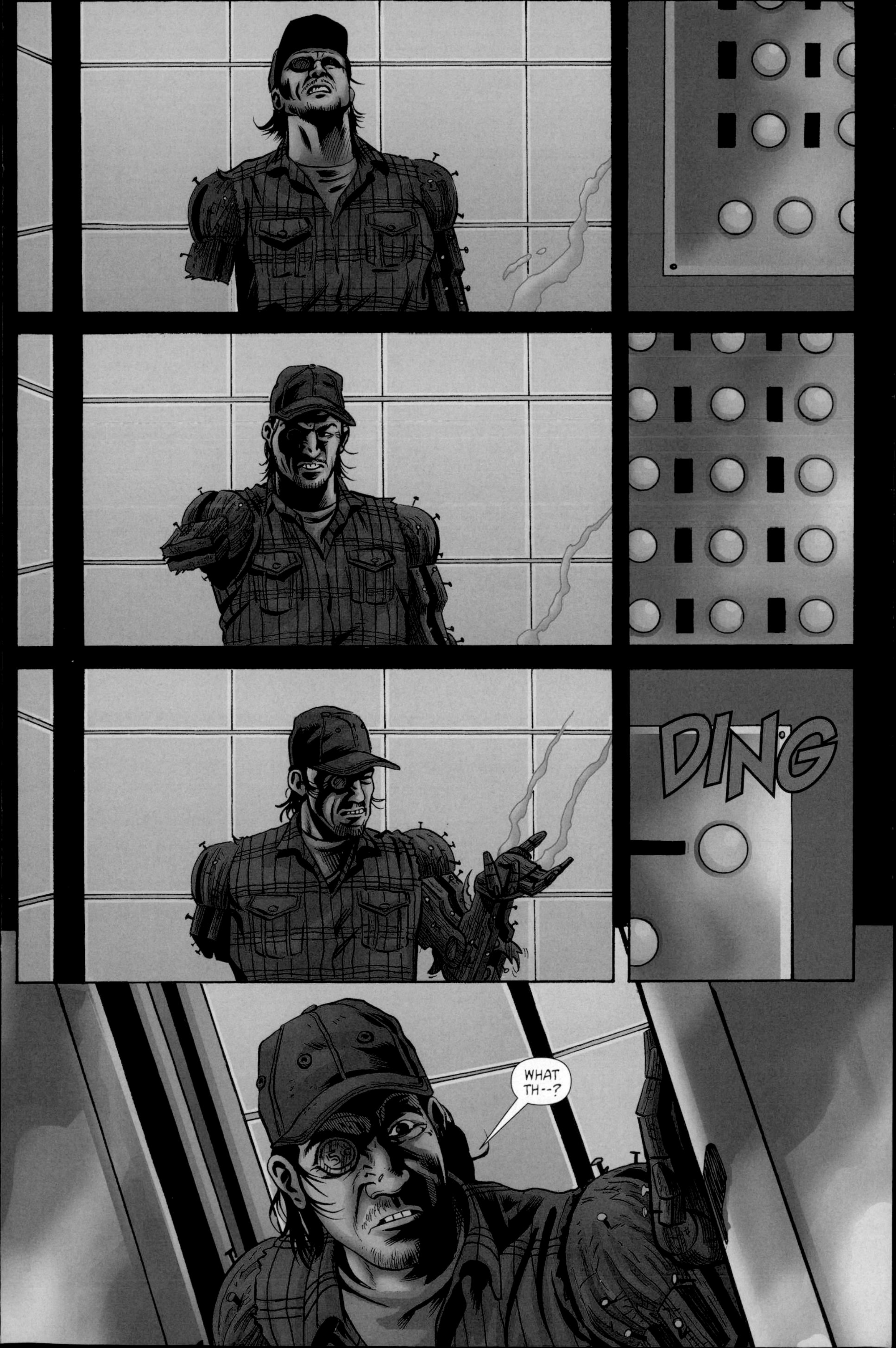
DING
WHAT TH--?

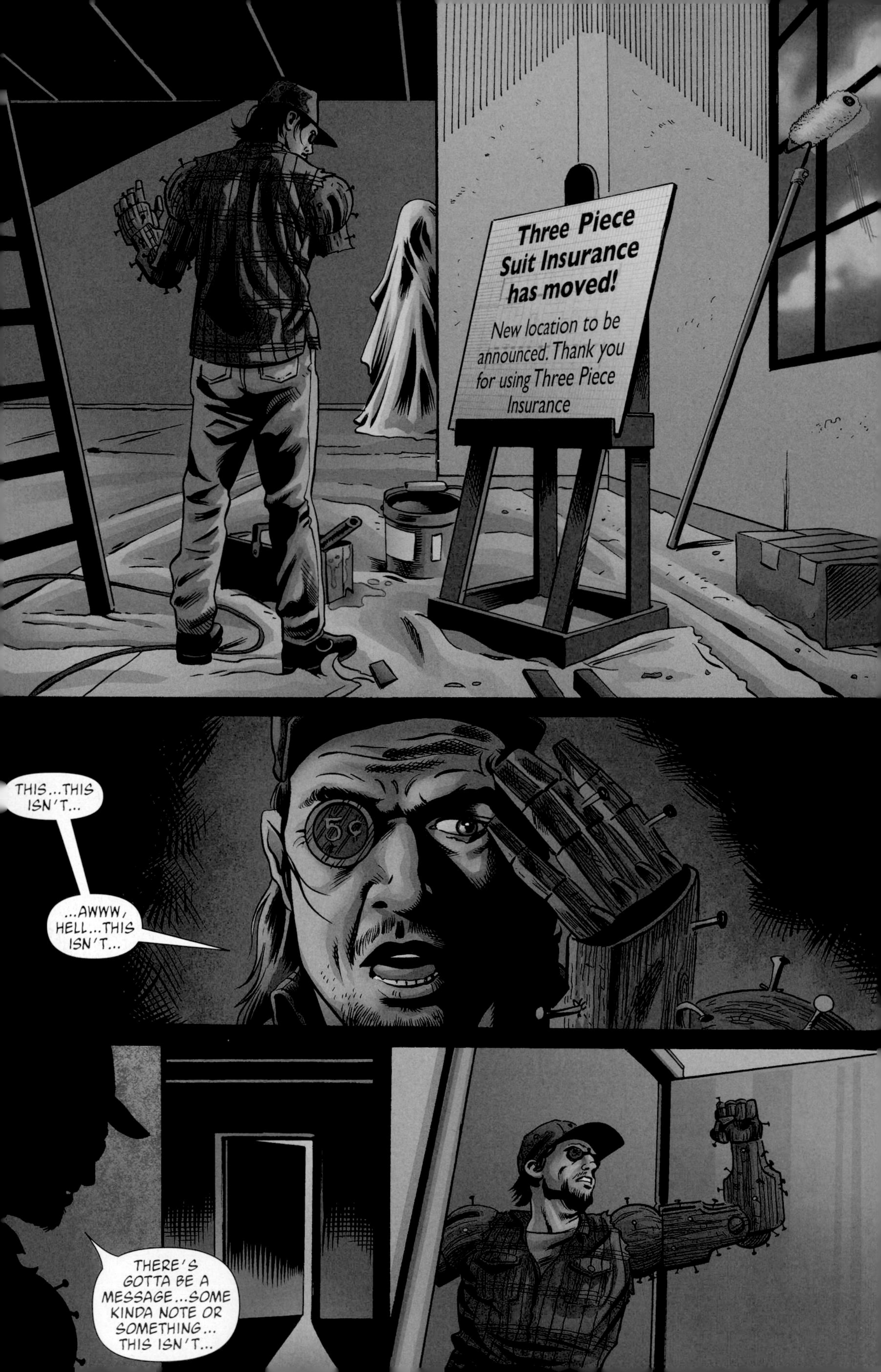

Three Piece
Suit Insurance
has moved!
New location to be announced. Thank you for using Three Piece Insurance
THIS...THIS ISN'T...
...AWWW, HELL...THIS ISN'T...
THERE'S GOTTA BE A MESSAGE...SOME KINDA NOTE OR SOMETHING... THIS ISN'T...

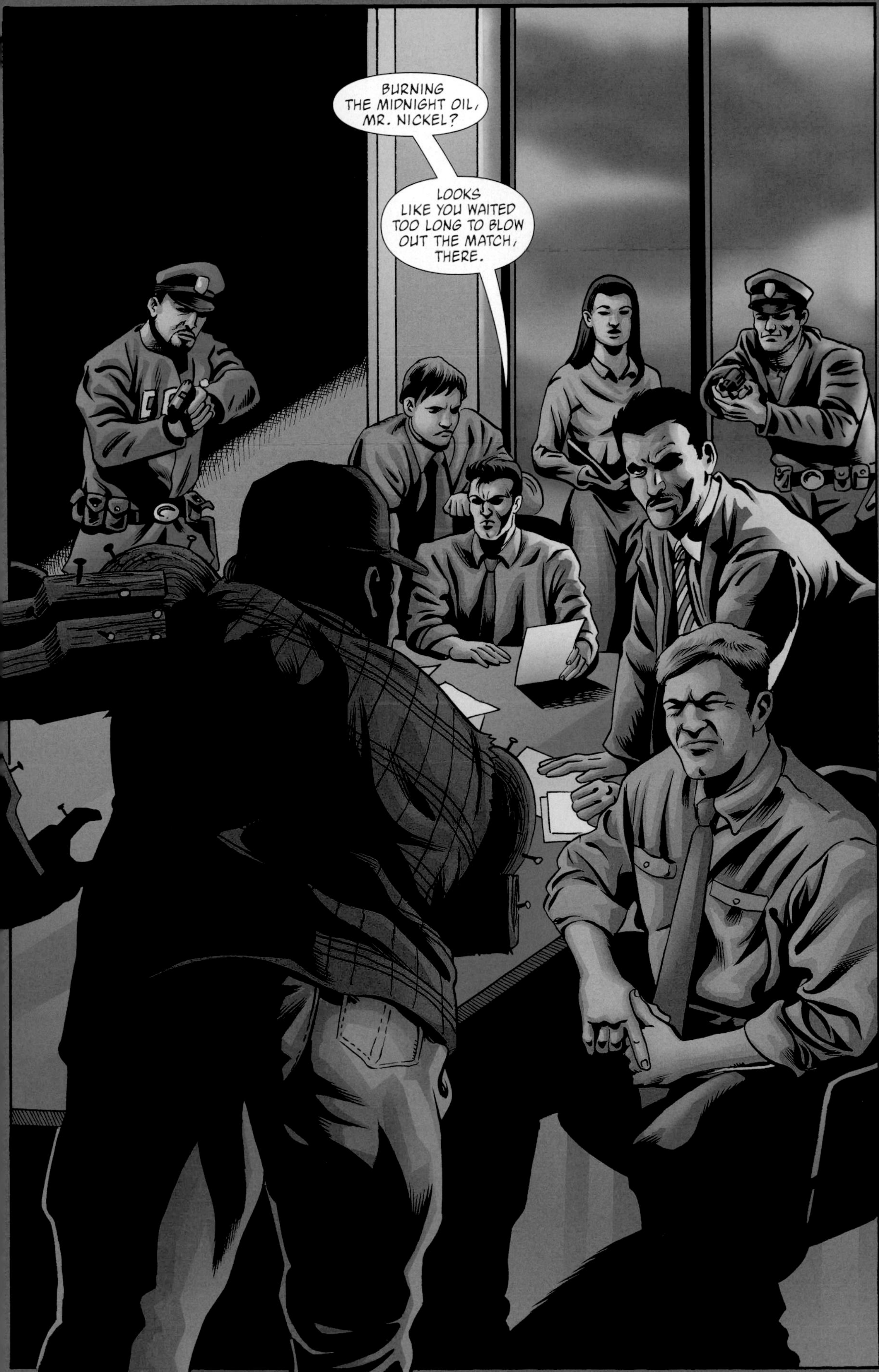
BURNING THE MIDNIGHT OIL, MR. NICKEL?
LOOKS LIKE YOU WAITED TOO LONG TO BLOW OUT THE MATCH, THERE.

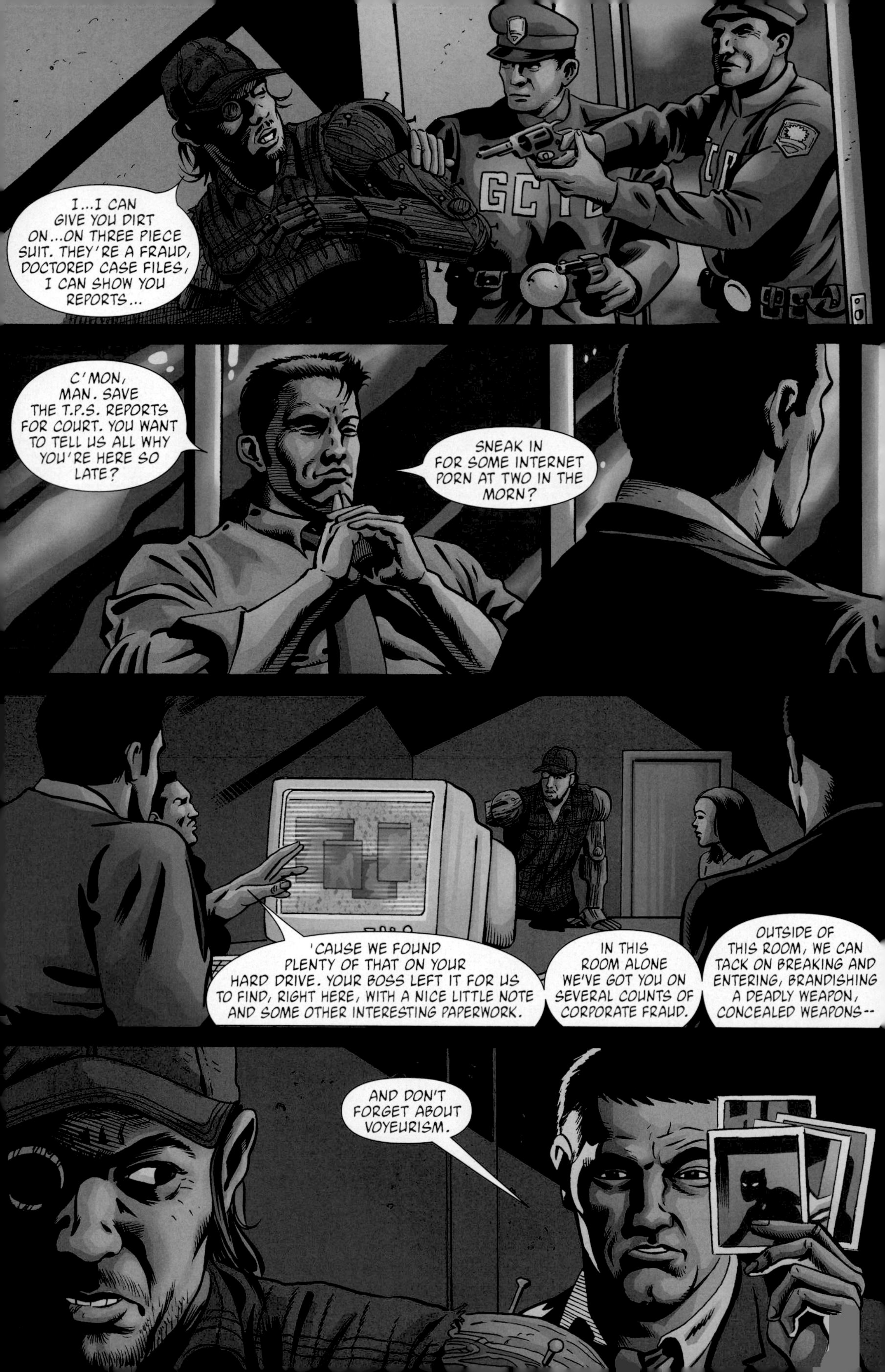
I...I CAN GIVE YOU DIRT ON...ON THREE PIECE SUIT. THEY'RE A FRAUD, DOCTORED CASE FILES, I CAN SHOW YOU REPORTS...
C'MON, MAN. SAVE THE T.P.S. REPORTS FOR COURT. YOU WANT TO TELL US ALL WHY YOU'RE HERE SO LATE?
SNEAK IN FOR SOME INTERNET PORN AT TWO IN THE MORN?
'CAUSE WE FOUND PLENTY OF THAT ON YOUR HARD DRIVE. YOUR BOSS LEFT IT FOR US TO FIND, RIGHT HERE, WITH A NICE LITTLE NOTE AND SOME OTHER INTERESTING PAPERWORK.
IN THIS ROOM ALONE WE'VE GOT YOU ON SEVERAL COUNTS OF CORPORATE FRAUD.
OUTSIDE OF THIS ROOM, WE CAN TACK ON BREAKING AND ENTERING, BRANDISHING A DEADLY WEAPON, CONCEALED WEAPONS--
AND DON'T FORGET ABOUT VOYEURISM.

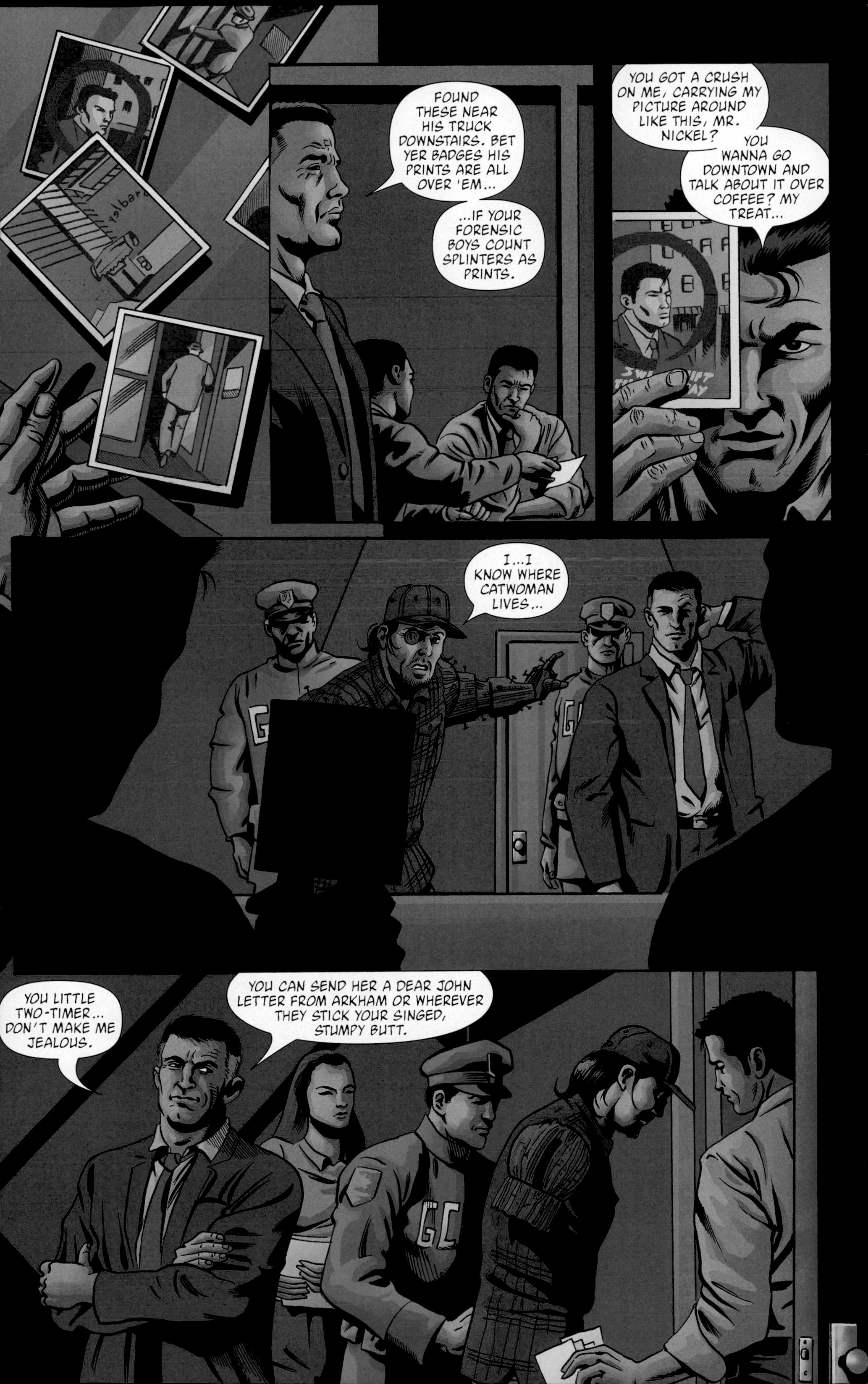
FOUND THESE NEAR HIS TRUCK DOWNSTAIRS. BET YER BADGES HIS PRINTS ARE ALL OVER 'EM...
...IF YOUR FORENSIC BOYS COUNT SPLINTERS AS PRINTS.
YOU GOT A CRUSH ON ME, CARRYING MY PICTURE AROUND LIKE THIS, MR. NICKEL?
YOU WANNA GO DOWNTOWN AND TALK ABOUT IT OVER COFFEE? MY TREAT...
I...I KNOW WHERE CATWOMAN LIVES...
YOU LITTLE TWO-TIMER... DON'T MAKE ME JEALOUS.
YOU CAN SEND HER A DEAR JOHN LETTER FROM ARKHAM OR WHEREVER THEY STICK YOUR SINGED, STUMPY BUTT.

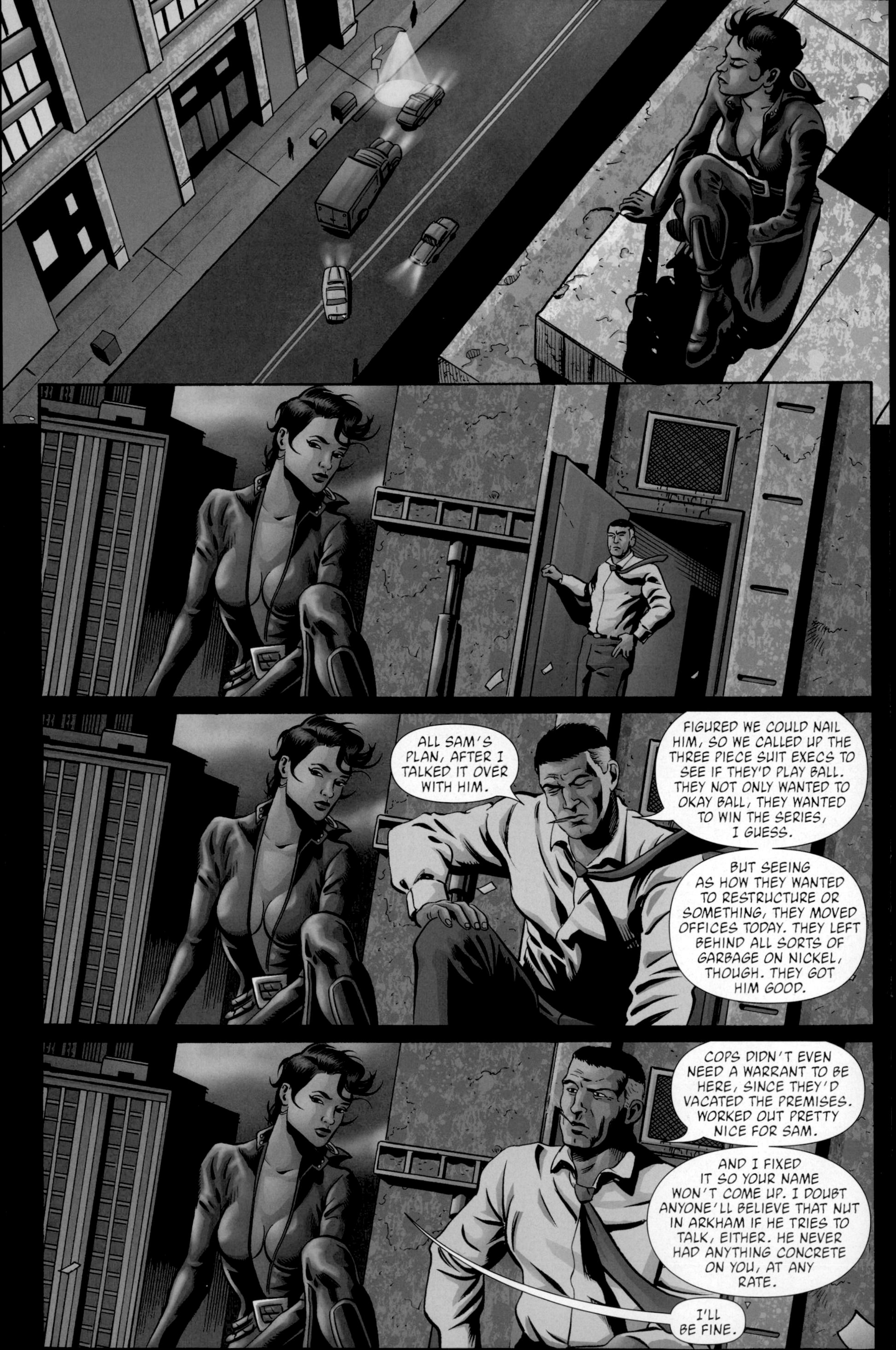
ALL SAM'S PLAN, AFTER I TALKED IT OVER WITH HIM.
FIGURED WE COULD NAIL HIM, SO WE CALLED UP THE THREE PIECE SUIT EXECS TO SEE IF THEY'D PLAY BALL. THEY NOT ONLY WANTED TO OKAY BALL, THEY WANTED TO WIN THE SERIES, I GUESS.
BUT SEEING AS HOW THEY WANTED TO RESTRUCTURE OR SOMETHING, THEY MOVED OFFICES TODAY. THEY LEFT BEHIND ALL SORTS OF GARBAGE ON NICKEL, THOUGH. THEY GOT HIM GOOD.
COPS DIDN'T EVEN NEED A WARRANT TO BE HERE, SINCE THEY'D VACATED THE PREMISES. WORKED OUT PRETTY NICE FOR SAM.
AND I FIXED IT SO YOUR NAME WON'T COME UP. I DOUBT ANYONE'LL BELIEVE THAT NUT IN ARKHAM IF HE TRIES TO TALK, EITHER. HE NEVER HAD ANYTHING CONCRETE ON YOU, AT ANY RATE.
I'LL BE FINE.

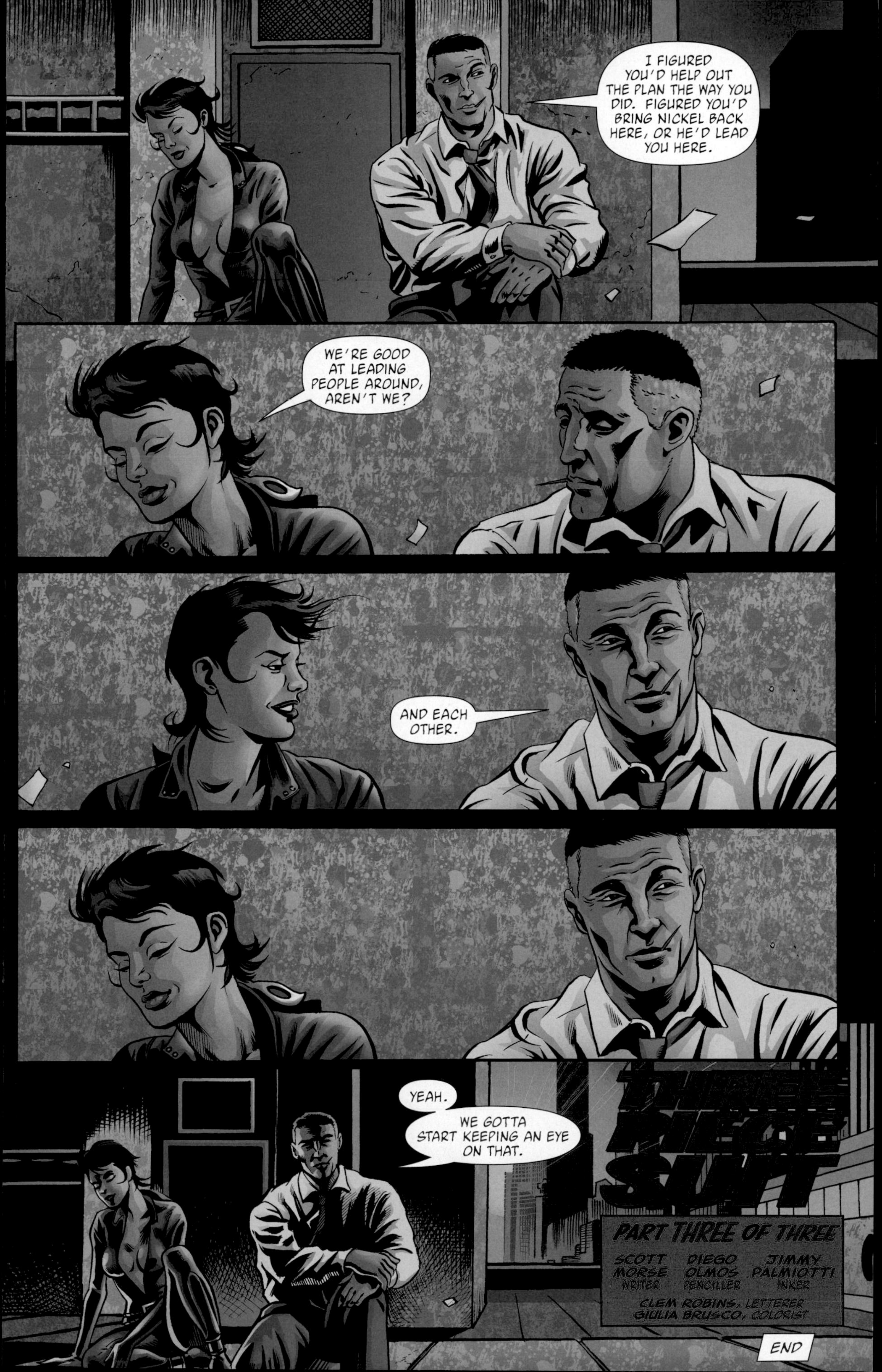
I FIGURED YOU'D HELP OUT THE PLAN THE WAY YOU DID. FIGURED YOU'D BRING NICKEL BACK HERE, OR HE'D LEAD YOU HERE.
WE'RE GOOD AT LEADING PEOPLE AROUND, AREN'T WE?
AND EACH OTHER.
YEAH.
WE GOTTA START KEEPING AN EYE ON THAT.
THREE PIECE SUIT
PART THREE OF THREE
SCOTT MORSE WRITER
DIEGO OLMOS PENCILLER
JIMMY PALMIOTTI INKER
CLEM ROBINS, LETTERER
GIULIA BRUSCO, COLORIST
END

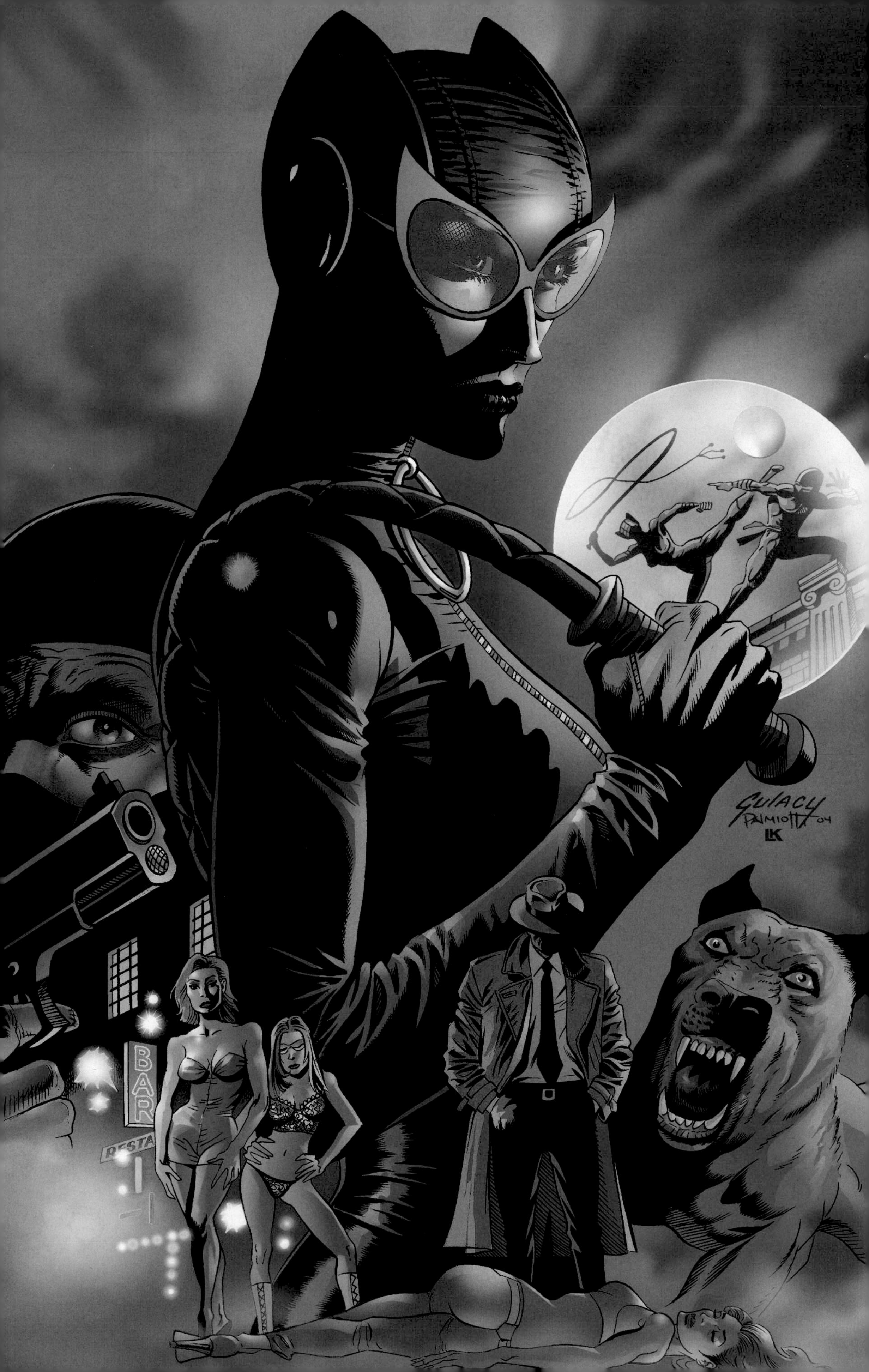
GULACY
PALMIOTTI '04
LK
BAR
RESTA

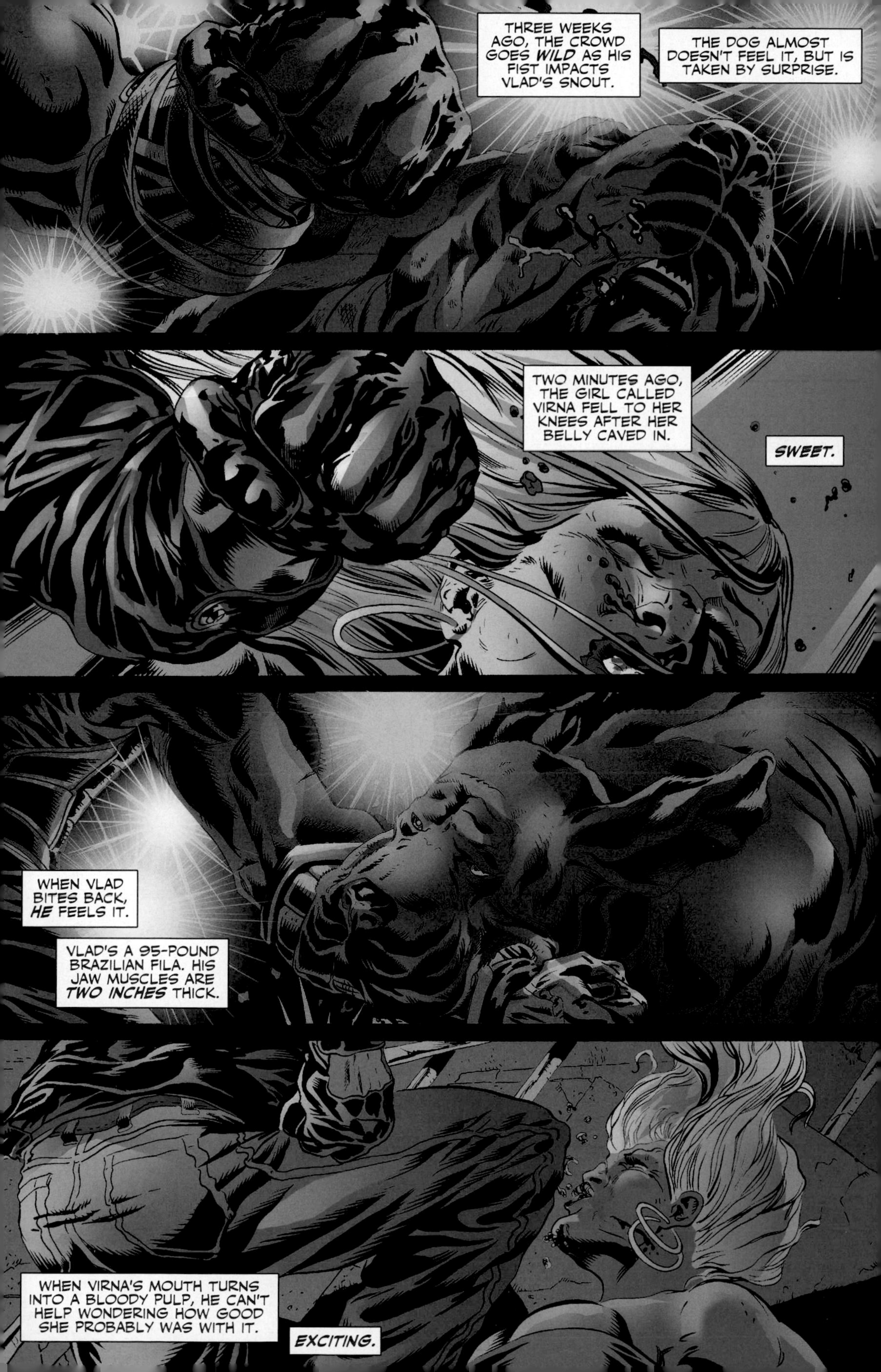
THREE WEEKS AGO, THE CROWD GOES WILD AS HIS FIST IMPACTS VLAD'S SNOUT.
THE DOG ALMOST DOESN'T FEEL IT, BUT IS TAKEN BY SURPRISE.
TWO MINUTES AGO, THE GIRL CALLED VIRNA FELL TO HER KNEES AFTER HER BELLY CAVED IN.
SWEET.
WHEN VLAD BITES BACK, HE FEELS IT.
VLAD'S A 95-POUND BRAZILIAN FILA. HIS JAW MUSCLES ARE TWO INCHES THICK.
WHEN VIRNA'S MOUTH TURNS INTO A BLOODY PULP, HE CAN'T HELP WONDERING HOW GOOD SHE PROBABLY WAS WITH IT.
EXCITING.

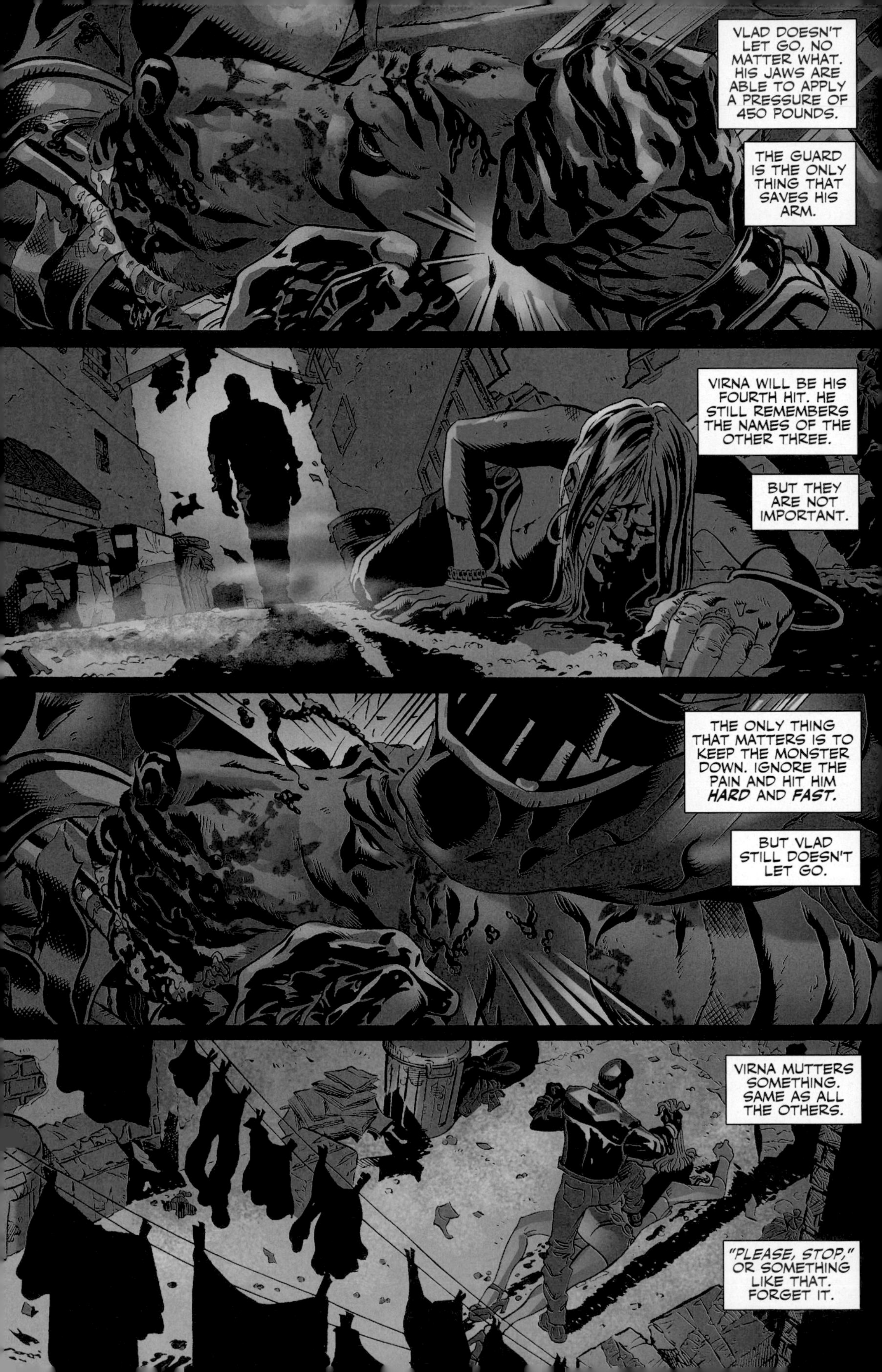
VLAD DOESN'T LET GO, NO MATTER WHAT. HIS JAWS ARE ABLE TO APPLY A PRESSURE OF 450 POUNDS.
THE GUARD IS THE ONLY THING THAT SAVES HIS ARM.
VIRNA WILL BE HIS FOURTH HIT. HE STILL REMEMBERS THE NAMES OF THE OTHER THREE.
BUT THEY ARE NOT IMPORTANT.
THE ONLY THING THAT MATTERS IS TO KEEP THE MONSTER DOWN. IGNORE THE PAIN AND HIT HIM *HARD* AND *FAST.*
BUT VLAD STILL DOESN'T LET GO.
VIRNA MUTTERS SOMETHING. SAME AS ALL THE OTHERS.
"PLEASE, STOP," OR SOMETHING LIKE THAT. FORGET IT.

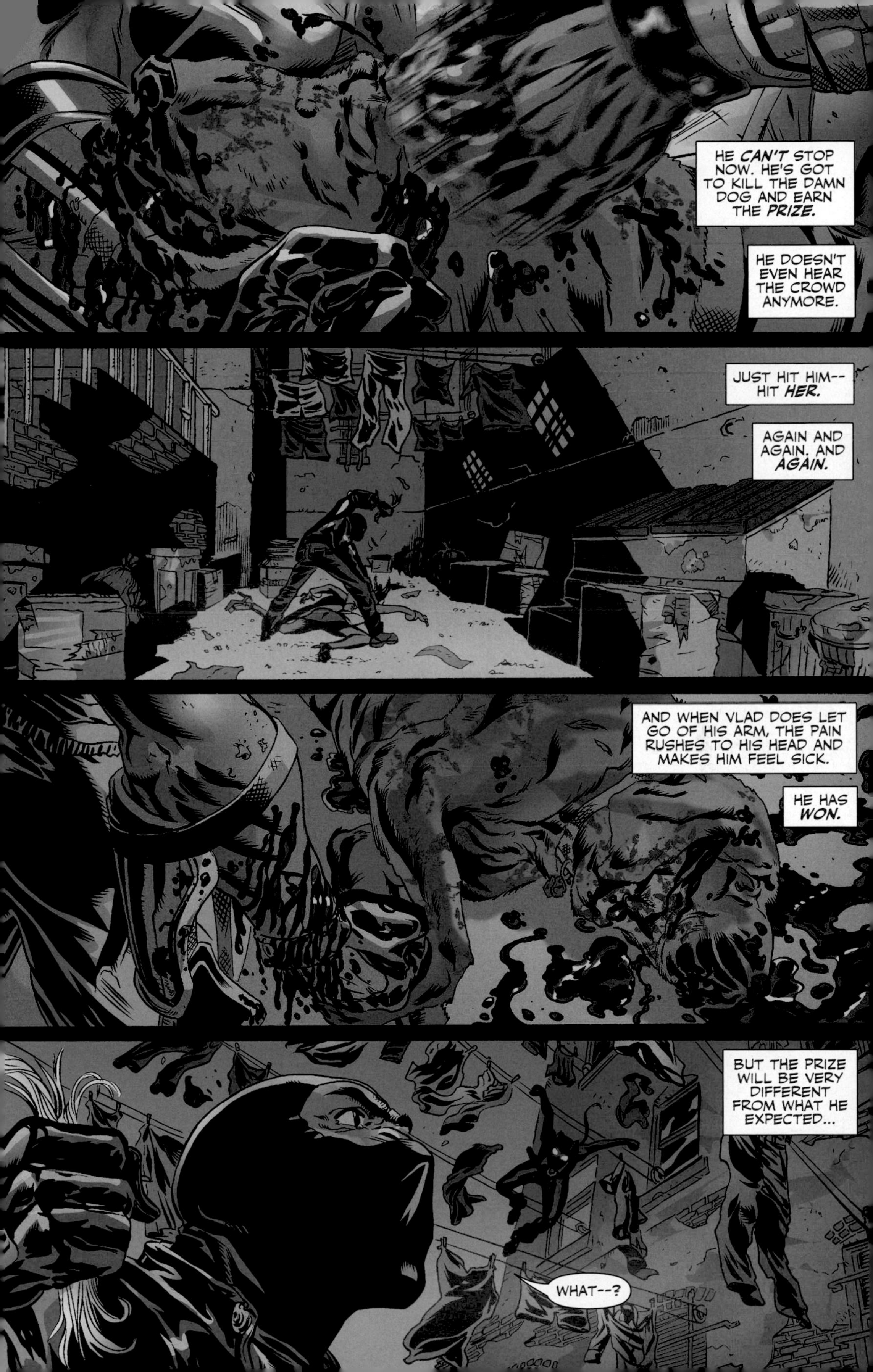
HE CAN'T STOP NOW. HE'S GOT TO KILL THE DAMN DOG AND EARN THE PRIZE.
HE DOESN'T EVEN HEAR THE CROWD ANYMORE.
JUST HIT HIM-- HIT HER.
AGAIN AND AGAIN. AND AGAIN.
AND WHEN VLAD DOES LET GO OF HIS ARM, THE PAIN RUSHES TO HIS HEAD AND MAKES HIM FEEL SICK.
HE HAS WON.
BUT THE PRIZE WILL BE VERY DIFFERENT FROM WHAT HE EXPECTED...
WHAT--?

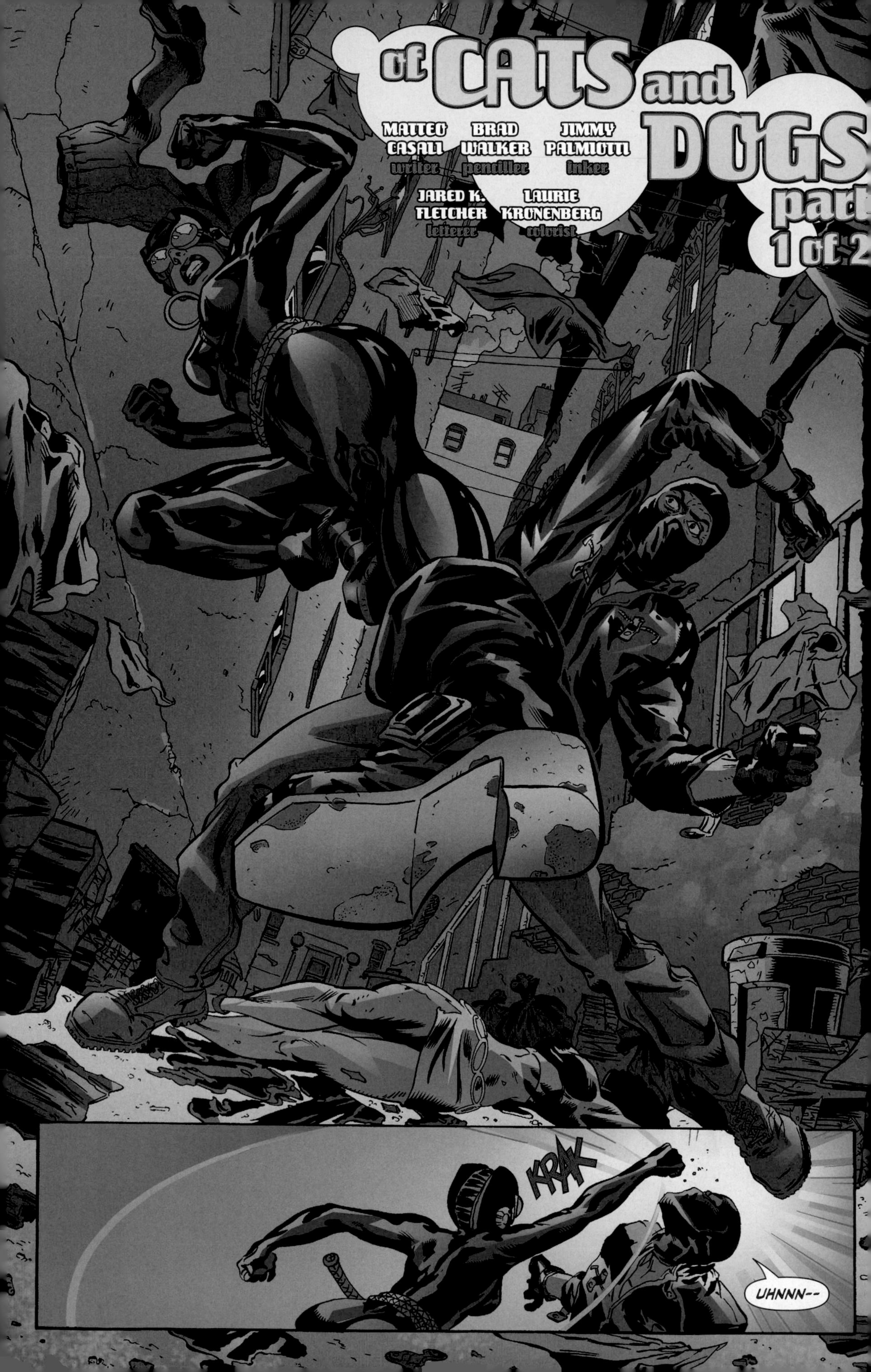
of CATS and DOGS part 1 of 2
MATTEO CASALI writer
BRAD WALKER penciller
JIMMY PALMIOTTI inker
JARED K. FLETCHER letterer
LAURIE KRONENBERG colorist
KRAK
UHNNN--

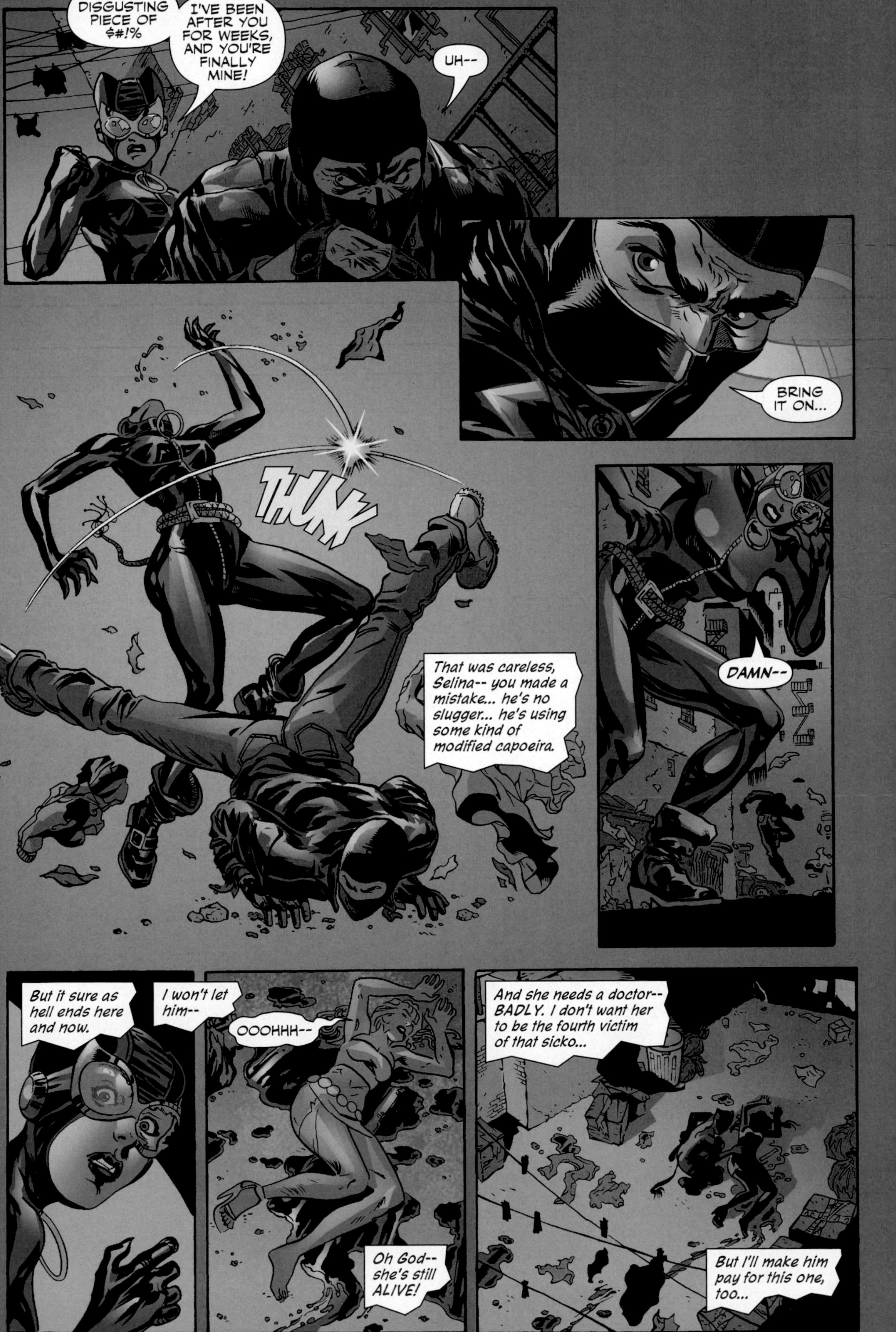

YOU DISGUSTING PIECE OF $#!%
I'VE BEEN AFTER YOU FOR WEEKS, AND YOU'RE FINALLY MINE!
UH--
BRING IT ON...
THUNK
That was careless, Selina-- you made a mistake... he's no slugger... he's using some kind of modified capoeira.
DAMN--
But it sure as hell ends here and now.
I won't let him--
OOOHHH--
Oh God-- she's still ALIVE!
And she needs a doctor-- BADLY. I don't want her to be the fourth victim of that sicko...
But I'll make him pay for this one, too...

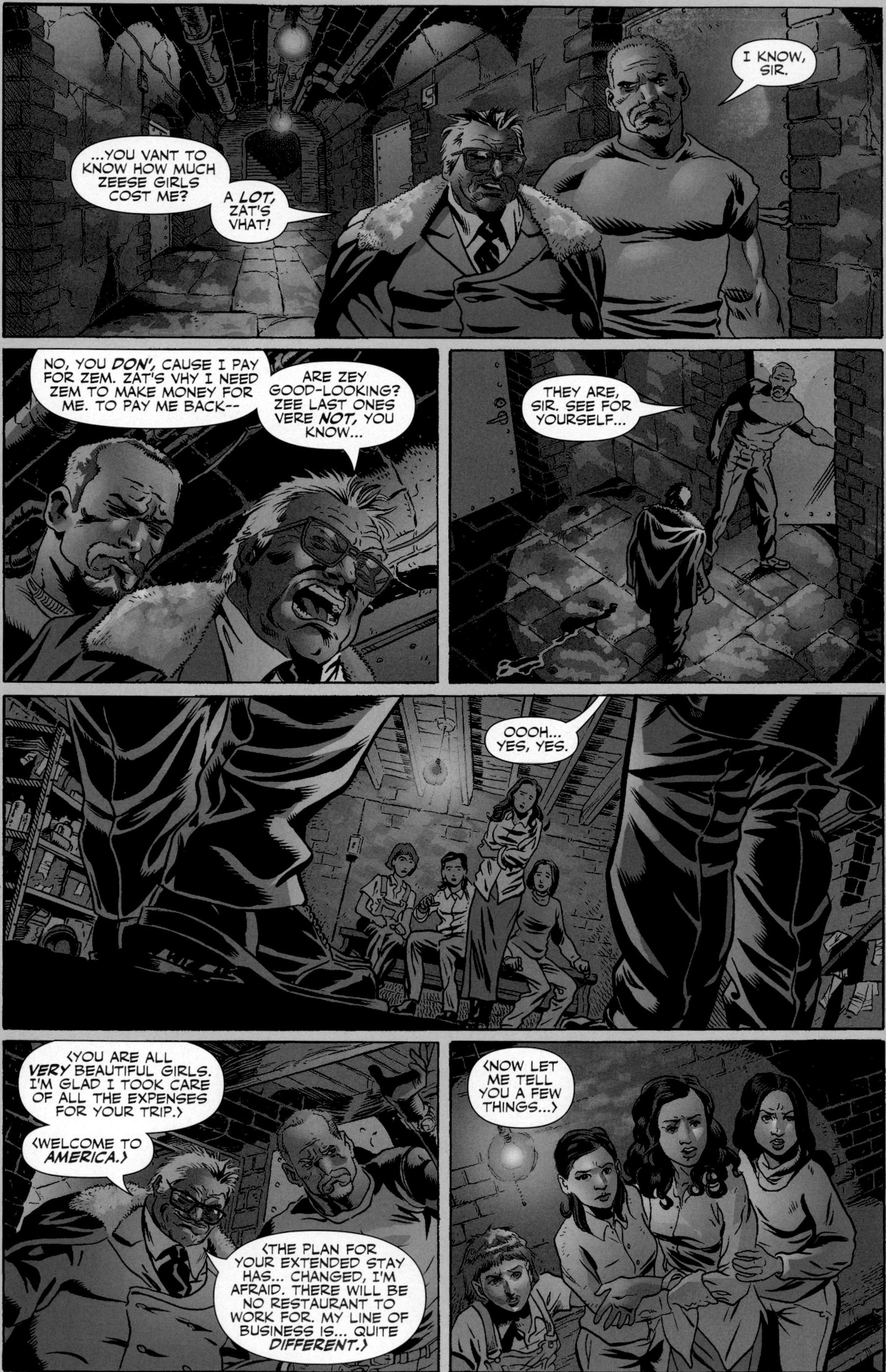
...YOU VANT TO KNOW HOW MUCH ZEESE GIRLS COST ME?
A LOT, ZAT'S VHAT!
I KNOW, SIR.
NO, YOU DON', CAUSE I PAY FOR ZEM. ZAT'S VHY I NEED ZEM TO MAKE MONEY FOR ME. TO PAY ME BACK--
ARE ZEY GOOD-LOOKING? ZEE LAST ONES VERE NOT, YOU KNOW...
THEY ARE, SIR. SEE FOR YOURSELF...
OOOH... YES, YES.
‹YOU ARE ALL VERY BEAUTIFUL GIRLS. I'M GLAD I TOOK CARE OF ALL THE EXPENSES FOR YOUR TRIP.›
‹WELCOME TO AMERICA.›
‹THE PLAN FOR YOUR EXTENDED STAY HAS... CHANGED, I'M AFRAID. THERE WILL BE NO RESTAURANT TO WORK FOR. MY LINE OF BUSINESS IS... QUITE DIFFERENT.›
‹NOW LET ME TELL YOU A FEW THINGS...›

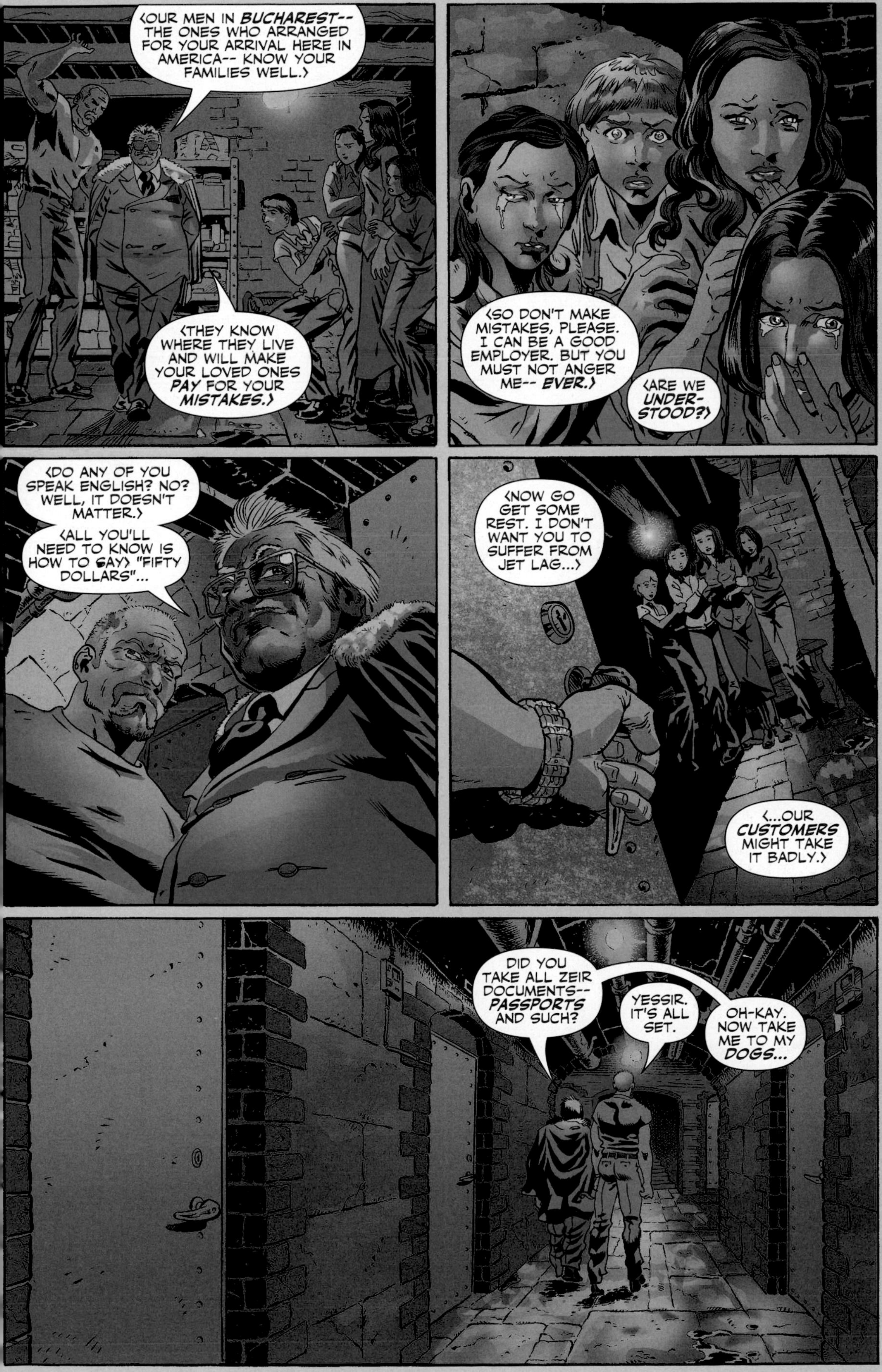

‹OUR MEN IN BUCHAREST-- THE ONES WHO ARRANGED FOR YOUR ARRIVAL HERE IN AMERICA-- KNOW YOUR FAMILIES WELL.›
‹THEY KNOW WHERE THEY LIVE AND WILL MAKE YOUR LOVED ONES PAY FOR YOUR MISTAKES.›
‹SO DON'T MAKE MISTAKES, PLEASE. I CAN BE A GOOD EMPLOYER. BUT YOU MUST NOT ANGER ME-- EVER.›
‹ARE WE UNDER-STOOD?›
‹DO ANY OF YOU SPEAK ENGLISH? NO? WELL, IT DOESN'T MATTER.›
‹ALL YOU'LL NEED TO KNOW IS HOW TO SAY› "FIFTY DOLLARS"...
‹NOW GO GET SOME REST. I DON'T WANT YOU TO SUFFER FROM JET LAG...›
‹...OUR CUSTOMERS MIGHT TAKE IT BADLY.›
DID YOU TAKE ALL ZEIR DOCUMENTS-- PASSPORTS AND SUCH?
YESSIR. IT'S ALL SET.
OH-KAY. NOW TAKE ME TO MY DOGS...

--LOOK AT HIM! IT'S BEAUTIFUL, RIGHT? OH, YES...

...VONDERFUL...

SEE ZOSE *SCARS?* HE IS A FIGHTER, ZIS ONE. A PUREBRED BRAZILIAN FILA. LIKE MY BELOVED VLAD.

MY *POOR,* BELOVED VLAD, YES.

YOU KNOW VHERE THE NAME "FILA" COMES FROM?

NO, SIR.

ZESE DOGS VERE USED BY THE *SLAVERS* OF BRAZIL TO CATCH ZEE BLACKS VHEN THEY RAN AWAY.

"FILA" MEANS *"TO HOLD"* IN ANCIENT PORTUGUESE. ONCE HE HAS YOU IN HIS JAWS... ZERE IS *NO* VAY OUT, MY FRIEND.

YESSIR. GUILLERMO IS IN HIS ROOM, RESTING AND GETTING READY FOR TONIGHT'S FIGHT.

SIR, DID YOU HEAR ABOUT--

IT VAS *VERY* PAINFUL FOR ME TO LOSE VLAD. HE VAS A GOOD DOG. HE VAS VORTH 40,000 DOLLARS.

AND THE MAN WHO KILLED HIM VILL PAY ME BACK. IN *FULL.* IS HE--?

YES. VIRNA VAS A GOOD ONE. I HEARD CATVOMAN SAVED HER, BUT SHE IS LOST TO US. ZAT *MURDERER* TOOK ANOZER OF MY GIRLS...

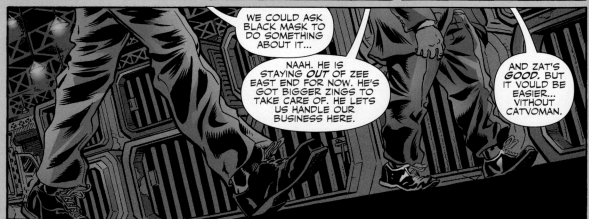

WE COULD ASK BLACK MASK TO DO SOMETHING ABOUT IT...

NAAH. HE IS STAYING *OUT* OF ZEE EAST END FOR NOW. HE'S GOT BIGGER ZINGS TO TAKE CARE OF. HE LETS US HANDLE OUR BUSINESS HERE.

AND ZAT'S *GOOD.* BUT IT VOULD BE EASIER... VITHOUT CATVOMAN.

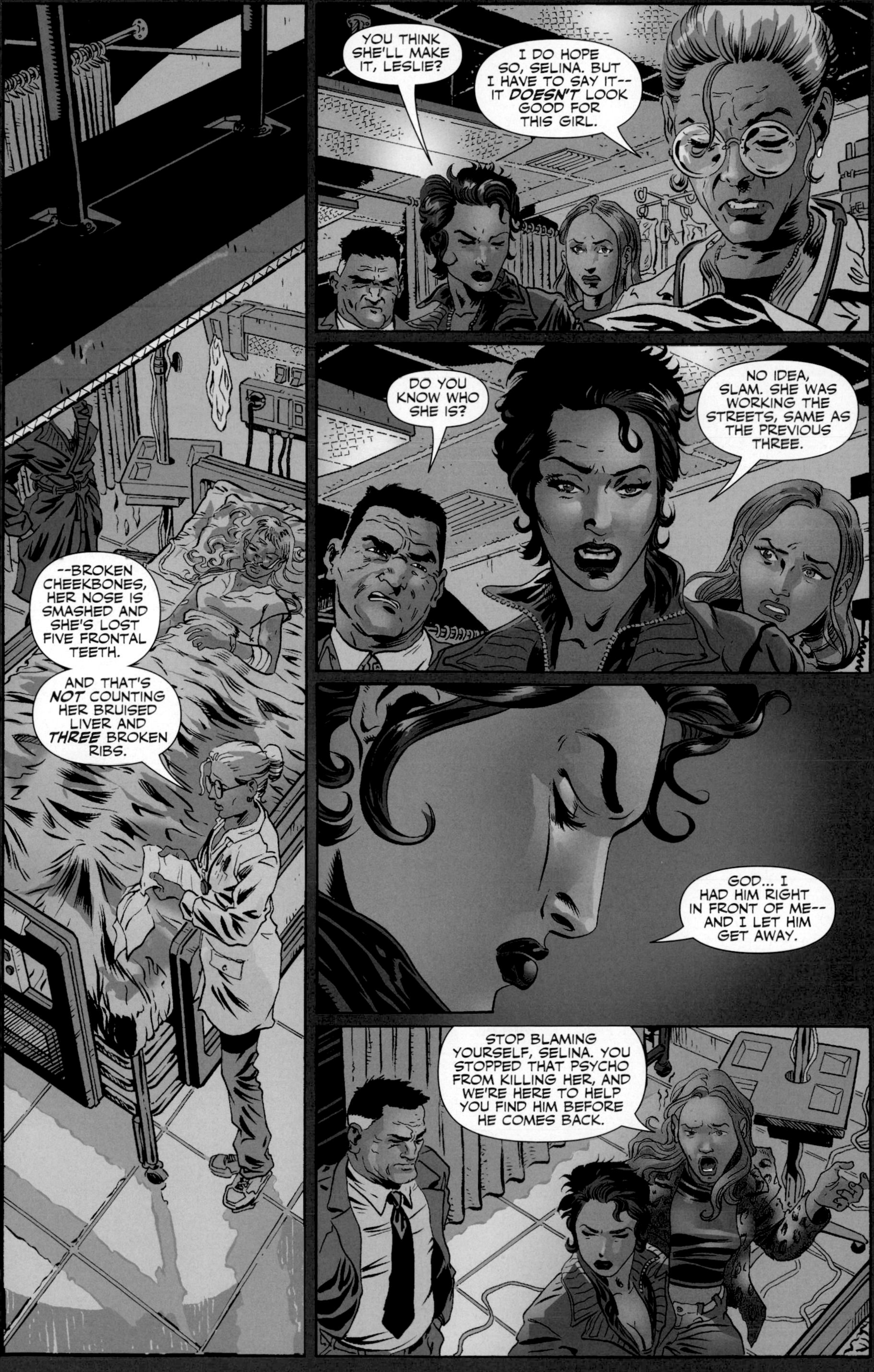
YOU THINK SHE'LL MAKE IT, LESLIE?
I DO HOPE SO, SELINA. BUT I HAVE TO SAY IT-- IT DOESN'T LOOK GOOD FOR THIS GIRL.
--BROKEN CHEEKBONES, HER NOSE IS SMASHED AND SHE'S LOST FIVE FRONTAL TEETH.
AND THAT'S NOT COUNTING HER BRUISED LIVER AND THREE BROKEN RIBS.
DO YOU KNOW WHO SHE IS?
NO IDEA, SLAM. SHE WAS WORKING THE STREETS, SAME AS THE PREVIOUS THREE.
GOD... I HAD HIM RIGHT IN FRONT OF ME-- AND I LET HIM GET AWAY.
STOP BLAMING YOURSELF, SELINA. YOU STOPPED THAT PSYCHO FROM KILLING HER, AND WE'RE HERE TO HELP YOU FIND HIM BEFORE HE COMES BACK.

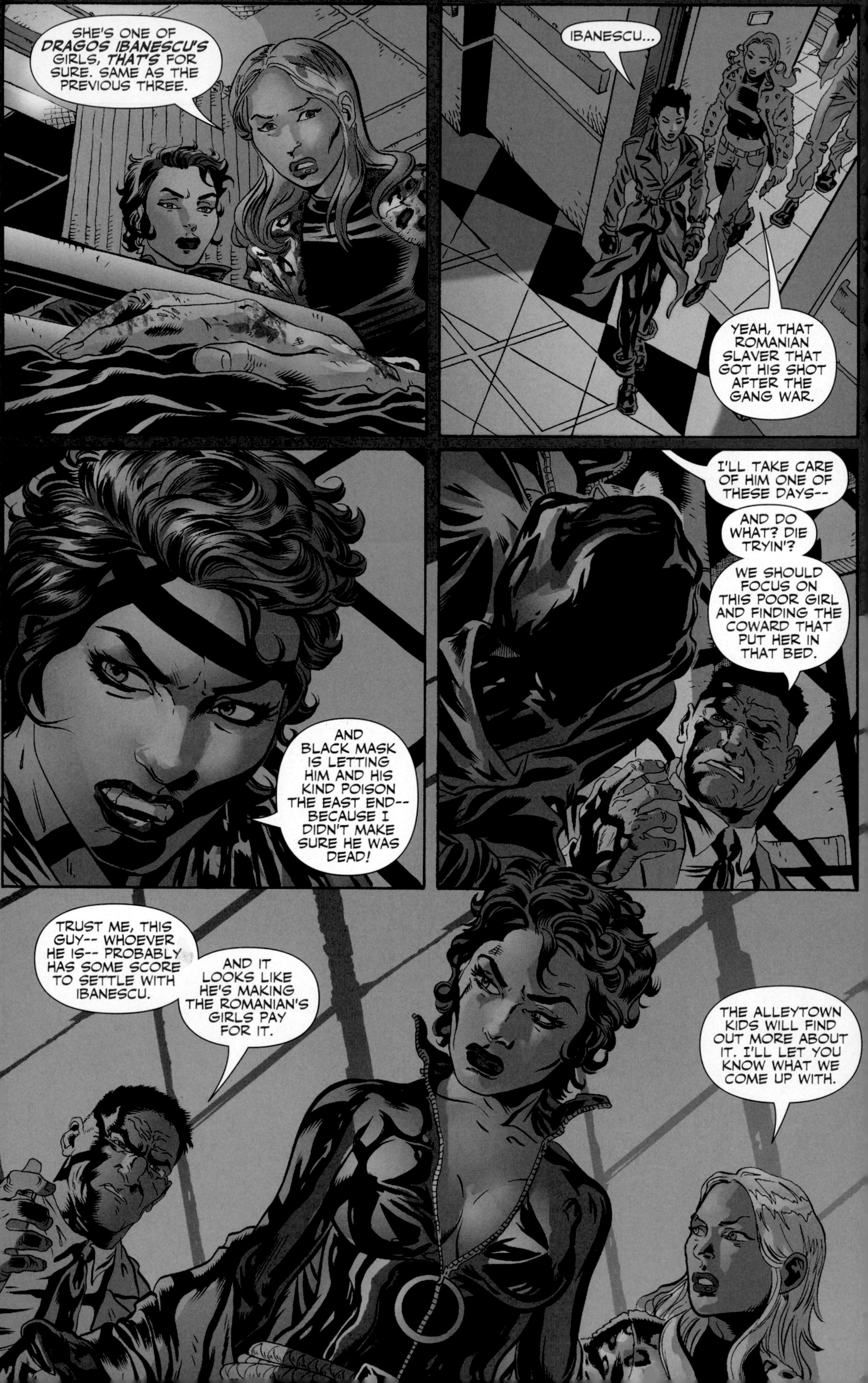
SHE'S ONE OF *DRAGOS IBANESCU'S* GIRLS, *THAT'S* FOR SURE. SAME AS THE PREVIOUS THREE.
IBANESCU...
YEAH, THAT ROMANIAN SLAVER THAT GOT HIS SHOT AFTER THE GANG WAR.
AND BLACK MASK IS LETTING HIM AND HIS KIND POISON THE EAST END-- BECAUSE I DIDN'T MAKE SURE HE WAS DEAD!
I'LL TAKE CARE OF HIM ONE OF THESE DAYS--
AND DO WHAT? DIE TRYIN'?
WE SHOULD FOCUS ON THIS POOR GIRL AND FINDING THE COWARD THAT PUT HER IN THAT BED.
TRUST ME, THIS GUY-- WHOEVER HE IS-- PROBABLY HAS SOME SCORE TO SETTLE WITH IBANESCU.
AND IT LOOKS LIKE HE'S MAKING THE ROMANIAN'S GIRLS PAY FOR IT.
THE ALLEYTOWN KIDS WILL FIND OUT MORE ABOUT IT. I'LL LET YOU KNOW WHAT WE COME UP WITH.

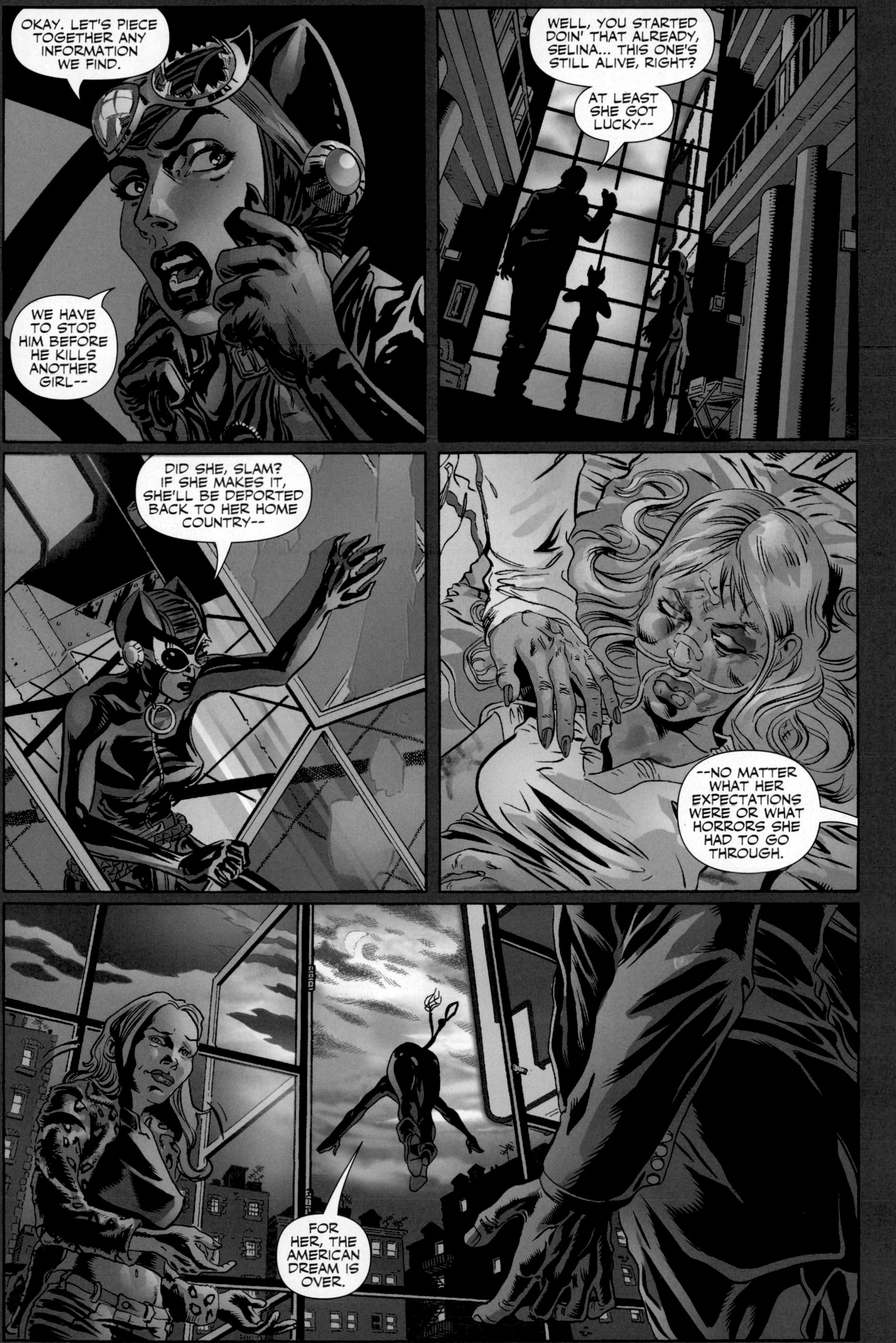
OKAY. LET'S PIECE TOGETHER ANY INFORMATION WE FIND.
WE HAVE TO STOP HIM BEFORE HE KILLS ANOTHER GIRL--
WELL, YOU STARTED DOIN' THAT ALREADY, SELINA... THIS ONE'S STILL ALIVE, RIGHT?
AT LEAST SHE GOT LUCKY--
DID SHE, SLAM? IF SHE MAKES IT, SHE'LL BE DEPORTED BACK TO HER HOME COUNTRY--
--NO MATTER WHAT HER EXPECTATIONS WERE OR WHAT HORRORS SHE HAD TO GO THROUGH.
FOR HER, THE AMERICAN DREAM IS OVER.

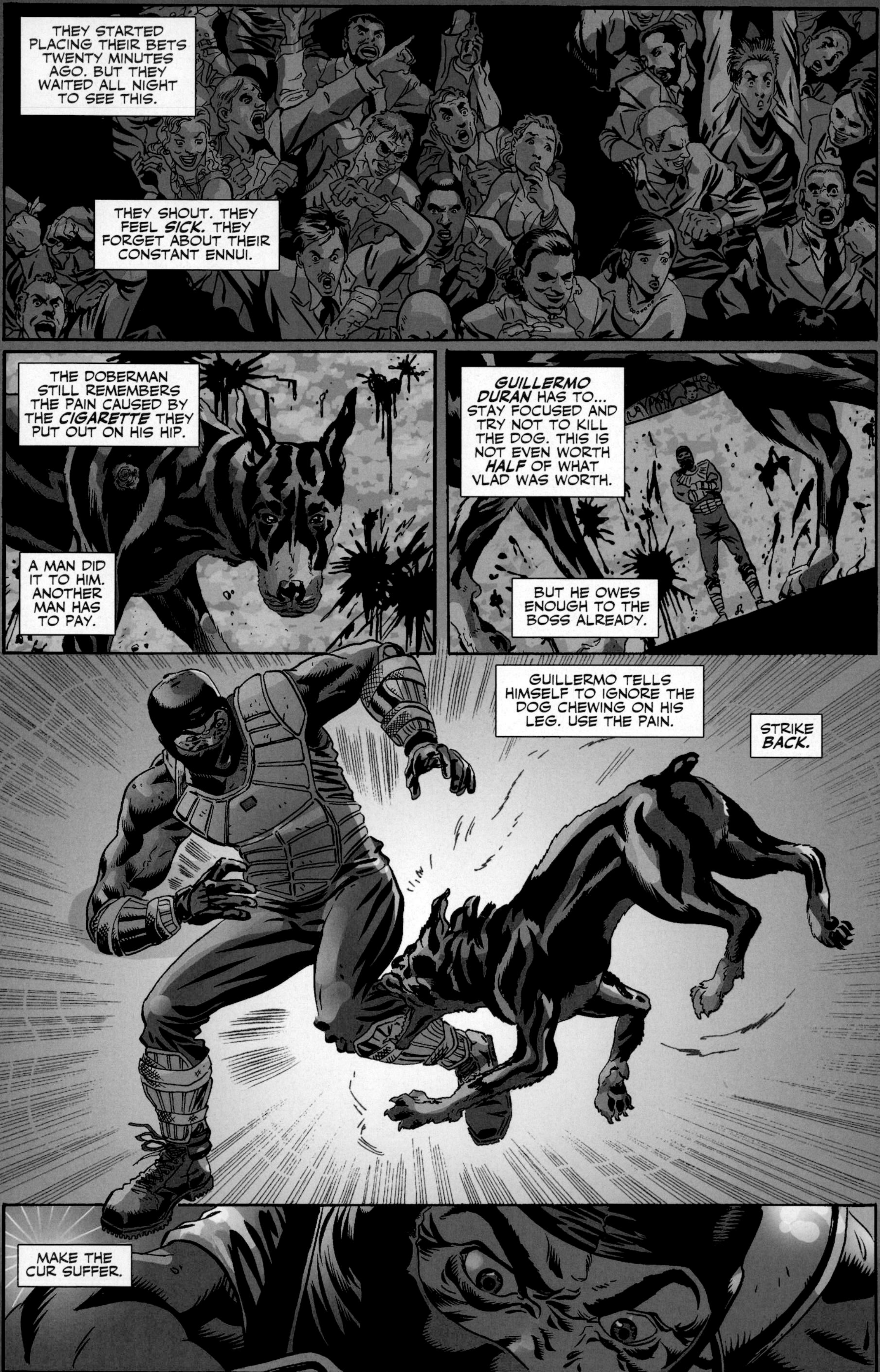
THEY STARTED PLACING THEIR BETS TWENTY MINUTES AGO. BUT THEY WAITED ALL NIGHT TO SEE THIS.
THEY SHOUT. THEY FEEL SICK. THEY FORGET ABOUT THEIR CONSTANT ENNUI.
THE DOBERMAN STILL REMEMBERS THE PAIN CAUSED BY THE CIGARETTE THEY PUT OUT ON HIS HIP.
A MAN DID IT TO HIM. ANOTHER MAN HAS TO PAY.
GUILLERMO DURAN HAS TO... STAY FOCUSED AND TRY NOT TO KILL THE DOG. THIS IS NOT EVEN WORTH HALF OF WHAT VLAD WAS WORTH.
BUT HE OWES ENOUGH TO THE BOSS ALREADY.
GUILLERMO TELLS HIMSELF TO IGNORE THE DOG CHEWING ON HIS LEG. USE THE PAIN.
STRIKE BACK.
MAKE THE CUR SUFFER.

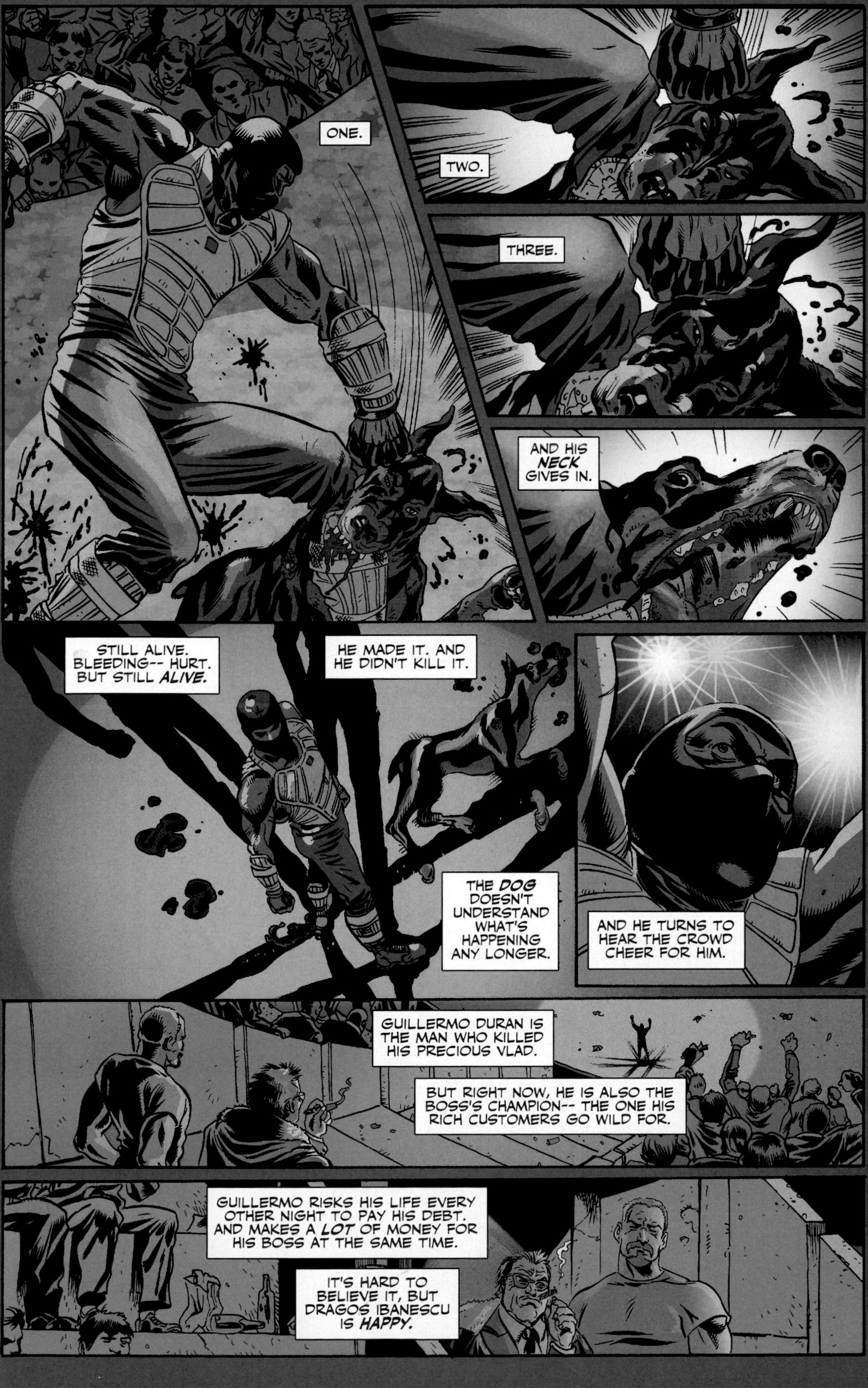
ONE.
TWO.
THREE.
AND HIS NECK GIVES IN.
STILL ALIVE. BLEEDING-- HURT. BUT STILL ALIVE.
HE MADE IT. AND HE DIDN'T KILL IT.
THE DOG DOESN'T UNDERSTAND WHAT'S HAPPENING ANY LONGER.
AND HE TURNS TO HEAR THE CROWD CHEER FOR HIM.
GUILLERMO DURAN IS THE MAN WHO KILLED HIS PRECIOUS VLAD.
BUT RIGHT NOW, HE IS ALSO THE BOSS'S CHAMPION-- THE ONE HIS RICH CUSTOMERS GO WILD FOR.
GUILLERMO RISKS HIS LIFE EVERY OTHER NIGHT TO PAY HIS DEBT. AND MAKES A LOT OF MONEY FOR HIS BOSS AT THE SAME TIME.
IT'S HARD TO BELIEVE IT, BUT DRAGOS IBANESCU IS HAPPY.

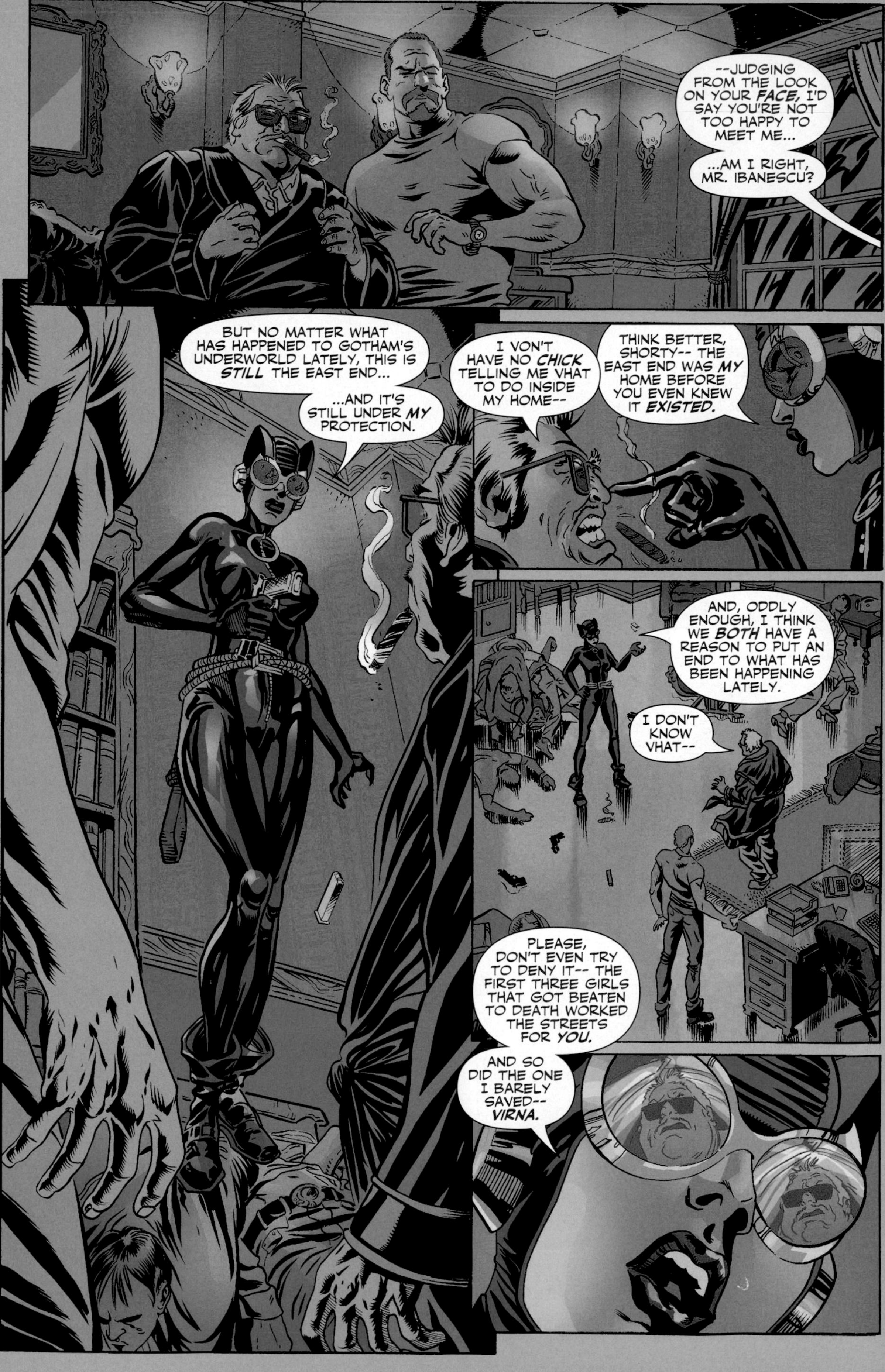
--JUDGING FROM THE LOOK ON YOUR FACE, I'D SAY YOU'RE NOT TOO HAPPY TO MEET ME...
...AM I RIGHT, MR. IBANESCU?
BUT NO MATTER WHAT HAS HAPPENED TO GOTHAM'S UNDERWORLD LATELY, THIS IS STILL THE EAST END...
...AND IT'S STILL UNDER MY PROTECTION.
I VON'T HAVE NO CHICK TELLING ME VHAT TO DO INSIDE MY HOME--
THINK BETTER, SHORTY-- THE EAST END WAS MY HOME BEFORE YOU EVEN KNEW IT EXISTED.
AND, ODDLY ENOUGH, I THINK WE BOTH HAVE A REASON TO PUT AN END TO WHAT HAS BEEN HAPPENING LATELY.
I DON'T KNOW VHAT--
PLEASE, DON'T EVEN TRY TO DENY IT-- THE FIRST THREE GIRLS THAT GOT BEATEN TO DEATH WORKED THE STREETS FOR YOU.
AND SO DID THE ONE I BARELY SAVED-- VIRNA.

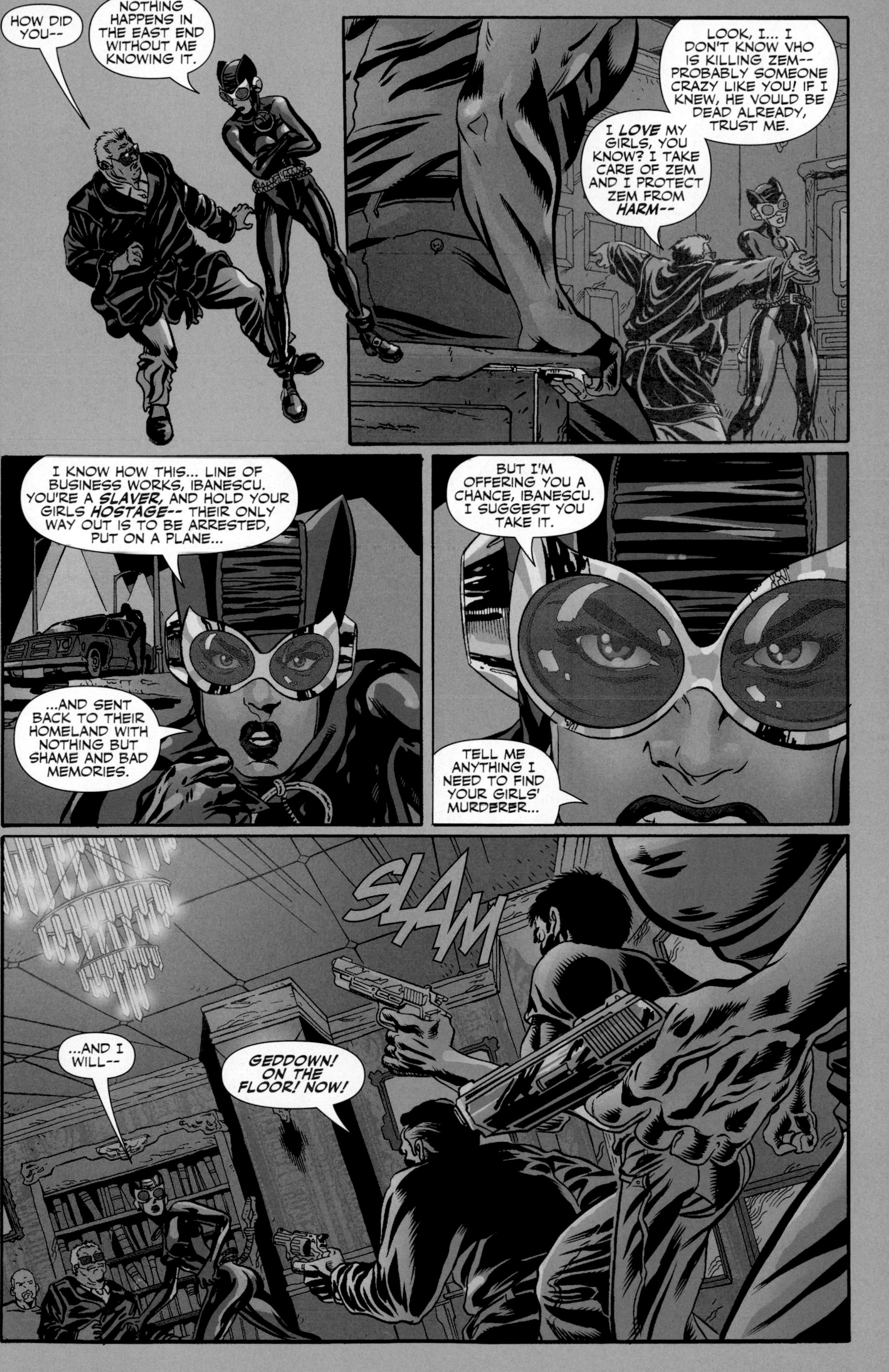
HOW DID YOU--
NOTHING HAPPENS IN THE EAST END WITHOUT ME KNOWING IT.
LOOK, I... I DON'T KNOW VHO IS KILLING ZEM-- PROBABLY SOMEONE CRAZY LIKE YOU! IF I KNEW, HE VOULD BE DEAD ALREADY, TRUST ME.
I LOVE MY GIRLS, YOU KNOW? I TAKE CARE OF ZEM AND I PROTECT ZEM FROM HARM--
I KNOW HOW THIS... LINE OF BUSINESS WORKS, IBANESCU. YOU'RE A SLAVER, AND HOLD YOUR GIRLS HOSTAGE-- THEIR ONLY WAY OUT IS TO BE ARRESTED, PUT ON A PLANE...
...AND SENT BACK TO THEIR HOMELAND WITH NOTHING BUT SHAME AND BAD MEMORIES.
BUT I'M OFFERING YOU A CHANCE, IBANESCU. I SUGGEST YOU TAKE IT.
TELL ME ANYTHING I NEED TO FIND YOUR GIRLS' MURDERER...
SLAM
...AND I WILL--
GEDDOWN! ON THE FLOOR! NOW!

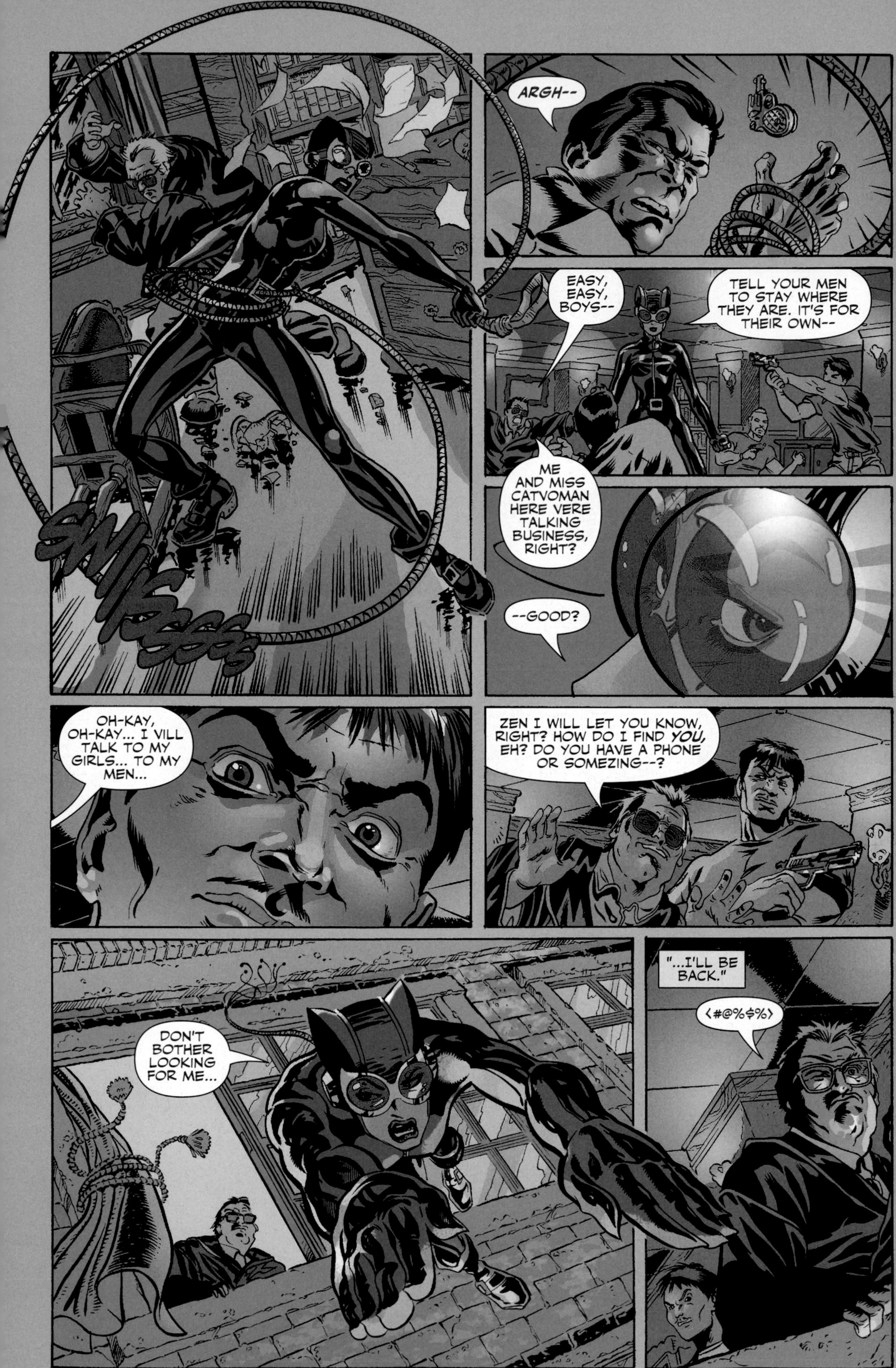
SWISSSS
ARGH--
EASY, EASY, BOYS--
TELL YOUR MEN TO STAY WHERE THEY ARE. IT'S FOR THEIR OWN--
ME AND MISS CATVOMAN HERE VERE TALKING BUSINESS, RIGHT?
--GOOD?
OH-KAY, OH-KAY... I VILL TALK TO MY GIRLS... TO MY MEN...
ZEN I WILL LET YOU KNOW, RIGHT? HOW DO I FIND *YOU,* EH? DO YOU HAVE A PHONE OR SOMEZING--?
DON'T BOTHER LOOKING FOR ME...
"...I'LL BE BACK."
<#@%$%>

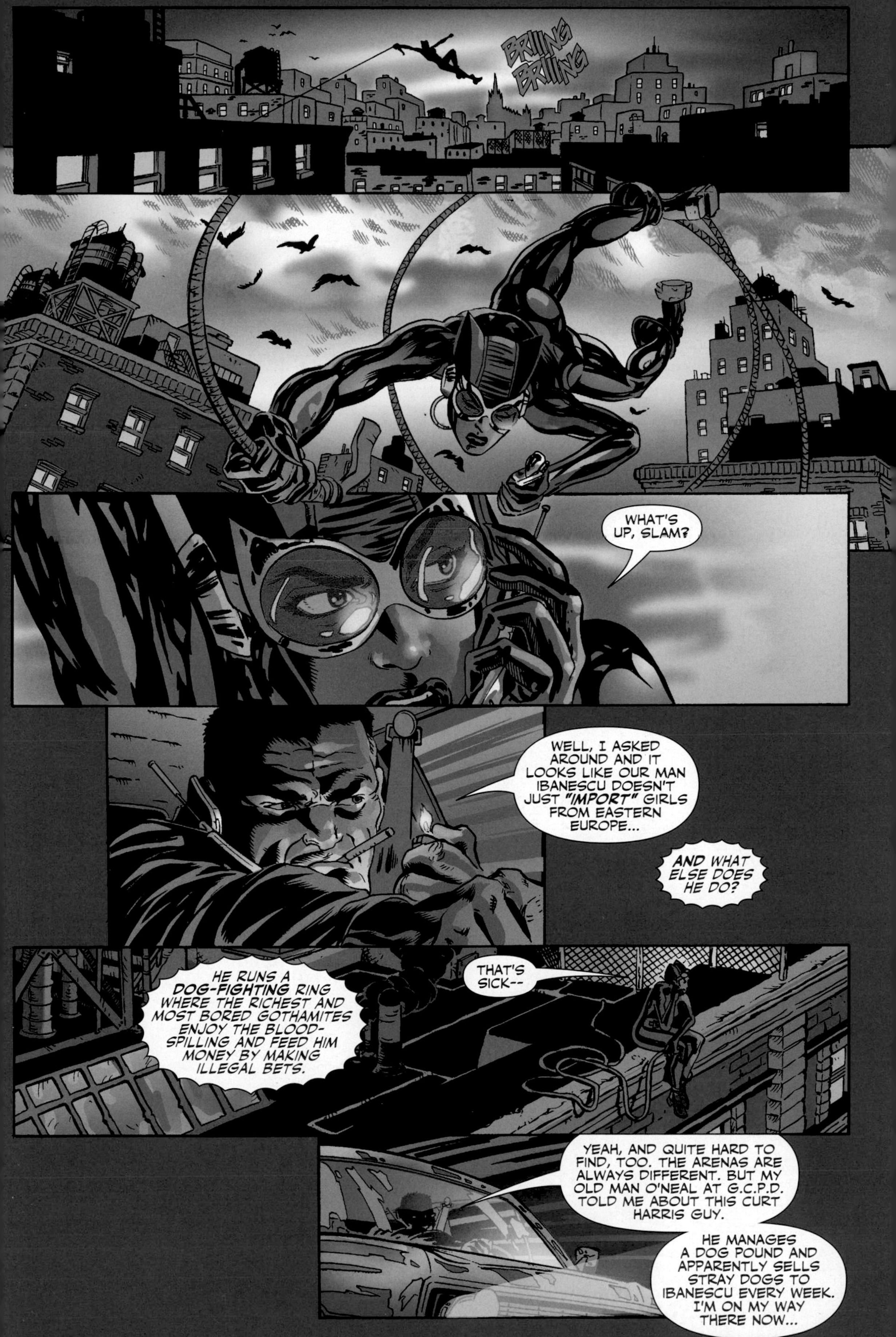
BRIIING BRIIING
WHAT'S UP, SLAM?
WELL, I ASKED AROUND AND IT LOOKS LIKE OUR MAN IBANESCU DOESN'T JUST "IMPORT" GIRLS FROM EASTERN EUROPE...
AND WHAT ELSE DOES HE DO?
HE RUNS A DOG-FIGHTING RING WHERE THE RICHEST AND MOST BORED GOTHAMITES ENJOY THE BLOOD-SPILLING AND FEED HIM MONEY BY MAKING ILLEGAL BETS.
THAT'S SICK--
YEAH, AND QUITE HARD TO FIND, TOO. THE ARENAS ARE ALWAYS DIFFERENT. BUT MY OLD MAN O'NEAL AT G.C.P.D. TOLD ME ABOUT THIS CURT HARRIS GUY.
HE MANAGES A DOG POUND AND APPARENTLY SELLS STRAY DOGS TO IBANESCU EVERY WEEK. I'M ON MY WAY THERE NOW...

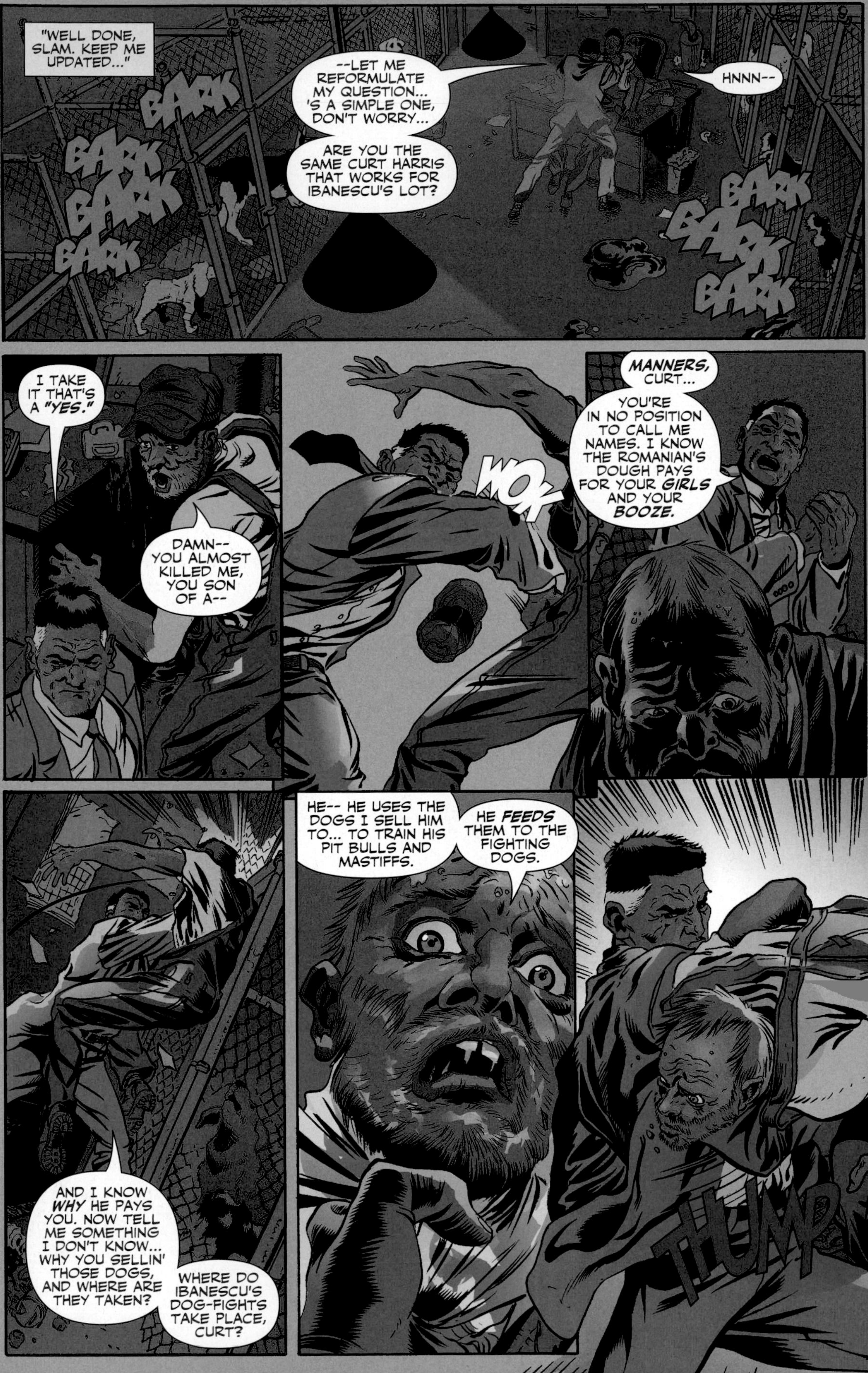
"WELL DONE, SLAM. KEEP ME UPDATED..."
--LET ME REFORMULATE MY QUESTION... 'S A SIMPLE ONE, DON'T WORRY...
ARE YOU THE SAME CURT HARRIS THAT WORKS FOR IBANESCU'S LOT?
HNNN--
BARK BARK BARK BARK
BARK BARK BARK BARK
I TAKE IT THAT'S A "YES."
DAMN-- YOU ALMOST KILLED ME, YOU SON OF A--
WOK
MANNERS, CURT...
YOU'RE IN NO POSITION TO CALL ME NAMES. I KNOW THE ROMANIAN'S DOUGH PAYS FOR YOUR GIRLS AND YOUR BOOZE.
AND I KNOW WHY HE PAYS YOU. NOW TELL ME SOMETHING I DON'T KNOW... WHY YOU SELLIN' THOSE DOGS, AND WHERE ARE THEY TAKEN?
WHERE DO IBANESCU'S DOG-FIGHTS TAKE PLACE, CURT?
HE-- HE USES THE DOGS I SELL HIM TO... TO TRAIN HIS PIT BULLS AND MASTIFFS.
HE FEEDS THEM TO THE FIGHTING DOGS.
THUMP

O-OOUUGH-- S-STOP IT...

SORRY, CURT. I GOT CARRIED AWAY. YOU'RE ONE *DISGUSTING* SHARPER, I'M TELLIN' YOU.

GO ON.

J-JESUS-- DO I LOOK LIKE I'M MAKING MONEY OUT OF SELLIN' HIM A HANDFUL OF MUTTS PER WEEK?

NO, YOU DON'T. SO WHAT?

THE *DOG-FIGHTING* MAKES IBANESCU *MORE MONEY* THAN THE GIRLS HE SENDS ON THE STREETS!

GOTHAM HIGHER-UPS *POUR* MONEY IN HIS POCKETS WITH THEIR BETS.

ARE YOU ONE OF THE BETTING MEN, CURT?

OH, YEAH-- AN' I GET THE "PRIVILEGE" TO WATCH THE FIGHTS... AND GIVE HIM BACK THE MONEY HE PAYS ME WITH BECAUSE OF THAT.

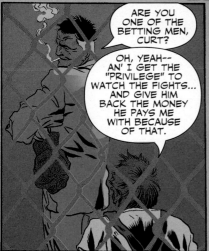

SO YOU KNOW *WHEN* AND *WHERE* THE NEXT SHOW'S GONNA BE, RIGHT?

Y-YEAH-- BUT... BUT WHY DO YOU WANT TO--?

SOMEONE'S KILLING THE ROMANIAN'S GIRLS. MAYBE IT HAS SOMETHING TO DO WITH HIS DOG-FIGHTING.

MY HUNCH IS IT'S A WAY TO SETTLE A SCORE WITH HIM, AND I WANNA FIND OUT *WHO'S* INVOLVED, AND *WHY* HE'S DOIN' IT.

NOW BE A *GOOD* PUPPY AND START SPILLIN' THE BEANS...

BARK BARK BARK

BARK BARK BARK

BARK BARK BARK

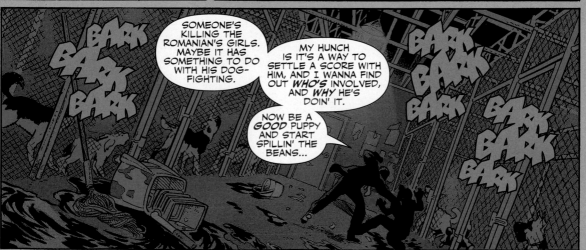

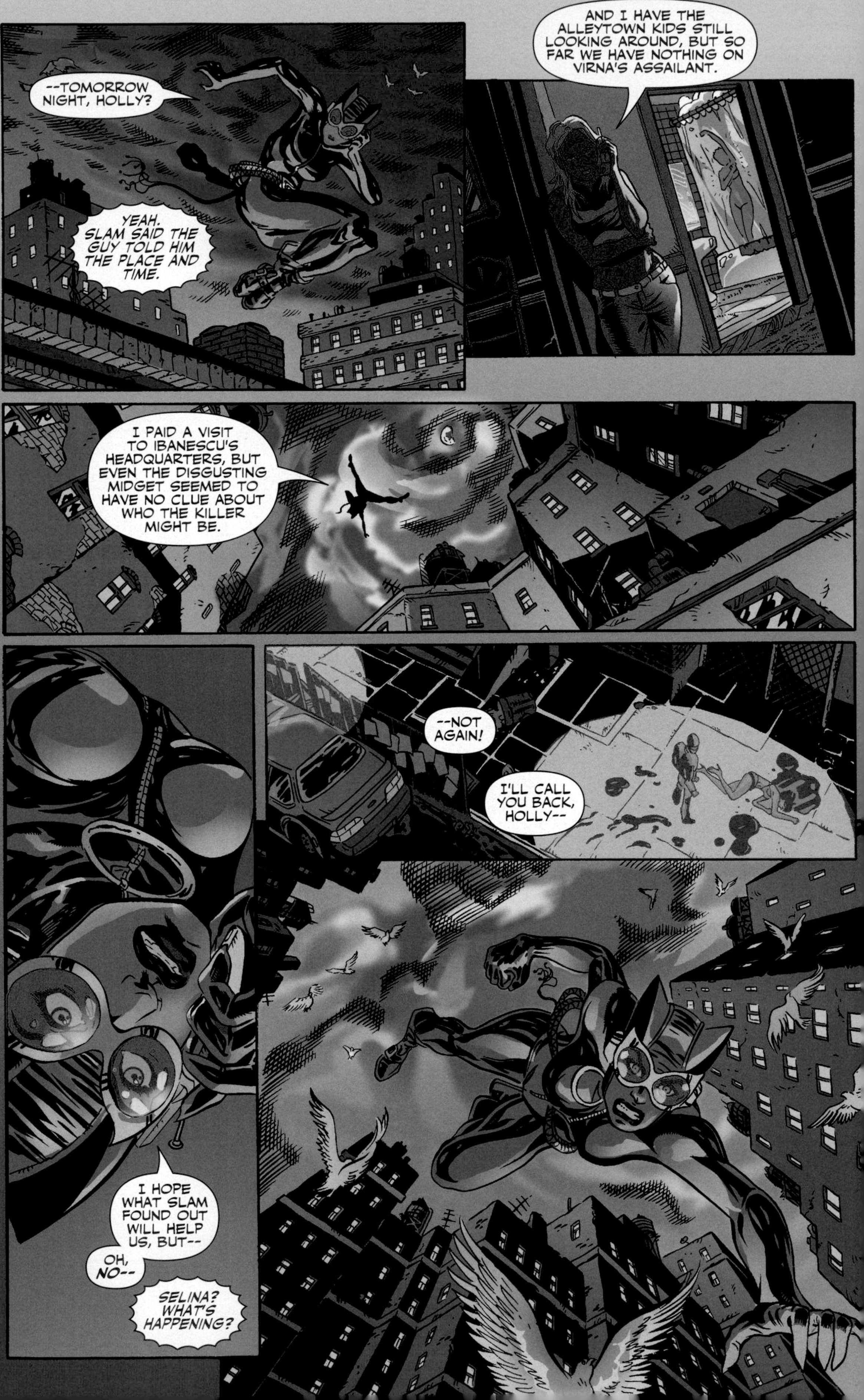
--TOMORROW NIGHT, HOLLY?
YEAH. SLAM SAID THE GUY TOLD HIM THE PLACE AND TIME.
AND I HAVE THE ALLEYTOWN KIDS STILL LOOKING AROUND, BUT SO FAR WE HAVE NOTHING ON VIRNA'S ASSAILANT.
I PAID A VISIT TO IBANESCU'S HEADQUARTERS, BUT EVEN THE DISGUSTING MIDGET SEEMED TO HAVE NO CLUE ABOUT WHO THE KILLER MIGHT BE.
I HOPE WHAT SLAM FOUND OUT WILL HELP US, BUT--
OH, NO--
SELINA? WHAT'S HAPPENING?
--NOT AGAIN!
I'LL CALL YOU BACK, HOLLY--

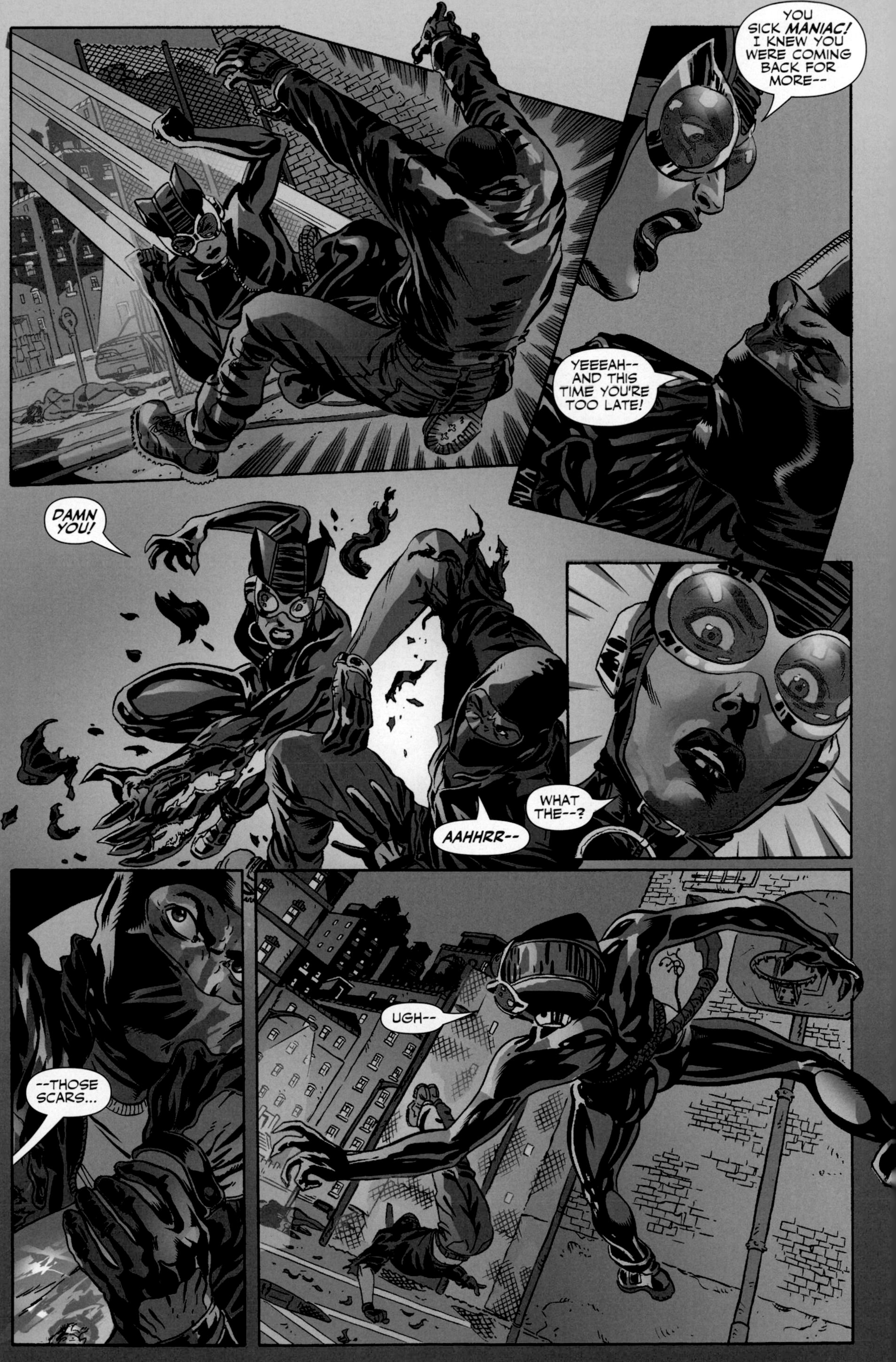

YOU SICK *MANIAC!* I KNEW YOU WERE COMING BACK FOR MORE--
YEEEAH-- AND THIS TIME YOU'RE TOO LATE!
DAMN YOU!
WHAT THE--?
AAHHRR--
--THOSE SCARS...
UGH--

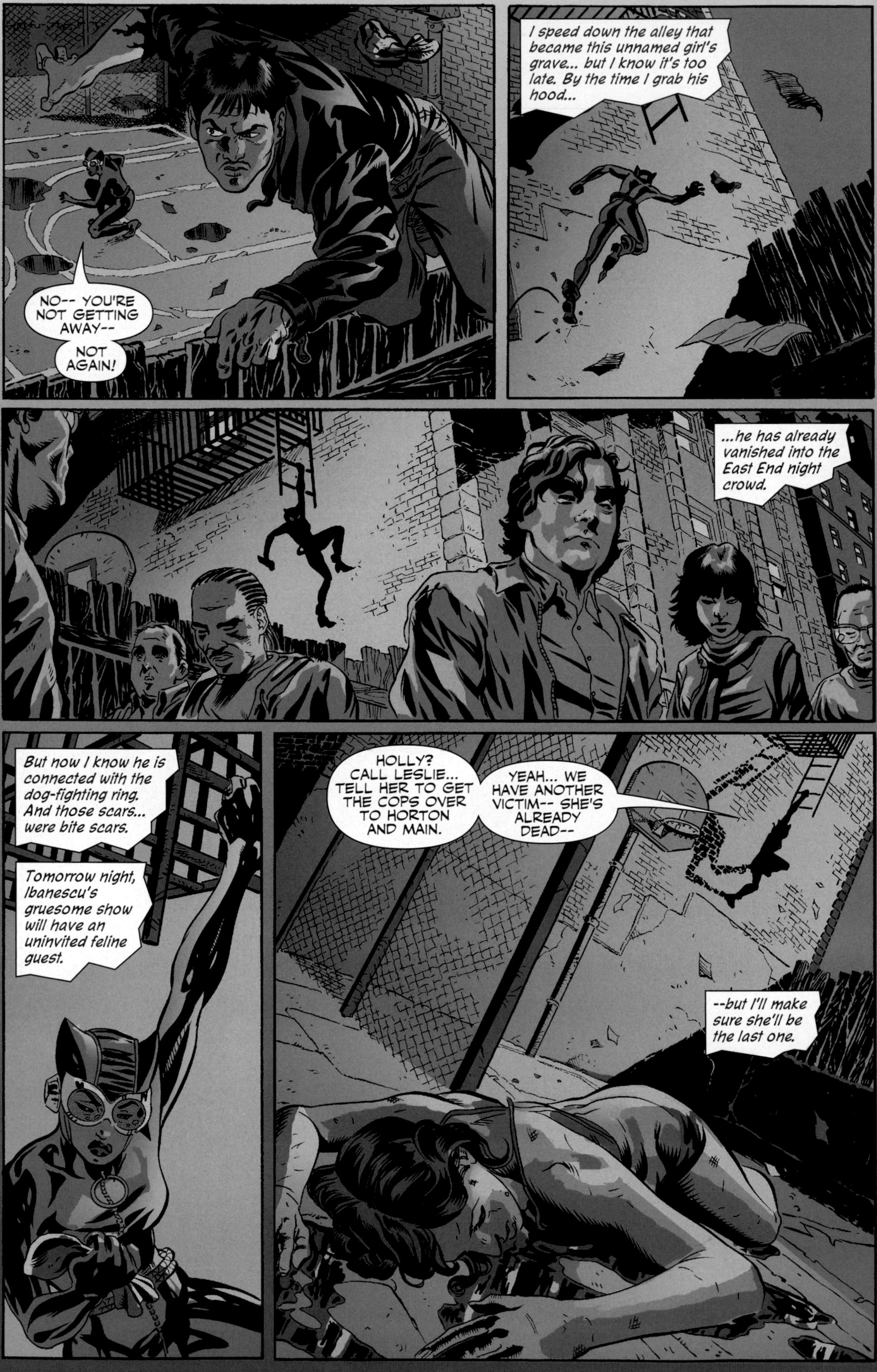
NO-- YOU'RE NOT GETTING AWAY--
NOT AGAIN!
I speed down the alley that became this unnamed girl's grave... but I know it's too late. By the time I grab his hood...
...he has already vanished into the East End night crowd.
But now I know he is connected with the dog-fighting ring. And those scars... were bite scars.
Tomorrow night, Ibanescu's gruesome show will have an uninvited feline guest.
HOLLY? CALL LESLIE... TELL HER TO GET THE COPS OVER TO HORTON AND MAIN.
YEAH... WE HAVE ANOTHER VICTIM-- SHE'S ALREADY DEAD--
--but I'll make sure she'll be the last one.

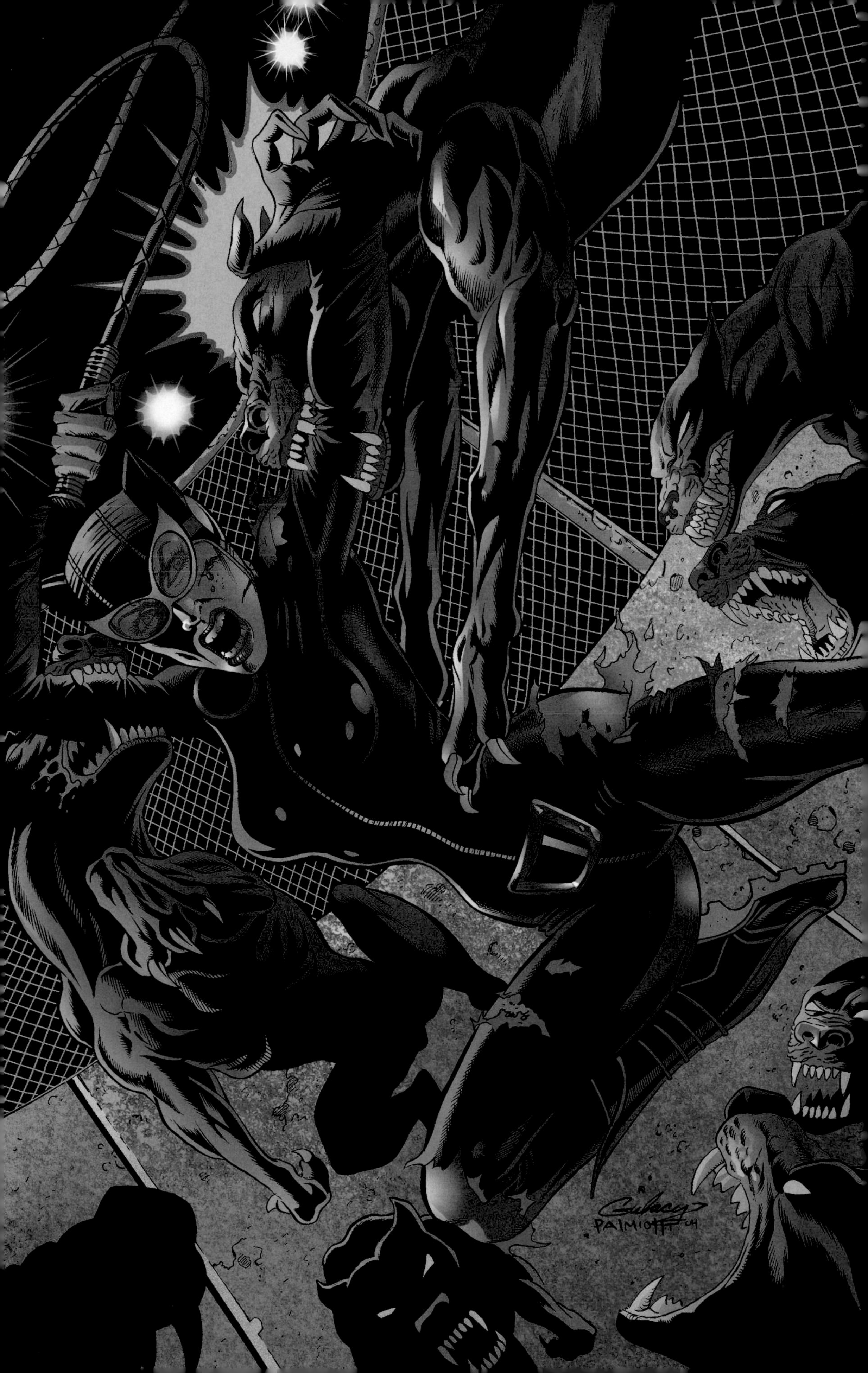

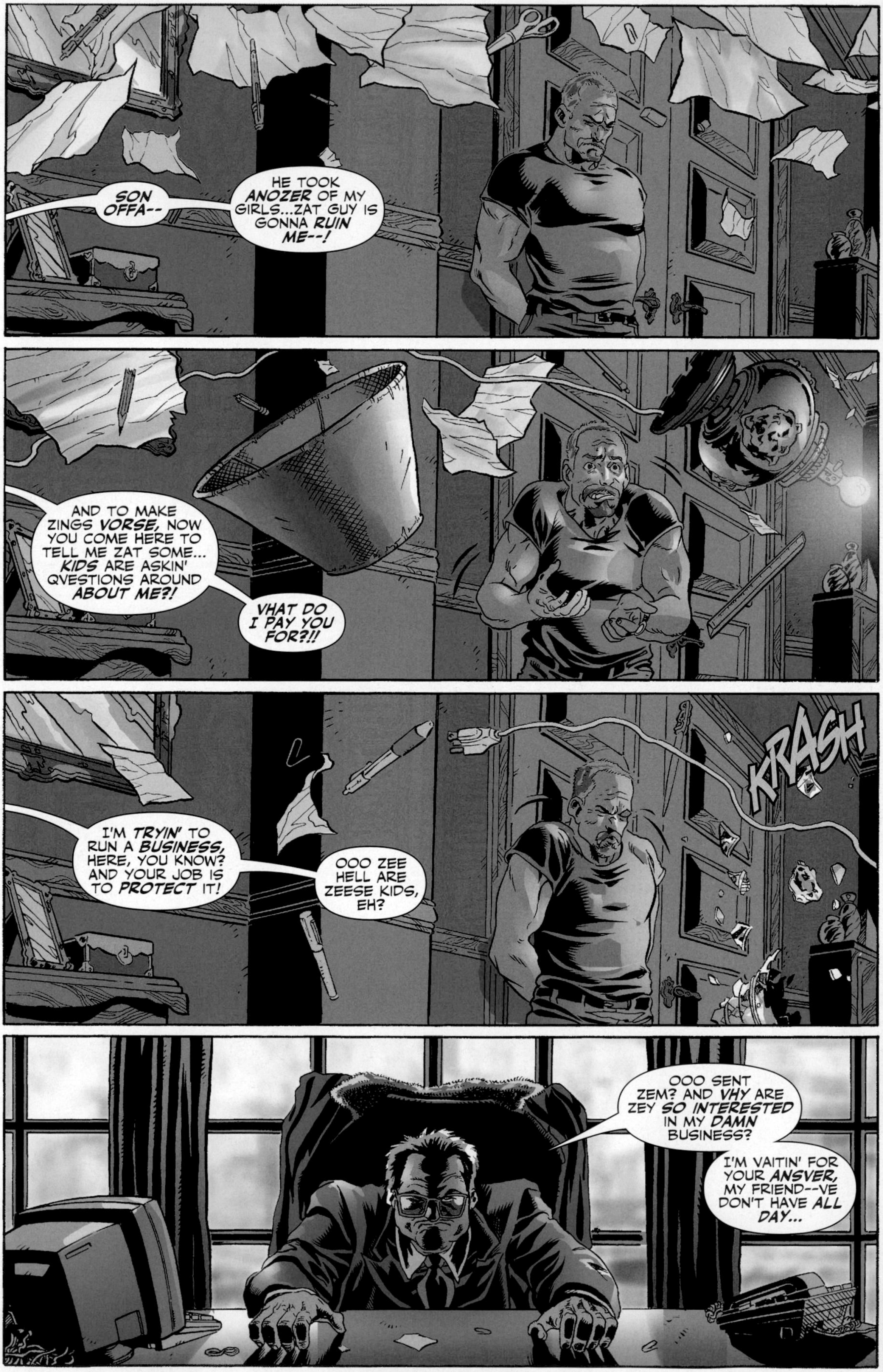
SON OFFA--
HE TOOK ANOZER OF MY GIRLS...ZAT GUY IS GONNA RUIN ME--!
AND TO MAKE ZINGS VORSE, NOW YOU COME HERE TO TELL ME ZAT SOME... KIDS ARE ASKIN' QVESTIONS AROUND ABOUT ME?!
VHAT DO I PAY YOU FOR?!!
KRASH
I'M TRYIN' TO RUN A BUSINESS, HERE, YOU KNOW? AND YOUR JOB IS TO PROTECT IT!
OOO ZEE HELL ARE ZEESE KIDS, EH?
OOO SENT ZEM? AND VHY ARE ZEY SO INTERESTED IN MY DAMN BUSINESS?
I'M VAITIN' FOR YOUR ANSVER, MY FRIEND--VE DON'T HAVE ALL DAY...

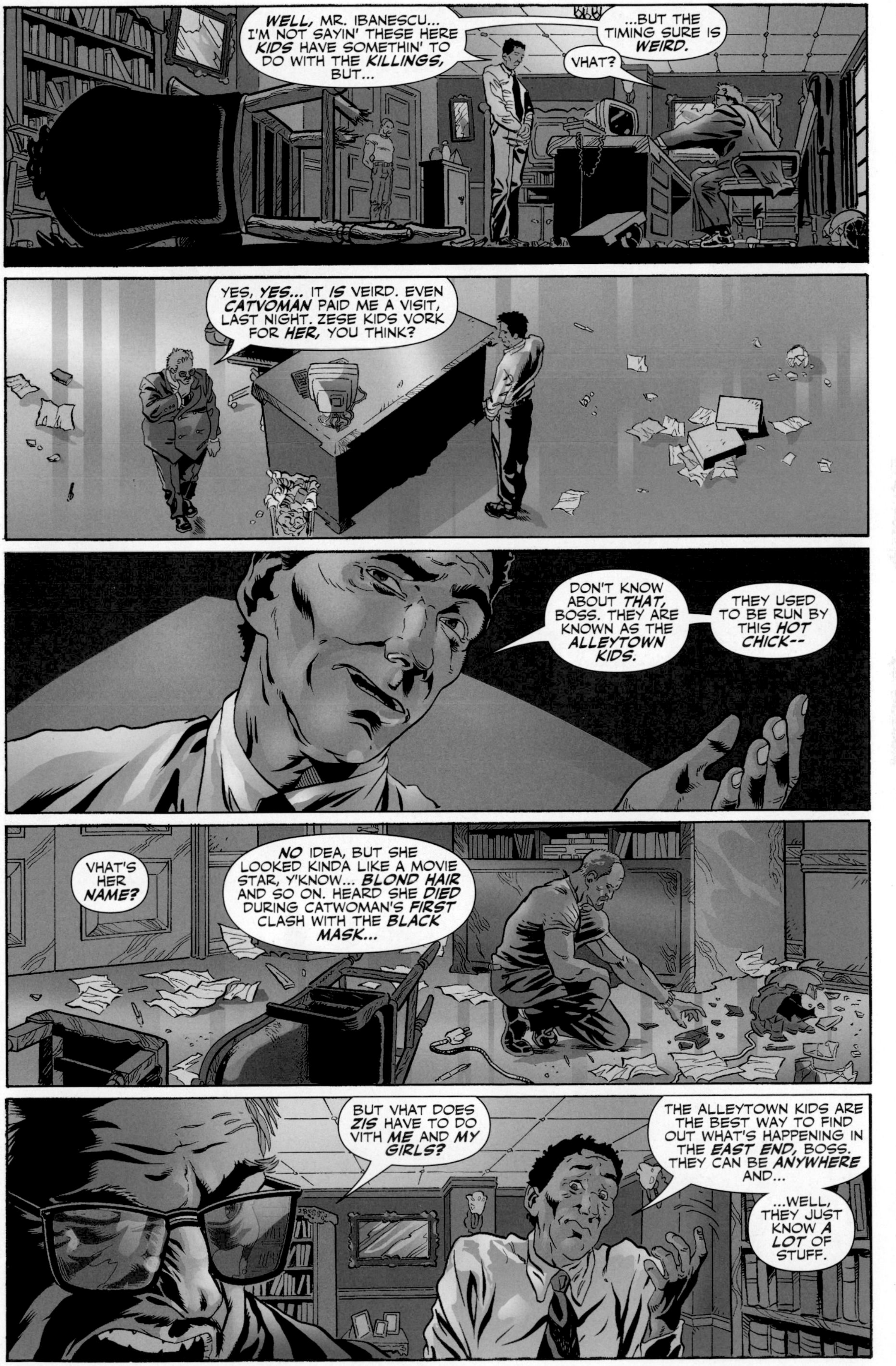
WELL, MR. IBANESCU... I'M NOT SAYIN' THESE HERE KIDS HAVE SOMETHIN' TO DO WITH THE KILLINGS, BUT...
...BUT THE TIMING SURE IS WEIRD.
VHAT?
YES, YES... IT IS VEIRD. EVEN CATVOMAN PAID ME A VISIT, LAST NIGHT. ZESE KIDS VORK FOR HER, YOU THINK?
DON'T KNOW ABOUT THAT, BOSS. THEY ARE KNOWN AS THE ALLEYTOWN KIDS.
THEY USED TO BE RUN BY THIS HOT CHICK--
VHAT'S HER NAME?
NO IDEA, BUT SHE LOOKED KINDA LIKE A MOVIE STAR, Y'KNOW... BLOND HAIR AND SO ON. HEARD SHE DIED DURING CATWOMAN'S FIRST CLASH WITH THE BLACK MASK...
BUT VHAT DOES ZIS HAVE TO DO VITH ME AND MY GIRLS?
THE ALLEYTOWN KIDS ARE THE BEST WAY TO FIND OUT WHAT'S HAPPENING IN THE EAST END, BOSS. THEY CAN BE ANYWHERE AND...
...WELL, THEY JUST KNOW A LOT OF STUFF.

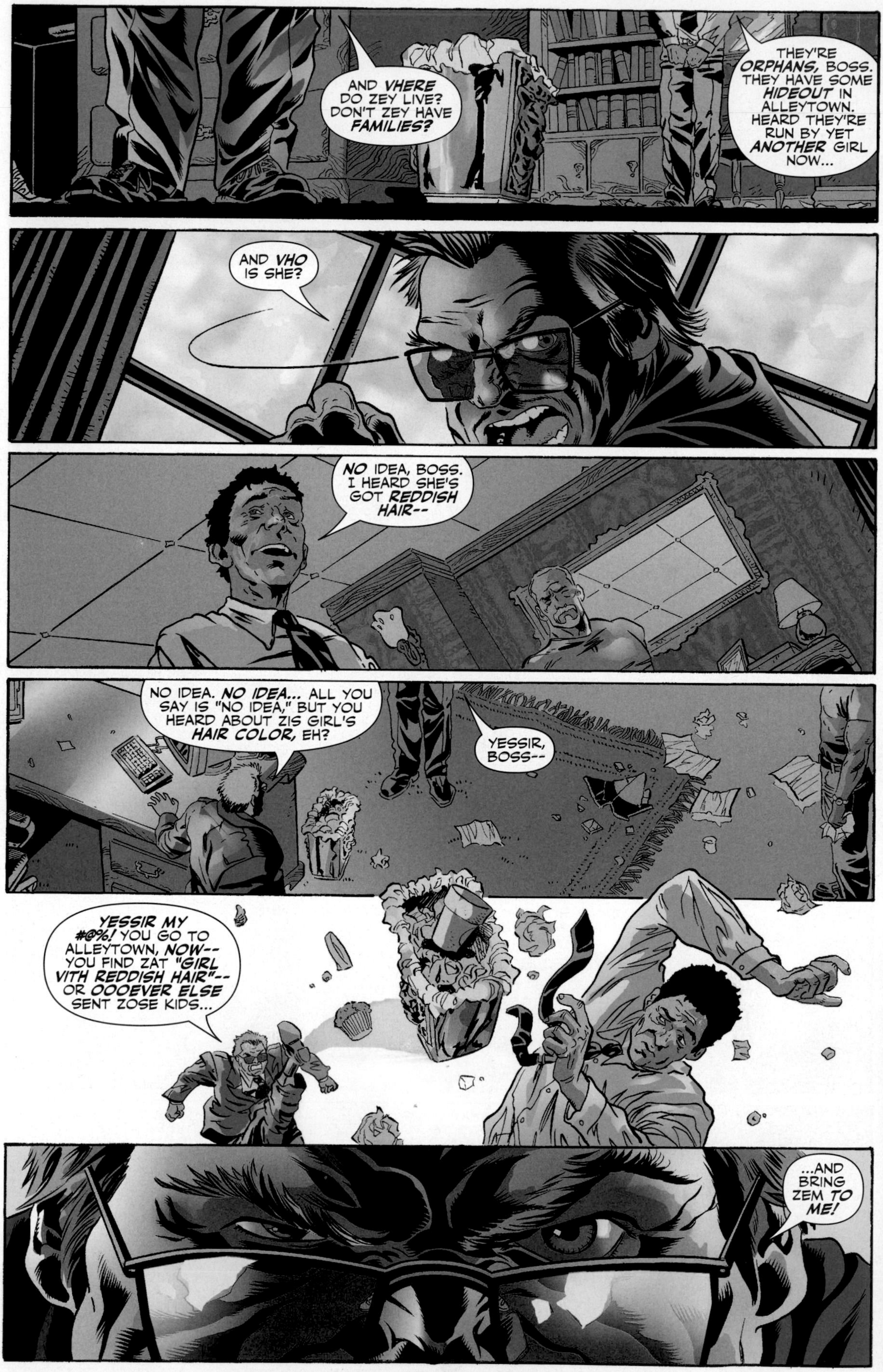
AND VHERE DO ZEY LIVE? DON'T ZEY HAVE FAMILIES?
THEY'RE ORPHANS, BOSS. THEY HAVE SOME HIDEOUT IN ALLEYTOWN. HEARD THEY'RE RUN BY YET ANOTHER GIRL NOW...
AND VHO IS SHE?
NO IDEA, BOSS. I HEARD SHE'S GOT REDDISH HAIR--
NO IDEA. NO IDEA... ALL YOU SAY IS "NO IDEA," BUT YOU HEARD ABOUT ZIS GIRL'S HAIR COLOR, EH?
YESSIR, BOSS--
YESSIR MY #@%! YOU GO TO ALLEYTOWN, NOW-- YOU FIND ZAT "GIRL VITH REDDISH HAIR"-- OR OOOEVER ELSE SENT ZOSE KIDS...
...AND BRING ZEM TO ME!

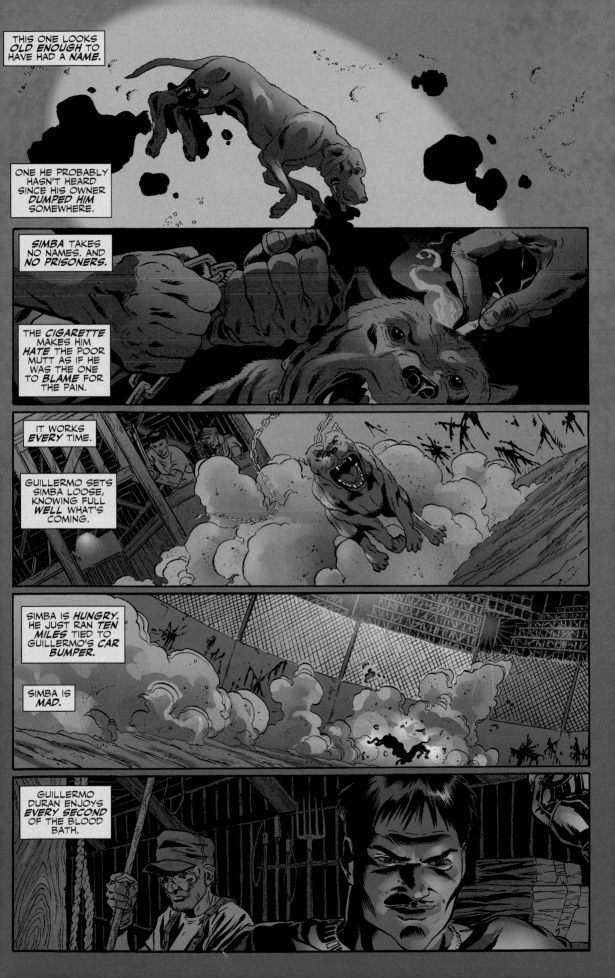

THIS ONE LOOKS *OLD ENOUGH* TO HAVE HAD A *NAME.*

ONE HE PROBABLY HASN'T HEARD SINCE HIS OWNER *DUMPED HIM* SOMEWHERE.

SIMBA TAKES NO NAMES. AND *NO PRISONERS.*

THE *CIGARETTE* MAKES HIM *HATE* THE POOR MUTT AS IF HE WAS THE ONE TO *BLAME* FOR THE PAIN.

IT WORKS *EVERY* TIME.

GUILLERMO SETS SIMBA LOOSE, KNOWING FULL *WELL* WHAT'S COMING.

SIMBA IS *HUNGRY.* HE JUST RAN *TEN MILES* TIED TO GUILLERMO'S *CAR BUMPER.*

SIMBA IS *MAD.*

GUILLERMO DURAN ENJOYS *EVERY SECOND* OF THE BLOOD BATH.

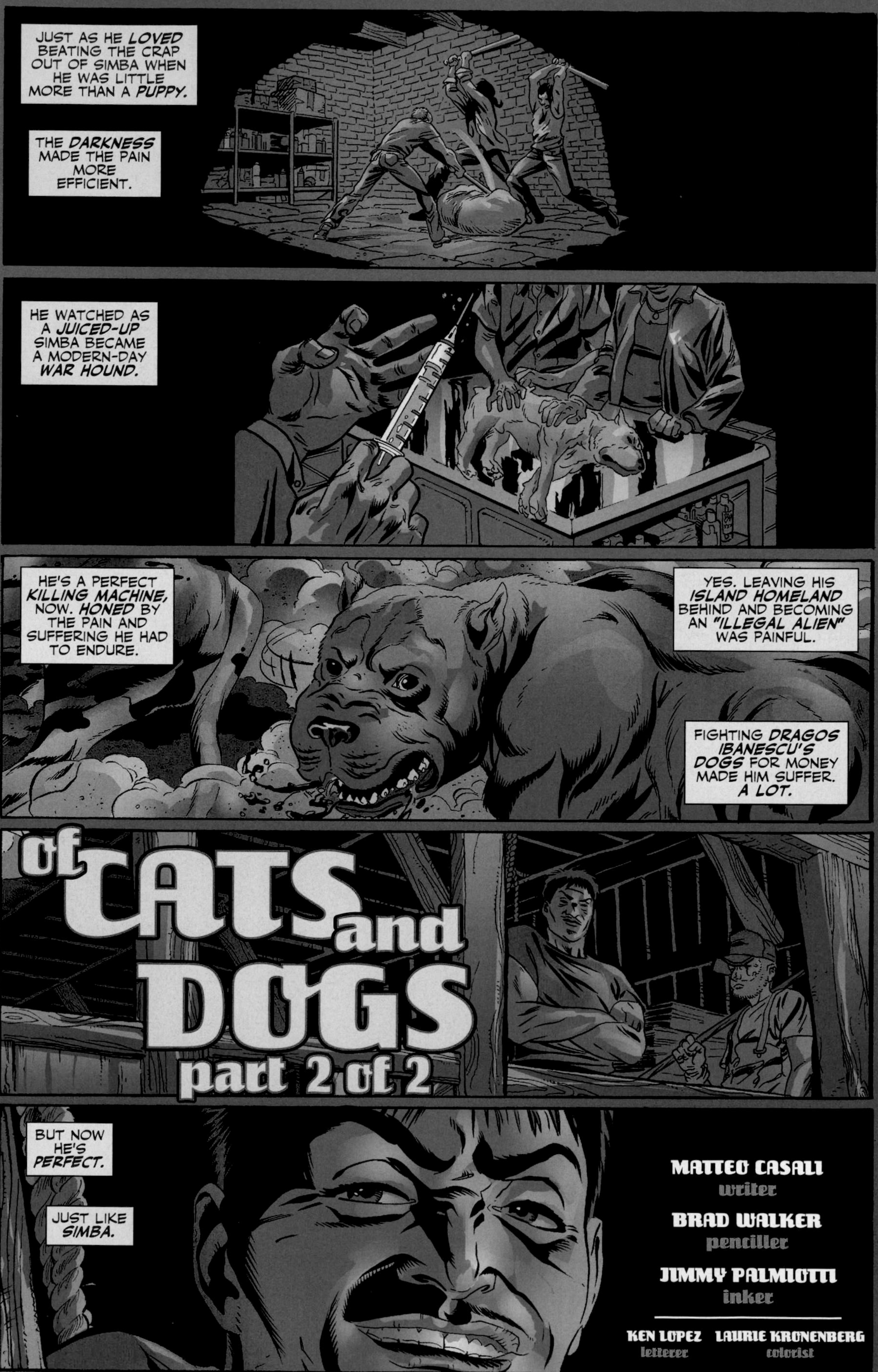
JUST AS HE LOVED BEATING THE CRAP OUT OF SIMBA WHEN HE WAS LITTLE MORE THAN A PUPPY.
THE DARKNESS MADE THE PAIN MORE EFFICIENT.
HE WATCHED AS A JUICED-UP SIMBA BECAME A MODERN-DAY WAR HOUND.
HE'S A PERFECT KILLING MACHINE, NOW. HONED BY THE PAIN AND SUFFERING HE HAD TO ENDURE.
YES. LEAVING HIS ISLAND HOMELAND BEHIND AND BECOMING AN "ILLEGAL ALIEN" WAS PAINFUL.
FIGHTING DRAGOS IBANESCU'S DOGS FOR MONEY MADE HIM SUFFER. A LOT.
of CATS and DOGS
part 2 of 2
BUT NOW HE'S PERFECT.
JUST LIKE SIMBA.
MATTEO CASALI
writer
BRAD WALKER
penciller
JIMMY PALMIOTTI
inker
KEN LOPEZ
letterer
LAURIE KRONENBERG
colorist

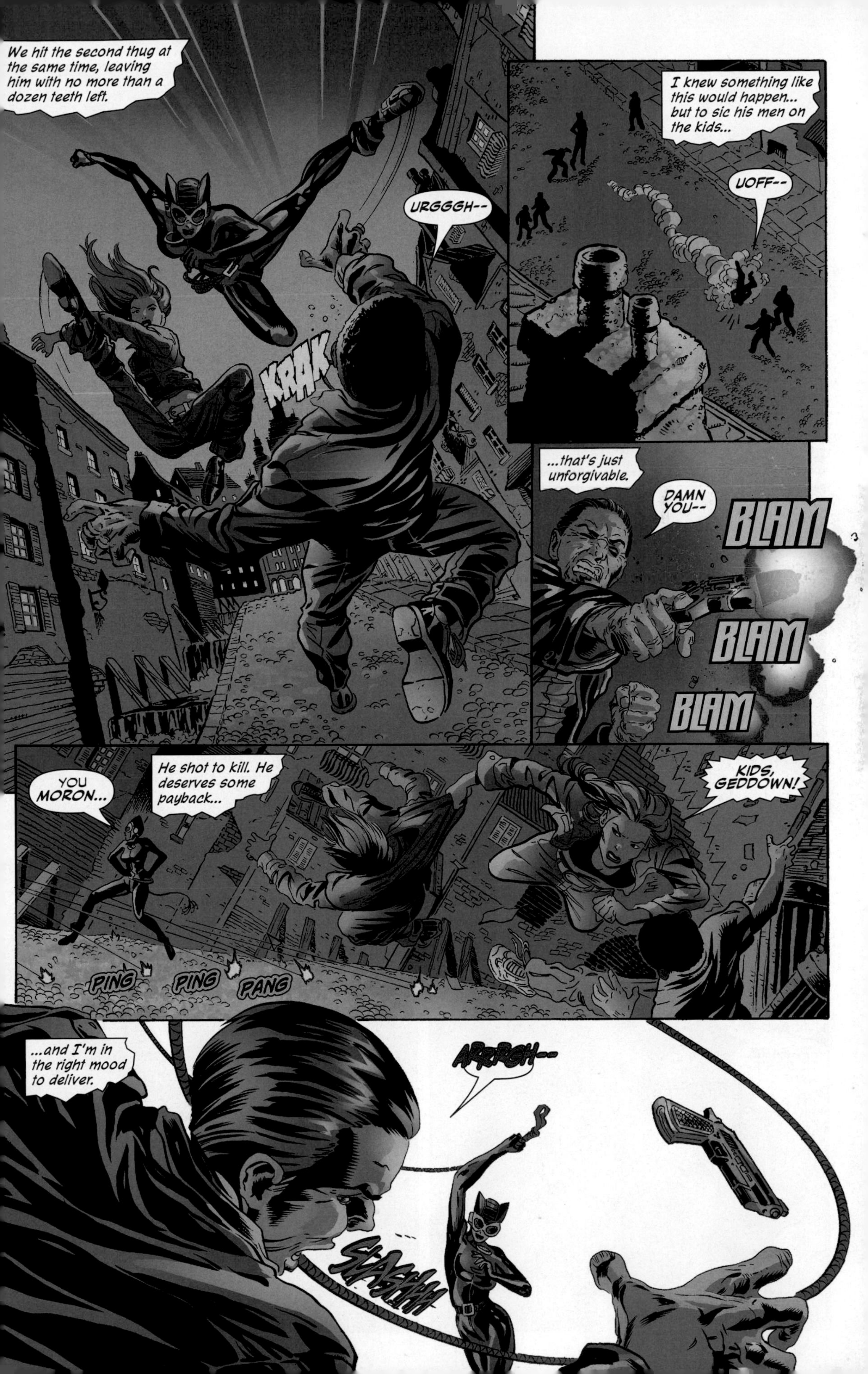
We hit the second thug at the same time, leaving him with no more than a dozen teeth left.
URGGGH--
KRAK
I knew something like this would happen... but to sic his men on the kids...
UOFF--
...that's just unforgivable.
DAMN YOU--
BLAM
BLAM
BLAM
YOU MORON...
He shot to kill. He deserves some payback...
KIDS, GEDDOWN!
PING
PING
PANG
...and I'm in the right mood to deliver.
ARRRGH--
SLASHHH

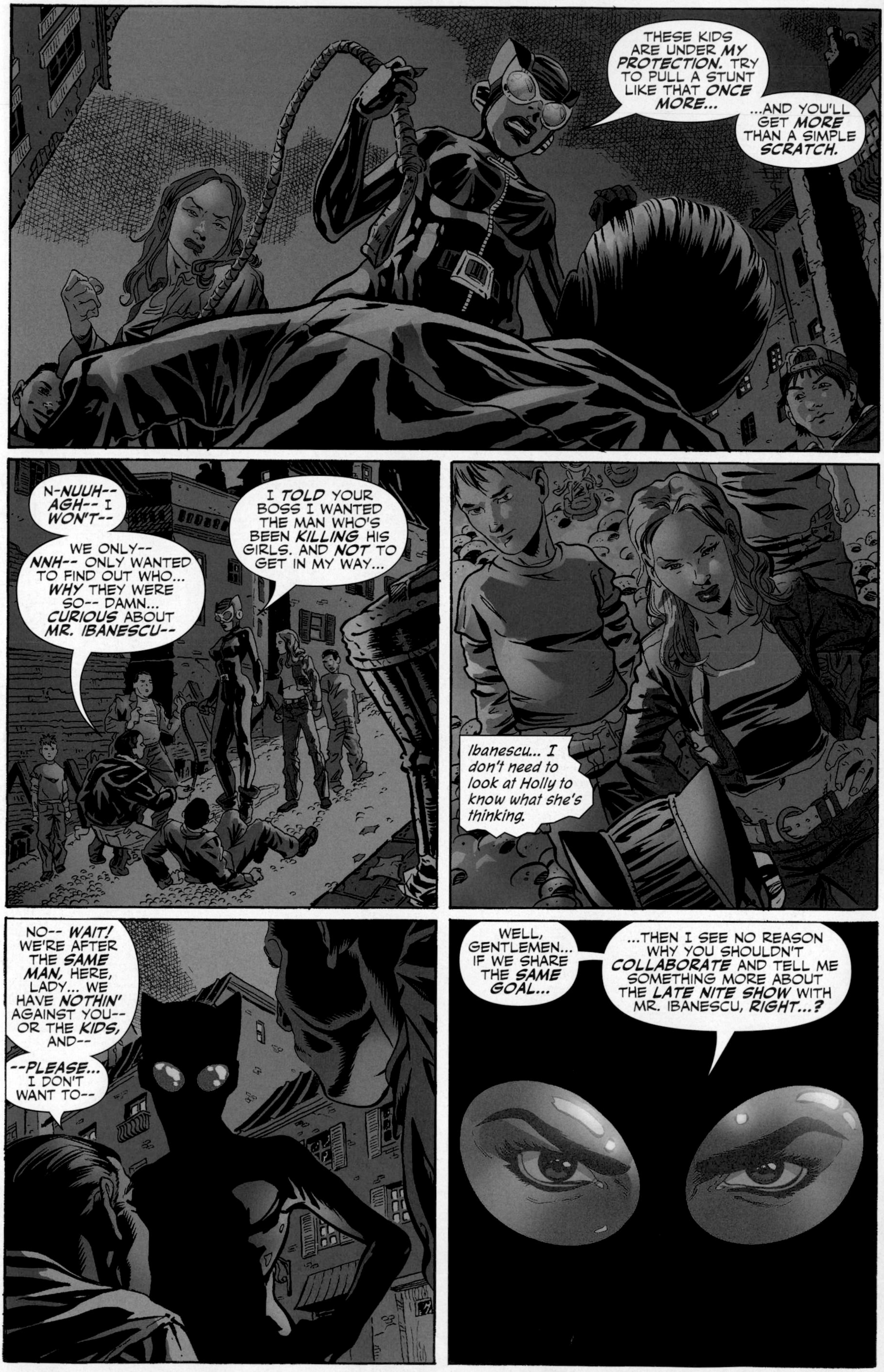

THESE KIDS ARE UNDER MY PROTECTION. TRY TO PULL A STUNT LIKE THAT ONCE MORE...
...AND YOU'LL GET MORE THAN A SIMPLE SCRATCH.
N-NUUH-- AGH-- I WON'T--
WE ONLY-- NNH-- ONLY WANTED TO FIND OUT WHO... WHY THEY WERE SO-- DAMN... CURIOUS ABOUT MR. IBANESCU--
I TOLD YOUR BOSS I WANTED THE MAN WHO'S BEEN KILLING HIS GIRLS. AND NOT TO GET IN MY WAY...
Ibanescu... I don't need to look at Holly to know what she's thinking.
NO-- WAIT! WE'RE AFTER THE SAME MAN, HERE, LADY... WE HAVE NOTHIN' AGAINST YOU-- OR THE KIDS, AND--
--PLEASE... I DON'T WANT TO--
WELL, GENTLEMEN... IF WE SHARE THE SAME GOAL...
...THEN I SEE NO REASON WHY YOU SHOULDN'T COLLABORATE AND TELL ME SOMETHING MORE ABOUT THE LATE NITE SHOW WITH MR. IBANESCU, RIGHT...?

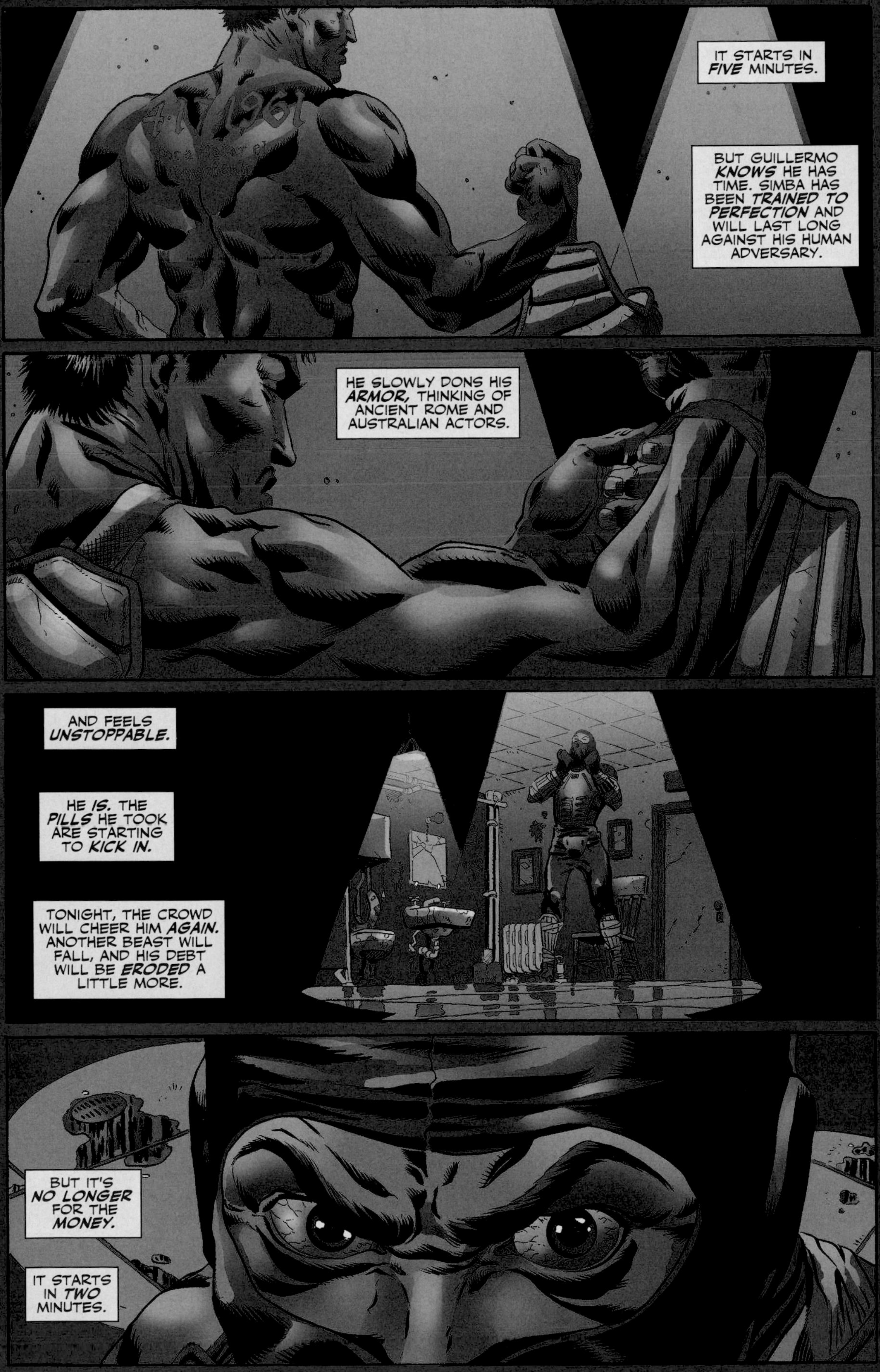
IT STARTS IN *FIVE* MINUTES.
BUT GUILLERMO *KNOWS* HE HAS TIME. SIMBA HAS BEEN *TRAINED TO PERFECTION* AND WILL LAST LONG AGAINST HIS HUMAN ADVERSARY.
HE SLOWLY DONS HIS *ARMOR,* THINKING OF ANCIENT ROME AND AUSTRALIAN ACTORS.
AND FEELS *UNSTOPPABLE.*
HE *IS.* THE *PILLS* HE TOOK ARE STARTING TO *KICK IN.*
TONIGHT, THE CROWD WILL CHEER HIM *AGAIN.* ANOTHER BEAST WILL FALL, AND HIS DEBT WILL BE *ERODED* A LITTLE MORE.
BUT IT'S *NO LONGER* FOR THE *MONEY.*
IT STARTS IN *TWO* MINUTES.

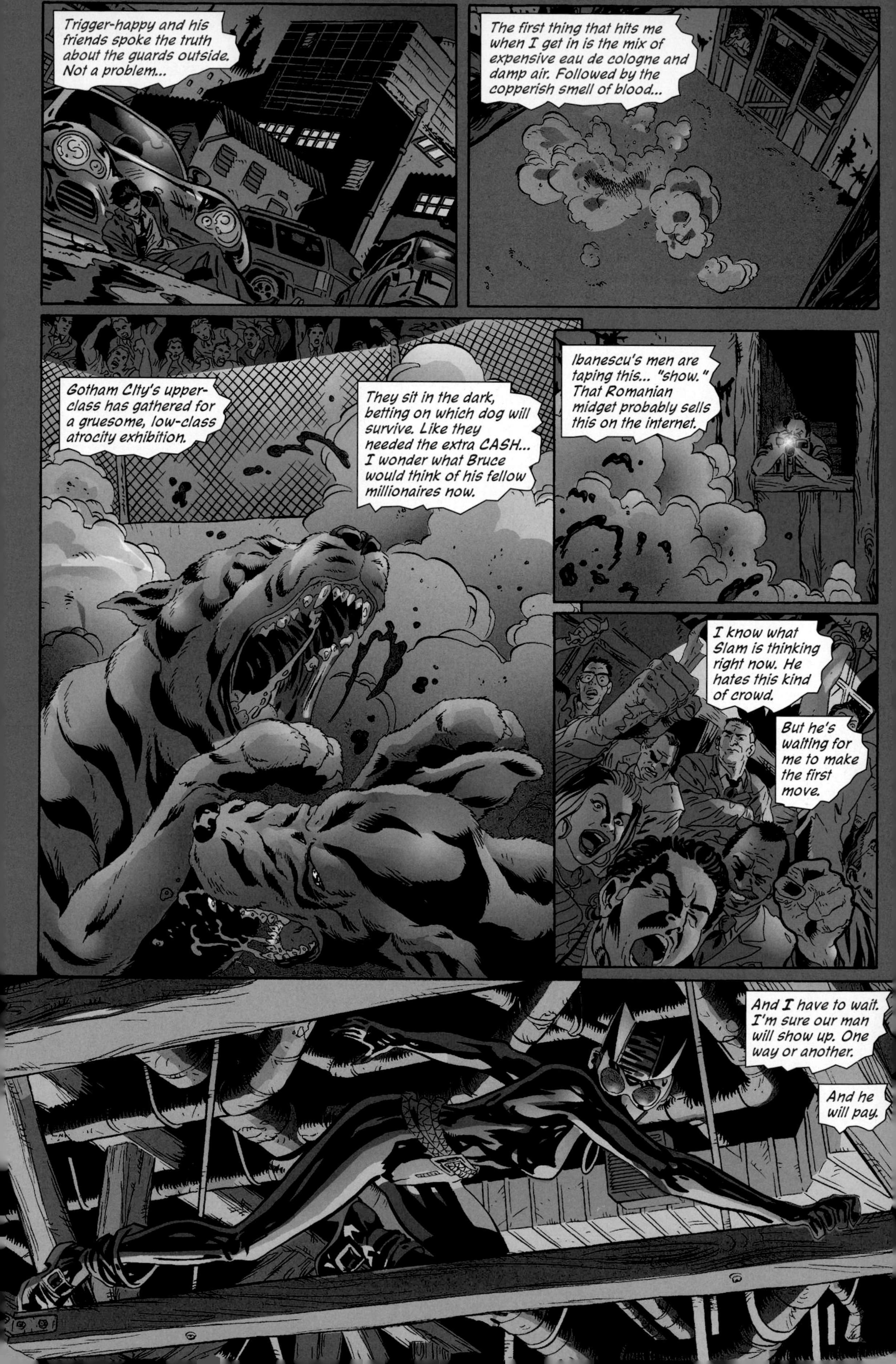
Trigger-happy and his friends spoke the truth about the guards outside. Not a problem...
The first thing that hits me when I get in is the mix of expensive eau de cologne and damp air. Followed by the copperish smell of blood...
Gotham City's upper-class has gathered for a gruesome, low-class atrocity exhibition.
They sit in the dark, betting on which dog will survive. Like they needed the extra CASH... I wonder what Bruce would think of his fellow millionaires now.
Ibanescu's men are taping this... "show." That Romanian midget probably sells this on the internet.
I know what Slam is thinking right now. He hates this kind of crowd.
But he's waiting for me to make the first move.
And I have to wait. I'm sure our man will show up. One way or another.
And he will pay.

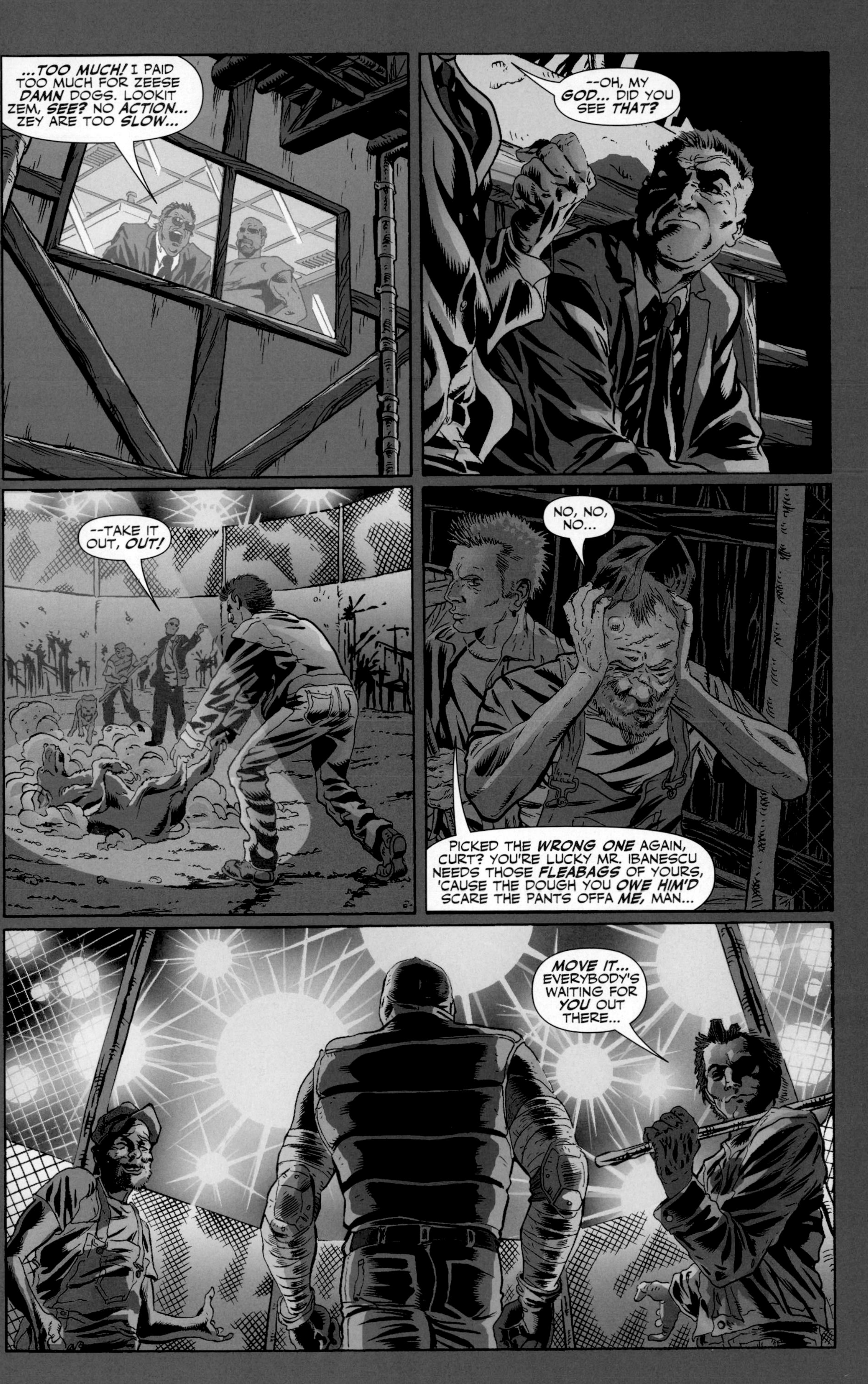

...TOO MUCH! I PAID TOO MUCH FOR ZEESE DAMN DOGS. LOOKIT ZEM, SEE? NO ACTION... ZEY ARE TOO SLOW...
--OH, MY GOD... DID YOU SEE THAT?
--TAKE IT OUT, OUT!
NO, NO, NO...
PICKED THE WRONG ONE AGAIN, CURT? YOU'RE LUCKY MR. IBANESCU NEEDS THOSE FLEABAGS OF YOURS, 'CAUSE THE DOUGH YOU OWE HIM'D SCARE THE PANTS OFFA ME, MAN...
MOVE IT... EVERYBODY'S WAITING FOR YOU OUT THERE...

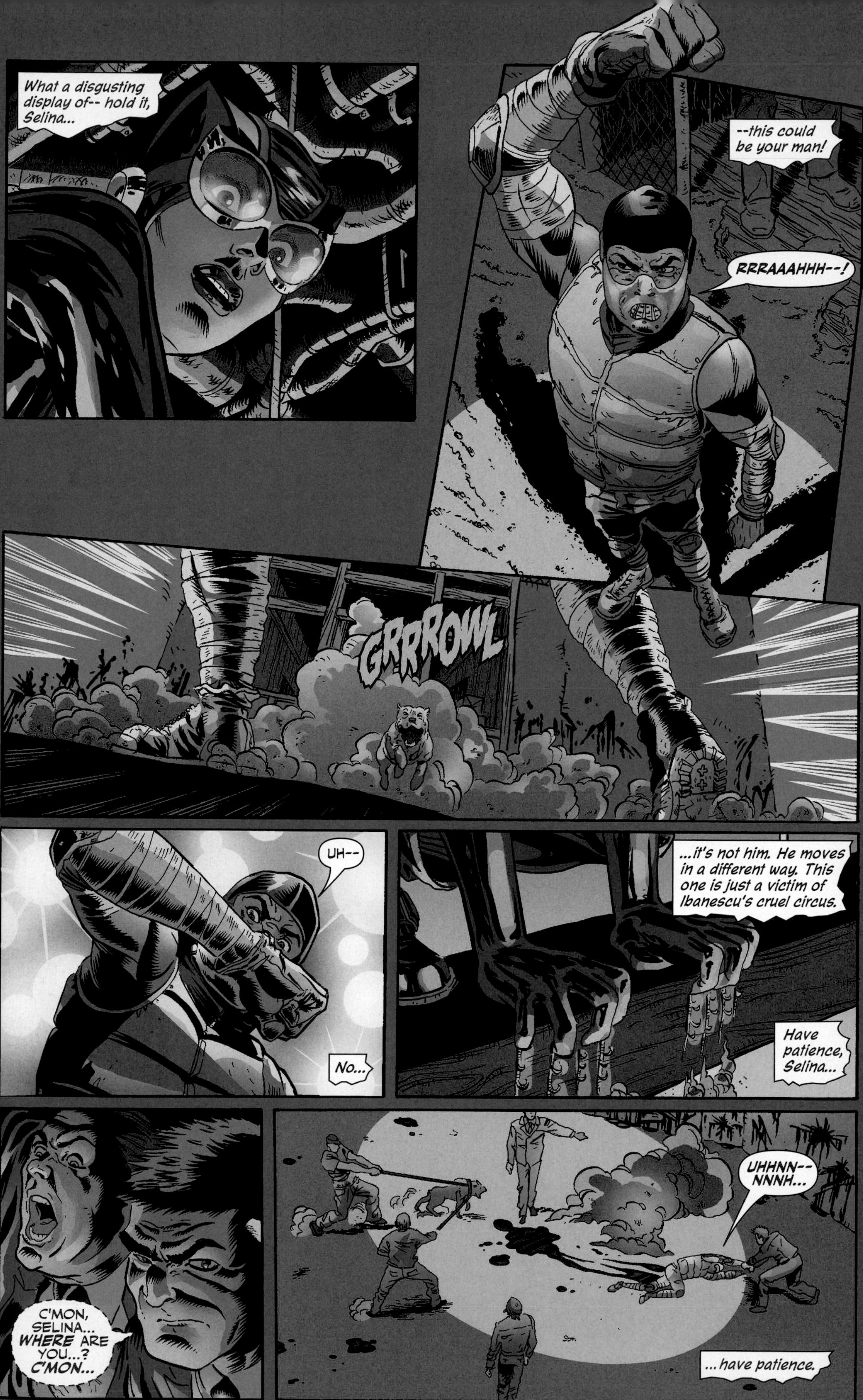
What a disgusting display of-- hold it, Selina...
--this could be your man!
RRRAAAHHH--!
GRRROWL
UH--
No...
...it's not him. He moves in a different way. This one is just a victim of Ibanescu's cruel circus.
Have patience, Selina...
C'MON, SELINA... WHERE ARE YOU...? C'MON...
UHHNN-- NNNH...
...have patience.

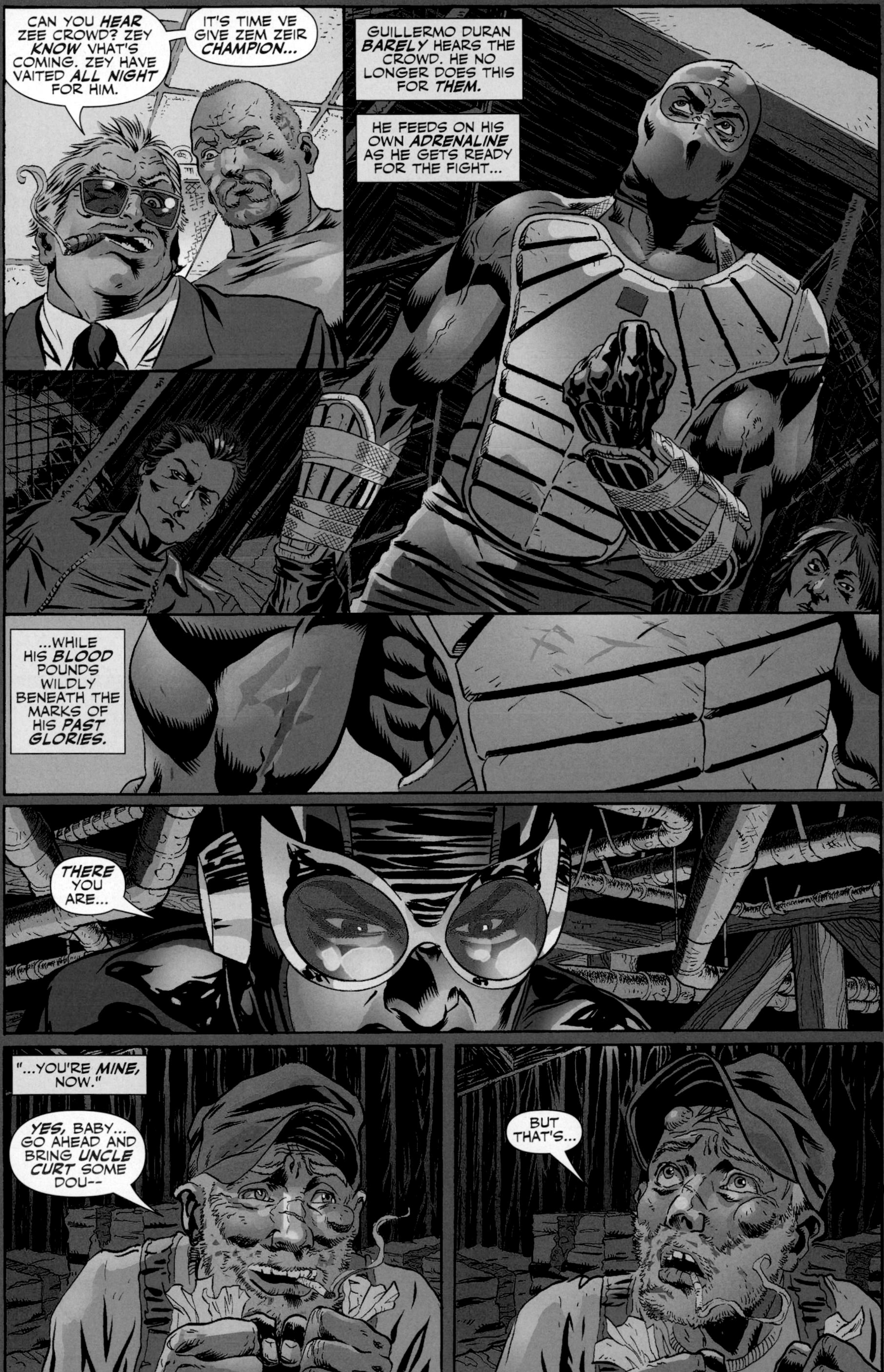
CAN YOU HEAR ZEE CROWD? ZEY KNOW VHAT'S COMING. ZEY HAVE VAITED ALL NIGHT FOR HIM.
IT'S TIME VE GIVE ZEM ZEIR CHAMPION...
GUILLERMO DURAN BARELY HEARS THE CROWD. HE NO LONGER DOES THIS FOR THEM.
HE FEEDS ON HIS OWN ADRENALINE AS HE GETS READY FOR THE FIGHT...
...WHILE HIS BLOOD POUNDS WILDLY BENEATH THE MARKS OF HIS PAST GLORIES.
THERE YOU ARE...
"...YOU'RE MINE, NOW."
YES, BABY... GO AHEAD AND BRING UNCLE CURT SOME DOU--
BUT THAT'S...

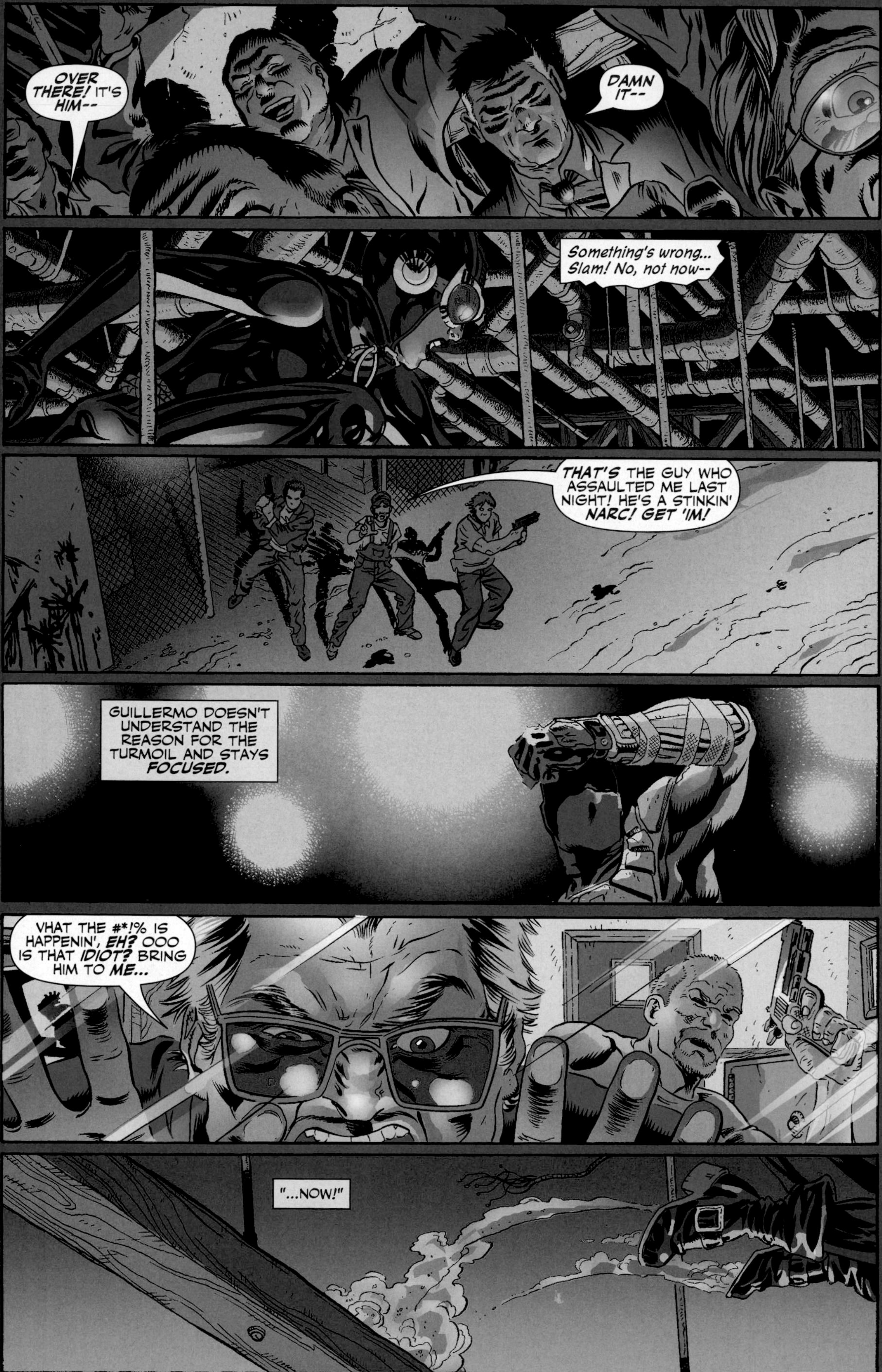
OVER THERE! IT'S HIM--
DAMN IT--
Something's wrong... Slam! No, not now--
THAT'S THE GUY WHO ASSAULTED ME LAST NIGHT! HE'S A STINKIN' NARC! GET 'IM!
GUILLERMO DOESN'T UNDERSTAND THE REASON FOR THE TURMOIL AND STAYS FOCUSED.
VHAT THE #*!% IS HAPPENIN', EH? OOO IS THAT IDIOT? BRING HIM TO ME...
"...NOW!"

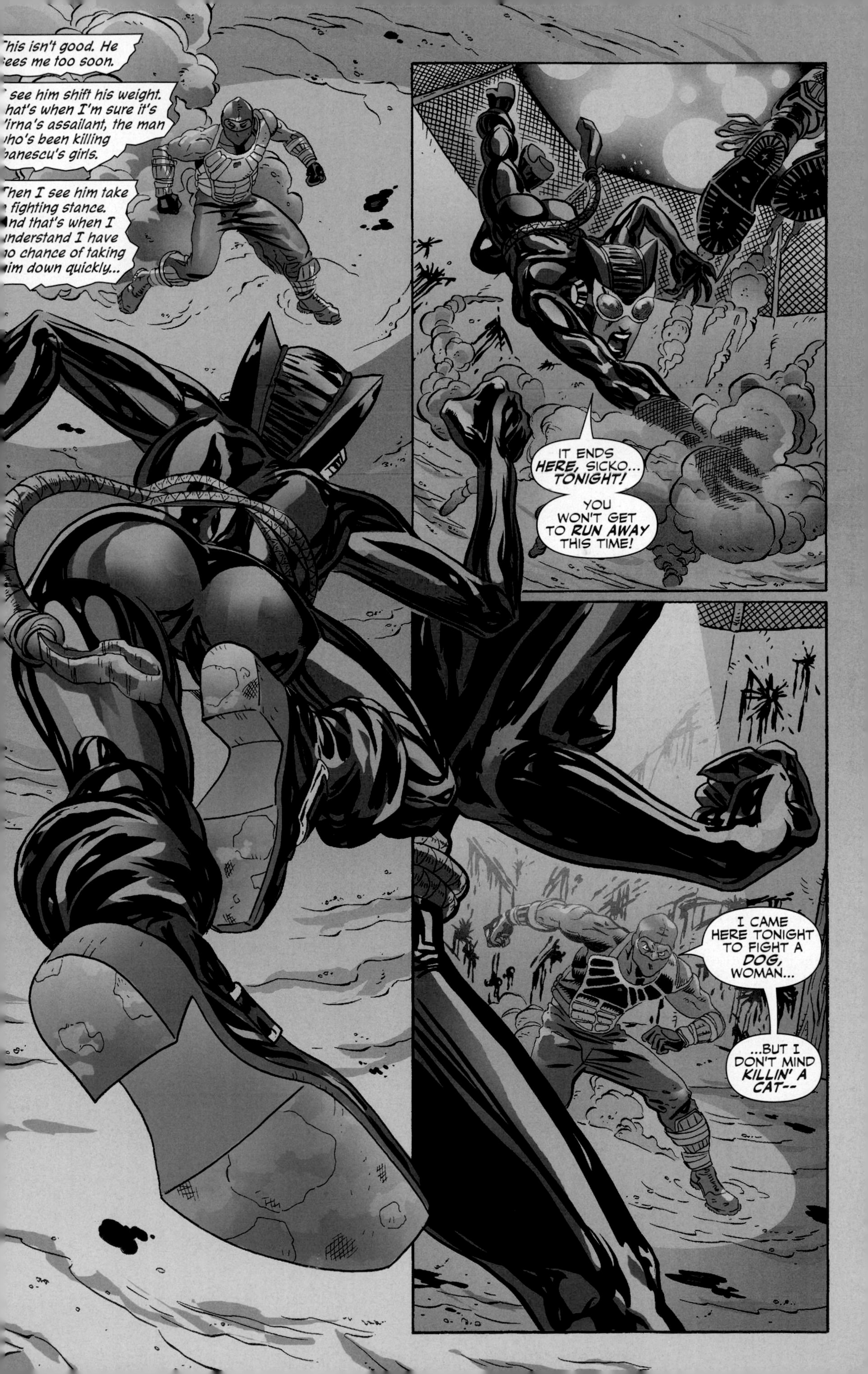
This isn't good. He sees me too soon.
I see him shift his weight. That's when I'm sure it's Virna's assailant, the man who's been killing Ioanescu's girls.
Then I see him take a fighting stance. And that's when I understand I have no chance of taking him down quickly...
IT ENDS HERE, SICKO... TONIGHT!
YOU WON'T GET TO RUN AWAY THIS TIME!
I CAME HERE TONIGHT TO FIGHT A DOG, WOMAN...
...BUT I DON'T MIND KILLIN' A CAT--

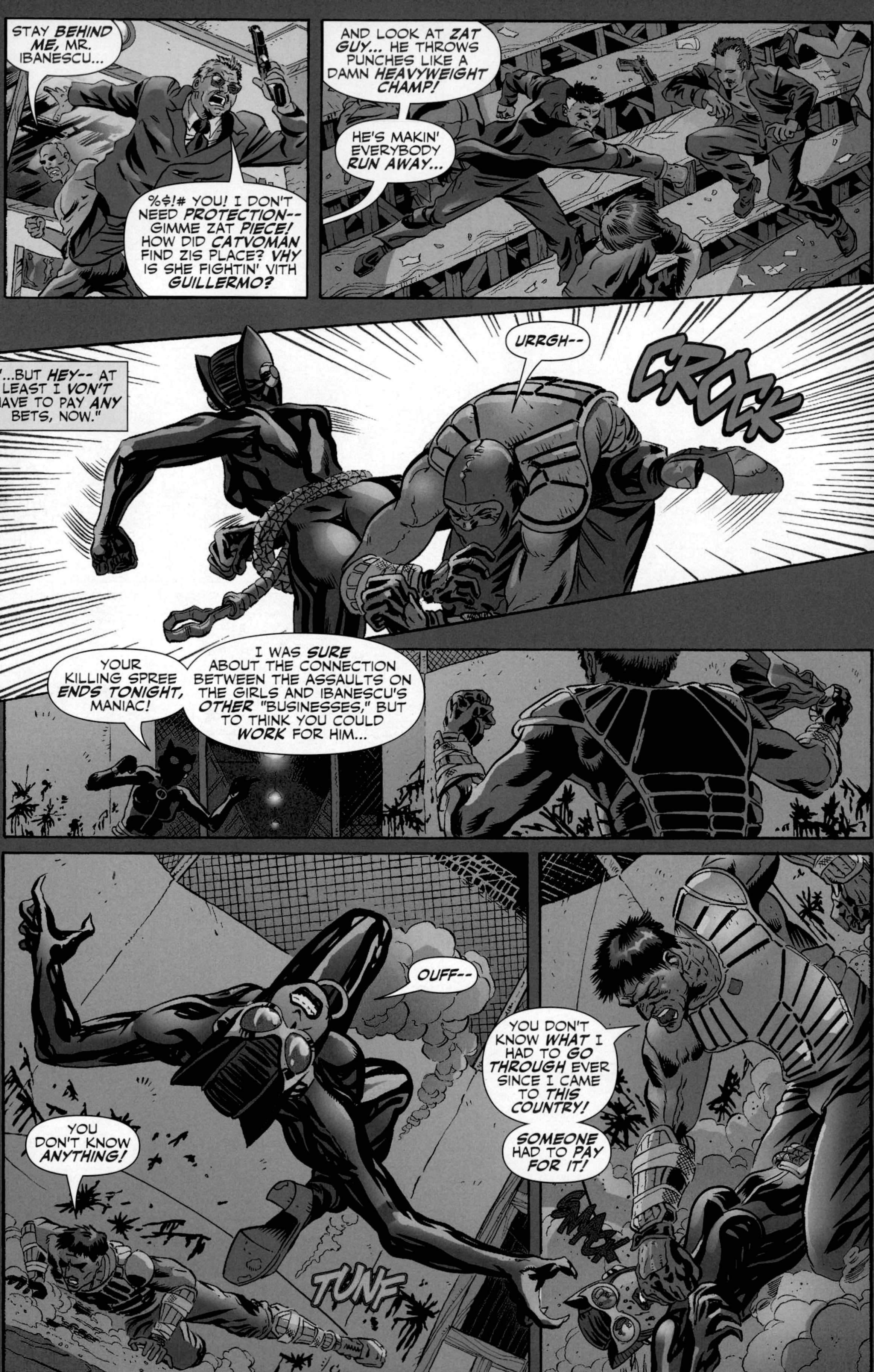
STAY BEHIND ME, MR. IBANESCU...
%$!# YOU! I DON'T NEED PROTECTION-- GIMME ZAT PIECE! HOW DID CATVOMAN FIND ZIS PLACE? VHY IS SHE FIGHTIN' VITH GUILLERMO?
AND LOOK AT ZAT GUY... HE THROWS PUNCHES LIKE A DAMN HEAVYWEIGHT CHAMP!
HE'S MAKIN' EVERYBODY RUN AWAY...
"...BUT HEY-- AT LEAST I VON'T HAVE TO PAY ANY BETS, NOW."
URRGH--
CROCK
YOUR KILLING SPREE ENDS TONIGHT, MANIAC!
I WAS SURE ABOUT THE CONNECTION BETWEEN THE ASSAULTS ON THE GIRLS AND IBANESCU'S OTHER "BUSINESSES," BUT TO THINK YOU COULD WORK FOR HIM...
OUFF--
YOU DON'T KNOW ANYTHING!
TUNF
YOU DON'T KNOW WHAT I HAD TO GO THROUGH EVER SINCE I CAME TO THIS COUNTRY!
SOMEONE HAD TO PAY FOR IT!
SMACK

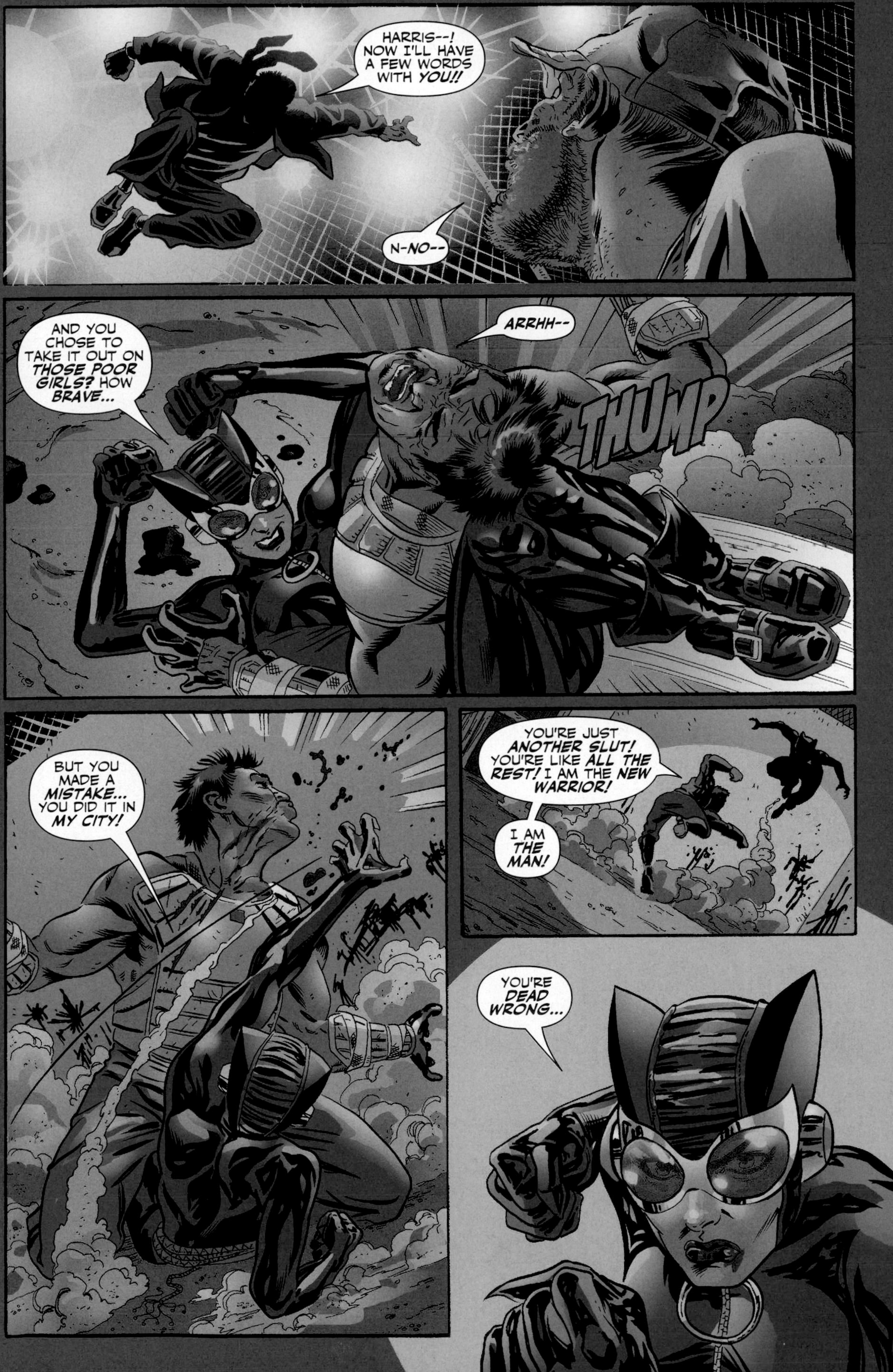
HARRIS--! NOW I'LL HAVE A FEW WORDS WITH YOU!!
N-NO--
AND YOU CHOSE TO TAKE IT OUT ON THOSE POOR GIRLS? HOW BRAVE...
ARRHH--
THUMP
BUT YOU MADE A MISTAKE... YOU DID IT IN MY CITY!
YOU'RE JUST ANOTHER SLUT! YOU'RE LIKE ALL THE REST! I AM THE NEW WARRIOR!
I AM THE MAN!
YOU'RE DEAD WRONG...

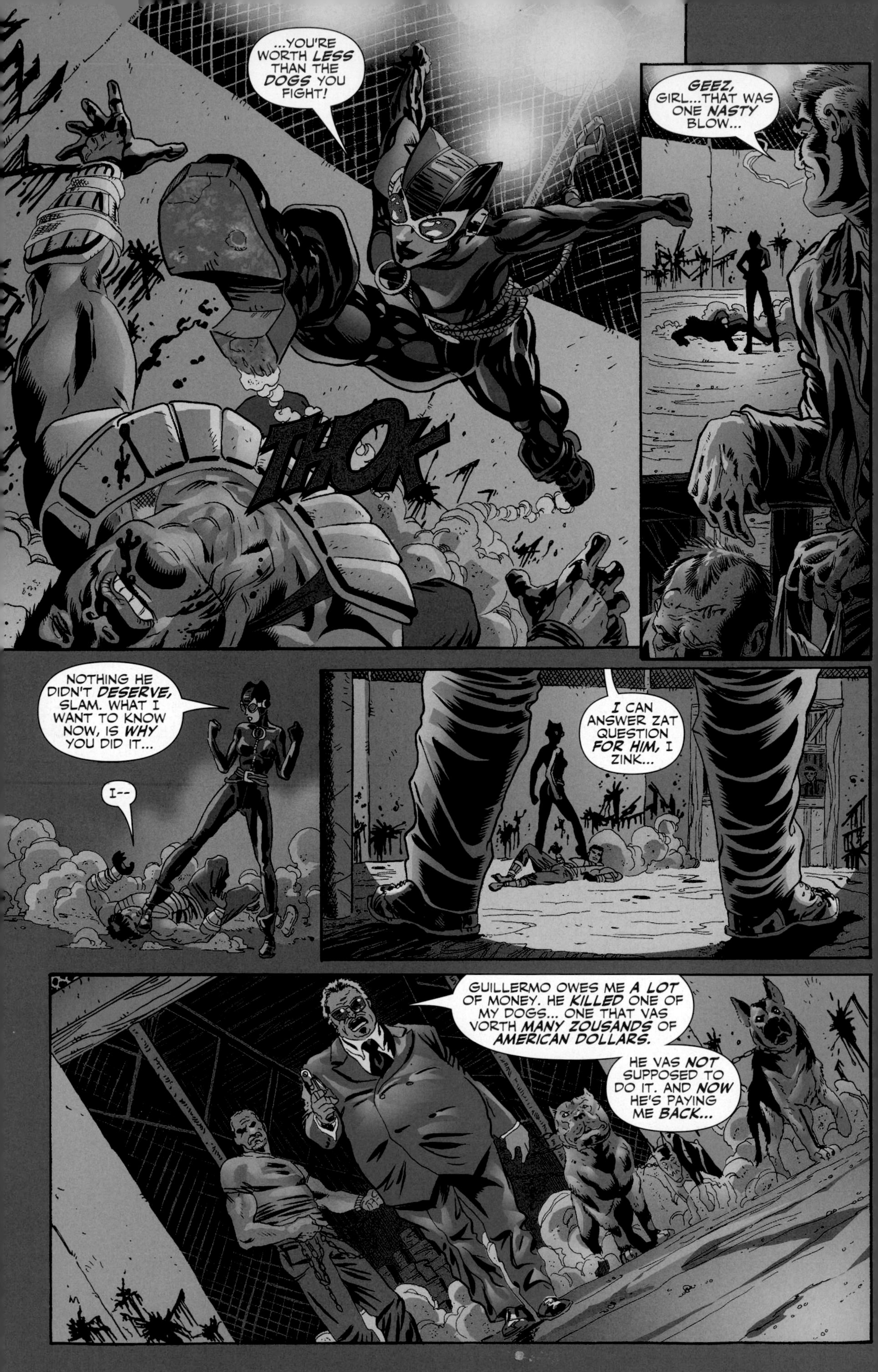
...YOU'RE WORTH LESS THAN THE DOGS YOU FIGHT!
THOK
GEEZ, GIRL...THAT WAS ONE NASTY BLOW...
NOTHING HE DIDN'T DESERVE, SLAM. WHAT I WANT TO KNOW NOW, IS WHY YOU DID IT...
I--
I CAN ANSWER ZAT QUESTION FOR HIM, I ZINK...
GUILLERMO OWES ME A LOT OF MONEY. HE KILLED ONE OF MY DOGS... ONE THAT VAS VORTH MANY ZOUSANDS OF AMERICAN DOLLARS.
HE VAS NOT SUPPOSED TO DO IT. AND NOW HE'S PAYING ME BACK...

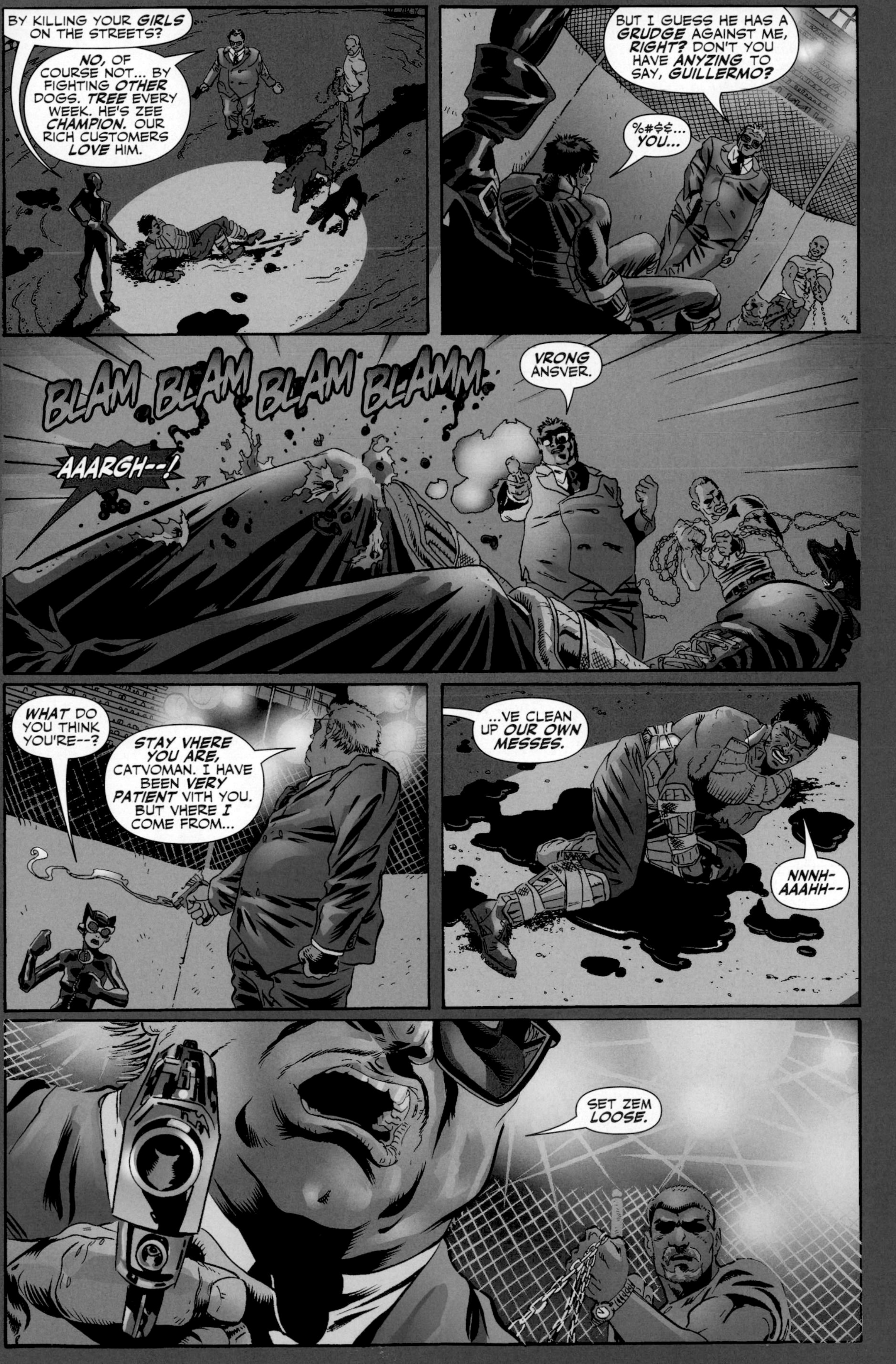
BY KILLING YOUR GIRLS ON THE STREETS?
NO, OF COURSE NOT... BY FIGHTING OTHER DOGS. TREE EVERY WEEK. HE'S ZEE CHAMPION. OUR RICH CUSTOMERS LOVE HIM.
BUT I GUESS HE HAS A GRUDGE AGAINST ME, RIGHT? DON'T YOU HAVE ANYZING TO SAY, GUILLERMO?
%#$$... YOU...
BLAM BLAM BLAM BLAMM
VRONG ANSVER.
AAARGH--!
WHAT DO YOU THINK YOU'RE--?
STAY VHERE YOU ARE, CATVOMAN. I HAVE BEEN VERY PATIENT VITH YOU. BUT VHERE I COME FROM...
...VE CLEAN UP OUR OWN MESSES.
NNNH-AAAHH--
SET ZEM LOOSE.

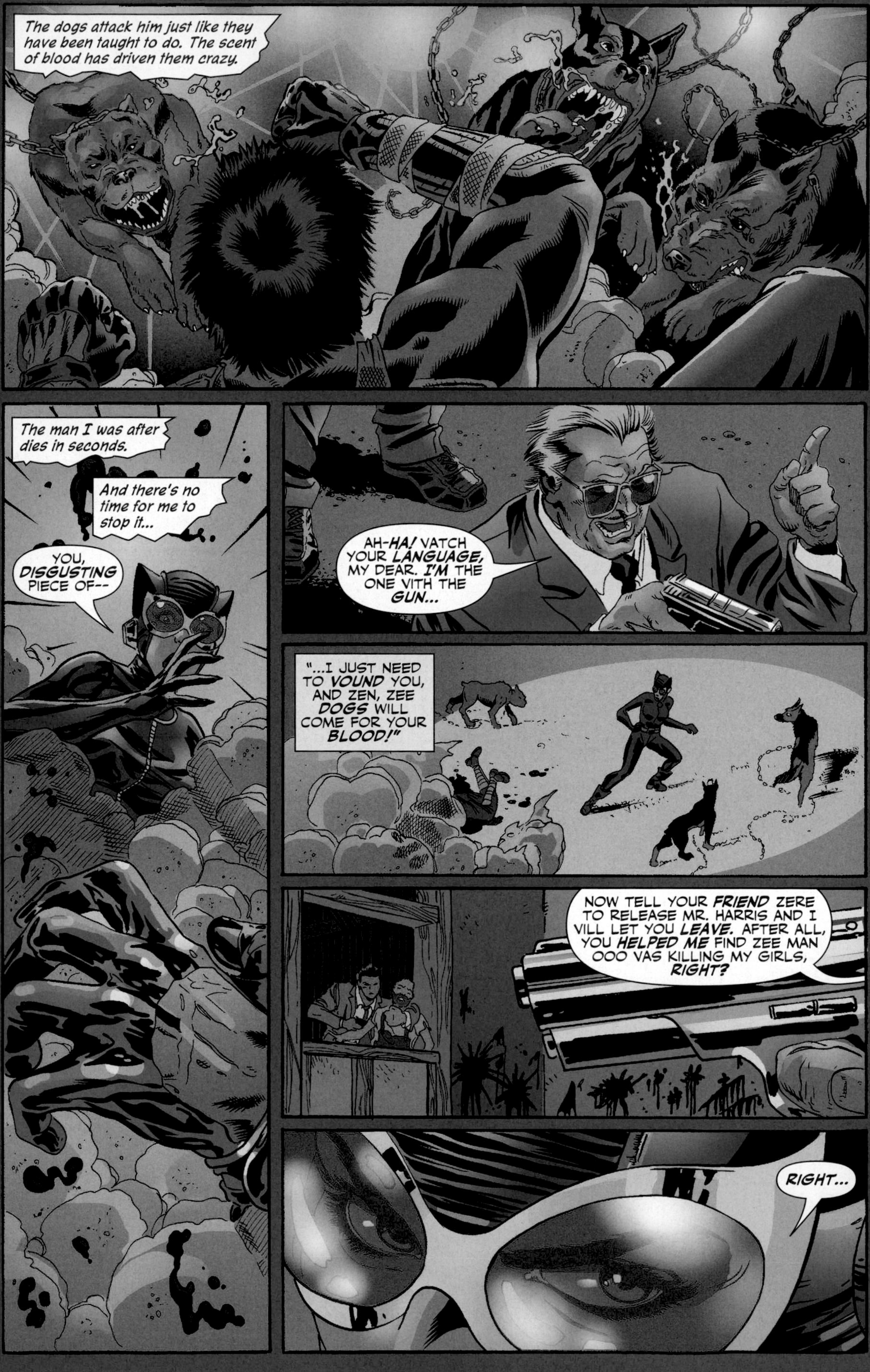
The dogs attack him just like they have been taught to do. The scent of blood has driven them crazy.
The man I was after dies in seconds.
And there's no time for me to stop it...
YOU, DISGUSTING PIECE OF--
AH-HA! VATCH YOUR LANGUAGE, MY DEAR. I'M THE ONE VITH THE GUN...
"...I JUST NEED TO VOUND YOU, AND ZEN, ZEE DOGS WILL COME FOR YOUR BLOOD!"
NOW TELL YOUR FRIEND ZERE TO RELEASE MR. HARRIS AND I VILL LET YOU LEAVE. AFTER ALL, YOU HELPED ME FIND ZEE MAN OOO VAS KILLING MY GIRLS, RIGHT?
RIGHT...

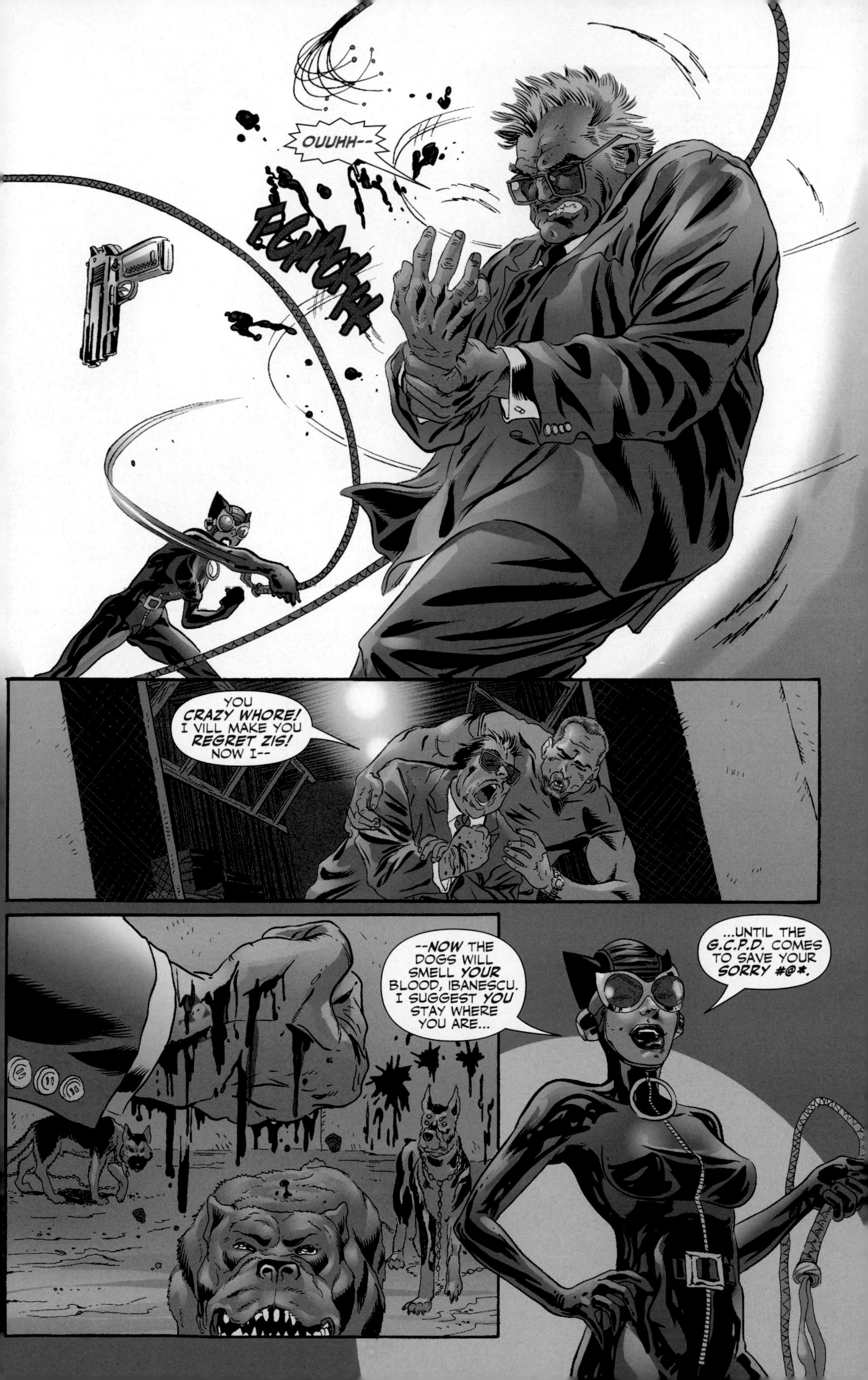
OUUHH--
TCHUCKKK
YOU CRAZY WHORE! I VILL MAKE YOU REGRET ZIS! NOW I--
--NOW THE DOGS WILL SMELL YOUR BLOOD, IBANESCU. I SUGGEST YOU STAY WHERE YOU ARE...
...UNTIL THE G.C.P.D. COMES TO SAVE YOUR SORRY #@*.

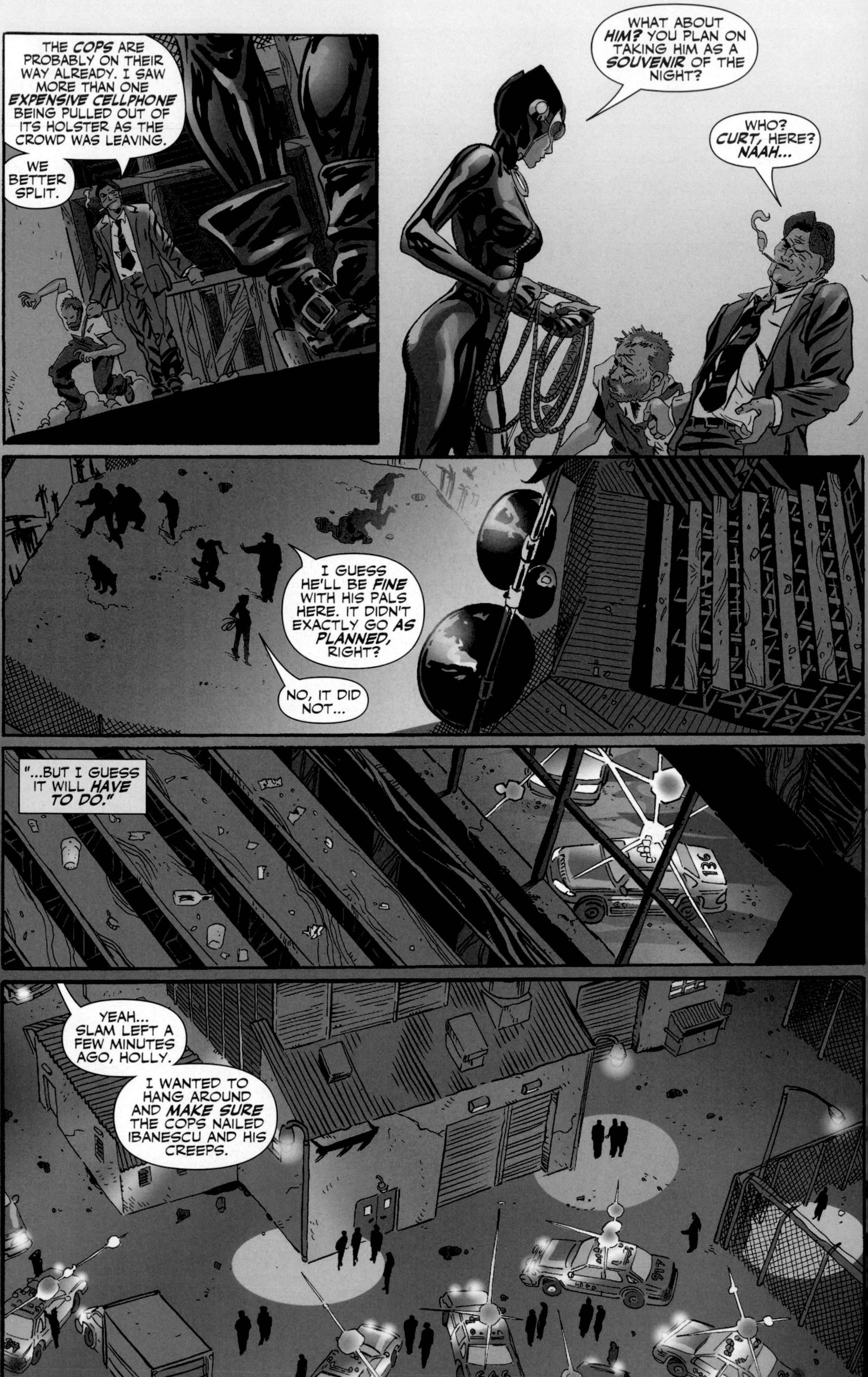
THE COPS ARE PROBABLY ON THEIR WAY ALREADY. I SAW MORE THAN ONE EXPENSIVE CELLPHONE BEING PULLED OUT OF ITS HOLSTER AS THE CROWD WAS LEAVING.
WE BETTER SPLIT.
WHAT ABOUT HIM? YOU PLAN ON TAKING HIM AS A SOUVENIR OF THE NIGHT?
WHO? CURT, HERE? NAAH...
I GUESS HE'LL BE FINE WITH HIS PALS HERE. IT DIDN'T EXACTLY GO AS PLANNED, RIGHT?
NO, IT DID NOT...
"...BUT I GUESS IT WILL HAVE TO DO."
136
YEAH... SLAM LEFT A FEW MINUTES AGO, HOLLY.
I WANTED TO HANG AROUND AND MAKE SURE THE COPS NAILED IBANESCU AND HIS CREEPS.

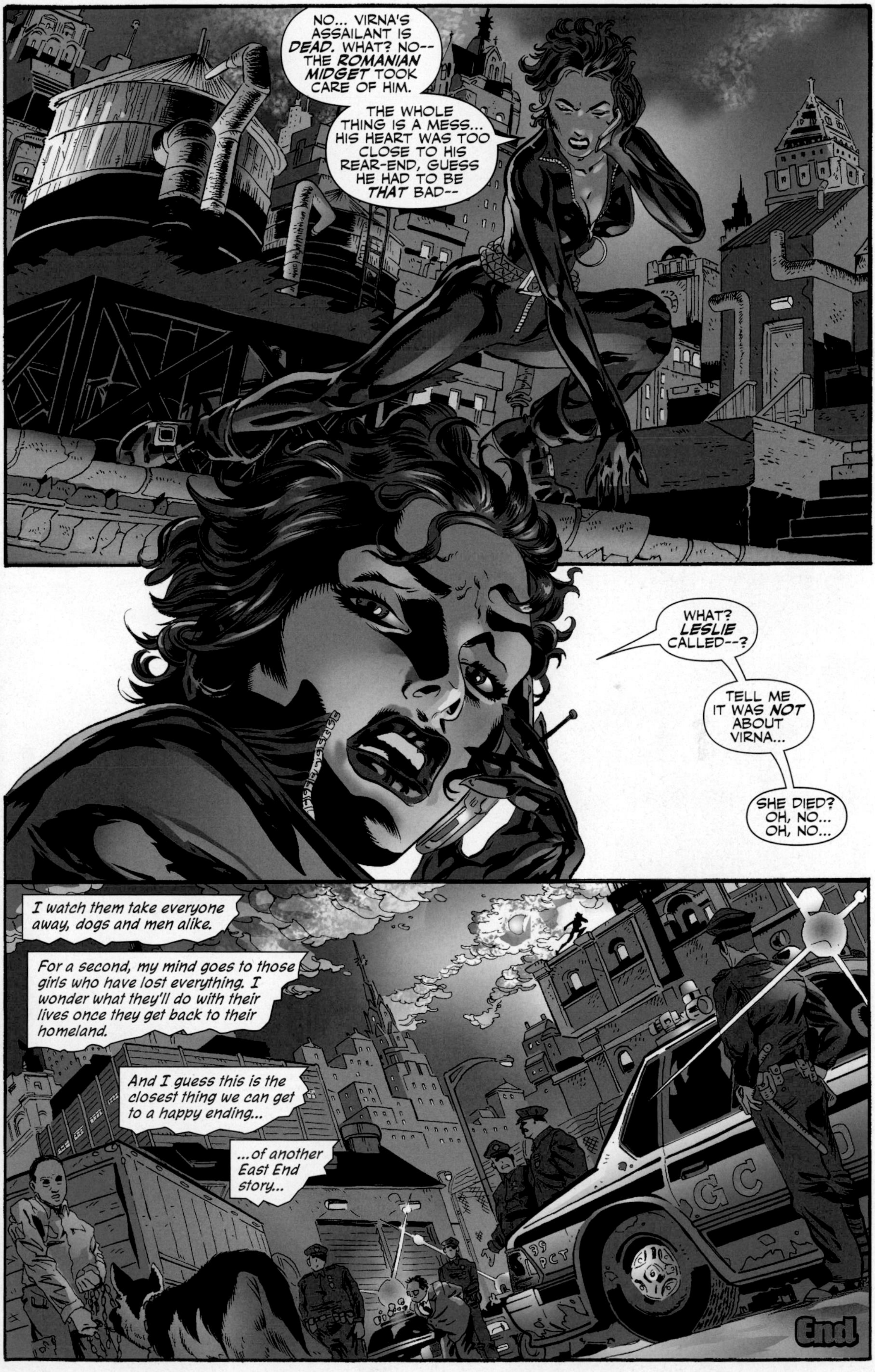
NO... VIRNA'S ASSAILANT IS DEAD. WHAT? NO-- THE ROMANIAN MIDGET TOOK CARE OF HIM.
THE WHOLE THING IS A MESS... HIS HEART WAS TOO CLOSE TO HIS REAR-END, GUESS HE HAD TO BE THAT BAD--
WHAT? LESLIE CALLED--?
TELL ME IT WAS NOT ABOUT VIRNA...
SHE DIED? OH, NO... OH, NO...
I watch them take everyone away, dogs and men alike.
For a second, my mind goes to those girls who have lost everything. I wonder what they'll do with their lives once they get back to their homeland.
And I guess this is the closest thing we can get to a happy ending...
...of another East End story...
GC
39 PCT
End

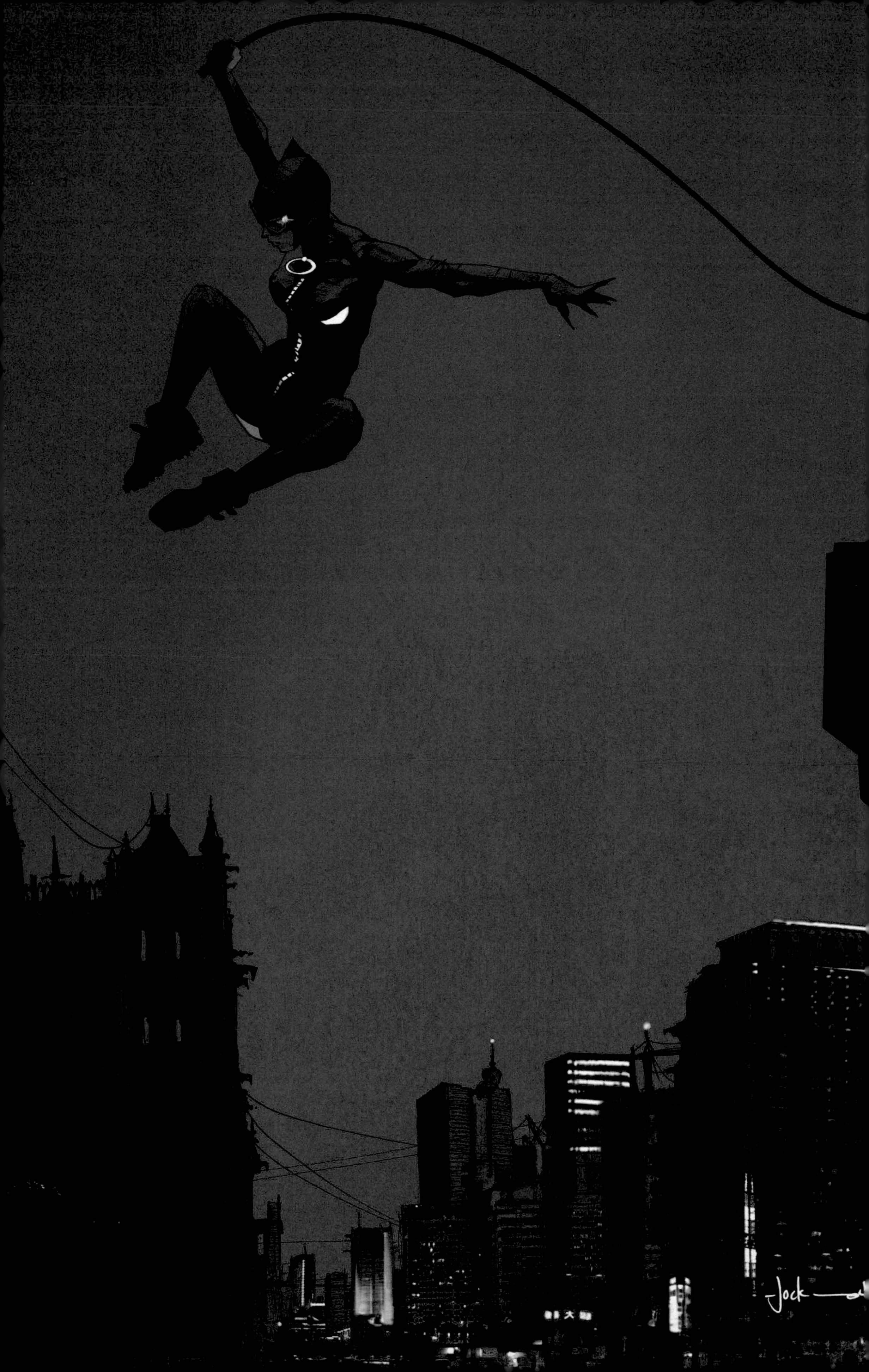
Jock

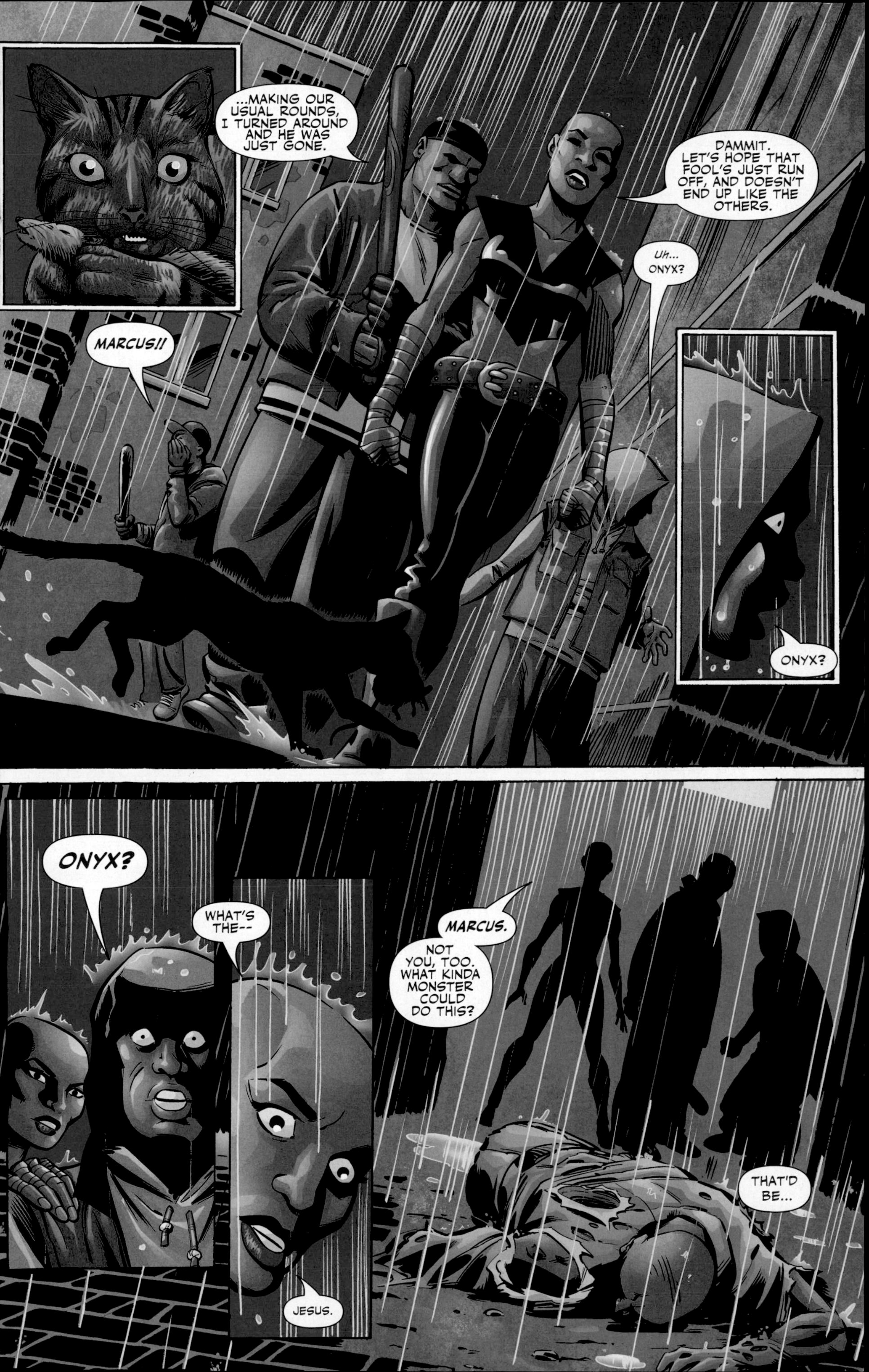
...MAKING OUR USUAL ROUNDS, I TURNED AROUND AND HE WAS JUST GONE.
DAMMIT. LET'S HOPE THAT FOOL'S JUST RUN OFF, AND DOESN'T END UP LIKE THE OTHERS.
Uh... ONYX?
MARCUS!!
ONYX?
ONYX?
WHAT'S THE--
JESUS.
MARCUS.
NOT YOU, TOO. WHAT KINDA MONSTER COULD DO THIS?
THAT'D BE...

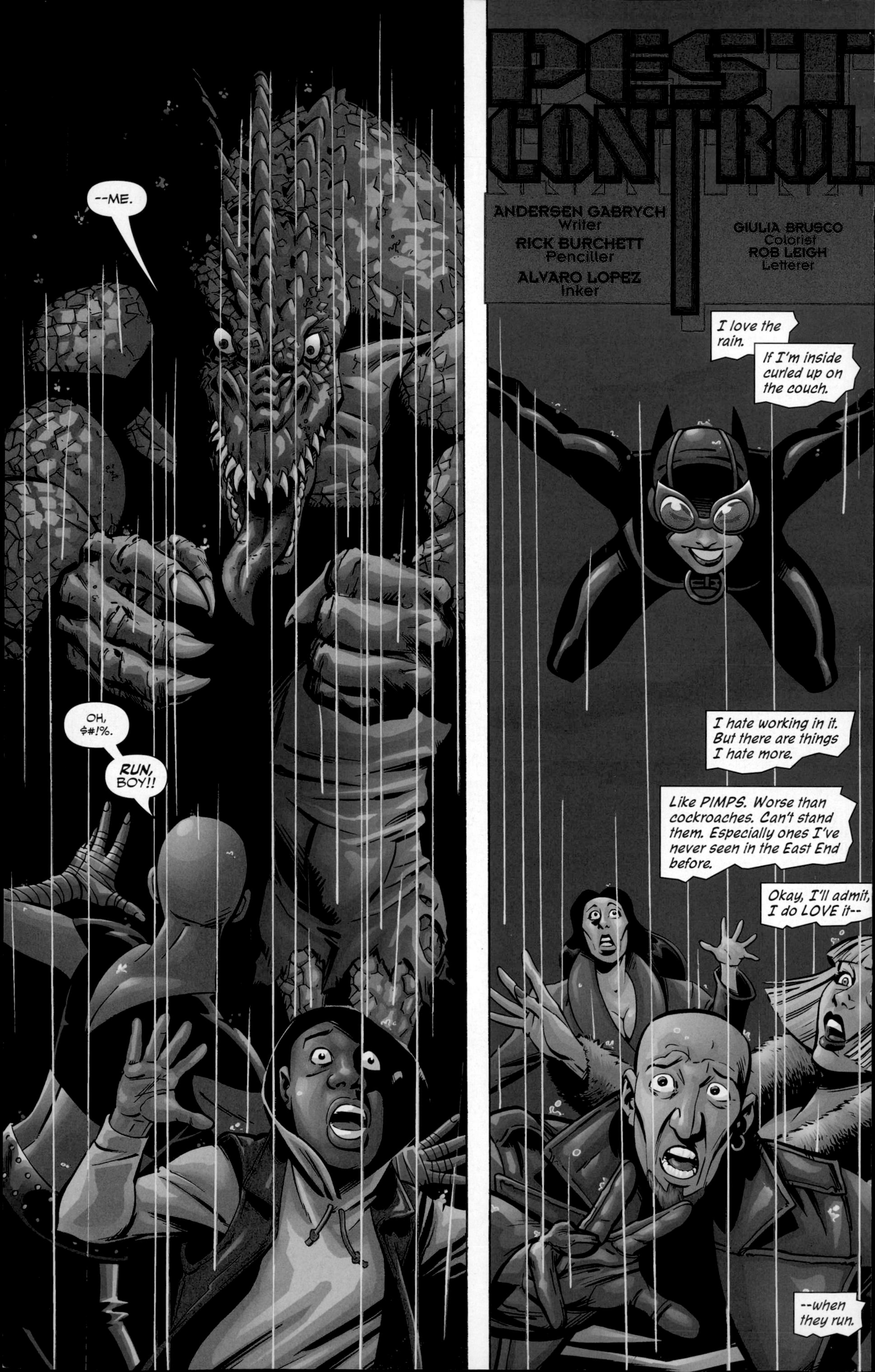
--ME.
OH, $#!%.
RUN, BOY!!
PEST CONTROL
ANDERSEN GABRYCH Writer
RICK BURCHETT Penciller
ALVARO LOPEZ Inker
GIULIA BRUSCO Colorist
ROB LEIGH Letterer
I love the rain.
If I'm inside curled up on the couch.
I hate working in it. But there are things I hate more.
Like PIMPS. Worse than cockroaches. Can't stand them. Especially ones I've never seen in the East End before.
Okay, I'll admit, I do LOVE it--
--when they run.

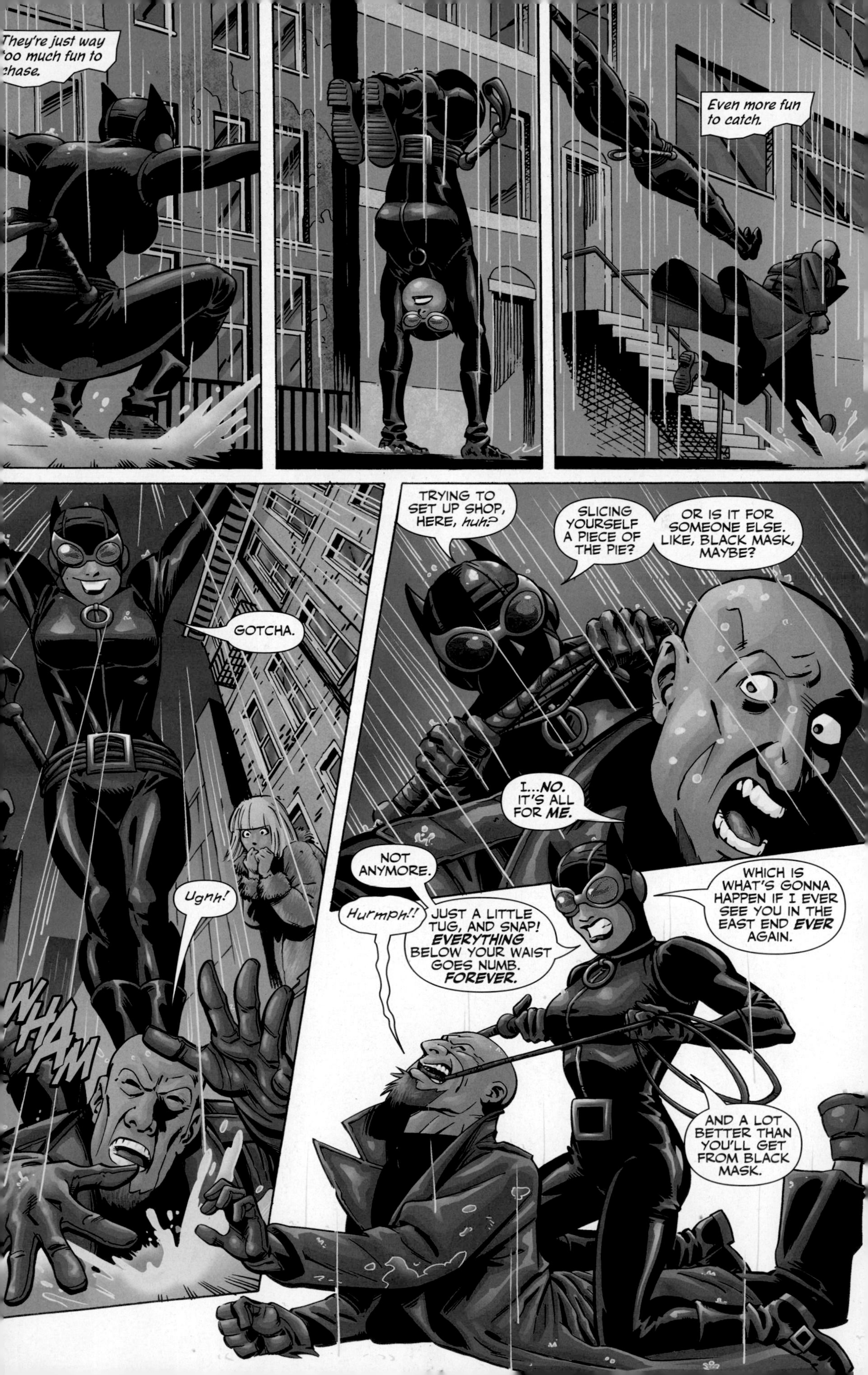
They're just way too much fun to chase.
Even more fun to catch.
GOTCHA.
Ugnh!
WHAM
TRYING TO SET UP SHOP, HERE, *huh?*
SLICING YOURSELF A PIECE OF THE PIE?
OR IS IT FOR SOMEONE ELSE. LIKE, BLACK MASK, MAYBE?
I...*NO.* IT'S ALL FOR *ME.*
NOT ANYMORE.
Hurmph!!
JUST A LITTLE TUG, AND SNAP! *EVERYTHING* BELOW YOUR WAIST GOES NUMB. *FOREVER.*
WHICH IS WHAT'S GONNA HAPPEN IF I EVER SEE YOU IN THE EAST END *EVER* AGAIN.
AND A LOT BETTER THAN YOU'LL GET FROM BLACK MASK.

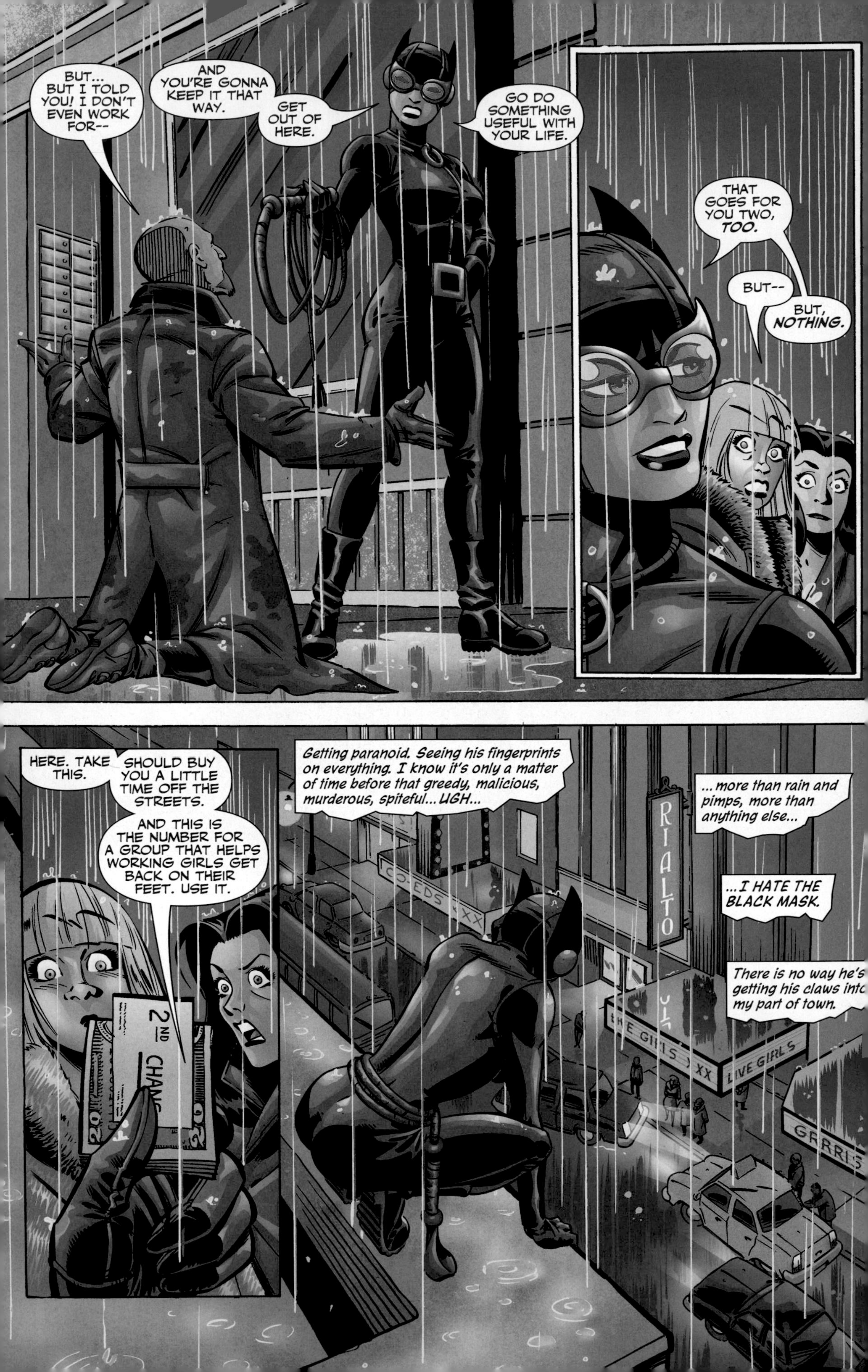
BUT... BUT I TOLD YOU! I DON'T EVEN WORK FOR--
AND YOU'RE GONNA KEEP IT THAT WAY.
GET OUT OF HERE.
GO DO SOMETHING USEFUL WITH YOUR LIFE.
THAT GOES FOR YOU TWO, *TOO.*
BUT--
BUT, *NOTHING.*
HERE. TAKE THIS.
SHOULD BUY YOU A LITTLE TIME OFF THE STREETS.
AND THIS IS THE NUMBER FOR A GROUP THAT HELPS WORKING GIRLS GET BACK ON THEIR FEET. USE IT.
2ND CHANC
Getting paranoid. Seeing his fingerprints on everything. I know it's only a matter of time before that greedy, malicious, murderous, spiteful... UGH...
...more than rain and pimps, more than anything else...
...I HATE THE BLACK MASK.
There is no way he's getting his claws into my part of town.
RIALTO
CO-EDS XXX
LIVE GIRLS
GRRRLS

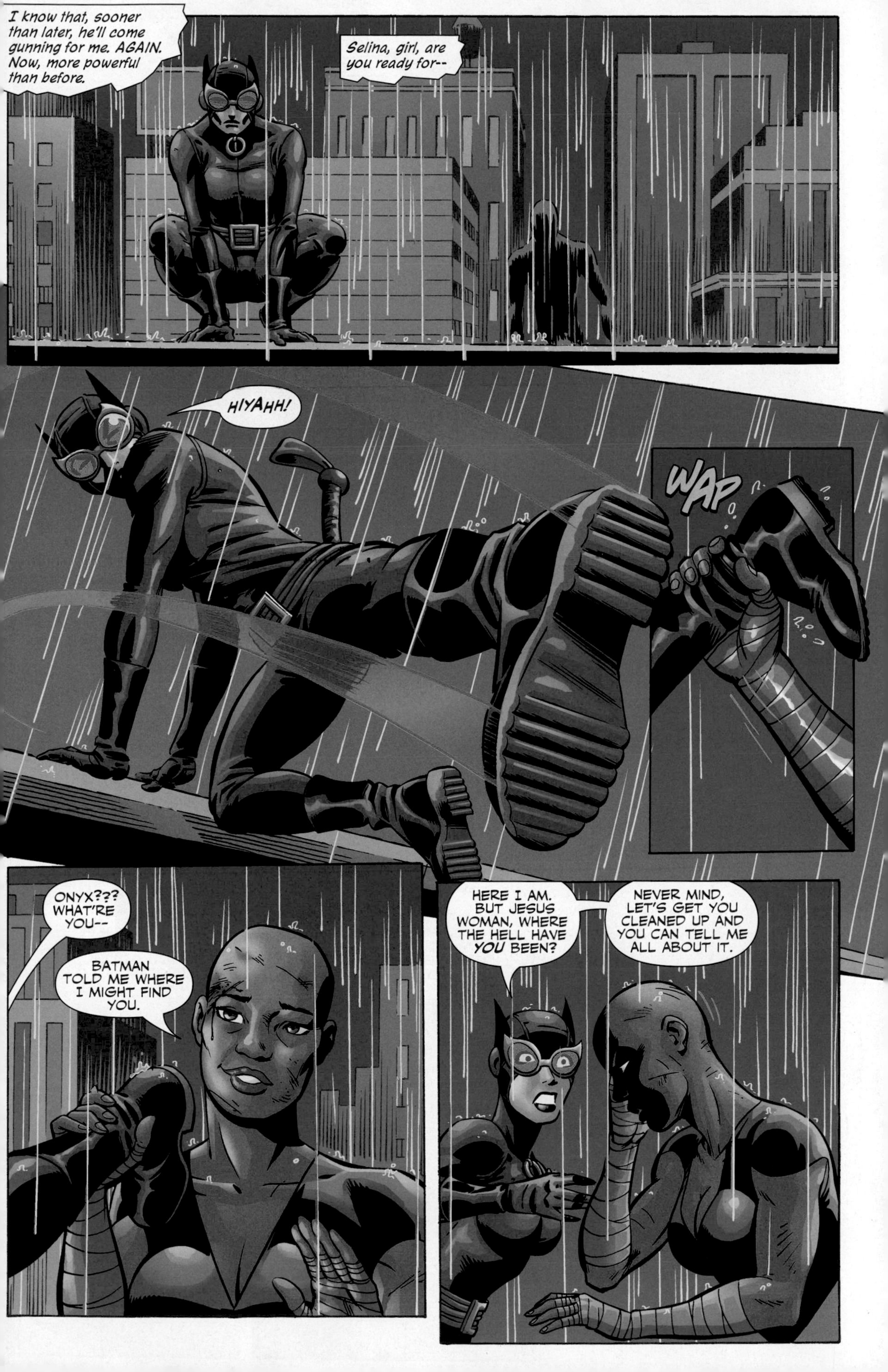
I know that, sooner than later, he'll come gunning for me. AGAIN. Now, more powerful than before.
Selina, girl, are you ready for--
HIYAHH!
WAP
ONYX??? WHAT'RE YOU--
BATMAN TOLD ME WHERE I MIGHT FIND YOU.
HERE I AM. BUT JESUS WOMAN, WHERE THE HELL HAVE YOU BEEN?
NEVER MIND, LET'S GET YOU CLEANED UP AND YOU CAN TELL ME ALL ABOUT IT.

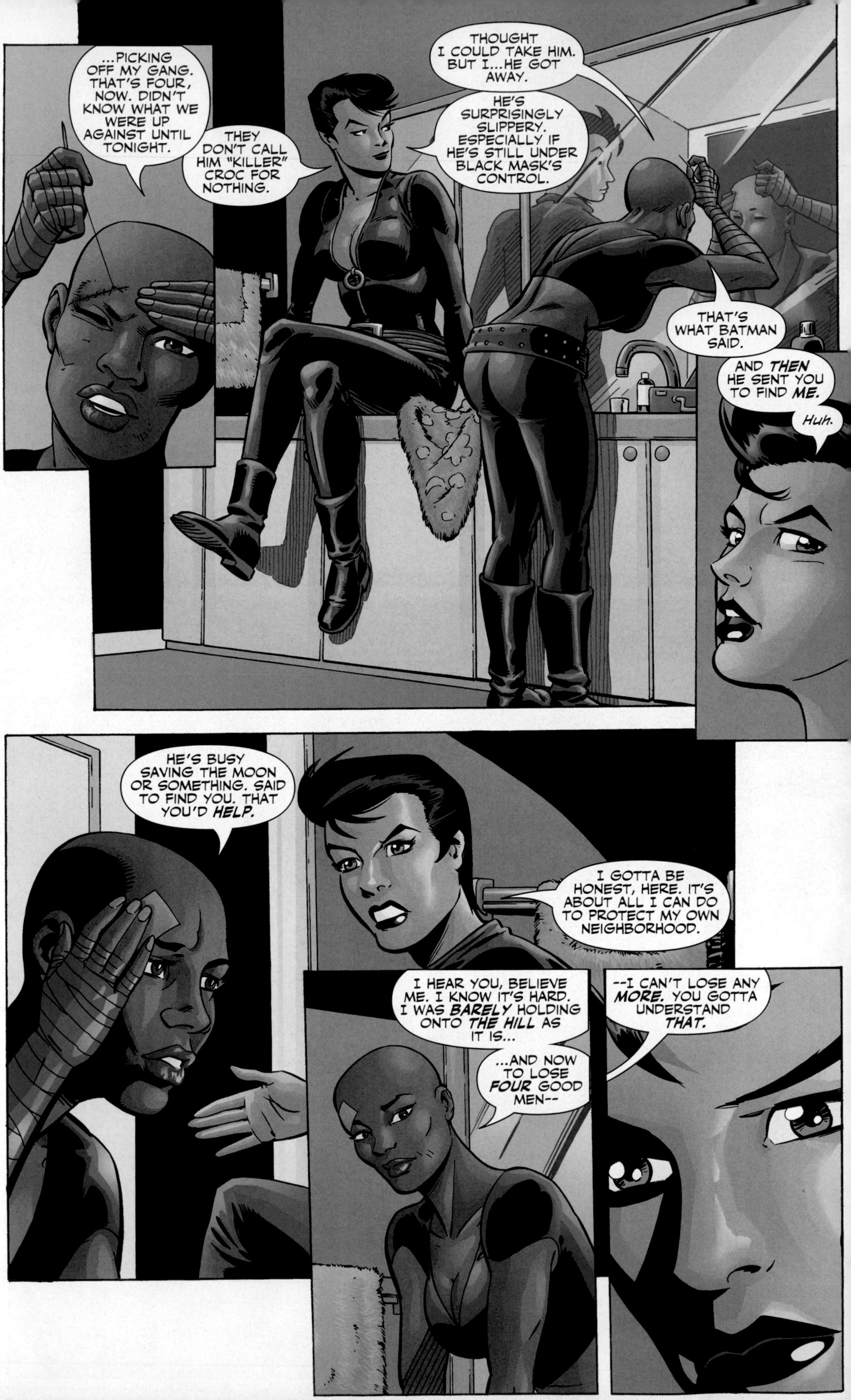
...PICKING OFF MY GANG. THAT'S FOUR, NOW. DIDN'T KNOW WHAT WE WERE UP AGAINST UNTIL TONIGHT.
THEY DON'T CALL HIM "KILLER" CROC FOR NOTHING.
THOUGHT I COULD TAKE HIM. BUT I...HE GOT AWAY.
HE'S SURPRISINGLY SLIPPERY. ESPECIALLY IF HE'S STILL UNDER BLACK MASK'S CONTROL.
THAT'S WHAT BATMAN SAID.
AND THEN HE SENT YOU TO FIND ME.
Huh.
HE'S BUSY SAVING THE MOON OR SOMETHING. SAID TO FIND YOU. THAT YOU'D HELP.
I GOTTA BE HONEST, HERE. IT'S ABOUT ALL I CAN DO TO PROTECT MY OWN NEIGHBORHOOD.
I HEAR YOU, BELIEVE ME. I KNOW IT'S HARD. I WAS BARELY HOLDING ONTO THE HILL AS IT IS...
...AND NOW TO LOSE FOUR GOOD MEN--
--I CAN'T LOSE ANY MORE. YOU GOTTA UNDERSTAND THAT.

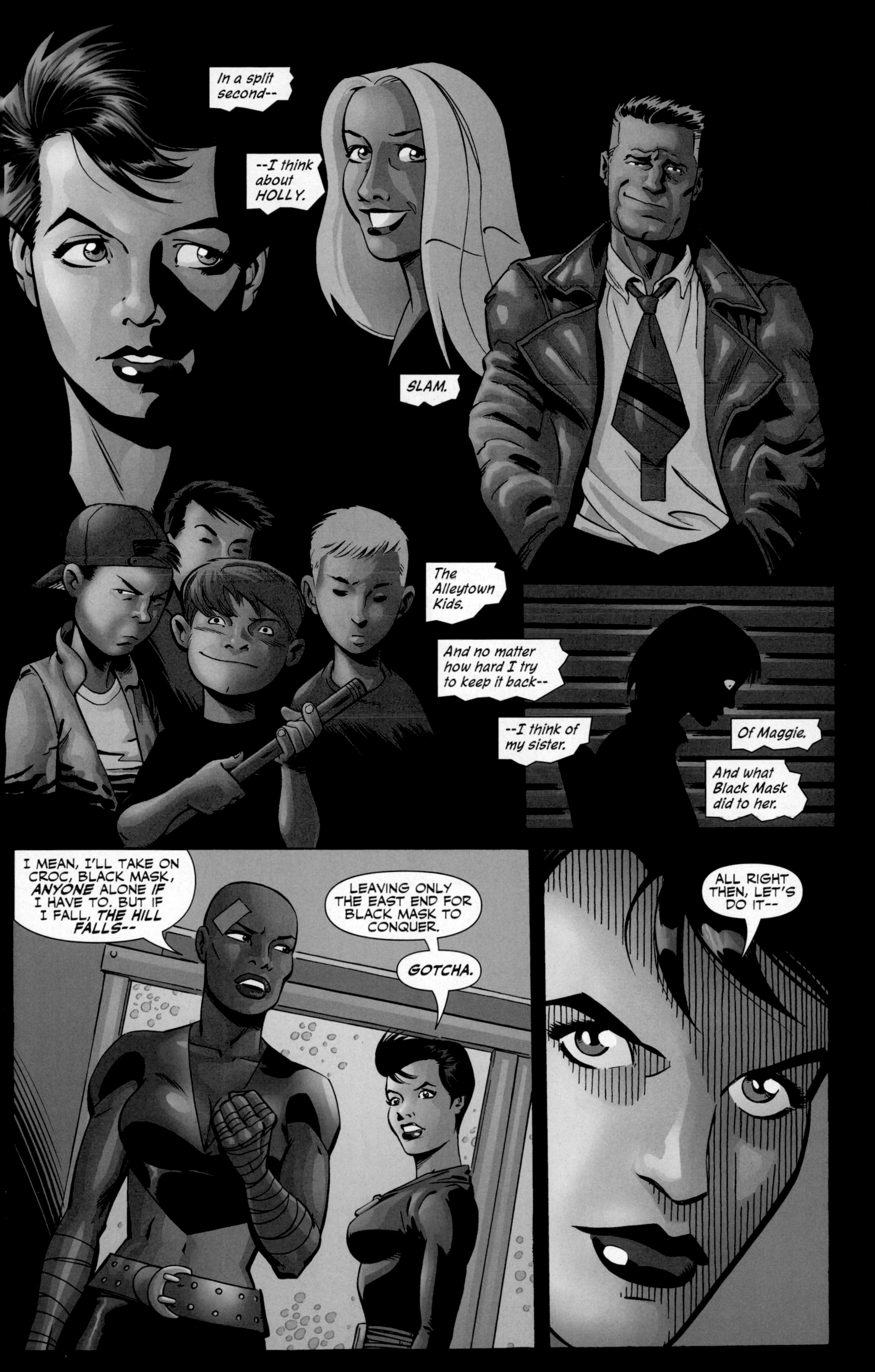
In a split second--
--I think about HOLLY.
SLAM.
The Alleytown Kids.
And no matter how hard I try to keep it back--
--I think of my sister.
Of Maggie.
And what Black Mask did to her.
I MEAN, I'LL TAKE ON CROC, BLACK MASK, ANYONE ALONE IF I HAVE TO. BUT IF I FALL, THE HILL FALLS--
LEAVING ONLY THE EAST END FOR BLACK MASK TO CONQUER.
GOTCHA.
ALL RIGHT THEN, LET'S DO IT--

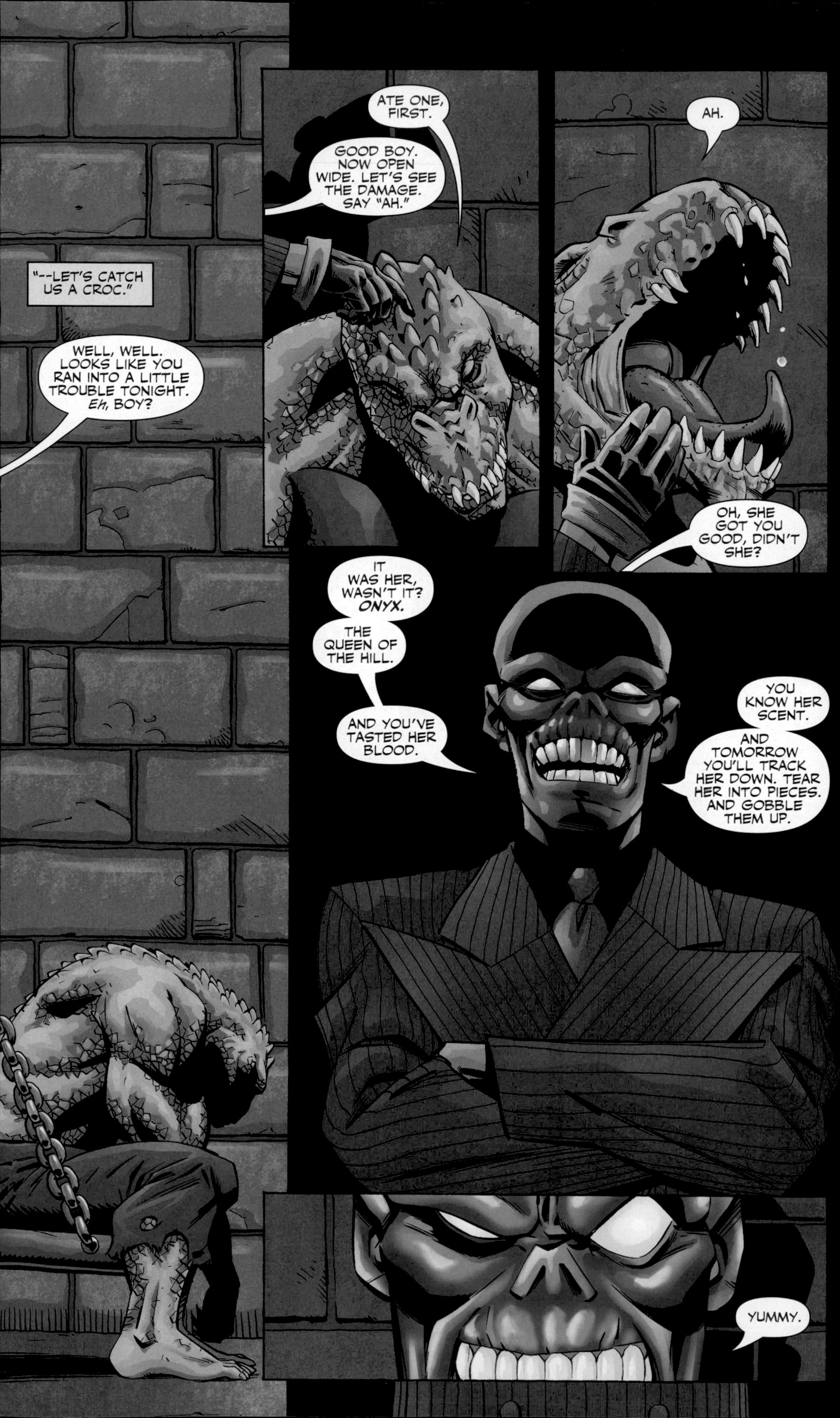
"--LET'S CATCH US A CROC."
WELL, WELL. LOOKS LIKE YOU RAN INTO A LITTLE TROUBLE TONIGHT. *Eh*, BOY?
ATE ONE, FIRST.
GOOD BOY. NOW OPEN WIDE. LET'S SEE THE DAMAGE. SAY "AH."
AH.
OH, SHE GOT YOU GOOD, DIDN'T SHE?
IT WAS HER, WASN'T IT? *ONYX.*
THE QUEEN OF THE HILL.
AND YOU'VE TASTED HER BLOOD.
YOU KNOW HER SCENT.
AND TOMORROW YOU'LL TRACK HER DOWN. TEAR HER INTO PIECES. AND GOBBLE THEM UP.
YUMMY.

Onyx and I spend half the night coming up with a plan. A plan that begins at the bank.

GOOD MORNING, MS. WINDER-MERE.

HELLO, *CRAIG.* I NEED TO GET INTO MY BOX.

RIGHT THIS WAY, MS. WINDER-MERE.

I remember the day I picked this up. Capri. Six years ago. Plucked it off the neck of the Duchess of Markovia in broad daylight.

She's renowned not only for her beauty and JEWELRY, but also her flagrant use of the N-WORD.

It almost seems like a crime...

...That some people don't prefer CASH.

HERE YA GO.

We call him the Tailor. Arms dealer and costume designer rolled into one.

OH, YEAH. THESE'RE PERFECT FOR MY NEW LENSES.

GOOD. I'LL BE BACK FOR *THESE* AT SIX.

Bank. Check. Tailor's. Check. Hardware store...

Wheet-whoo!

AND HOW!

PLEASE. I'D TEAR YOU APART, COWBOY.

...EVERYTHING DELIVERED UP TO 4457 CLASSON BY THIS AFTERNOON.

Uh... OKAY. THAT'S IN THE, uh... HILL?

SURE IS.

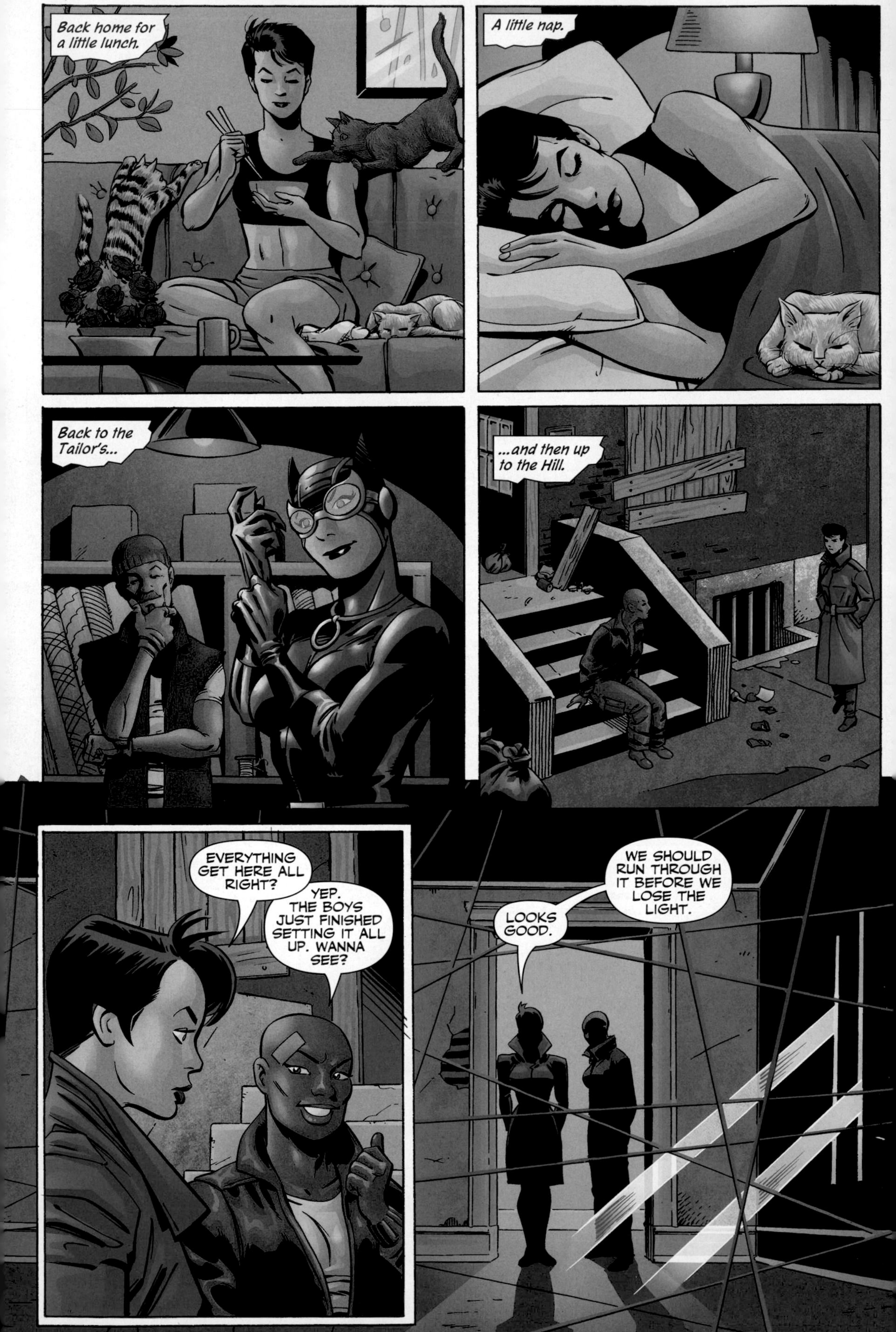
Back home for a little lunch.
A little nap.
Back to the Tailor's...
...and then up to the Hill.
EVERYTHING GET HERE ALL RIGHT?
YEP. THE BOYS JUST FINISHED SETTING IT ALL UP. WANNA SEE?
LOOKS GOOD.
WE SHOULD RUN THROUGH IT BEFORE WE LOSE THE LIGHT.

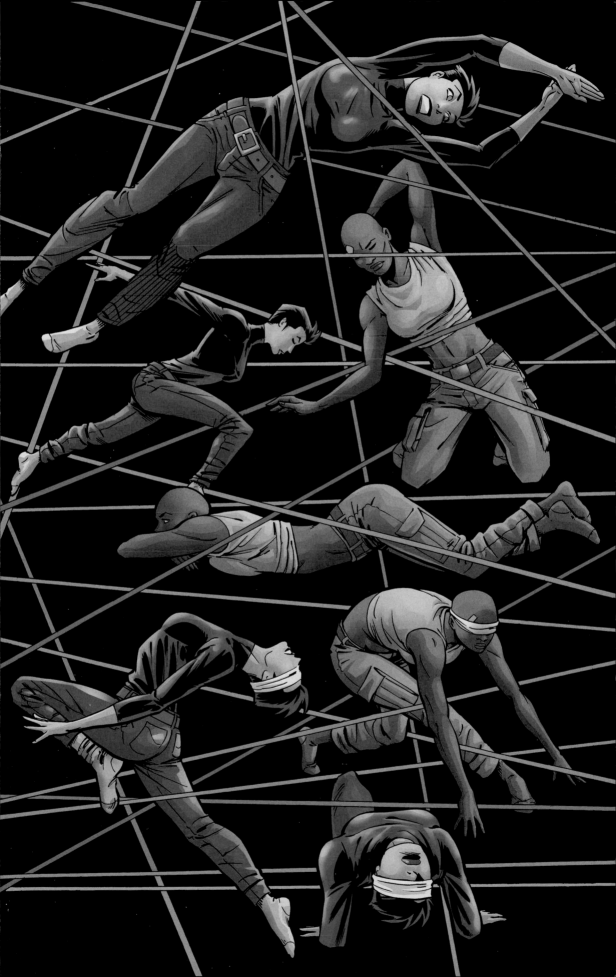

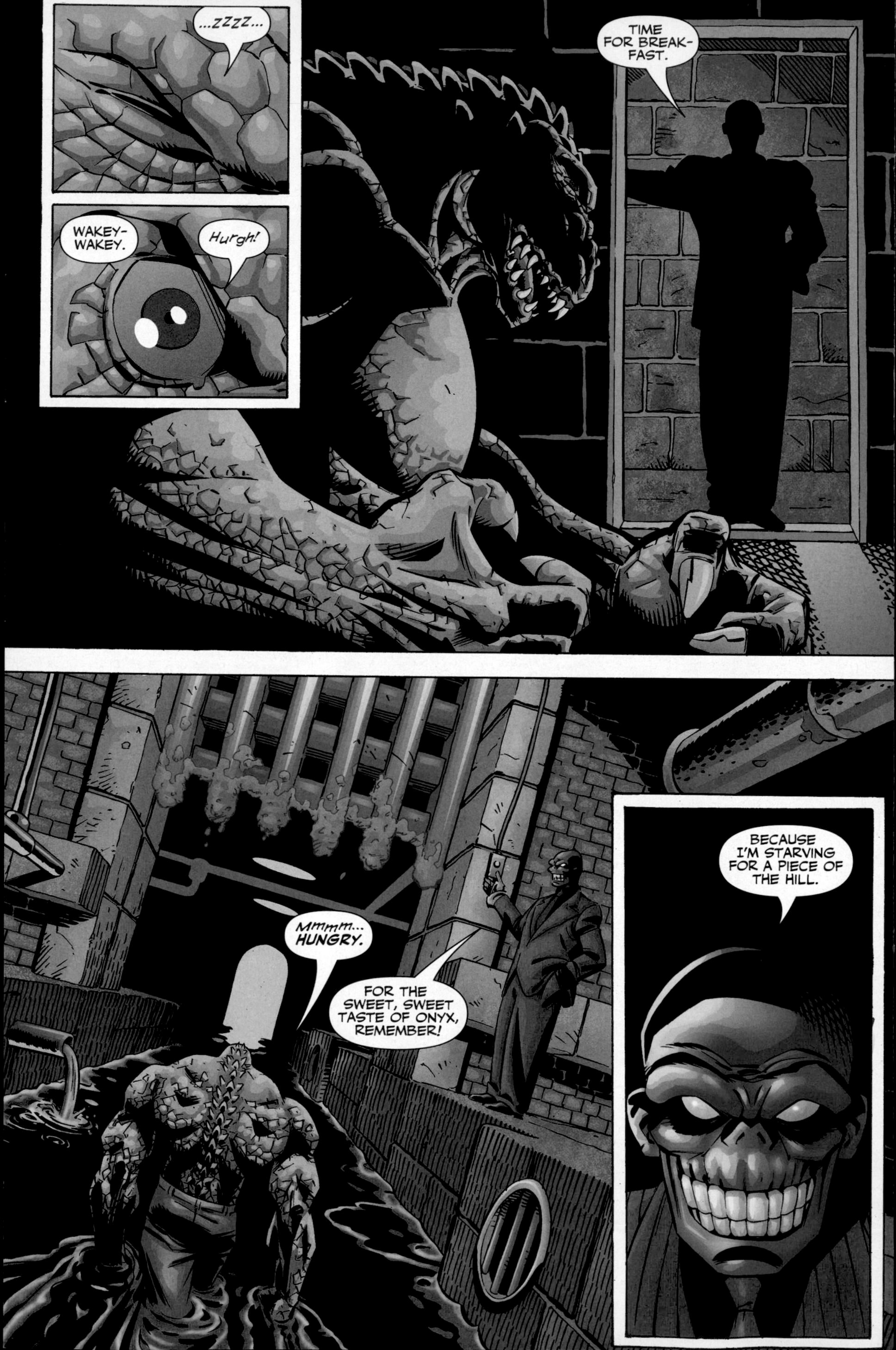
...ZZZZ...
WAKEY-WAKEY.
Hurgh!
TIME FOR BREAK-FAST.
Mmmmm... HUNGRY.
FOR THE SWEET, SWEET TASTE OF ONYX, REMEMBER!
BECAUSE I'M STARVING FOR A PIECE OF THE HILL.

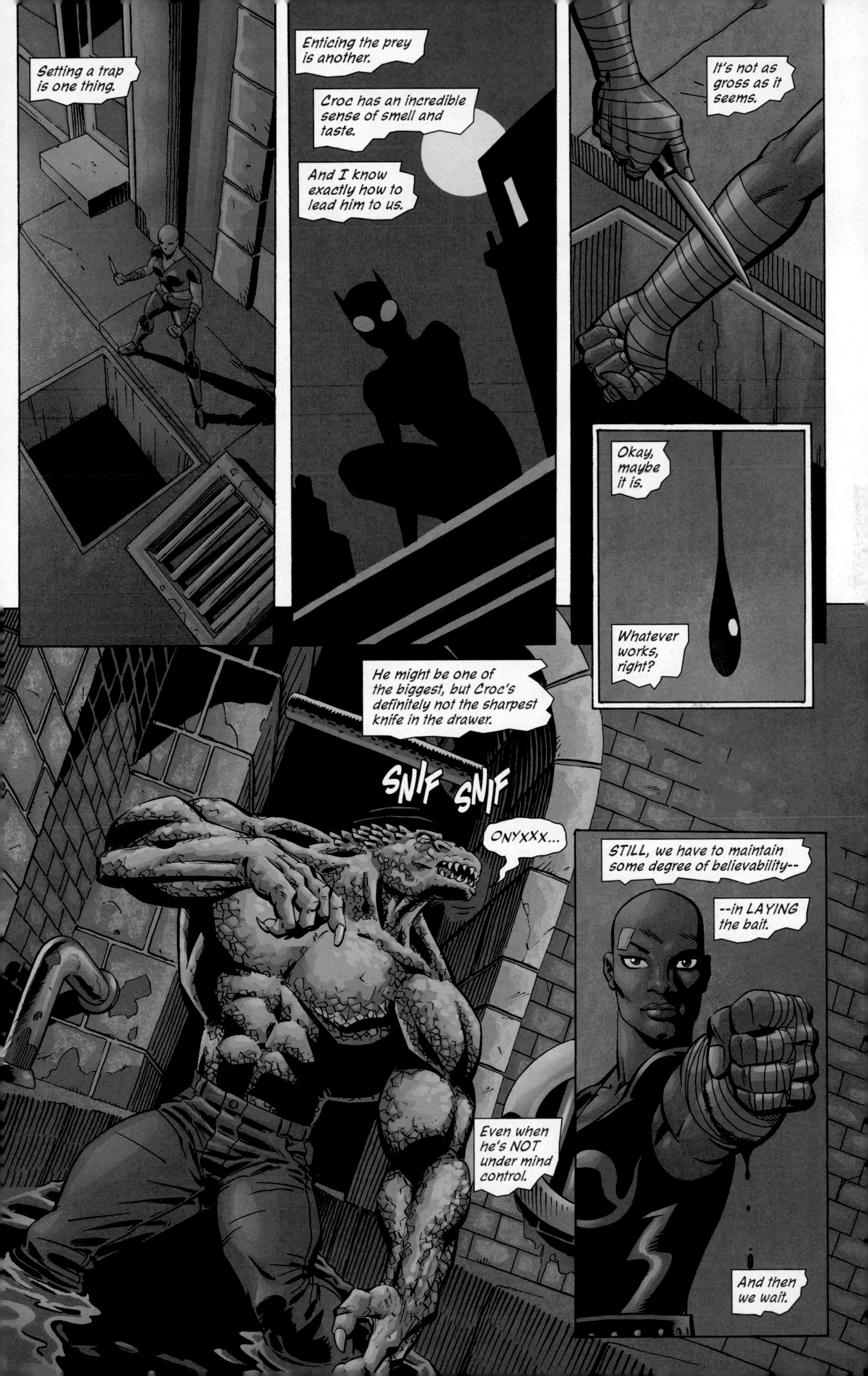
Setting a trap is one thing.
Enticing the prey is another.
Croc has an incredible sense of smell and taste.
And I know exactly how to lead him to us.
It's not as gross as it seems.
Okay, maybe it is.
Whatever works, right?
He might be one of the biggest, but Croc's definitely not the sharpest knife in the drawer.
SNIF SNIF
ONYXXX...
Even when he's NOT under mind control.
STILL, we have to maintain some degree of believability--
--in LAYING the bait.
And then we wait.

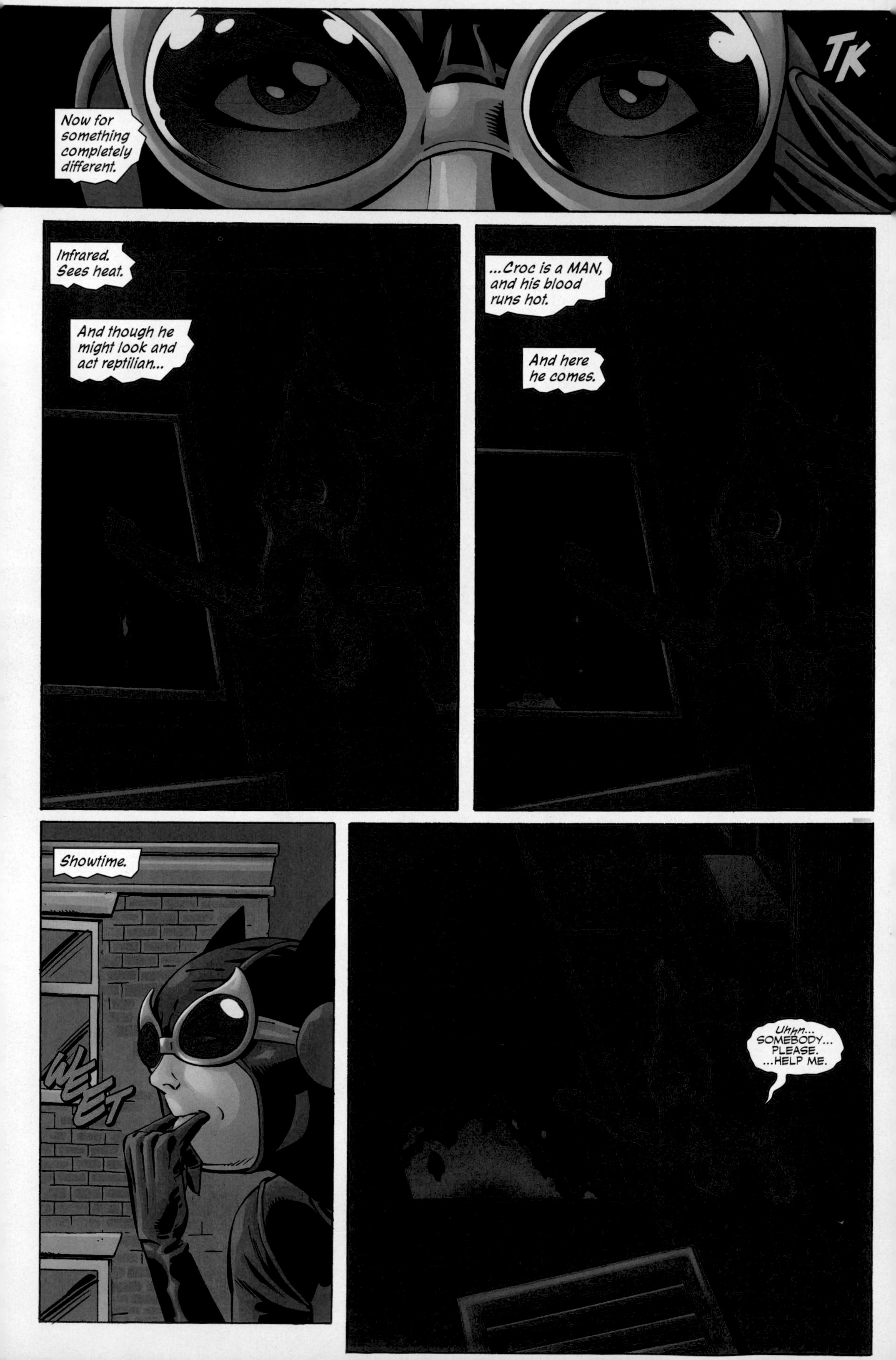
TK
Now for something completely different.
Infrared. Sees heat.
And though he might look and act reptilian...
...Croc is a MAN, and his blood runs hot.
And here he comes.
Showtime.
WEET
Uhhn... SOMEBODY... PLEASE. ...HELP ME.

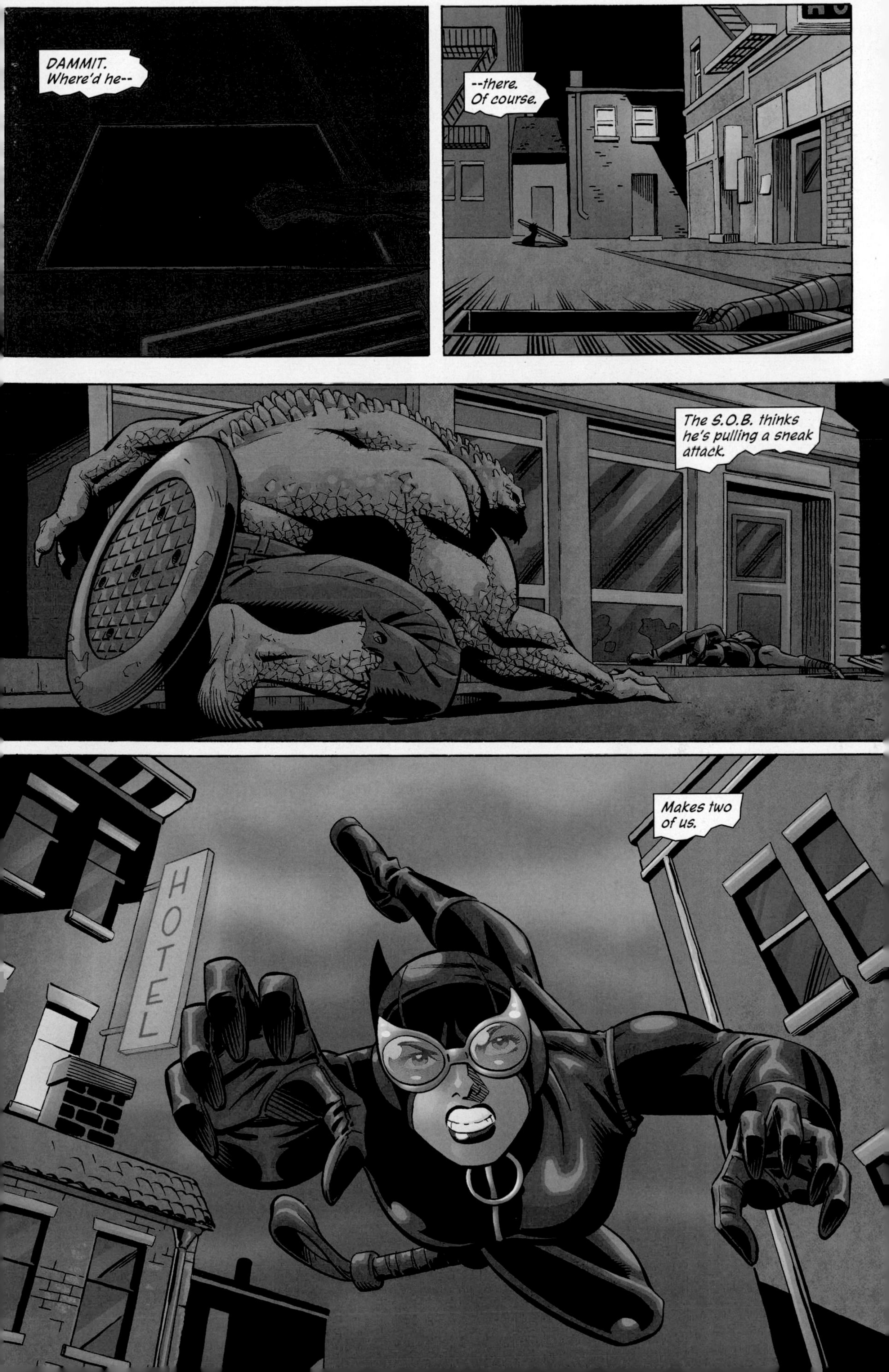
DAMMIT. Where'd he--
--there. Of course.
The S.O.B. thinks he's pulling a sneak attack.
HOTEL
Makes two of us.

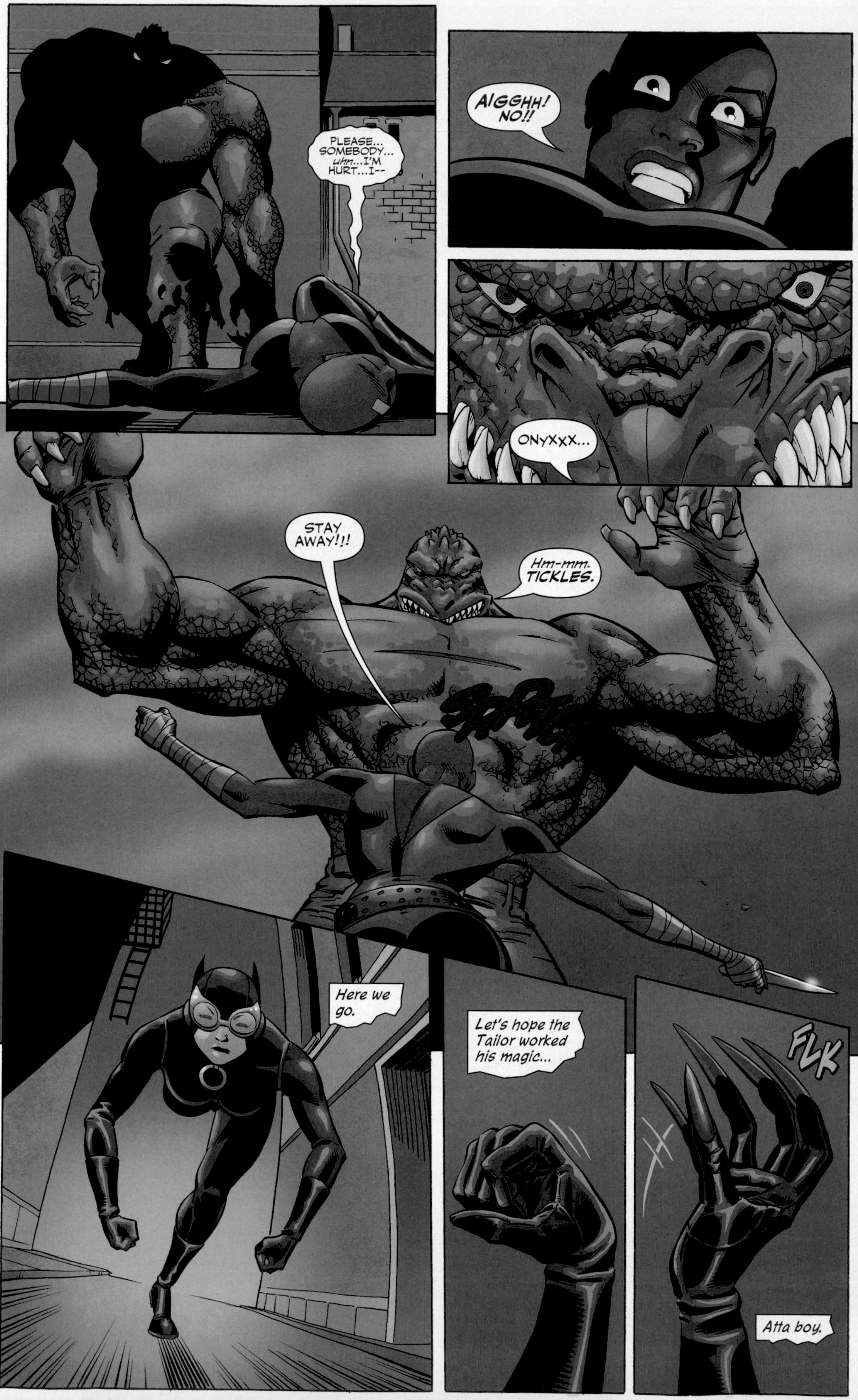
PLEASE... SOMEBODY... uhn...I'M HURT...I--
AIGGHH! NO!!
ONYXXX...
STAY AWAY!!!
Hm-mm. TICKLES.
Here we go.
Let's hope the Tailor worked his magic...
FLK
Atta boy.

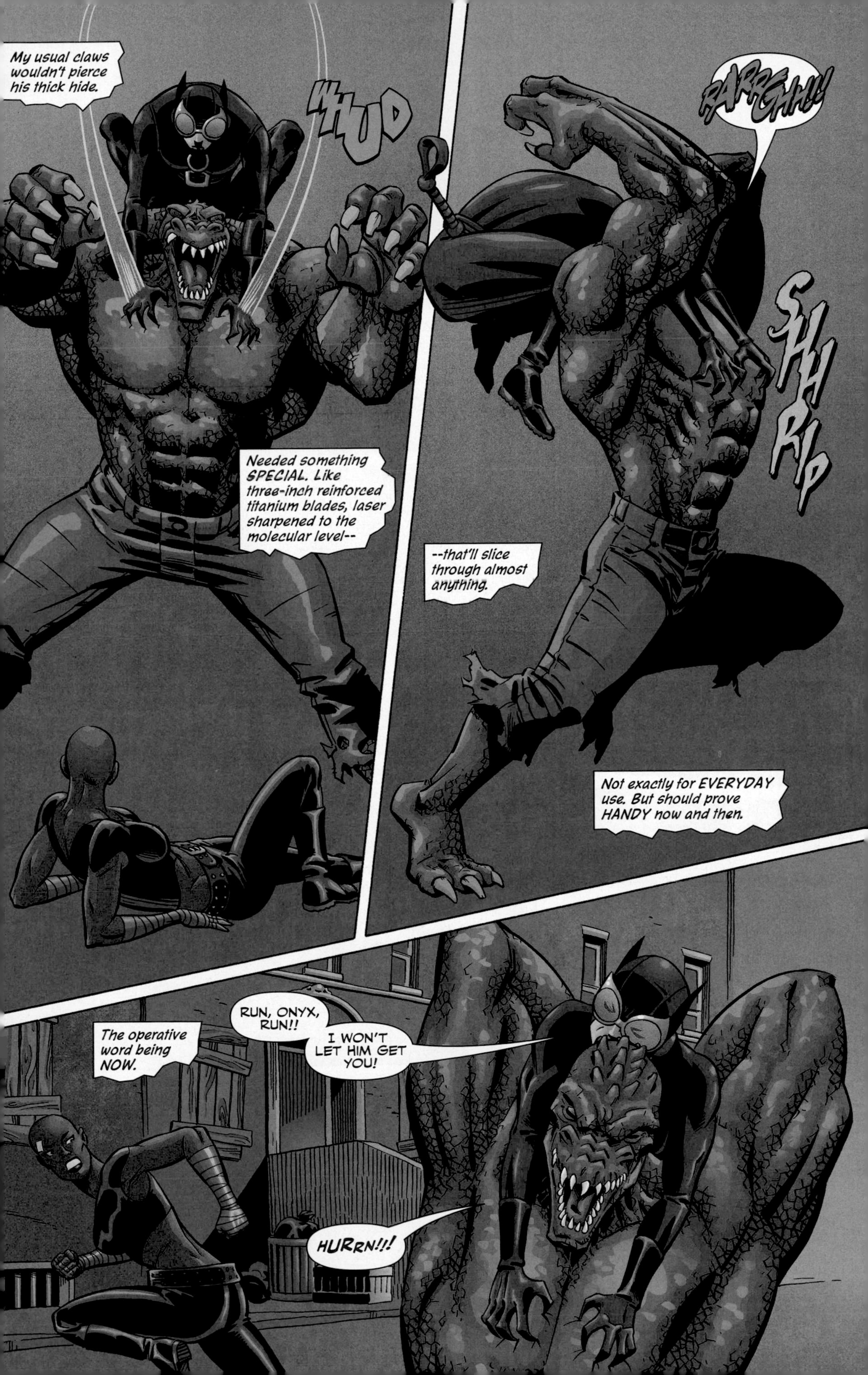
My usual claws wouldn't pierce his thick hide.
WHUD
Needed something SPECIAL. Like three-inch reinforced titanium blades, laser sharpened to the molecular level--
RARRGHH!!
SHHRIP
--that'll slice through almost anything.
Not exactly for EVERYDAY use. But should prove HANDY now and then.
The operative word being NOW.
RUN, ONYX, RUN!!
I WON'T LET HIM GET YOU!
HURRN!!!

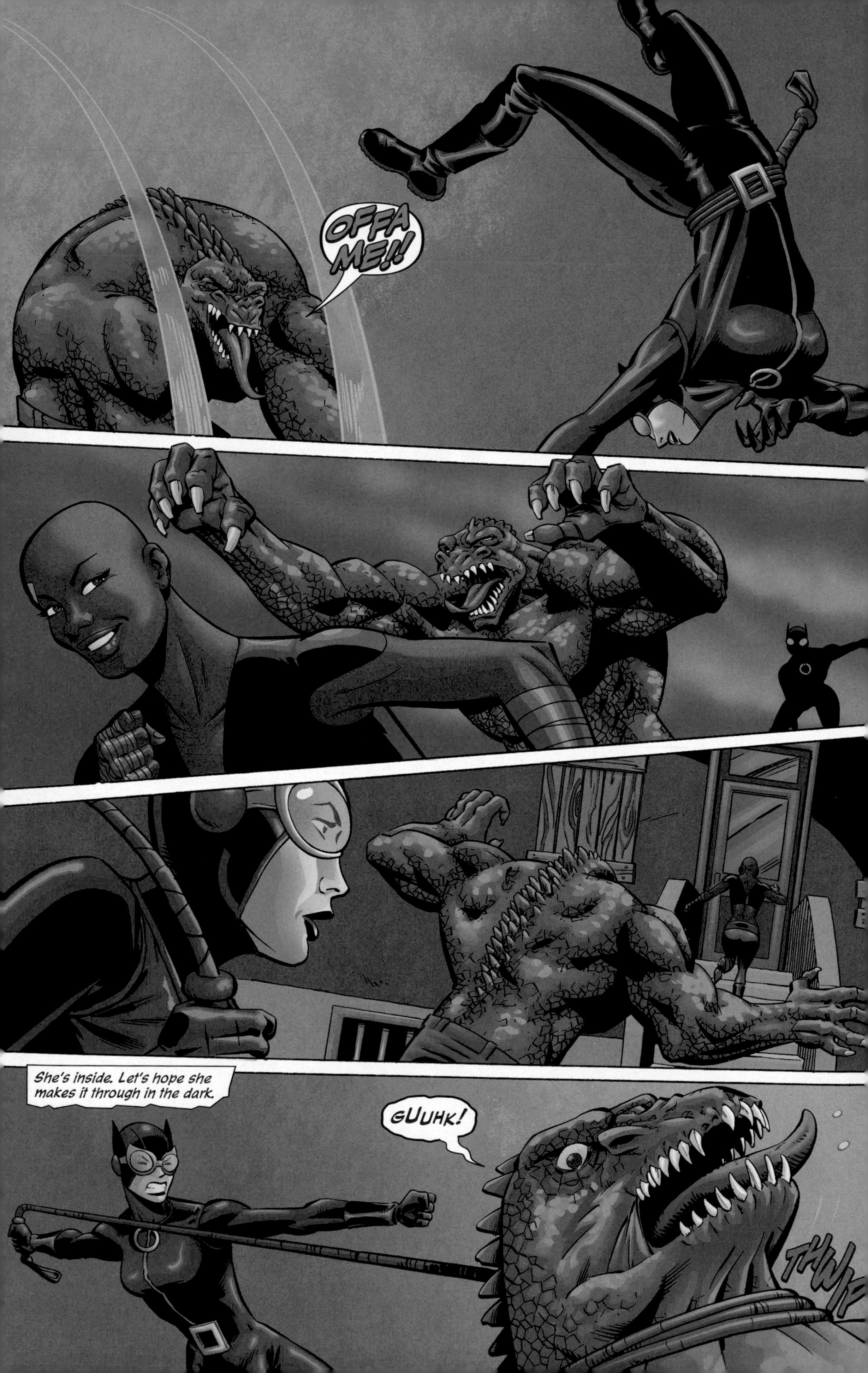
OFFA ME!!
She's inside. Let's hope she makes it through in the dark.
GUUHK!
THWIP

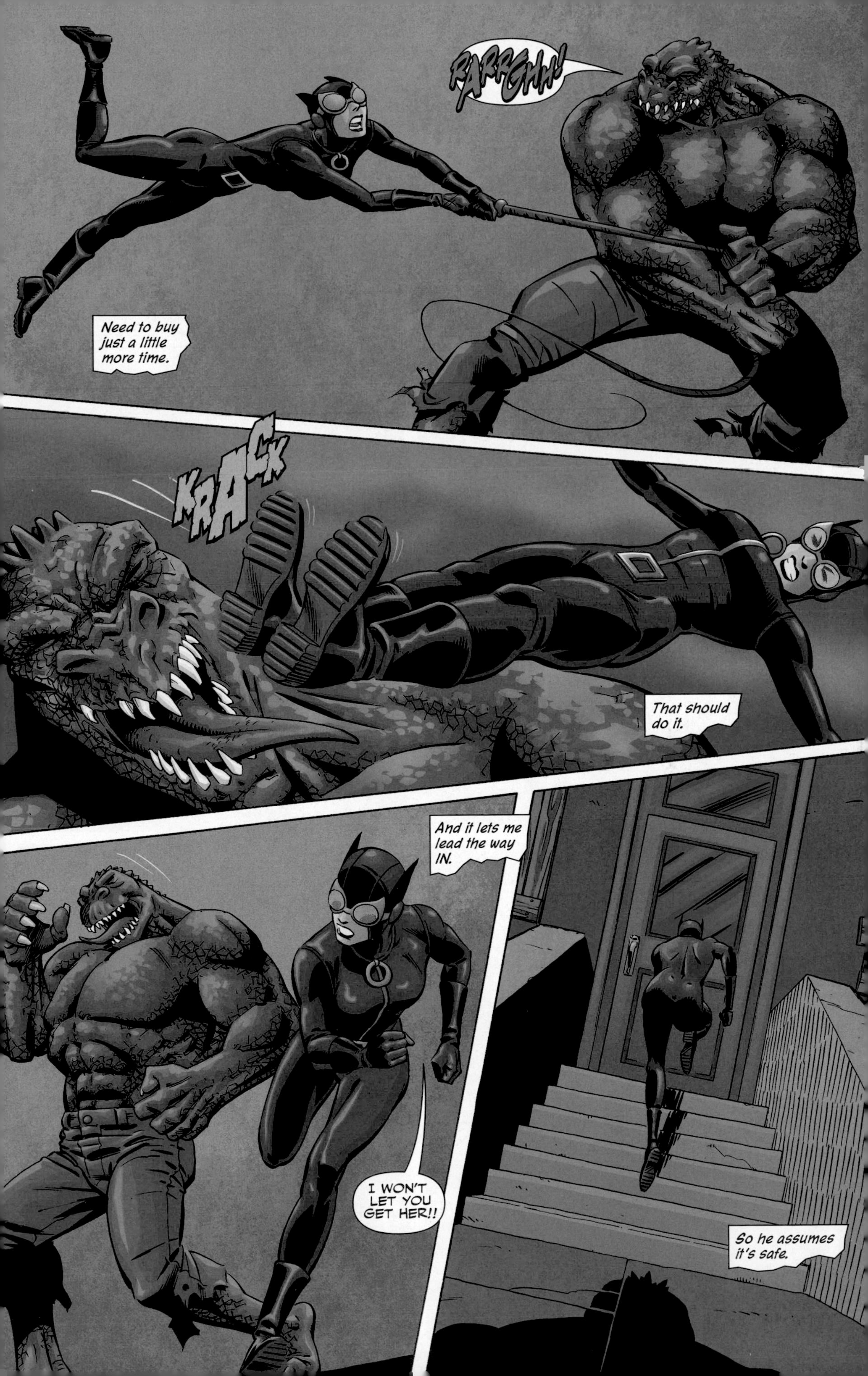
RARRGHH!
Need to buy just a little more time.
KRACK
That should do it.
And it lets me lead the way IN.
I WON'T LET YOU GET HER!!
So he assumes it's safe.

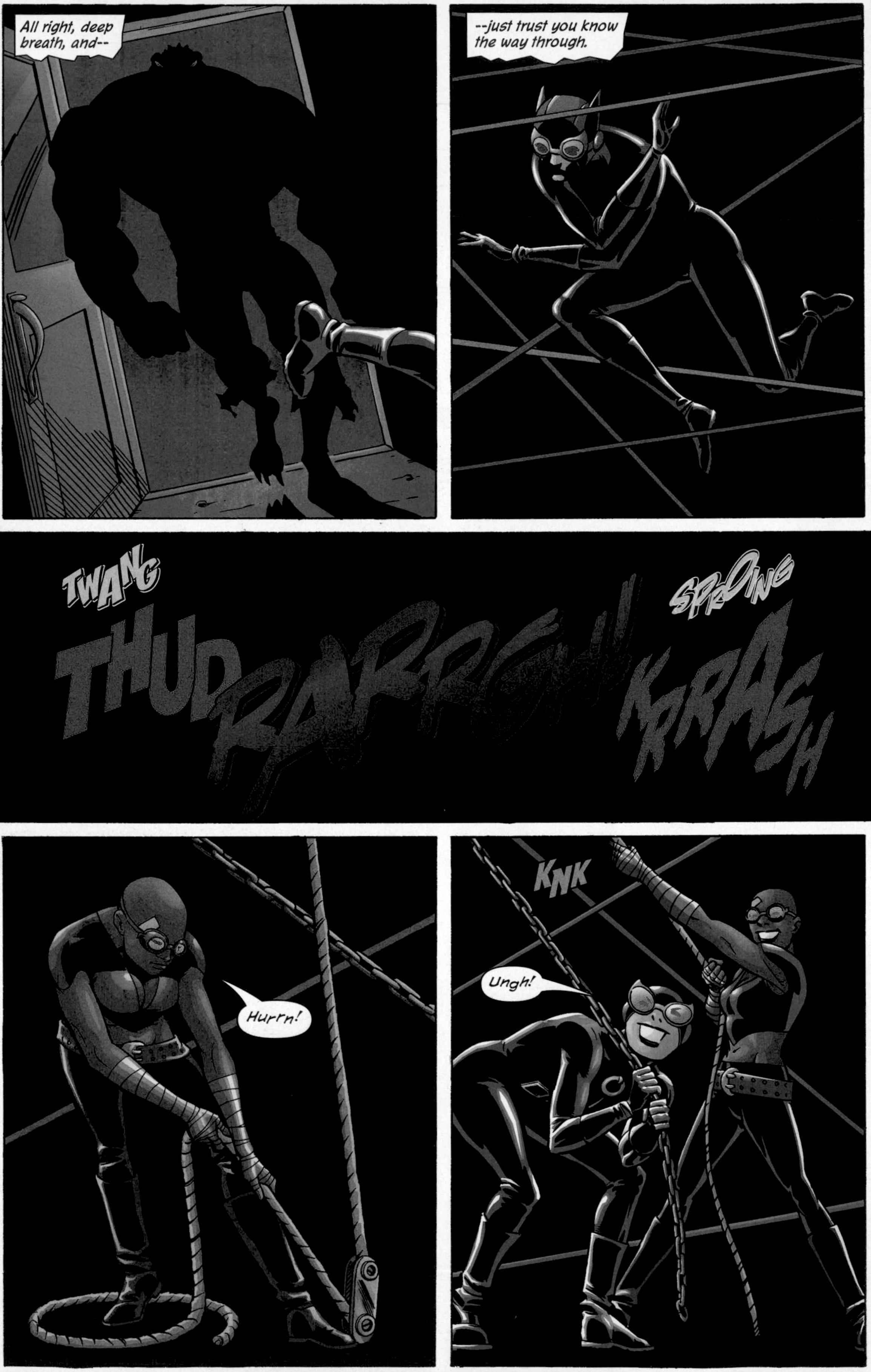
All right, deep breath, and--
--just trust you know the way through.
TWANG
THUD
RARRRGH!!
SPRONG
KRRASH
Hurrn!
KNK
Ungh!

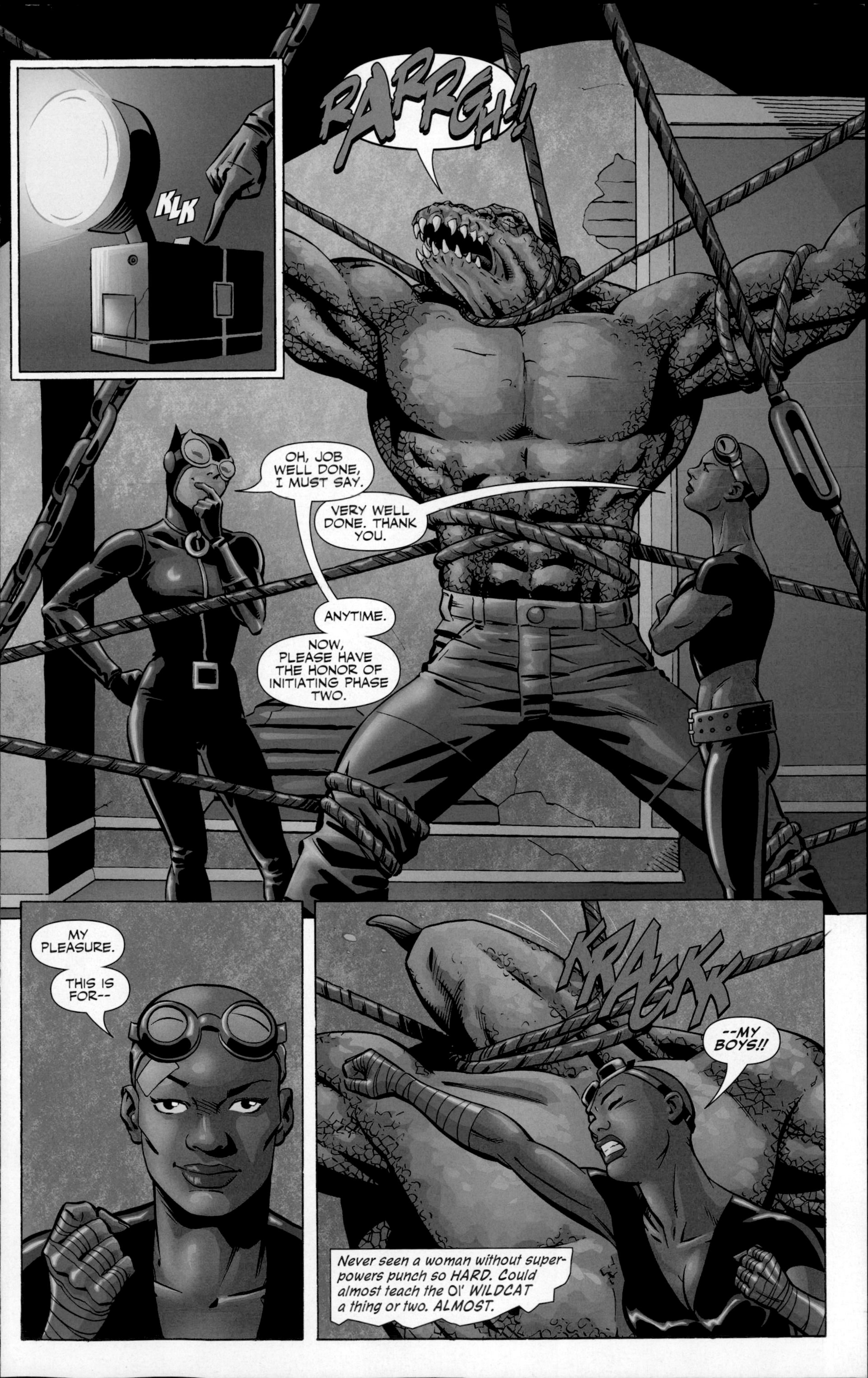
KLK
RARRGH!!
OH, JOB WELL DONE, I MUST SAY.
VERY WELL DONE. THANK YOU.
ANYTIME.
NOW, PLEASE HAVE THE HONOR OF INITIATING PHASE TWO.
MY PLEASURE.
THIS IS FOR--
KRAK
--MY BOYS!!
Never seen a woman without super-powers punch so HARD. Could almost teach the Ol' WILDCAT a thing or two. ALMOST.

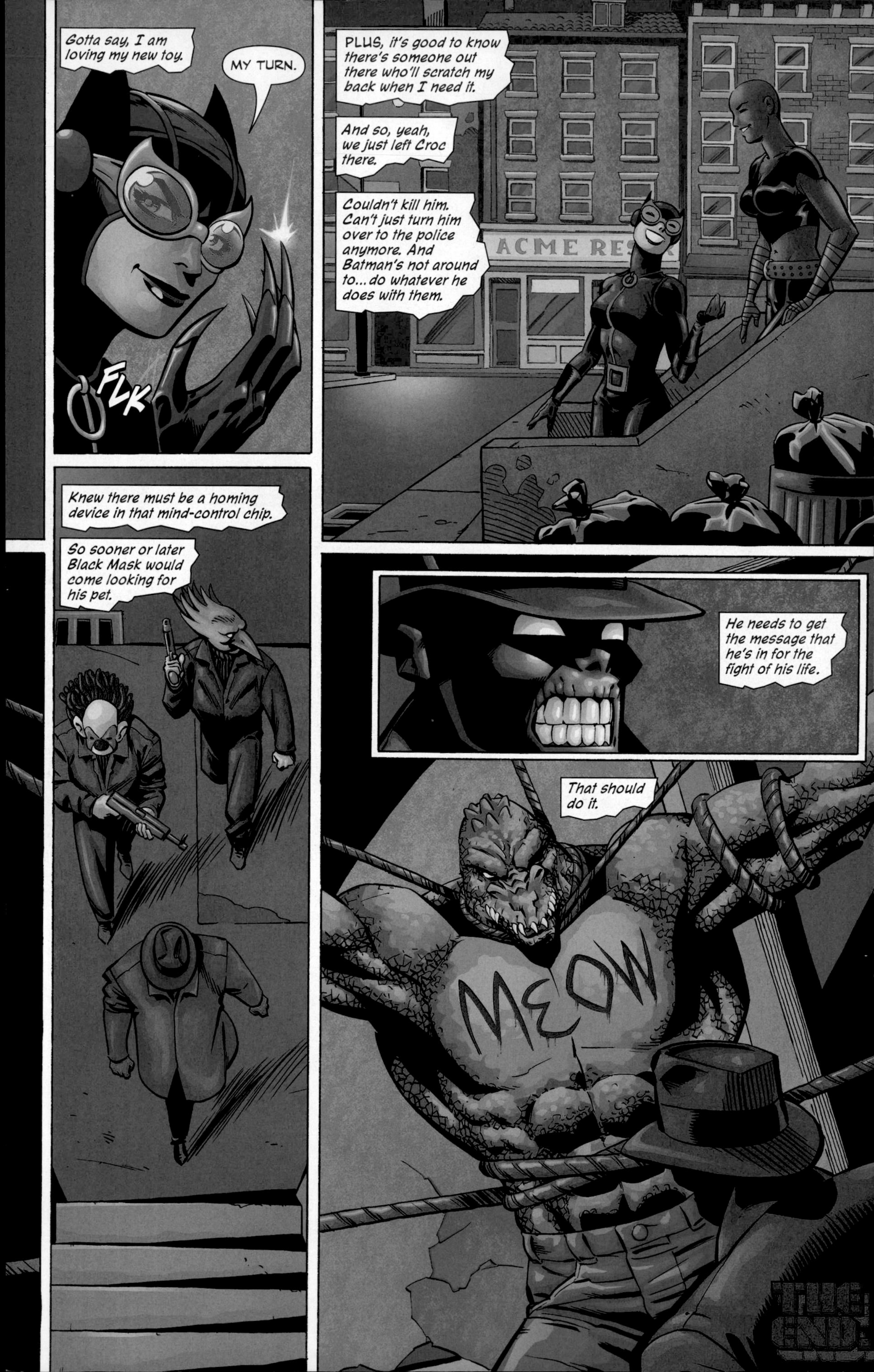
Gotta say, I am loving my new toy.
MY TURN.
FLK
PLUS, it's good to know there's someone out there who'll scratch my back when I need it.
And so, yeah, we just left Croc there.
Couldn't kill him. Can't just turn him over to the police anymore. And Batman's not around to... do whatever he does with them.
ACME RES
Knew there must be a homing device in that mind-control chip.
So sooner or later Black Mask would come looking for his pet.
He needs to get the message that he's in for the fight of his life.
That should do it.
MEOW
THE END

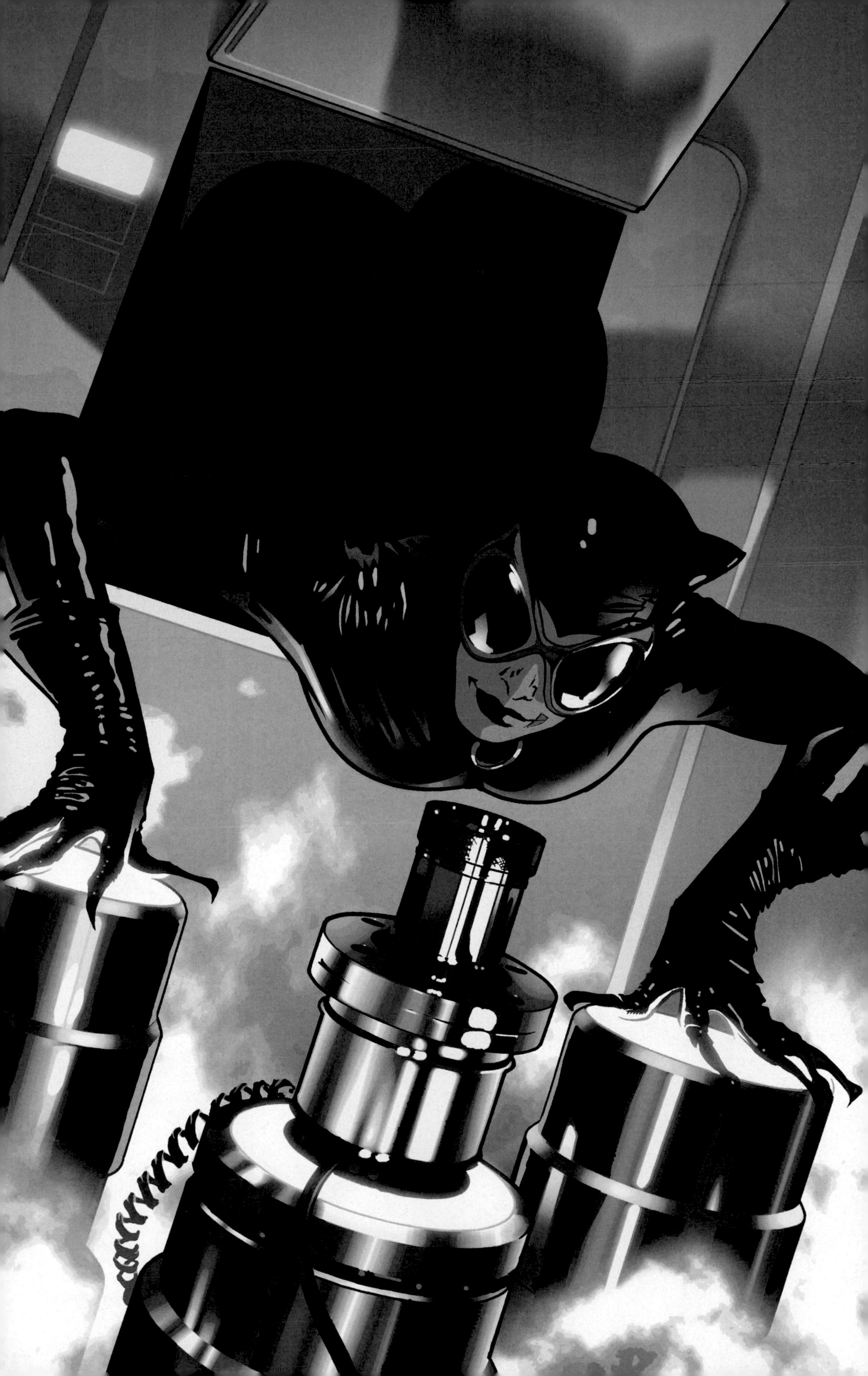

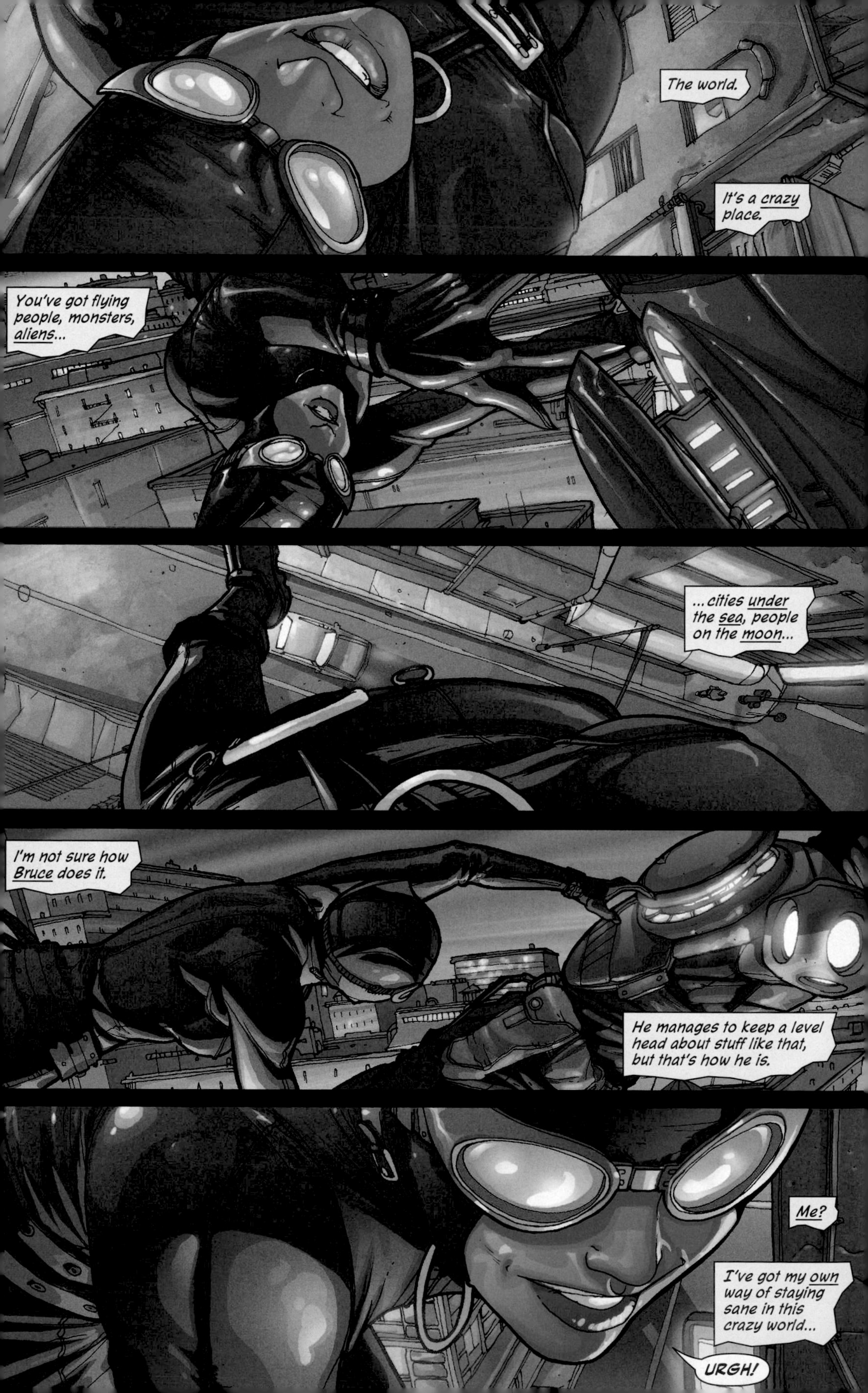
The world.
It's a crazy place.
You've got flying people, monsters, aliens...
...cities under the sea, people on the moon...
I'm not sure how Bruce does it.
He manages to keep a level head about stuff like that, but that's how he is.
Me?
I've got my own way of staying sane in this crazy world...
URGH!

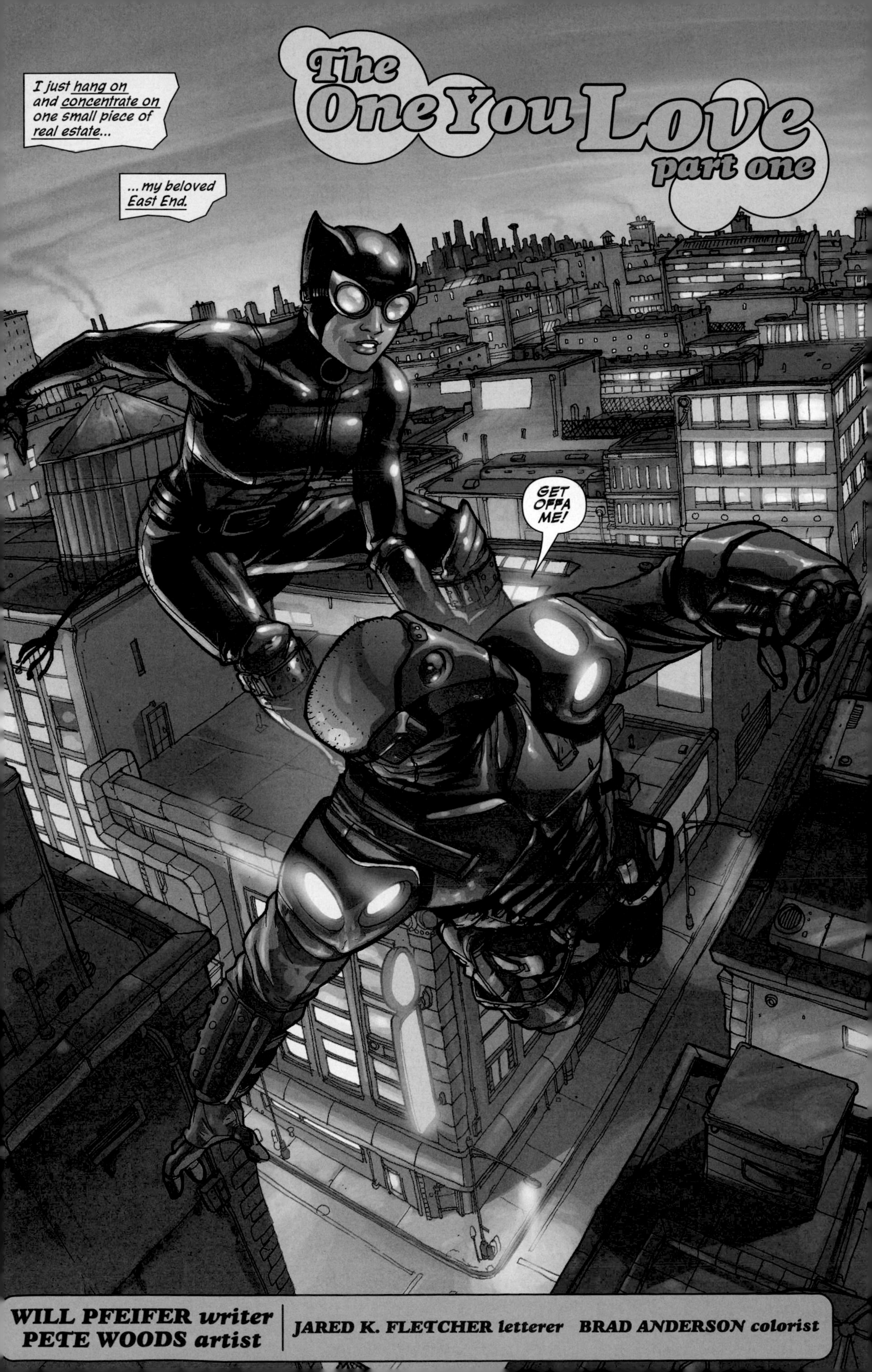
I just hang on and concentrate on one small piece of real estate...
The One You Love part one
... my beloved East End.
GET OFFA ME!
WILL PFEIFER writer
PETE WOODS artist
JARED K. FLETCHER letterer
BRAD ANDERSON colorist

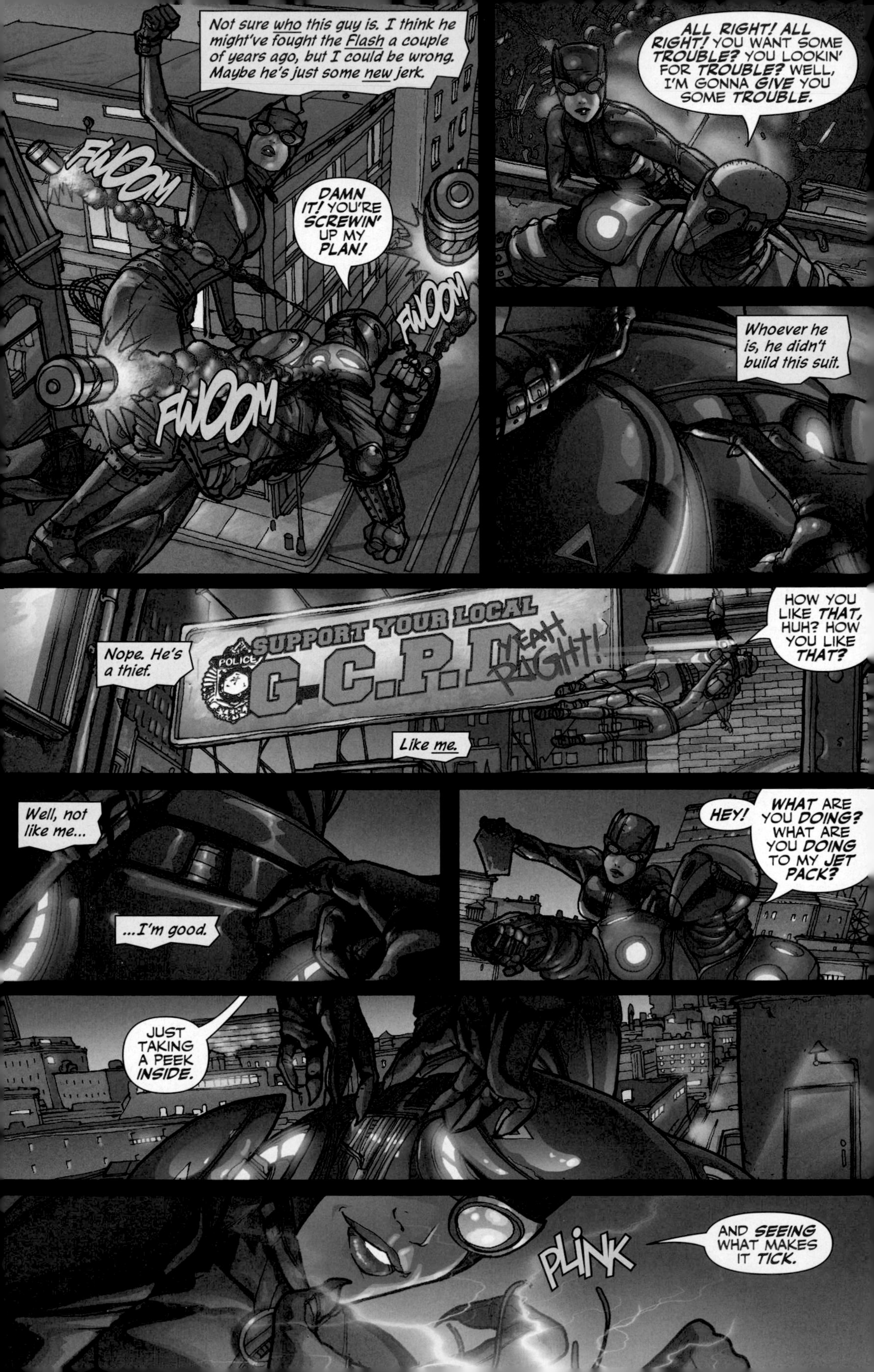

Not sure who this guy is. I think he might've fought the Flash a couple of years ago, but I could be wrong. Maybe he's just some new jerk.
FWOOM
DAMN IT! YOU'RE SCREWIN' UP MY PLAN!
FWOOM
FWOOM
ALL RIGHT! ALL RIGHT! YOU WANT SOME TROUBLE? YOU LOOKIN' FOR TROUBLE? WELL, I'M GONNA GIVE YOU SOME TROUBLE.
Whoever he is, he didn't build this suit.
Nope. He's a thief.
SUPPORT YOUR LOCAL
POLICE
G.C.P.D.
YEAH RIGHT!
HOW YOU LIKE THAT, HUH? HOW YOU LIKE THAT?
Like me.
Well, not like me...
...I'm good.
HEY!
WHAT ARE YOU DOING? WHAT ARE YOU DOING TO MY JET PACK?
JUST TAKING A PEEK INSIDE.
PLINK
AND SEEING WHAT MAKES IT TICK.

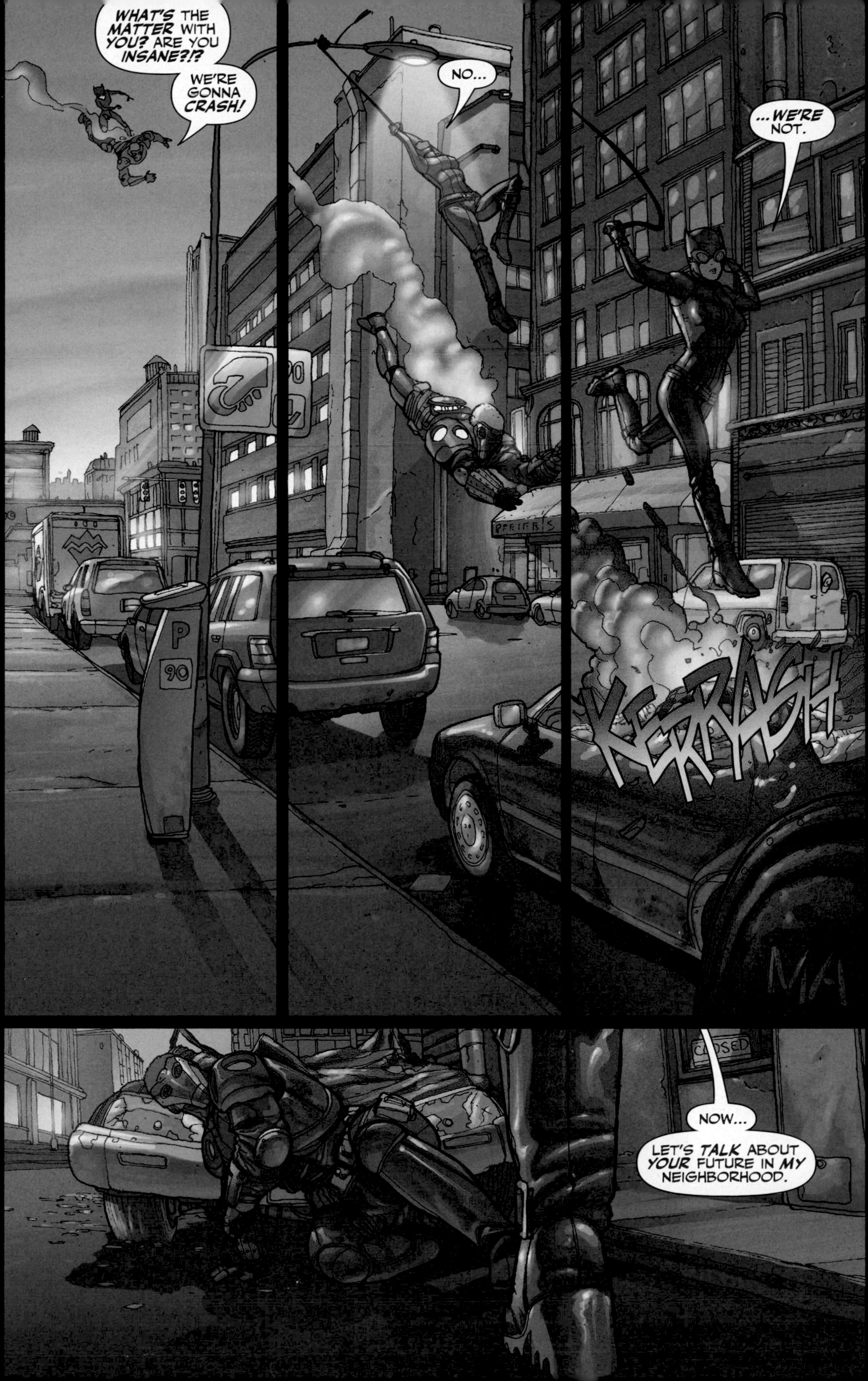

WHAT'S THE MATTER WITH YOU? ARE YOU INSANE?!?
WE'RE GONNA CRASH!
NO...
...WE'RE NOT.
KERRASH
NOW...
LET'S TALK ABOUT YOUR FUTURE IN MY NEIGHBORHOOD.

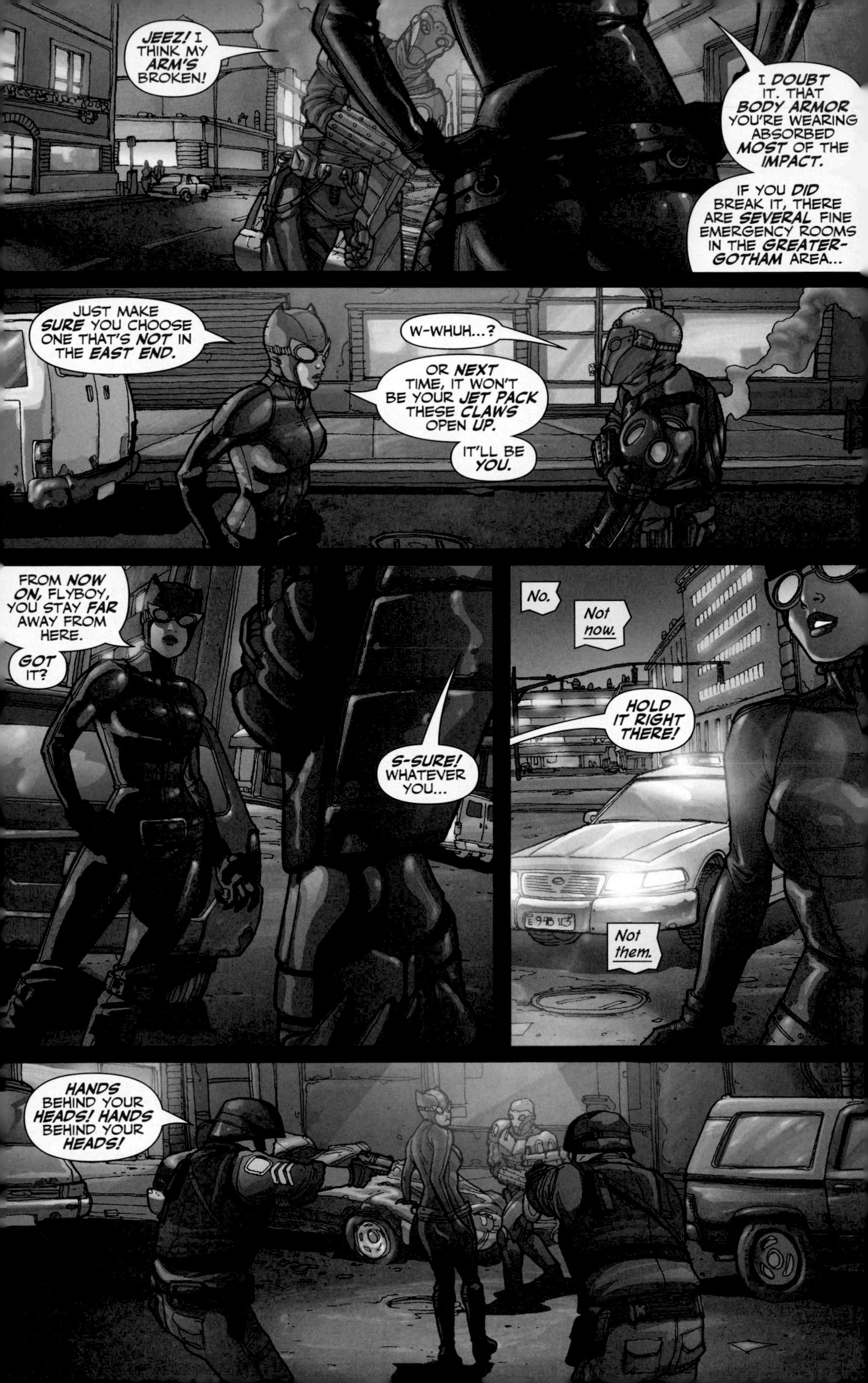
JEEZ! I THINK MY ARM'S BROKEN!
I DOUBT IT. THAT BODY ARMOR YOU'RE WEARING ABSORBED MOST OF THE IMPACT.
IF YOU DID BREAK IT, THERE ARE SEVERAL FINE EMERGENCY ROOMS IN THE GREATER-GOTHAM AREA...
JUST MAKE SURE YOU CHOOSE ONE THAT'S NOT IN THE EAST END.
W-WHUH...?
OR NEXT TIME, IT WON'T BE YOUR JET PACK THESE CLAWS OPEN UP.
IT'LL BE YOU.
FROM NOW ON, FLYBOY, YOU STAY FAR AWAY FROM HERE.
GOT IT?
S-SURE! WHATEVER YOU...
No.
Not now.
HOLD IT RIGHT THERE!
Not them.
HANDS BEHIND YOUR HEADS! HANDS BEHIND YOUR HEADS!

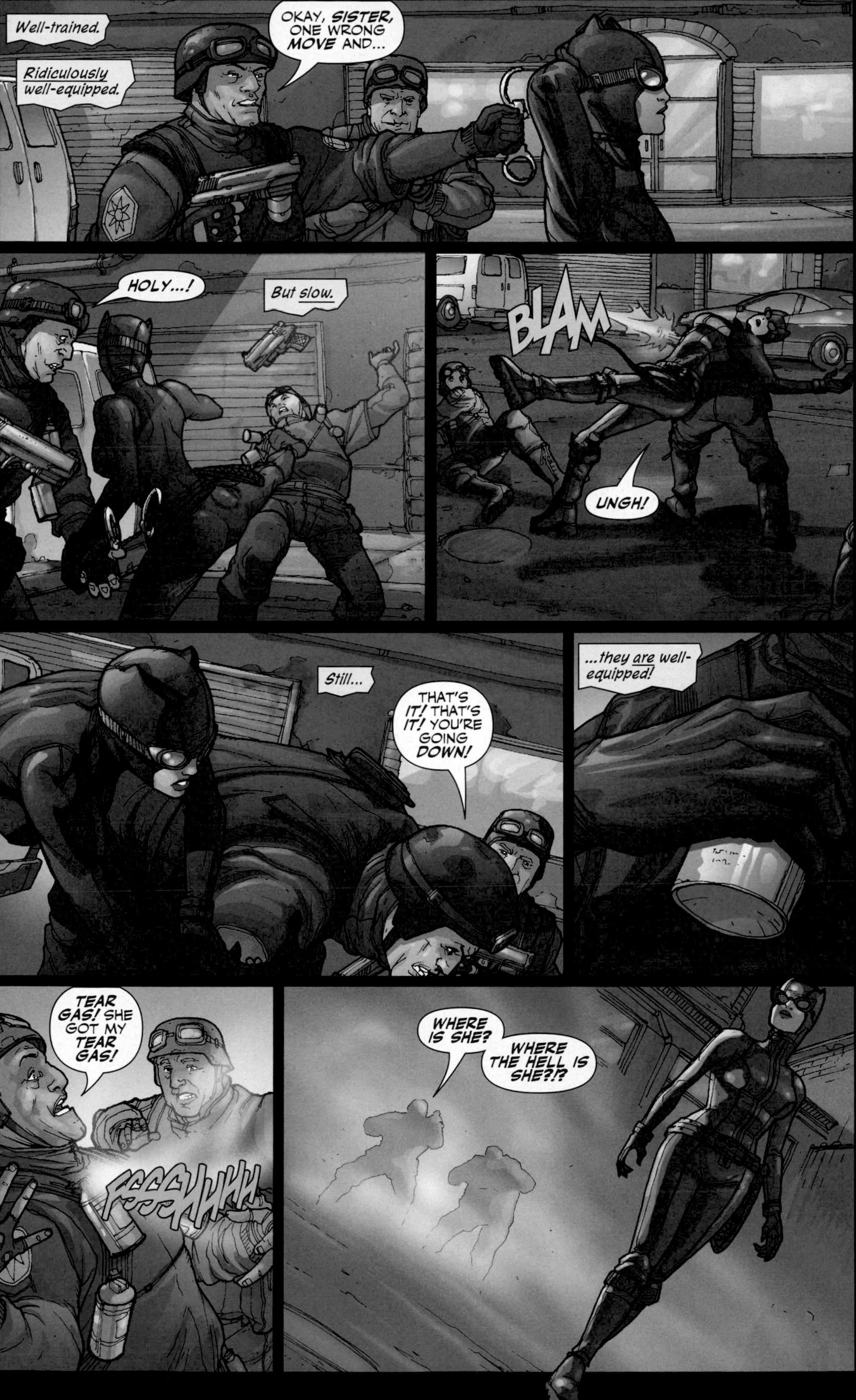

Well-trained.
Ridiculously well-equipped.
OKAY, SISTER, ONE WRONG MOVE AND...
HOLY...!
But slow.
BLAM
UNGH!
Still...
THAT'S IT! THAT'S IT! YOU'RE GOING DOWN!
...they are well-equipped!
TEAR GAS! SHE GOT MY TEAR GAS!
FSSSHHHH
WHERE IS SHE?
WHERE THE HELL IS SHE?!?

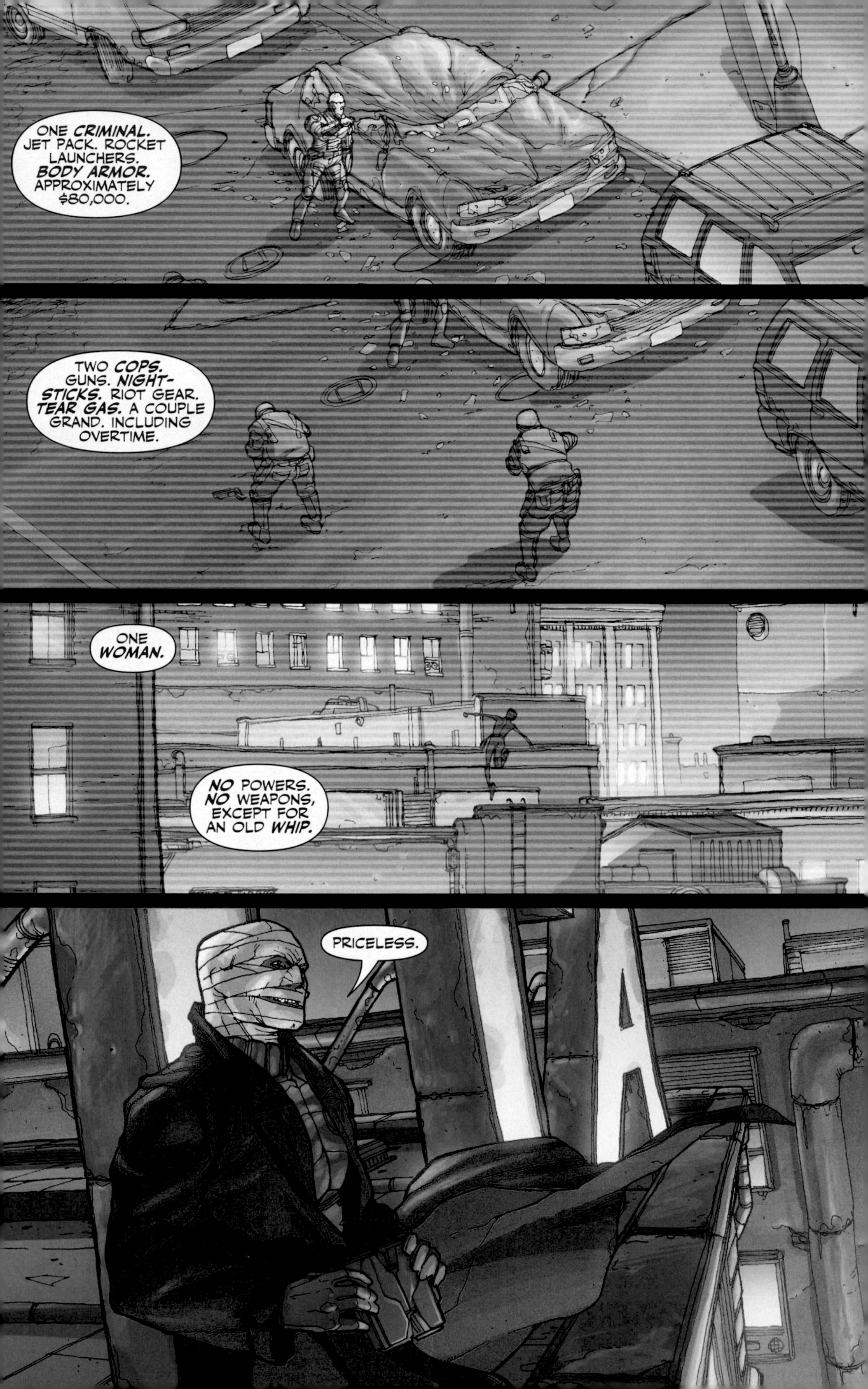
ONE CRIMINAL. JET PACK. ROCKET LAUNCHERS. BODY ARMOR. APPROXIMATELY $80,000.
TWO COPS. GUNS. NIGHT-STICKS. RIOT GEAR. TEAR GAS. A COUPLE GRAND. INCLUDING OVERTIME.
ONE WOMAN.
NO POWERS. NO WEAPONS, EXCEPT FOR AN OLD WHIP.
PRICELESS.

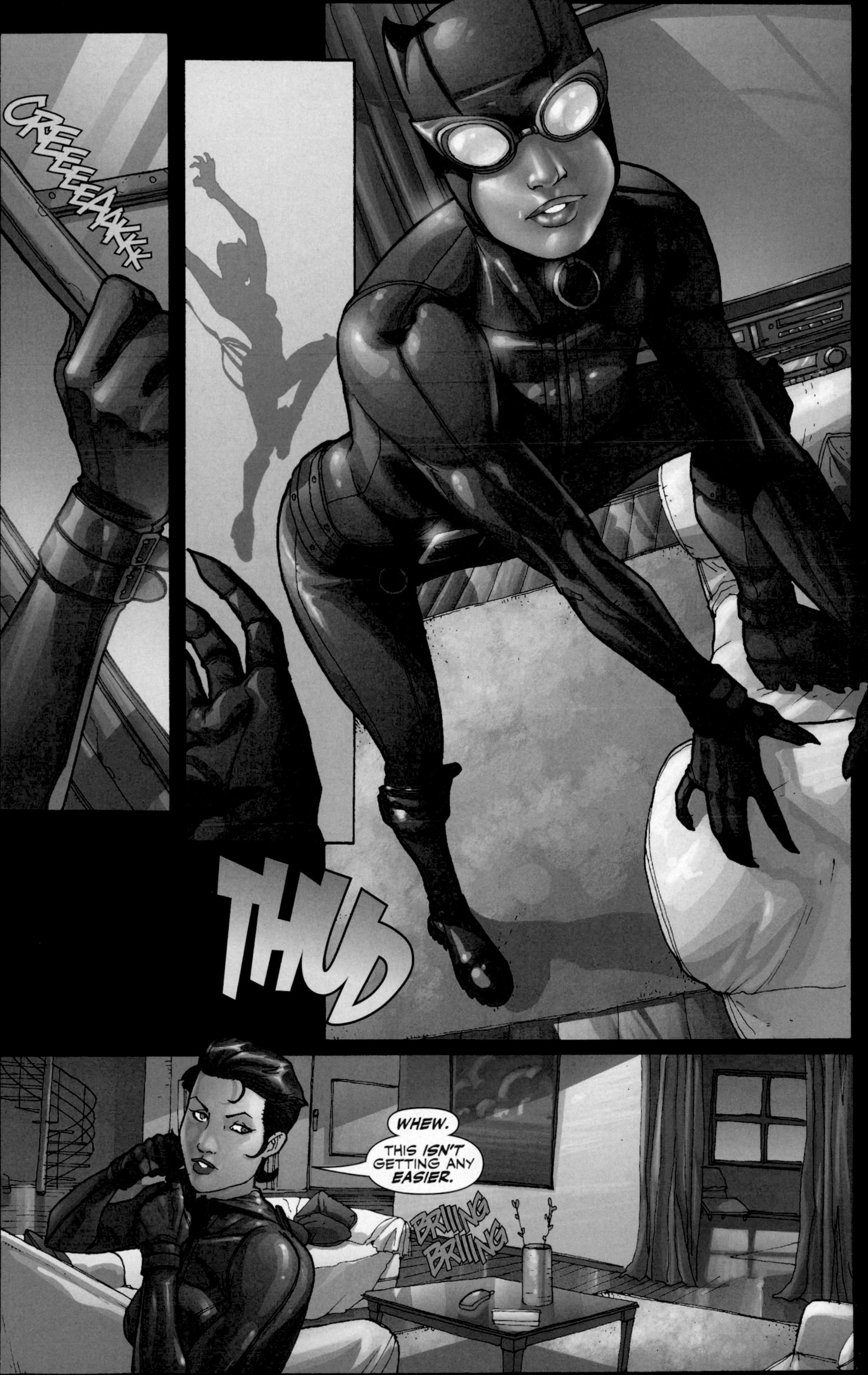
CREEEEAAKKK
THUD
WHEW.
THIS ISN'T GETTING ANY EASIER.
BRIIING BRIIING

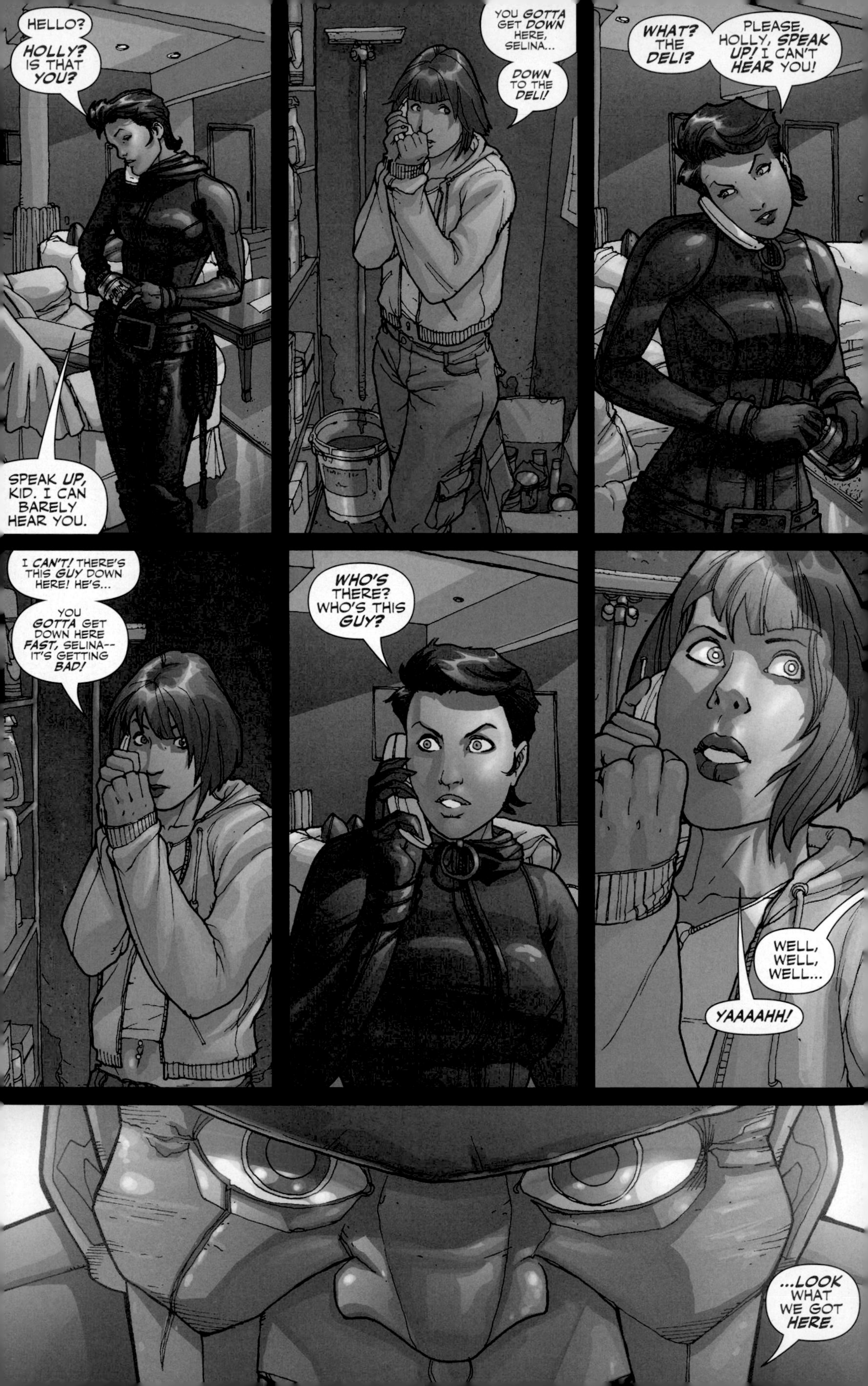
HELLO? HOLLY? IS THAT YOU?
SPEAK UP, KID. I CAN BARELY HEAR YOU.
YOU GOTTA GET DOWN HERE, SELINA...
DOWN TO THE DELI!
WHAT? THE DELI?
PLEASE, HOLLY, SPEAK UP! I CAN'T HEAR YOU!
I CAN'T! THERE'S THIS GUY DOWN HERE! HE'S...
YOU GOTTA GET DOWN HERE FAST, SELINA-- IT'S GETTING BAD!
WHO'S THERE? WHO'S THIS GUY?
WELL, WELL, WELL...
YAAAAHH!
...LOOK WHAT WE GOT HERE.

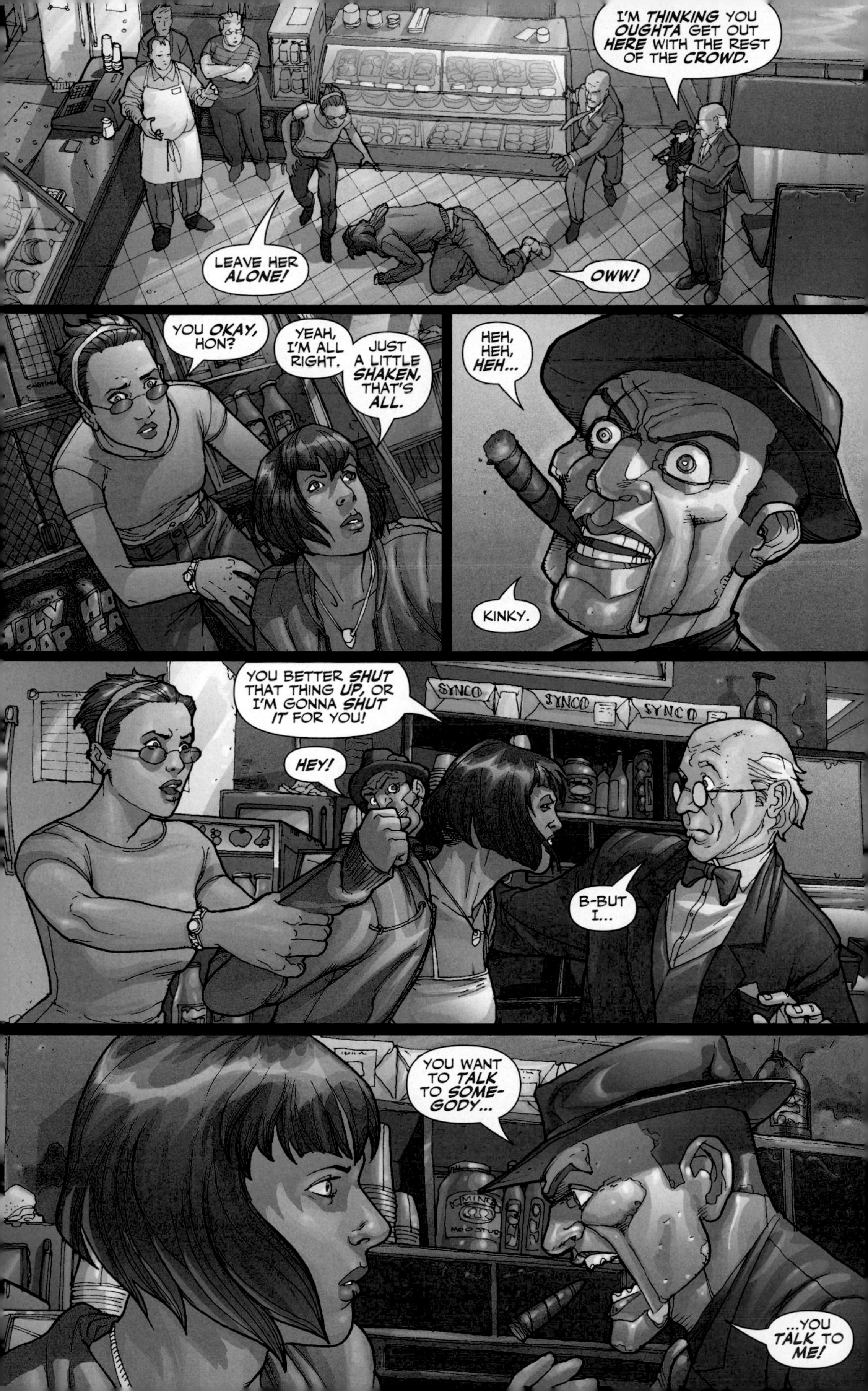
I'M THINKING YOU OUGHTA GET OUT HERE WITH THE REST OF THE CROWD.
LEAVE HER ALONE!
OWW!
YOU OKAY, HON?
YEAH, I'M ALL RIGHT.
JUST A LITTLE SHAKEN, THAT'S ALL.
HEH, HEH, HEH...
KINKY.
YOU BETTER SHUT THAT THING UP, OR I'M GONNA SHUT IT FOR YOU!
HEY!
B-BUT I...
YOU WANT TO TALK TO SOME-BODY...
...YOU TALK TO ME!

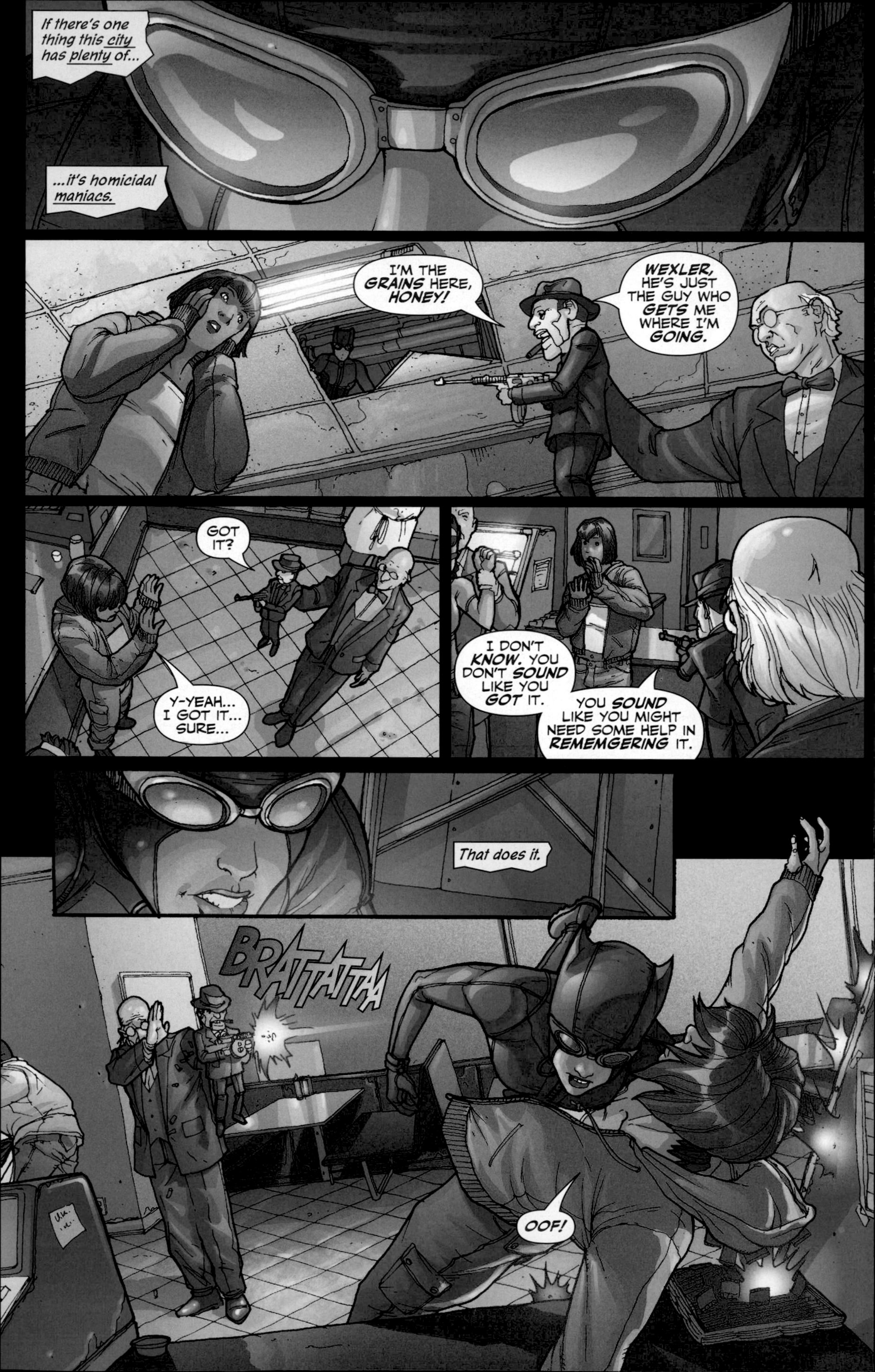

If there's one thing this city has plenty of...
...it's homicidal maniacs.
I'M THE GRAINS HERE, HONEY!
WEXLER, HE'S JUST THE GUY WHO GETS ME WHERE I'M GOING.
GOT IT?
Y-YEAH... I GOT IT... SURE...
I DON'T KNOW. YOU DON'T SOUND LIKE YOU GOT IT.
YOU SOUND LIKE YOU MIGHT NEED SOME HELP IN REMEMGERING IT.
That does it.
BRATTATTAA
OOF!

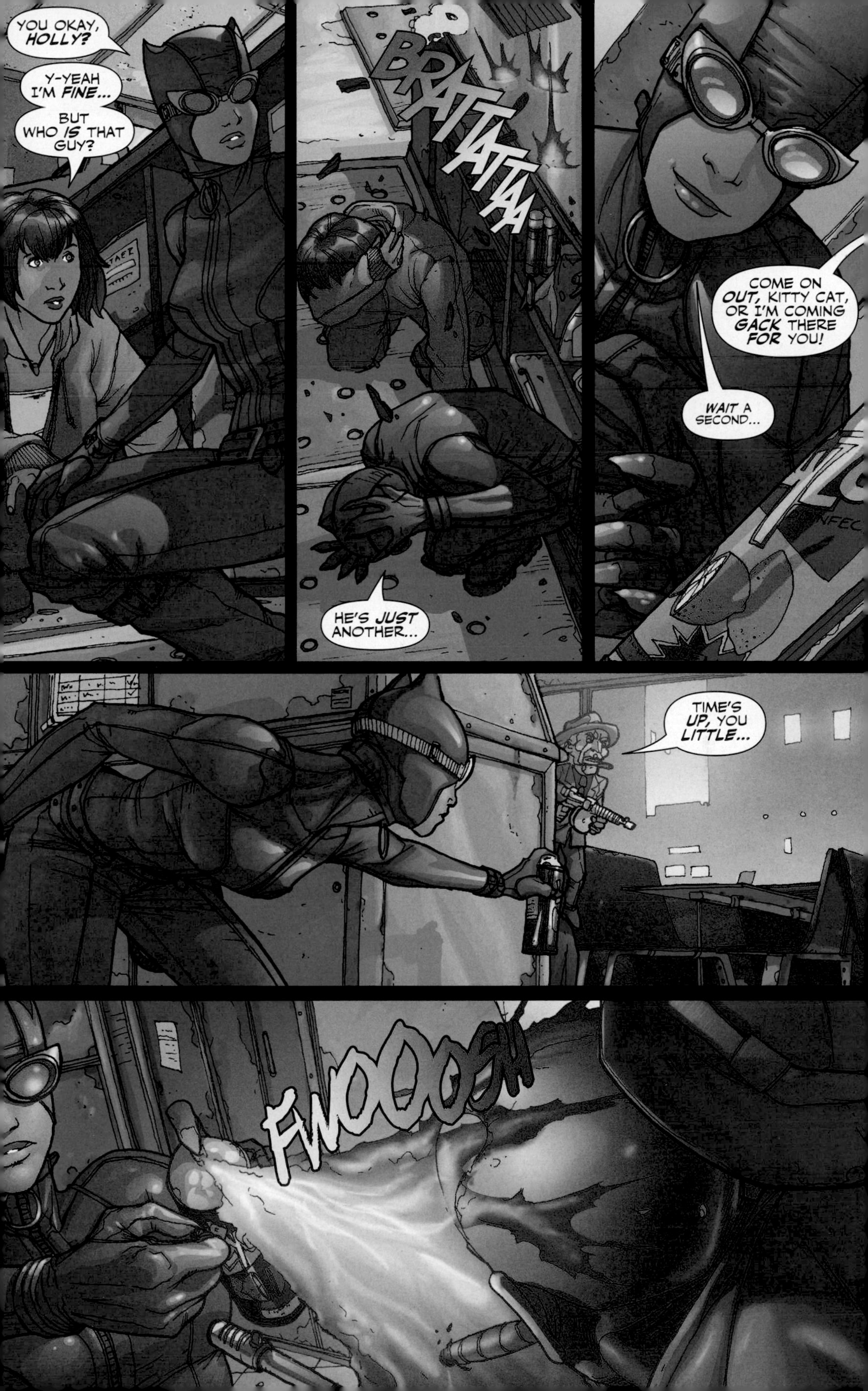
YOU OKAY, HOLLY?
Y-YEAH I'M FINE...
BUT WHO IS THAT GUY?
BRATTATTAA
HE'S JUST ANOTHER...
COME ON OUT, KITTY CAT, OR I'M COMING GACK THERE FOR YOU!
WAIT A SECOND...
TIME'S UP, YOU LITTLE...
FWOOOSH

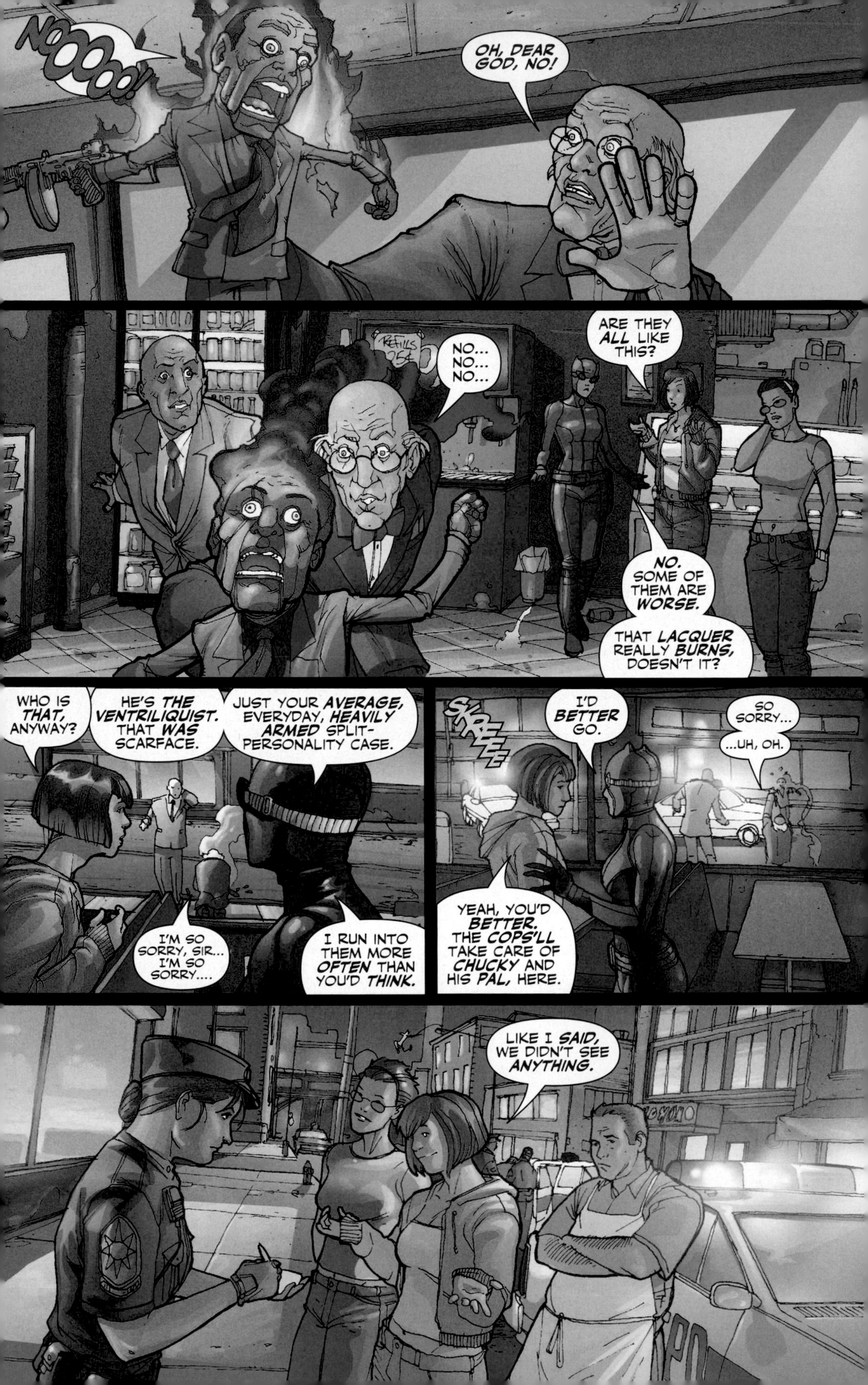
NOOOOOO!
OH, DEAR GOD, NO!
NO... NO... NO...
REFILLS 25¢
ARE THEY ALL LIKE THIS?
NO. SOME OF THEM ARE WORSE.
THAT LACQUER REALLY BURNS, DOESN'T IT?
WHO IS THAT, ANYWAY?
HE'S THE VENTRILIQUIST. THAT WAS SCARFACE.
JUST YOUR AVERAGE, EVERYDAY, HEAVILY ARMED SPLIT-PERSONALITY CASE.
I'M SO SORRY, SIR... I'M SO SORRY....
I RUN INTO THEM MORE OFTEN THAN YOU'D THINK.
SKREEE
I'D BETTER GO.
SO SORRY...
...UH, OH.
YEAH, YOU'D BETTER. THE COPS'LL TAKE CARE OF CHUCKY AND HIS PAL, HERE.
LIKE I SAID, WE DIDN'T SEE ANYTHING.

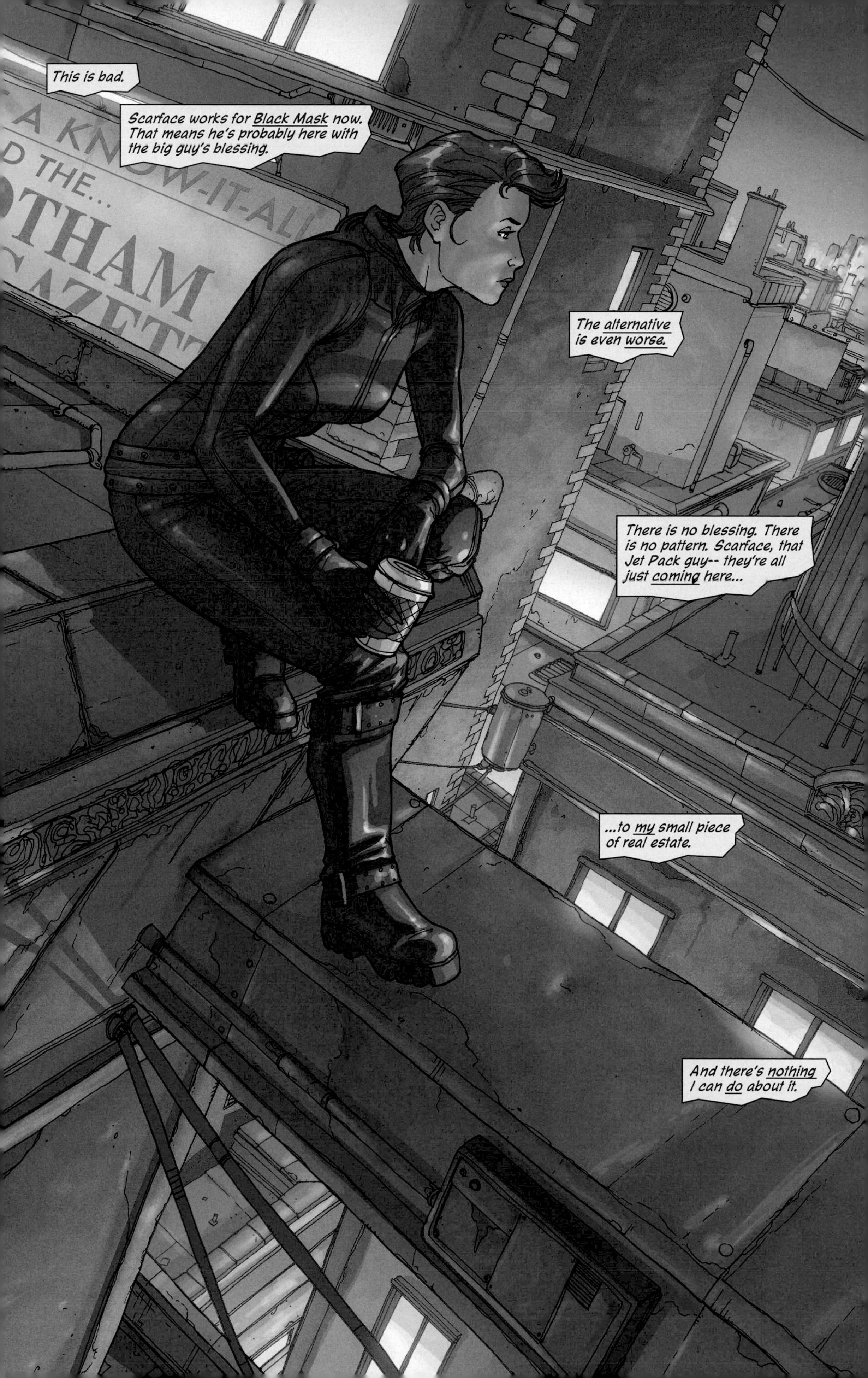
This is bad.
Scarface works for Black Mask now. That means he's probably here with the big guy's blessing.
The alternative is even worse.
There is no blessing. There is no pattern. Scarface, that Jet Pack guy-- they're all just coming here...
...to my small piece of real estate.
And there's nothing I can do about it.

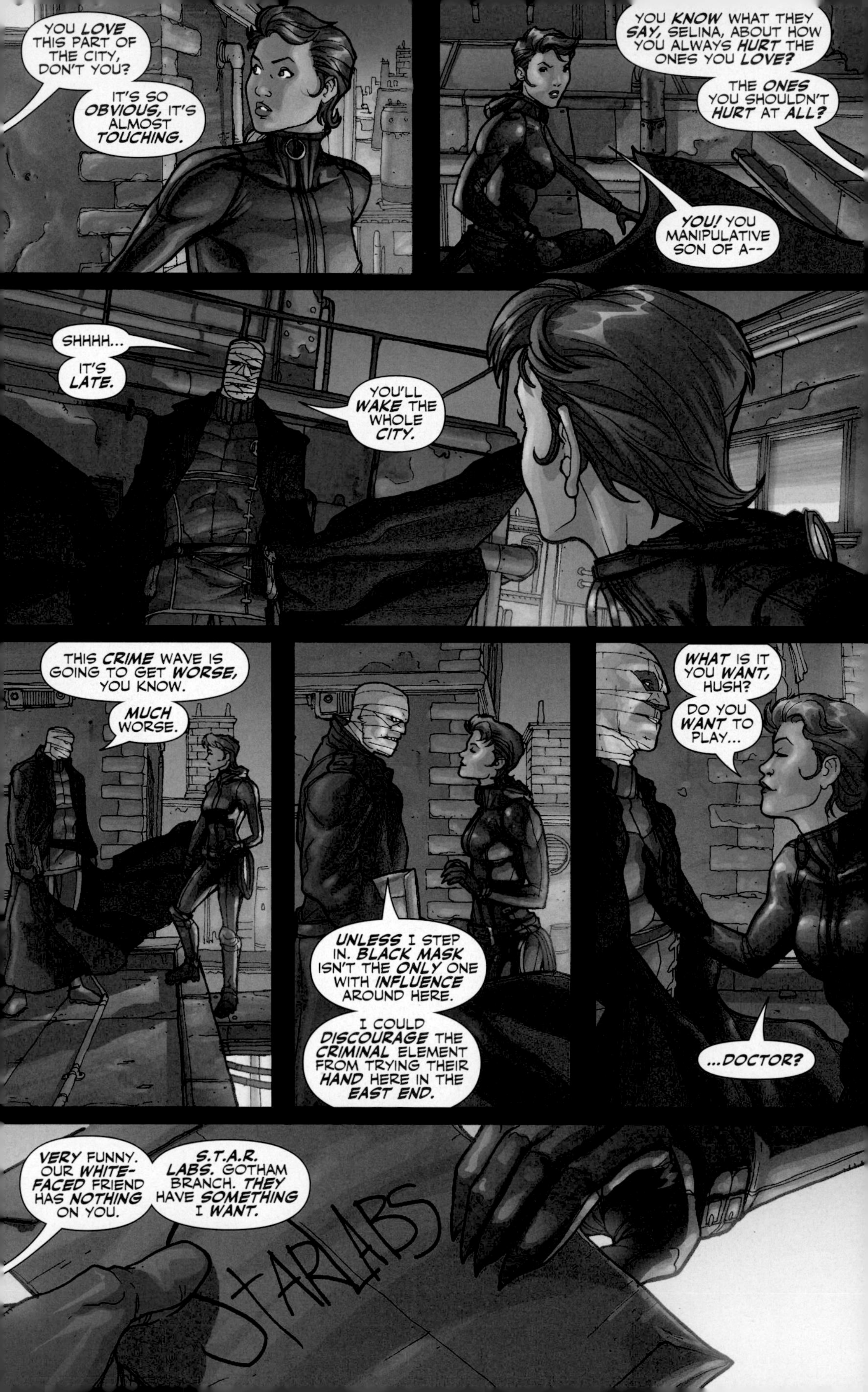

YOU LOVE THIS PART OF THE CITY, DON'T YOU?
IT'S SO OBVIOUS, IT'S ALMOST TOUCHING.
YOU KNOW WHAT THEY SAY, SELINA, ABOUT HOW YOU ALWAYS HURT THE ONES YOU LOVE?
THE ONES YOU SHOULDN'T HURT AT ALL?
YOU! YOU MANIPULATIVE SON OF A--
SHHHH...
IT'S LATE.
YOU'LL WAKE THE WHOLE CITY.
THIS CRIME WAVE IS GOING TO GET WORSE, YOU KNOW.
MUCH WORSE.
UNLESS I STEP IN. BLACK MASK ISN'T THE ONLY ONE WITH INFLUENCE AROUND HERE.
I COULD DISCOURAGE THE CRIMINAL ELEMENT FROM TRYING THEIR HAND HERE IN THE EAST END.
WHAT IS IT YOU WANT, HUSH?
DO YOU WANT TO PLAY...
...DOCTOR?
VERY FUNNY. OUR WHITE-FACED FRIEND HAS NOTHING ON YOU.
S.T.A.R. LABS. GOTHAM BRANCH. THEY HAVE SOMETHING I WANT.
STARLABS

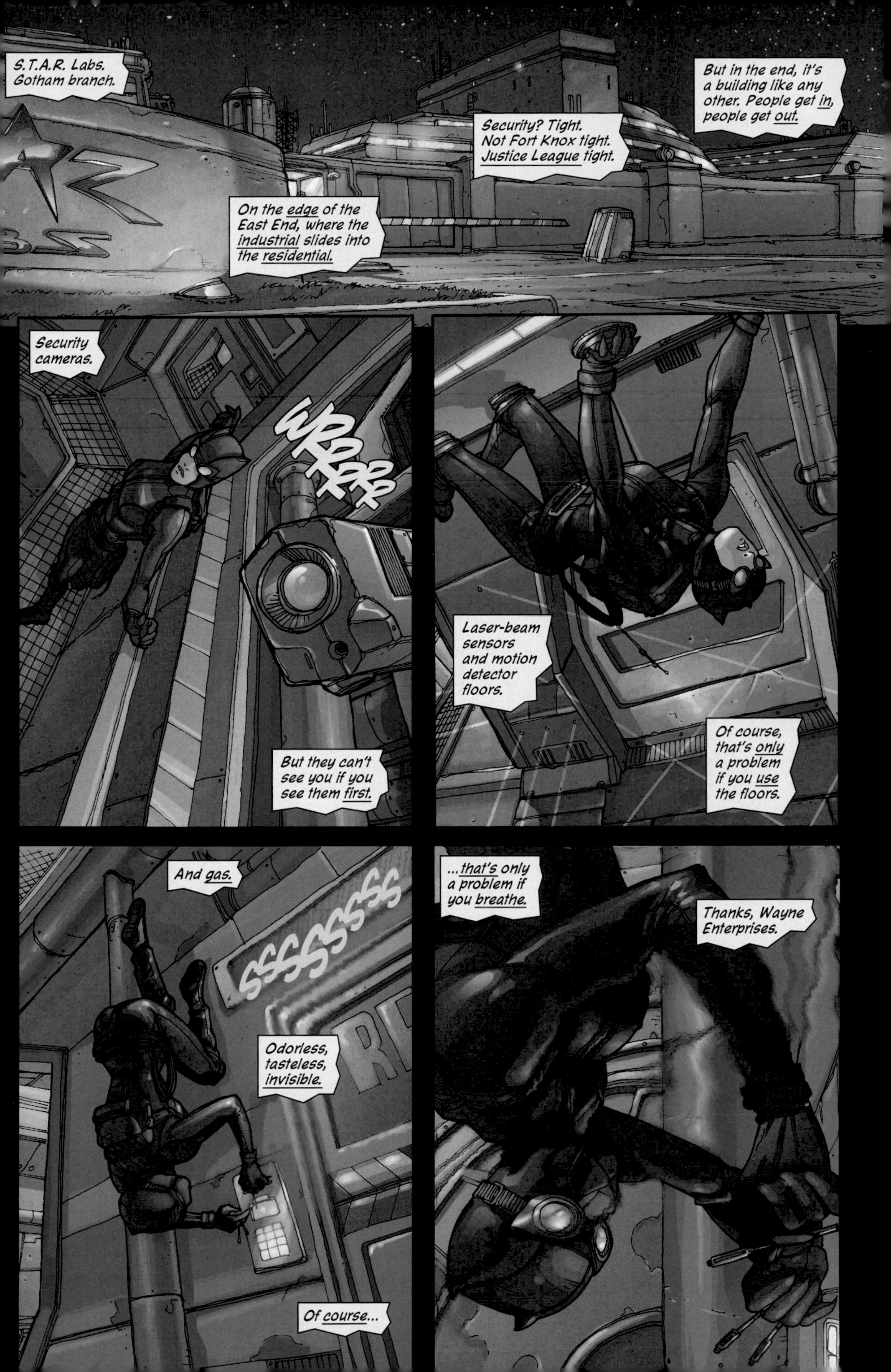
S.T.A.R. Labs. Gotham branch.
On the edge of the East End, where the industrial slides into the residential.
Security? Tight. Not Fort Knox tight. Justice League tight.
But in the end, it's a building like any other. People get in, people get out.
Security cameras.
WRRRRR
But they can't see you if you see them first.
Laser-beam sensors and motion detector floors.
Of course, that's only a problem if you use the floors.
And gas.
SSSSSSSS
Odorless, tasteless, invisible.
Of course...
...that's only a problem if you breathe.
Thanks, Wayne Enterprises.

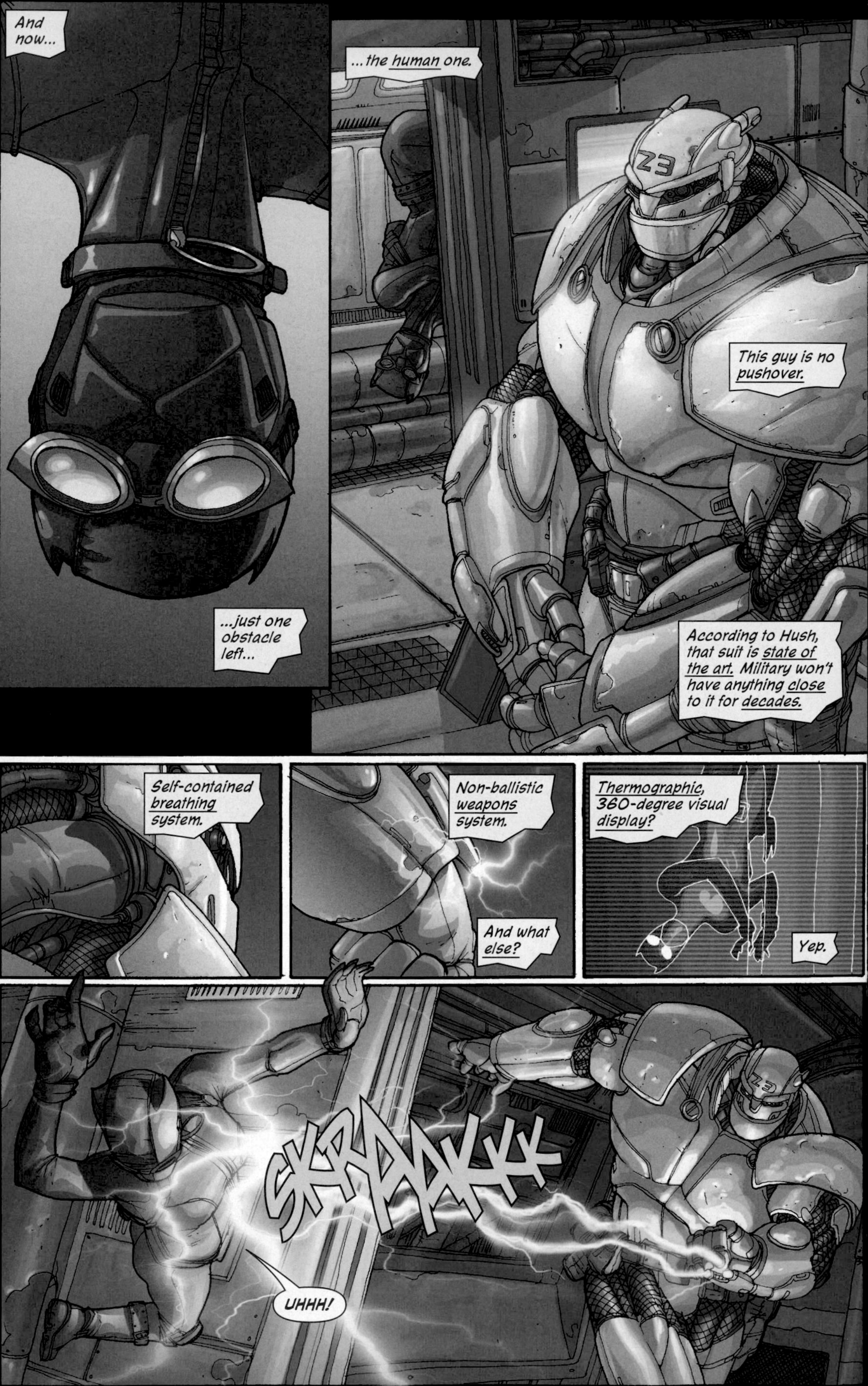

And now...
...just one obstacle left...
...the human one.
This guy is no pushover.
According to Hush, that suit is state of the art. Military won't have anything close to it for decades.
Self-contained breathing system.
Non-ballistic weapons system.
And what else?
Thermographic, 360-degree visual display?
Yep.
SKRAAKKK
UHHH!

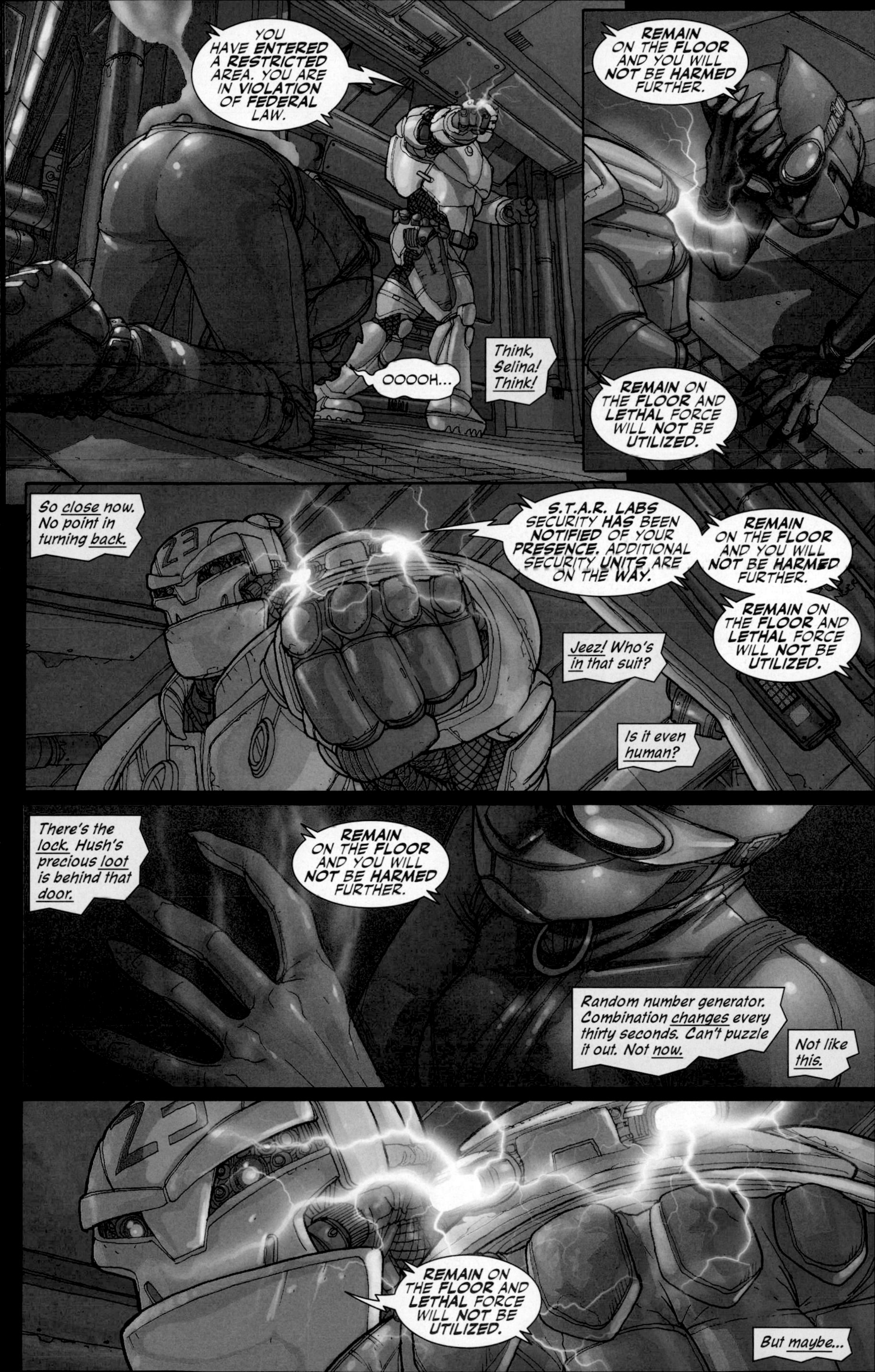

YOU HAVE ENTERED A RESTRICTED AREA. YOU ARE IN VIOLATION OF FEDERAL LAW.
OOOOH...
Think, Selina! Think!
REMAIN ON THE FLOOR AND YOU WILL NOT BE HARMED FURTHER.
REMAIN ON THE FLOOR AND LETHAL FORCE WILL NOT BE UTILIZED.
So close now. No point in turning back.
S.T.A.R. LABS SECURITY HAS BEEN NOTIFIED OF YOUR PRESENCE. ADDITIONAL SECURITY UNITS ARE ON THE WAY.
REMAIN ON THE FLOOR AND YOU WILL NOT BE HARMED FURTHER.
REMAIN ON THE FLOOR AND LETHAL FORCE WILL NOT BE UTILIZED.
Jeez! Who's in that suit?
Is it even human?
There's the lock. Hush's precious loot is behind that door.
REMAIN ON THE FLOOR AND YOU WILL NOT BE HARMED FURTHER.
Random number generator. Combination changes every thirty seconds. Can't puzzle it out. Not now.
Not like this.
REMAIN ON THE FLOOR AND LETHAL FORCE WILL NOT BE UTILIZED.
But maybe...

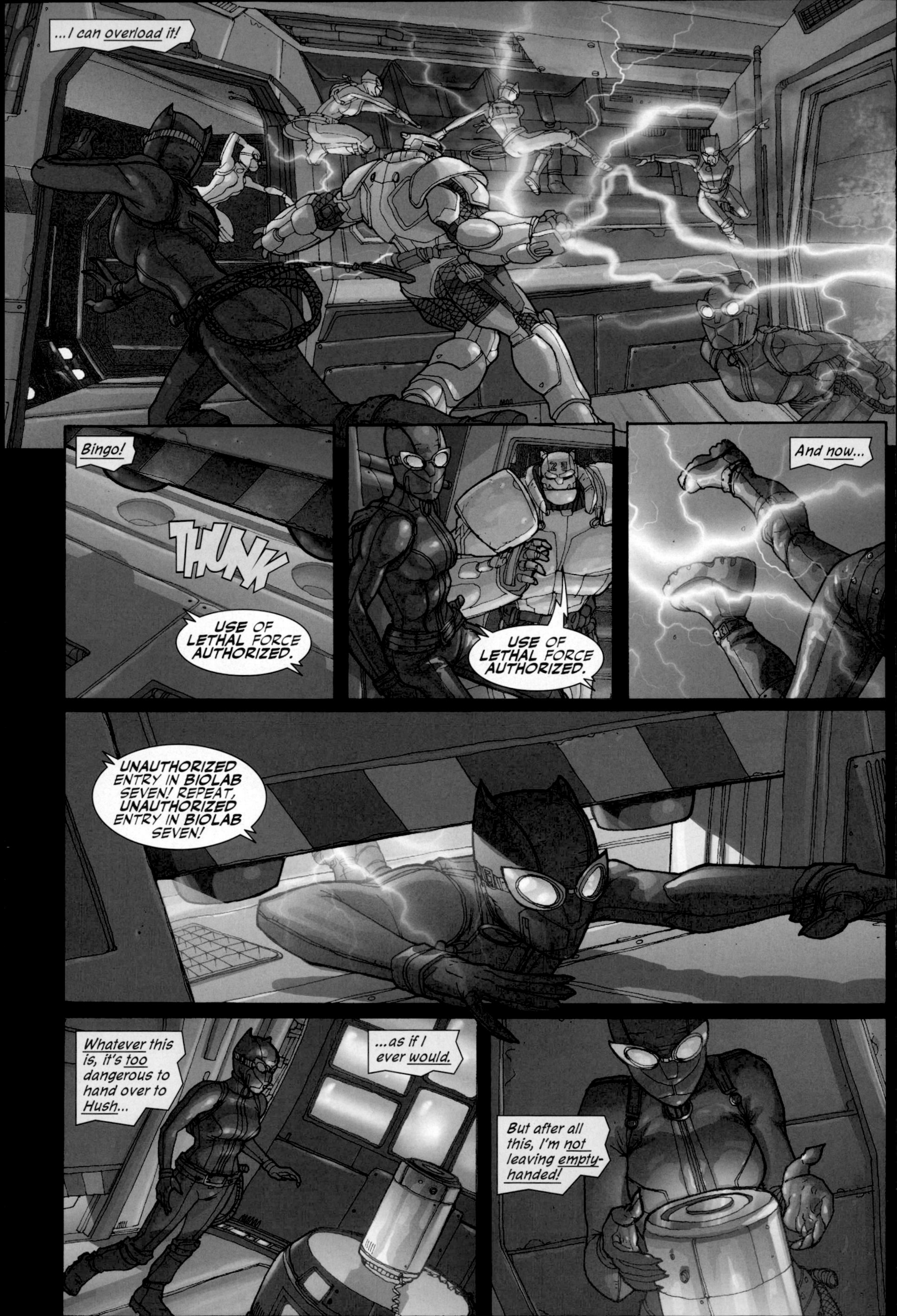
...I can overload it!
Bingo!
THUNK
USE OF LETHAL FORCE AUTHORIZED.
USE OF LETHAL FORCE AUTHORIZED.
And now...
UNAUTHORIZED ENTRY IN BIOLAB SEVEN! REPEAT, UNAUTHORIZED ENTRY IN BIOLAB SEVEN!
Whatever this is, it's too dangerous to hand over to Hush...
...as if I ever would.
But after all this, I'm not leaving empty-handed!

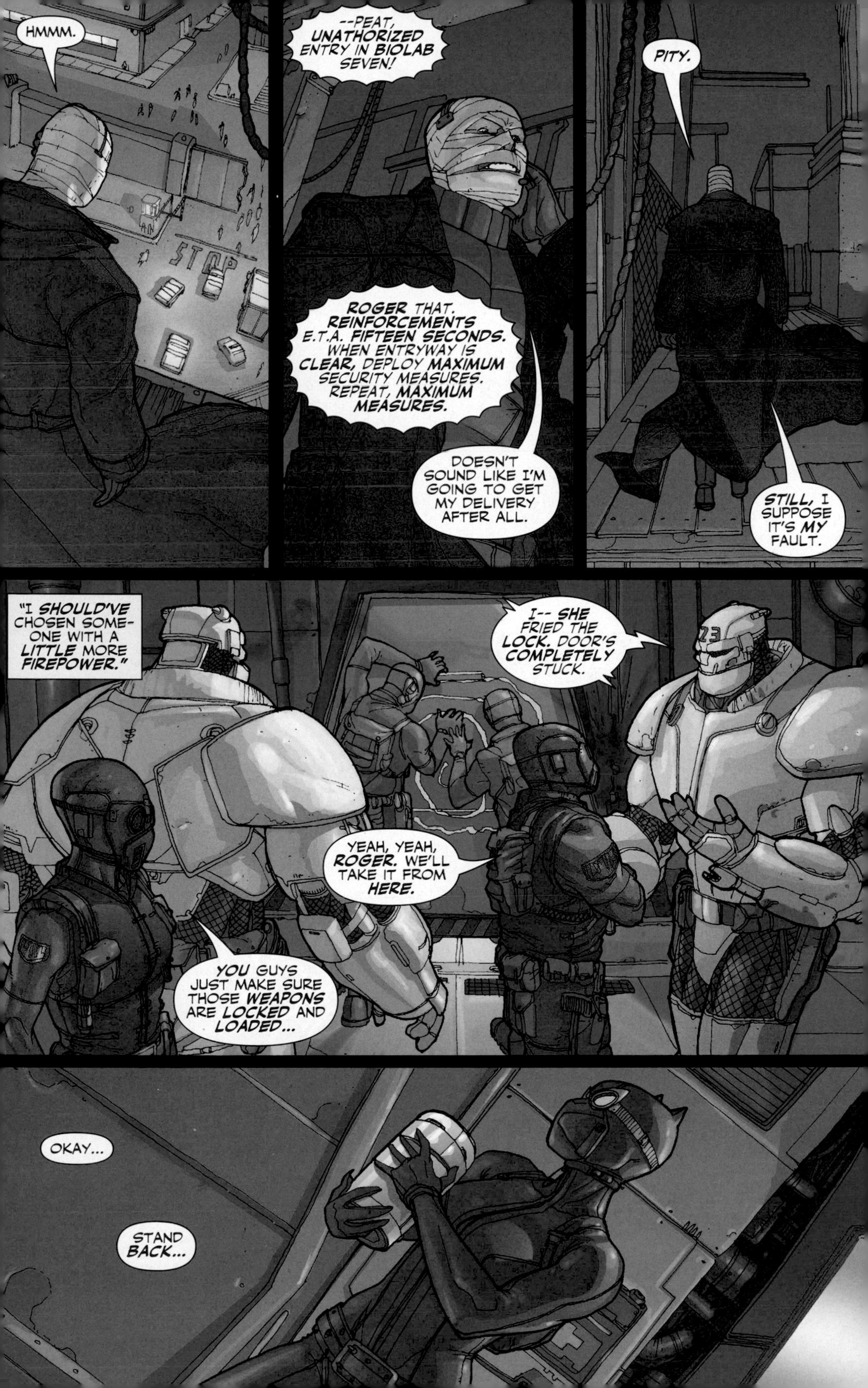
HMMM.
--PEAT, UNATHORIZED ENTRY IN BIOLAB SEVEN!
ROGER THAT. REINFORCEMENTS E.T.A. FIFTEEN SECONDS. WHEN ENTRYWAY IS CLEAR, DEPLOY MAXIMUM SECURITY MEASURES. REPEAT, MAXIMUM MEASURES.
DOESN'T SOUND LIKE I'M GOING TO GET MY DELIVERY AFTER ALL.
PITY.
STILL, I SUPPOSE IT'S MY FAULT.
"I SHOULD'VE CHOSEN SOMEONE WITH A LITTLE MORE FIREPOWER."
I-- SHE FRIED THE LOCK. DOOR'S COMPLETELY STUCK.
YEAH, YEAH, ROGER. WE'LL TAKE IT FROM HERE.
YOU GUYS JUST MAKE SURE THOSE WEAPONS ARE LOCKED AND LOADED...
OKAY...
STAND BACK...

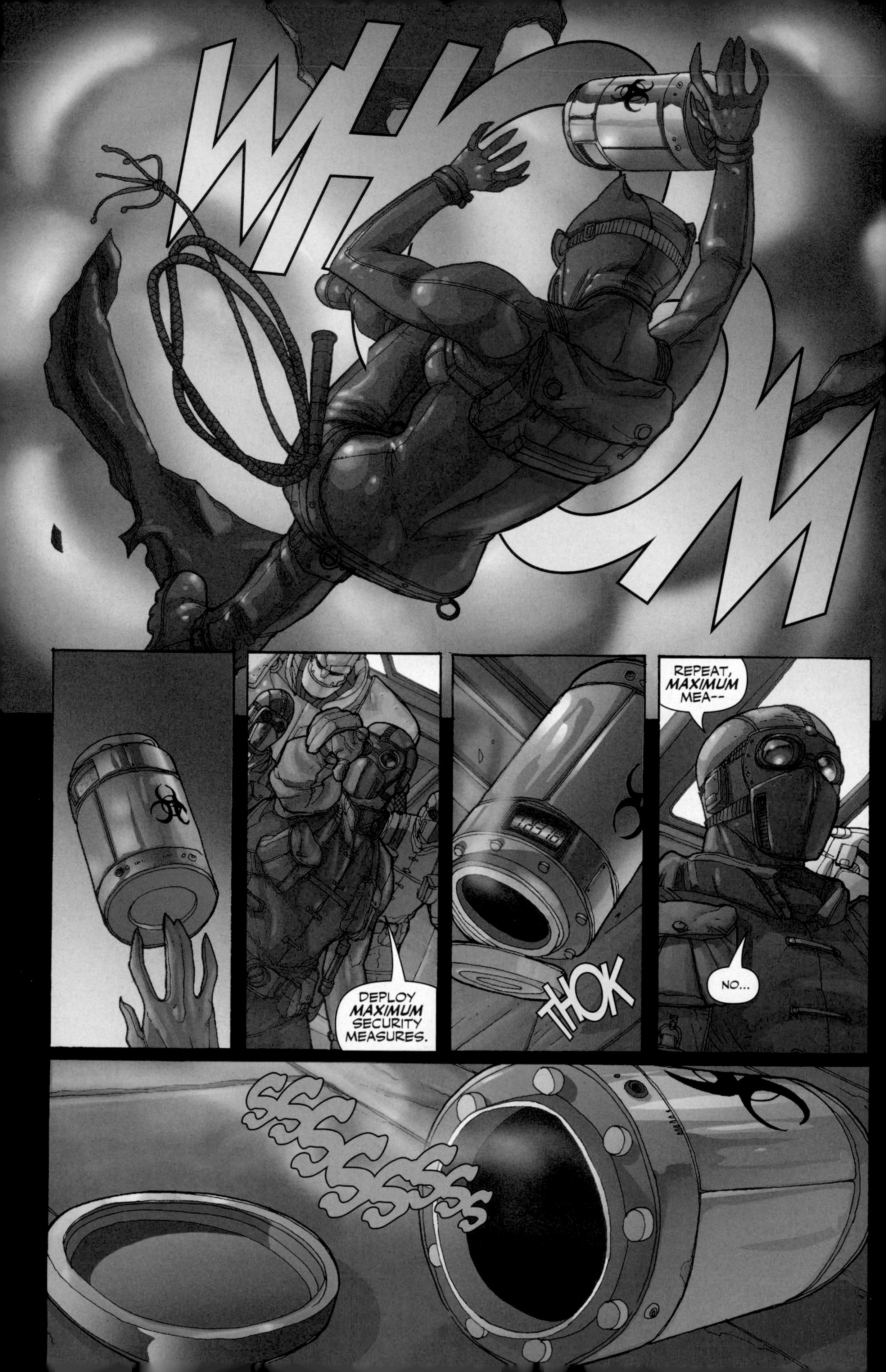
WHOOM
DEPLOY MAXIMUM SECURITY MEASURES.
THOK
REPEAT, MAXIMUM MEA--
NO...
SSSSSSSS

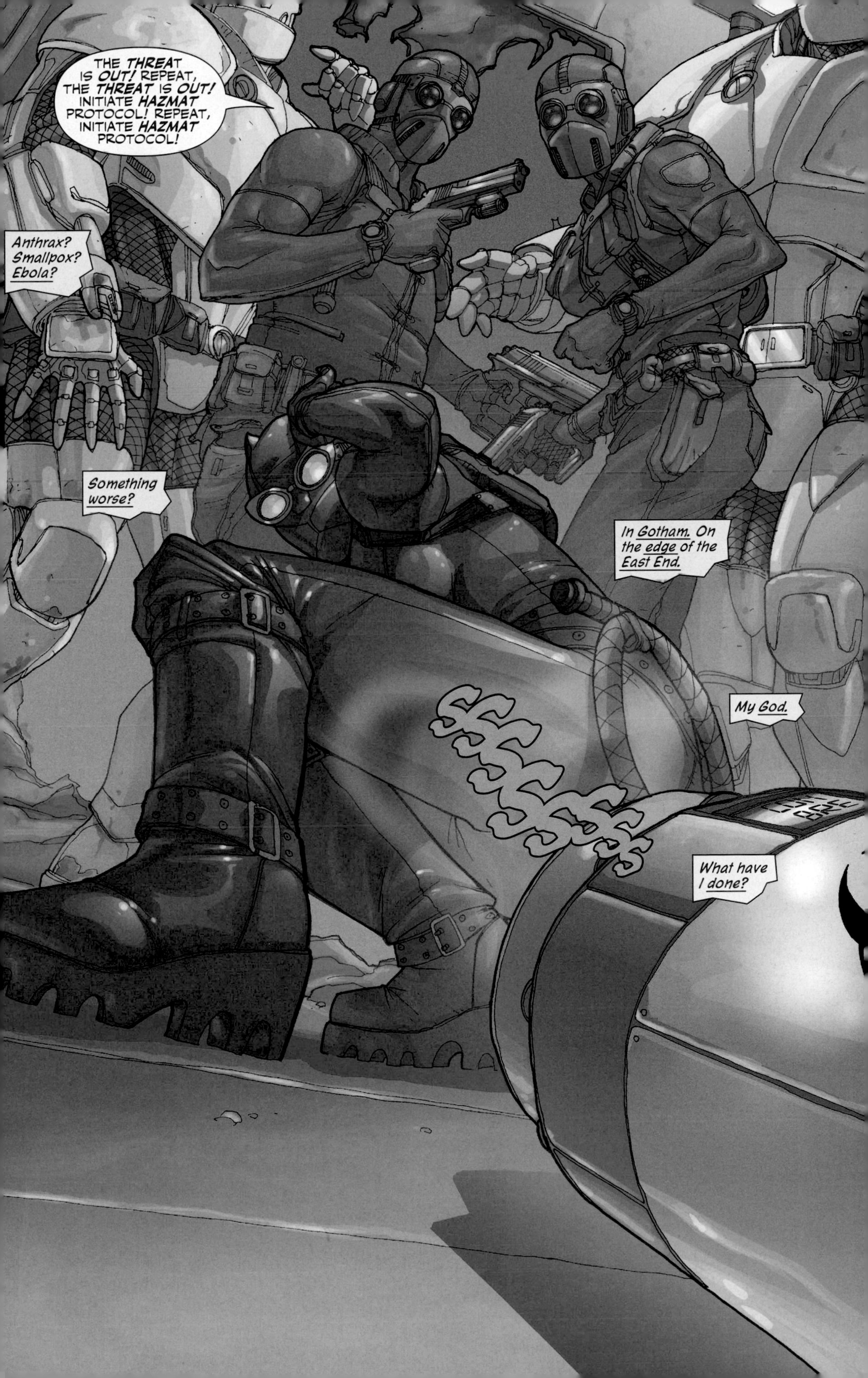
THE THREAT IS OUT! REPEAT, THE THREAT IS OUT! INITIATE HAZMAT PROTOCOL! REPEAT, INITIATE HAZMAT PROTOCOL!
Anthrax? Smallpox? Ebola?
Something worse?
In Gotham. On the edge of the East End.
SSSSSSSS
My God.
What have I done?

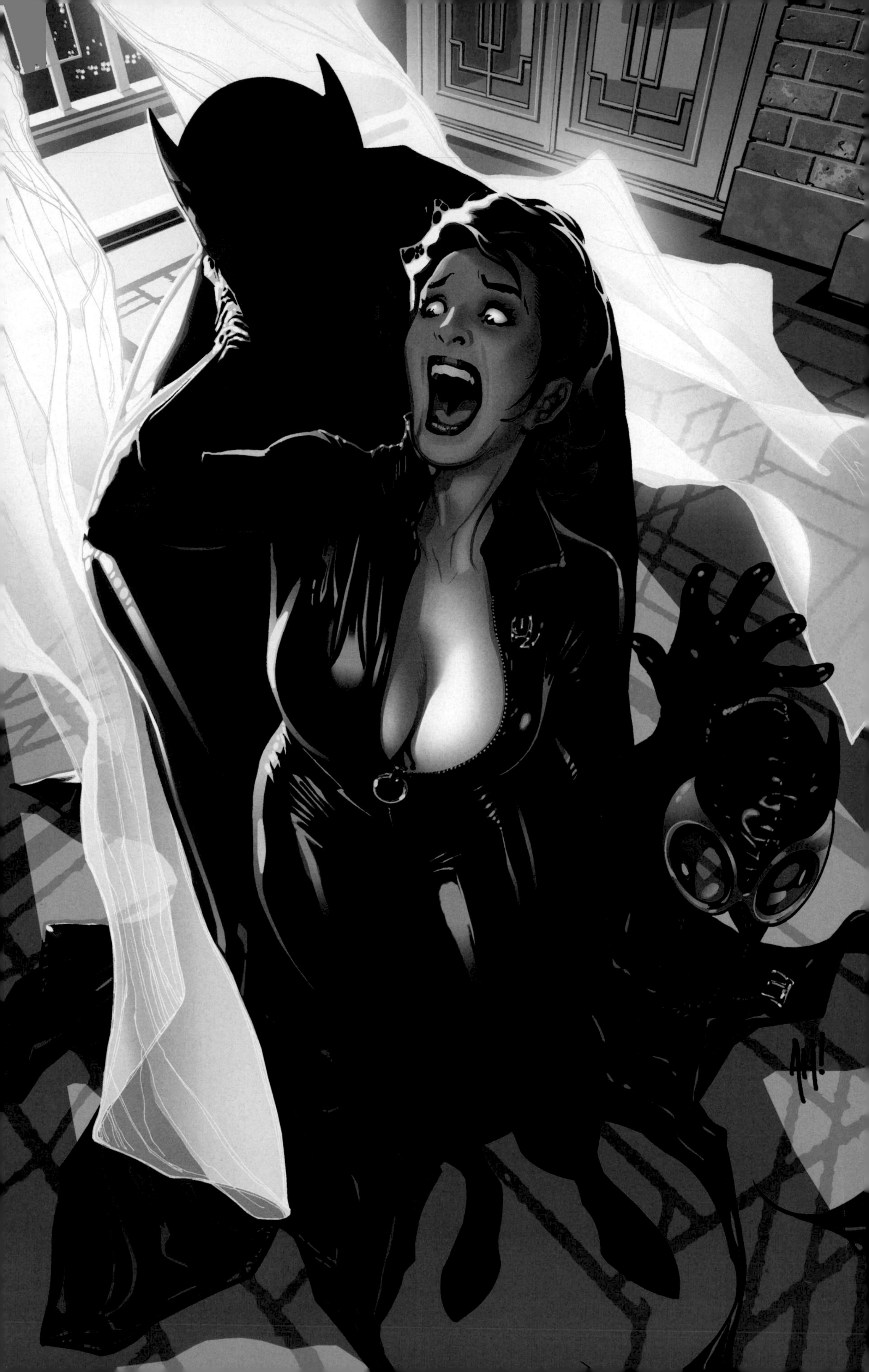

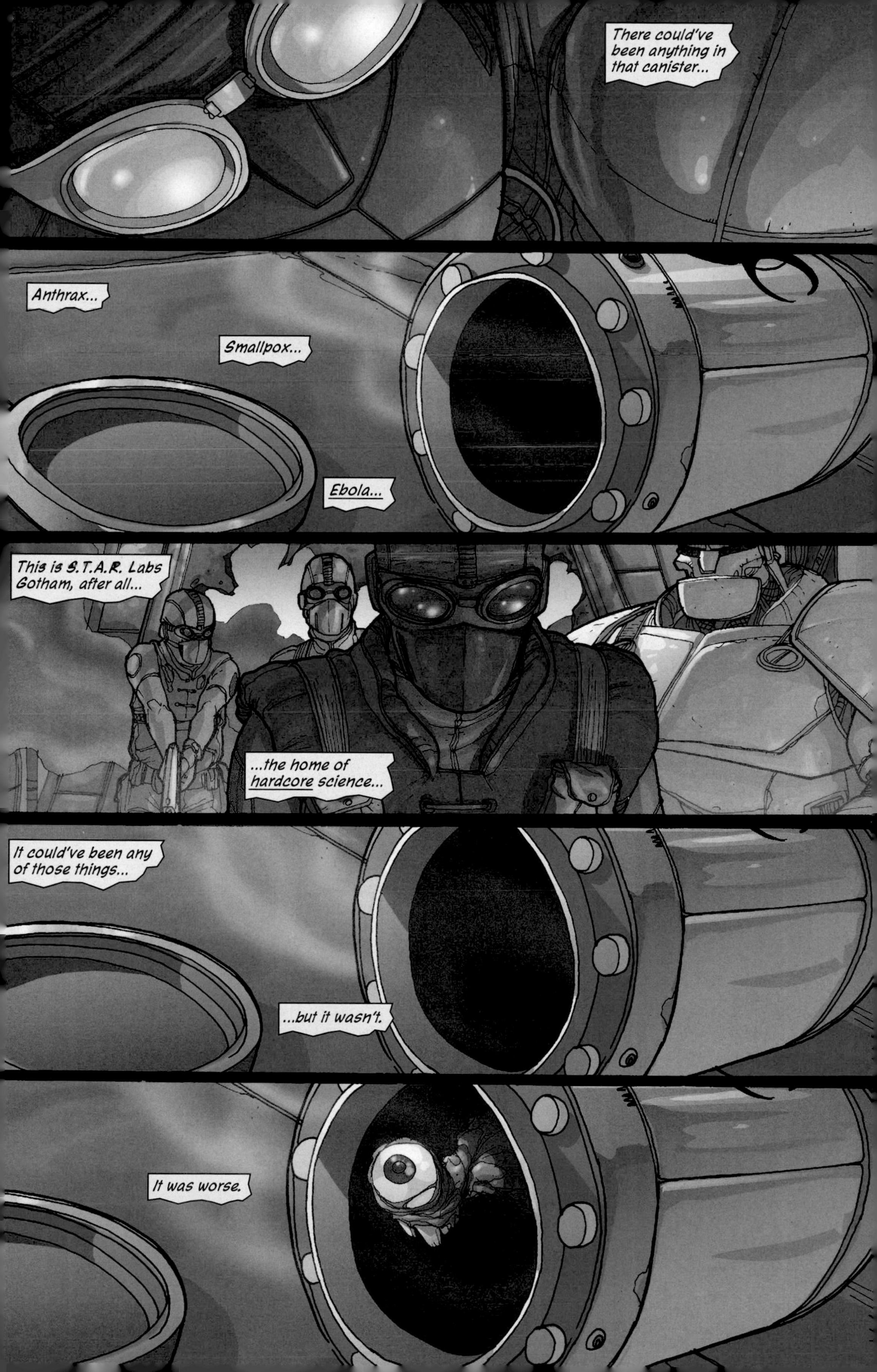
There could've been anything in that canister...
Anthrax...
Smallpox...
Ebola...
This is S.T.A.R. Labs Gotham, after all...
...the home of hardcore science...
It could've been any of those things...
...but it wasn't.
It was worse.

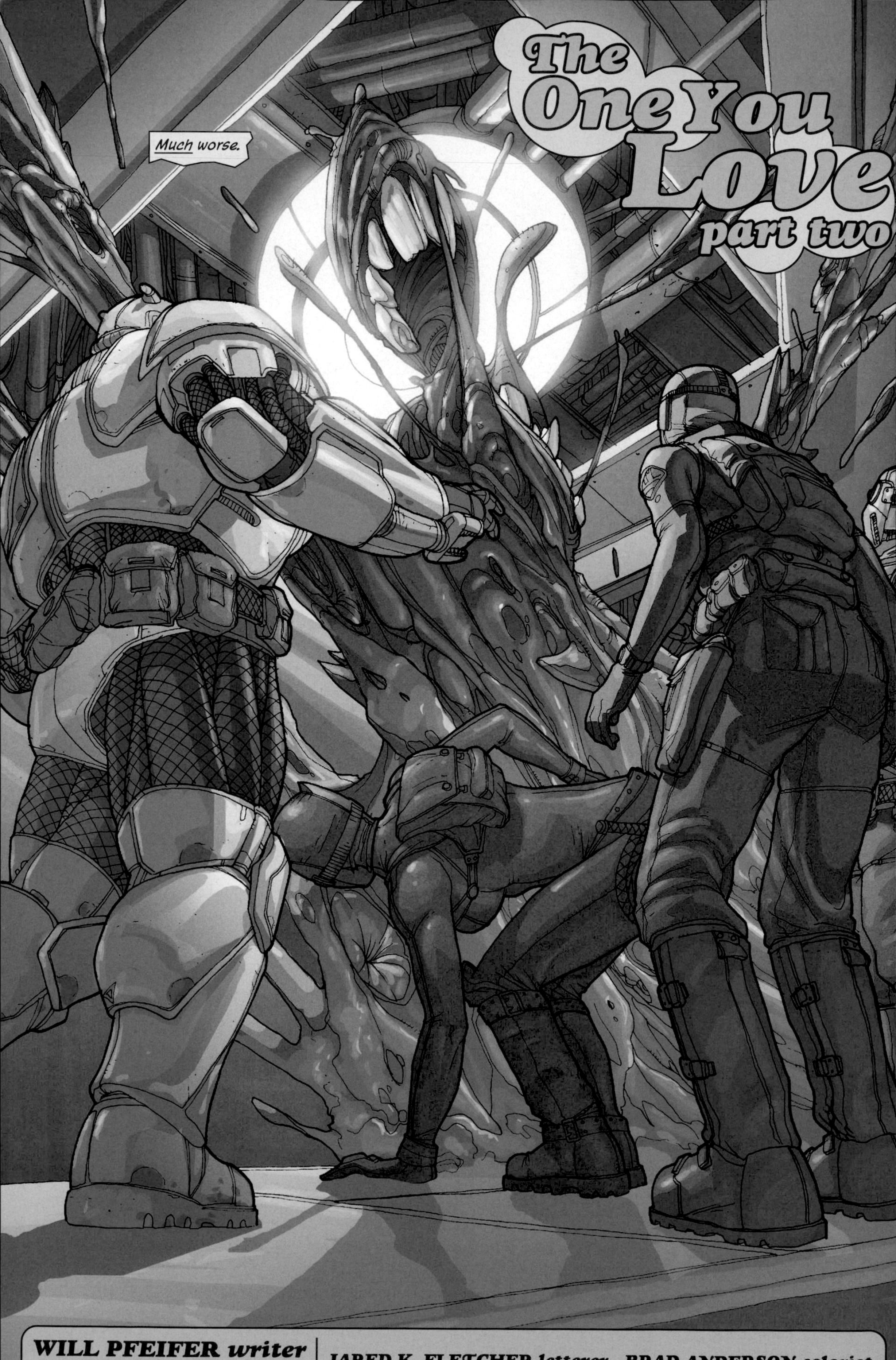

Much worse.
The One You Love
part two

WILL PFEIFER *writer*
PETE WOODS *artist*
JARED K. FLETCHER *letterer* **BRAD ANDERSON** *colorist*

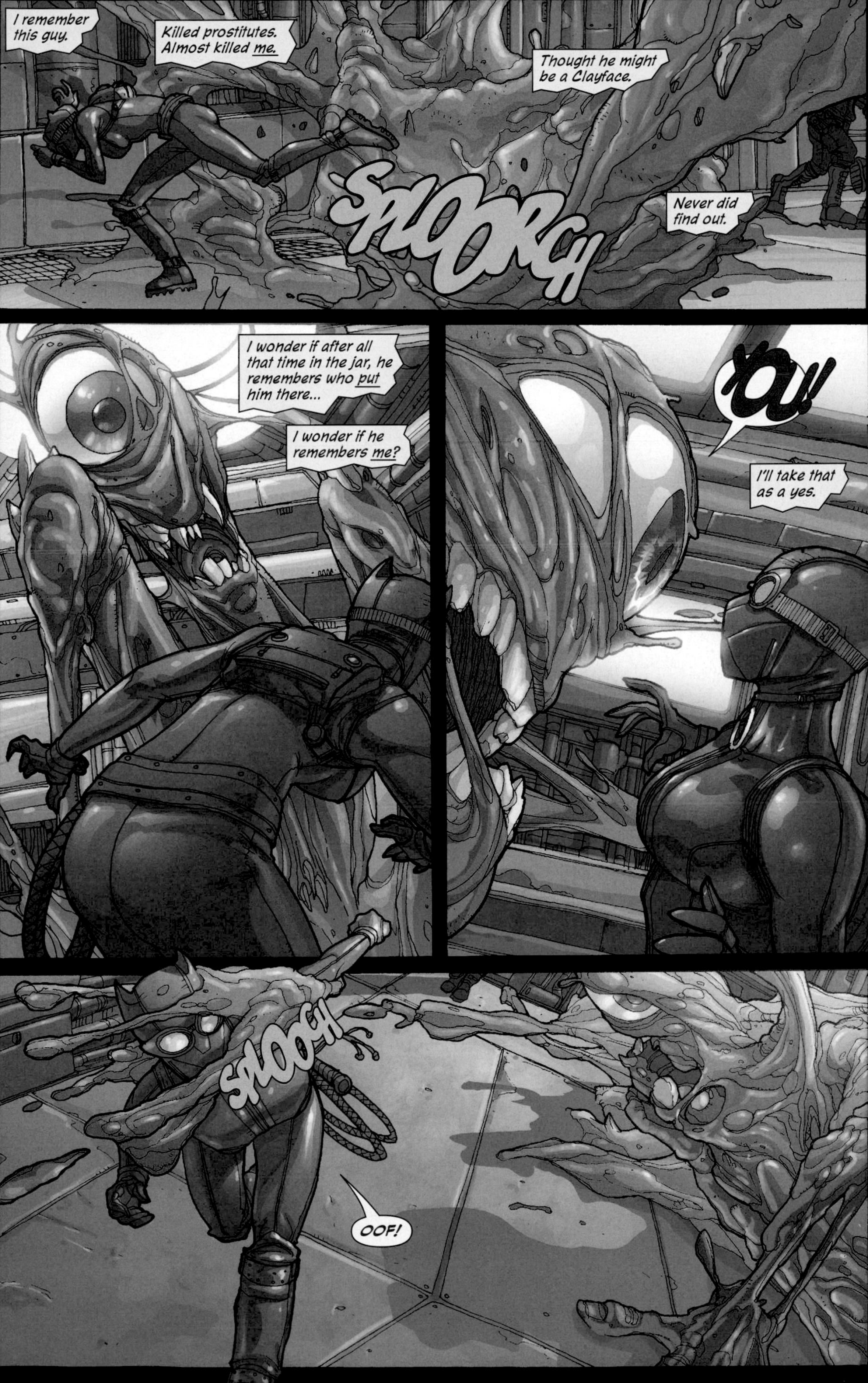
I remember this guy.
Killed prostitutes. Almost killed me.
Thought he might be a Clayface.
SPLOORCH
Never did find out.
I wonder if after all that time in the jar, he remembers who put him there...
I wonder if he remembers me?
YOU!
I'll take that as a yes.
SPLOOCH
OOF!

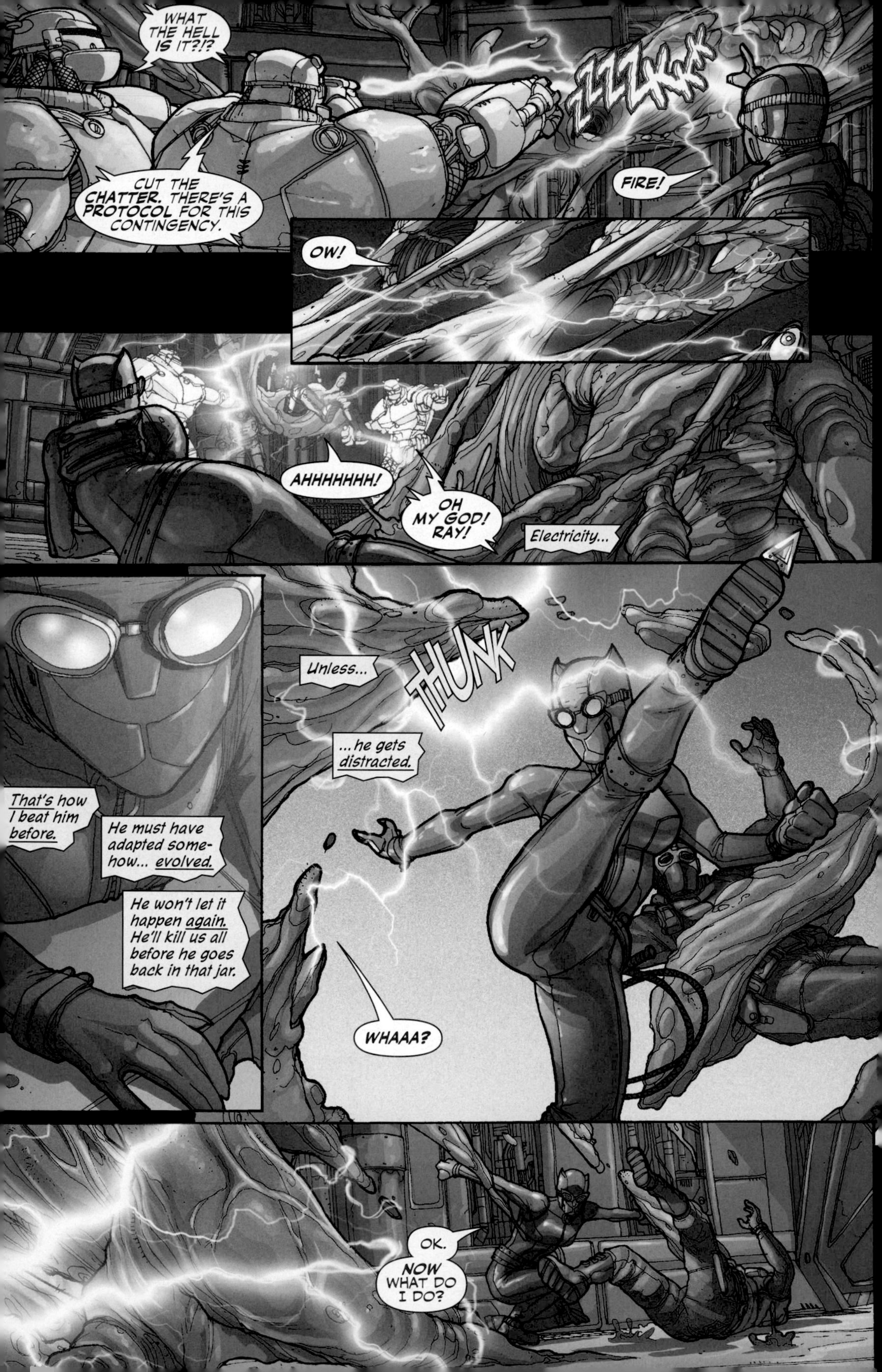
WHAT THE HELL IS IT?!?
CUT THE CHATTER. THERE'S A PROTOCOL FOR THIS CONTINGENCY.
ZZZZKKT
FIRE!
OW!
AHHHHHHH!
OH MY GOD! RAY!
Electricity...
Unless...
THUNK
...he gets distracted.
That's how I beat him before.
He must have adapted somehow... evolved.
He won't let it happen again. He'll kill us all before he goes back in that jar.
WHAAA?
OK. NOW WHAT DO I DO?

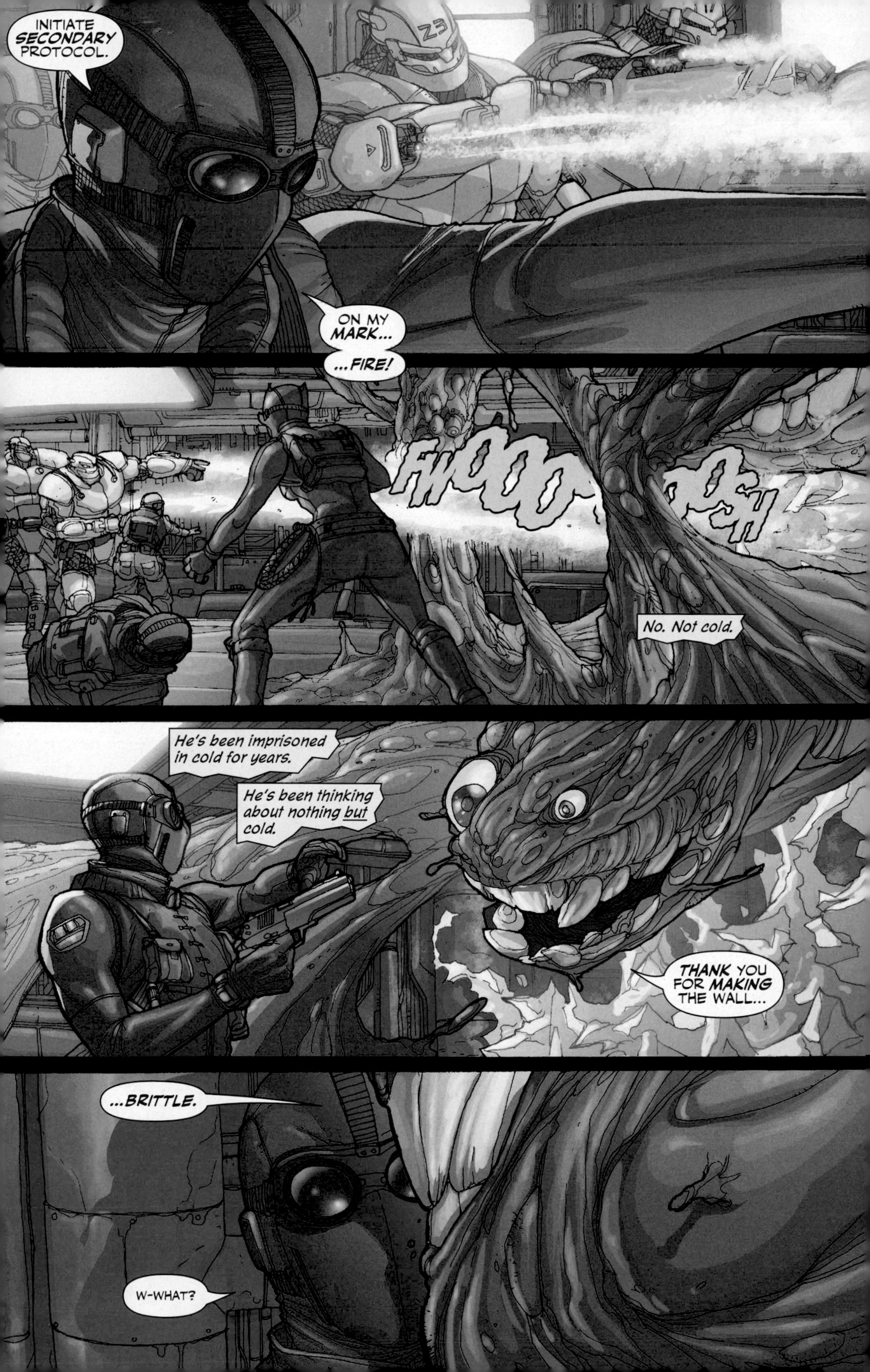
INITIATE SECONDARY PROTOCOL.
ON MY MARK...
...FIRE!
FWOOOOOOSH
No. Not cold.
He's been imprisoned in cold for years.
He's been thinking about nothing but cold.
THANK YOU FOR MAKING THE WALL...
...BRITTLE.
W-WHAT?

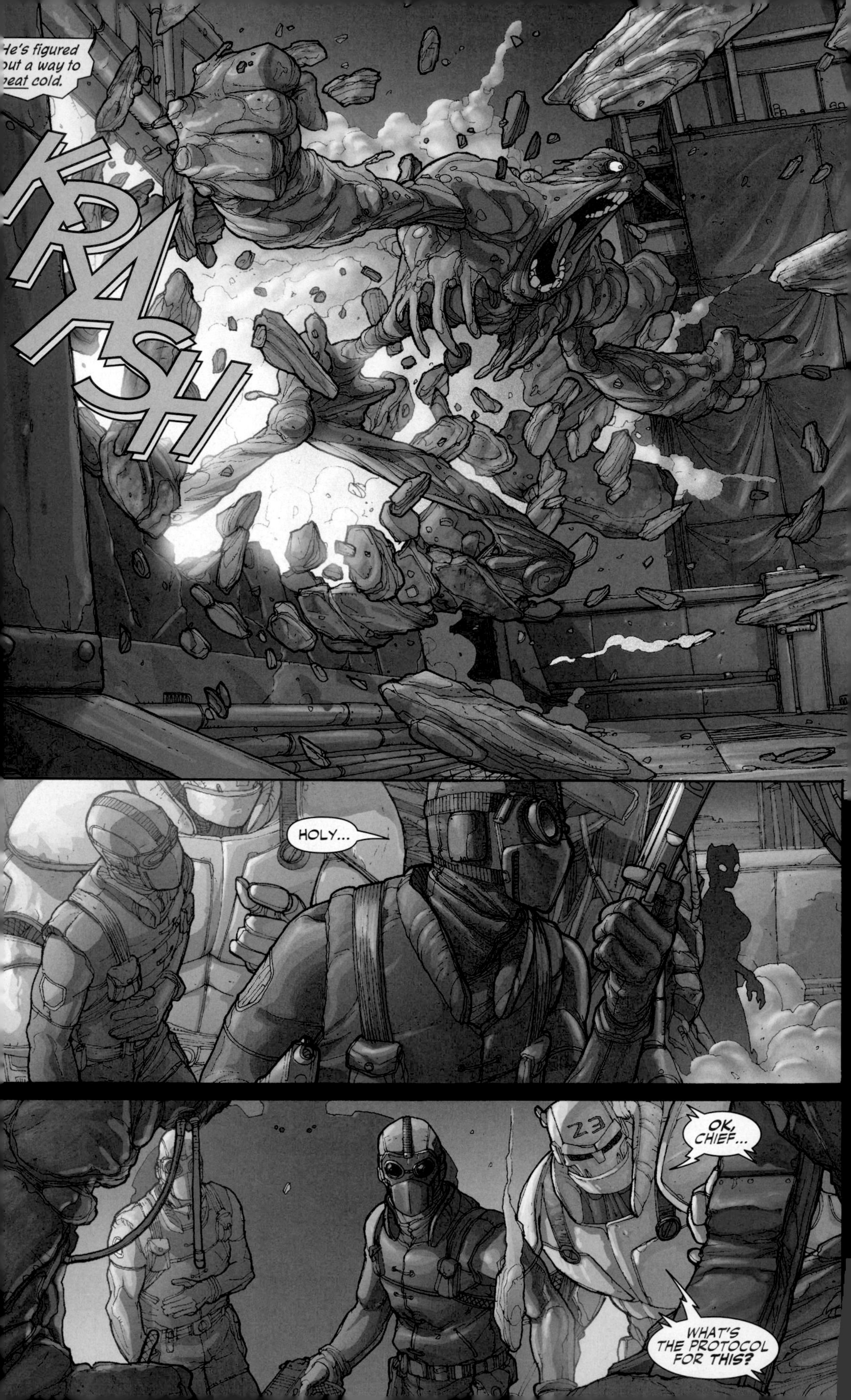
He's figured
out a way to
heat cold.
KRASH
HOLY...
OK,
CHIEF...
WHAT'S
THE PROTOCOL
FOR THIS?

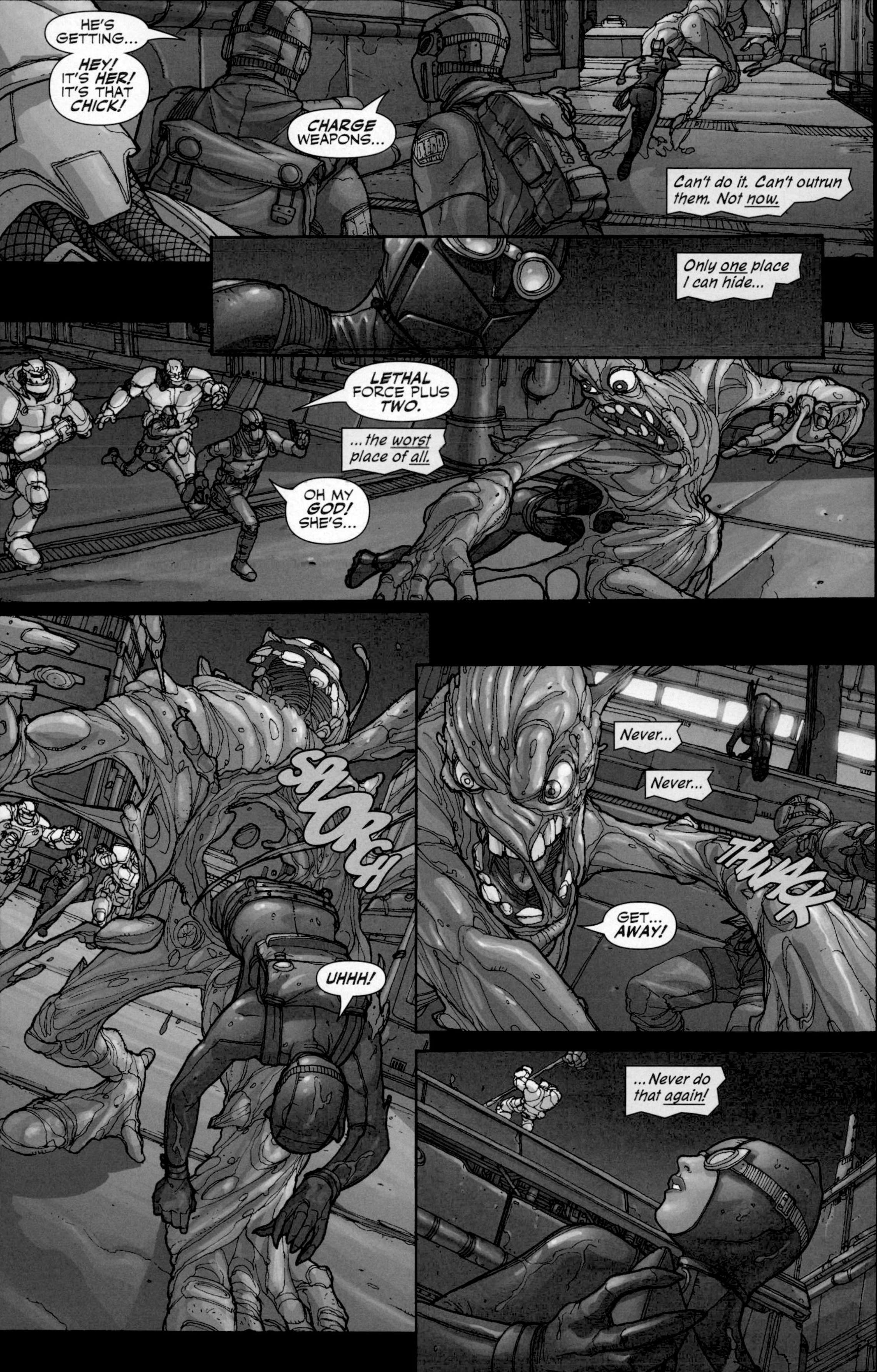
HE'S GETTING...
HEY! IT'S HER! IT'S THAT CHICK!
CHARGE WEAPONS...
Can't do it. Can't outrun them. Not now.
Only one place I can hide...
LETHAL FORCE PLUS TWO.
...the worst place of all.
OH MY GOD! SHE'S...
SPLORCH
UHHH!
Never...
Never...
THWACK
GET... AWAY!
...Never do that again!

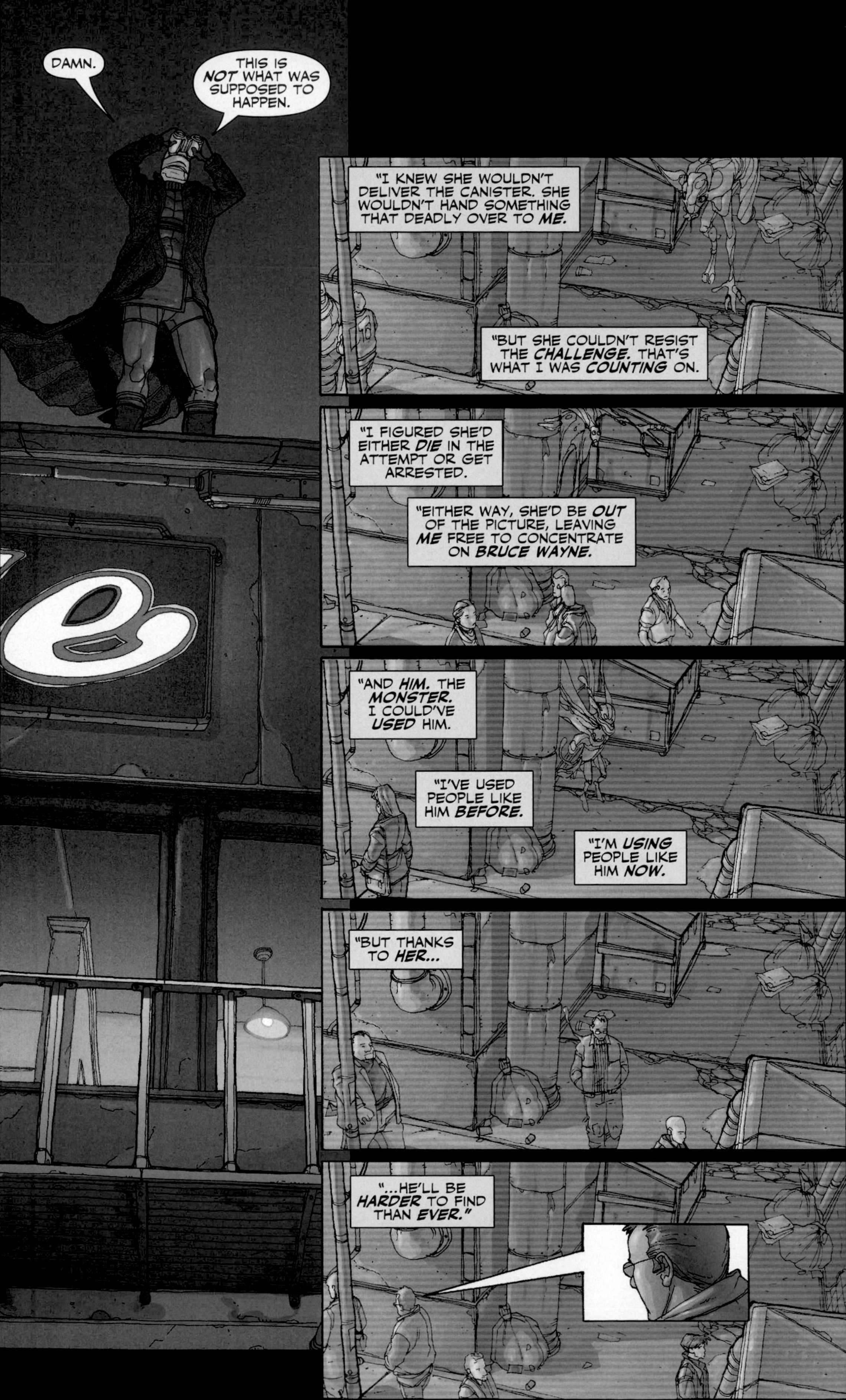
DAMN.
THIS IS NOT WHAT WAS SUPPOSED TO HAPPEN.
"I KNEW SHE WOULDN'T DELIVER THE CANISTER. SHE WOULDN'T HAND SOMETHING THAT DEADLY OVER TO ME.
"BUT SHE COULDN'T RESIST THE CHALLENGE. THAT'S WHAT I WAS COUNTING ON.
"I FIGURED SHE'D EITHER DIE IN THE ATTEMPT OR GET ARRESTED.
"EITHER WAY, SHE'D BE OUT OF THE PICTURE, LEAVING ME FREE TO CONCENTRATE ON BRUCE WAYNE.
"AND HIM. THE MONSTER. I COULD'VE USED HIM.
"I'VE USED PEOPLE LIKE HIM BEFORE.
"I'M USING PEOPLE LIKE HIM NOW.
"BUT THANKS TO HER...
"...HE'LL BE HARDER TO FIND THAN EVER."

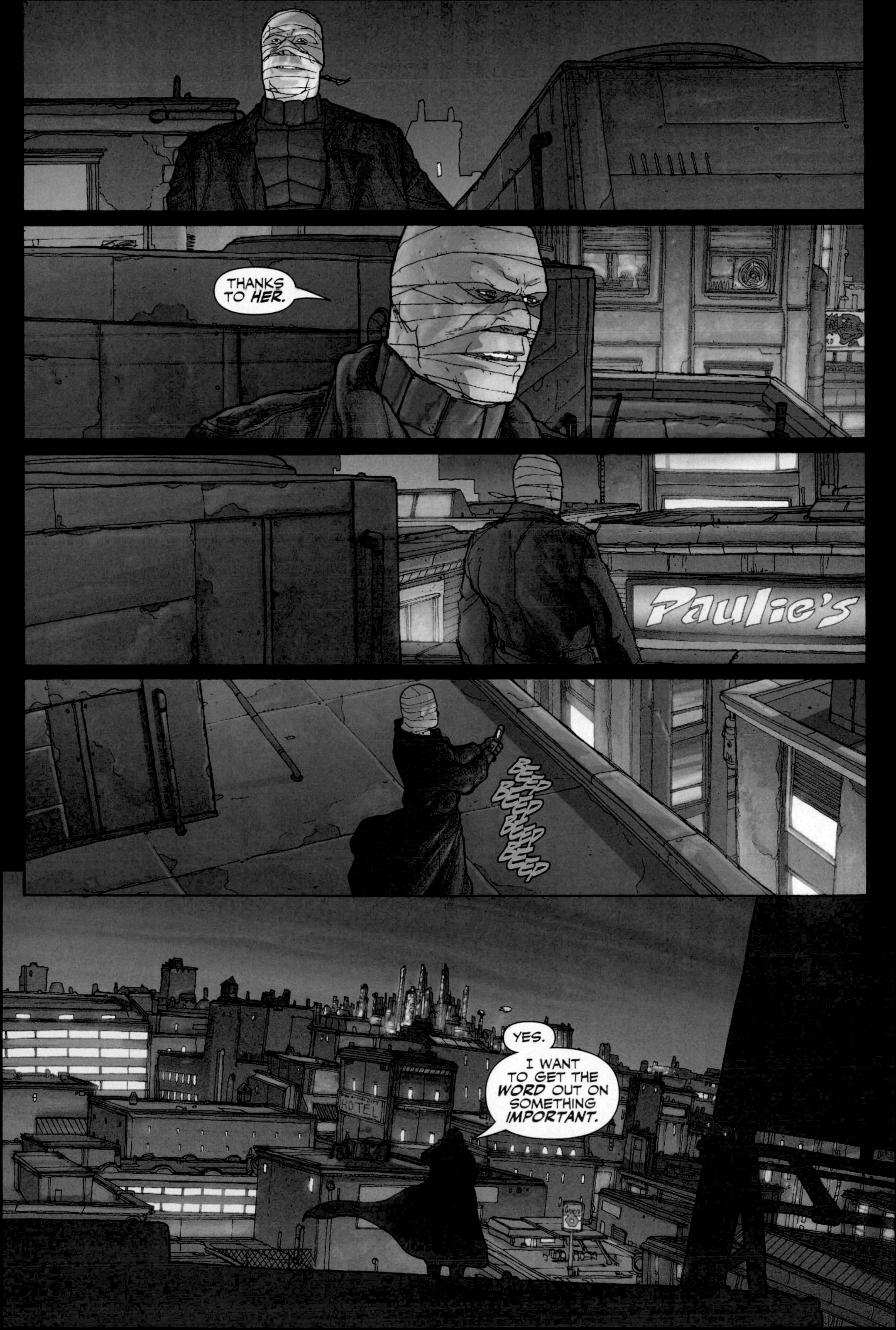
THANKS TO HER.
Paulie's
BEEP BEEP BEEP BEEP BEEP
YES.
I WANT TO GET THE WORD OUT ON SOMETHING IMPORTANT.

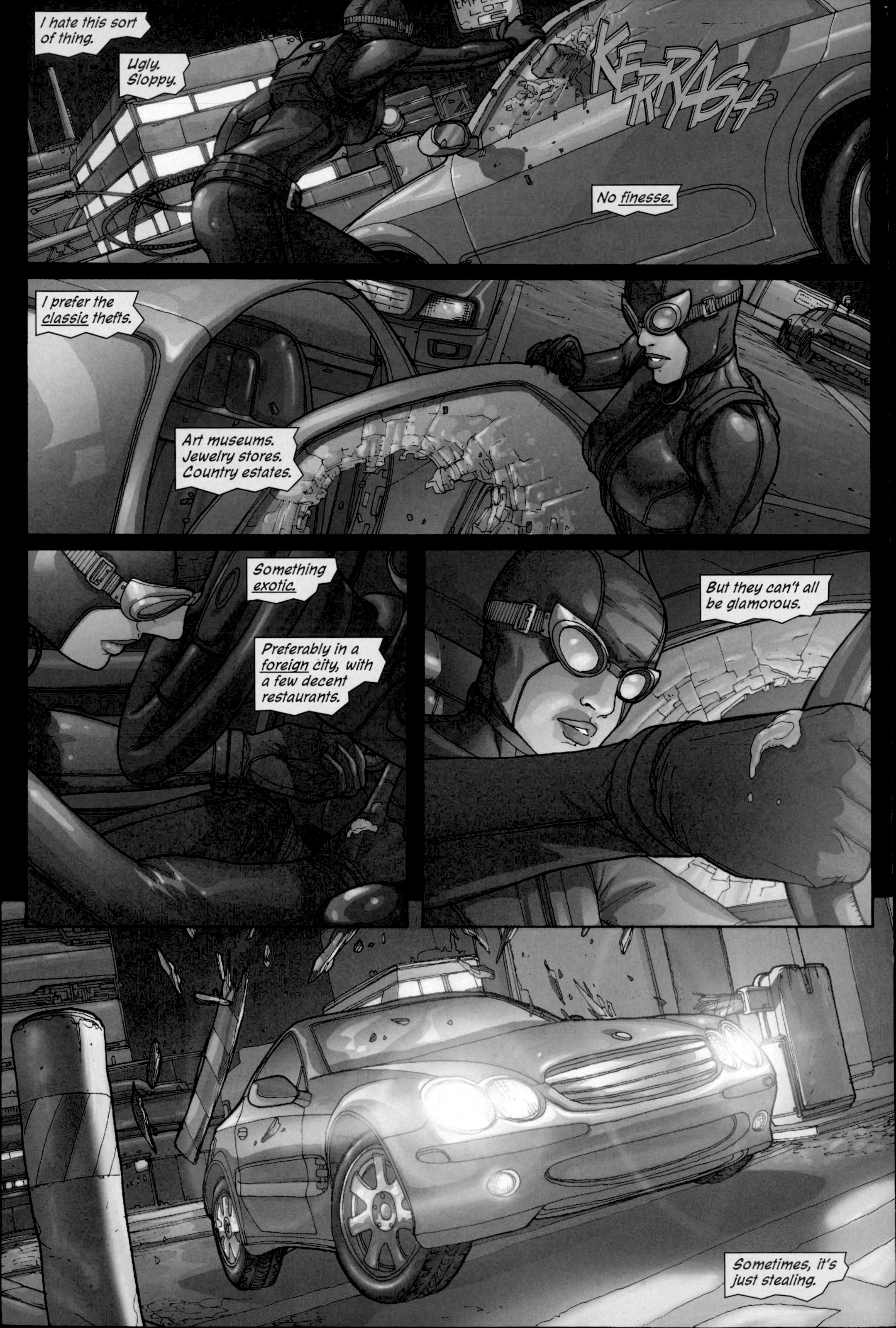

I hate this sort of thing.
Ugly. Sloppy.
KERRASH
No finesse.
I prefer the classic thefts.
Art museums. Jewelry stores. Country estates.
Something exotic.
Preferably in a foreign city, with a few decent restaurants.
But they can't all be glamorous.
Sometimes, it's just stealing.

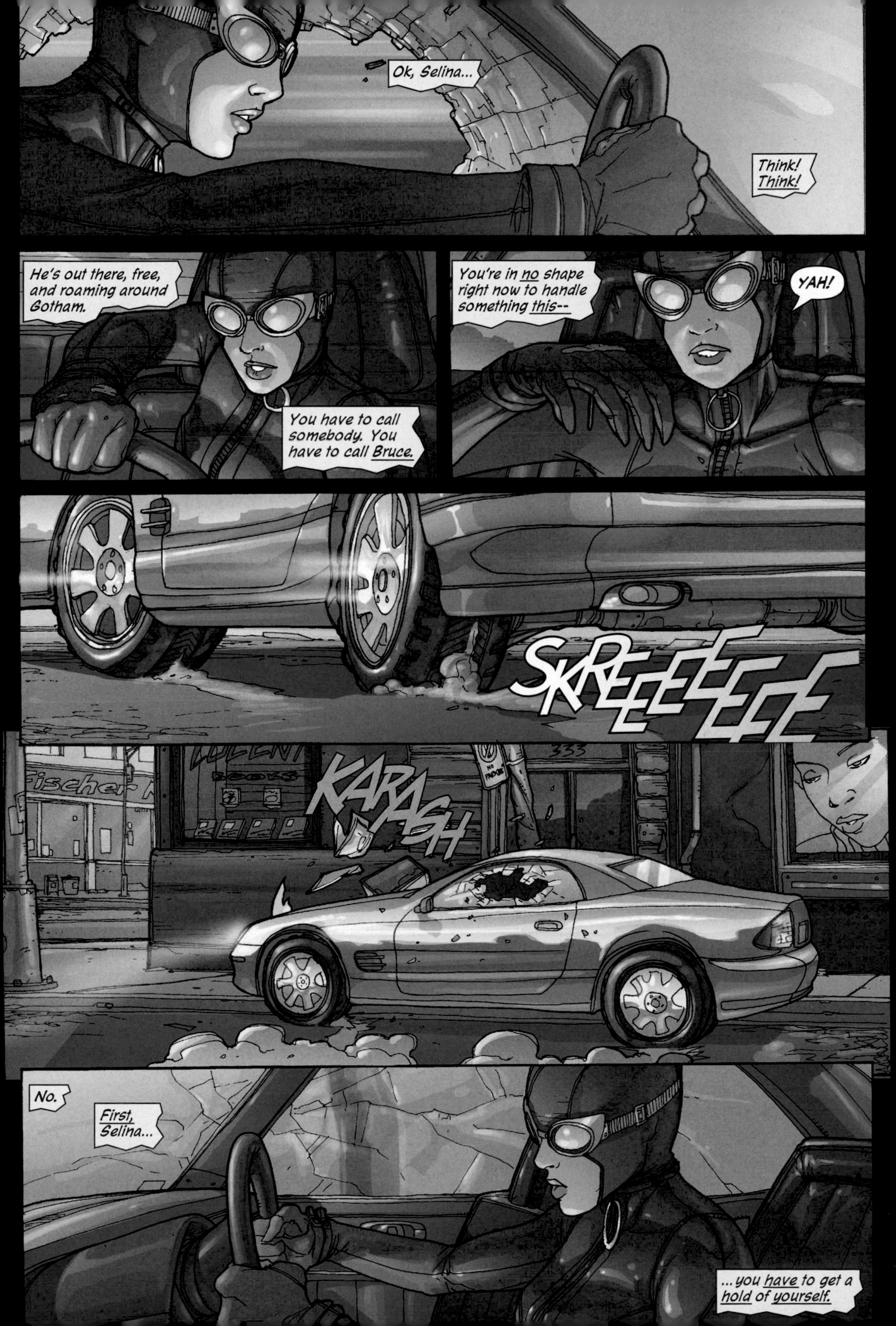

Ok, Selina...
Think! Think!
He's out there, free, and roaming around Gotham.
You have to call somebody. You have to call Bruce.
You're in no shape right now to handle something this--
YAH!
SKREEEEEEEE
KARASH
No.
First, Selina...
...you have to get a hold of yourself.

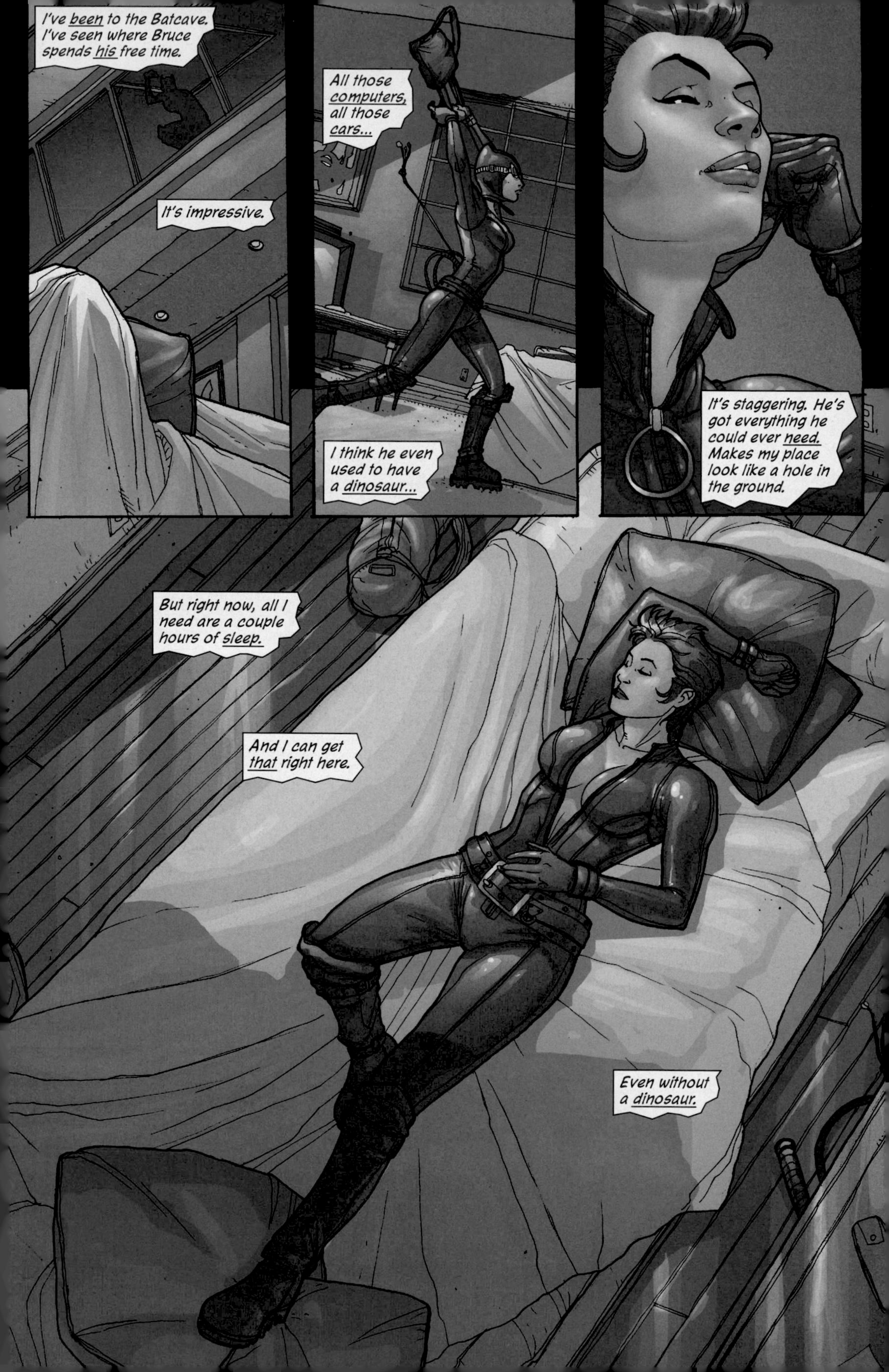
I've been to the Batcave. I've seen where Bruce spends his free time.
It's impressive.
All those computers, all those cars...
I think he even used to have a dinosaur...
It's staggering. He's got everything he could ever need. Makes my place look like a hole in the ground.
But right now, all I need are a couple hours of sleep.
And I can get that right here.
Even without a dinosaur.

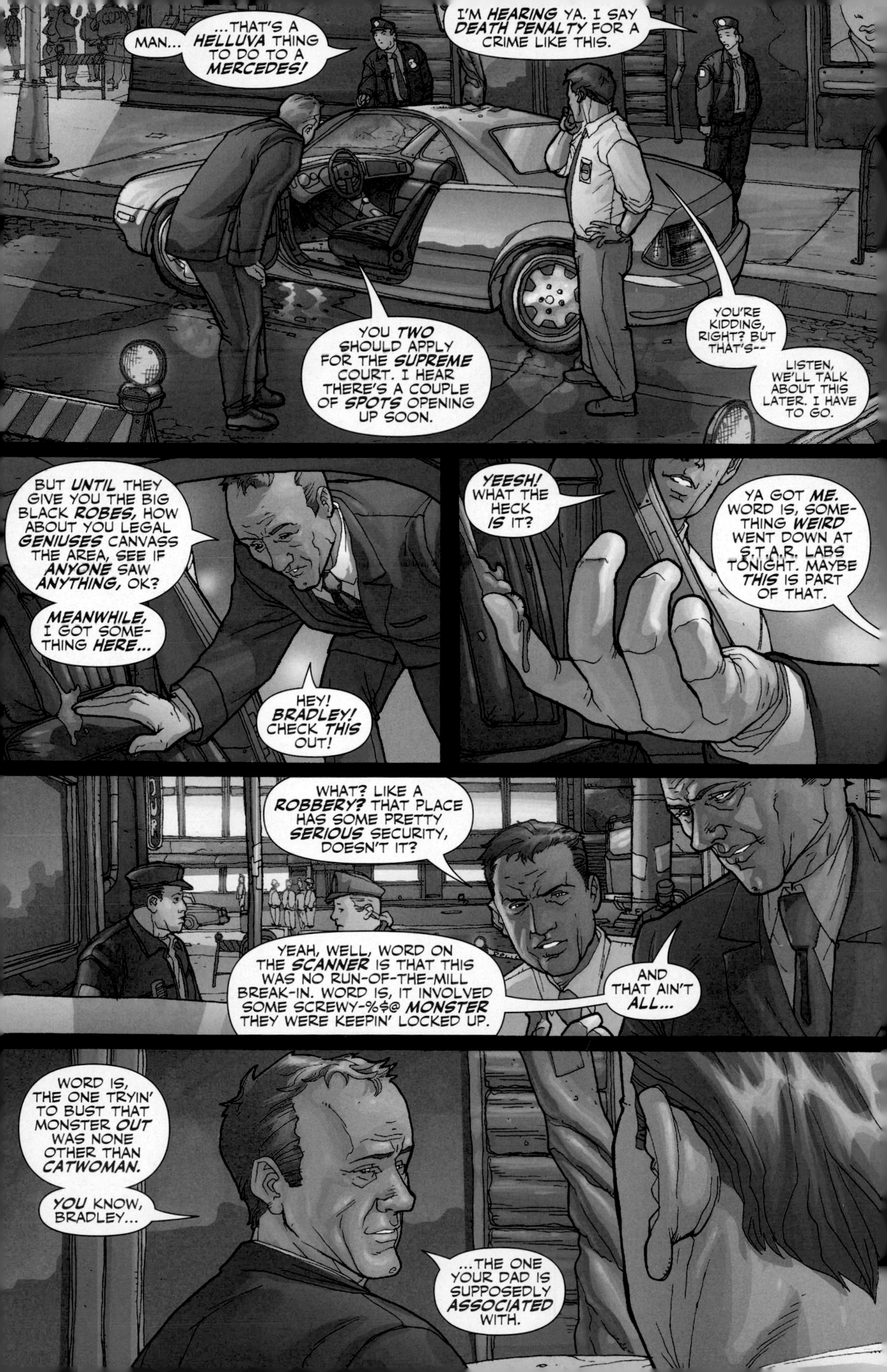
MAN...
...THAT'S A HELLUVA THING TO DO TO A MERCEDES!
I'M HEARING YA. I SAY DEATH PENALTY FOR A CRIME LIKE THIS.
YOU TWO SHOULD APPLY FOR THE SUPREME COURT. I HEAR THERE'S A COUPLE OF SPOTS OPENING UP SOON.
YOU'RE KIDDING, RIGHT? BUT THAT'S--
LISTEN, WE'LL TALK ABOUT THIS LATER. I HAVE TO GO.
BUT UNTIL THEY GIVE YOU THE BIG BLACK ROBES, HOW ABOUT YOU LEGAL GENIUSES CANVASS THE AREA, SEE IF ANYONE SAW ANYTHING, OK?
MEANWHILE, I GOT SOMETHING HERE...
HEY! BRADLEY! CHECK THIS OUT!
YEESH! WHAT THE HECK IS IT?
YA GOT ME. WORD IS, SOMETHING WEIRD WENT DOWN AT S.T.A.R. LABS TONIGHT. MAYBE THIS IS PART OF THAT.
WHAT? LIKE A ROBBERY? THAT PLACE HAS SOME PRETTY SERIOUS SECURITY, DOESN'T IT?
YEAH, WELL, WORD ON THE SCANNER IS THAT THIS WAS NO RUN-OF-THE-MILL BREAK-IN. WORD IS, IT INVOLVED SOME SCREWY-%$@ MONSTER THEY WERE KEEPIN' LOCKED UP.
AND THAT AIN'T ALL...
WORD IS, THE ONE TRYIN' TO BUST THAT MONSTER OUT WAS NONE OTHER THAN CATWOMAN.
YOU KNOW, BRADLEY...
...THE ONE YOUR DAD IS SUPPOSEDLY ASSOCIATED WITH.

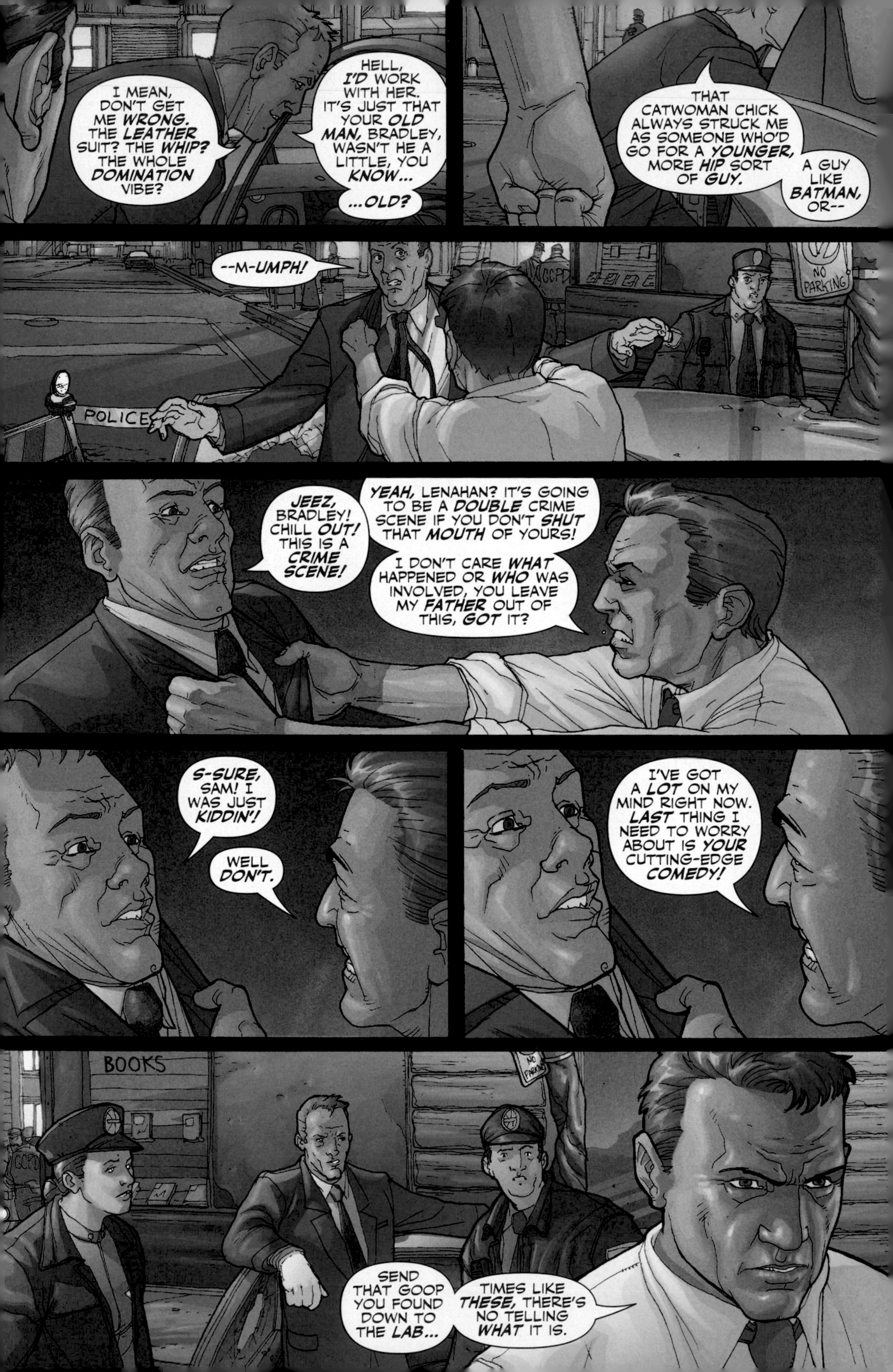

I MEAN, DON'T GET ME WRONG. THE LEATHER SUIT? THE WHIP? THE WHOLE DOMINATION VIBE?
HELL, I'D WORK WITH HER. IT'S JUST THAT YOUR OLD MAN, BRADLEY, WASN'T HE A LITTLE, YOU KNOW...
...OLD?
THAT CATWOMAN CHICK ALWAYS STRUCK ME AS SOMEONE WHO'D GO FOR A YOUNGER, MORE HIP SORT OF GUY.
A GUY LIKE BATMAN, OR--
--M-UMPH!
GCPD
NO PARKING
POLICE
JEEZ, BRADLEY! CHILL OUT! THIS IS A CRIME SCENE!
YEAH, LENAHAN? IT'S GOING TO BE A DOUBLE CRIME SCENE IF YOU DON'T SHUT THAT MOUTH OF YOURS!
I DON'T CARE WHAT HAPPENED OR WHO WAS INVOLVED, YOU LEAVE MY FATHER OUT OF THIS, GOT IT?
S-SURE, SAM! I WAS JUST KIDDIN'!
WELL DON'T.
I'VE GOT A LOT ON MY MIND RIGHT NOW. LAST THING I NEED TO WORRY ABOUT IS YOUR CUTTING-EDGE COMEDY!
BOOKS
NO PARKING
GCPD
SEND THAT GOOP YOU FOUND DOWN TO THE LAB...
TIMES LIKE THESE, THERE'S NO TELLING WHAT IT IS.

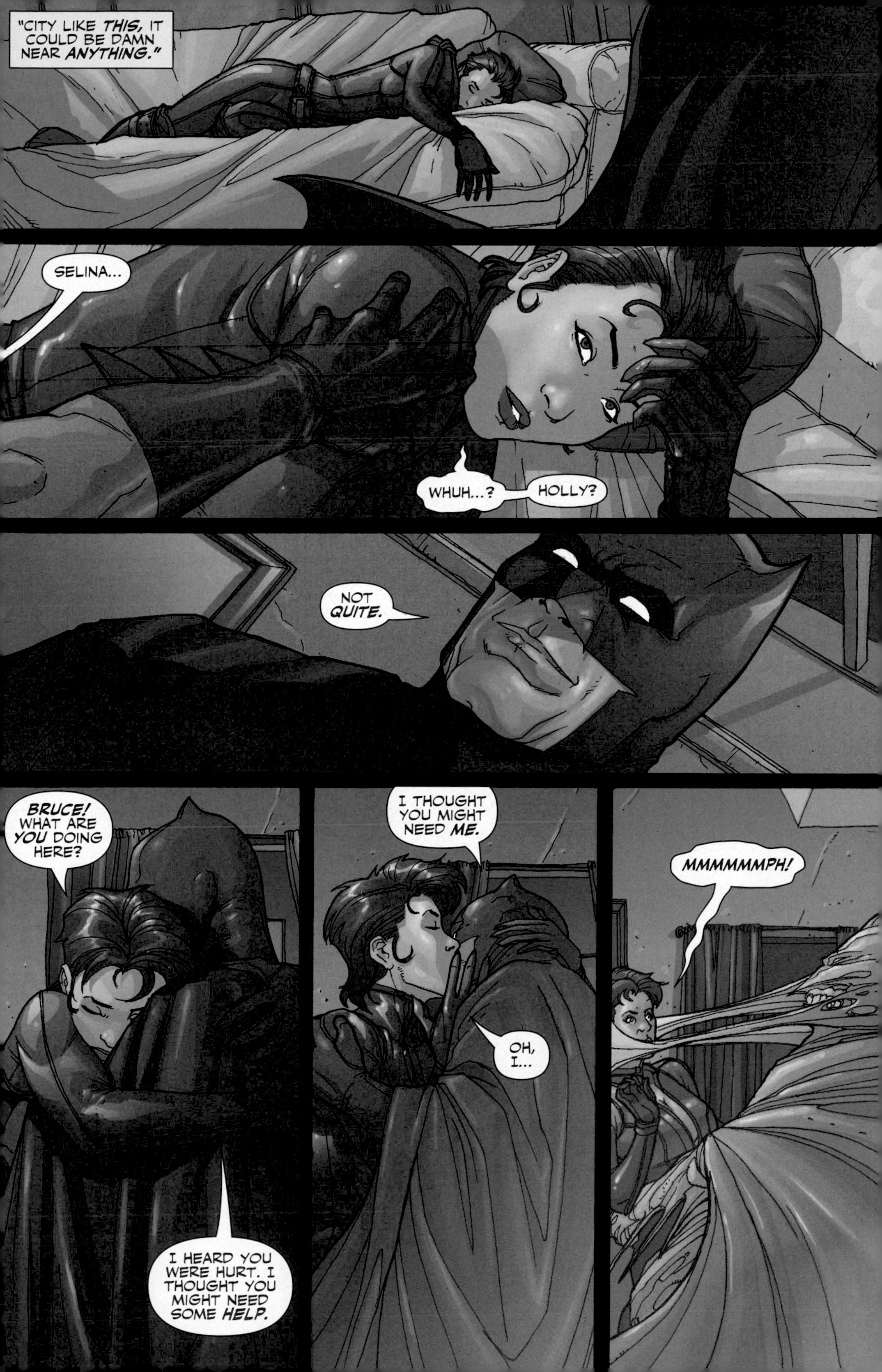
"CITY LIKE THIS, IT COULD BE DAMN NEAR ANYTHING."
SELINA...
WHUH...?
HOLLY?
NOT QUITE.
BRUCE! WHAT ARE YOU DOING HERE?
I HEARD YOU WERE HURT. I THOUGHT YOU MIGHT NEED SOME HELP.
I THOUGHT YOU MIGHT NEED ME.
OH, I...
MMMMMMPH!

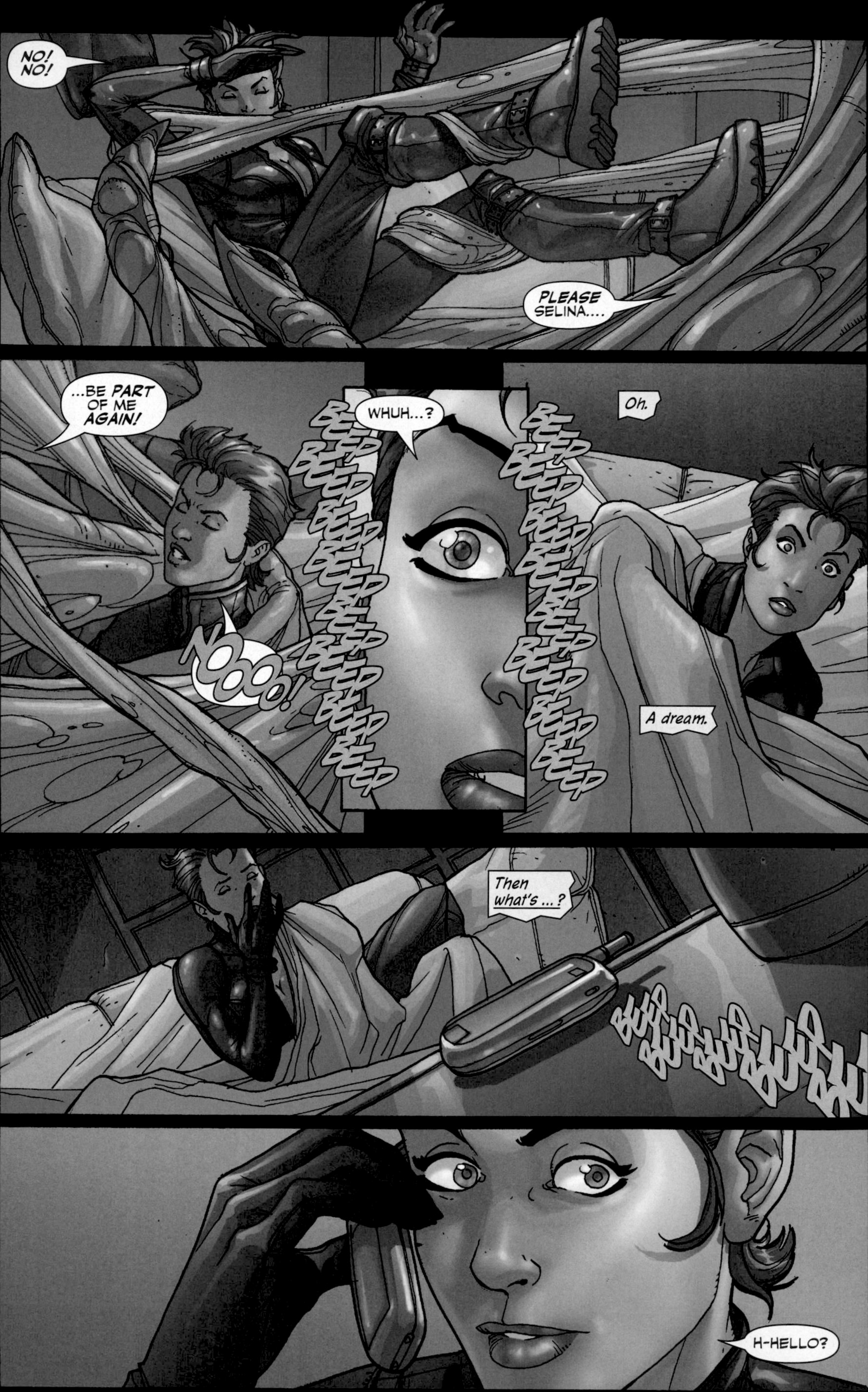

NO! NO!
PLEASE SELINA....
...BE PART OF ME AGAIN!
NOOOO!
WHUH...?
BEEP BEEP BEEP BEEP BEEP BEEP BEEP BEEP BEEP BEEP BEEP BEEP
BEEP BEEP BEEP BEEP BEEP BEEP BEEP BEEP BEEP BEEP BEEP BEEP
Oh.
A dream.
Then what's ...?
H-HELLO?

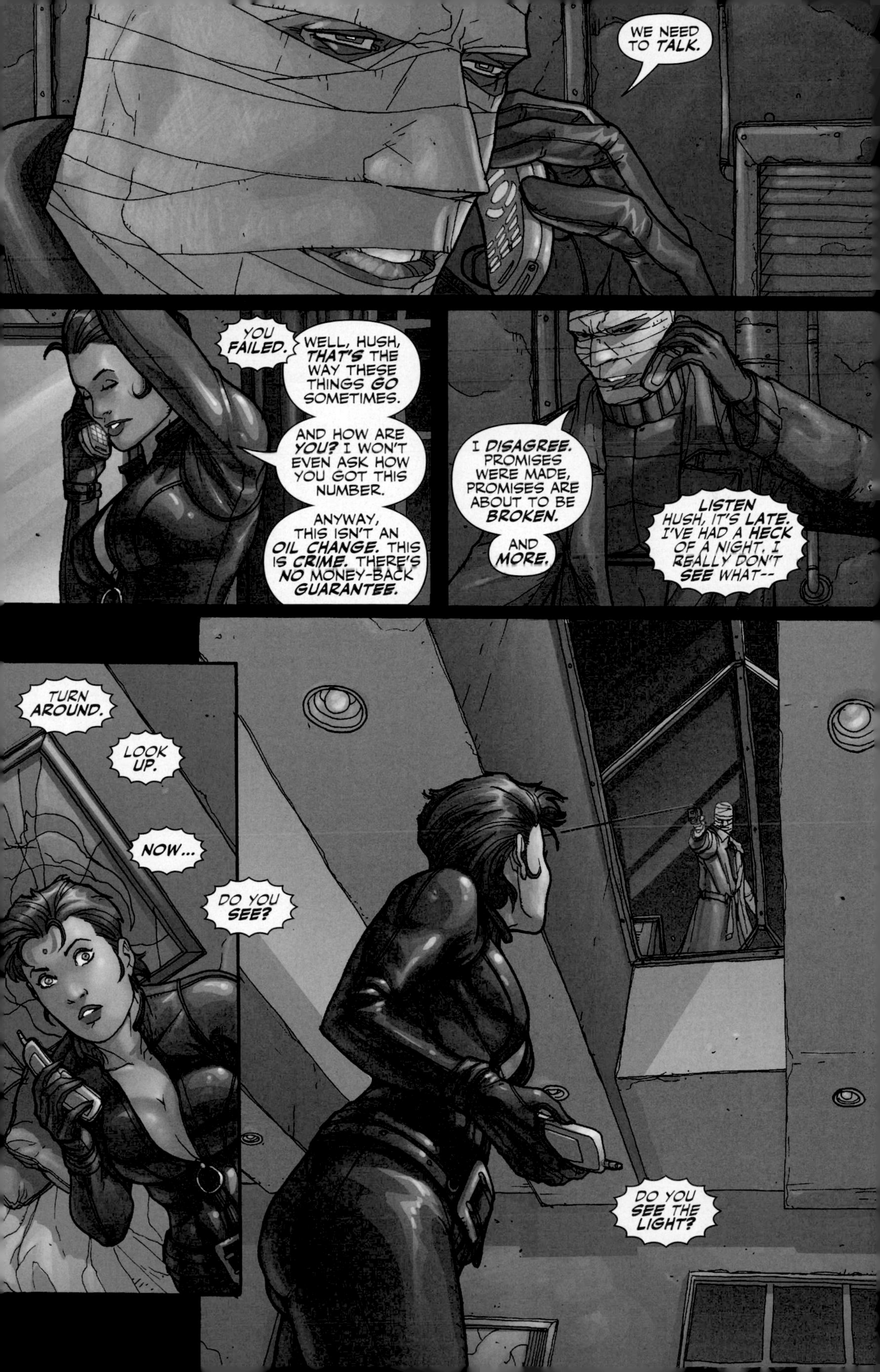
WE NEED TO TALK.
YOU FAILED.
WELL, HUSH, THAT'S THE WAY THESE THINGS GO SOMETIMES.
AND HOW ARE YOU? I WON'T EVEN ASK HOW YOU GOT THIS NUMBER.
ANYWAY, THIS ISN'T AN OIL CHANGE. THIS IS CRIME. THERE'S NO MONEY-BACK GUARANTEE.
I DISAGREE. PROMISES WERE MADE, PROMISES ARE ABOUT TO BE BROKEN.
AND MORE.
LISTEN HUSH, IT'S LATE. I'VE HAD A HECK OF A NIGHT. I REALLY DON'T SEE WHAT--
TURN AROUND.
LOOK UP.
NOW...
DO YOU SEE?
DO YOU SEE THE LIGHT?

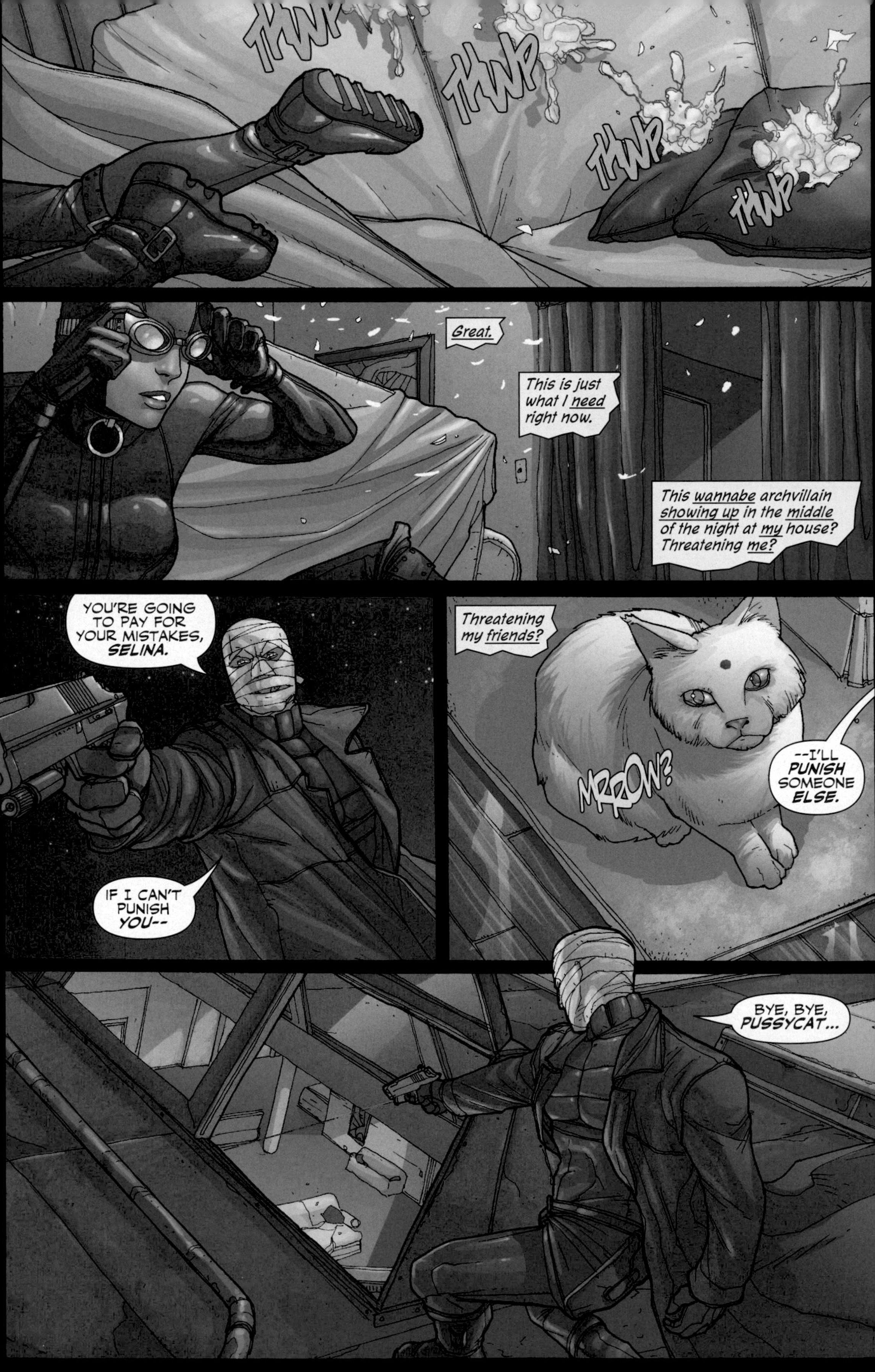

THWP
THWP
THWP
THWP
Great.
This is just what I need right now.
This wannabe archvillain showing up in the middle of the night at my house? Threatening me?
YOU'RE GOING TO PAY FOR YOUR MISTAKES, SELINA.
IF I CAN'T PUNISH YOU--
Threatening my friends?
MRROW?
--I'LL PUNISH SOMEONE ELSE.
BYE, BYE, PUSSYCAT...

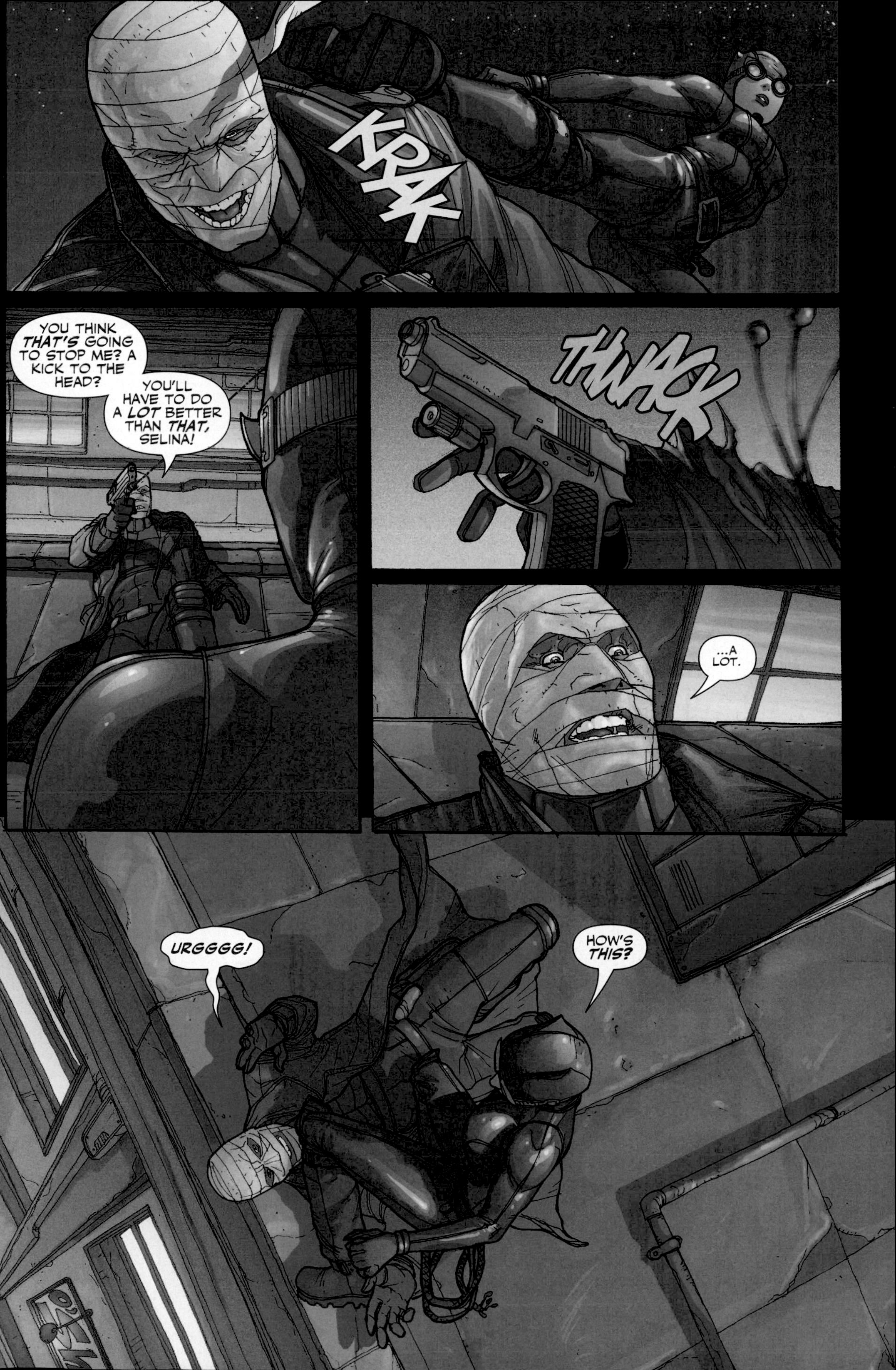
KRAK
YOU THINK THAT'S GOING TO STOP ME? A KICK TO THE HEAD?
YOU'LL HAVE TO DO A LOT BETTER THAN THAT, SELINA!
THWACK
...A LOT.
URGGGG!
HOW'S THIS?

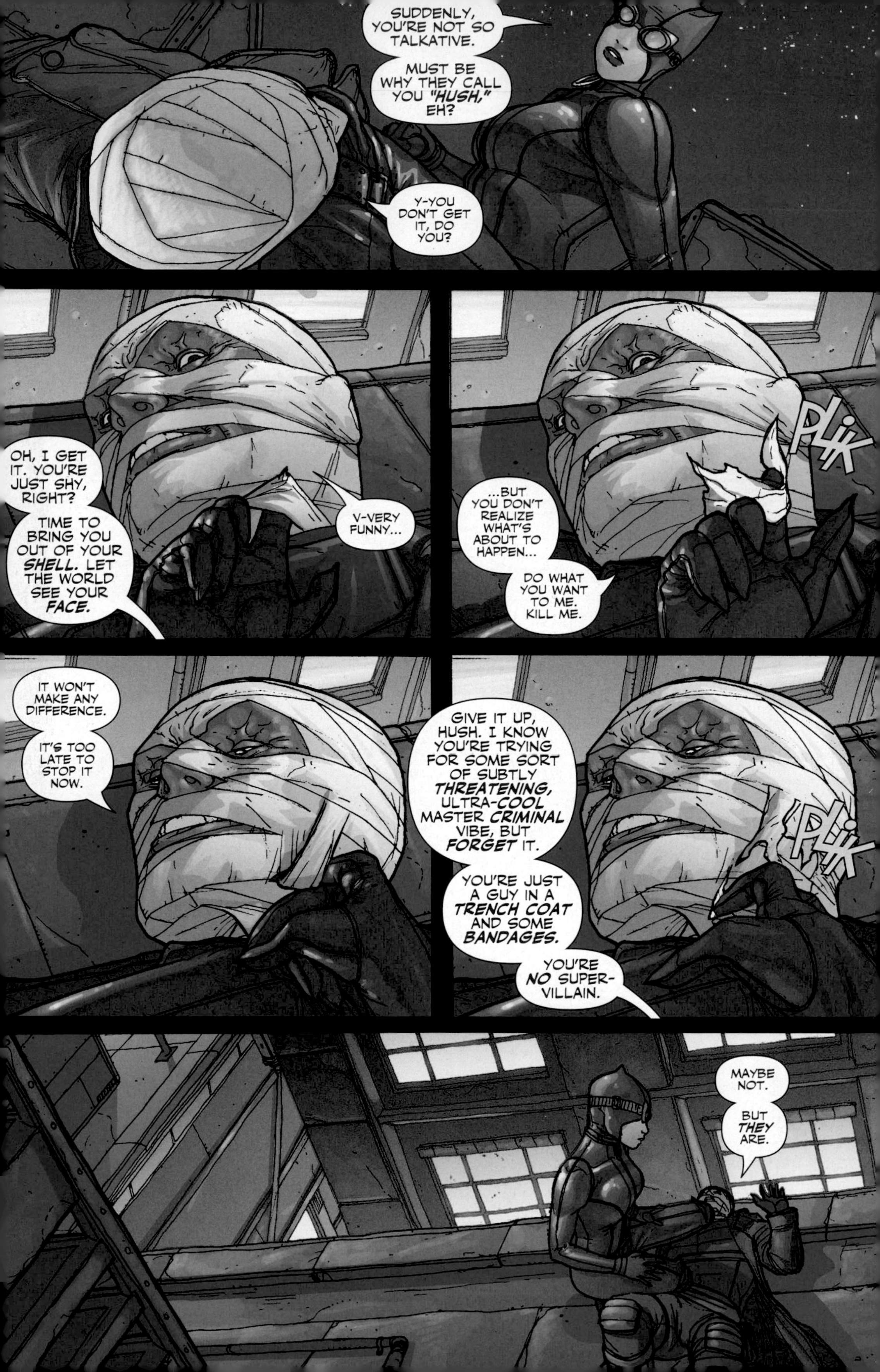

SUDDENLY, YOU'RE NOT SO TALKATIVE.
MUST BE WHY THEY CALL YOU "HUSH," EH?
Y-YOU DON'T GET IT, DO YOU?
OH, I GET IT. YOU'RE JUST SHY, RIGHT?
TIME TO BRING YOU OUT OF YOUR SHELL. LET THE WORLD SEE YOUR FACE.
V-VERY FUNNY...
...BUT YOU DON'T REALIZE WHAT'S ABOUT TO HAPPEN...
PLIK
DO WHAT YOU WANT TO ME. KILL ME.
IT WON'T MAKE ANY DIFFERENCE.
IT'S TOO LATE TO STOP IT NOW.
GIVE IT UP, HUSH. I KNOW YOU'RE TRYING FOR SOME SORT OF SUBTLY THREATENING, ULTRA-COOL MASTER CRIMINAL VIBE, BUT FORGET IT.
YOU'RE JUST A GUY IN A TRENCH COAT AND SOME BANDAGES.
YOU'RE NO SUPER-VILLAIN.
PLIK
MAYBE NOT.
BUT THEY ARE.

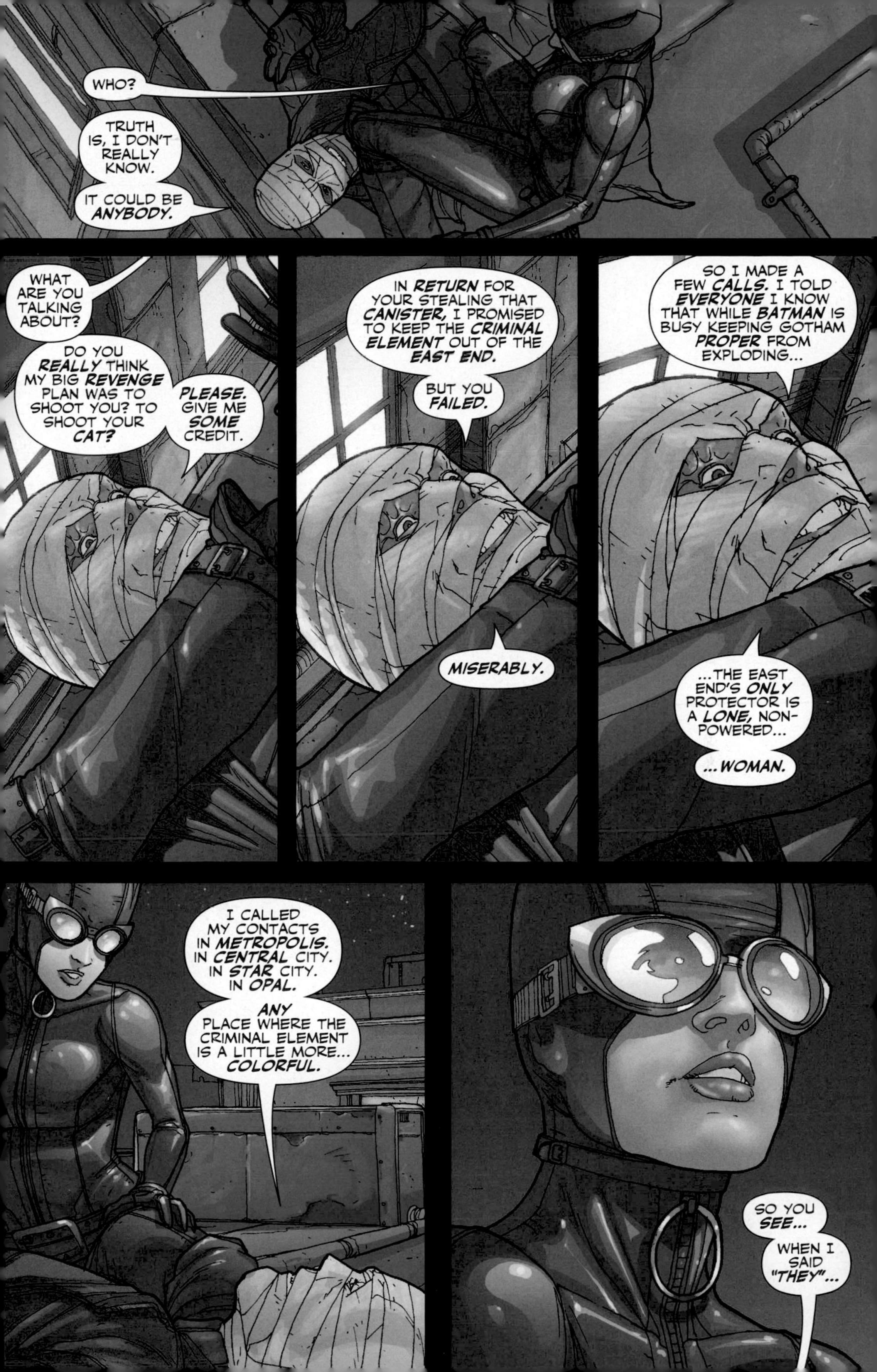
WHO?
TRUTH IS, I DON'T REALLY KNOW.
IT COULD BE ANYBODY.
WHAT ARE YOU TALKING ABOUT?
DO YOU REALLY THINK MY BIG REVENGE PLAN WAS TO SHOOT YOU? TO SHOOT YOUR CAT?
PLEASE. GIVE ME SOME CREDIT.
IN RETURN FOR YOUR STEALING THAT CANISTER, I PROMISED TO KEEP THE CRIMINAL ELEMENT OUT OF THE EAST END.
BUT YOU FAILED.
MISERABLY.
SO I MADE A FEW CALLS. I TOLD EVERYONE I KNOW THAT WHILE BATMAN IS BUSY KEEPING GOTHAM PROPER FROM EXPLODING...
...THE EAST END'S ONLY PROTECTOR IS A LONE, NON-POWERED...
...WOMAN.
I CALLED MY CONTACTS IN METROPOLIS. IN CENTRAL CITY. IN STAR CITY. IN OPAL.
ANY PLACE WHERE THE CRIMINAL ELEMENT IS A LITTLE MORE... COLORFUL.
SO YOU SEE...
WHEN I SAID "THEY"...

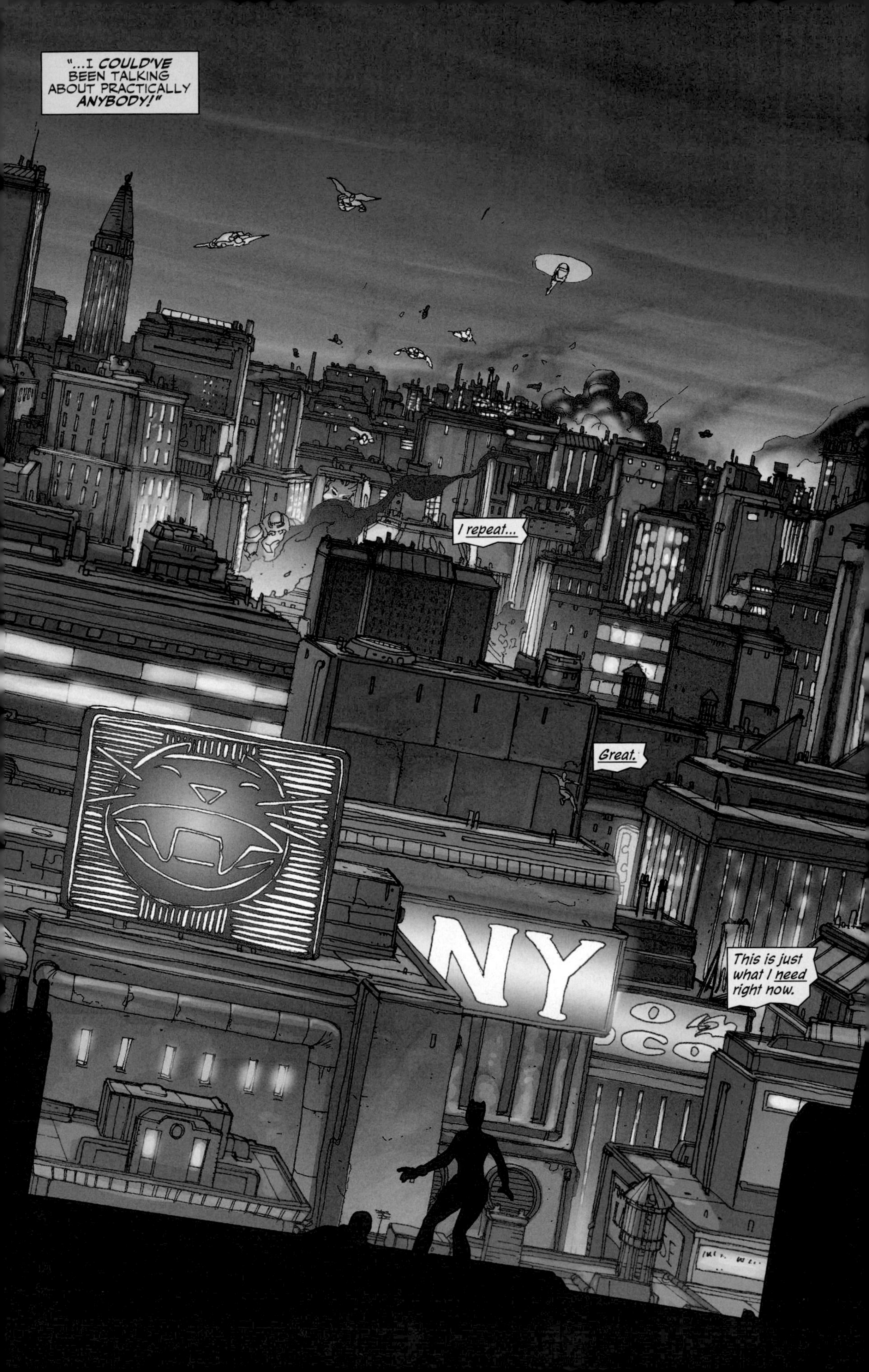
"...I COULD'VE BEEN TALKING ABOUT PRACTICALLY ANYBODY!"
I repeat...
Great.
This is just what I need right now.
NY

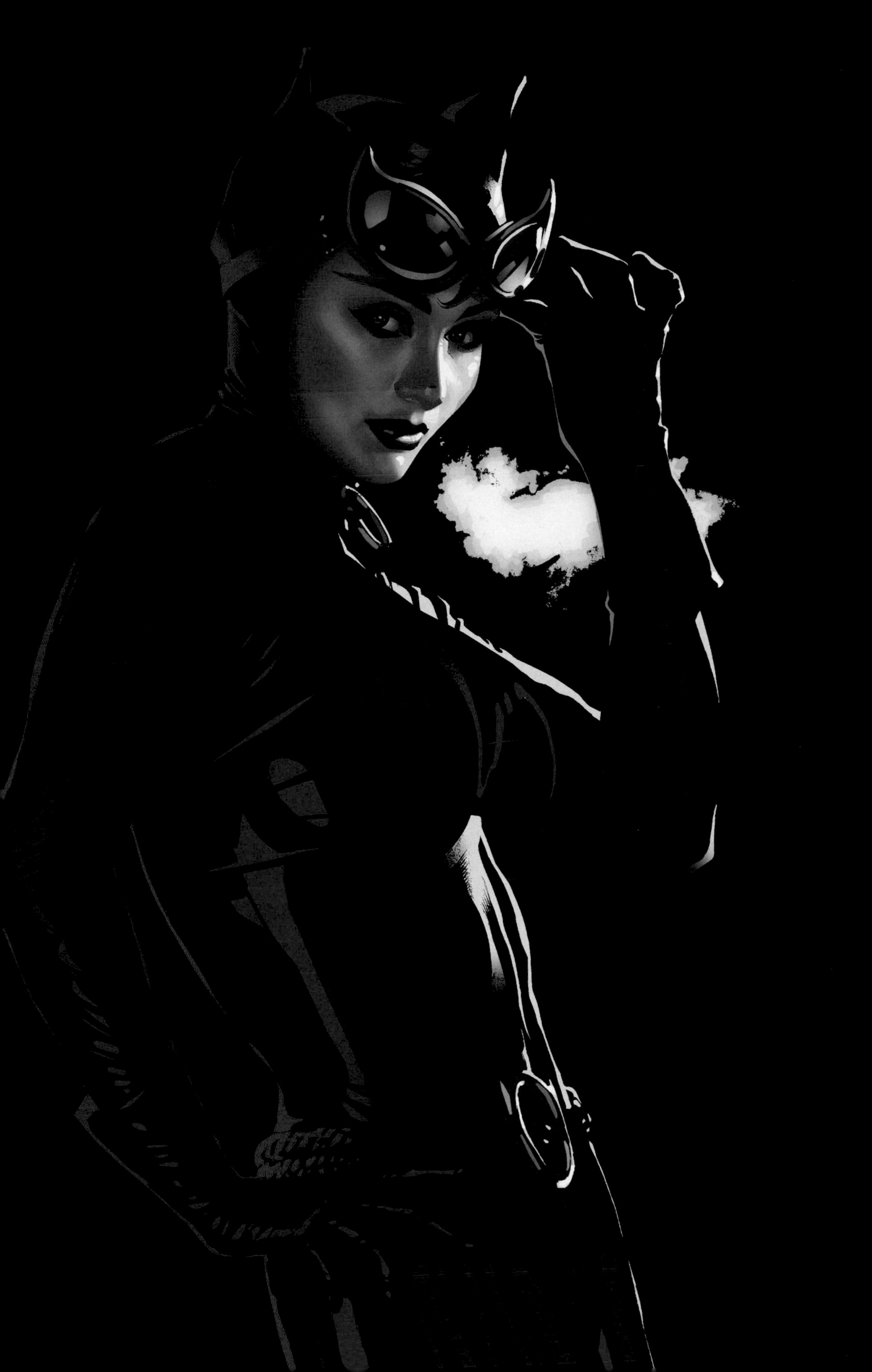

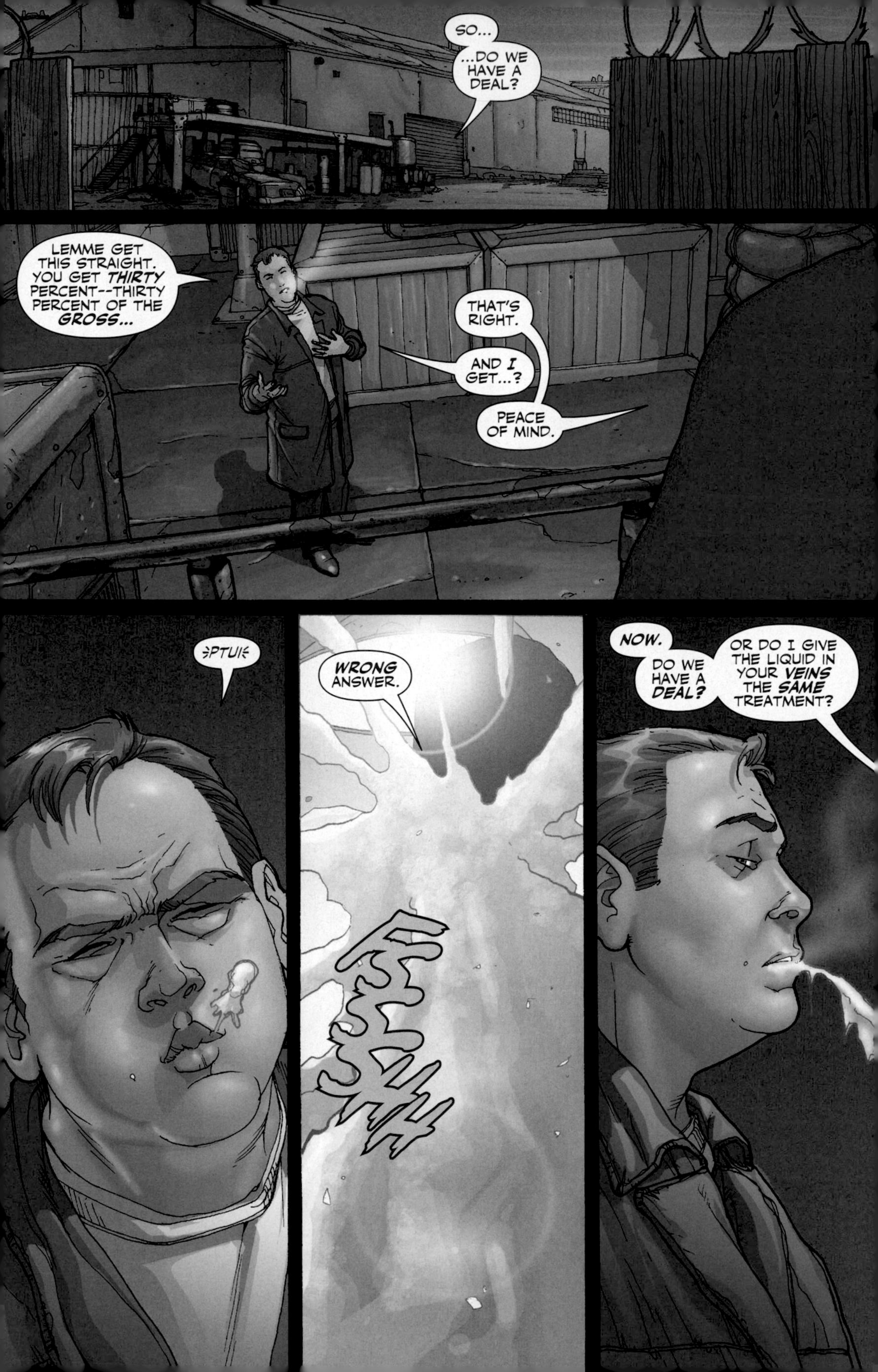
SO...
...DO WE HAVE A DEAL?
LEMME GET THIS STRAIGHT. YOU GET THIRTY PERCENT--THIRTY PERCENT OF THE GROSS...
THAT'S RIGHT.
AND I GET...?
PEACE OF MIND.
PTUI
WRONG ANSWER.
FSSSHHH
NOW.
DO WE HAVE A DEAL?
OR DO I GIVE THE LIQUID IN YOUR VEINS THE SAME TREATMENT?

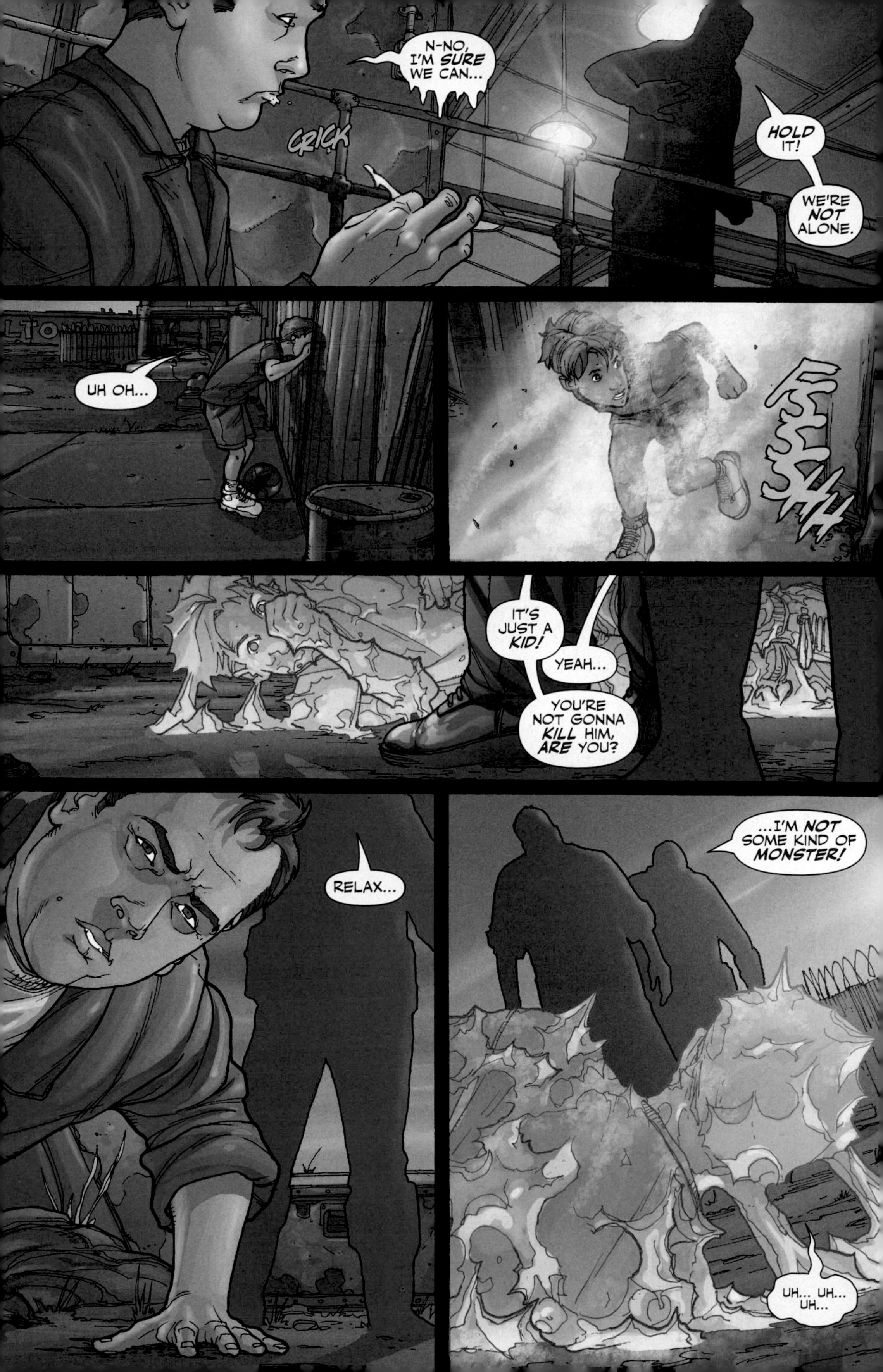
N-NO, I'M SURE WE CAN...
CRICK
HOLD IT!
WE'RE NOT ALONE.
LTO
UH OH...
FSSSHH
IT'S JUST A KID!
YEAH...
YOU'RE NOT GONNA KILL HIM, ARE YOU?
RELAX...
...I'M NOT SOME KIND OF MONSTER!
UH... UH... UH...

The One You Love part three

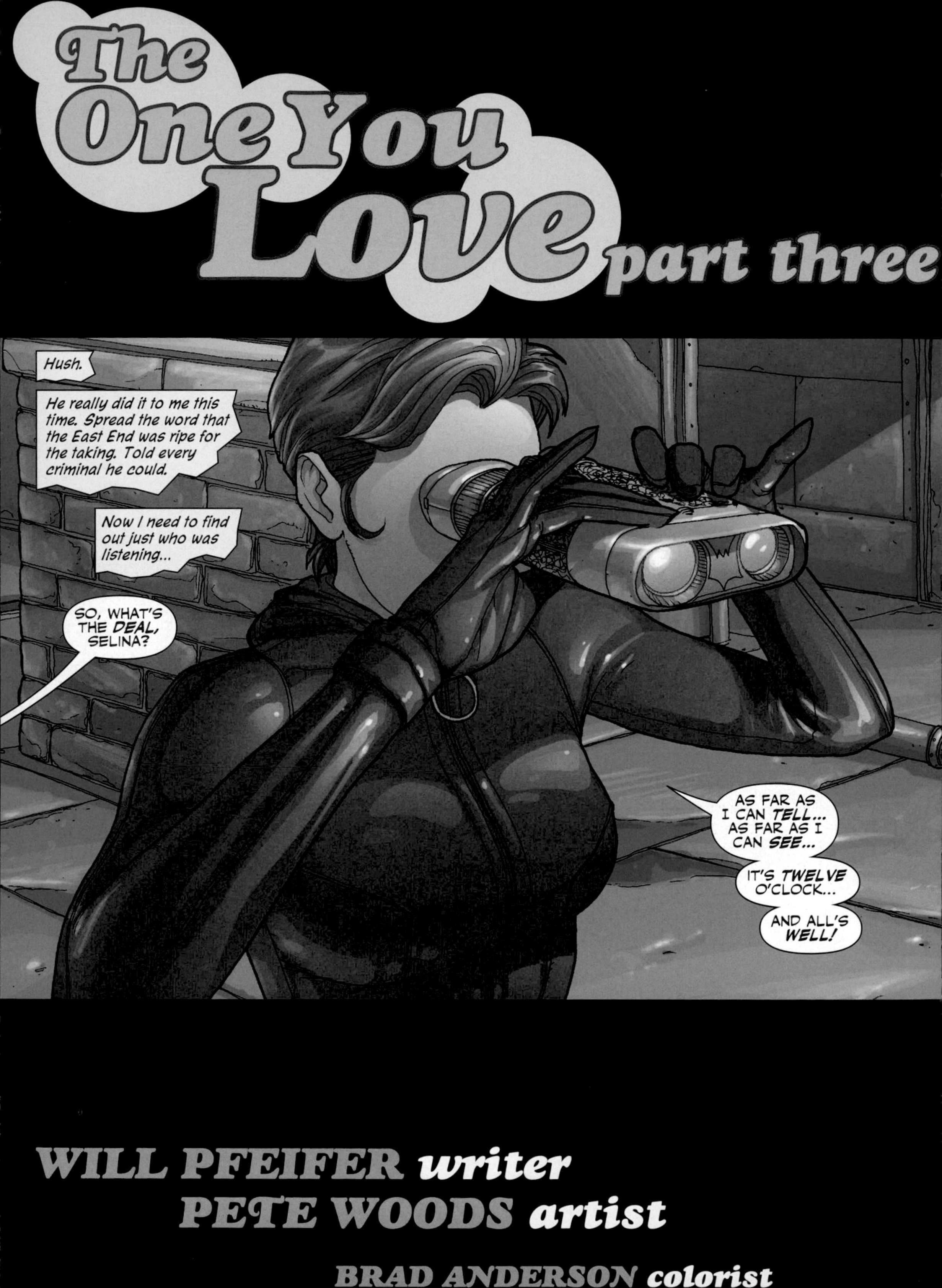
Hush.
He really did it to me this time. Spread the word that the East End was ripe for the taking. Told every criminal he could.
Now I need to find out just who was listening...
SO, WHAT'S THE DEAL, SELINA?
AS FAR AS I CAN TELL... AS FAR AS I CAN SEE...
IT'S TWELVE O'CLOCK...
AND ALL'S WELL!

WILL PFEIFER *writer*
PETE WOODS *artist*
BRAD ANDERSON *colorist*

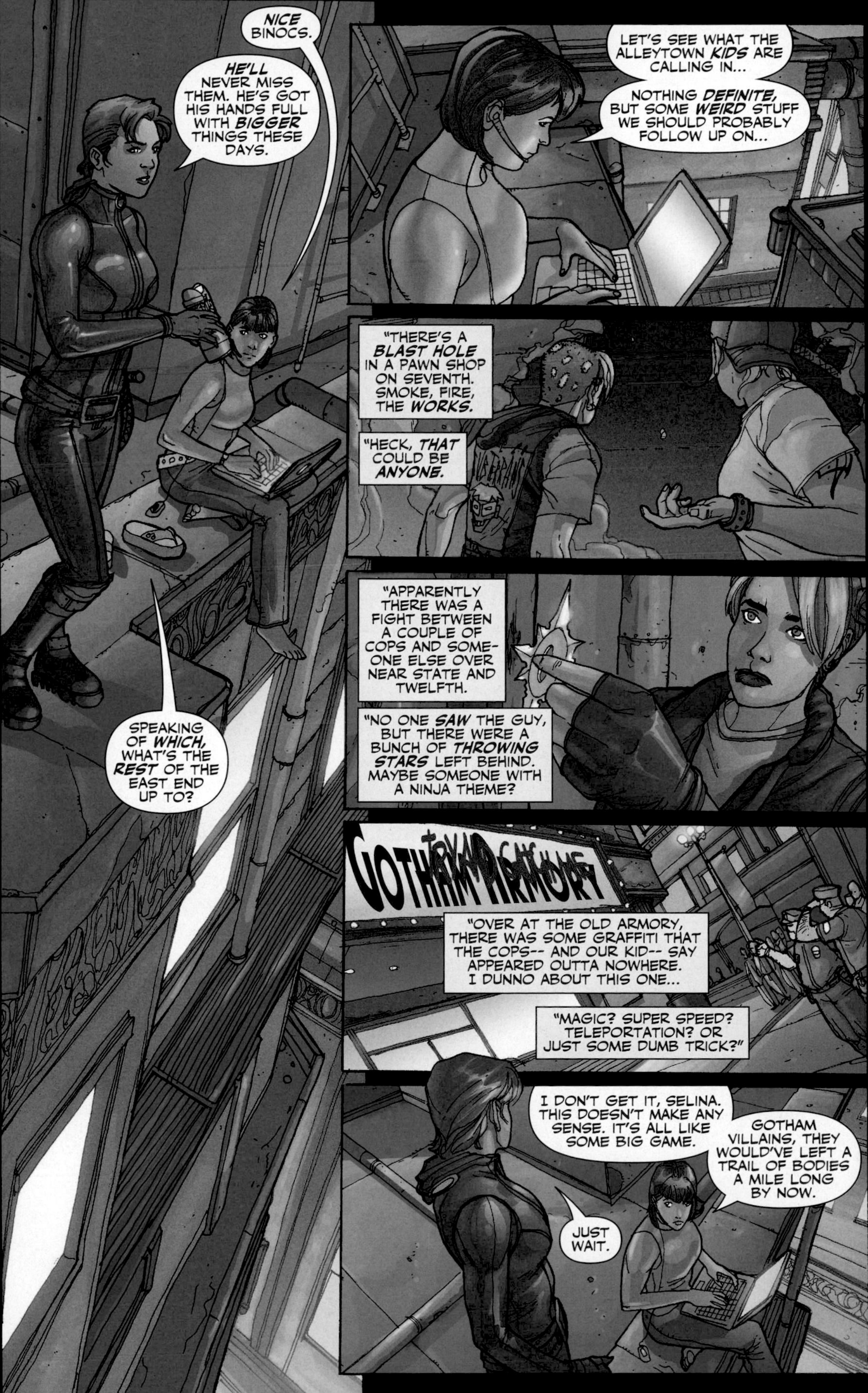
NICE BINOCS.
HE'LL NEVER MISS THEM. HE'S GOT HIS HANDS FULL WITH BIGGER THINGS THESE DAYS.
LET'S SEE WHAT THE ALLEYTOWN KIDS ARE CALLING IN...
NOTHING DEFINITE, BUT SOME WEIRD STUFF WE SHOULD PROBABLY FOLLOW UP ON...
"THERE'S A BLAST HOLE IN A PAWN SHOP ON SEVENTH. SMOKE, FIRE, THE WORKS.
"HECK, THAT COULD BE ANYONE.
"APPARENTLY THERE WAS A FIGHT BETWEEN A COUPLE OF COPS AND SOME-ONE ELSE OVER NEAR STATE AND TWELFTH.
"NO ONE SAW THE GUY, BUT THERE WERE A BUNCH OF THROWING STARS LEFT BEHIND. MAYBE SOMEONE WITH A NINJA THEME?
SPEAKING OF WHICH, WHAT'S THE REST OF THE EAST END UP TO?
GOTHAM ARMORY
"OVER AT THE OLD ARMORY, THERE WAS SOME GRAFFITI THAT THE COPS-- AND OUR KID-- SAY APPEARED OUTTA NOWHERE. I DUNNO ABOUT THIS ONE...
"MAGIC? SUPER SPEED? TELEPORTATION? OR JUST SOME DUMB TRICK?"
I DON'T GET IT, SELINA. THIS DOESN'T MAKE ANY SENSE. IT'S ALL LIKE SOME BIG GAME.
GOTHAM VILLAINS, THEY WOULD'VE LEFT A TRAIL OF BODIES A MILE LONG BY NOW.
JUST WAIT.

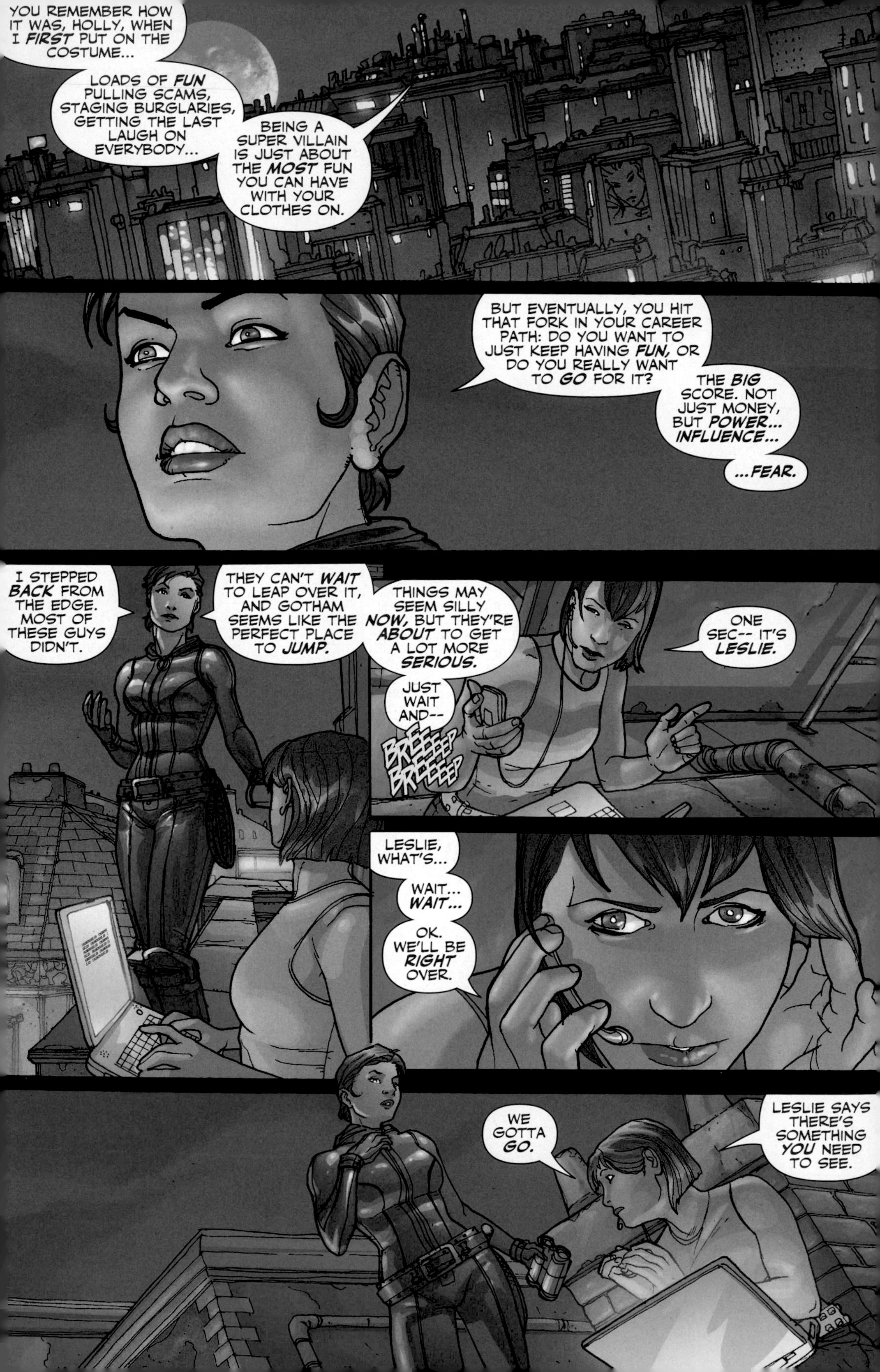

YOU REMEMBER HOW IT WAS, HOLLY, WHEN I FIRST PUT ON THE COSTUME...
LOADS OF FUN PULLING SCAMS, STAGING BURGLARIES, GETTING THE LAST LAUGH ON EVERYBODY...
BEING A SUPER VILLAIN IS JUST ABOUT THE MOST FUN YOU CAN HAVE WITH YOUR CLOTHES ON.
BUT EVENTUALLY, YOU HIT THAT FORK IN YOUR CAREER PATH: DO YOU WANT TO JUST KEEP HAVING FUN, OR DO YOU REALLY WANT TO GO FOR IT?
THE BIG SCORE. NOT JUST MONEY, BUT POWER... INFLUENCE...
...FEAR.
I STEPPED BACK FROM THE EDGE. MOST OF THESE GUYS DIDN'T.
THEY CAN'T WAIT TO LEAP OVER IT, AND GOTHAM SEEMS LIKE THE PERFECT PLACE TO JUMP.
THINGS MAY SEEM SILLY NOW, BUT THEY'RE ABOUT TO GET A LOT MORE SERIOUS.
JUST WAIT AND--
BREEEEEP BREEEEEP
ONE SEC-- IT'S LESLIE.
LESLIE, WHAT'S...
WAIT... WAIT...
OK. WE'LL BE RIGHT OVER.
WE GOTTA GO.
LESLIE SAYS THERE'S SOMETHING YOU NEED TO SEE.

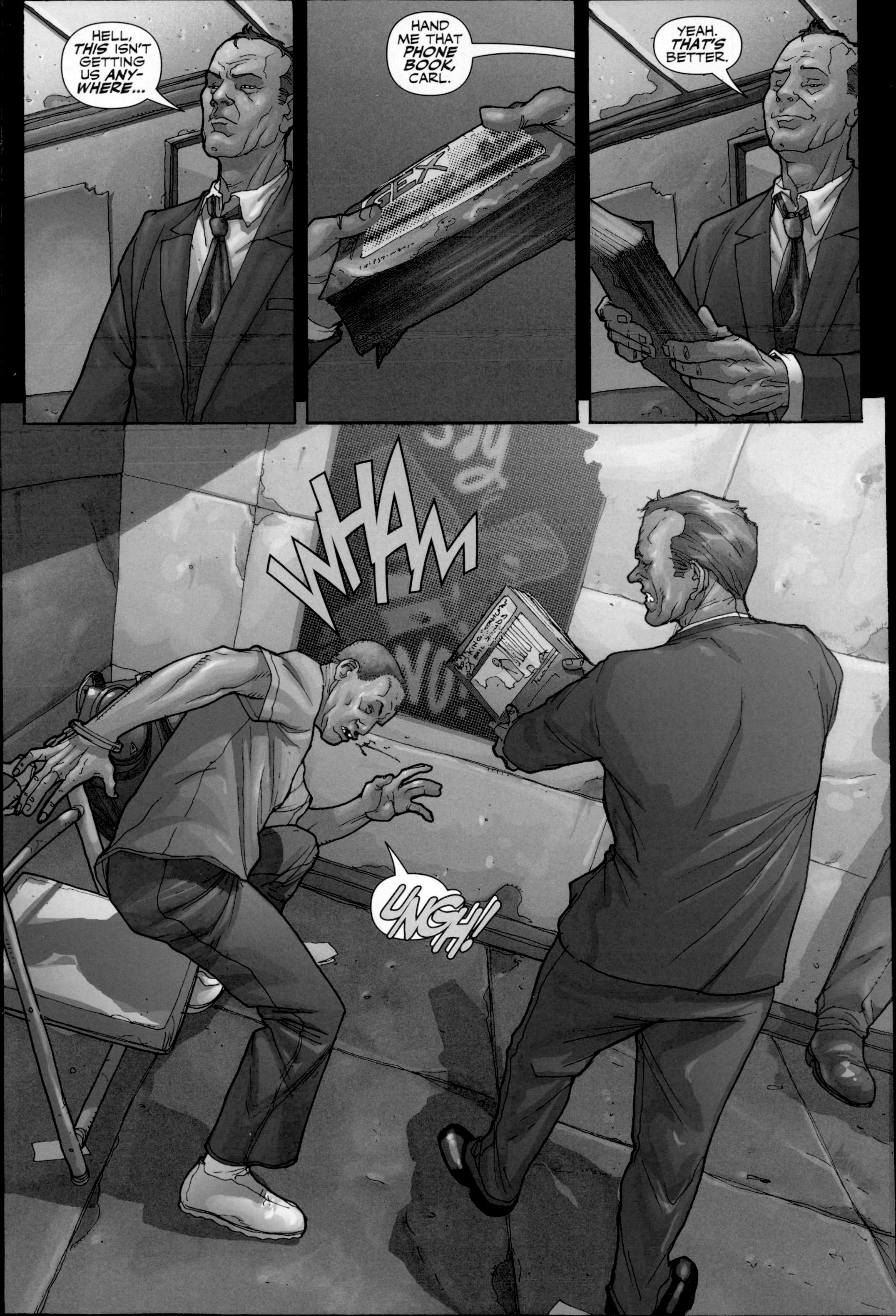
HELL, THIS ISN'T GETTING US ANY-WHERE...
HAND ME THAT PHONE BOOK, CARL.
YEAH. THAT'S BETTER.
WHAM
UNGH!

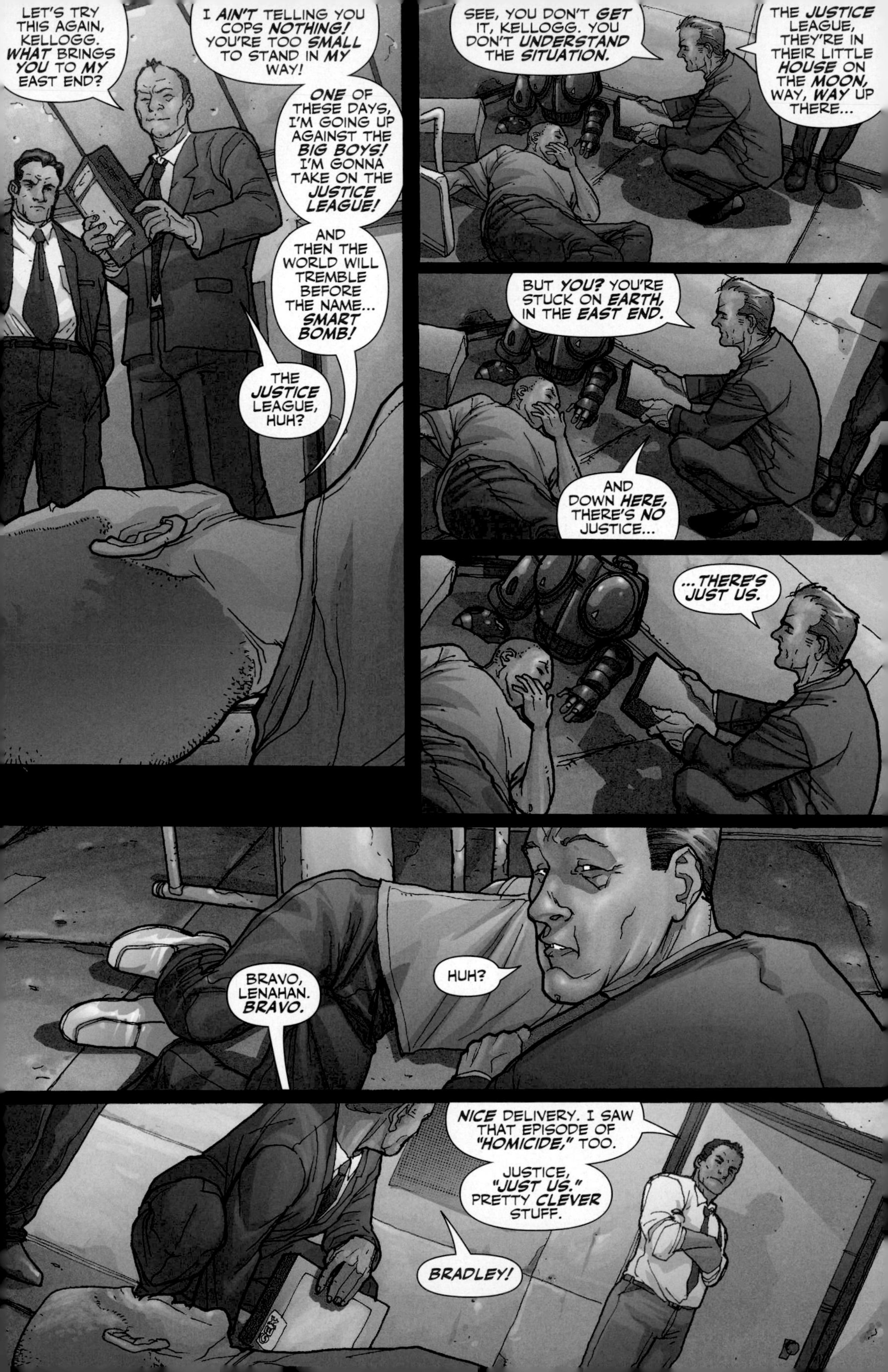
LET'S TRY THIS AGAIN, KELLOGG. WHAT BRINGS YOU TO MY EAST END?
I AIN'T TELLING YOU COPS NOTHING! YOU'RE TOO SMALL TO STAND IN MY WAY!
ONE OF THESE DAYS, I'M GOING UP AGAINST THE BIG BOYS! I'M GONNA TAKE ON THE JUSTICE LEAGUE!
AND THEN THE WORLD WILL TREMBLE BEFORE THE NAME... SMART BOMB!
THE JUSTICE LEAGUE, HUH?
SEE, YOU DON'T GET IT, KELLOGG. YOU DON'T UNDERSTAND THE SITUATION.
THE JUSTICE LEAGUE, THEY'RE IN THEIR LITTLE HOUSE ON THE MOON, WAY, WAY UP THERE...
BUT YOU? YOU'RE STUCK ON EARTH, IN THE EAST END.
AND DOWN HERE, THERE'S NO JUSTICE...
...THERE'S JUST US.
BRAVO, LENAHAN. BRAVO.
HUH?
NICE DELIVERY. I SAW THAT EPISODE OF "HOMICIDE," TOO.
JUSTICE, "JUST US." PRETTY CLEVER STUFF.
BRADLEY!

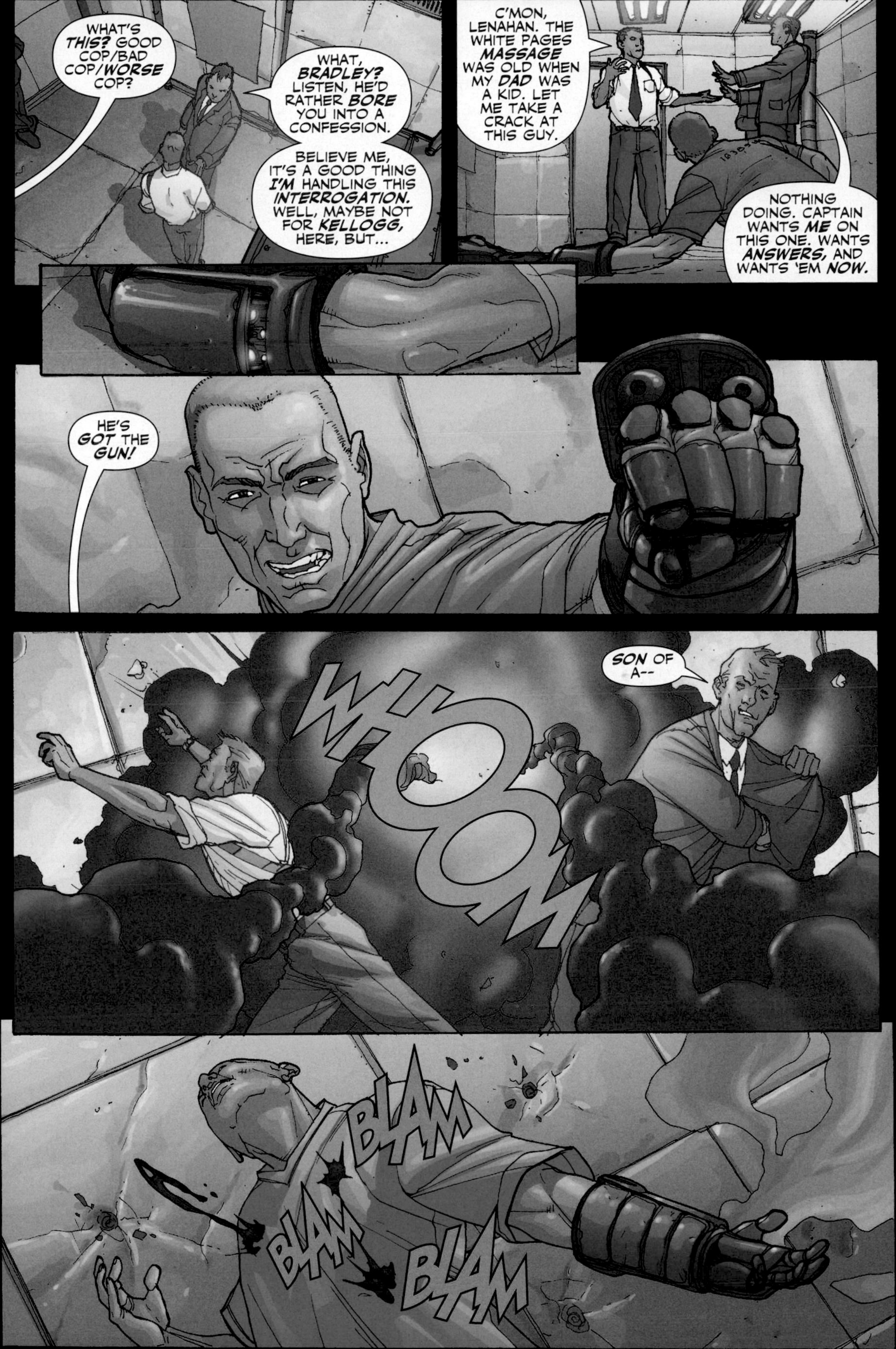
WHAT'S THIS? GOOD COP/BAD COP/WORSE COP?
WHAT, BRADLEY? LISTEN, HE'D RATHER BORE YOU INTO A CONFESSION.
BELIEVE ME, IT'S A GOOD THING I'M HANDLING THIS INTERROGATION. WELL, MAYBE NOT FOR KELLOGG, HERE, BUT...
C'MON, LENAHAN. THE WHITE PAGES MASSAGE WAS OLD WHEN MY DAD WAS A KID. LET ME TAKE A CRACK AT THIS GUY.
NOTHING DOING. CAPTAIN WANTS ME ON THIS ONE. WANTS ANSWERS, AND WANTS 'EM NOW.
HE'S GOT THE GUN!
SON OF A--
WHOOM
BLAM
BLAM
BLAM

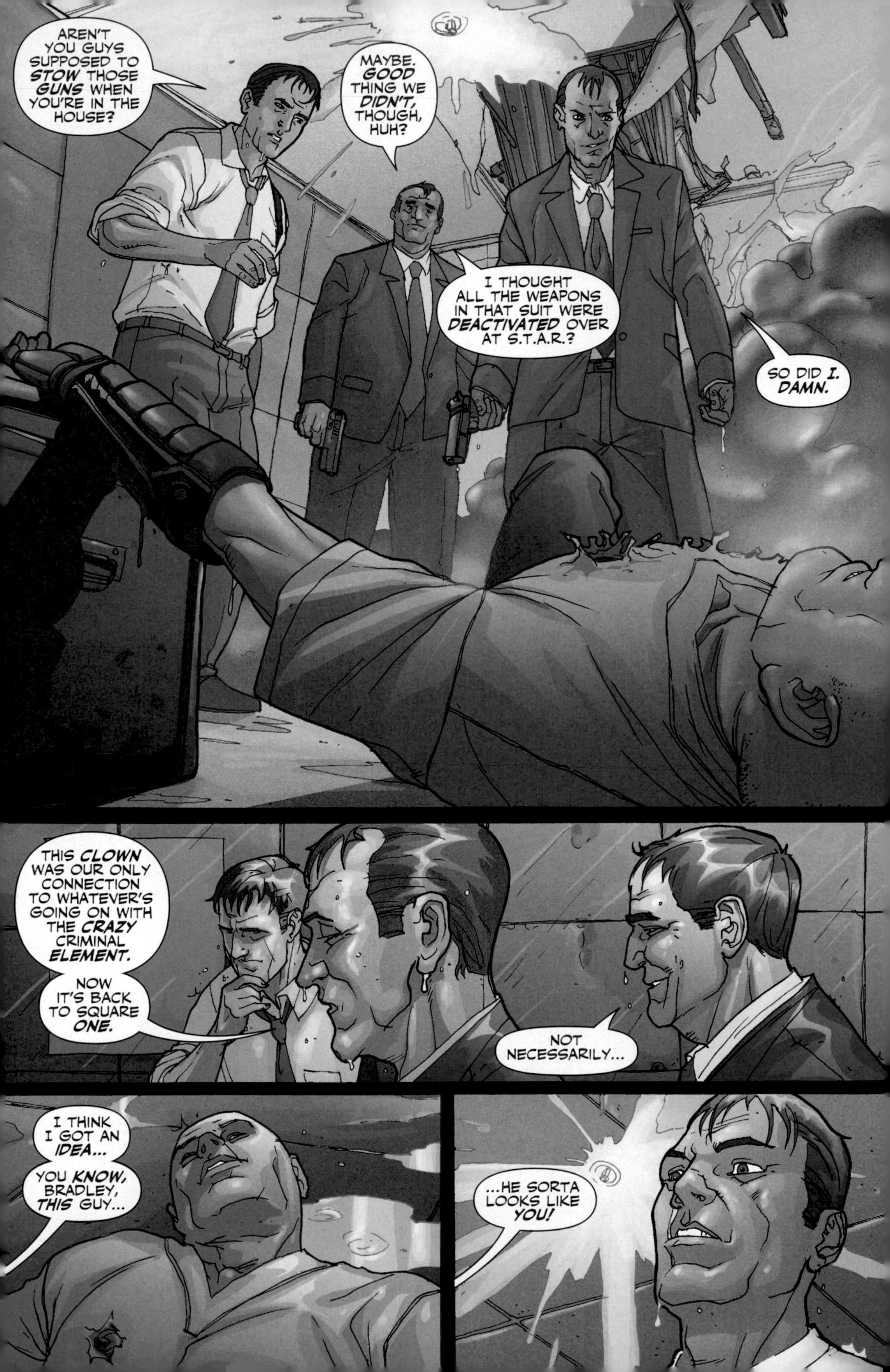
AREN'T YOU GUYS SUPPOSED TO STOW THOSE GUNS WHEN YOU'RE IN THE HOUSE?
MAYBE. GOOD THING WE DIDN'T, THOUGH, HUH?
I THOUGHT ALL THE WEAPONS IN THAT SUIT WERE DEACTIVATED OVER AT S.T.A.R.?
SO DID I. DAMN.
THIS CLOWN WAS OUR ONLY CONNECTION TO WHATEVER'S GOING ON WITH THE CRAZY CRIMINAL ELEMENT.
NOW IT'S BACK TO SQUARE ONE.
NOT NECESSARILY...
I THINK I GOT AN IDEA...
YOU KNOW, BRADLEY, THIS GUY...
...HE SORTA LOOKS LIKE YOU!

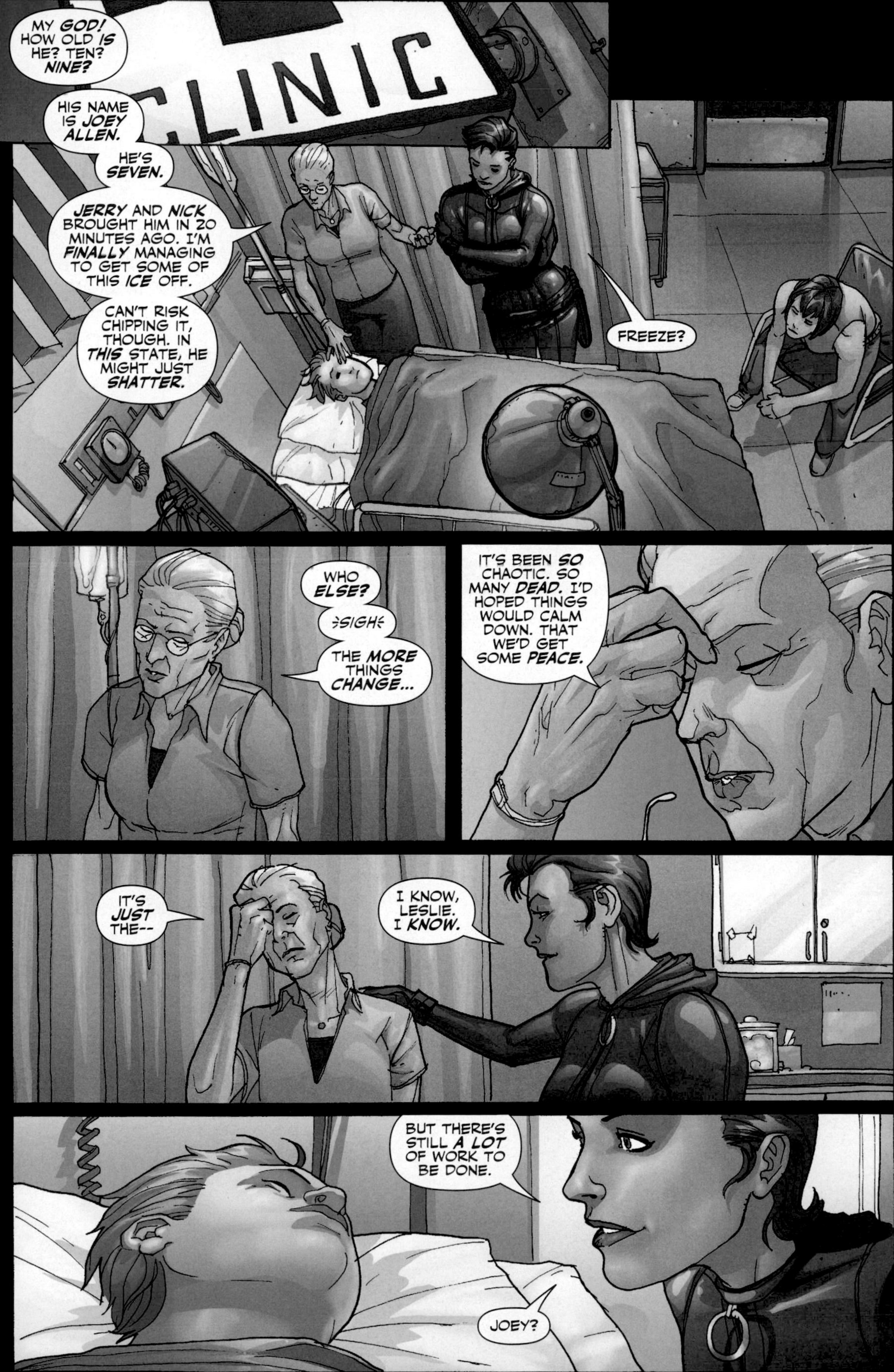
MY GOD! HOW OLD IS HE? TEN? NINE?
CLINIC
HIS NAME IS JOEY ALLEN.
HE'S SEVEN.
JERRY AND NICK BROUGHT HIM IN 20 MINUTES AGO. I'M FINALLY MANAGING TO GET SOME OF THIS ICE OFF.
CAN'T RISK CHIPPING IT, THOUGH. IN THIS STATE, HE MIGHT JUST SHATTER.
FREEZE?
WHO ELSE?
SIGH
THE MORE THINGS CHANGE...
IT'S BEEN SO CHAOTIC. SO MANY DEAD. I'D HOPED THINGS WOULD CALM DOWN. THAT WE'D GET SOME PEACE.
IT'S JUST THE--
I KNOW, LESLIE. I KNOW.
BUT THERE'S STILL A LOT OF WORK TO BE DONE.
JOEY?

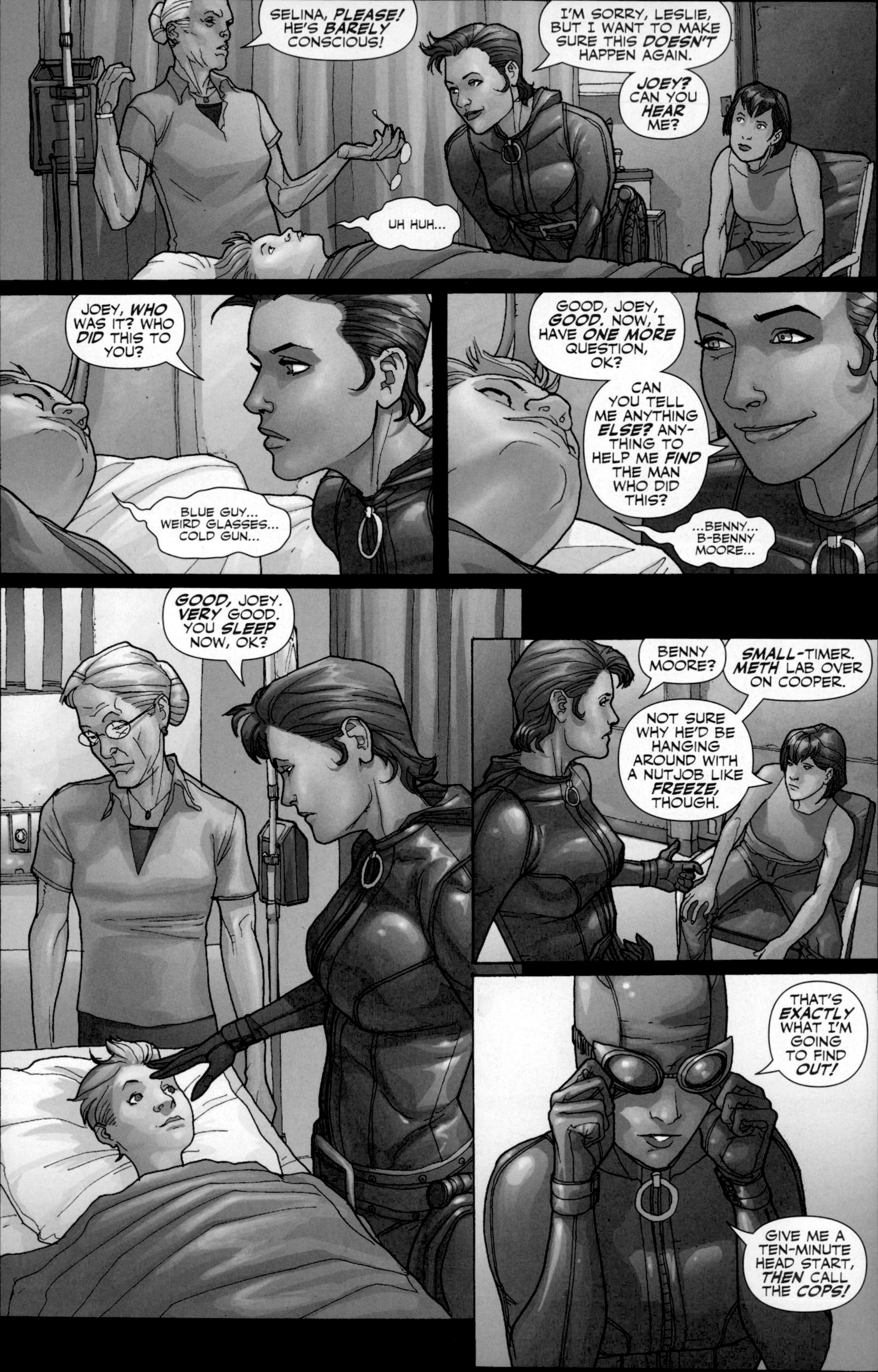
SELINA, PLEASE! HE'S BARELY CONSCIOUS!
I'M SORRY, LESLIE, BUT I WANT TO MAKE SURE THIS DOESN'T HAPPEN AGAIN.
JOEY? CAN YOU HEAR ME?
UH HUH...
JOEY, WHO WAS IT? WHO DID THIS TO YOU?
BLUE GUY... WEIRD GLASSES... COLD GUN...
GOOD, JOEY, GOOD. NOW, I HAVE ONE MORE QUESTION, OK?
CAN YOU TELL ME ANYTHING ELSE? ANY-THING TO HELP ME FIND THE MAN WHO DID THIS?
...BENNY... B-BENNY MOORE...
GOOD, JOEY. VERY GOOD. YOU SLEEP NOW, OK?
BENNY MOORE?
SMALL-TIMER. METH LAB OVER ON COOPER.
NOT SURE WHY HE'D BE HANGING AROUND WITH A NUTJOB LIKE FREEZE, THOUGH.
THAT'S EXACTLY WHAT I'M GOING TO FIND OUT!
GIVE ME A TEN-MINUTE HEAD START, THEN CALL THE COPS!

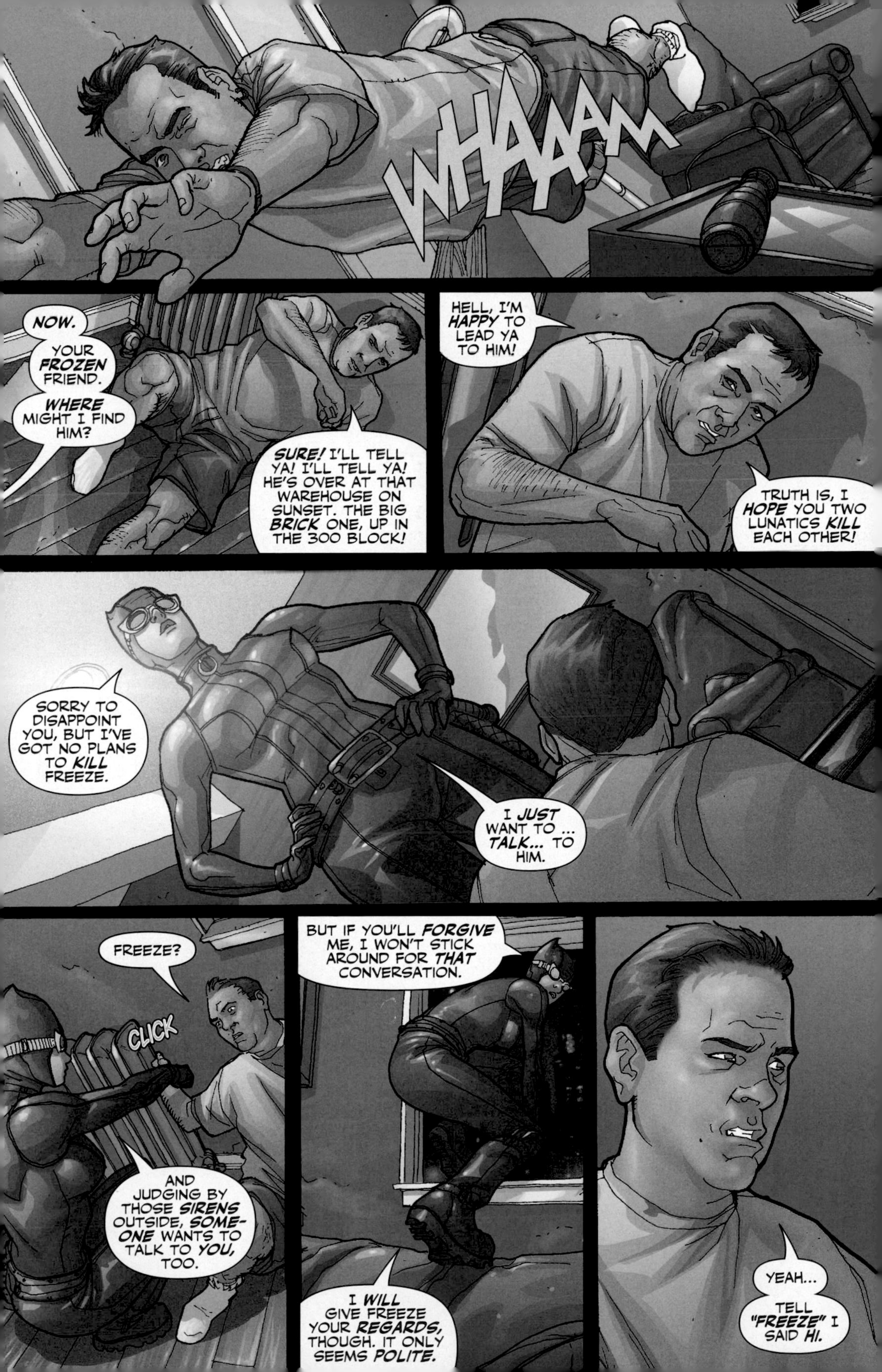
WHAAAM
NOW.
YOUR FROZEN FRIEND.
WHERE MIGHT I FIND HIM?
SURE! I'LL TELL YA! I'LL TELL YA! HE'S OVER AT THAT WAREHOUSE ON SUNSET. THE BIG BRICK ONE, UP IN THE 300 BLOCK!
HELL, I'M HAPPY TO LEAD YA TO HIM!
TRUTH IS, I HOPE YOU TWO LUNATICS KILL EACH OTHER!
SORRY TO DISAPPOINT YOU, BUT I'VE GOT NO PLANS TO KILL FREEZE.
I JUST WANT TO ... TALK... TO HIM.
FREEZE?
CLICK
AND JUDGING BY THOSE SIRENS OUTSIDE, SOME-ONE WANTS TO TALK TO YOU, TOO.
BUT IF YOU'LL FORGIVE ME, I WON'T STICK AROUND FOR THAT CONVERSATION.
I WILL GIVE FREEZE YOUR REGARDS, THOUGH. IT ONLY SEEMS POLITE.
YEAH...
TELL "FREEZE" I SAID HI.

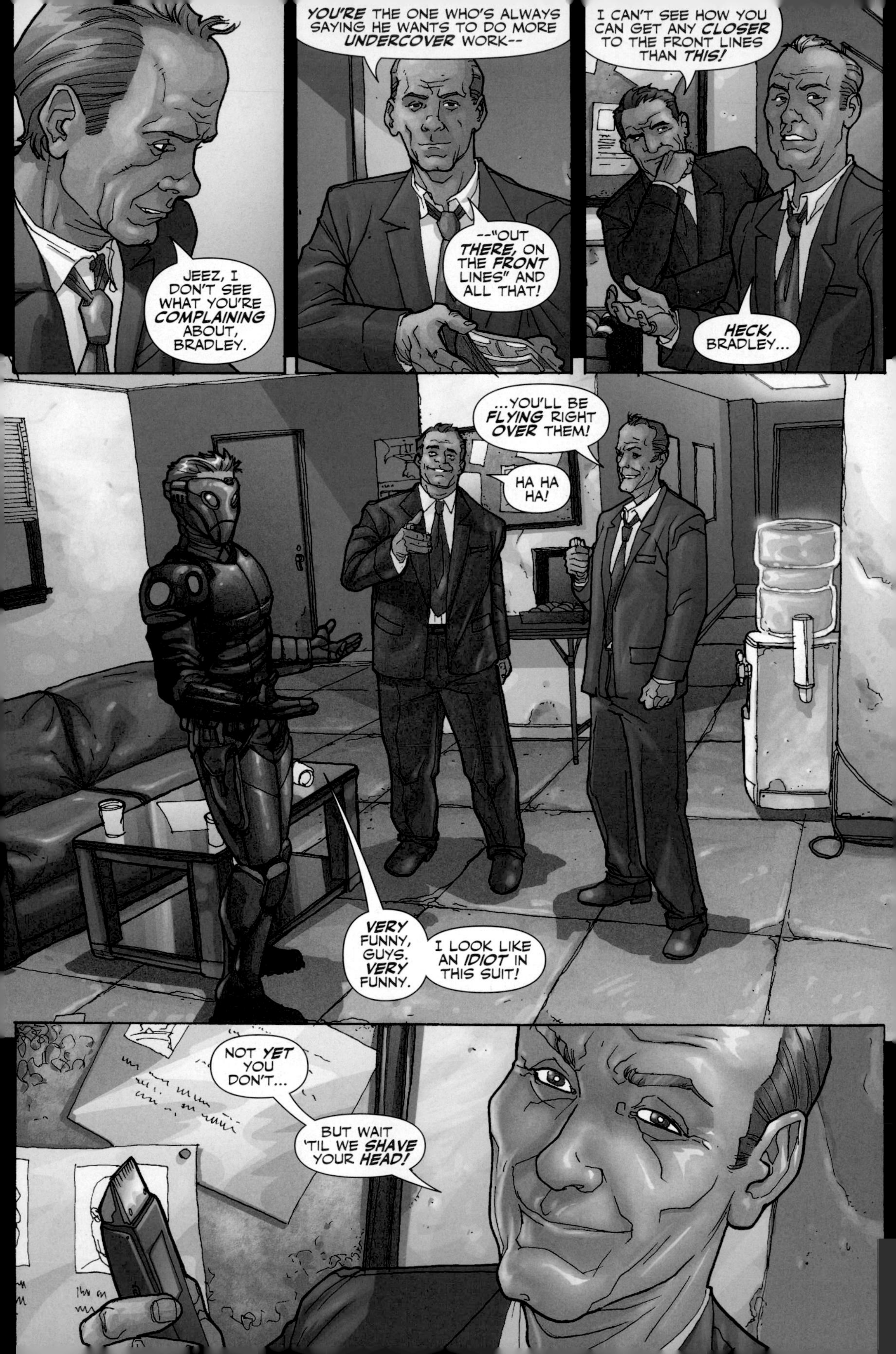
JEEZ, I DON'T SEE WHAT YOU'RE COMPLAINING ABOUT, BRADLEY.
YOU'RE THE ONE WHO'S ALWAYS SAYING HE WANTS TO DO MORE UNDERCOVER WORK--
--"OUT THERE, ON THE FRONT LINES" AND ALL THAT!
I CAN'T SEE HOW YOU CAN GET ANY CLOSER TO THE FRONT LINES THAN THIS!
HECK, BRADLEY...
...YOU'LL BE FLYING RIGHT OVER THEM!
HA HA HA!
VERY FUNNY, GUYS. VERY FUNNY.
I LOOK LIKE AN IDIOT IN THIS SUIT!
NOT YET YOU DON'T...
BUT WAIT 'TIL WE SHAVE YOUR HEAD!

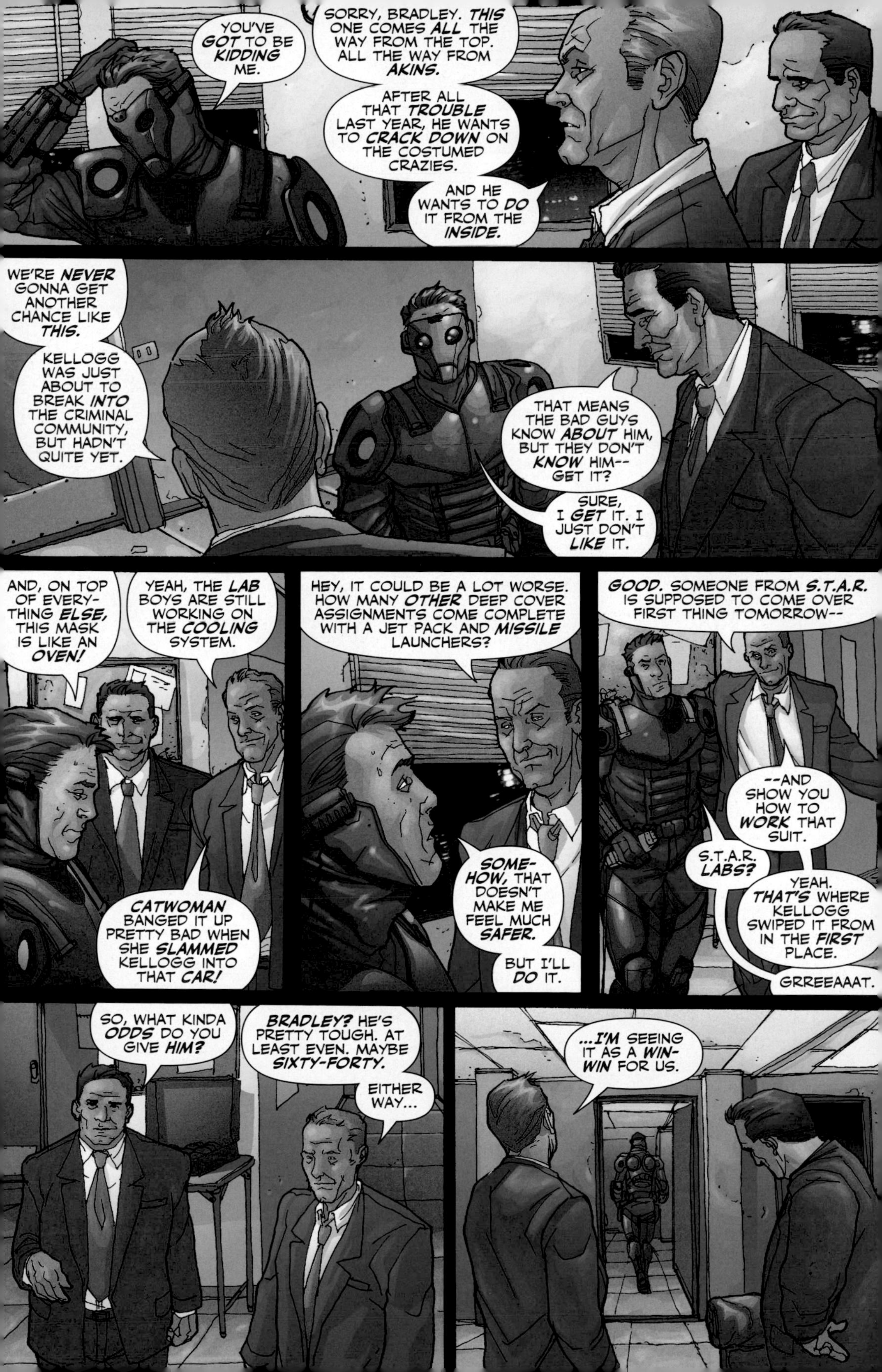
YOU'VE GOT TO BE KIDDING ME.
SORRY, BRADLEY. THIS ONE COMES ALL THE WAY FROM THE TOP. ALL THE WAY FROM AKINS.
AFTER ALL THAT TROUBLE LAST YEAR, HE WANTS TO CRACK DOWN ON THE COSTUMED CRAZIES.
AND HE WANTS TO DO IT FROM THE INSIDE.
WE'RE NEVER GONNA GET ANOTHER CHANCE LIKE THIS.
KELLOGG WAS JUST ABOUT TO BREAK INTO THE CRIMINAL COMMUNITY, BUT HADN'T QUITE YET.
THAT MEANS THE BAD GUYS KNOW ABOUT HIM, BUT THEY DON'T KNOW HIM-- GET IT?
SURE, I GET IT. I JUST DON'T LIKE IT.
AND, ON TOP OF EVERY-THING ELSE, THIS MASK IS LIKE AN OVEN!
YEAH, THE LAB BOYS ARE STILL WORKING ON THE COOLING SYSTEM.
CATWOMAN BANGED IT UP PRETTY BAD WHEN SHE SLAMMED KELLOGG INTO THAT CAR!
HEY, IT COULD BE A LOT WORSE. HOW MANY OTHER DEEP COVER ASSIGNMENTS COME COMPLETE WITH A JET PACK AND MISSILE LAUNCHERS?
SOME-HOW, THAT DOESN'T MAKE ME FEEL MUCH SAFER.
BUT I'LL DO IT.
GOOD. SOMEONE FROM S.T.A.R. IS SUPPOSED TO COME OVER FIRST THING TOMORROW--
--AND SHOW YOU HOW TO WORK THAT SUIT.
S.T.A.R. LABS?
YEAH. THAT'S WHERE KELLOGG SWIPED IT FROM IN THE FIRST PLACE.
GRREEAAAT.
SO, WHAT KINDA ODDS DO YOU GIVE HIM?
BRADLEY? HE'S PRETTY TOUGH. AT LEAST EVEN. MAYBE SIXTY-FORTY.
EITHER WAY...
...I'M SEEING IT AS A WIN-WIN FOR US.

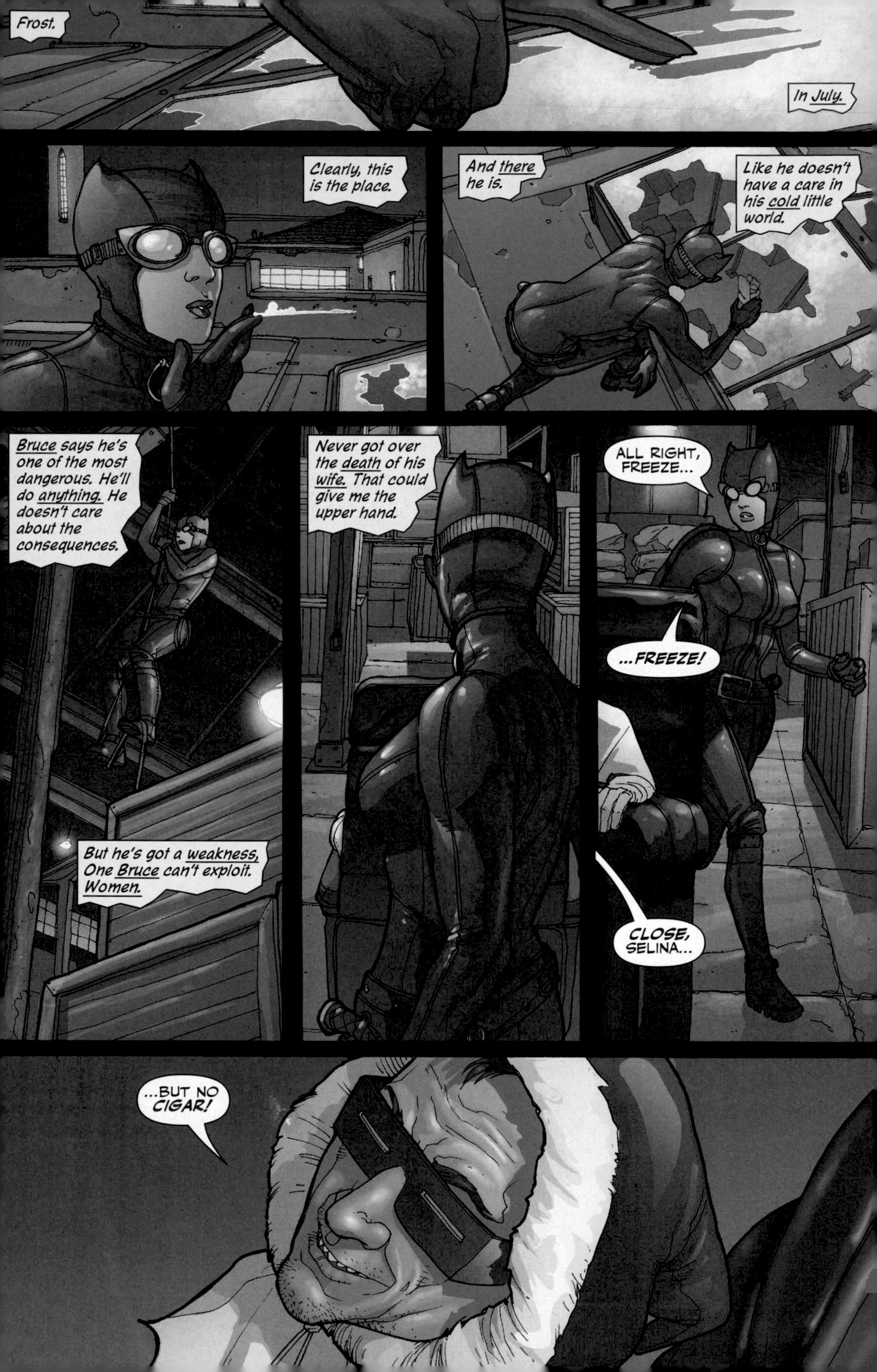
Frost.
In July.
Clearly, this is the place.
And there he is.
Like he doesn't have a care in his cold little world.
Bruce says he's one of the most dangerous. He'll do anything. He doesn't care about the consequences.
But he's got a weakness, One Bruce can't exploit. Women.
Never got over the death of his wife. That could give me the upper hand.
ALL RIGHT, FREEZE...
...FREEZE!
CLOSE, SELINA...
...BUT NO CIGAR!

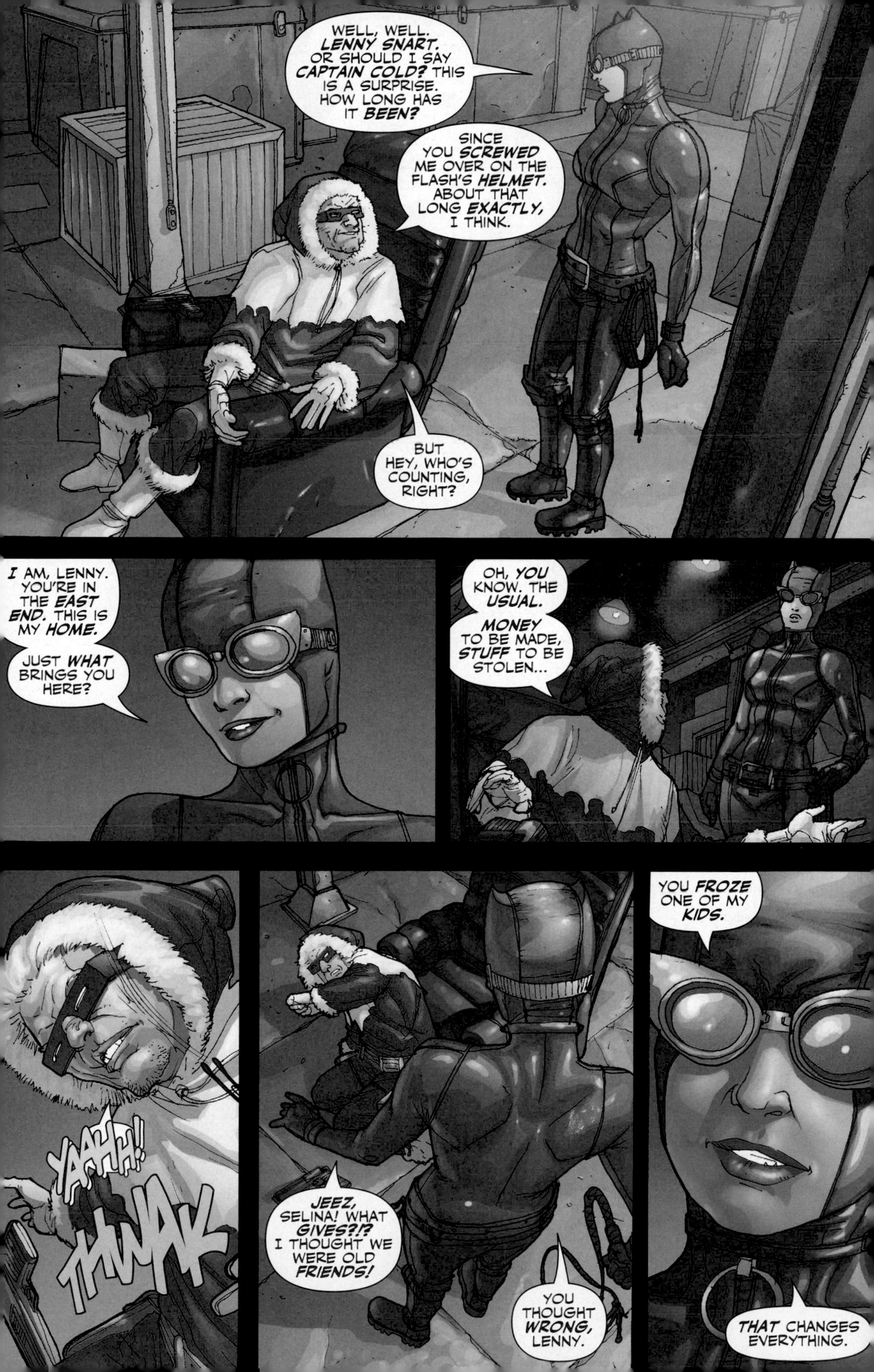

WELL, WELL. LENNY SNART. OR SHOULD I SAY CAPTAIN COLD? THIS IS A SURPRISE. HOW LONG HAS IT BEEN?
SINCE YOU SCREWED ME OVER ON THE FLASH'S HELMET. ABOUT THAT LONG EXACTLY, I THINK.
BUT HEY, WHO'S COUNTING, RIGHT?
I AM, LENNY. YOU'RE IN THE EAST END. THIS IS MY HOME.
JUST WHAT BRINGS YOU HERE?
OH, YOU KNOW. THE USUAL.
MONEY TO BE MADE, STUFF TO BE STOLEN...
YAAHH!!
THWAK
JEEZ, SELINA! WHAT GIVES?!? I THOUGHT WE WERE OLD FRIENDS!
YOU THOUGHT WRONG, LENNY.
YOU FROZE ONE OF MY KIDS.
THAT CHANGES EVERYTHING.

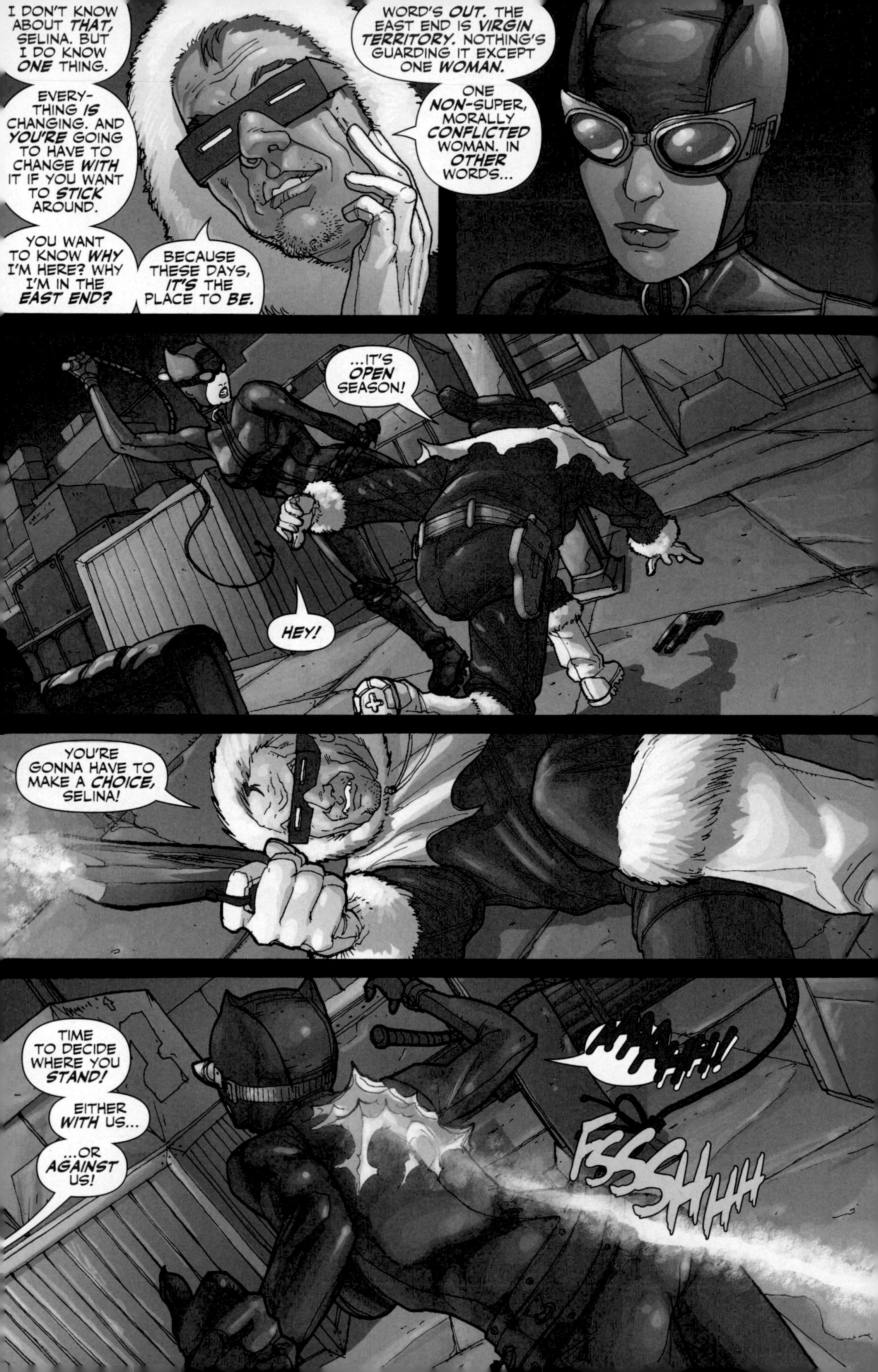

I DON'T KNOW ABOUT THAT, SELINA. BUT I DO KNOW ONE THING.
EVERY-THING IS CHANGING. AND YOU'RE GOING TO HAVE TO CHANGE WITH IT IF YOU WANT TO STICK AROUND.
YOU WANT TO KNOW WHY I'M HERE? WHY I'M IN THE EAST END?
BECAUSE THESE DAYS, IT'S THE PLACE TO BE.
WORD'S OUT. THE EAST END IS VIRGIN TERRITORY. NOTHING'S GUARDING IT EXCEPT ONE WOMAN.
ONE NON-SUPER, MORALLY CONFLICTED WOMAN. IN OTHER WORDS...
...IT'S OPEN SEASON!
HEY!
YOU'RE GONNA HAVE TO MAKE A CHOICE, SELINA!
TIME TO DECIDE WHERE YOU STAND!
EITHER WITH US...
...OR AGAINST US!
FSSSHHH

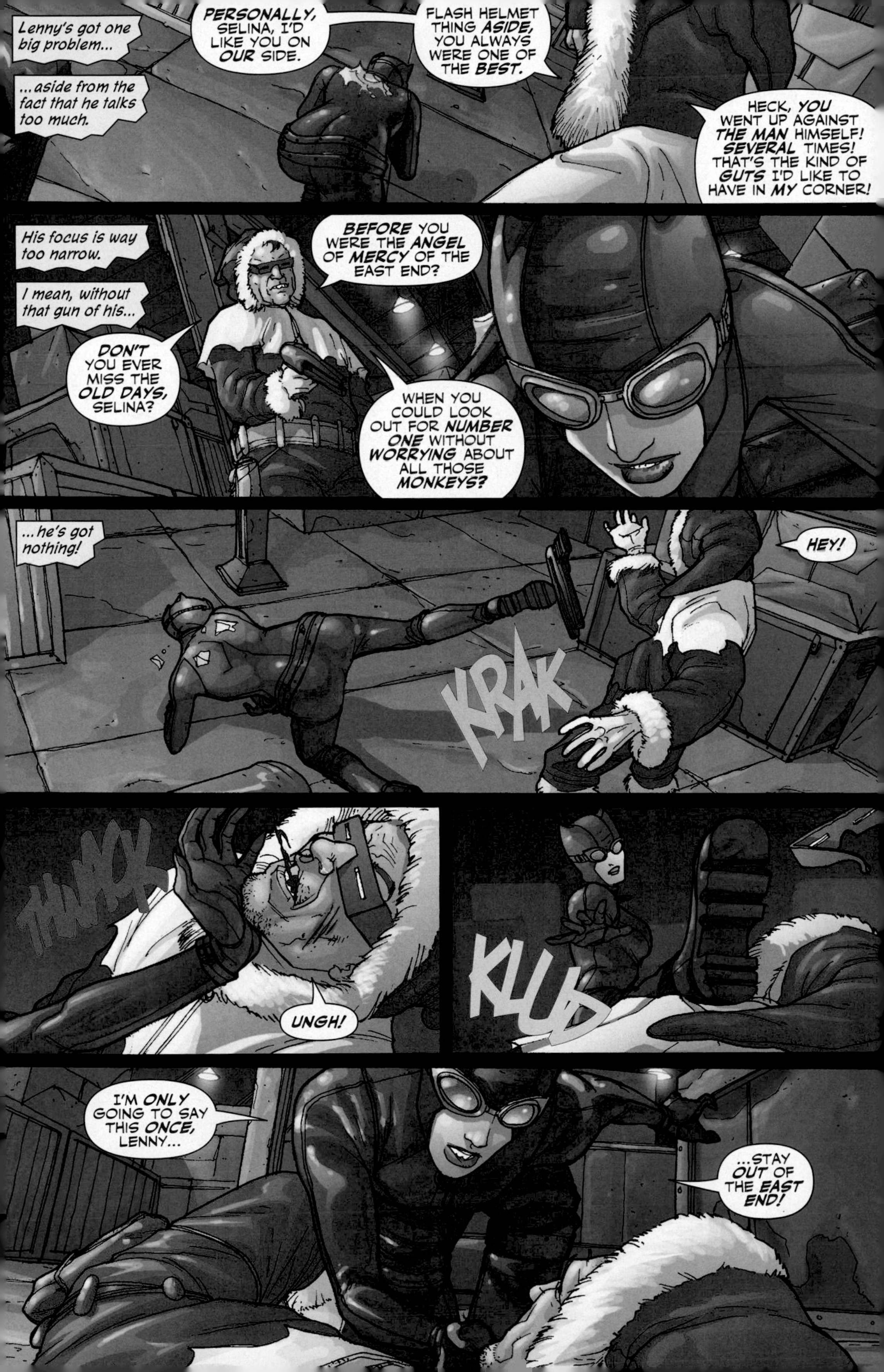

Lenny's got one big problem...
...aside from the fact that he talks too much.
PERSONALLY, SELINA, I'D LIKE YOU ON OUR SIDE.
FLASH HELMET THING ASIDE, YOU ALWAYS WERE ONE OF THE BEST.
HECK, YOU WENT UP AGAINST THE MAN HIMSELF! SEVERAL TIMES! THAT'S THE KIND OF GUTS I'D LIKE TO HAVE IN MY CORNER!
His focus is way too narrow.
I mean, without that gun of his...
BEFORE YOU WERE THE ANGEL OF MERCY OF THE EAST END?
DON'T YOU EVER MISS THE OLD DAYS, SELINA?
WHEN YOU COULD LOOK OUT FOR NUMBER ONE WITHOUT WORRYING ABOUT ALL THOSE MONKEYS?
...he's got nothing!
HEY!
KRAK
THWACK
UNGH!
KLUD
I'M ONLY GOING TO SAY THIS ONCE, LENNY...
...STAY OUT OF THE EAST END!

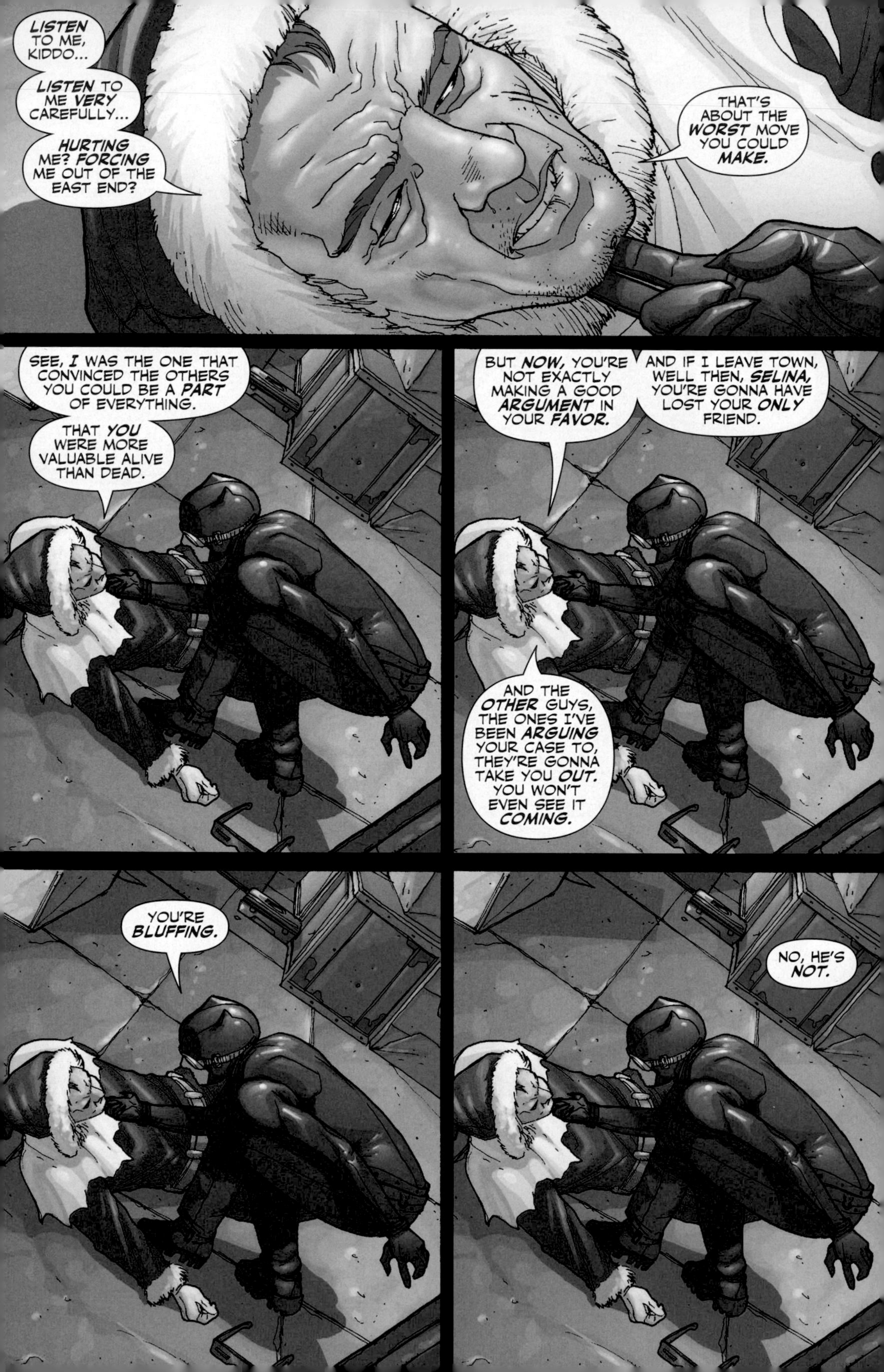
LISTEN TO ME, KIDDO...
LISTEN TO ME VERY CAREFULLY...
HURTING ME? FORCING ME OUT OF THE EAST END?
THAT'S ABOUT THE WORST MOVE YOU COULD MAKE.
SEE, I WAS THE ONE THAT CONVINCED THE OTHERS YOU COULD BE A PART OF EVERYTHING.
THAT YOU WERE MORE VALUABLE ALIVE THAN DEAD.
BUT NOW, YOU'RE NOT EXACTLY MAKING A GOOD ARGUMENT IN YOUR FAVOR.
AND IF I LEAVE TOWN, WELL THEN, SELINA, YOU'RE GONNA HAVE LOST YOUR ONLY FRIEND.
AND THE OTHER GUYS, THE ONES I'VE BEEN ARGUING YOUR CASE TO, THEY'RE GONNA TAKE YOU OUT. YOU WON'T EVEN SEE IT COMING.
YOU'RE BLUFFING.
NO, HE'S NOT.

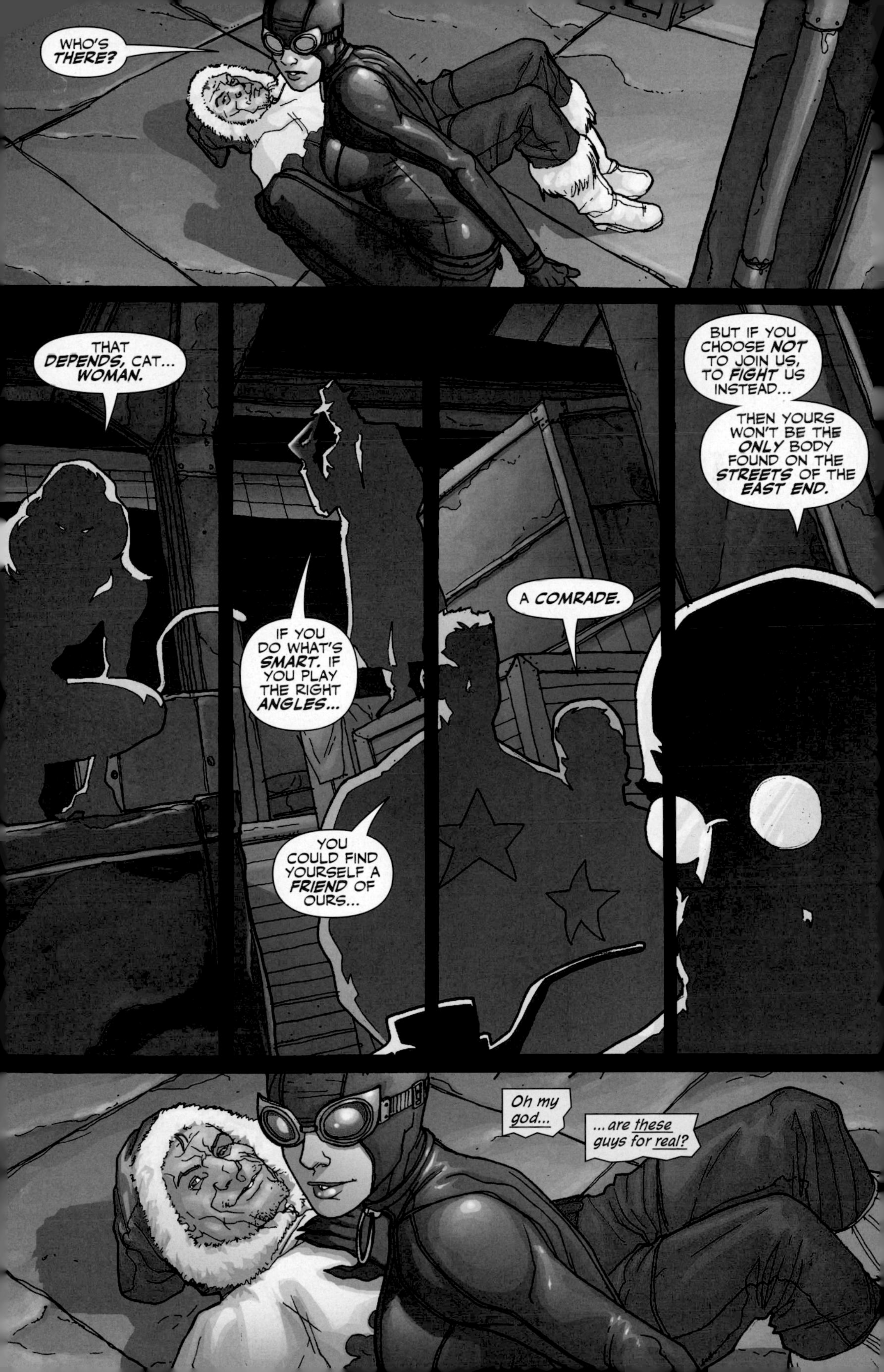
WHO'S THERE?
THAT DEPENDS, CAT... WOMAN.
IF YOU DO WHAT'S SMART. IF YOU PLAY THE RIGHT ANGLES...
YOU COULD FIND YOURSELF A FRIEND OF OURS...
A COMRADE.
BUT IF YOU CHOOSE NOT TO JOIN US, TO FIGHT US INSTEAD...
THEN YOURS WON'T BE THE ONLY BODY FOUND ON THE STREETS OF THE EAST END.
Oh my god...
...are these guys for real?

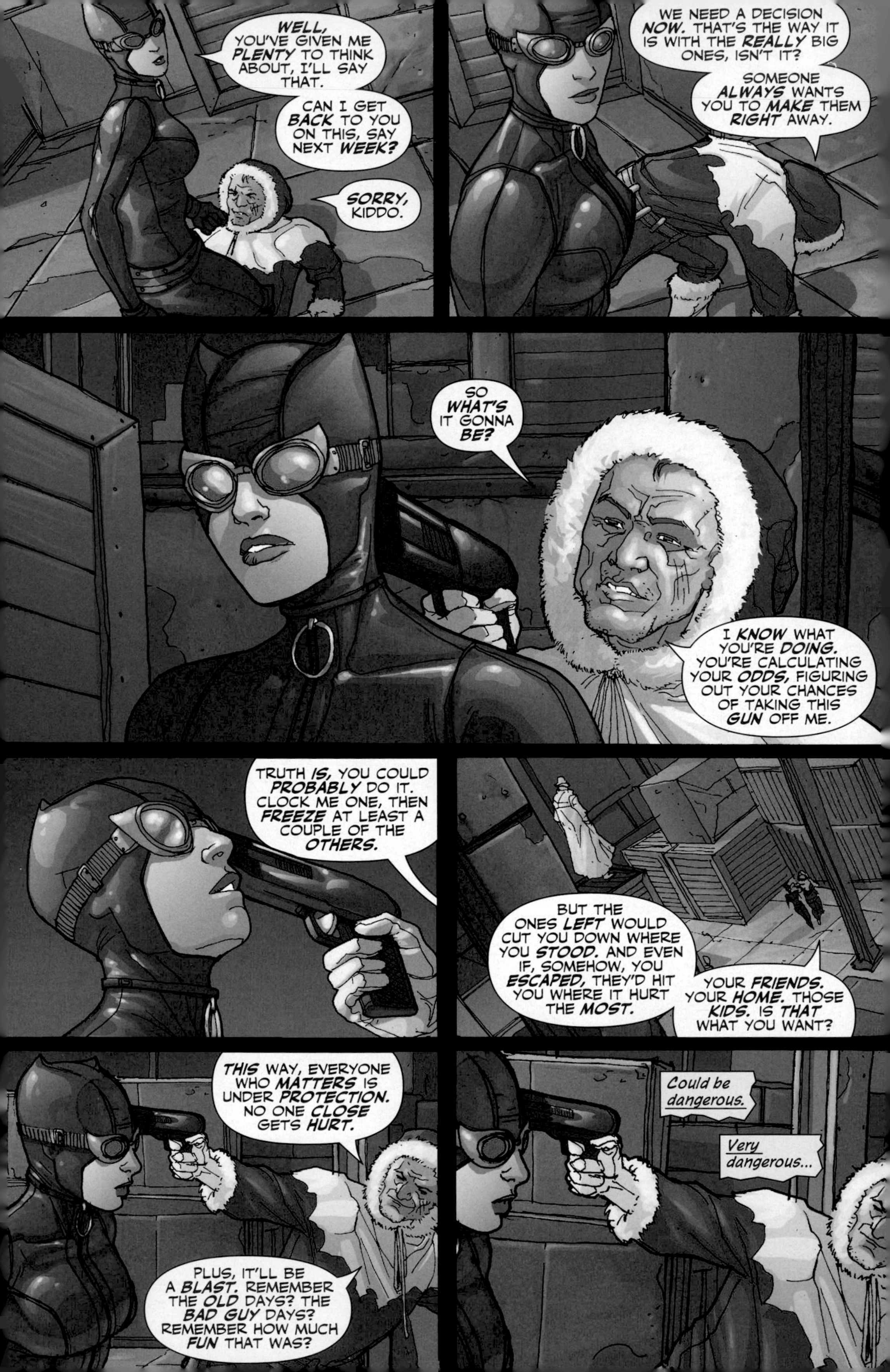
WELL, YOU'VE GIVEN ME PLENTY TO THINK ABOUT, I'LL SAY THAT.
CAN I GET BACK TO YOU ON THIS, SAY NEXT WEEK?
SORRY, KIDDO.
WE NEED A DECISION NOW. THAT'S THE WAY IT IS WITH THE REALLY BIG ONES, ISN'T IT?
SOMEONE ALWAYS WANTS YOU TO MAKE THEM RIGHT AWAY.
SO WHAT'S IT GONNA BE?
I KNOW WHAT YOU'RE DOING. YOU'RE CALCULATING YOUR ODDS, FIGURING OUT YOUR CHANCES OF TAKING THIS GUN OFF ME.
TRUTH IS, YOU COULD PROBABLY DO IT. CLOCK ME ONE, THEN FREEZE AT LEAST A COUPLE OF THE OTHERS.
BUT THE ONES LEFT WOULD CUT YOU DOWN WHERE YOU STOOD. AND EVEN IF, SOMEHOW, YOU ESCAPED, THEY'D HIT YOU WHERE IT HURT THE MOST.
YOUR FRIENDS. YOUR HOME. THOSE KIDS. IS THAT WHAT YOU WANT?
THIS WAY, EVERYONE WHO MATTERS IS UNDER PROTECTION. NO ONE CLOSE GETS HURT.
PLUS, IT'LL BE A BLAST. REMEMBER THE OLD DAYS? THE BAD GUY DAYS? REMEMBER HOW MUCH FUN THAT WAS?
Could be dangerous.
Very dangerous...

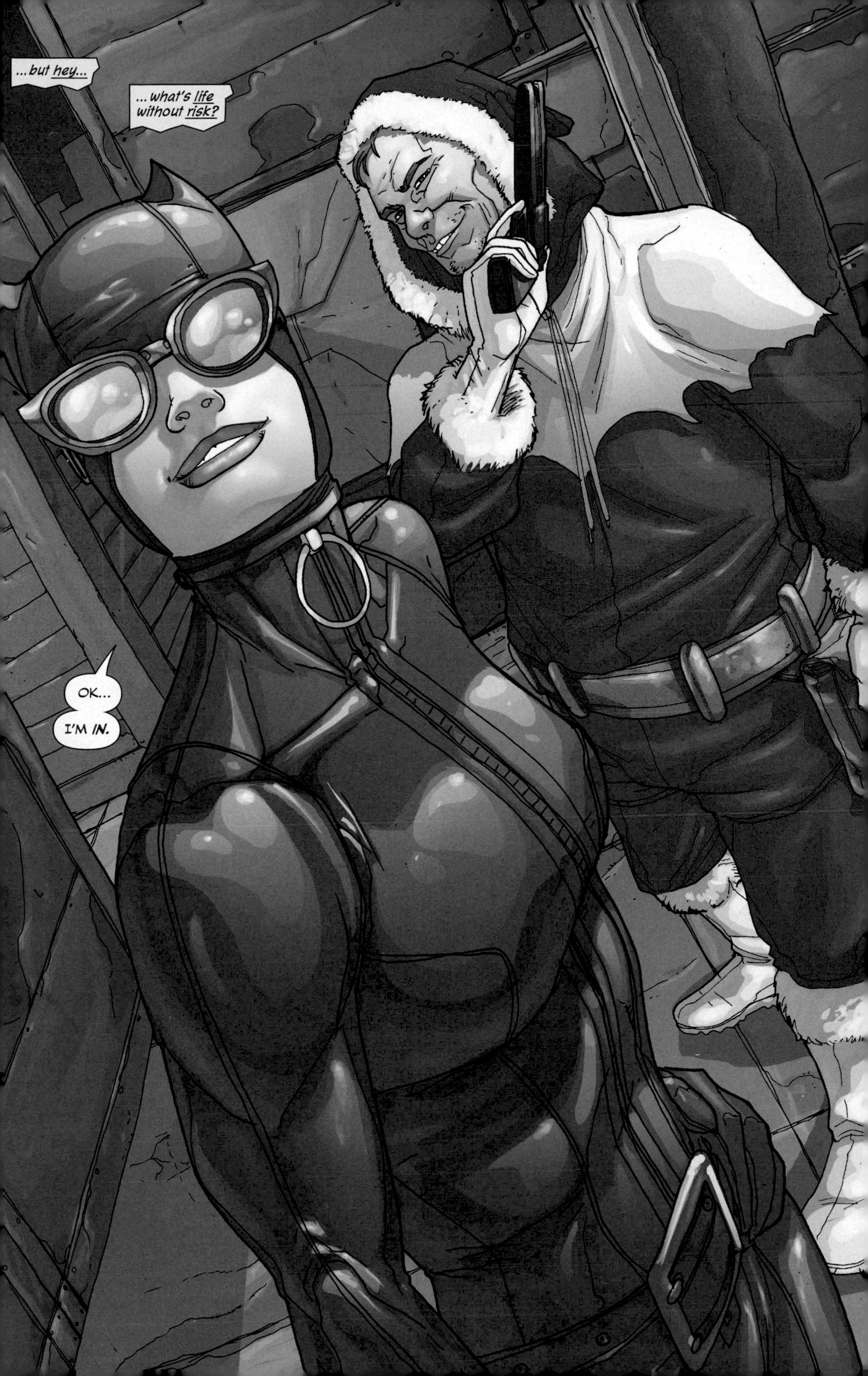
...but hey...
...what's life without risk?
OK... I'M IN.

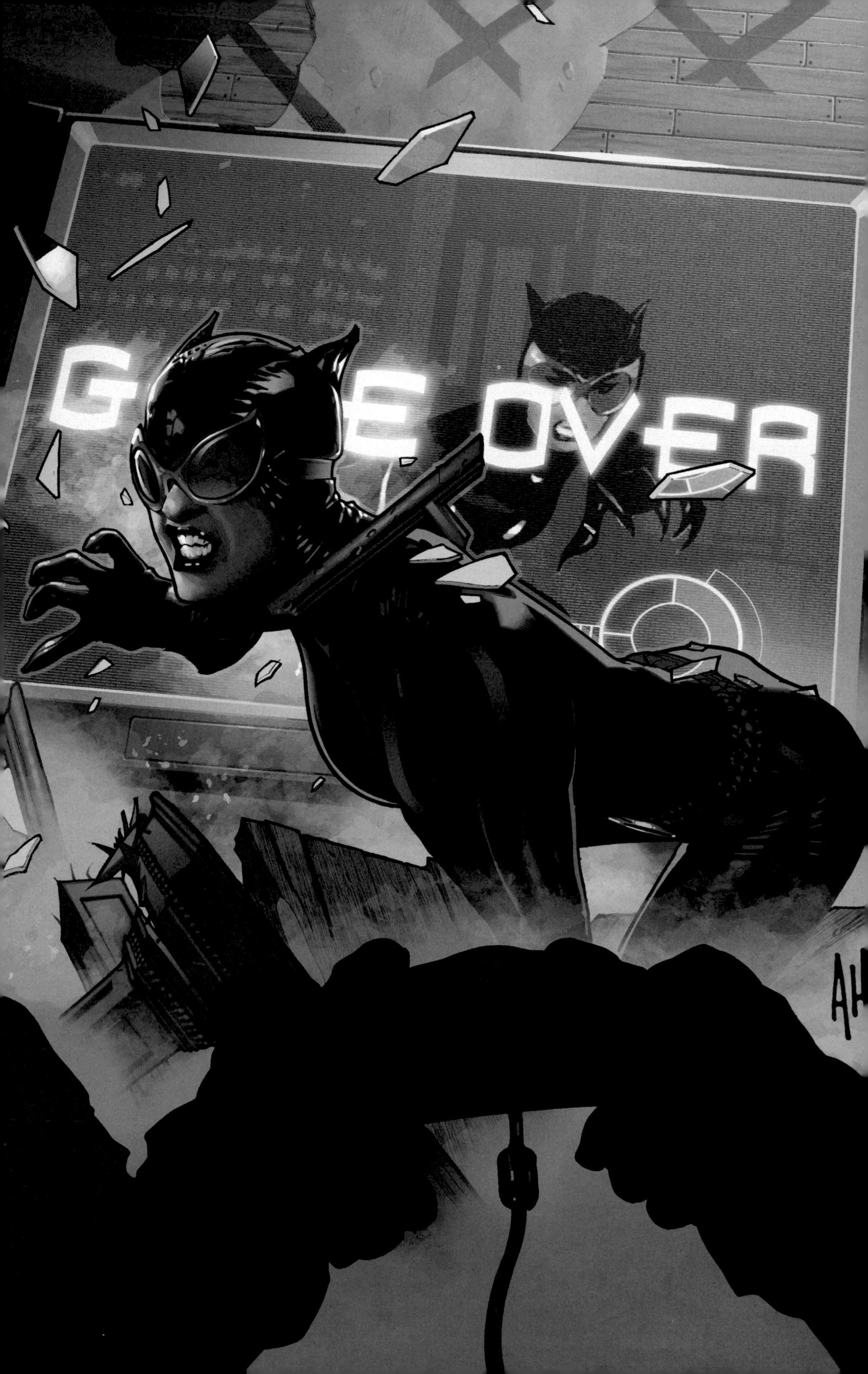
G E OVER

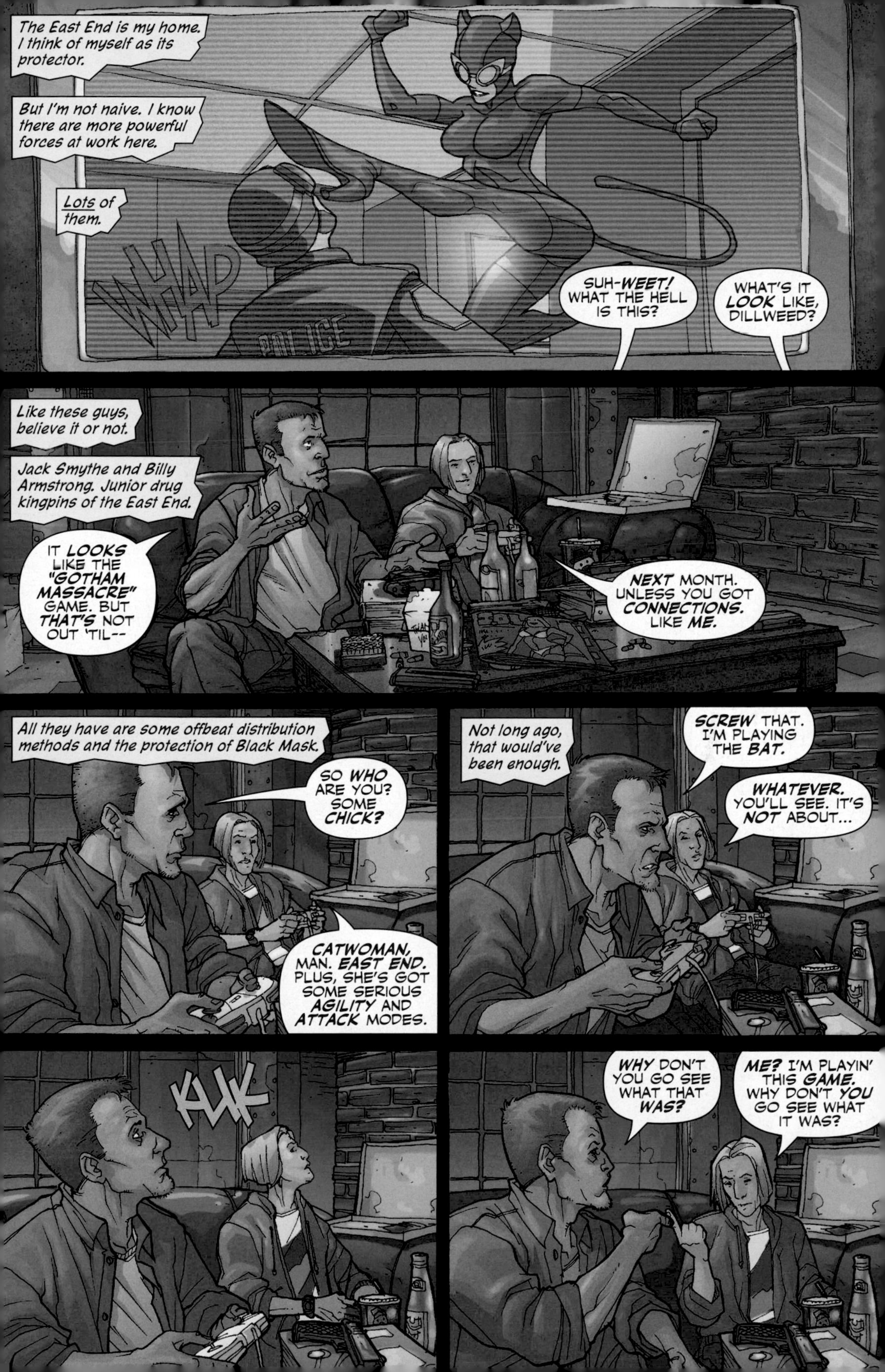
The East End is my home. I think of myself as its protector.
But I'm not naive. I know there are more powerful forces at work here.
Lots of them.
WHAP
SUH-WEET! WHAT THE HELL IS THIS?
WHAT'S IT LOOK LIKE, DILLWEED?
Like these guys, believe it or not.
Jack Smythe and Billy Armstrong. Junior drug kingpins of the East End.
IT LOOKS LIKE THE "GOTHAM MASSACRE" GAME. BUT THAT'S NOT OUT 'TIL--
NEXT MONTH. UNLESS YOU GOT CONNECTIONS. LIKE ME.
All they have are some offbeat distribution methods and the protection of Black Mask.
SO WHO ARE YOU? SOME CHICK?
CATWOMAN, MAN. EAST END. PLUS, SHE'S GOT SOME SERIOUS AGILITY AND ATTACK MODES.
Not long ago, that would've been enough.
SCREW THAT. I'M PLAYING THE BAT.
WHATEVER. YOU'LL SEE. IT'S NOT ABOUT...
KLIK
WHY DON'T YOU GO SEE WHAT THAT WAS?
ME? I'M PLAYIN' THIS GAME. WHY DON'T YOU GO SEE WHAT IT WAS?

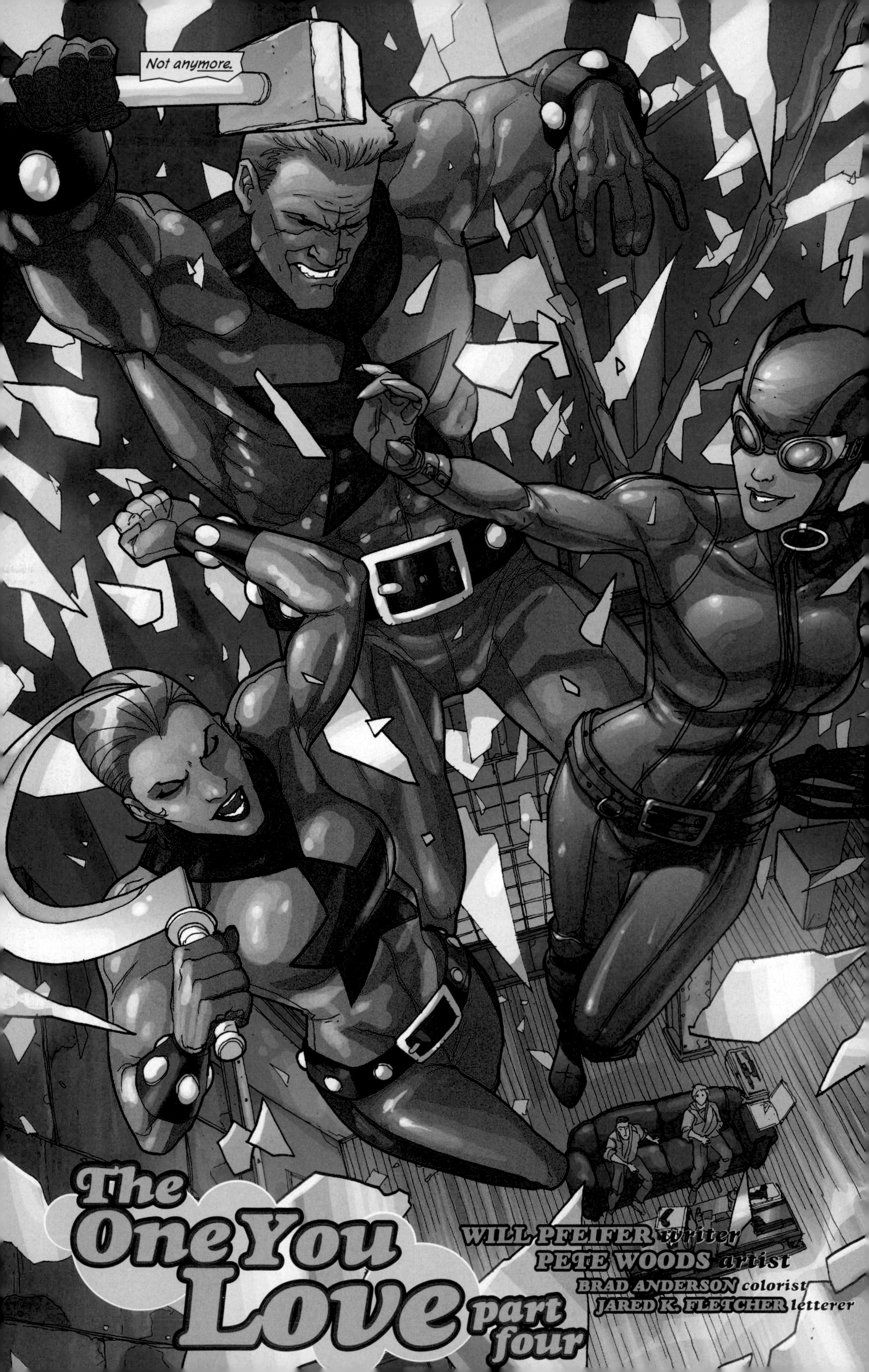
Not anymore.
The One You Love part four
WILL PFEIFER writer
PETE WOODS artist
BRAD ANDERSON colorist
JARED K. FLETCHER letterer

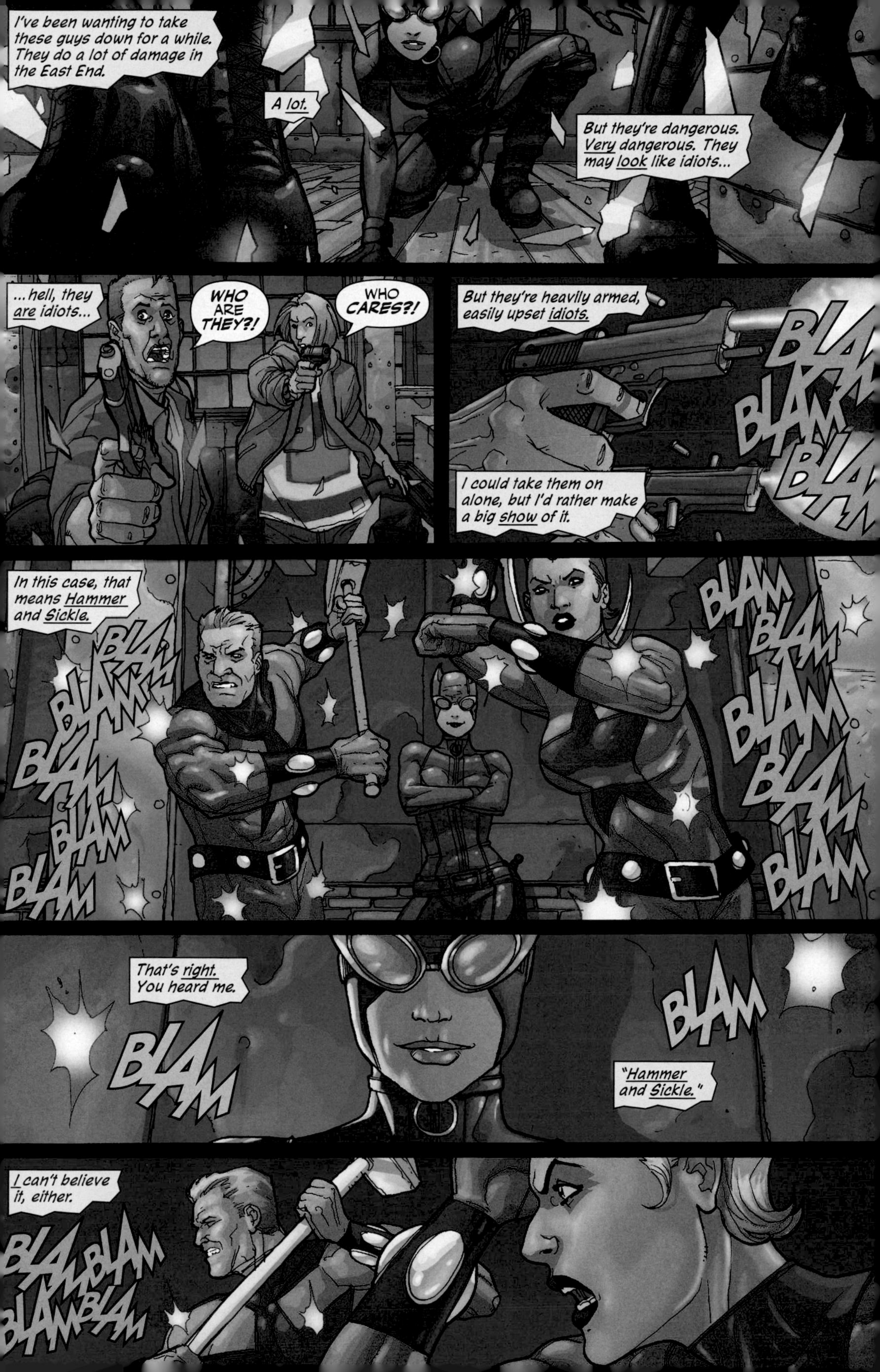
I've been wanting to take these guys down for a while. They do a lot of damage in the East End.
A lot.
But they're dangerous. Very dangerous. They may look like idiots...
...hell, they are idiots...
WHO ARE THEY?!
WHO CARES?!
But they're heavily armed, easily upset idiots.
BLAM BLAM BLAM BLAM
I could take them on alone, but I'd rather make a big show of it.
In this case, that means Hammer and Sickle.
BLAM BLAM BLAM BLAM BLAM
BLAM BLAM BLAM BLAM BLAM BLAM
That's right. You heard me.
BLAM
BLAM
"Hammer and Sickle."
I can't believe it, either.
BLAM BLAM BLAM BLAM

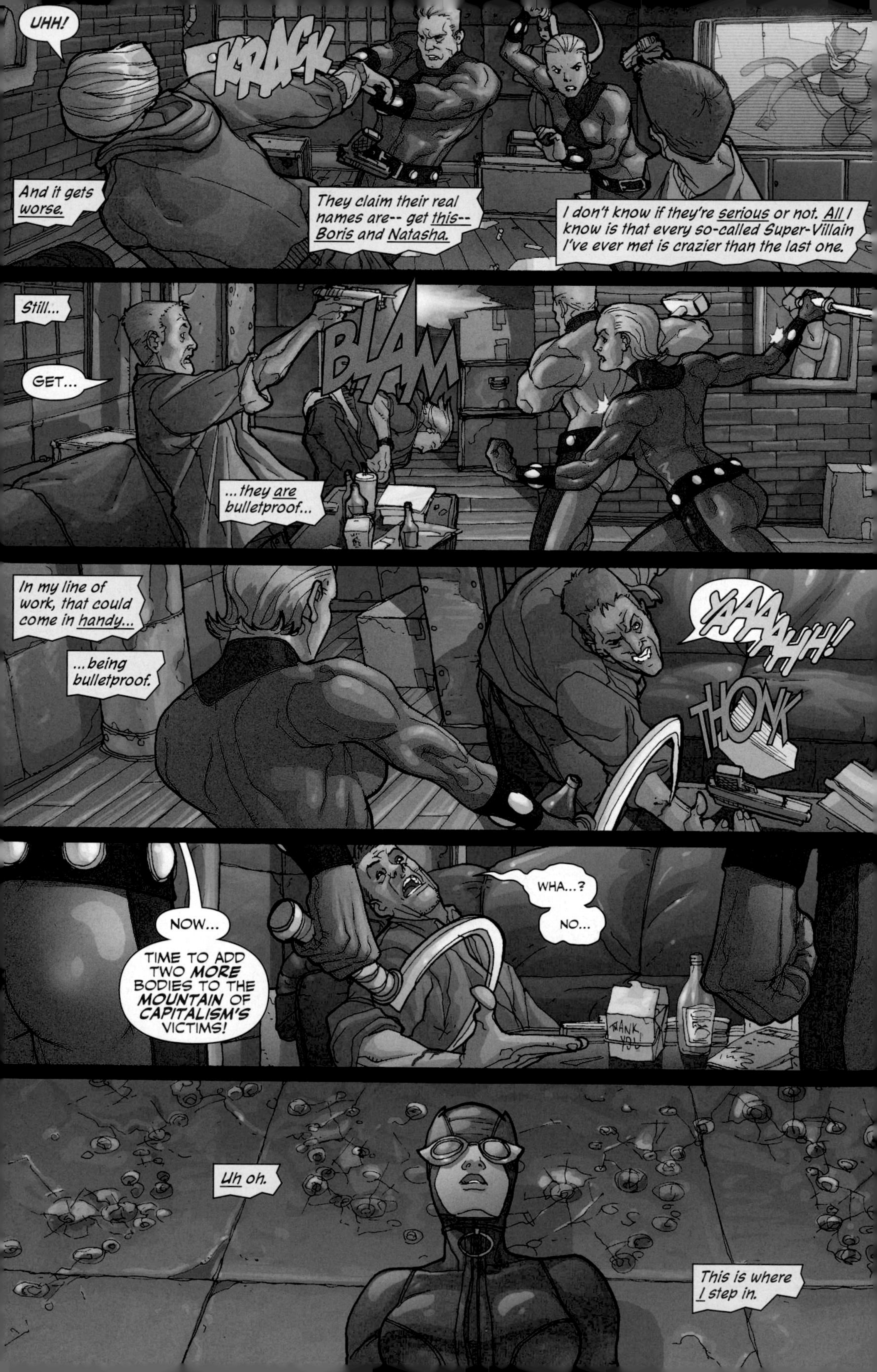
UHH!
KRACK
And it gets worse.
They claim their real names are-- get this-- Boris and Natasha.
I don't know if they're serious or not. All I know is that every so-called Super-Villain I've ever met is crazier than the last one.
Still...
GET...
BLAM
...they are bulletproof...
In my line of work, that could come in handy...
...being bulletproof.
YAAAAHH!
THONK
NOW...
TIME TO ADD TWO MORE BODIES TO THE MOUNTAIN OF CAPITALISM'S VICTIMS!
WHA...?
NO...
Uh oh.
This is where I step in.

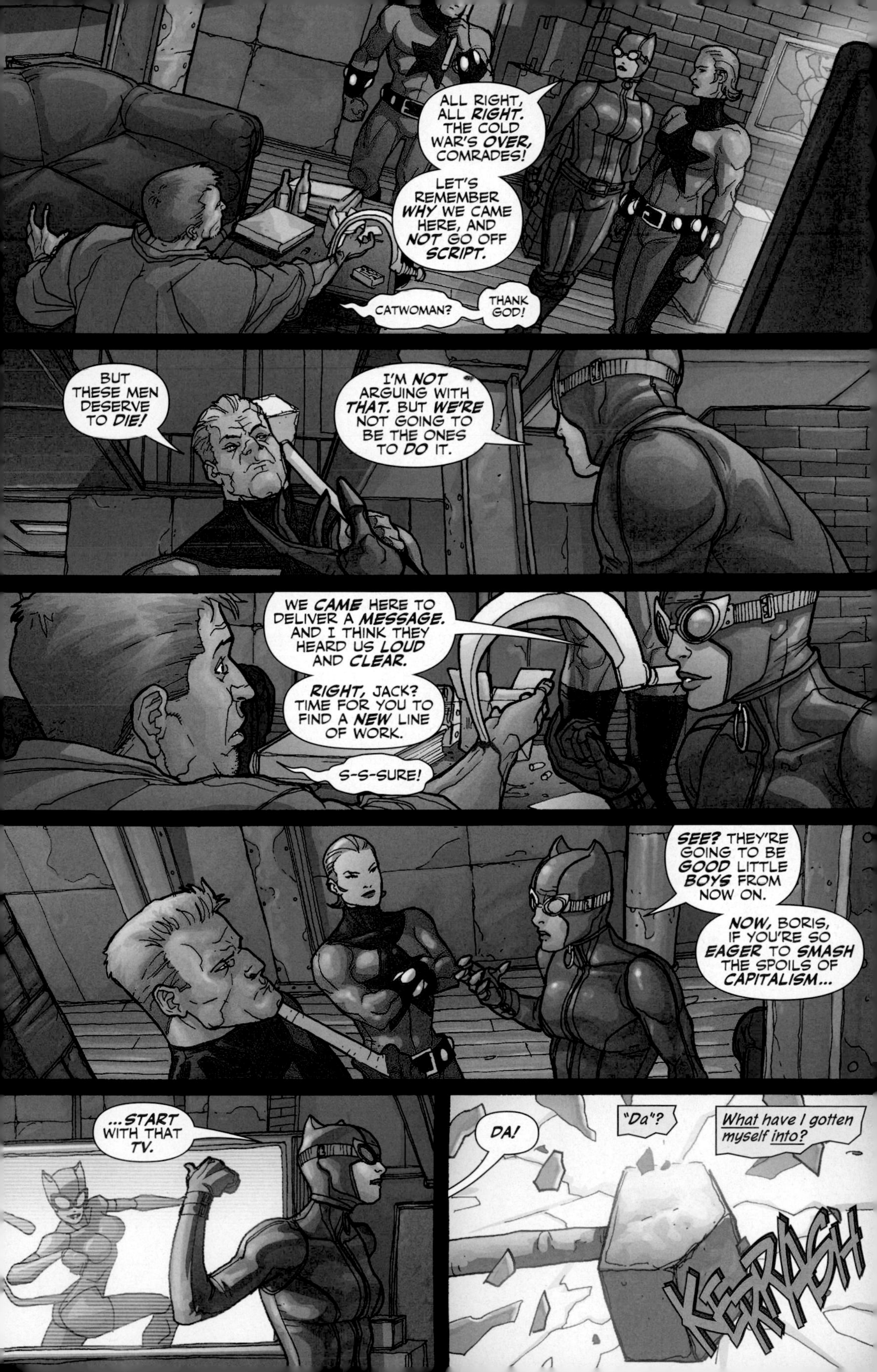
ALL RIGHT, ALL RIGHT. THE COLD WAR'S OVER, COMRADES!
LET'S REMEMBER WHY WE CAME HERE, AND NOT GO OFF SCRIPT.
CATWOMAN?
THANK GOD!
BUT THESE MEN DESERVE TO DIE!
I'M NOT ARGUING WITH THAT. BUT WE'RE NOT GOING TO BE THE ONES TO DO IT.
WE CAME HERE TO DELIVER A MESSAGE. AND I THINK THEY HEARD US LOUD AND CLEAR.
RIGHT, JACK? TIME FOR YOU TO FIND A NEW LINE OF WORK.
S-S-SURE!
SEE? THEY'RE GOING TO BE GOOD LITTLE BOYS FROM NOW ON.
NOW, BORIS, IF YOU'RE SO EAGER TO SMASH THE SPOILS OF CAPITALISM...
...START WITH THAT TV.
DA!
"Da"?
What have I gotten myself into?
KERRASH

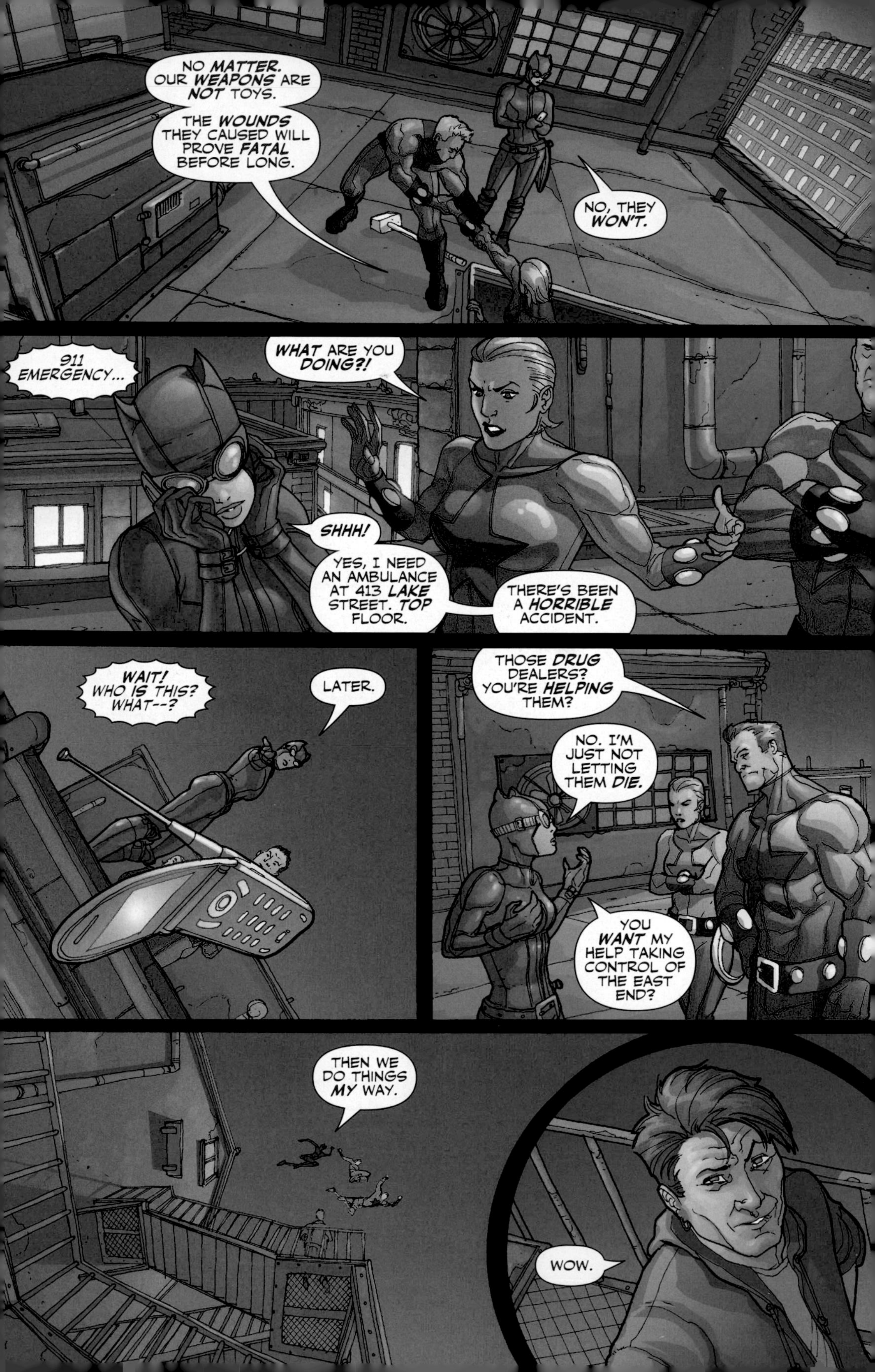
NO MATTER. OUR WEAPONS ARE NOT TOYS.
THE WOUNDS THEY CAUSED WILL PROVE FATAL BEFORE LONG.
NO, THEY WON'T.
911 EMERGENCY...
WHAT ARE YOU DOING?!
SHHH!
YES, I NEED AN AMBULANCE AT 413 LAKE STREET. TOP FLOOR.
THERE'S BEEN A HORRIBLE ACCIDENT.
WAIT! WHO IS THIS? WHAT--?
LATER.
THOSE DRUG DEALERS? YOU'RE HELPING THEM?
NO. I'M JUST NOT LETTING THEM DIE.
YOU WANT MY HELP TAKING CONTROL OF THE EAST END?
THEN WE DO THINGS MY WAY.
WOW.

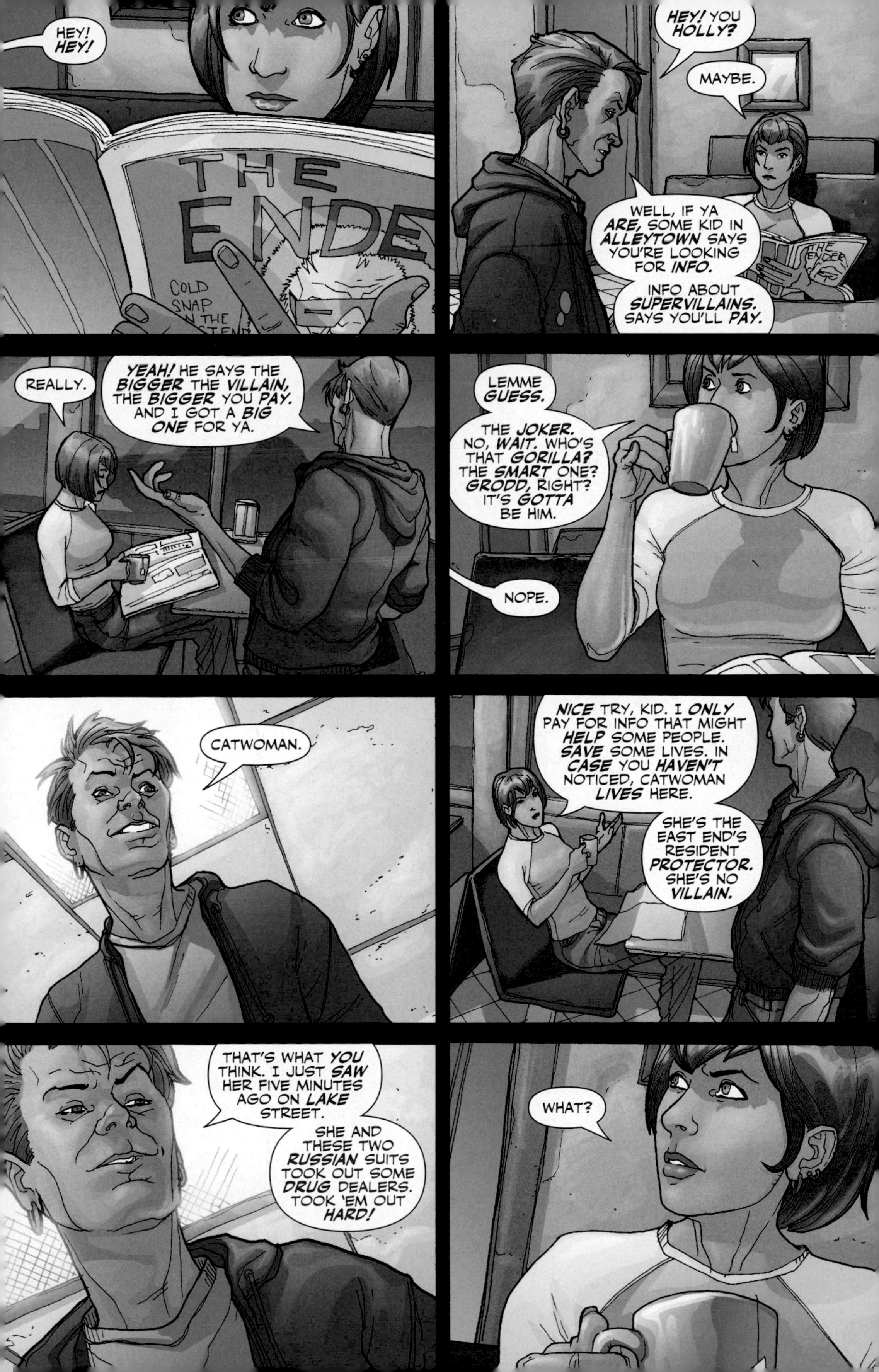
HEY! HEY!
THE ENDER
COLD SNAP
HEY! YOU HOLLY?
MAYBE.
WELL, IF YA ARE, SOME KID IN ALLEYTOWN SAYS YOU'RE LOOKING FOR INFO.
INFO ABOUT SUPERVILLAINS. SAYS YOU'LL PAY.
REALLY.
YEAH! HE SAYS THE BIGGER THE VILLAIN, THE BIGGER YOU PAY. AND I GOT A BIG ONE FOR YA.
LEMME GUESS.
THE JOKER. NO, WAIT. WHO'S THAT GORILLA? THE SMART ONE? GRODD, RIGHT? IT'S GOTTA BE HIM.
NOPE.
CATWOMAN.
NICE TRY, KID. I ONLY PAY FOR INFO THAT MIGHT HELP SOME PEOPLE. SAVE SOME LIVES. IN CASE YOU HAVEN'T NOTICED, CATWOMAN LIVES HERE.
SHE'S THE EAST END'S RESIDENT PROTECTOR. SHE'S NO VILLAIN.
THAT'S WHAT YOU THINK. I JUST SAW HER FIVE MINUTES AGO ON LAKE STREET.
SHE AND THESE TWO RUSSIAN SUITS TOOK OUT SOME DRUG DEALERS. TOOK 'EM OUT HARD!
WHAT?

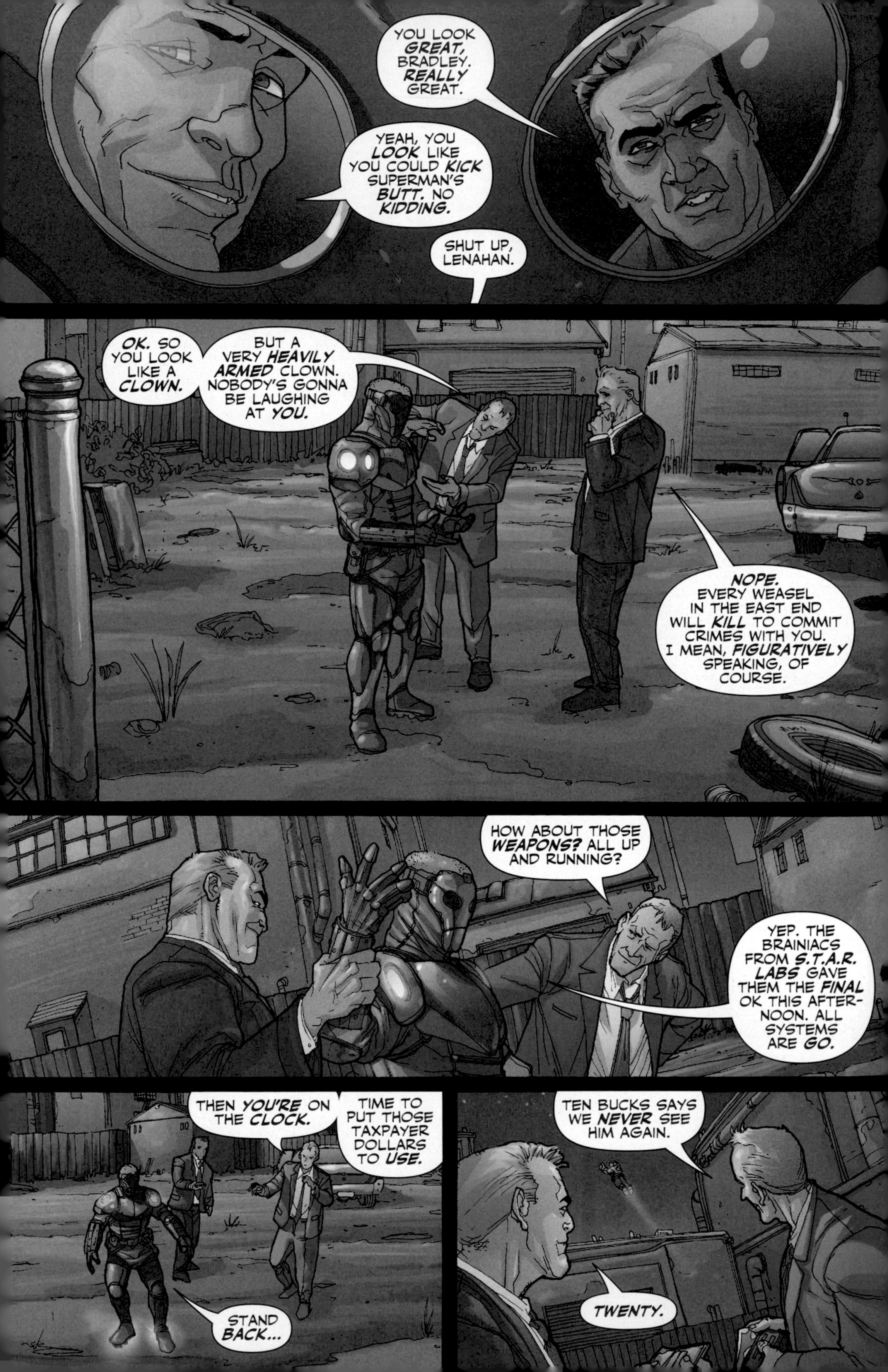
YOU LOOK GREAT, BRADLEY. REALLY GREAT.
YEAH, YOU LOOK LIKE YOU COULD KICK SUPERMAN'S BUTT. NO KIDDING.
SHUT UP, LENAHAN.
OK. SO YOU LOOK LIKE A CLOWN.
BUT A VERY HEAVILY ARMED CLOWN. NOBODY'S GONNA BE LAUGHING AT YOU.
NOPE. EVERY WEASEL IN THE EAST END WILL KILL TO COMMIT CRIMES WITH YOU. I MEAN, FIGURATIVELY SPEAKING, OF COURSE.
HOW ABOUT THOSE WEAPONS? ALL UP AND RUNNING?
YEP. THE BRAINIACS FROM S.T.A.R. LABS GAVE THEM THE FINAL OK THIS AFTER-NOON. ALL SYSTEMS ARE GO.
THEN YOU'RE ON THE CLOCK.
TIME TO PUT THOSE TAXPAYER DOLLARS TO USE.
STAND BACK...
TEN BUCKS SAYS WE NEVER SEE HIM AGAIN.
TWENTY.

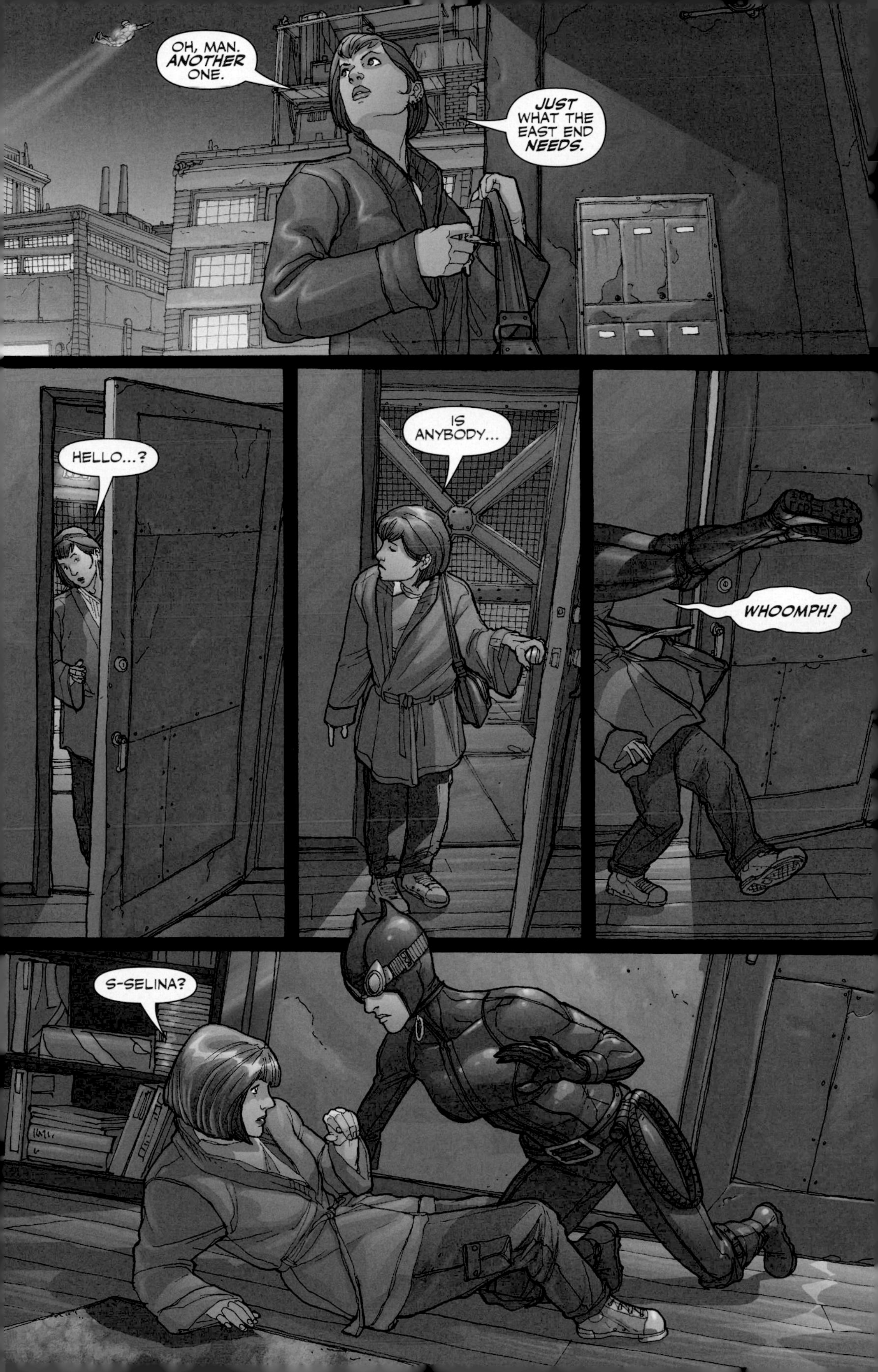
OH, MAN. ANOTHER ONE.
JUST WHAT THE EAST END NEEDS.
HELLO...?
IS ANYBODY...
WHOOMPH!
S-SELINA?

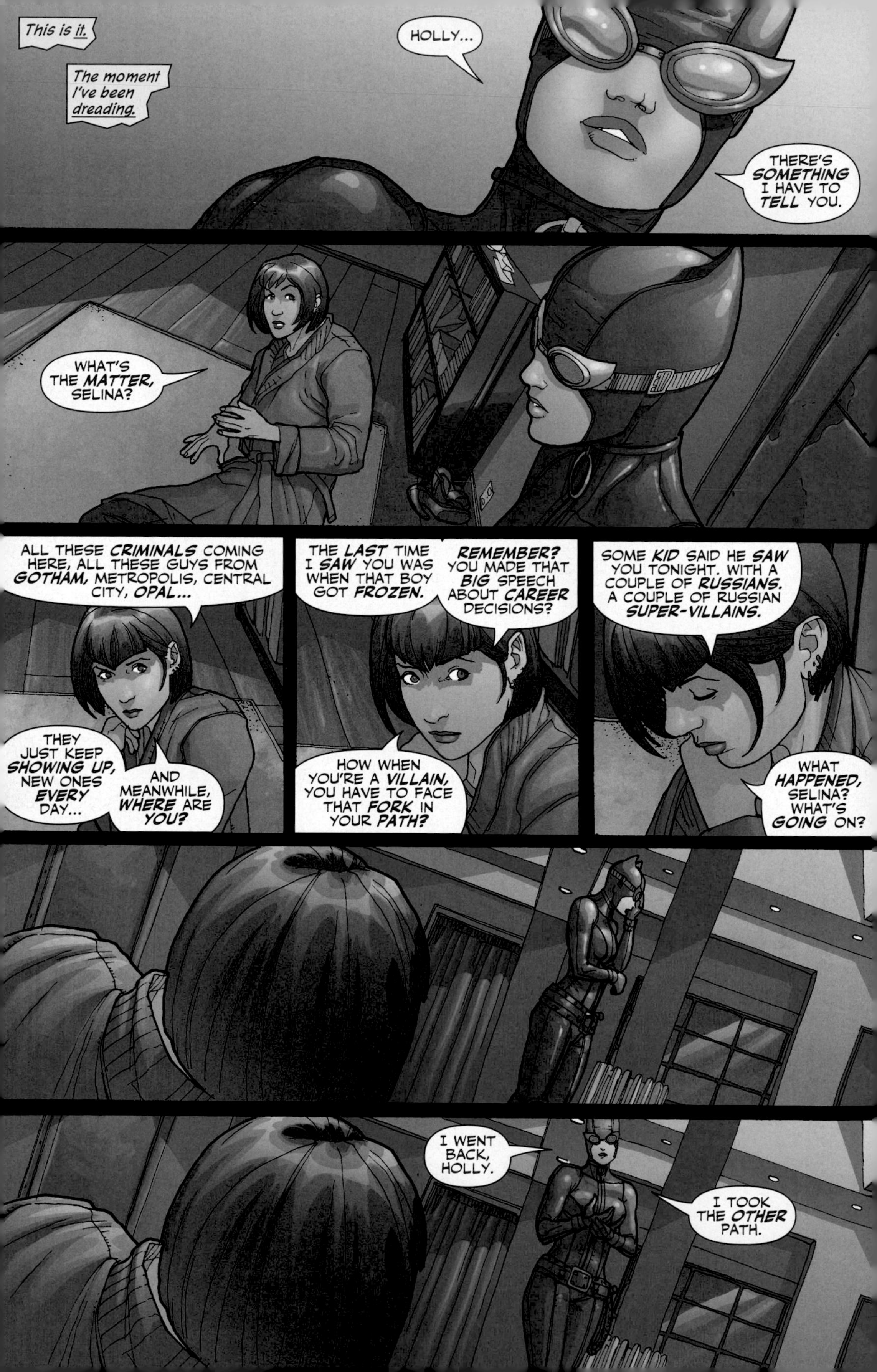
This is it.
The moment I've been dreading.
HOLLY...
THERE'S SOMETHING I HAVE TO TELL YOU.
WHAT'S THE MATTER, SELINA?
ALL THESE CRIMINALS COMING HERE, ALL THESE GUYS FROM GOTHAM, METROPOLIS, CENTRAL CITY, OPAL...
THEY JUST KEEP SHOWING UP, NEW ONES EVERY DAY...
AND MEANWHILE, WHERE ARE YOU?
THE LAST TIME I SAW YOU WAS WHEN THAT BOY GOT FROZEN.
REMEMBER? YOU MADE THAT BIG SPEECH ABOUT CAREER DECISIONS?
HOW WHEN YOU'RE A VILLAIN, YOU HAVE TO FACE THAT FORK IN YOUR PATH?
SOME KID SAID HE SAW YOU TONIGHT. WITH A COUPLE OF RUSSIANS. A COUPLE OF RUSSIAN SUPER-VILLAINS.
WHAT HAPPENED, SELINA? WHAT'S GOING ON?
I WENT BACK, HOLLY.
I TOOK THE OTHER PATH.

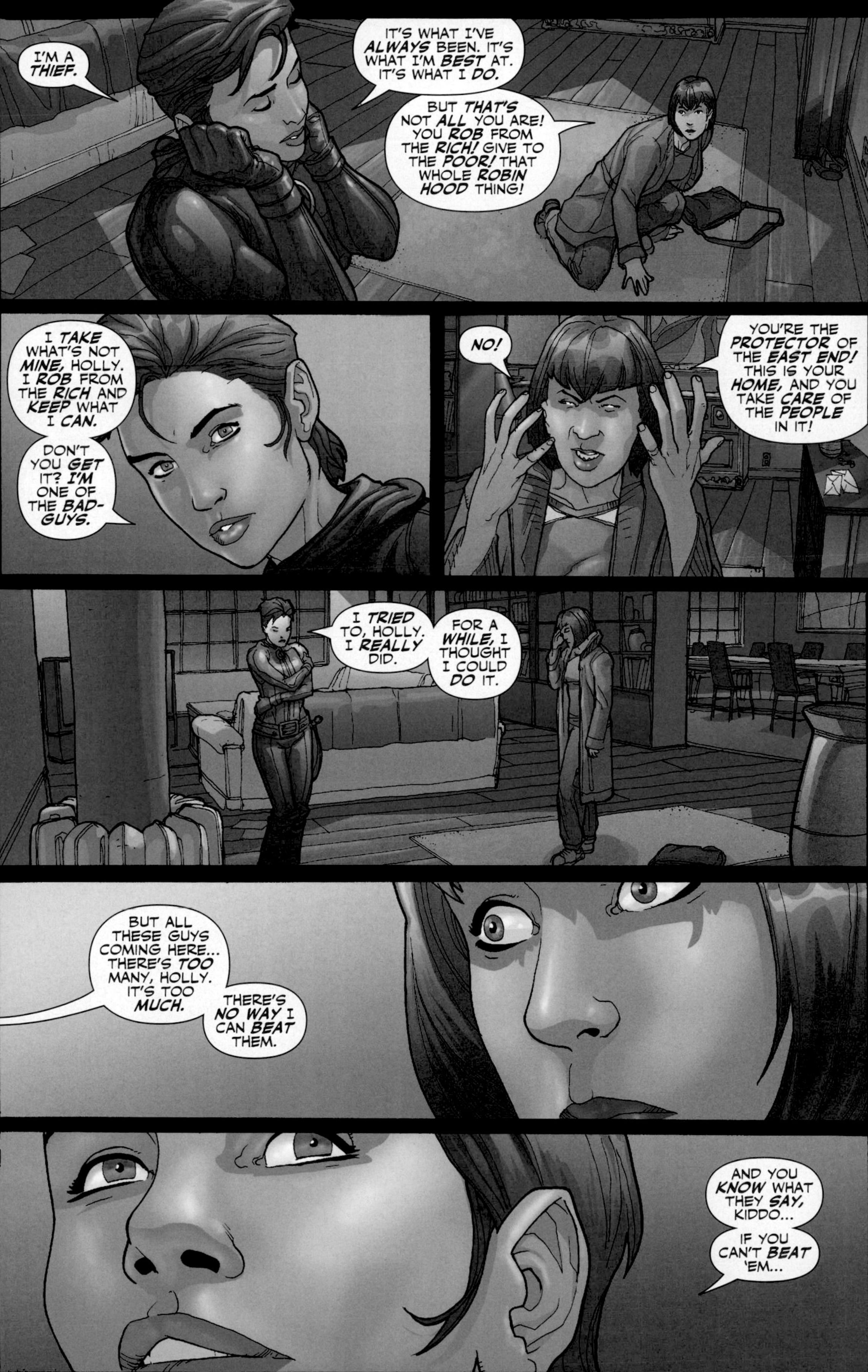
I'M A THIEF.
IT'S WHAT I'VE ALWAYS BEEN. IT'S WHAT I'M BEST AT. IT'S WHAT I DO.
BUT THAT'S NOT ALL YOU ARE! YOU ROB FROM THE RICH! GIVE TO THE POOR! THAT WHOLE ROBIN HOOD THING!
I TAKE WHAT'S NOT MINE, HOLLY. I ROB FROM THE RICH AND KEEP WHAT I CAN.
DON'T YOU GET IT? I'M ONE OF THE BAD-GUYS.
NO!
YOU'RE THE PROTECTOR OF THE EAST END! THIS IS YOUR HOME, AND YOU TAKE CARE OF THE PEOPLE IN IT!
I TRIED TO, HOLLY. I REALLY DID.
FOR A WHILE, I THOUGHT I COULD DO IT.
BUT ALL THESE GUYS COMING HERE... THERE'S TOO MANY, HOLLY. IT'S TOO MUCH.
THERE'S NO WAY I CAN BEAT THEM.
AND YOU KNOW WHAT THEY SAY, KIDDO...
IF YOU CAN'T BEAT 'EM...

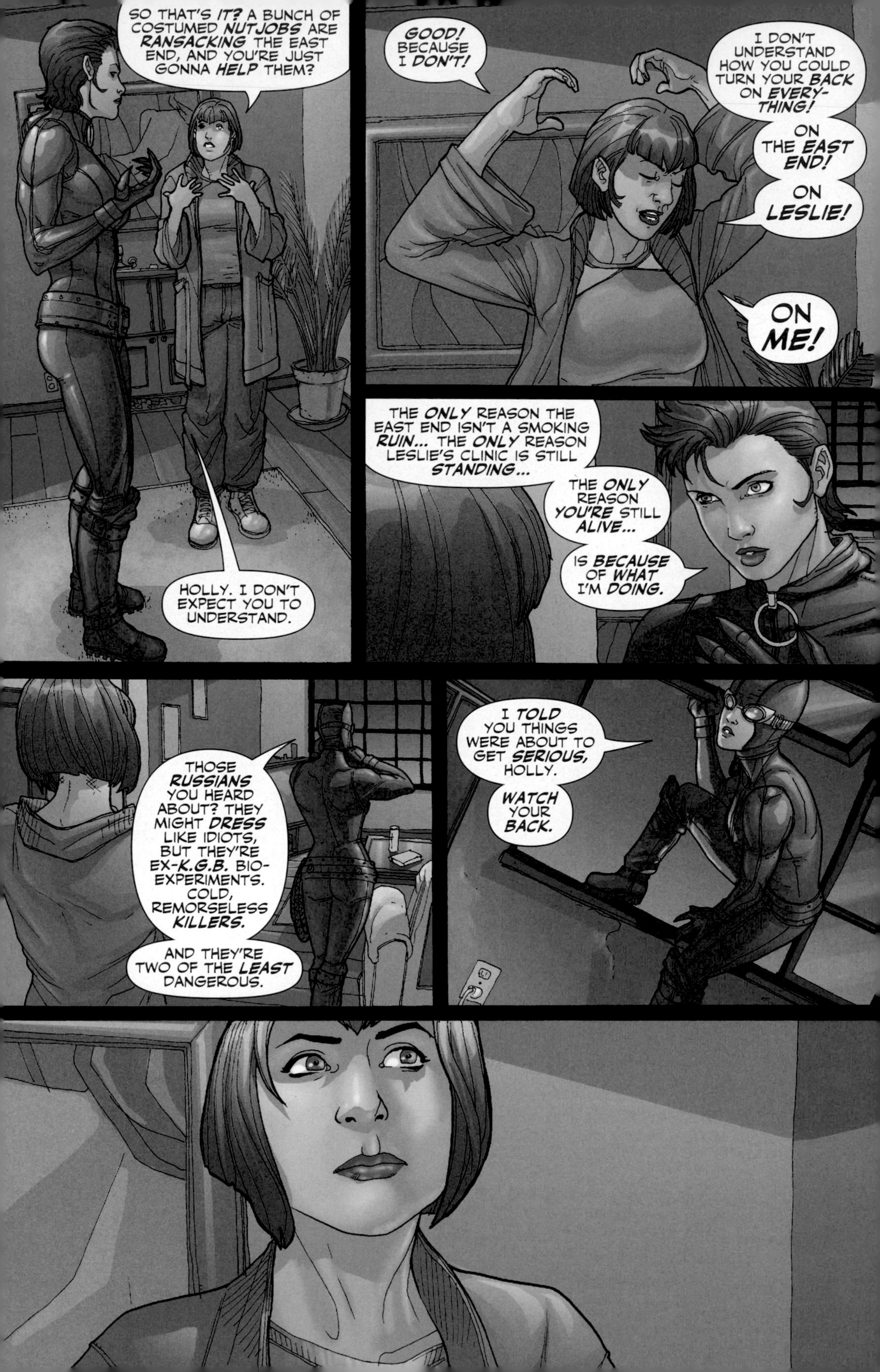
SO THAT'S IT? A BUNCH OF COSTUMED NUTJOBS ARE RANSACKING THE EAST END, AND YOU'RE JUST GONNA HELP THEM?
HOLLY. I DON'T EXPECT YOU TO UNDERSTAND.
GOOD! BECAUSE I DON'T!
I DON'T UNDERSTAND HOW YOU COULD TURN YOUR BACK ON EVERY-THING!
ON THE EAST END!
ON LESLIE!
ON ME!
THE ONLY REASON THE EAST END ISN'T A SMOKING RUIN... THE ONLY REASON LESLIE'S CLINIC IS STILL STANDING...
THE ONLY REASON YOU'RE STILL ALIVE...
IS BECAUSE OF WHAT I'M DOING.
THOSE RUSSIANS YOU HEARD ABOUT? THEY MIGHT DRESS LIKE IDIOTS, BUT THEY'RE EX-K.G.B. BIO-EXPERIMENTS. COLD, REMORSELESS KILLERS.
AND THEY'RE TWO OF THE LEAST DANGEROUS.
I TOLD YOU THINGS WERE ABOUT TO GET SERIOUS, HOLLY.
WATCH YOUR BACK.

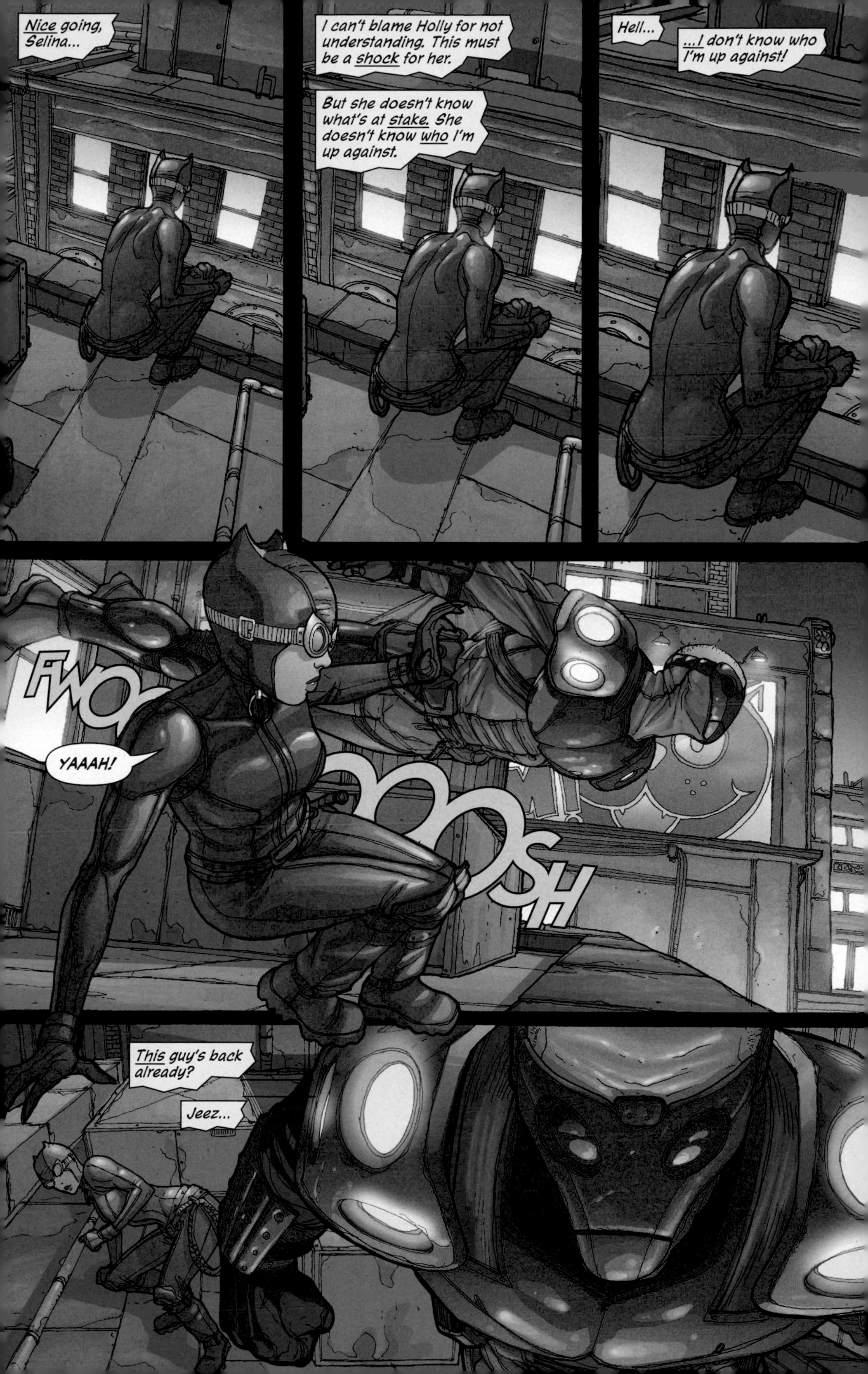
Nice going, Selina...
I can't blame Holly for not understanding. This must be a shock for her.
But she doesn't know what's at stake. She doesn't know who I'm up against.
Hell...
...I don't know who I'm up against!
FWOOOOOSH
YAAAH!
This guy's back already?
Jeez...

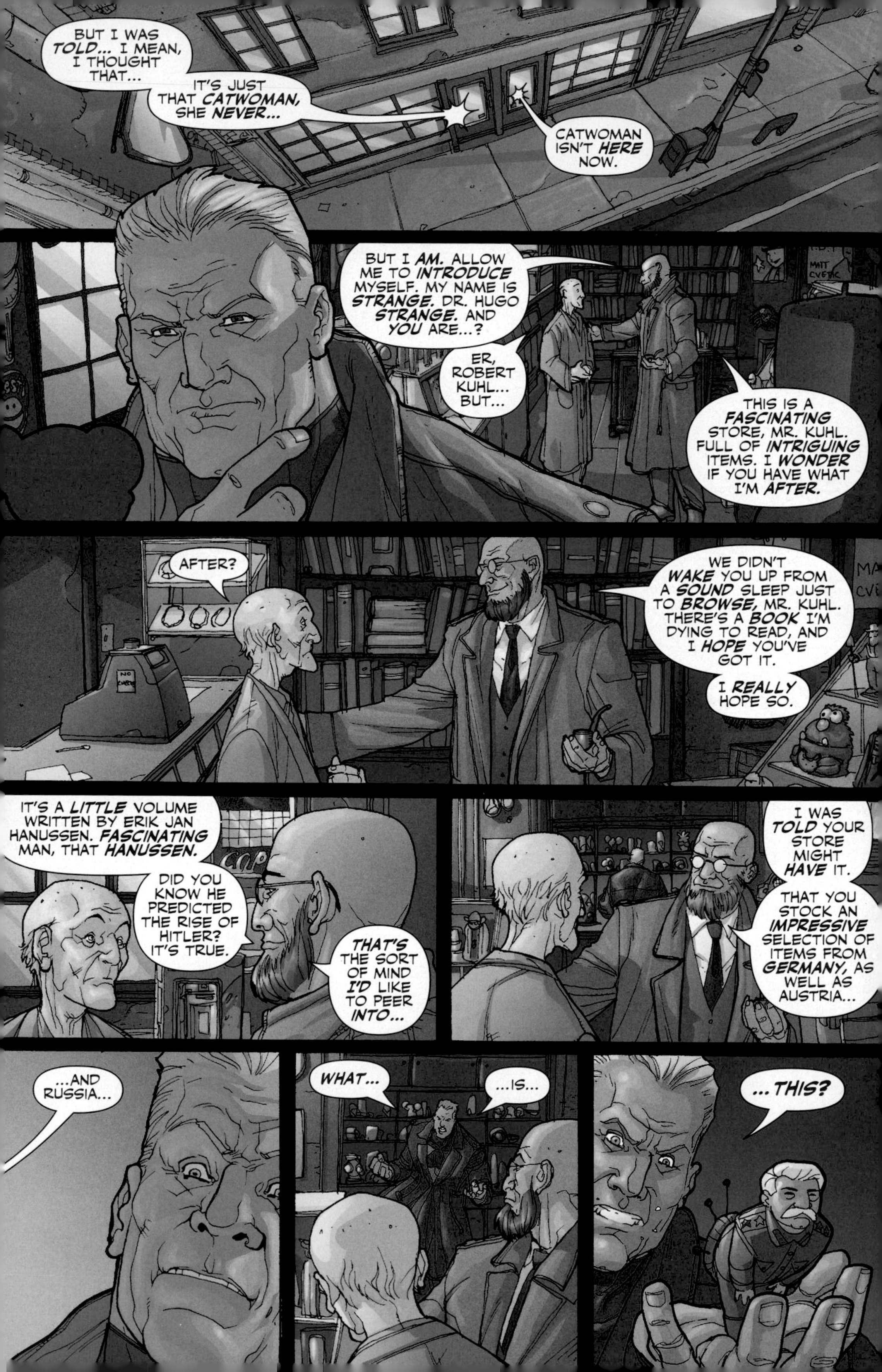

BUT I WAS TOLD... I MEAN, I THOUGHT THAT...
IT'S JUST THAT CATWOMAN, SHE NEVER...
CATWOMAN ISN'T HERE NOW.
BUT I AM. ALLOW ME TO INTRODUCE MYSELF. MY NAME IS STRANGE. DR. HUGO STRANGE. AND YOU ARE...?
ER, ROBERT KUHL... BUT...
THIS IS A FASCINATING STORE, MR. KUHL. FULL OF INTRIGUING ITEMS. I WONDER IF YOU HAVE WHAT I'M AFTER.
AFTER?
WE DIDN'T WAKE YOU UP FROM A SOUND SLEEP JUST TO BROWSE, MR. KUHL. THERE'S A BOOK I'M DYING TO READ, AND I HOPE YOU'VE GOT IT.
I REALLY HOPE SO.
IT'S A LITTLE VOLUME WRITTEN BY ERIK JAN HANUSSEN. FASCINATING MAN, THAT HANUSSEN.
DID YOU KNOW HE PREDICTED THE RISE OF HITLER? IT'S TRUE.
THAT'S THE SORT OF MIND I'D LIKE TO PEER INTO...
I WAS TOLD YOUR STORE MIGHT HAVE IT.
THAT YOU STOCK AN IMPRESSIVE SELECTION OF ITEMS FROM GERMANY, AS WELL AS AUSTRIA...
...AND RUSSIA...
WHAT...
...IS...
...THIS?

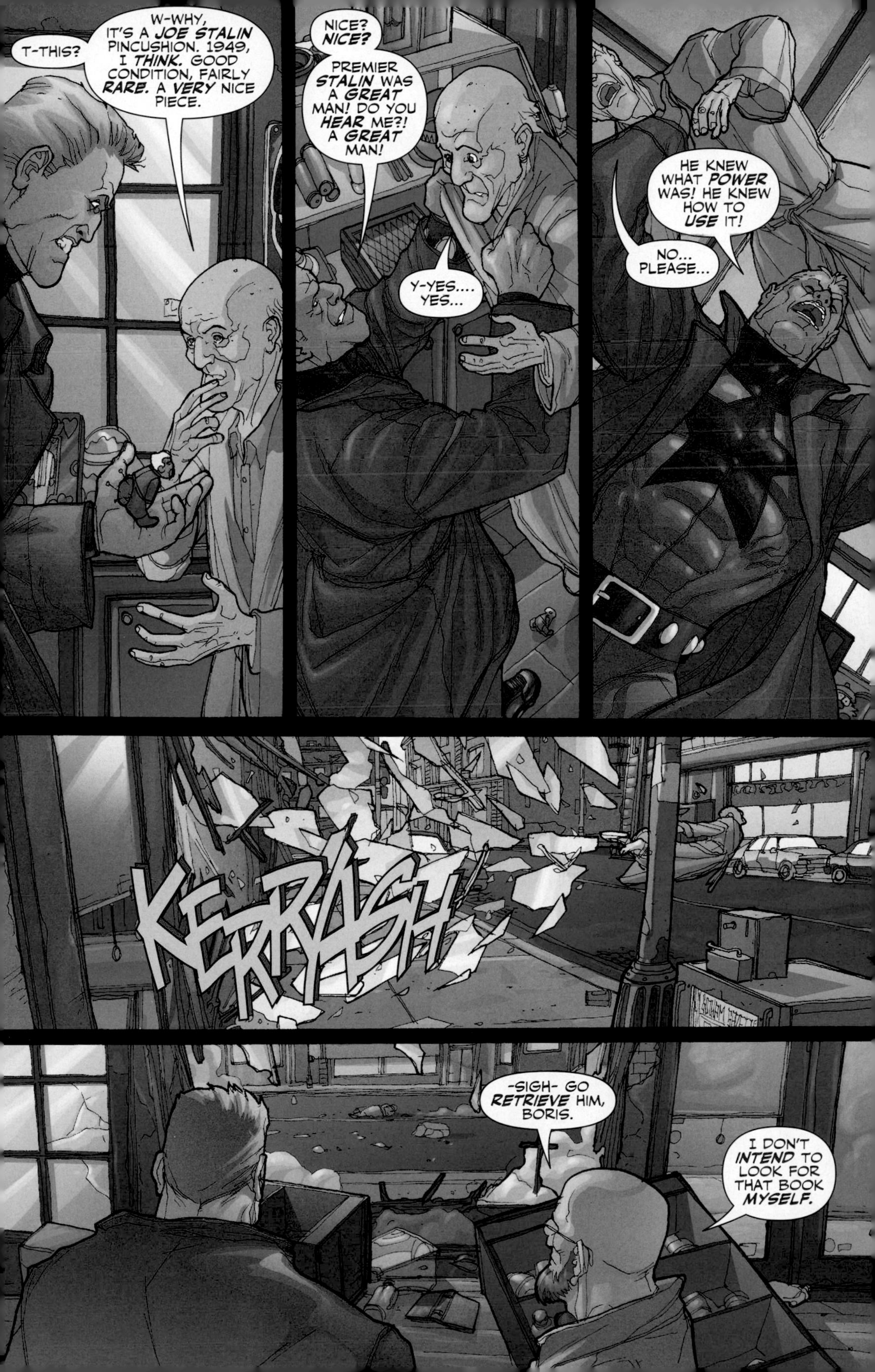
T-THIS?
W-WHY, IT'S A JOE STALIN PINCUSHION. 1949, I THINK. GOOD CONDITION, FAIRLY RARE. A VERY NICE PIECE.
NICE? NICE?
PREMIER STALIN WAS A GREAT MAN! DO YOU HEAR ME?! A GREAT MAN!
Y-YES.... YES...
HE KNEW WHAT POWER WAS! HE KNEW HOW TO USE IT!
NO... PLEASE...
KERRASH
-SIGH- GO RETRIEVE HIM, BORIS.
I DON'T INTEND TO LOOK FOR THAT BOOK MYSELF.

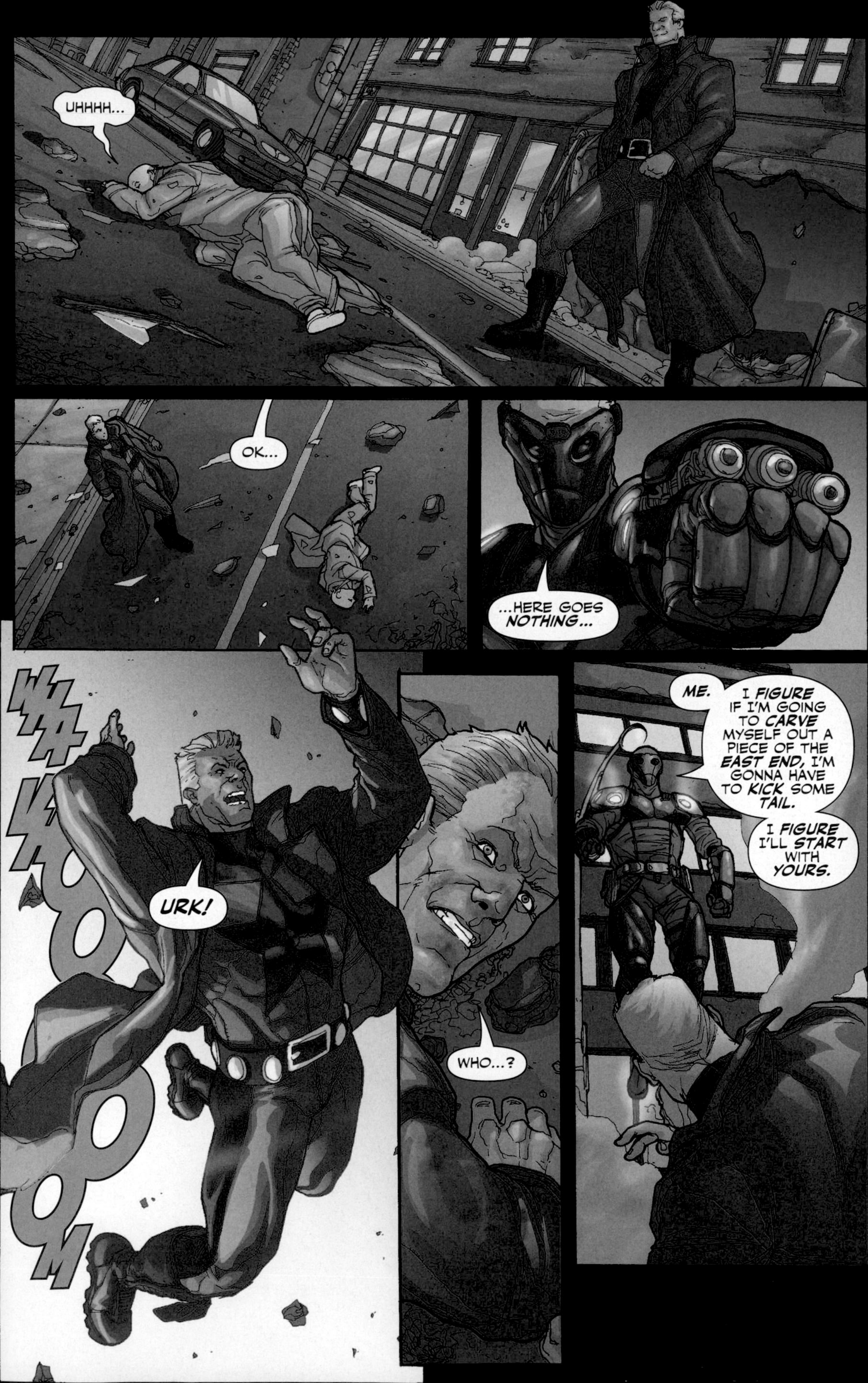
UHHHH...
OK...
...HERE GOES NOTHING...
WHAKOOOOOM
URK!
WHO...?
ME.
I FIGURE IF I'M GOING TO CARVE MYSELF OUT A PIECE OF THE EAST END, I'M GONNA HAVE TO KICK SOME TAIL.
I FIGURE I'LL START WITH YOURS.

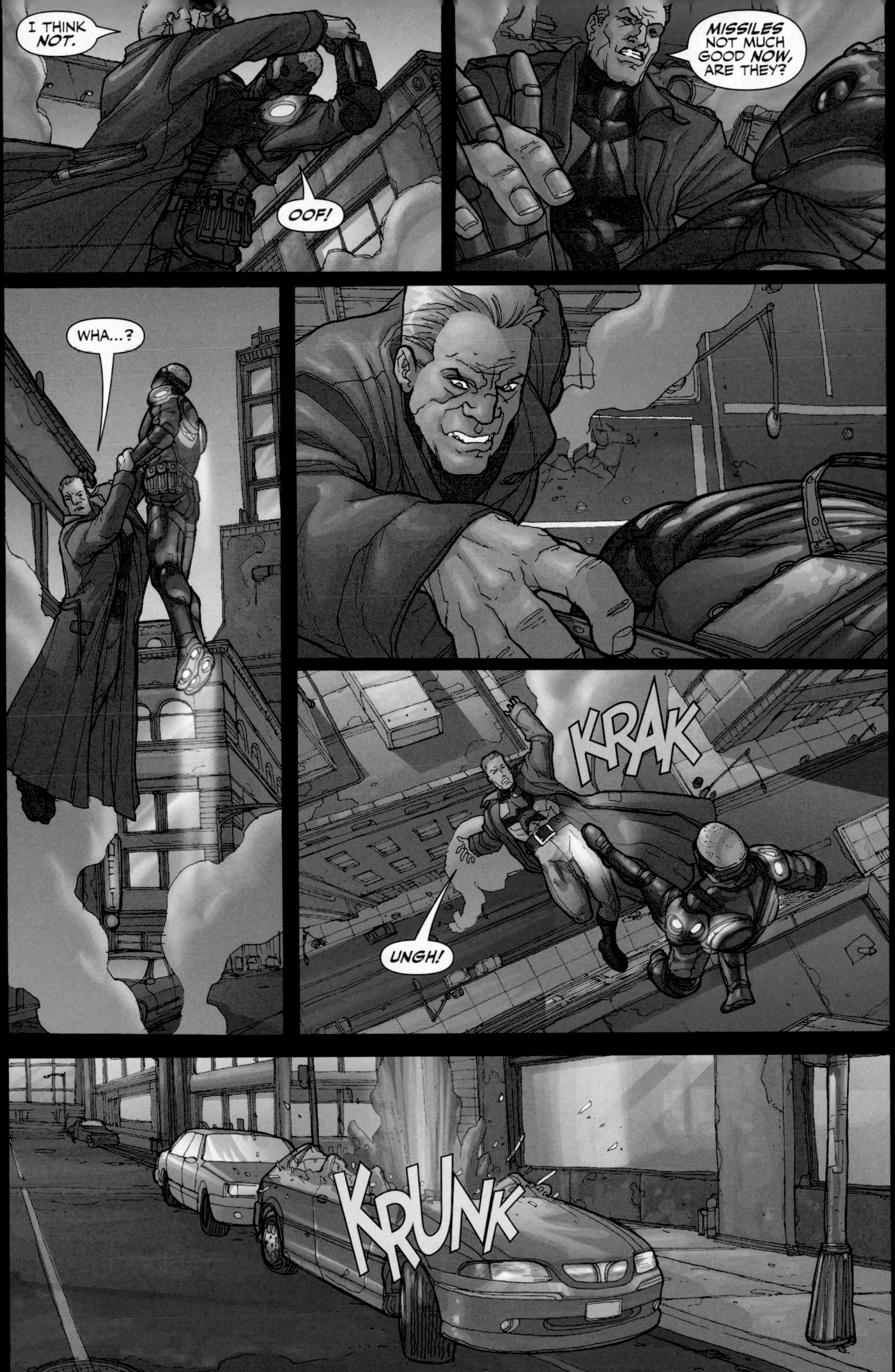
I THINK NOT.
OOF!
MISSILES NOT MUCH GOOD NOW, ARE THEY?
WHA...?
KRAK
UNGH!
KRUNK

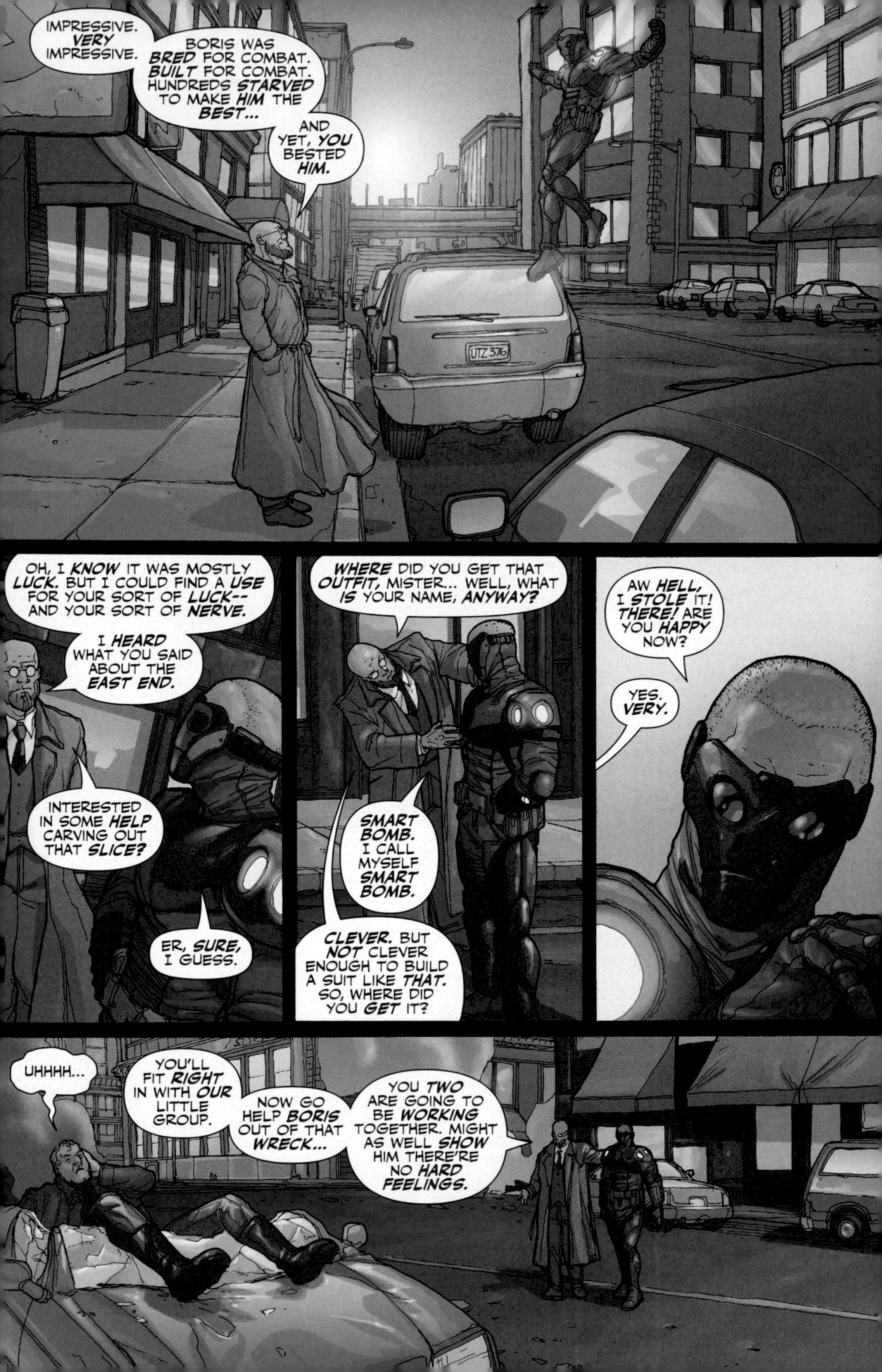

IMPRESSIVE. VERY IMPRESSIVE.
BORIS WAS BRED FOR COMBAT. BUILT FOR COMBAT. HUNDREDS STARVED TO MAKE HIM THE BEST...
AND YET, YOU BESTED HIM.
UTZ 376
OH, I KNOW IT WAS MOSTLY LUCK. BUT I COULD FIND A USE FOR YOUR SORT OF LUCK-- AND YOUR SORT OF NERVE.
I HEARD WHAT YOU SAID ABOUT THE EAST END.
INTERESTED IN SOME HELP CARVING OUT THAT SLICE?
ER, SURE, I GUESS.
WHERE DID YOU GET THAT OUTFIT, MISTER... WELL, WHAT IS YOUR NAME, ANYWAY?
SMART BOMB. I CALL MYSELF SMART BOMB.
CLEVER. BUT NOT CLEVER ENOUGH TO BUILD A SUIT LIKE THAT. SO, WHERE DID YOU GET IT?
AW HELL, I STOLE IT! THERE! ARE YOU HAPPY NOW?
YES. VERY.
UHHHH...
YOU'LL FIT RIGHT IN WITH OUR LITTLE GROUP.
NOW GO HELP BORIS OUT OF THAT WRECK...
YOU TWO ARE GOING TO BE WORKING TOGETHER. MIGHT AS WELL SHOW HIM THERE'RE NO HARD FEELINGS.

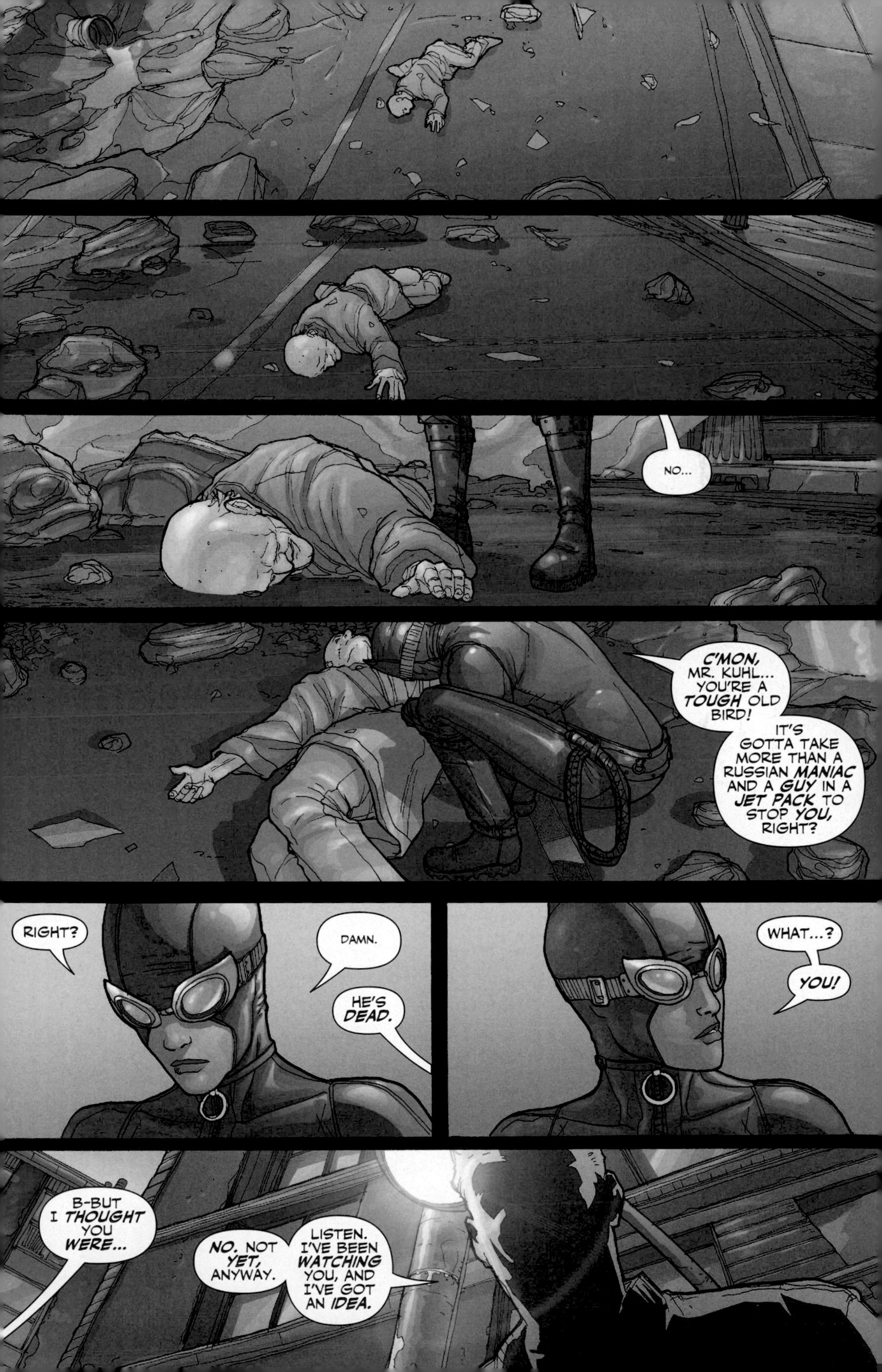
NO...
C'MON, MR. KUHL... YOU'RE A TOUGH OLD BIRD!
IT'S GOTTA TAKE MORE THAN A RUSSIAN MANIAC AND A GUY IN A JET PACK TO STOP YOU, RIGHT?
RIGHT?
DAMN.
HE'S DEAD.
WHAT...?
YOU!
B-BUT I THOUGHT YOU WERE...
NO. NOT YET, ANYWAY.
LISTEN. I'VE BEEN WATCHING YOU, AND I'VE GOT AN IDEA.

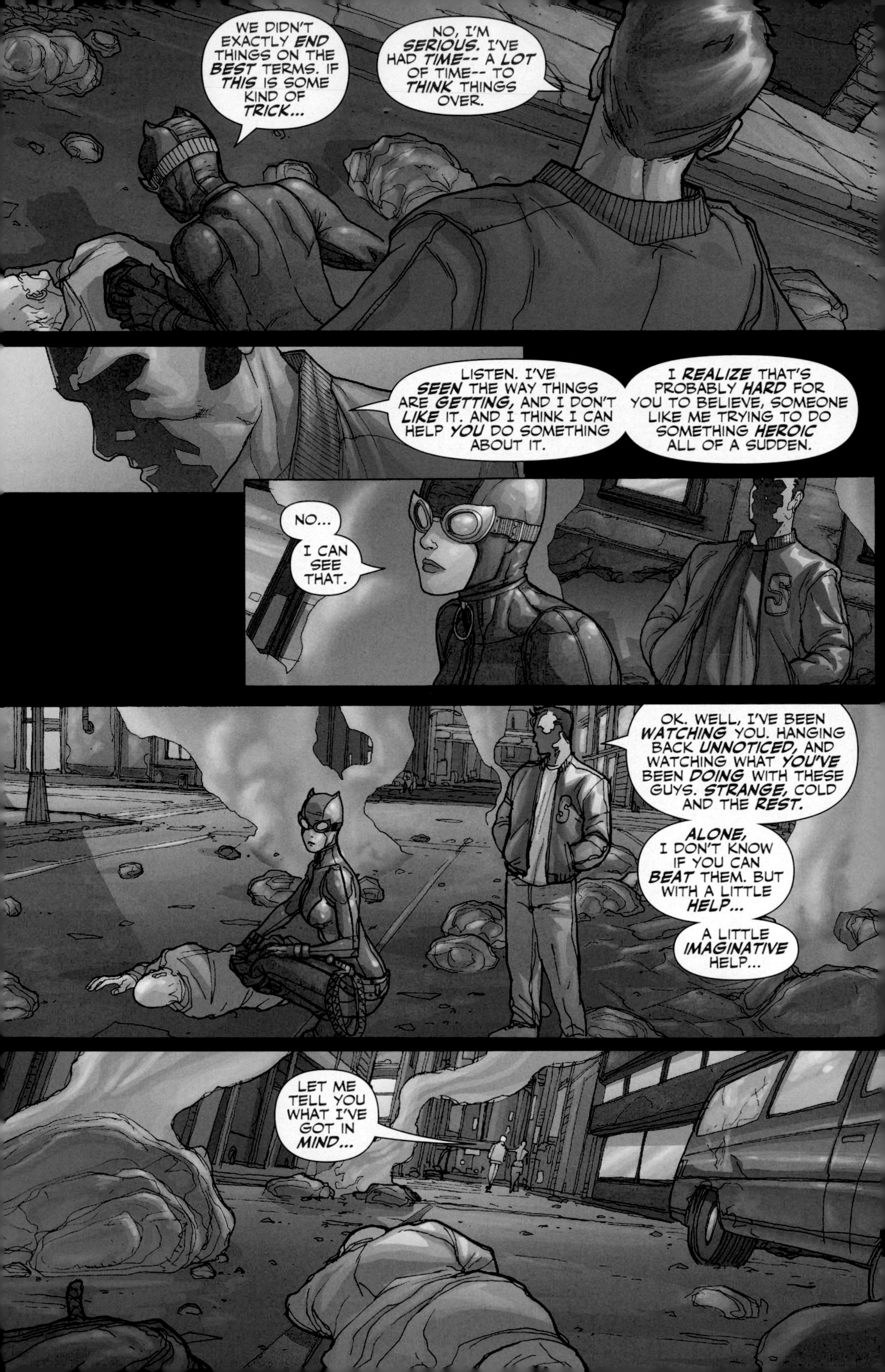

WE DIDN'T EXACTLY END THINGS ON THE BEST TERMS. IF THIS IS SOME KIND OF TRICK...
NO, I'M SERIOUS. I'VE HAD TIME-- A LOT OF TIME-- TO THINK THINGS OVER.
LISTEN. I'VE SEEN THE WAY THINGS ARE GETTING, AND I DON'T LIKE IT. AND I THINK I CAN HELP YOU DO SOMETHING ABOUT IT.
I REALIZE THAT'S PROBABLY HARD FOR YOU TO BELIEVE, SOMEONE LIKE ME TRYING TO DO SOMETHING HEROIC ALL OF A SUDDEN.
NO...
I CAN SEE THAT.
OK. WELL, I'VE BEEN WATCHING YOU. HANGING BACK UNNOTICED, AND WATCHING WHAT YOU'VE BEEN DOING WITH THESE GUYS. STRANGE, COLD AND THE REST.
ALONE, I DON'T KNOW IF YOU CAN BEAT THEM. BUT WITH A LITTLE HELP...
A LITTLE IMAGINATIVE HELP...
LET ME TELL YOU WHAT I'VE GOT IN MIND...

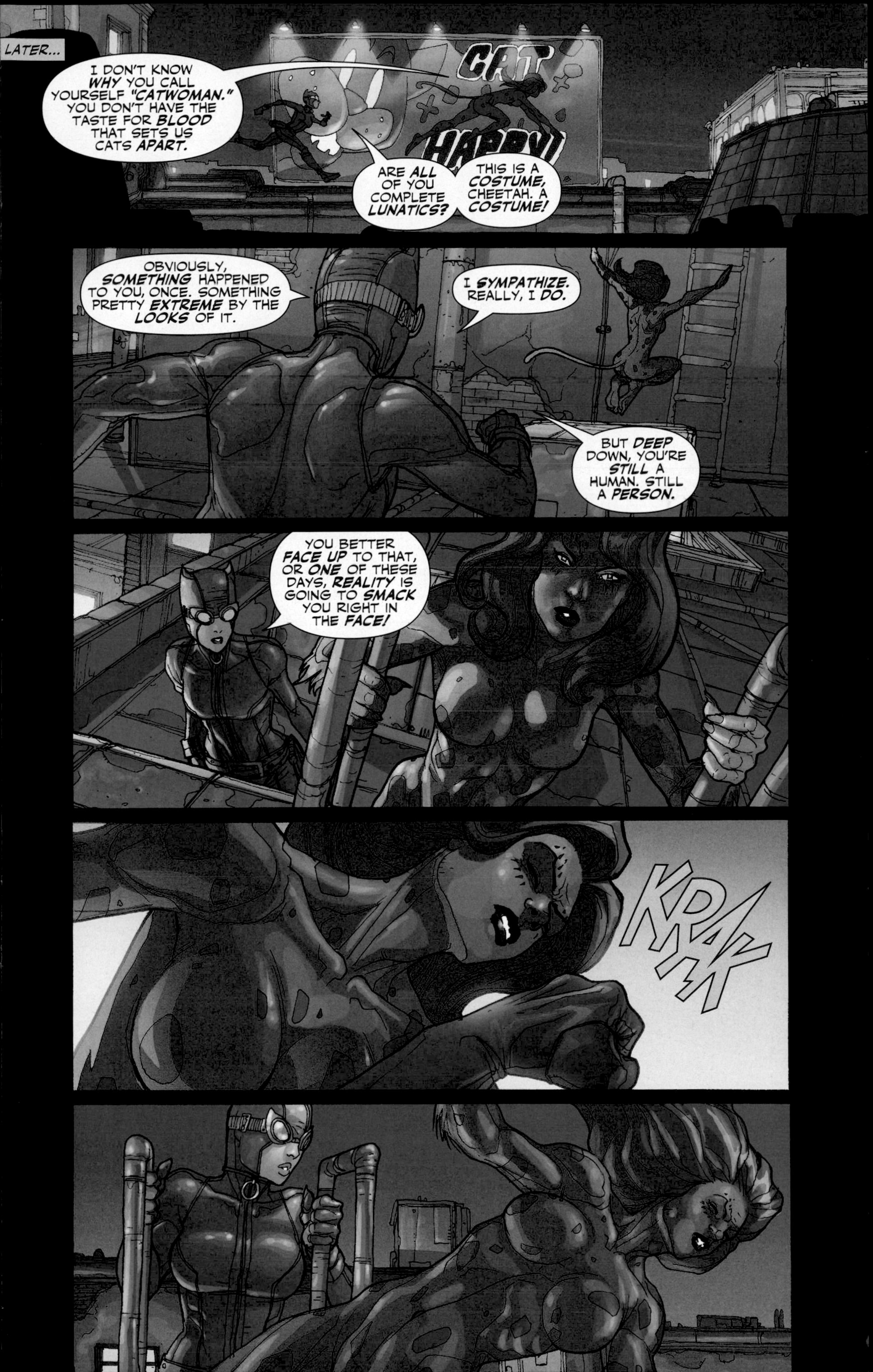
LATER...
I DON'T KNOW WHY YOU CALL YOURSELF "CATWOMAN." YOU DON'T HAVE THE TASTE FOR BLOOD THAT SETS US CATS APART.
ARE ALL OF YOU COMPLETE LUNATICS?
THIS IS A COSTUME, CHEETAH. A COSTUME!
OBVIOUSLY, SOMETHING HAPPENED TO YOU, ONCE. SOMETHING PRETTY EXTREME BY THE LOOKS OF IT.
I SYMPATHIZE. REALLY, I DO.
BUT DEEP DOWN, YOU'RE STILL A HUMAN. STILL A PERSON.
YOU BETTER FACE UP TO THAT, OR ONE OF THESE DAYS, REALITY IS GOING TO SMACK YOU RIGHT IN THE FACE!
KRAK

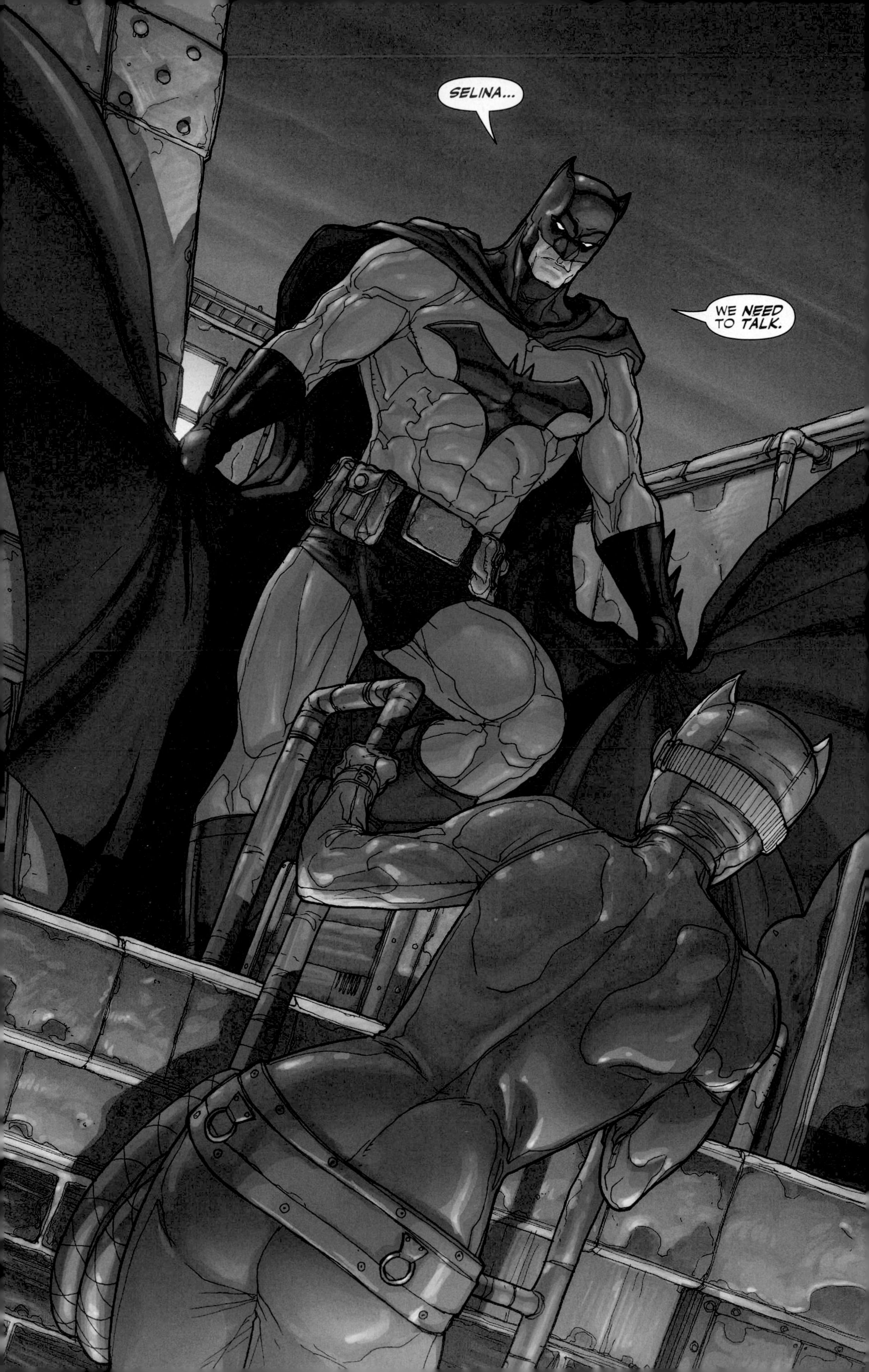
SELINA...
WE NEED TO TALK.

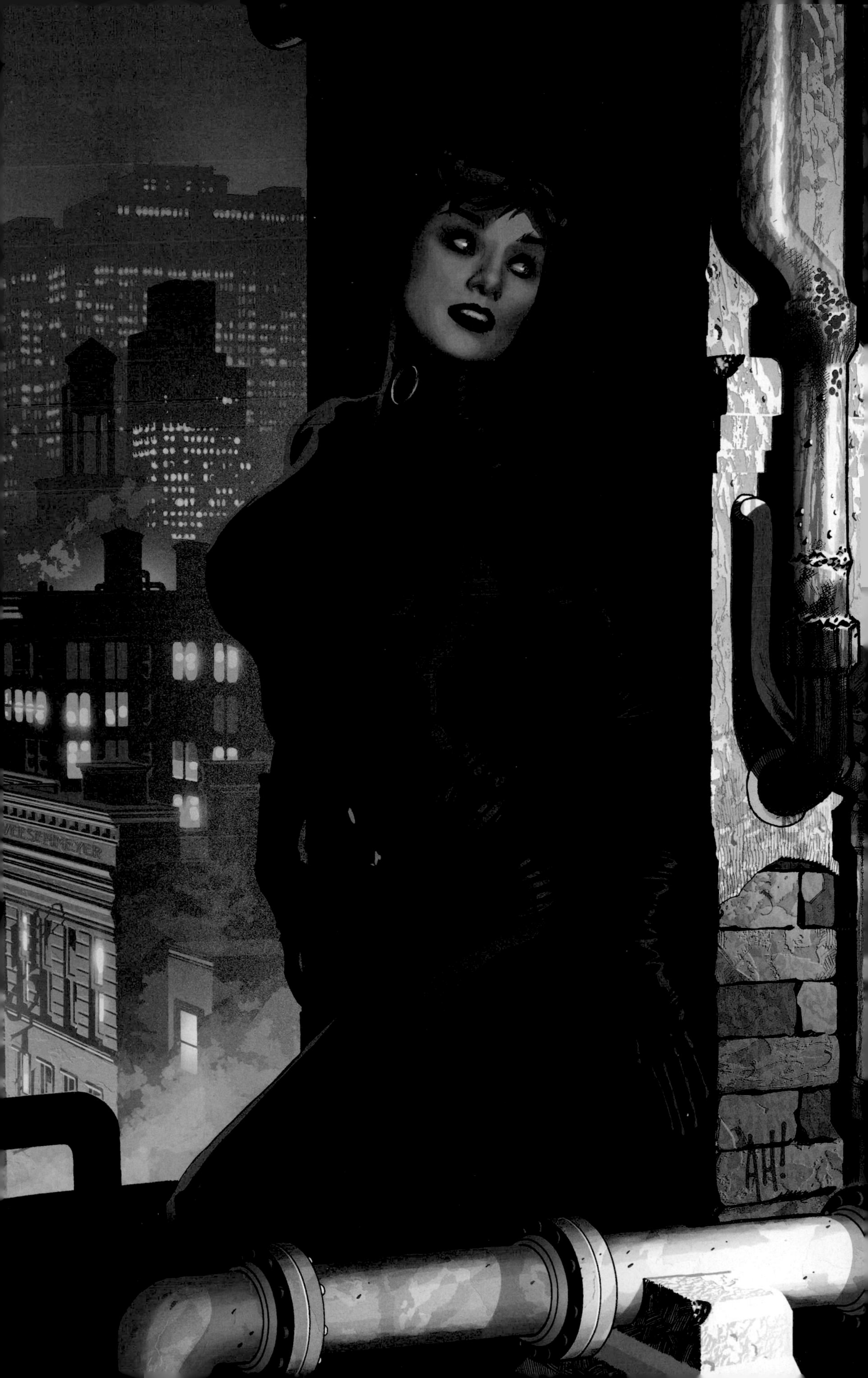
AH!

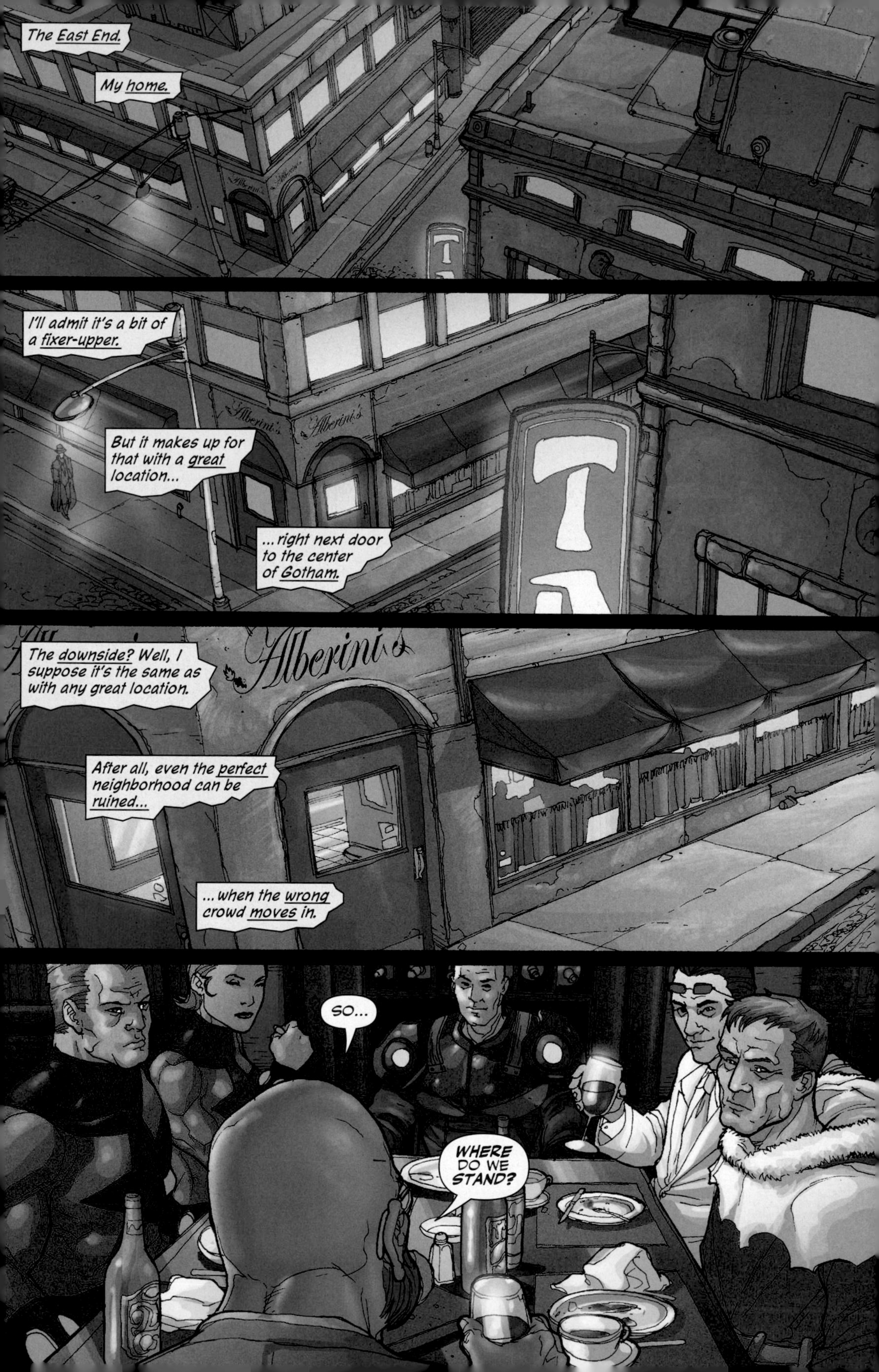
The East End.
My home.
I'll admit it's a bit of a fixer-upper.
But it makes up for that with a great location...
...right next door to the center of Gotham.
Alberini's
The downside? Well, I suppose it's the same as with any great location.
After all, even the perfect neighborhood can be ruined...
...when the wrong crowd moves in.
SO...
WHERE DO WE STAND?

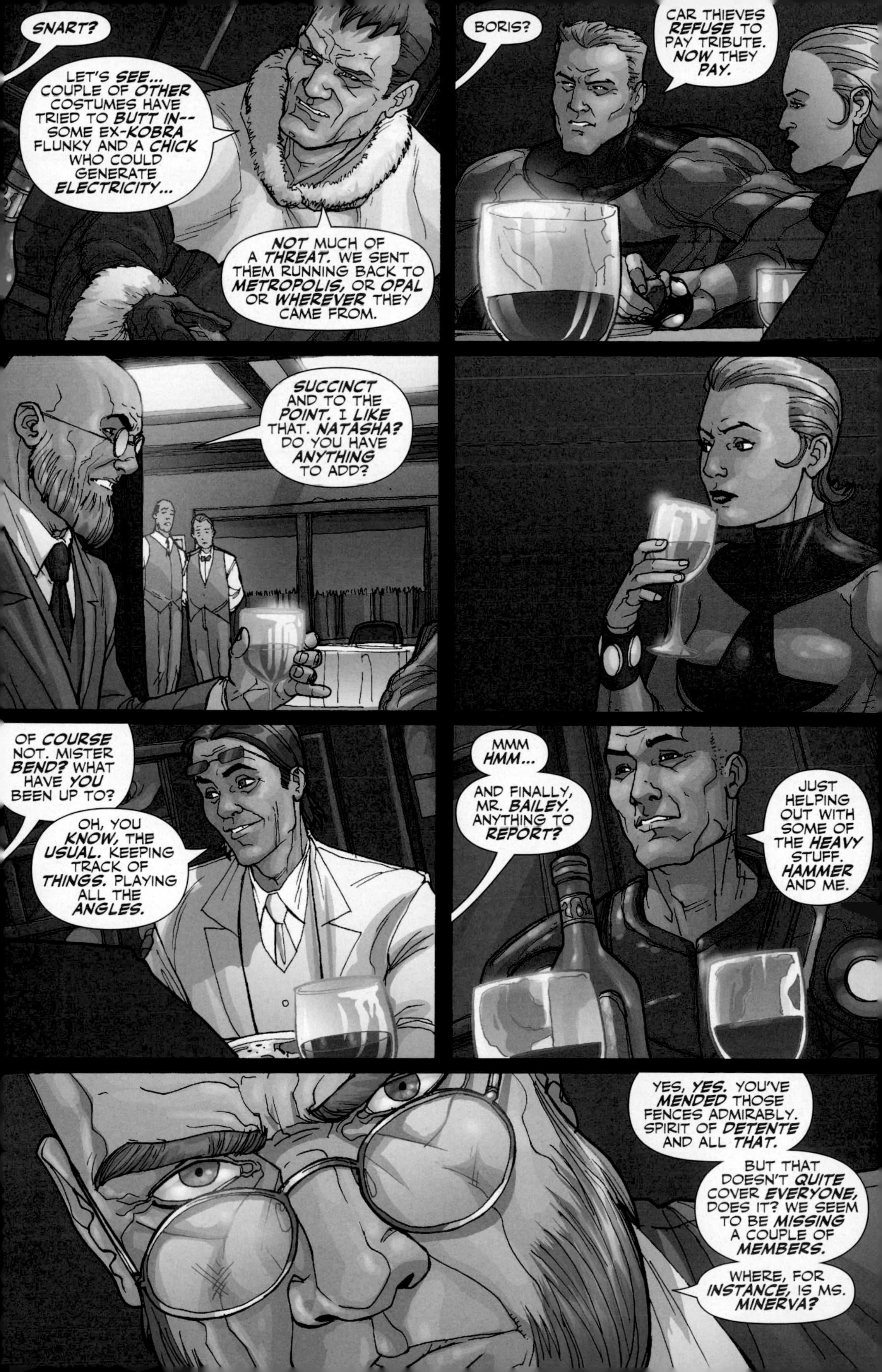
SNART?
LET'S SEE... COUPLE OF OTHER COSTUMES HAVE TRIED TO BUTT IN-- SOME EX-KOBRA FLUNKY AND A CHICK WHO COULD GENERATE ELECTRICITY...
NOT MUCH OF A THREAT. WE SENT THEM RUNNING BACK TO METROPOLIS, OR OPAL OR WHEREVER THEY CAME FROM.
BORIS?
CAR THIEVES REFUSE TO PAY TRIBUTE. NOW THEY PAY.
SUCCINCT AND TO THE POINT. I LIKE THAT. NATASHA? DO YOU HAVE ANYTHING TO ADD?
OF COURSE NOT. MISTER BEND? WHAT HAVE YOU BEEN UP TO?
OH, YOU KNOW, THE USUAL. KEEPING TRACK OF THINGS. PLAYING ALL THE ANGLES.
MMM HMM...
AND FINALLY, MR. BAILEY. ANYTHING TO REPORT?
JUST HELPING OUT WITH SOME OF THE HEAVY STUFF. HAMMER AND ME.
YES, YES. YOU'VE MENDED THOSE FENCES ADMIRABLY. SPIRIT OF DETENTE AND ALL THAT.
BUT THAT DOESN'T QUITE COVER EVERYONE, DOES IT? WE SEEM TO BE MISSING A COUPLE OF MEMBERS.
WHERE, FOR INSTANCE, IS MS. MINERVA?

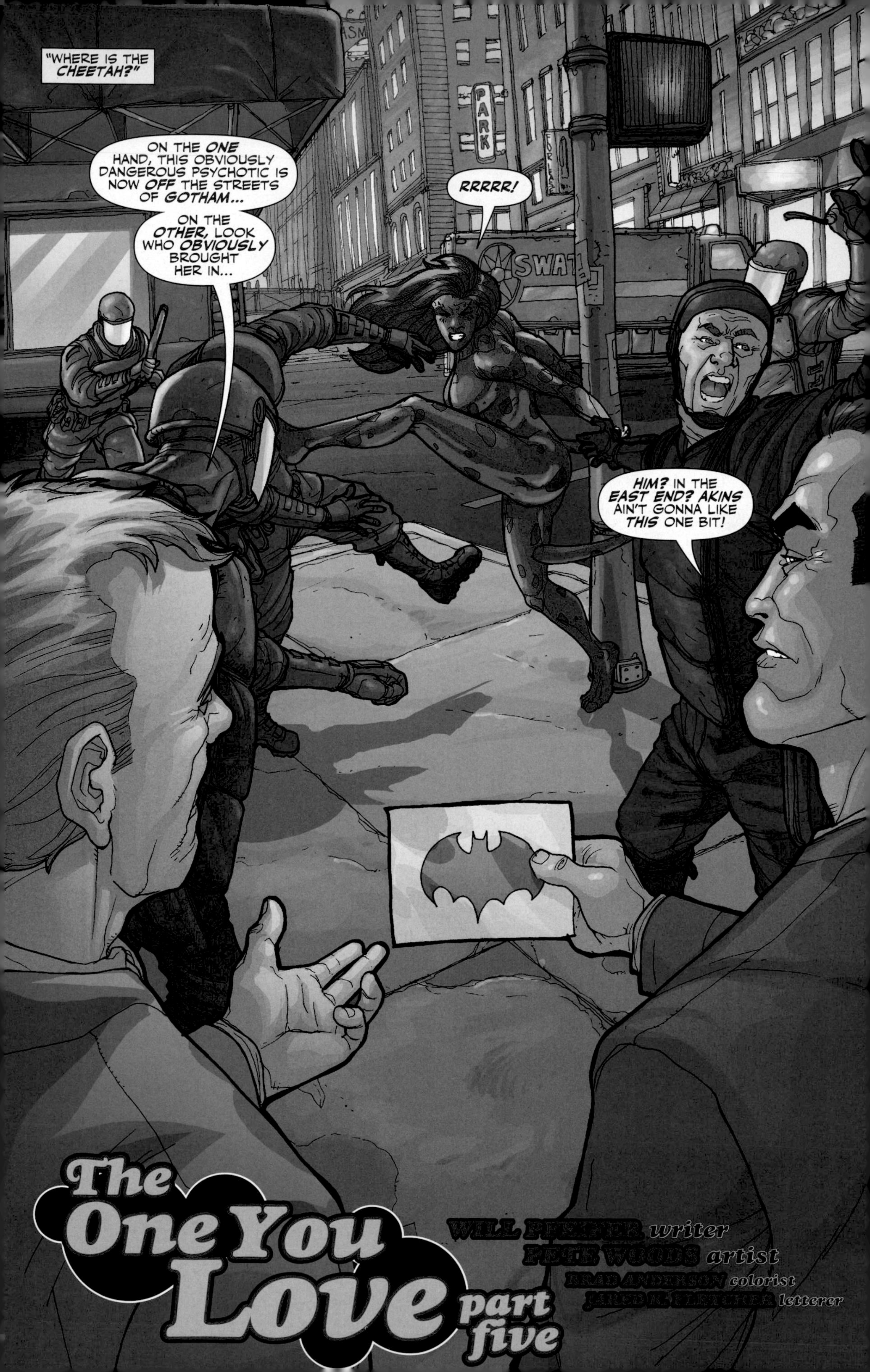
"WHERE IS THE CHEETAH?"
ON THE ONE HAND, THIS OBVIOUSLY DANGEROUS PSYCHOTIC IS NOW OFF THE STREETS OF GOTHAM...
ON THE OTHER, LOOK WHO OBVIOUSLY BROUGHT HER IN...
RRRRR!
HIM? IN THE EAST END? AKINS AIN'T GONNA LIKE THIS ONE BIT!
The One You Love part five
WILL PFEIFER writer
PETE WOODS artist
BRAD ANDERSON colorist
JARED K. FLETCHER letterer

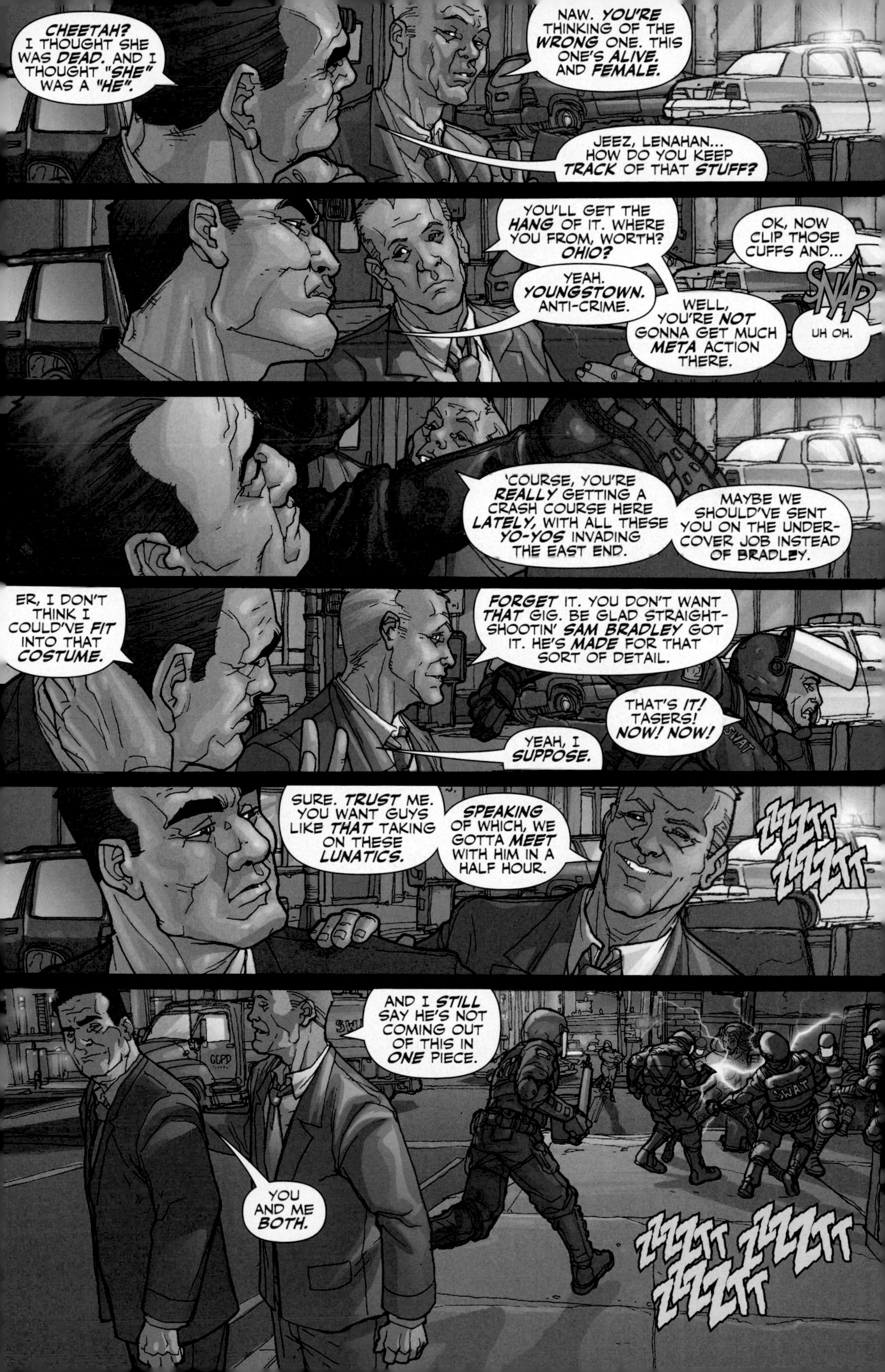
CHEETAH? I THOUGHT SHE WAS DEAD. AND I THOUGHT "SHE" WAS A "HE".
NAW. YOU'RE THINKING OF THE WRONG ONE. THIS ONE'S ALIVE. AND FEMALE.
JEEZ, LENAHAN... HOW DO YOU KEEP TRACK OF THAT STUFF?
YOU'LL GET THE HANG OF IT. WHERE YOU FROM, WORTH? OHIO?
YEAH. YOUNGSTOWN. ANTI-CRIME.
WELL, YOU'RE NOT GONNA GET MUCH META ACTION THERE.
OK, NOW CLIP THOSE CUFFS AND...
SNAP
UH OH.
'COURSE, YOU'RE REALLY GETTING A CRASH COURSE HERE LATELY, WITH ALL THESE YO-YOS INVADING THE EAST END.
MAYBE WE SHOULD'VE SENT YOU ON THE UNDER-COVER JOB INSTEAD OF BRADLEY.
ER, I DON'T THINK I COULD'VE FIT INTO THAT COSTUME.
FORGET IT. YOU DON'T WANT THAT GIG. BE GLAD STRAIGHT-SHOOTIN' SAM BRADLEY GOT IT. HE'S MADE FOR THAT SORT OF DETAIL.
YEAH, I SUPPOSE.
THAT'S IT! TASERS! NOW! NOW!
SURE. TRUST ME. YOU WANT GUYS LIKE THAT TAKING ON THESE LUNATICS.
SPEAKING OF WHICH, WE GOTTA MEET WITH HIM IN A HALF HOUR.
ZZZZTT ZZZZTT
AND I STILL SAY HE'S NOT COMING OUT OF THIS IN ONE PIECE.
YOU AND ME BOTH.
ZZZZTT ZZZZTT ZZZZTT ZZZZTT

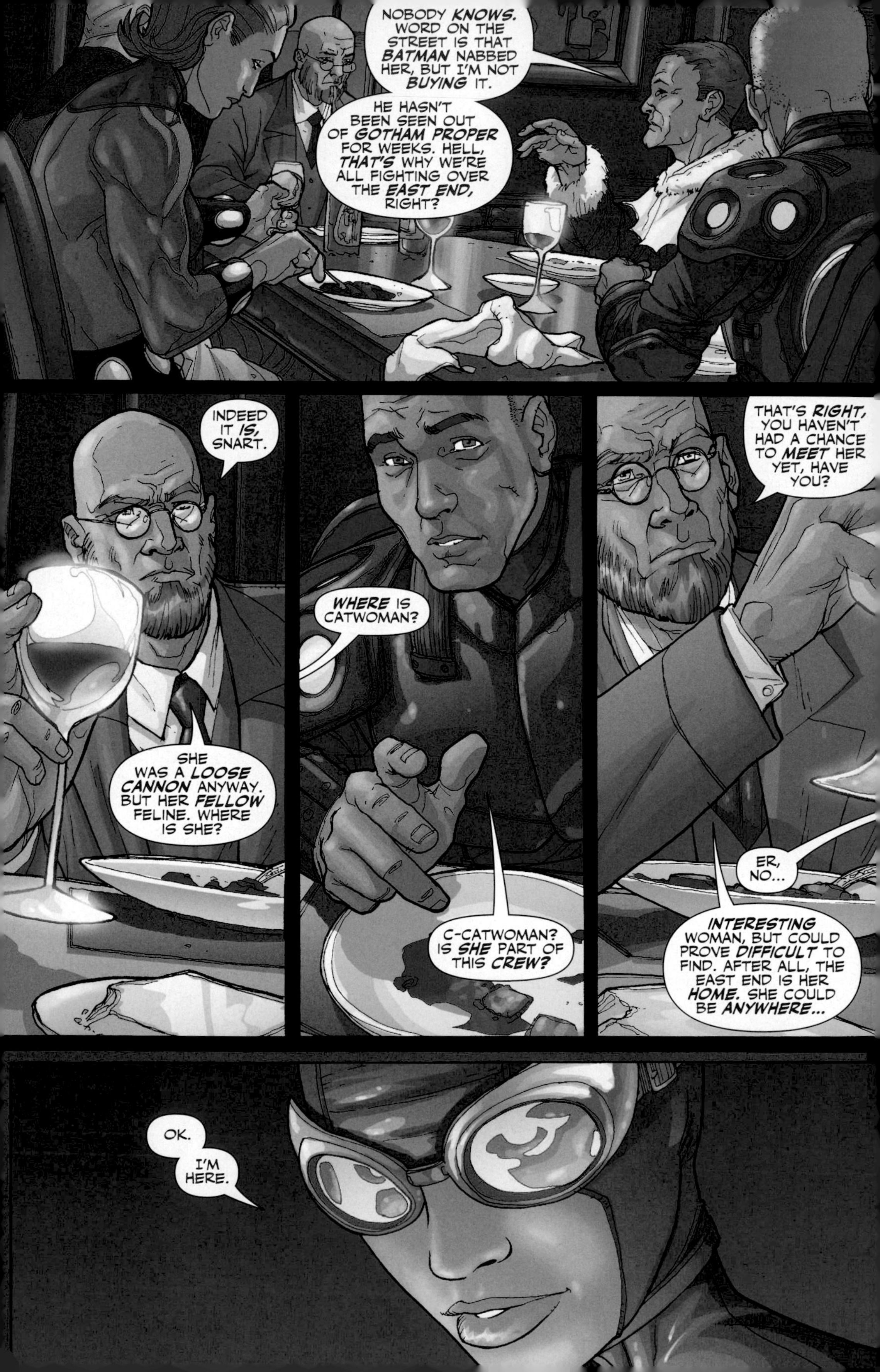
NOBODY KNOWS. WORD ON THE STREET IS THAT BATMAN NABBED HER, BUT I'M NOT BUYING IT.
HE HASN'T BEEN SEEN OUT OF GOTHAM PROPER FOR WEEKS. HELL, THAT'S WHY WE'RE ALL FIGHTING OVER THE EAST END, RIGHT?
INDEED IT IS, SNART.
SHE WAS A LOOSE CANNON ANYWAY. BUT HER FELLOW FELINE. WHERE IS SHE?
WHERE IS CATWOMAN?
C-CATWOMAN? IS SHE PART OF THIS CREW?
THAT'S RIGHT, YOU HAVEN'T HAD A CHANCE TO MEET HER YET, HAVE YOU?
ER, NO...
INTERESTING WOMAN, BUT COULD PROVE DIFFICULT TO FIND. AFTER ALL, THE EAST END IS HER HOME. SHE COULD BE ANYWHERE...
OK.
I'M HERE.

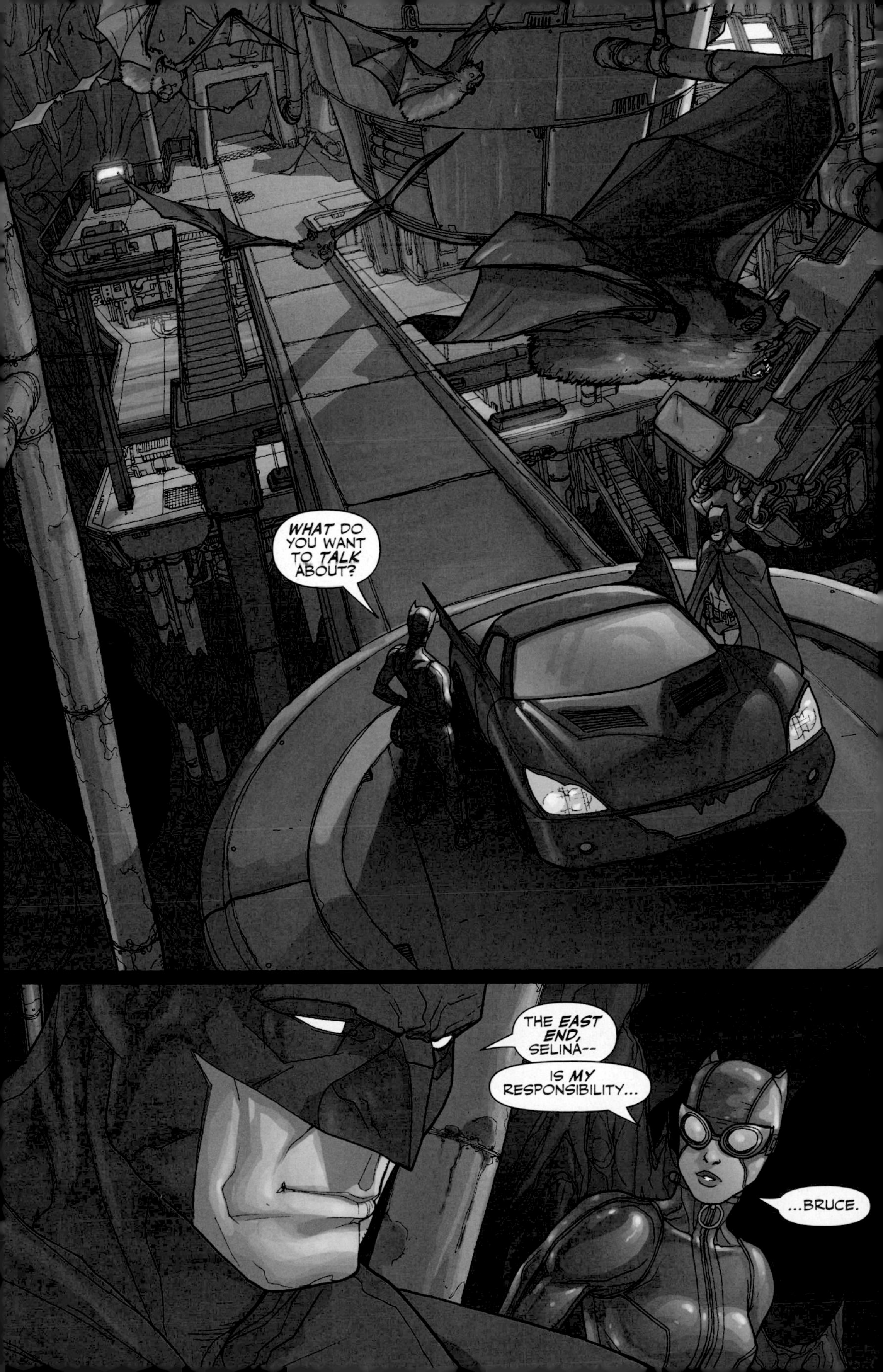
WHAT DO YOU WANT TO TALK ABOUT?
THE EAST END, SELINA--
IS MY RESPONSIBILITY...
...BRUCE.

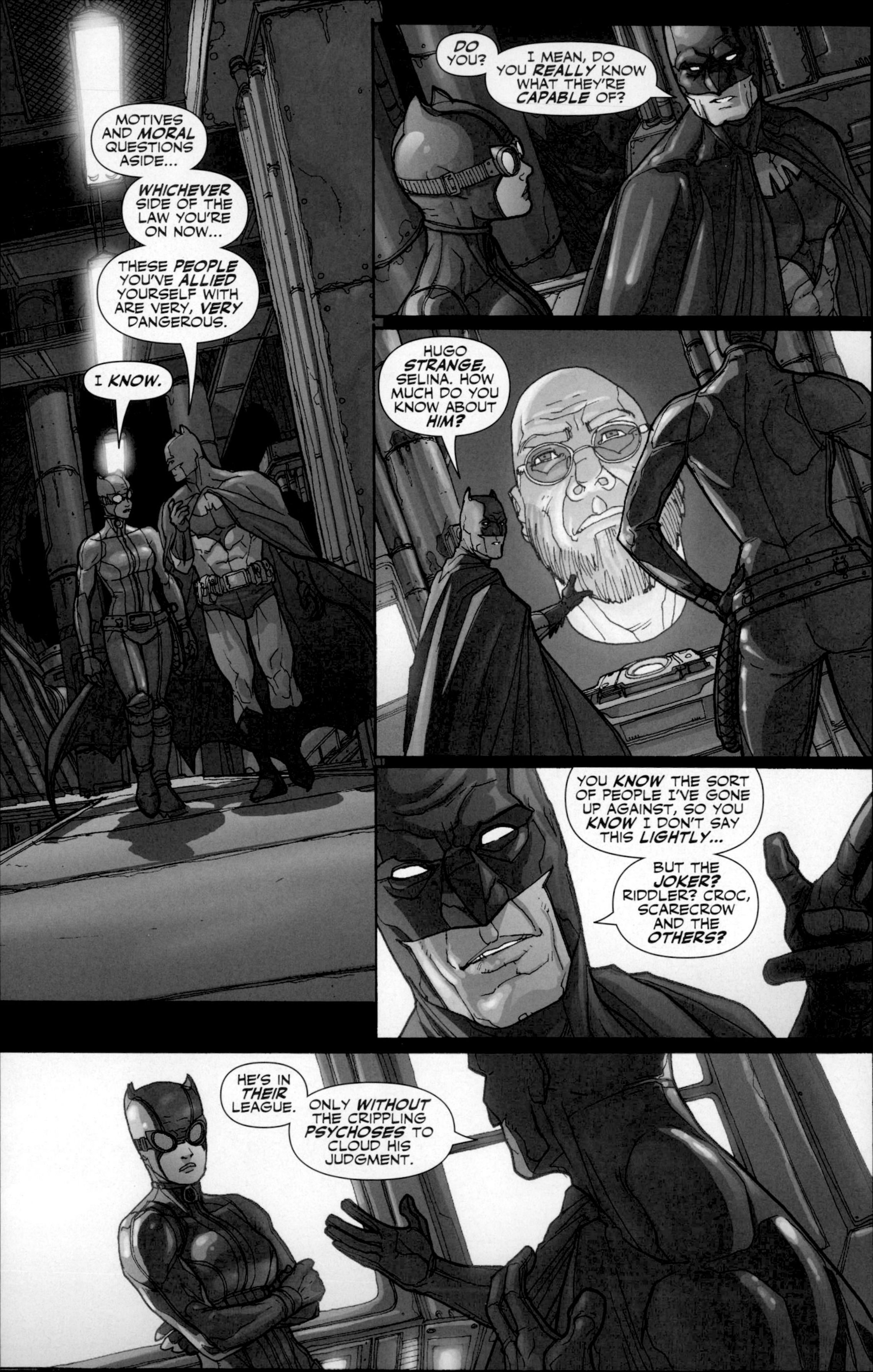
MOTIVES AND MORAL QUESTIONS ASIDE...
WHICHEVER SIDE OF THE LAW YOU'RE ON NOW...
THESE PEOPLE YOU'VE ALLIED YOURSELF WITH ARE VERY, VERY DANGEROUS.
I KNOW.
DO YOU?
I MEAN, DO YOU REALLY KNOW WHAT THEY'RE CAPABLE OF?
HUGO STRANGE, SELINA. HOW MUCH DO YOU KNOW ABOUT HIM?
YOU KNOW THE SORT OF PEOPLE I'VE GONE UP AGAINST, SO YOU KNOW I DON'T SAY THIS LIGHTLY...
BUT THE JOKER? RIDDLER? CROC, SCARECROW AND THE OTHERS?
HE'S IN THEIR LEAGUE.
ONLY WITHOUT THE CRIPPLING PSYCHOSES TO CLOUD HIS JUDGMENT.

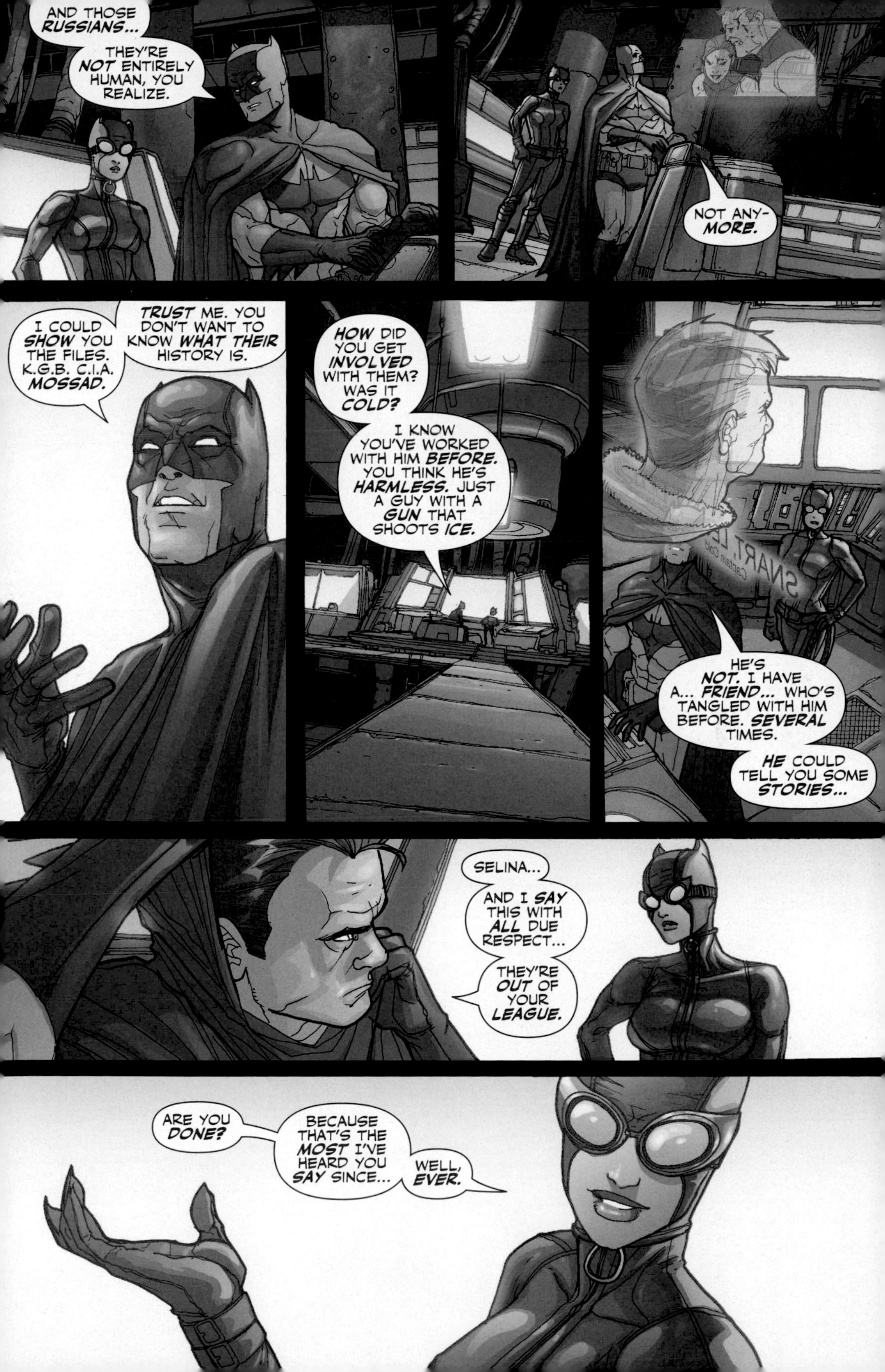
AND THOSE RUSSIANS...
THEY'RE NOT ENTIRELY HUMAN, YOU REALIZE.
NOT ANY-MORE.
I COULD SHOW YOU THE FILES. K.G.B. C.I.A. MOSSAD.
TRUST ME. YOU DON'T WANT TO KNOW WHAT THEIR HISTORY IS.
HOW DID YOU GET INVOLVED WITH THEM? WAS IT COLD?
I KNOW YOU'VE WORKED WITH HIM BEFORE. YOU THINK HE'S HARMLESS. JUST A GUY WITH A GUN THAT SHOOTS ICE.
HE'S NOT. I HAVE A... FRIEND... WHO'S TANGLED WITH HIM BEFORE. SEVERAL TIMES.
HE COULD TELL YOU SOME STORIES...
SELINA...
AND I SAY THIS WITH ALL DUE RESPECT...
THEY'RE OUT OF YOUR LEAGUE.
ARE YOU DONE?
BECAUSE THAT'S THE MOST I'VE HEARD YOU SAY SINCE...
WELL, EVER.

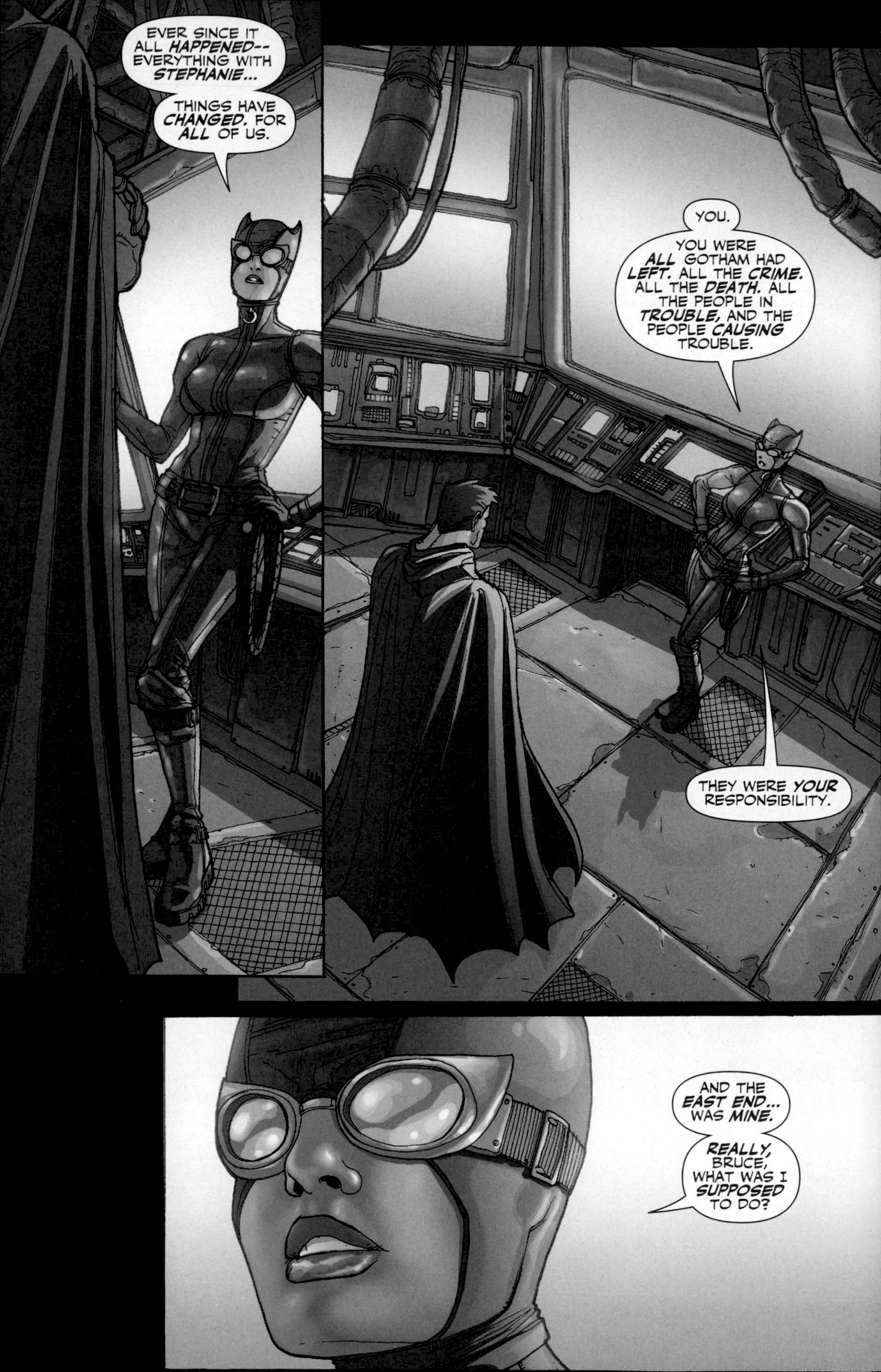
EVER SINCE IT ALL HAPPENED-- EVERYTHING WITH STEPHANIE...
THINGS HAVE CHANGED. FOR ALL OF US.
YOU.
YOU WERE ALL GOTHAM HAD LEFT. ALL THE CRIME. ALL THE DEATH. ALL THE PEOPLE IN TROUBLE, AND THE PEOPLE CAUSING TROUBLE.
THEY WERE YOUR RESPONSIBILITY.
AND THE EAST END... WAS MINE.
REALLY, BRUCE, WHAT WAS I SUPPOSED TO DO?

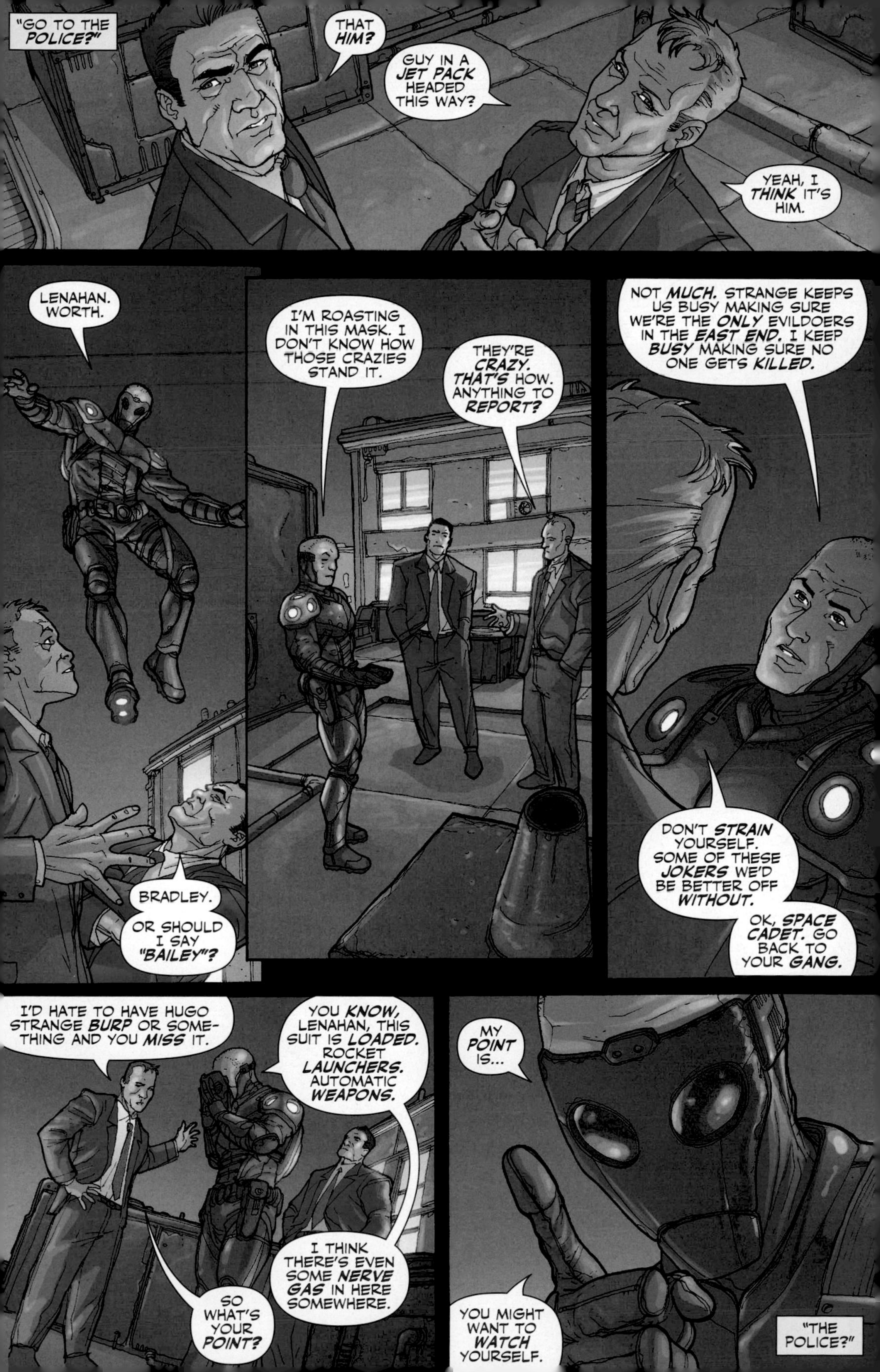
"GO TO THE POLICE?"
THAT HIM?
GUY IN A JET PACK HEADED THIS WAY?
YEAH, I THINK IT'S HIM.
LENAHAN. WORTH.
BRADLEY.
OR SHOULD I SAY "BAILEY"?
I'M ROASTING IN THIS MASK. I DON'T KNOW HOW THOSE CRAZIES STAND IT.
THEY'RE CRAZY. THAT'S HOW. ANYTHING TO REPORT?
NOT MUCH. STRANGE KEEPS US BUSY MAKING SURE WE'RE THE ONLY EVILDOERS IN THE EAST END. I KEEP BUSY MAKING SURE NO ONE GETS KILLED.
DON'T STRAIN YOURSELF. SOME OF THESE JOKERS WE'D BE BETTER OFF WITHOUT.
OK, SPACE CADET. GO BACK TO YOUR GANG.
I'D HATE TO HAVE HUGO STRANGE BURP OR SOME-THING AND YOU MISS IT.
YOU KNOW, LENAHAN, THIS SUIT IS LOADED. ROCKET LAUNCHERS. AUTOMATIC WEAPONS.
I THINK THERE'S EVEN SOME NERVE GAS IN HERE SOMEWHERE.
SO WHAT'S YOUR POINT?
MY POINT IS...
YOU MIGHT WANT TO WATCH YOURSELF.
"THE POLICE?"

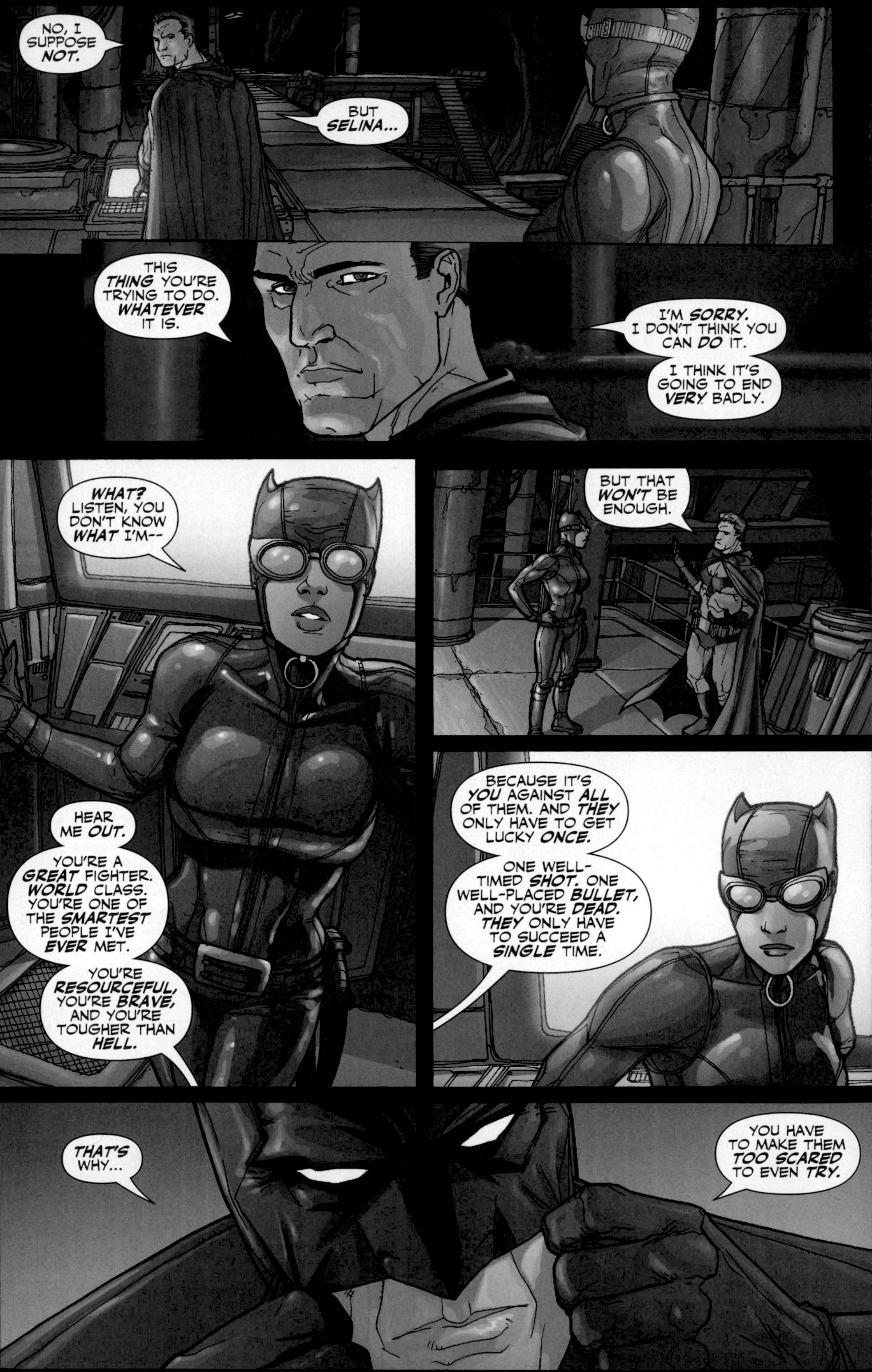

NO, I SUPPOSE NOT.
BUT SELINA...
THIS THING YOU'RE TRYING TO DO. WHATEVER IT IS.
I'M SORRY. I DON'T THINK YOU CAN DO IT.
I THINK IT'S GOING TO END VERY BADLY.
WHAT? LISTEN, YOU DON'T KNOW WHAT I'M--
HEAR ME OUT.
YOU'RE A GREAT FIGHTER. WORLD CLASS. YOU'RE ONE OF THE SMARTEST PEOPLE I'VE EVER MET.
YOU'RE RESOURCEFUL, YOU'RE BRAVE, AND YOU'RE TOUGHER THAN HELL.
BUT THAT WON'T BE ENOUGH.
BECAUSE IT'S YOU AGAINST ALL OF THEM. AND THEY ONLY HAVE TO GET LUCKY ONCE.
ONE WELL-TIMED SHOT. ONE WELL-PLACED BULLET, AND YOU'RE DEAD. THEY ONLY HAVE TO SUCCEED A SINGLE TIME.
THAT'S WHY...
YOU HAVE TO MAKE THEM TOO SCARED TO EVEN TRY.

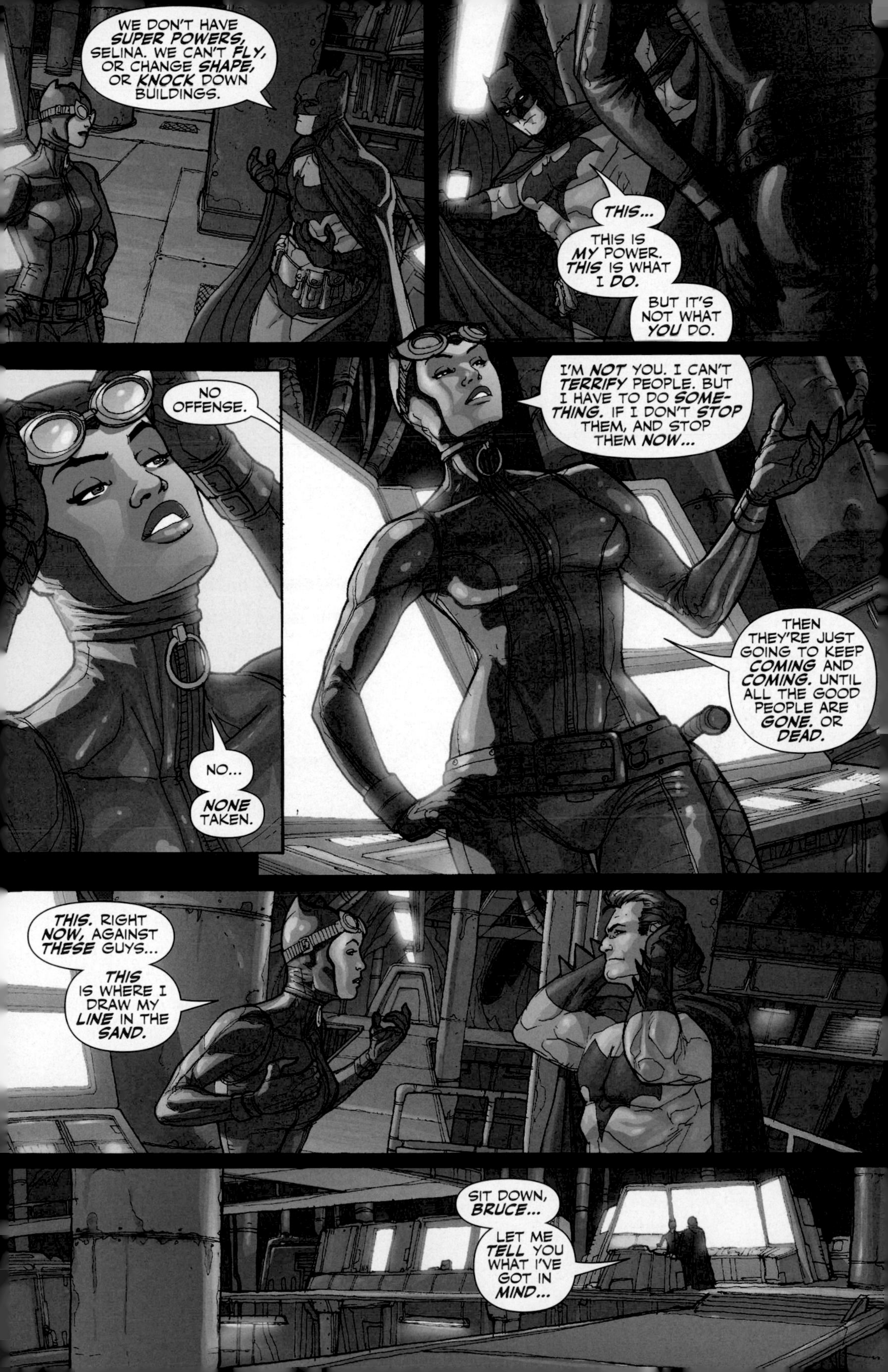
WE DON'T HAVE SUPER POWERS, SELINA. WE CAN'T FLY, OR CHANGE SHAPE, OR KNOCK DOWN BUILDINGS.
THIS...
THIS IS MY POWER. THIS IS WHAT I DO.
BUT IT'S NOT WHAT YOU DO.
NO OFFENSE.
NO...
NONE TAKEN.
I'M NOT YOU. I CAN'T TERRIFY PEOPLE. BUT I HAVE TO DO SOMETHING. IF I DON'T STOP THEM, AND STOP THEM NOW...
THEN THEY'RE JUST GOING TO KEEP COMING AND COMING. UNTIL ALL THE GOOD PEOPLE ARE GONE. OR DEAD.
THIS. RIGHT NOW, AGAINST THESE GUYS...
THIS IS WHERE I DRAW MY LINE IN THE SAND.
SIT DOWN, BRUCE...
LET ME TELL YOU WHAT I'VE GOT IN MIND...

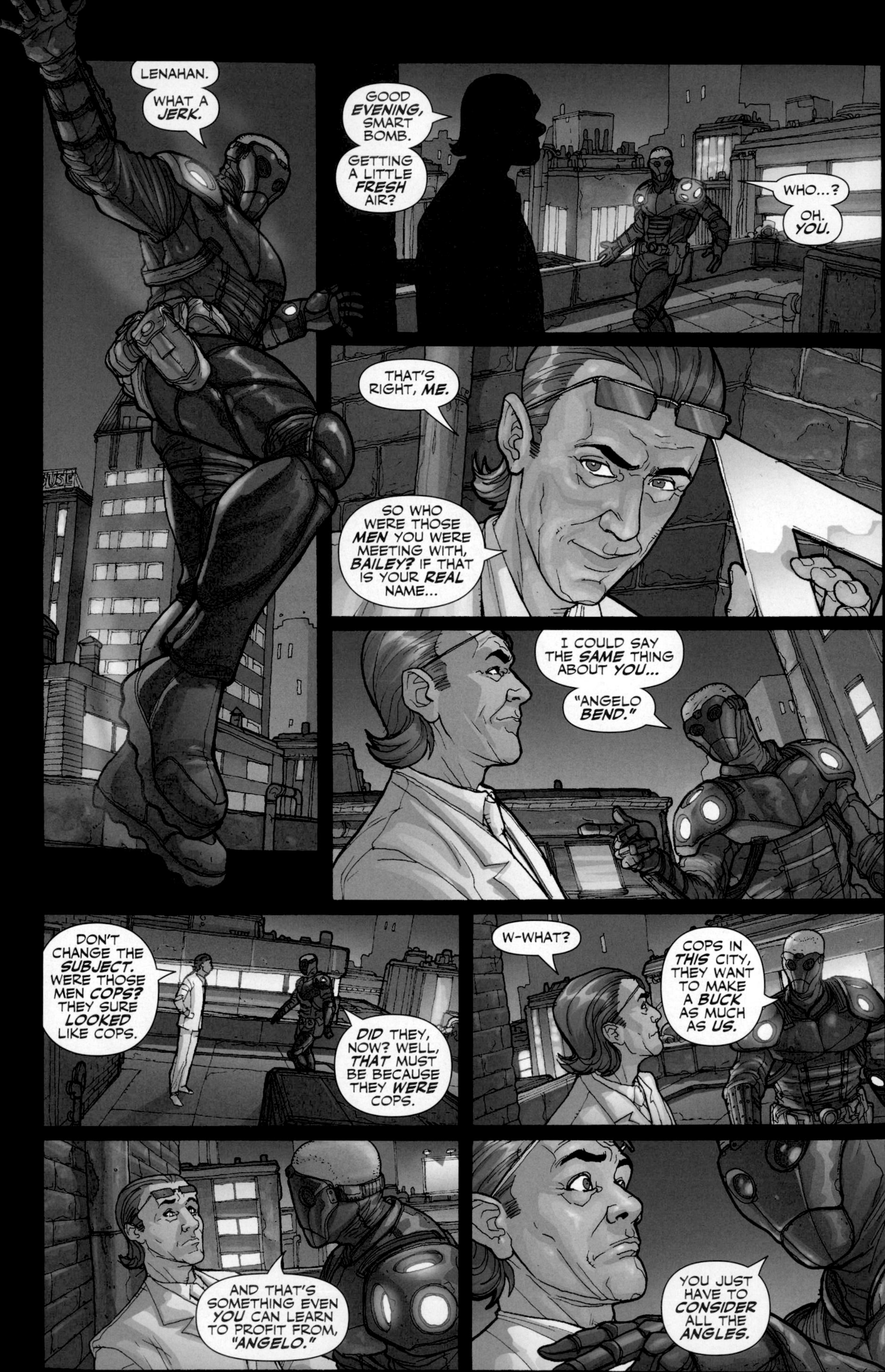
LENAHAN. WHAT A JERK.
GOOD EVENING, SMART BOMB.
GETTING A LITTLE FRESH AIR?
WHO...?
OH. YOU.
THAT'S RIGHT, ME.
SO WHO WERE THOSE MEN YOU WERE MEETING WITH, BAILEY? IF THAT IS YOUR REAL NAME...
I COULD SAY THE SAME THING ABOUT YOU...
"ANGELO BEND."
DON'T CHANGE THE SUBJECT. WERE THOSE MEN COPS? THEY SURE LOOKED LIKE COPS.
DID THEY, NOW? WELL, THAT MUST BE BECAUSE THEY WERE COPS.
W-WHAT?
COPS IN THIS CITY, THEY WANT TO MAKE A BUCK AS MUCH AS US.
AND THAT'S SOMETHING EVEN YOU CAN LEARN TO PROFIT FROM, "ANGELO."
YOU JUST HAVE TO CONSIDER ALL THE ANGLES.

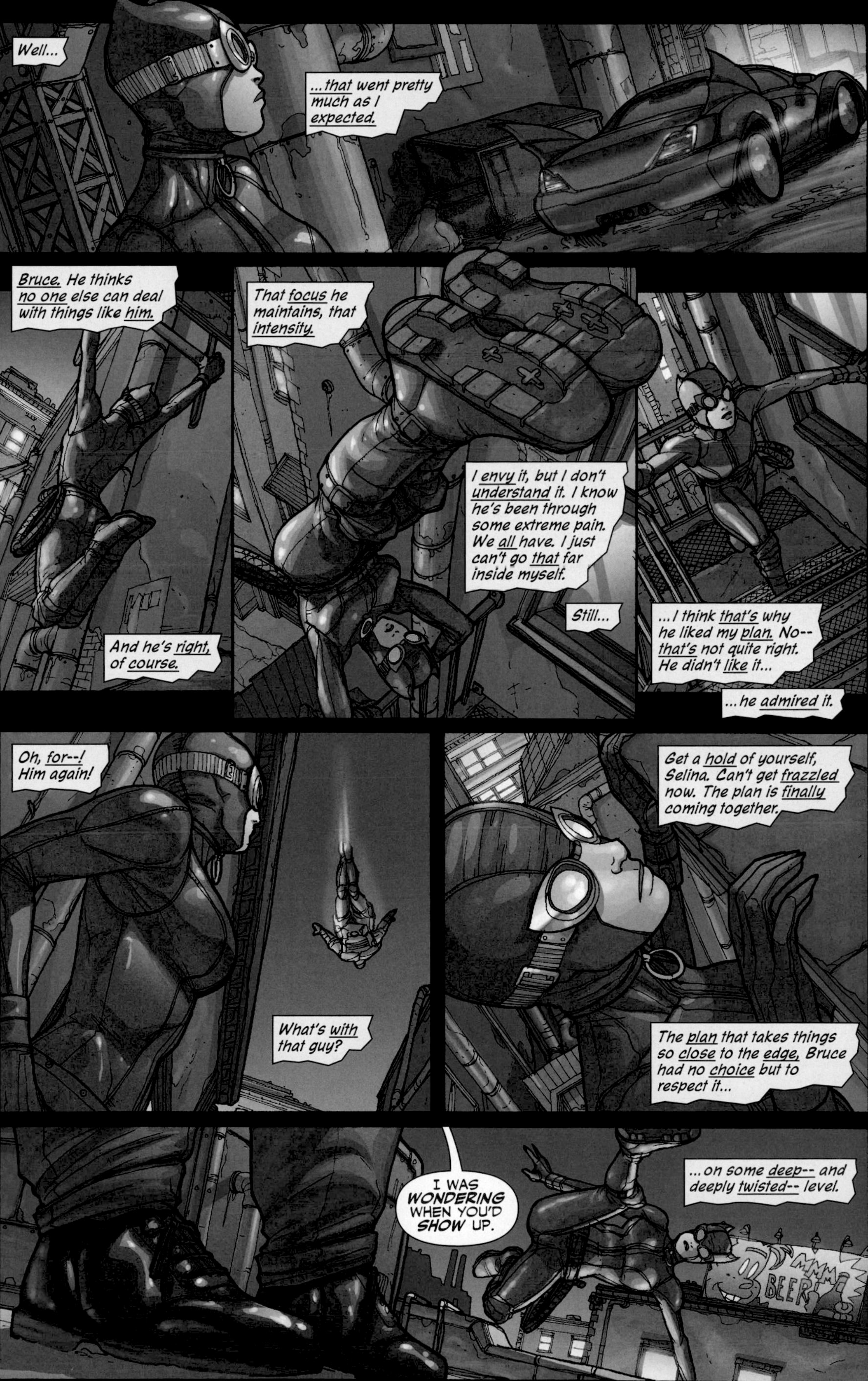
Well...
...that went pretty much as I expected.
Bruce. He thinks no one else can deal with things like him.
And he's right, of course.
That focus he maintains, that intensity.
I envy it, but I don't understand it. I know he's been through some extreme pain. We all have. I just can't go that far inside myself.
Still...
...I think that's why he liked my plan. No--that's not quite right. He didn't like it...
...he admired it.
Oh, for--! Him again!
What's with that guy?
Get a hold of yourself, Selina. Can't get frazzled now. The plan is finally coming together.
The plan that takes things so close to the edge, Bruce had no choice but to respect it...
I WAS WONDERING WHEN YOU'D SHOW UP.
...on some deep-- and deeply twisted-- level.
MMM BEER

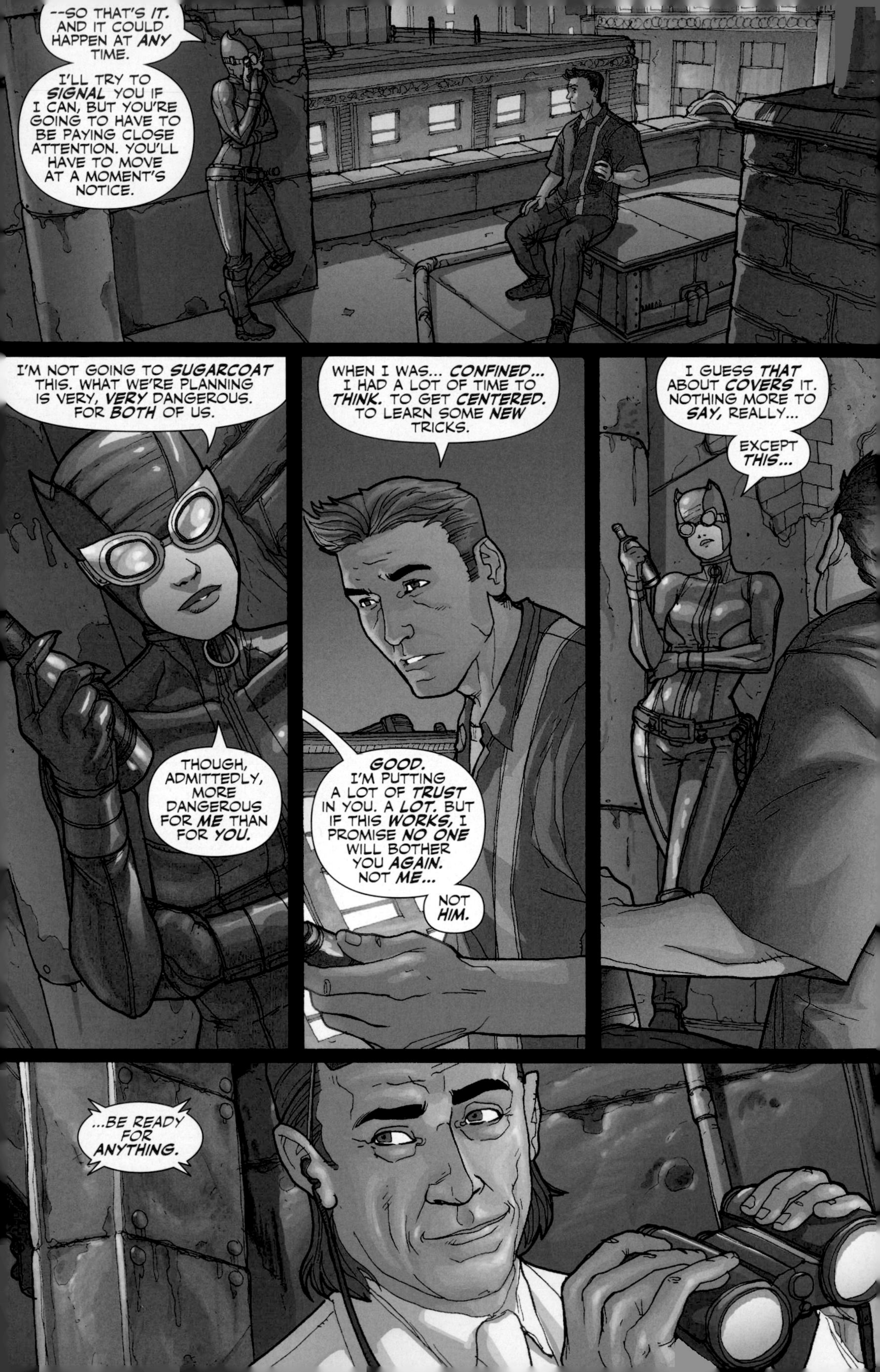
--SO THAT'S IT. AND IT COULD HAPPEN AT ANY TIME.
I'LL TRY TO SIGNAL YOU IF I CAN, BUT YOU'RE GOING TO HAVE TO BE PAYING CLOSE ATTENTION. YOU'LL HAVE TO MOVE AT A MOMENT'S NOTICE.
I'M NOT GOING TO SUGARCOAT THIS. WHAT WE'RE PLANNING IS VERY, VERY DANGEROUS. FOR BOTH OF US.
THOUGH, ADMITTEDLY, MORE DANGEROUS FOR ME THAN FOR YOU.
WHEN I WAS... CONFINED... I HAD A LOT OF TIME TO THINK. TO GET CENTERED. TO LEARN SOME NEW TRICKS.
GOOD. I'M PUTTING A LOT OF TRUST IN YOU. A LOT. BUT IF THIS WORKS, I PROMISE NO ONE WILL BOTHER YOU AGAIN. NOT ME...
NOT HIM.
I GUESS THAT ABOUT COVERS IT. NOTHING MORE TO SAY, REALLY...
EXCEPT THIS...
...BE READY FOR ANYTHING.

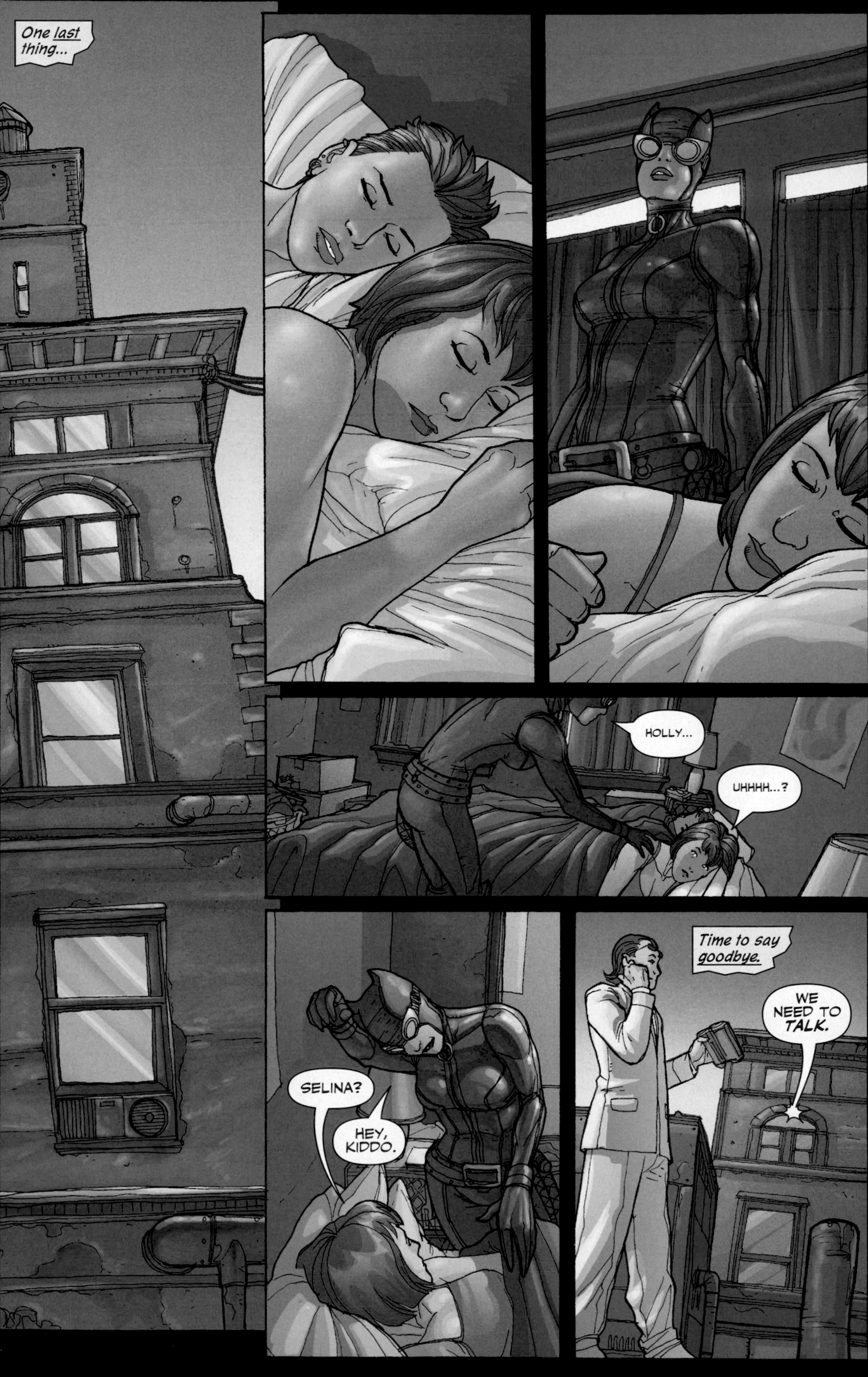
One last thing...
HOLLY...
UHHHH...?
SELINA?
HEY, KIDDO.
Time to say goodbye.
WE NEED TO TALK.

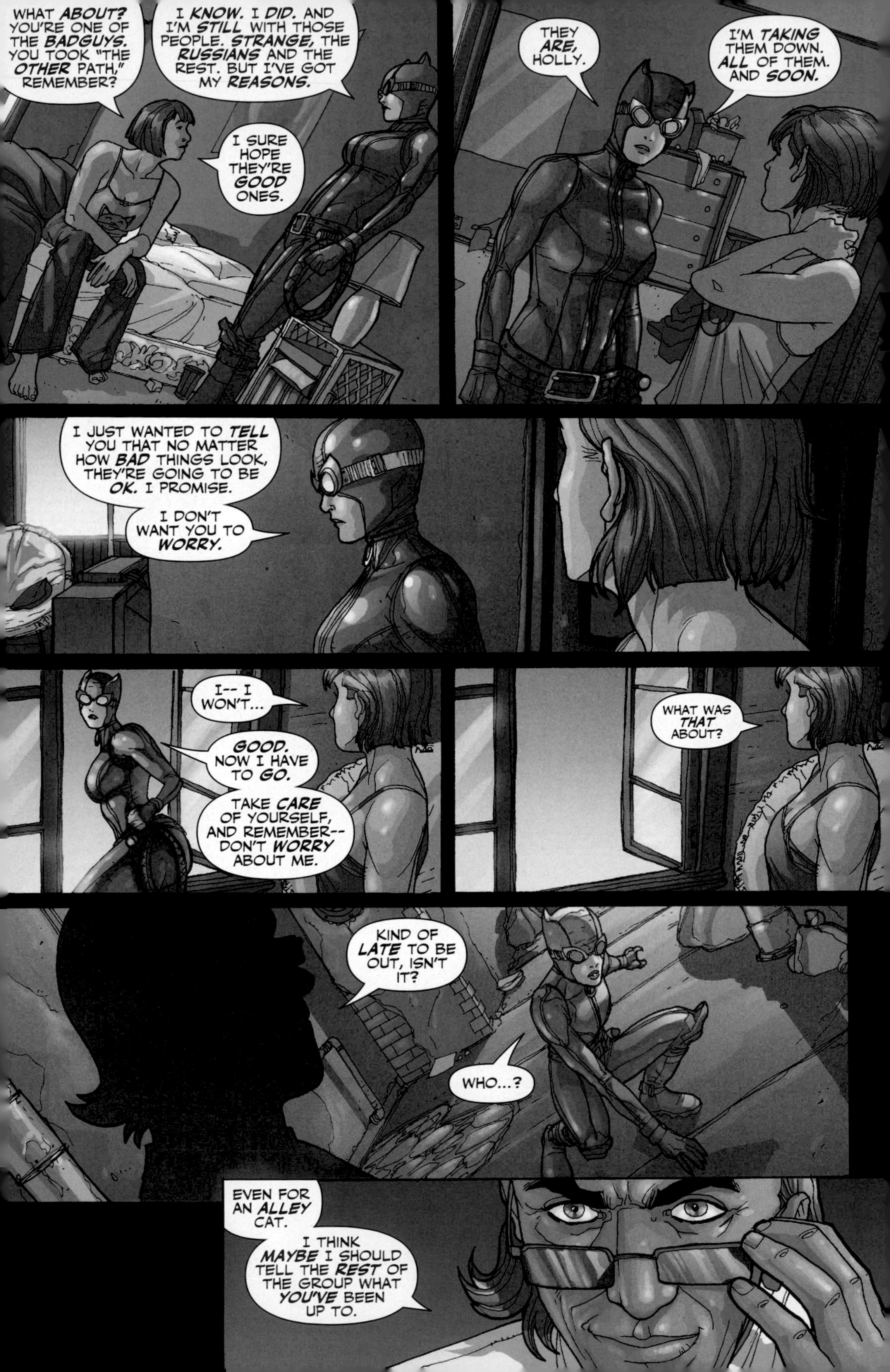
WHAT ABOUT? YOU'RE ONE OF THE BADGUYS. YOU TOOK "THE OTHER PATH," REMEMBER?
I KNOW. I DID. AND I'M STILL WITH THOSE PEOPLE. STRANGE, THE RUSSIANS AND THE REST. BUT I'VE GOT MY REASONS.
I SURE HOPE THEY'RE GOOD ONES.
THEY ARE, HOLLY.
I'M TAKING THEM DOWN. ALL OF THEM. AND SOON.
I JUST WANTED TO TELL YOU THAT NO MATTER HOW BAD THINGS LOOK, THEY'RE GOING TO BE OK. I PROMISE.
I DON'T WANT YOU TO WORRY.
I-- I WON'T...
GOOD. NOW I HAVE TO GO.
TAKE CARE OF YOURSELF, AND REMEMBER-- DON'T WORRY ABOUT ME.
WHAT WAS THAT ABOUT?
KIND OF LATE TO BE OUT, ISN'T IT?
WHO...?
EVEN FOR AN ALLEY CAT.
I THINK MAYBE I SHOULD TELL THE REST OF THE GROUP WHAT YOU'VE BEEN UP TO.

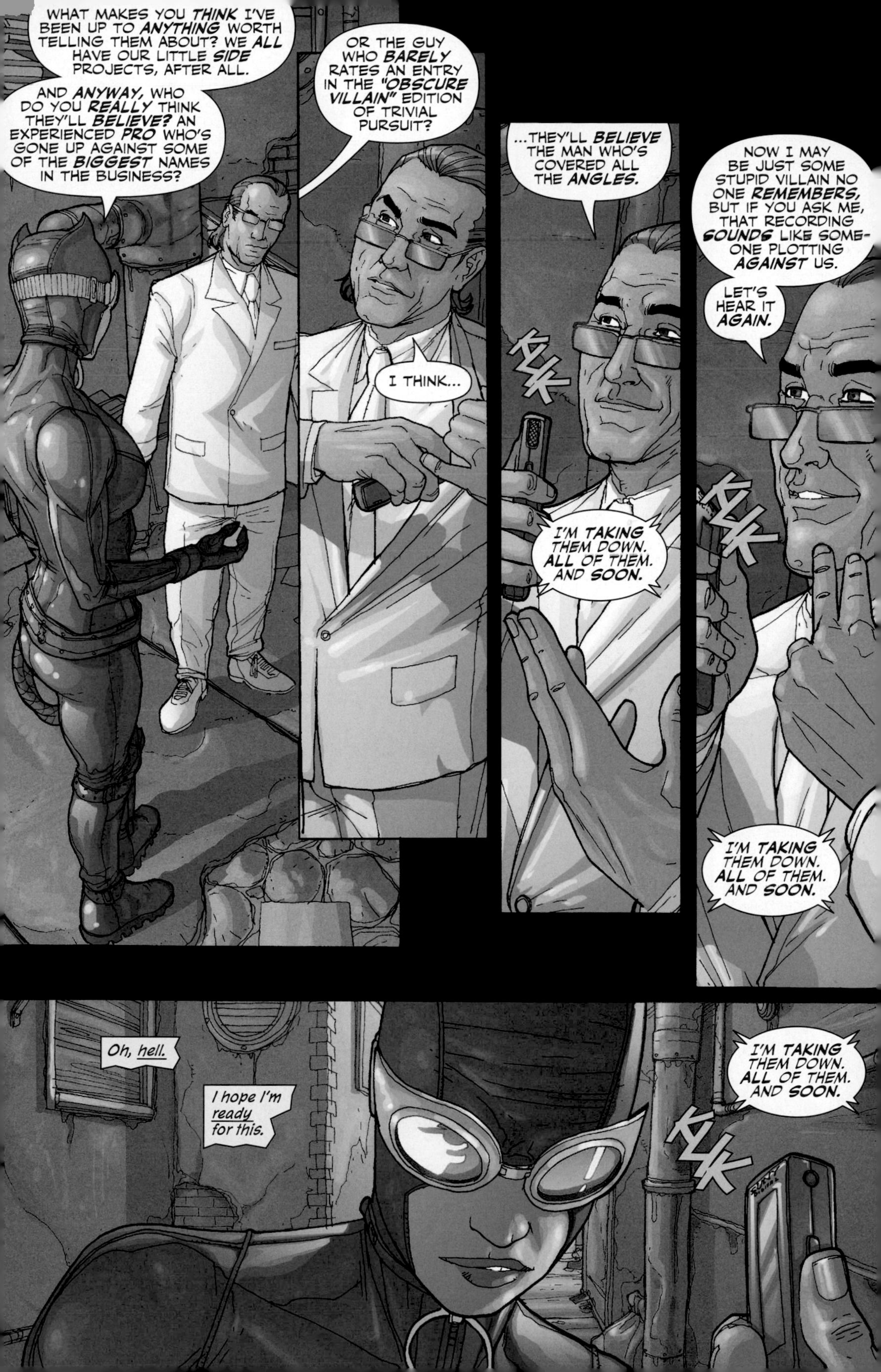
WHAT MAKES YOU THINK I'VE BEEN UP TO ANYTHING WORTH TELLING THEM ABOUT? WE ALL HAVE OUR LITTLE SIDE PROJECTS, AFTER ALL.
AND ANYWAY, WHO DO YOU REALLY THINK THEY'LL BELIEVE? AN EXPERIENCED PRO WHO'S GONE UP AGAINST SOME OF THE BIGGEST NAMES IN THE BUSINESS?
OR THE GUY WHO BARELY RATES AN ENTRY IN THE "OBSCURE VILLAIN" EDITION OF TRIVIAL PURSUIT?
I THINK...
...THEY'LL BELIEVE THE MAN WHO'S COVERED ALL THE ANGLES.
KLIK
I'M TAKING THEM DOWN. ALL OF THEM. AND SOON.
NOW I MAY BE JUST SOME STUPID VILLAIN NO ONE REMEMBERS, BUT IF YOU ASK ME, THAT RECORDING SOUNDS LIKE SOME-ONE PLOTTING AGAINST US.
LET'S HEAR IT AGAIN.
KLIK
I'M TAKING THEM DOWN. ALL OF THEM. AND SOON.
Oh, hell.
I hope I'm ready for this.
I'M TAKING THEM DOWN. ALL OF THEM. AND SOON.
KLIK

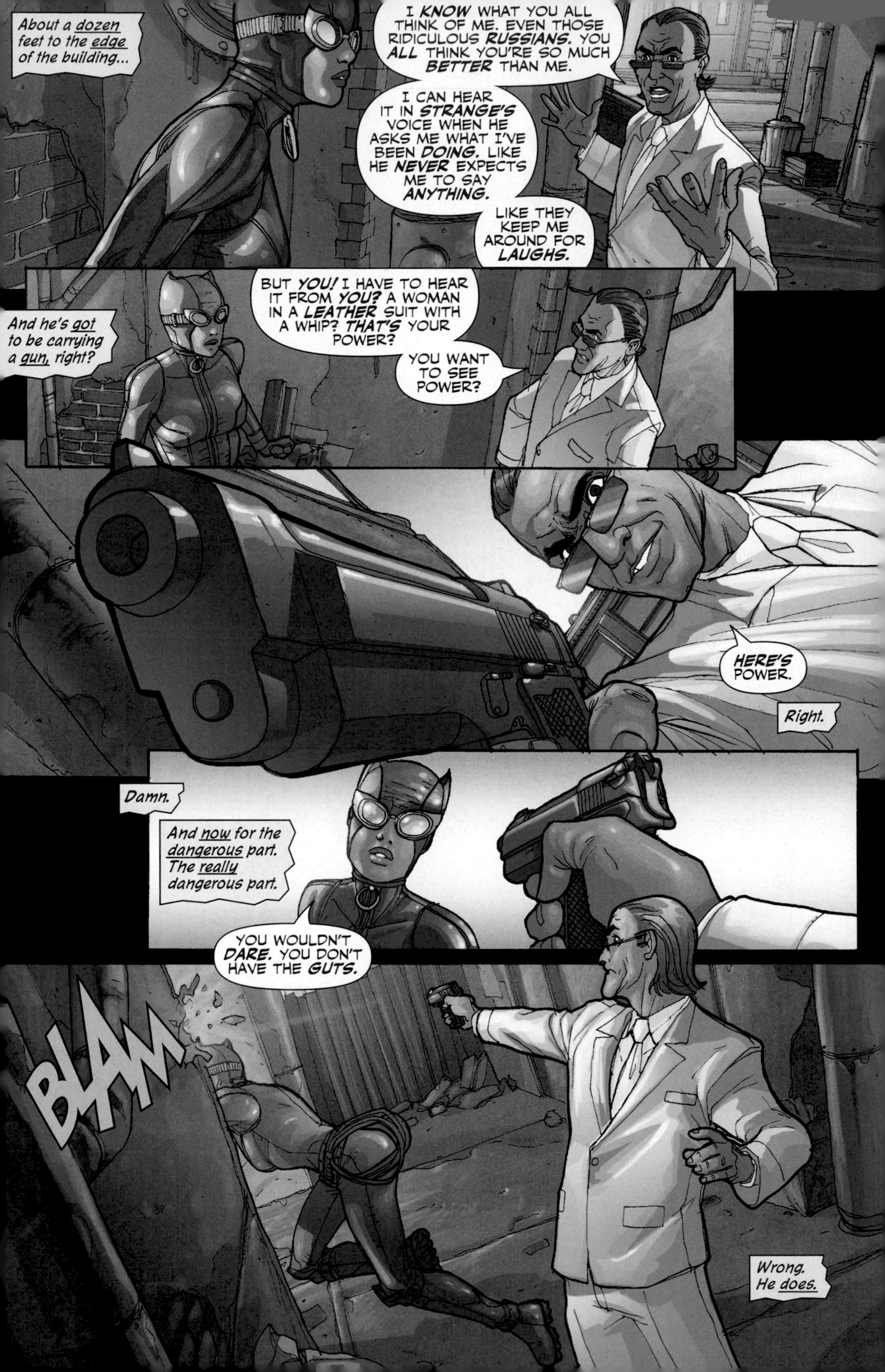
About a dozen feet to the edge of the building...
I KNOW WHAT YOU ALL THINK OF ME. EVEN THOSE RIDICULOUS RUSSIANS. YOU ALL THINK YOU'RE SO MUCH BETTER THAN ME.
I CAN HEAR IT IN STRANGE'S VOICE WHEN HE ASKS ME WHAT I'VE BEEN DOING. LIKE HE NEVER EXPECTS ME TO SAY ANYTHING.
LIKE THEY KEEP ME AROUND FOR LAUGHS.
And he's got to be carrying a gun, right?
BUT YOU! I HAVE TO HEAR IT FROM YOU? A WOMAN IN A LEATHER SUIT WITH A WHIP? THAT'S YOUR POWER?
YOU WANT TO SEE POWER?
HERE'S POWER.
Right.
Damn.
And now for the dangerous part. The really dangerous part.
YOU WOULDN'T DARE. YOU DON'T HAVE THE GUTS.
BLAM
Wrong. He does.

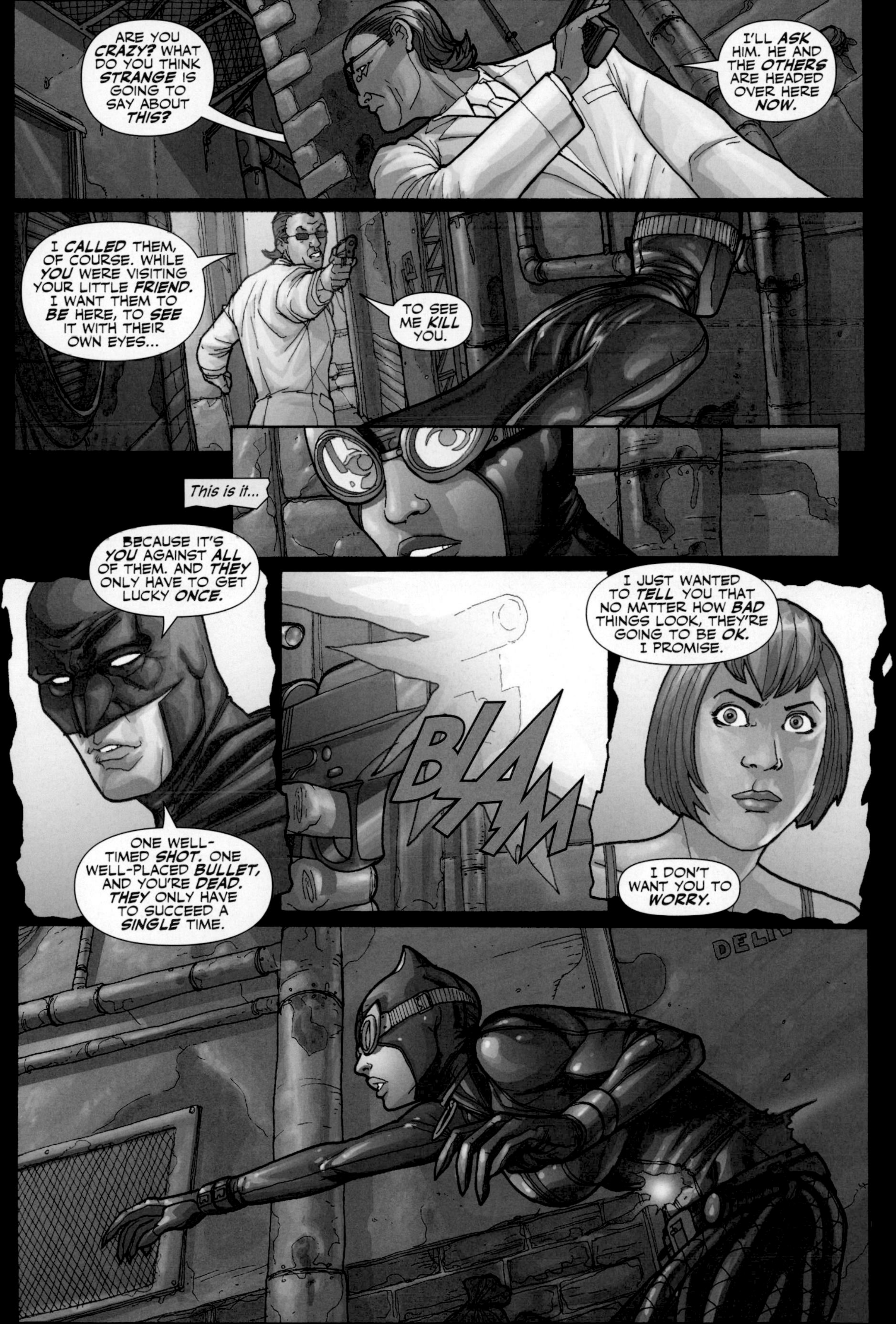
ARE YOU CRAZY? WHAT DO YOU THINK STRANGE IS GOING TO SAY ABOUT THIS?
I'LL ASK HIM. HE AND THE OTHERS ARE HEADED OVER HERE NOW.
I CALLED THEM, OF COURSE. WHILE YOU WERE VISITING YOUR LITTLE FRIEND. I WANT THEM TO BE HERE, TO SEE IT WITH THEIR OWN EYES...
TO SEE ME KILL YOU.
This is it...
BECAUSE IT'S YOU AGAINST ALL OF THEM. AND THEY ONLY HAVE TO GET LUCKY ONCE.
ONE WELL-TIMED SHOT. ONE WELL-PLACED BULLET, AND YOU'RE DEAD. THEY ONLY HAVE TO SUCCEED A SINGLE TIME.
BLAM
I JUST WANTED TO TELL YOU THAT NO MATTER HOW BAD THINGS LOOK, THEY'RE GOING TO BE OK. I PROMISE.
I DON'T WANT YOU TO WORRY.

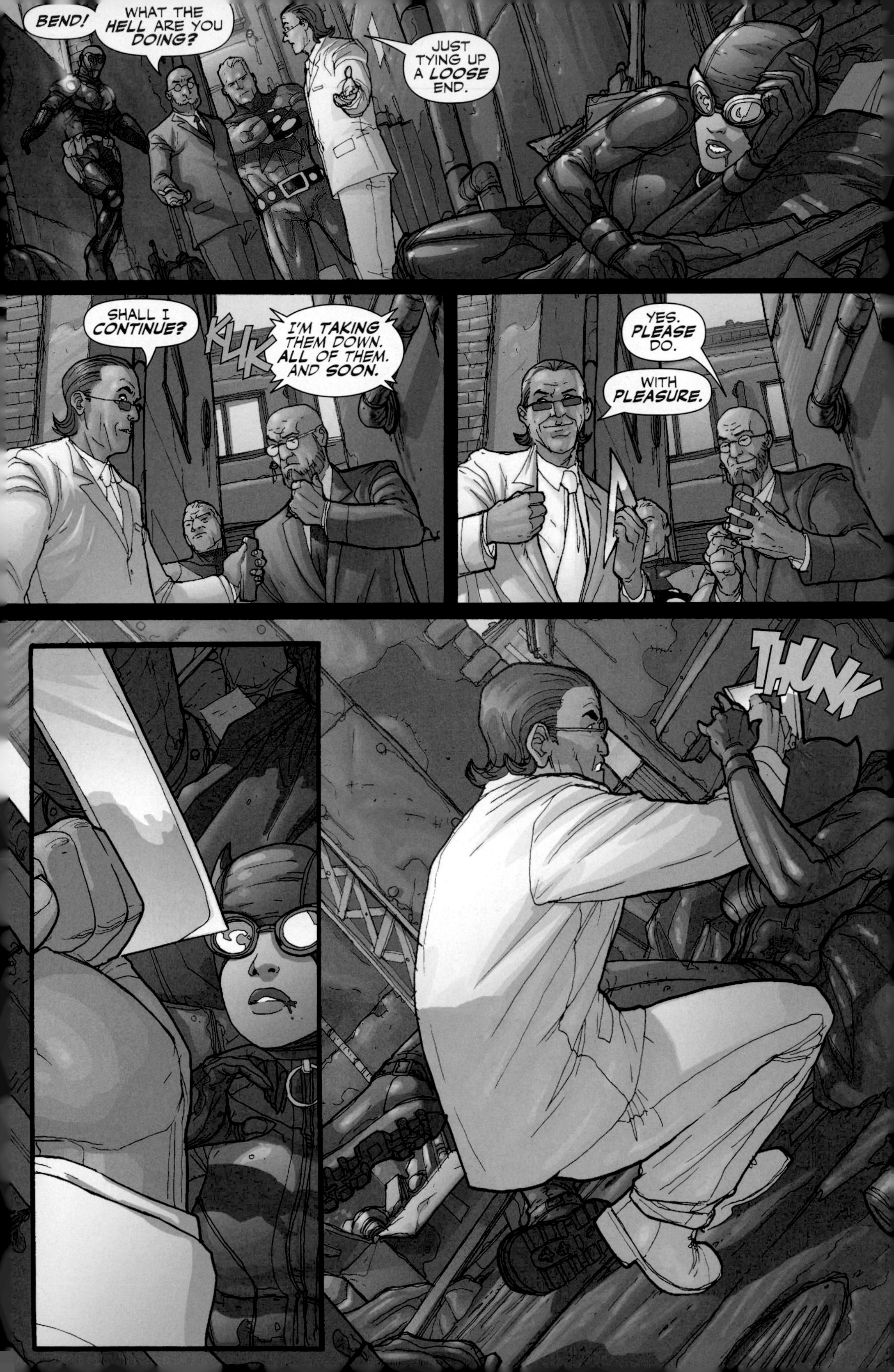
BEND!
WHAT THE HELL ARE YOU DOING?
JUST TYING UP A LOOSE END.
SHALL I CONTINUE?
KLIK
I'M TAKING THEM DOWN. ALL OF THEM. AND SOON.
YES. PLEASE DO.
WITH PLEASURE.
THUNK

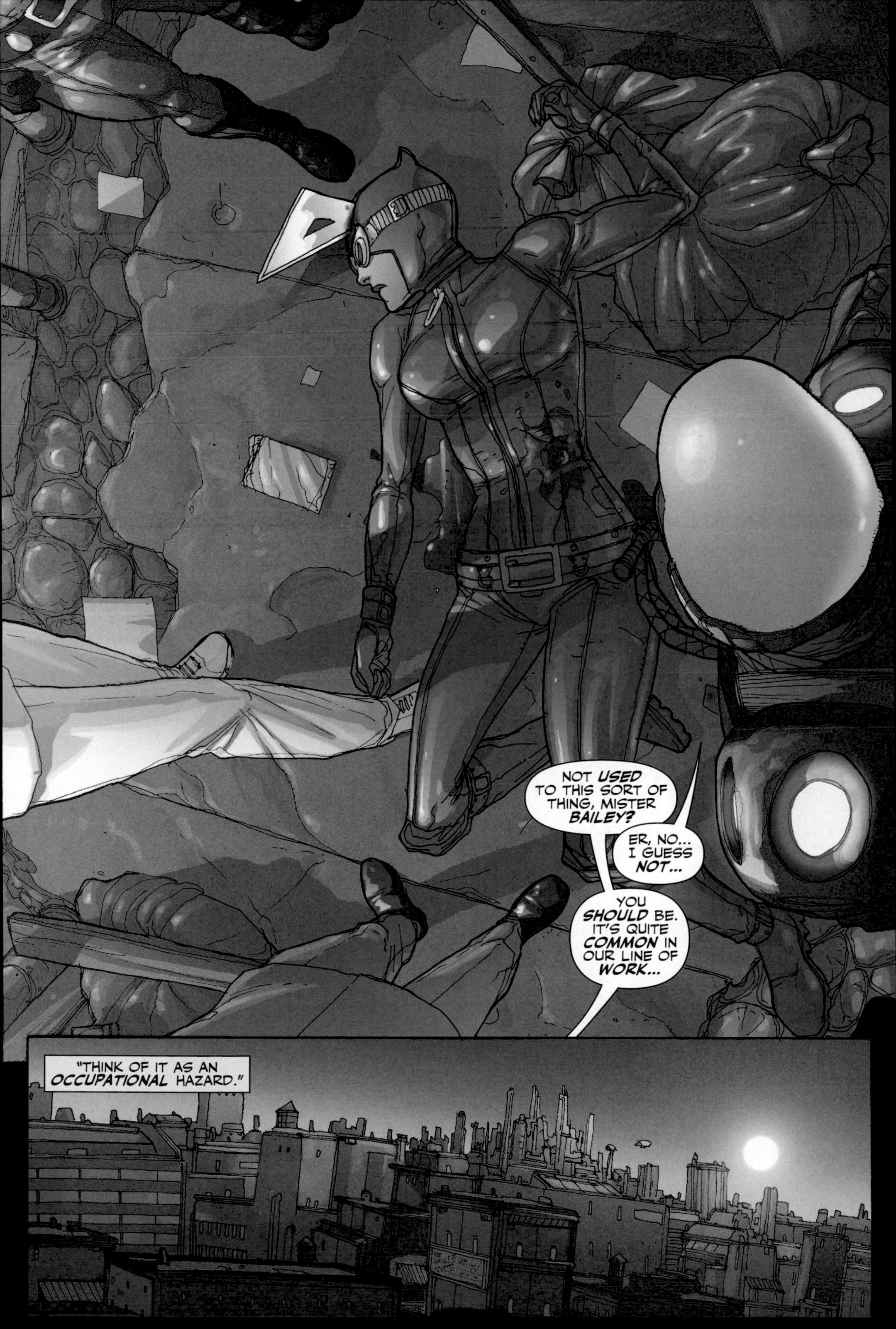
NOT USED TO THIS SORT OF THING, MISTER BAILEY?
ER, NO... I GUESS NOT...
YOU SHOULD BE. IT'S QUITE COMMON IN OUR LINE OF WORK...
"THINK OF IT AS AN OCCUPATIONAL HAZARD."

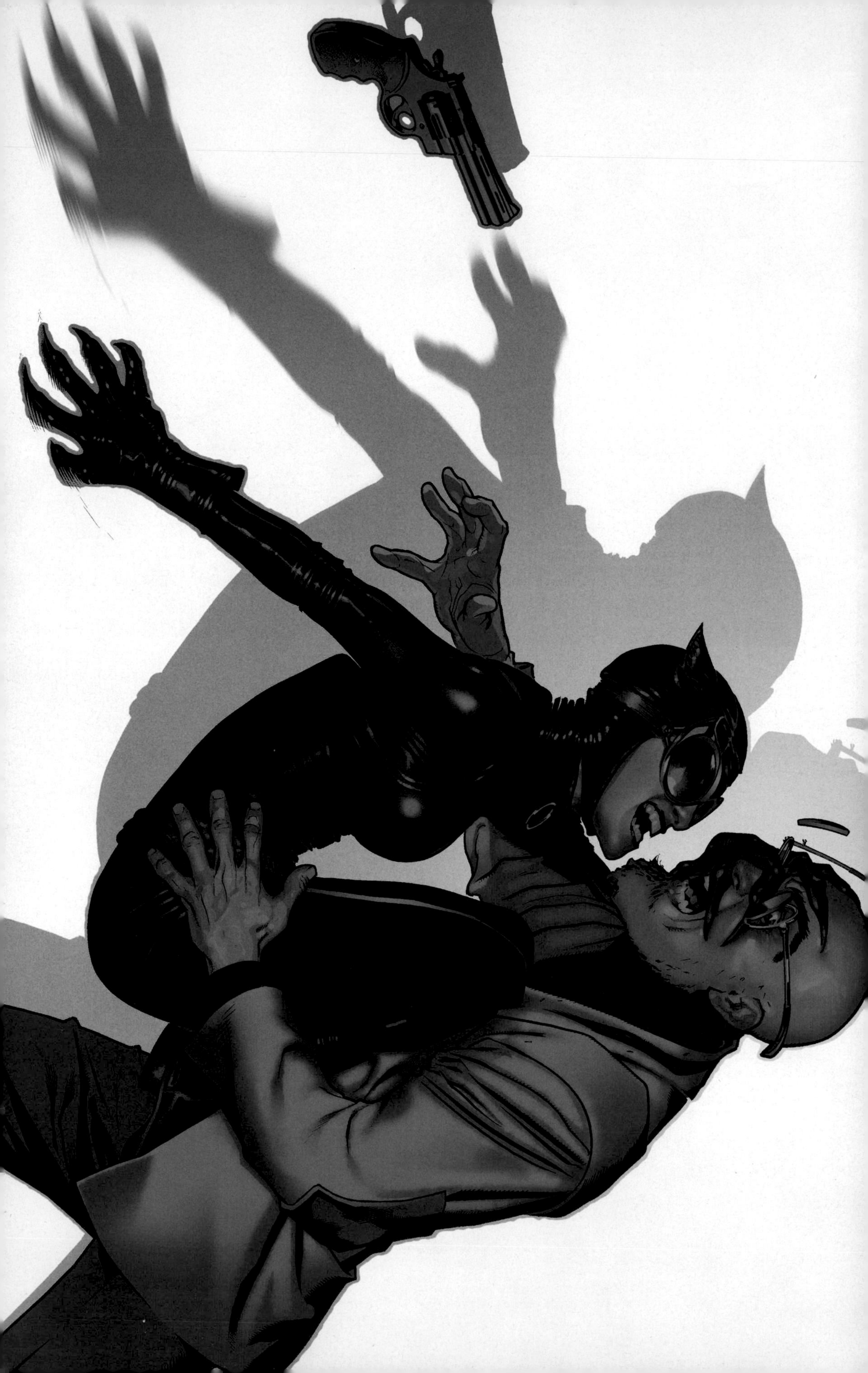

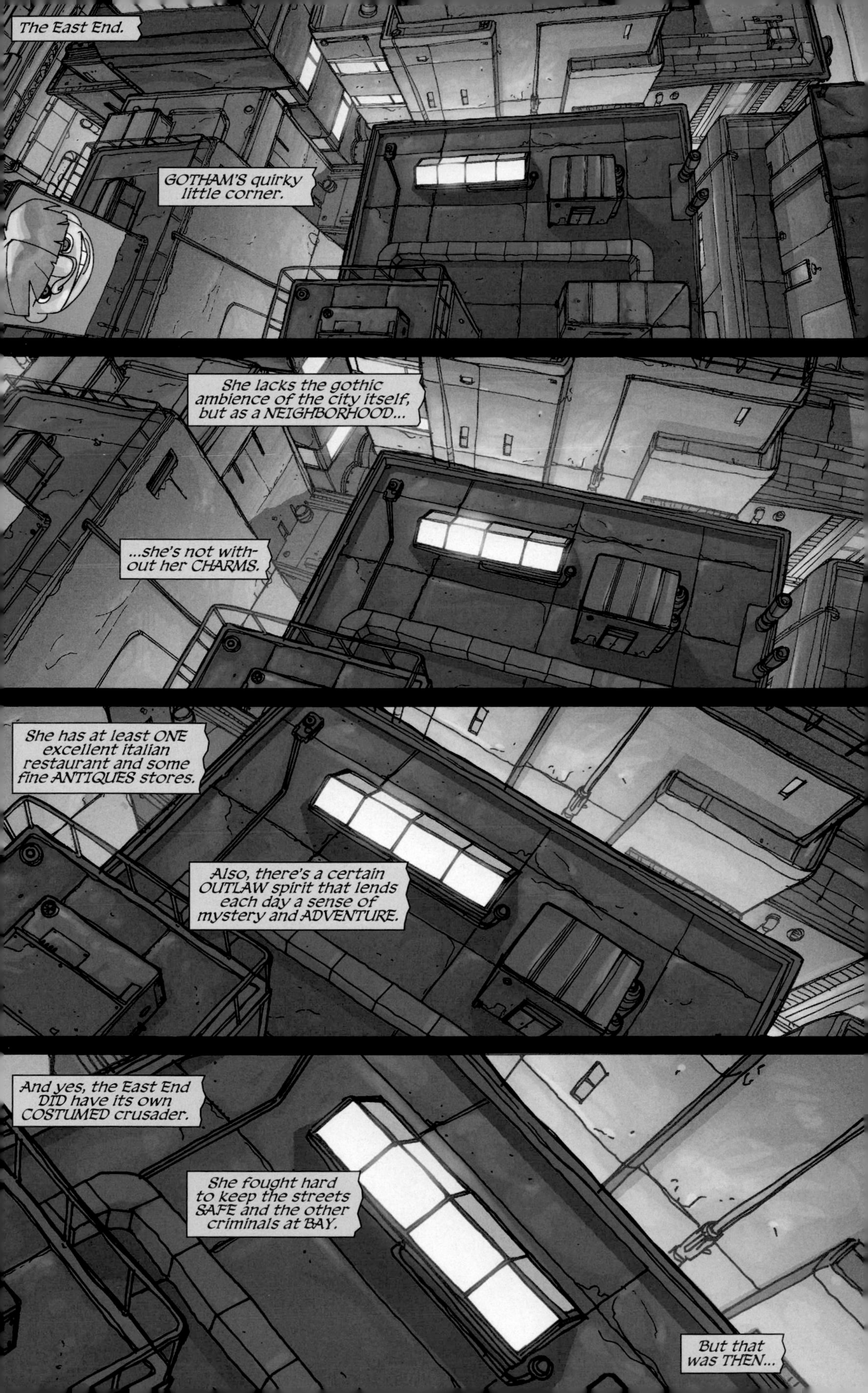
The East End.
GOTHAM'S quirky little corner.
She lacks the gothic ambience of the city itself, but as a NEIGHBORHOOD...
...she's not without her CHARMS.
She has at least ONE excellent italian restaurant and some fine ANTIQUES stores.
Also, there's a certain OUTLAW spirit that lends each day a sense of mystery and ADVENTURE.
And yes, the East End DID have its own COSTUMED crusader.
She fought hard to keep the streets SAFE and the other criminals at BAY.
But that was THEN...

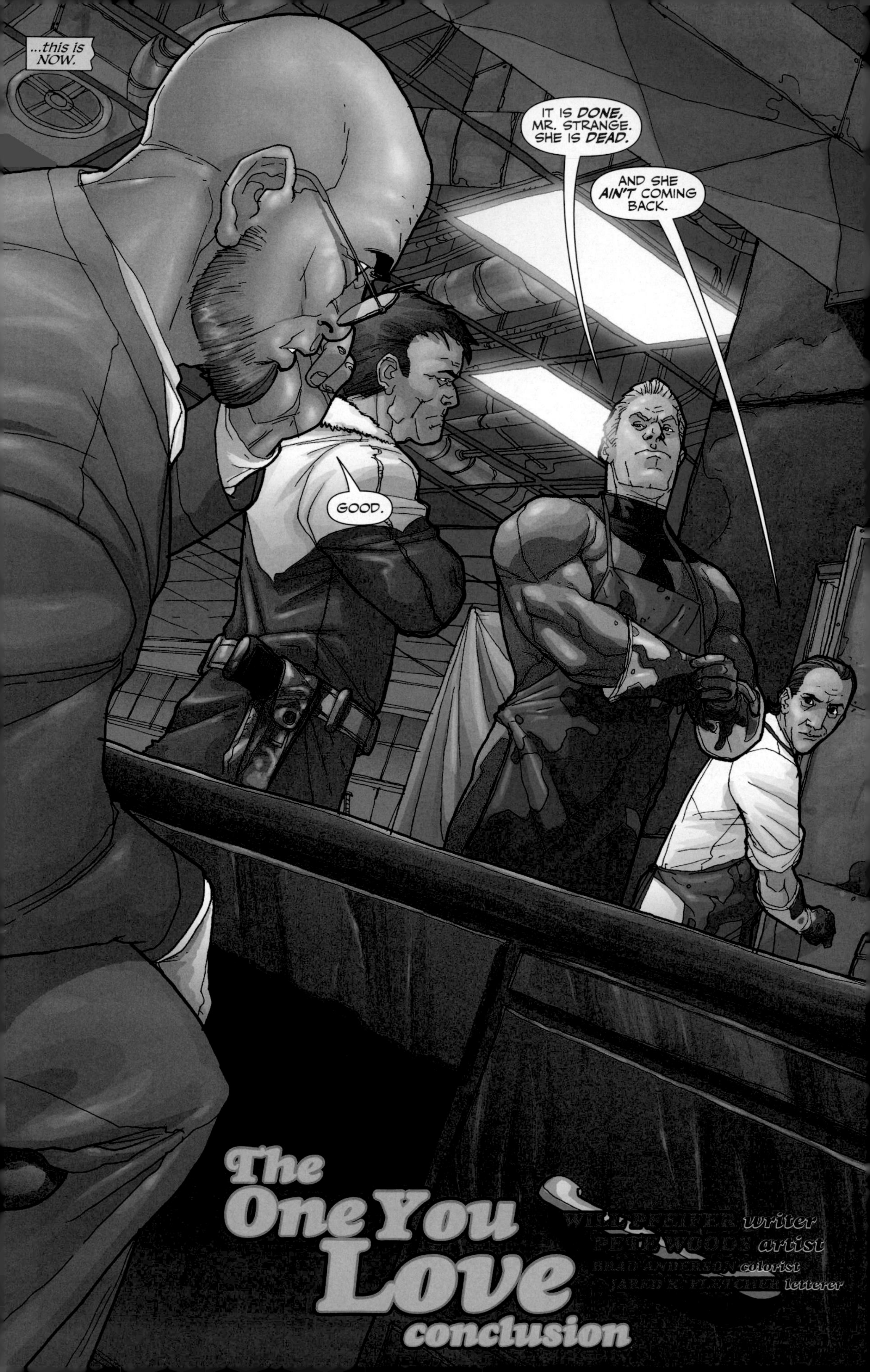

...this is NOW.
IT IS DONE, MR. STRANGE. SHE IS DEAD.
AND SHE AIN'T COMING BACK.
GOOD.
The One You Love conclusion
WILL PFEIFER writer
PETE WOODS artist
BRAD ANDERSON colorist
JARED K. FLETCHER letterer

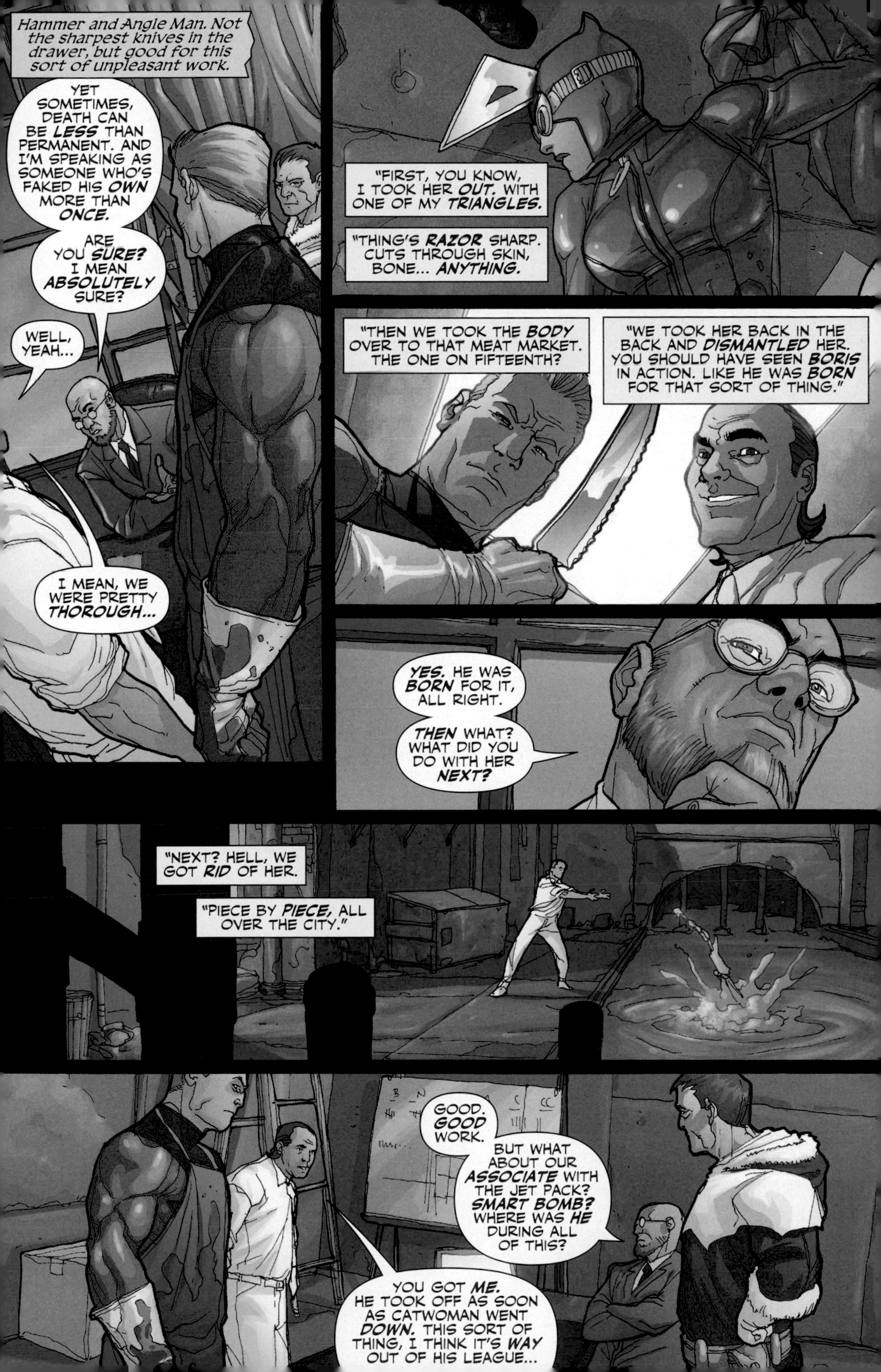
Hammer and Angle Man. Not the sharpest knives in the drawer, but good for this sort of unpleasant work.
YET SOMETIMES, DEATH CAN BE LESS THAN PERMANENT. AND I'M SPEAKING AS SOMEONE WHO'S FAKED HIS OWN MORE THAN ONCE.
ARE YOU SURE? I MEAN ABSOLUTELY SURE?
WELL, YEAH...
I MEAN, WE WERE PRETTY THOROUGH...
"FIRST, YOU KNOW, I TOOK HER OUT. WITH ONE OF MY TRIANGLES.
"THING'S RAZOR SHARP. CUTS THROUGH SKIN, BONE... ANYTHING.
"THEN WE TOOK THE BODY OVER TO THAT MEAT MARKET. THE ONE ON FIFTEENTH?
"WE TOOK HER BACK IN THE BACK AND DISMANTLED HER. YOU SHOULD HAVE SEEN BORIS IN ACTION. LIKE HE WAS BORN FOR THAT SORT OF THING."
YES. HE WAS BORN FOR IT, ALL RIGHT.
THEN WHAT? WHAT DID YOU DO WITH HER NEXT?
"NEXT? HELL, WE GOT RID OF HER.
"PIECE BY PIECE, ALL OVER THE CITY."
GOOD. GOOD WORK.
BUT WHAT ABOUT OUR ASSOCIATE WITH THE JET PACK? SMART BOMB? WHERE WAS HE DURING ALL OF THIS?
YOU GOT ME. HE TOOK OFF AS SOON AS CATWOMAN WENT DOWN. THIS SORT OF THING, I THINK IT'S WAY OUT OF HIS LEAGUE...

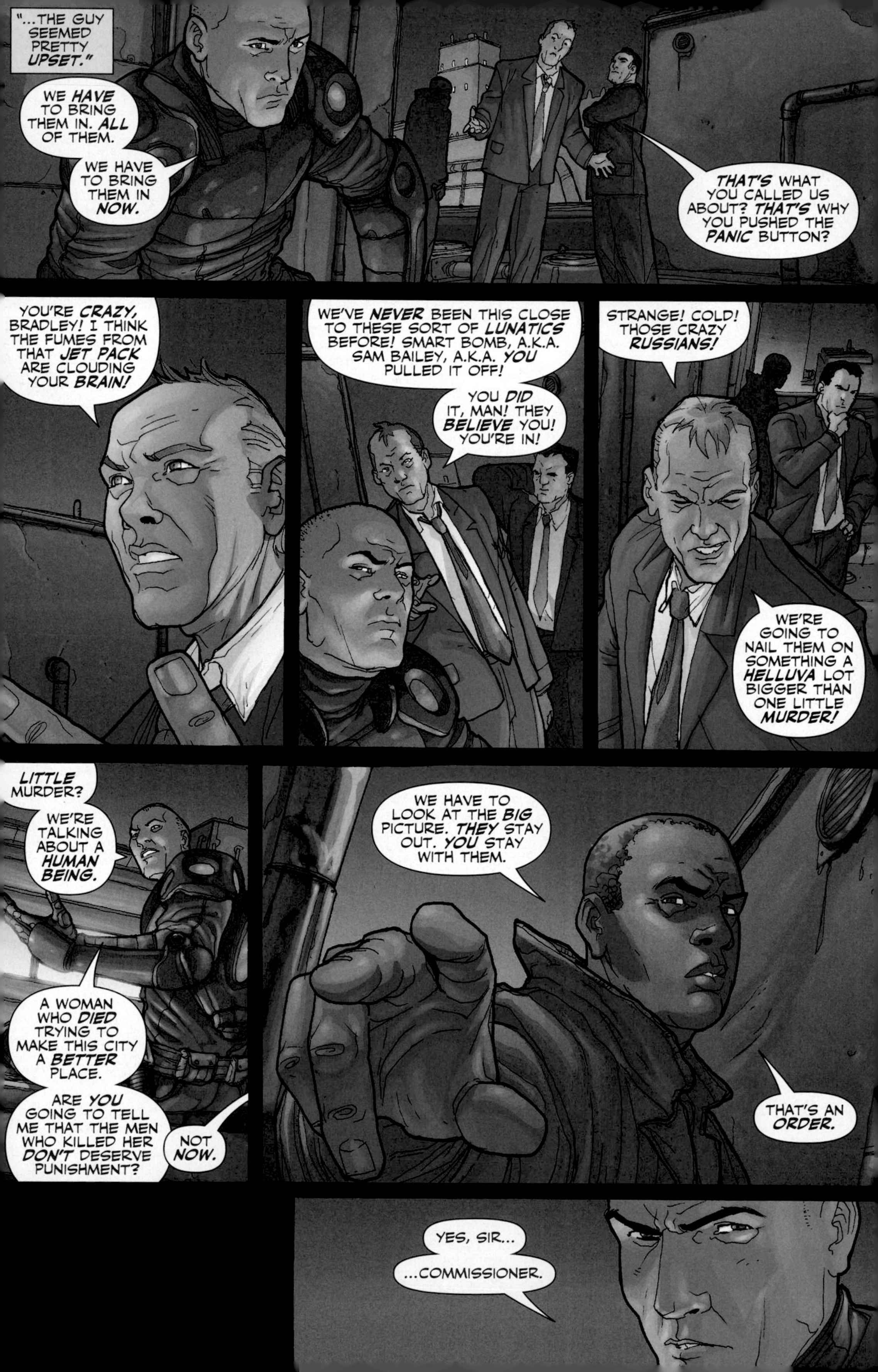
"...THE GUY SEEMED PRETTY *UPSET.*"
WE *HAVE* TO BRING THEM IN. *ALL* OF THEM.
WE HAVE TO BRING THEM IN *NOW.*
THAT'S WHAT YOU CALLED US ABOUT? *THAT'S* WHY YOU PUSHED THE *PANIC* BUTTON?
YOU'RE *CRAZY,* BRADLEY! I THINK THE FUMES FROM THAT *JET PACK* ARE CLOUDING YOUR *BRAIN!*
WE'VE *NEVER* BEEN THIS CLOSE TO THESE SORT OF *LUNATICS* BEFORE! SMART BOMB, A.K.A. SAM BAILEY, A.K.A. *YOU* PULLED IT OFF!
YOU *DID* IT, MAN! THEY *BELIEVE* YOU! YOU'RE IN!
STRANGE! COLD! THOSE CRAZY *RUSSIANS!*
WE'RE GOING TO NAIL THEM ON SOMETHING A *HELLUVA* LOT BIGGER THAN ONE LITTLE *MURDER!*
LITTLE MURDER?
WE'RE TALKING ABOUT A *HUMAN BEING.*
A WOMAN WHO *DIED* TRYING TO MAKE THIS CITY A *BETTER* PLACE.
ARE *YOU* GOING TO TELL ME THAT THE MEN WHO KILLED HER *DON'T* DESERVE PUNISHMENT?
NOT *NOW.*
WE HAVE TO LOOK AT THE *BIG* PICTURE. *THEY* STAY OUT. *YOU* STAY WITH THEM.
THAT'S AN *ORDER.*
YES, SIR...
...COMMISSIONER.

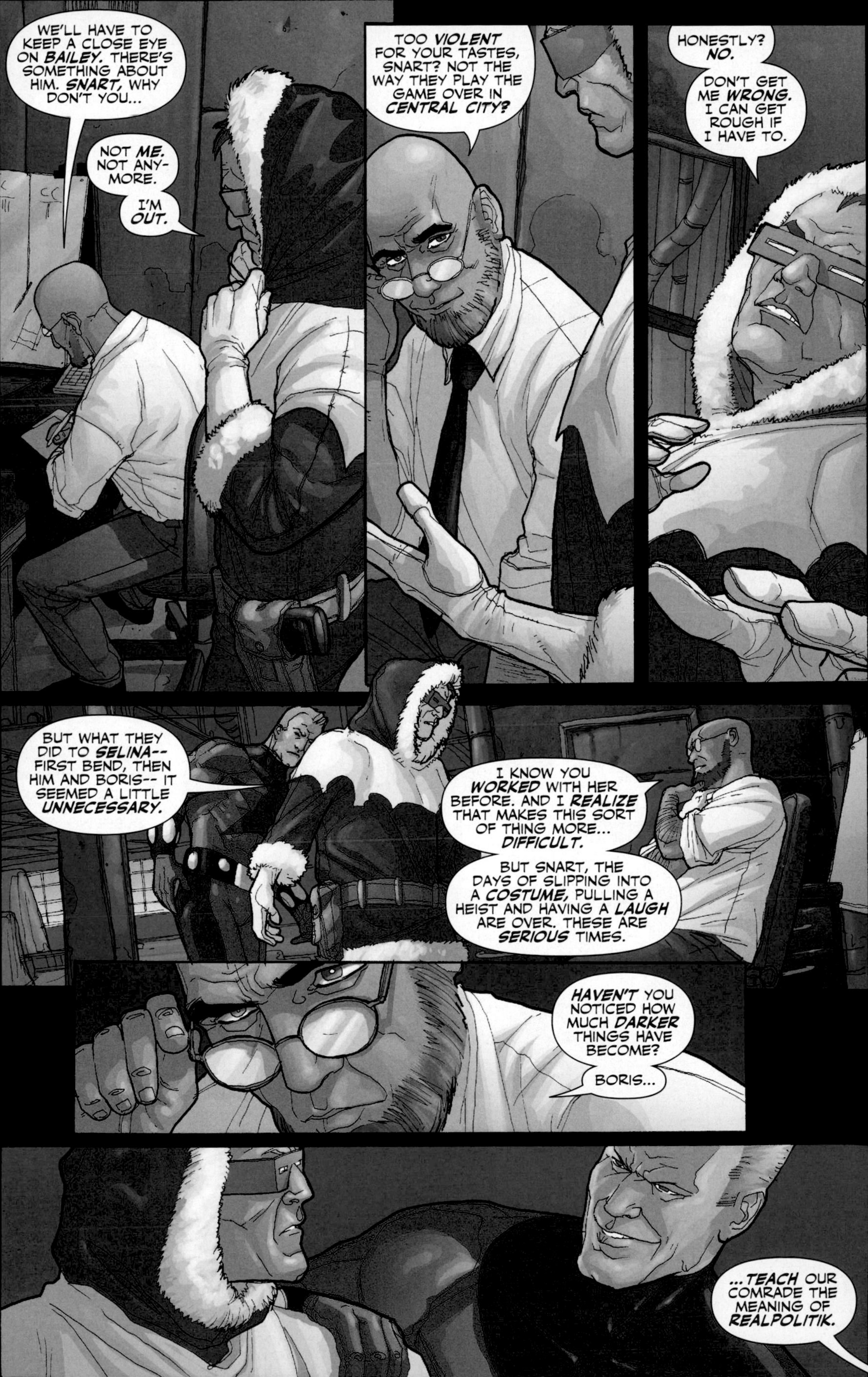
WE'LL HAVE TO KEEP A CLOSE EYE ON BAILEY. THERE'S SOMETHING ABOUT HIM. SNART, WHY DON'T YOU...
NOT ME. NOT ANY-MORE.
I'M OUT.
TOO VIOLENT FOR YOUR TASTES, SNART? NOT THE WAY THEY PLAY THE GAME OVER IN CENTRAL CITY?
HONESTLY? NO.
DON'T GET ME WRONG. I CAN GET ROUGH IF I HAVE TO.
BUT WHAT THEY DID TO SELINA-- FIRST BEND, THEN HIM AND BORIS-- IT SEEMED A LITTLE UNNECESSARY.
I KNOW YOU WORKED WITH HER BEFORE. AND I REALIZE THAT MAKES THIS SORT OF THING MORE... DIFFICULT.
BUT SNART, THE DAYS OF SLIPPING INTO A COSTUME, PULLING A HEIST AND HAVING A LAUGH ARE OVER. THESE ARE SERIOUS TIMES.
HAVEN'T YOU NOTICED HOW MUCH DARKER THINGS HAVE BECOME?
BORIS...
...TEACH OUR COMRADE THE MEANING OF REALPOLITIK.

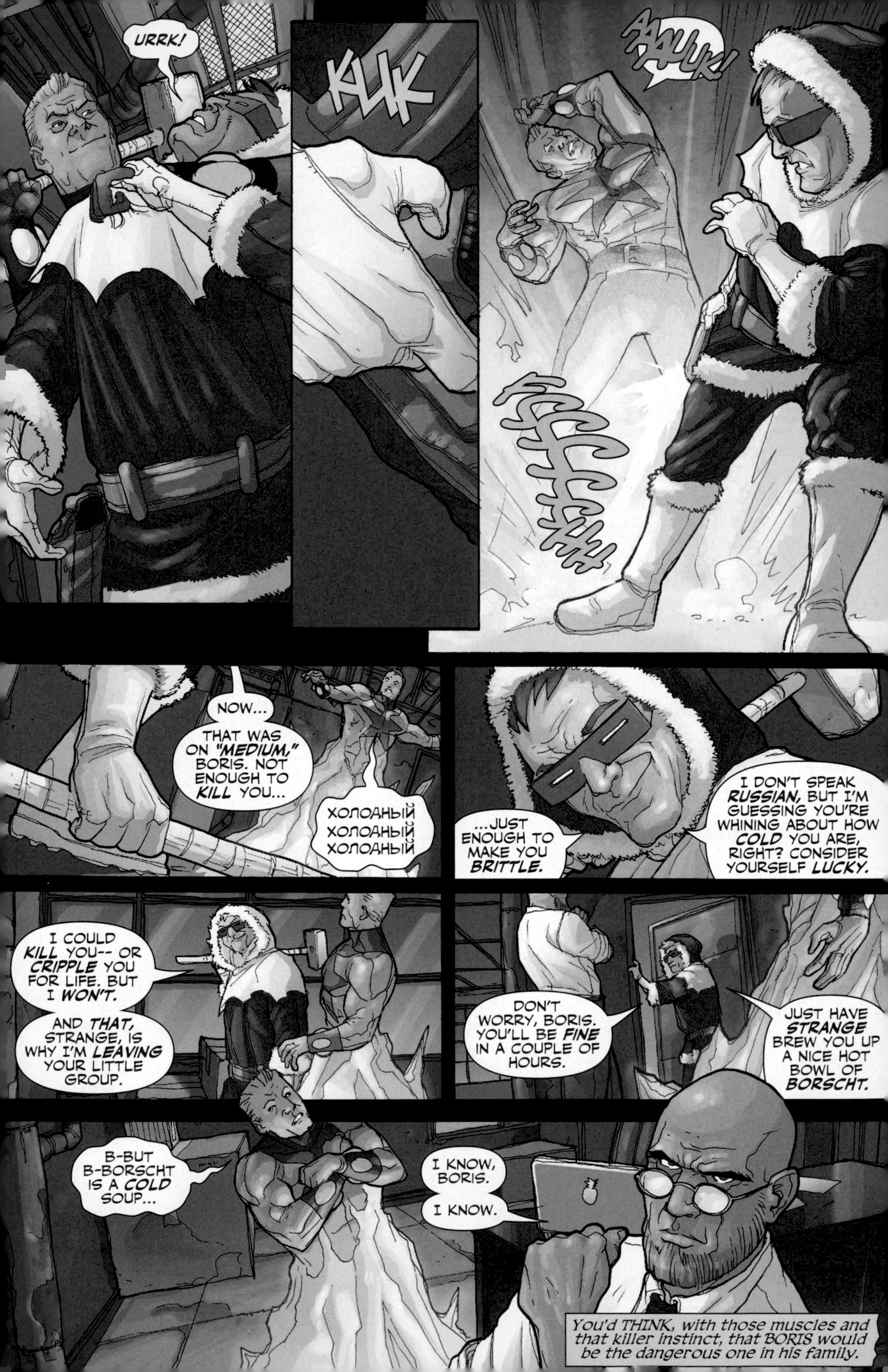
URRK!
KLUK
AAAUK!
KSSCCHHH
NOW...
THAT WAS ON "MEDIUM," BORIS. NOT ENOUGH TO KILL YOU...
ХОЛОДНЫЙ ХОЛОДНЫЙ ХОЛОДНЫЙ
...JUST ENOUGH TO MAKE YOU BRITTLE.
I DON'T SPEAK RUSSIAN, BUT I'M GUESSING YOU'RE WHINING ABOUT HOW COLD YOU ARE, RIGHT? CONSIDER YOURSELF LUCKY.
I COULD KILL YOU-- OR CRIPPLE YOU FOR LIFE. BUT I WON'T.
AND THAT, STRANGE, IS WHY I'M LEAVING YOUR LITTLE GROUP.
DON'T WORRY, BORIS. YOU'LL BE FINE IN A COUPLE OF HOURS.
JUST HAVE STRANGE BREW YOU UP A NICE HOT BOWL OF BORSCHT.
B-BUT B-BORSCHT IS A COLD SOUP...
I KNOW, BORIS.
I KNOW.
You'd THINK, with those muscles and that killer instinct, that BORIS would be the dangerous one in his family.

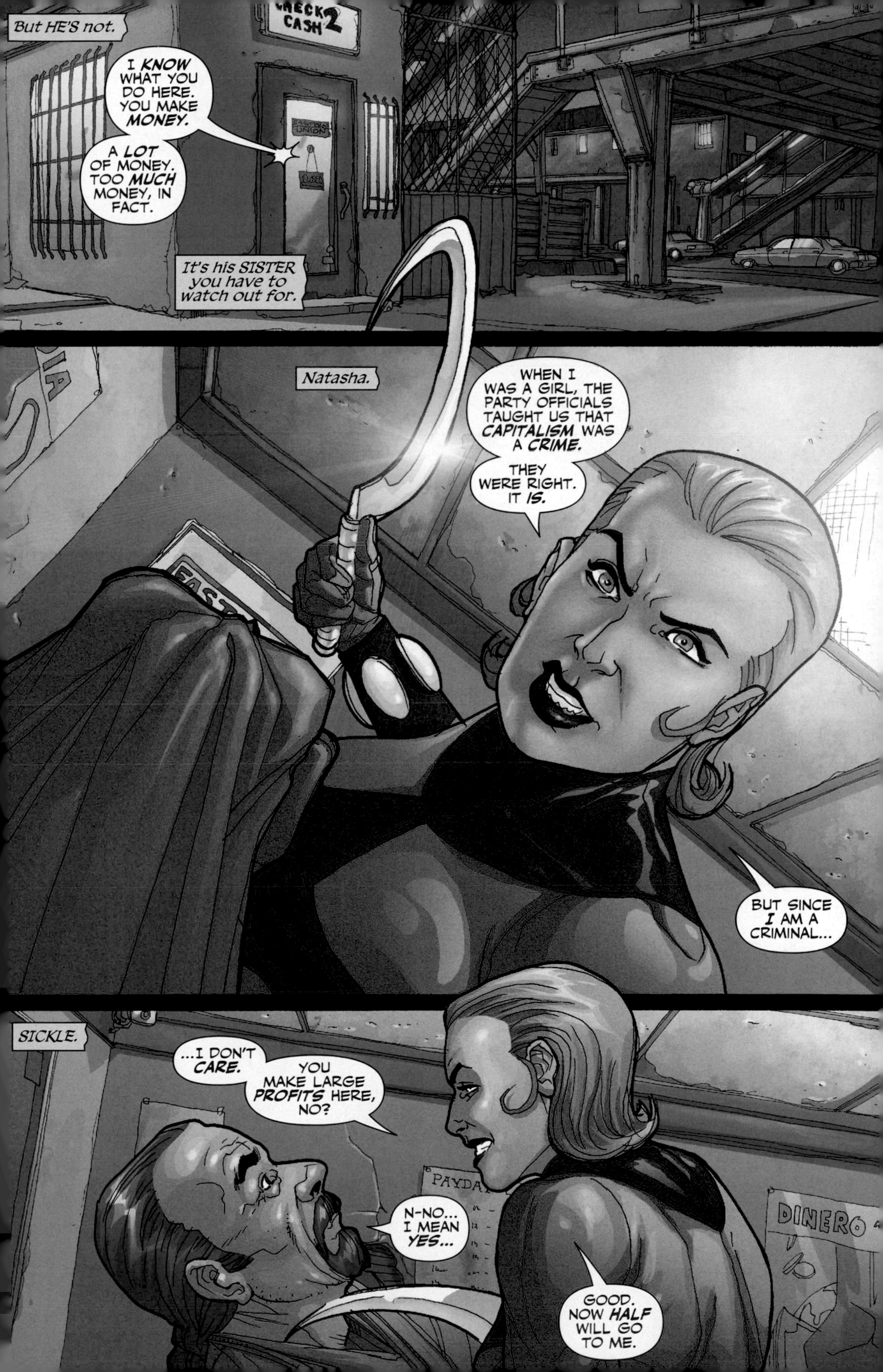

But HE'S not.
CHECK CASH 2
I KNOW WHAT YOU DO HERE. YOU MAKE MONEY.
A LOT OF MONEY. TOO MUCH MONEY, IN FACT.
CLOSED
It's his SISTER you have to watch out for.
Natasha.
WHEN I WAS A GIRL, THE PARTY OFFICIALS TAUGHT US THAT CAPITALISM WAS A CRIME.
THEY WERE RIGHT. IT IS.
BUT SINCE I AM A CRIMINAL...
SICKLE.
...I DON'T CARE.
YOU MAKE LARGE PROFITS HERE, NO?
PAYDAY
N-NO... I MEAN YES...
DINERO
GOOD. NOW HALF WILL GO TO ME.

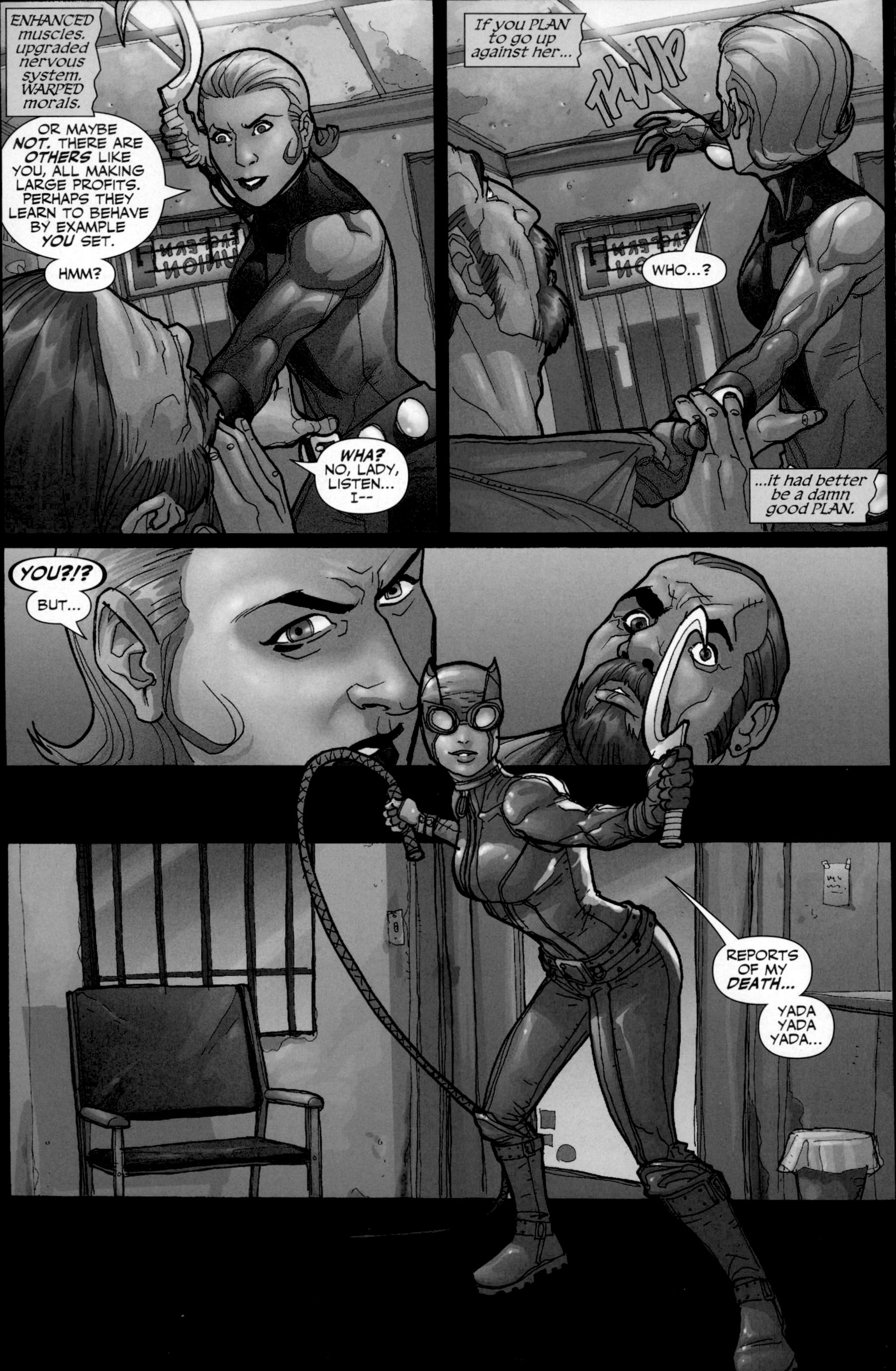

ENHANCED muscles. upgraded nervous system. WARPED morals.
OR MAYBE NOT. THERE ARE OTHERS LIKE YOU, ALL MAKING LARGE PROFITS. PERHAPS THEY LEARN TO BEHAVE BY EXAMPLE YOU SET.
HMM?
WHA? NO, LADY, LISTEN... I--
If you PLAN to go up against her...
THWIP
WHO...?
...it had better be a damn good PLAN.
YOU?!?
BUT...
REPORTS OF MY DEATH...
YADA YADA YADA...

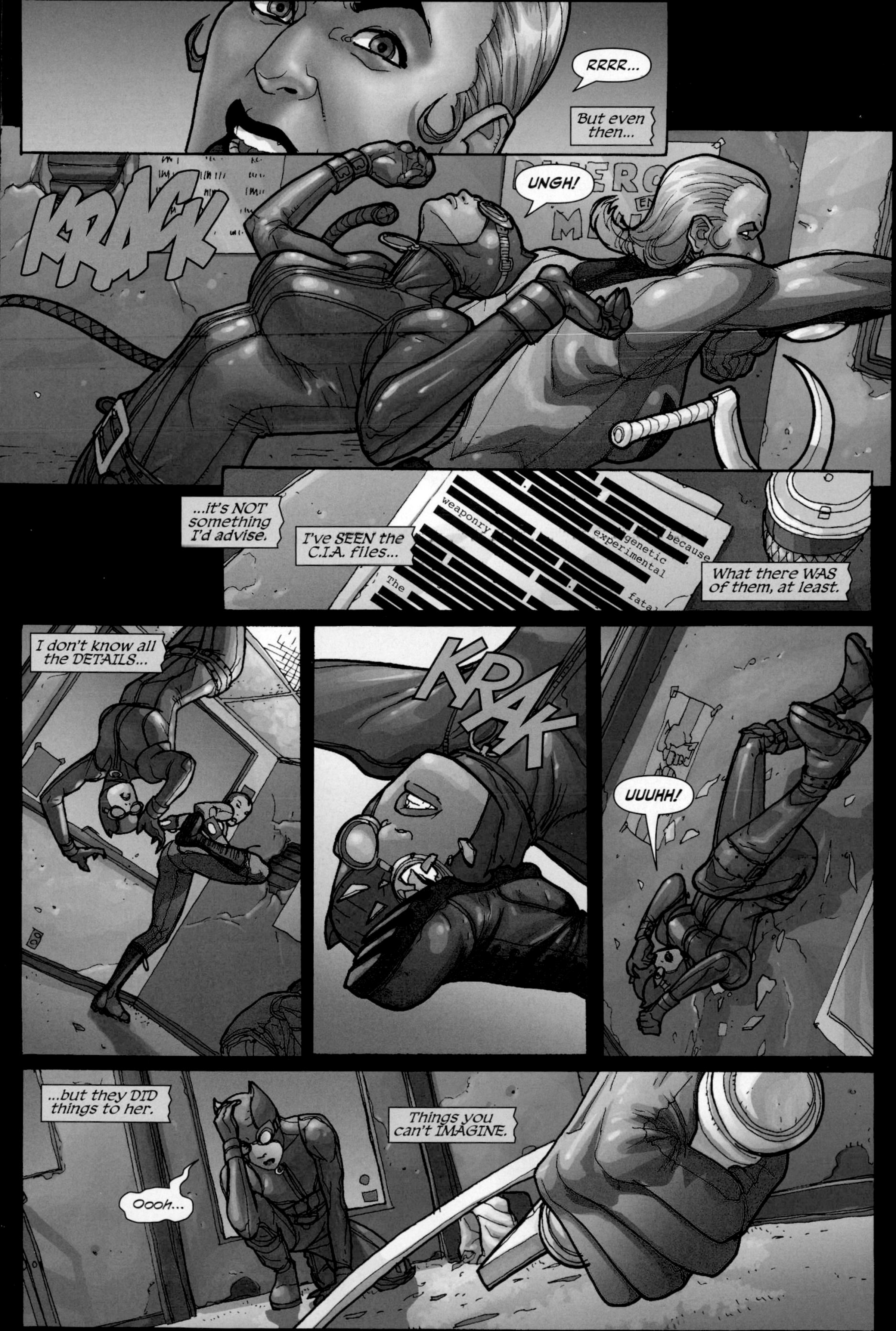
RRRR...
But even then...
KRACK
UNGH!
...it's NOT something I'd advise.
I've SEEN the C.I.A. files...
[redacted] weaponry [redacted] genetic [redacted] because experimental [redacted] The [redacted] fatal [redacted]
What there WAS of them, at least.
I don't know all the DETAILS...
KRAK
UUUHH!
...but they DID things to her.
Things you can't IMAGINE.
Oooh...

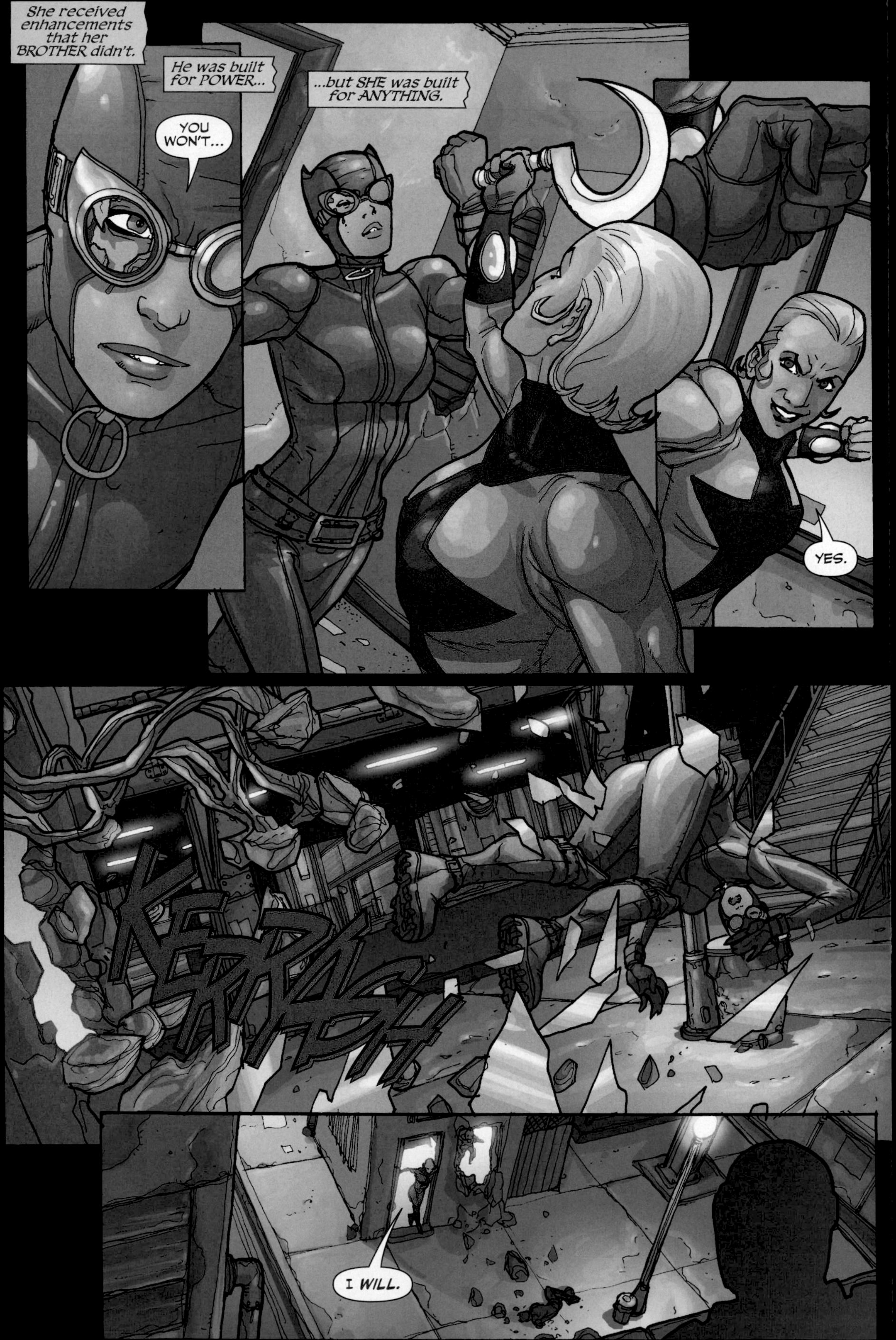
She received enhancements that her BROTHER didn't.
He was built for POWER...
...but SHE was built for ANYTHING.
YOU WON'T...
YES.
KERRASH
I WILL.

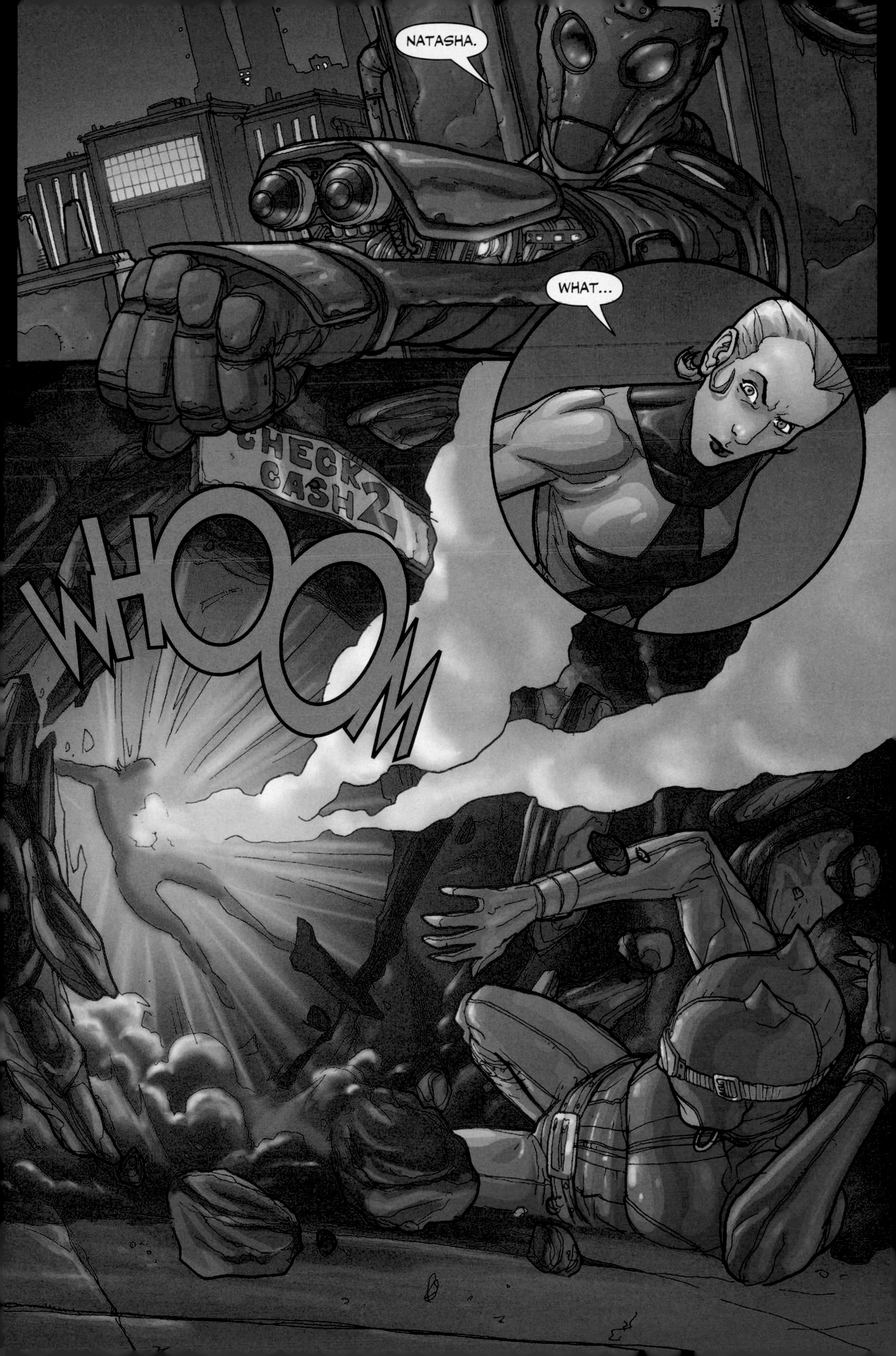
NATASHA.
WHAT...
CHECK CASH 2
WHOOM

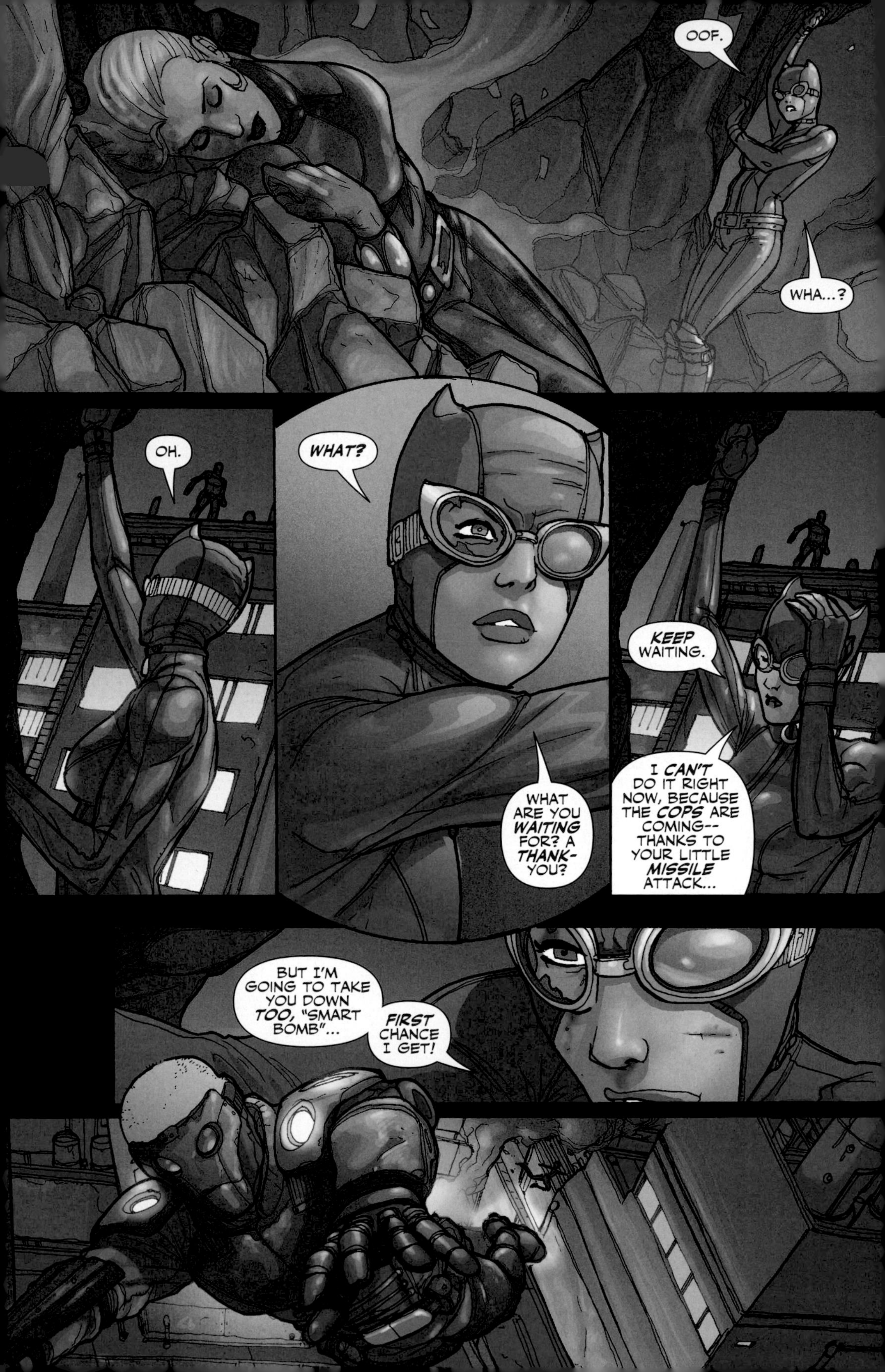
OOF.
WHA...?
OH.
WHAT?
WHAT ARE YOU WAITING FOR? A THANK-YOU?
KEEP WAITING.
I CAN'T DO IT RIGHT NOW, BECAUSE THE COPS ARE COMING-- THANKS TO YOUR LITTLE MISSILE ATTACK...
BUT I'M GOING TO TAKE YOU DOWN TOO, "SMART BOMB"...
FIRST CHANCE I GET!

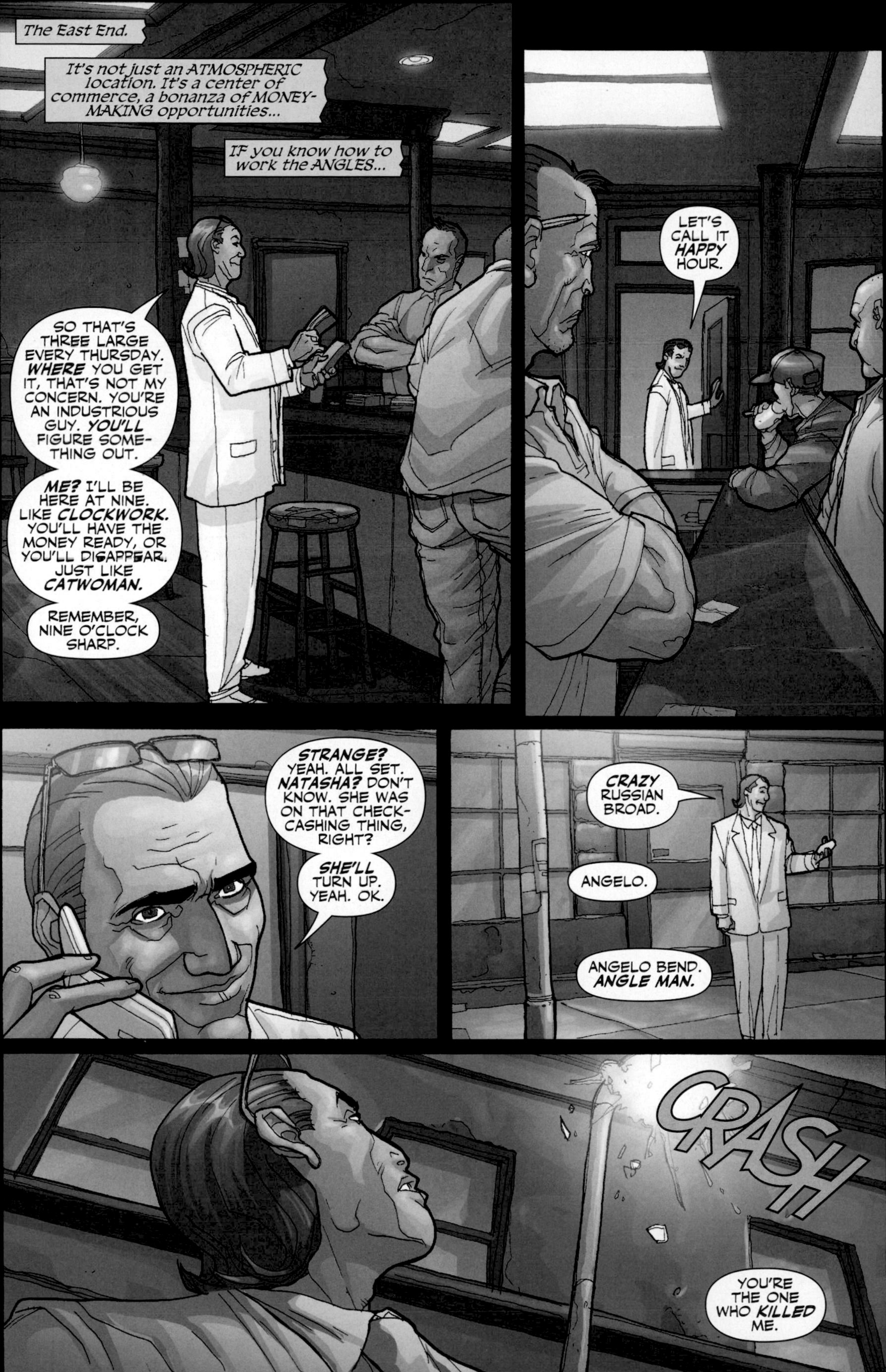
The East End.
It's not just an ATMOSPHERIC location. It's a center of commerce, a bonanza of MONEY-MAKING opportunities...
IF you know how to work the ANGLES...
SO THAT'S THREE LARGE EVERY THURSDAY. WHERE YOU GET IT, THAT'S NOT MY CONCERN. YOU'RE AN INDUSTRIOUS GUY. YOU'LL FIGURE SOMETHING OUT.
ME? I'LL BE HERE AT NINE. LIKE CLOCKWORK. YOU'LL HAVE THE MONEY READY, OR YOU'LL DISAPPEAR. JUST LIKE CATWOMAN.
REMEMBER, NINE O'CLOCK SHARP.
LET'S CALL IT HAPPY HOUR.
STRANGE? YEAH. ALL SET. NATASHA? DON'T KNOW. SHE WAS ON THAT CHECK-CASHING THING, RIGHT?
SHE'LL TURN UP. YEAH. OK.
CRAZY RUSSIAN BROAD.
ANGELO.
ANGELO BEND. ANGLE MAN.
CRASH
YOU'RE THE ONE WHO KILLED ME.

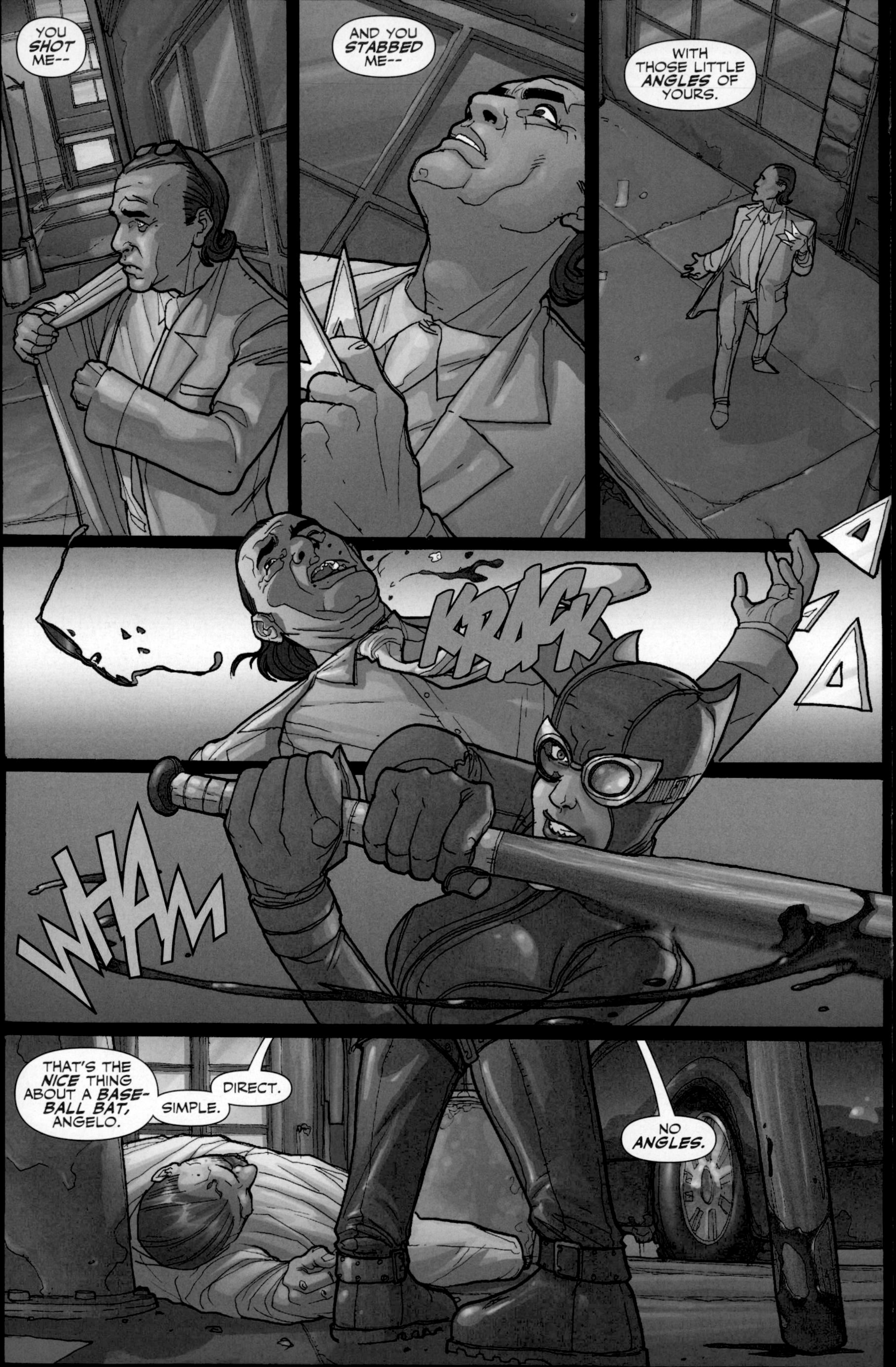

YOU SHOT ME--
AND YOU STABBED ME--
WITH THOSE LITTLE ANGLES OF YOURS.
KRACK
WHAM
THAT'S THE NICE THING ABOUT A BASE-BALL BAT, ANGELO.
SIMPLE.
DIRECT.
NO ANGLES.

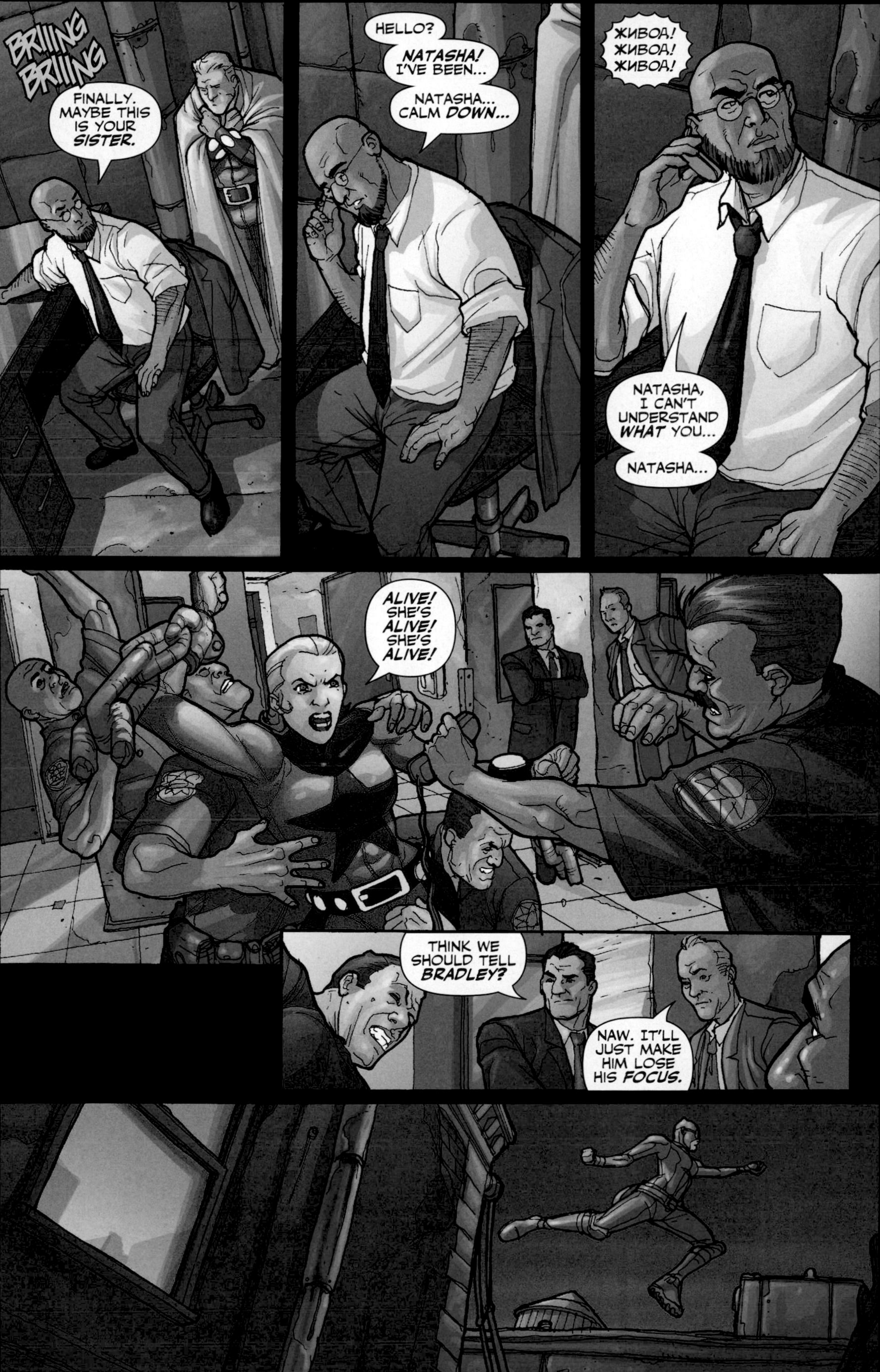
BRIIING BRIIING
FINALLY. MAYBE THIS IS YOUR SISTER.
HELLO?
NATASHA! I'VE BEEN...
NATASHA... CALM DOWN...
ЖИВОД! ЖИВОД! ЖИВОД!
NATASHA, I CAN'T UNDERSTAND WHAT YOU...
NATASHA...
ALIVE! SHE'S ALIVE! SHE'S ALIVE!
THINK WE SHOULD TELL BRADLEY?
NAW. IT'LL JUST MAKE HIM LOSE HIS FOCUS.

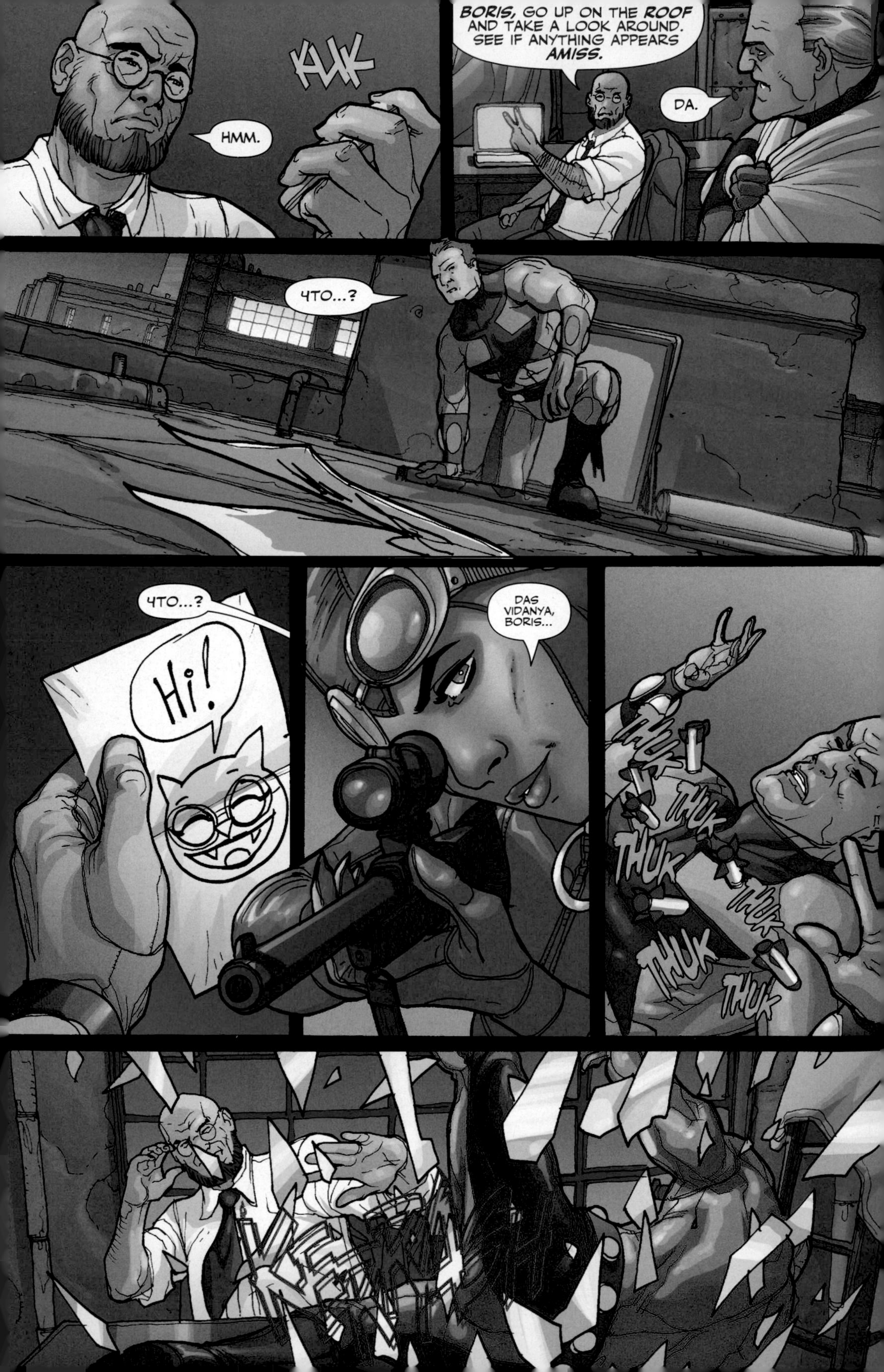
KLIK
HMM.
BORIS, GO UP ON THE ROOF AND TAKE A LOOK AROUND. SEE IF ANYTHING APPEARS AMISS.
DA.
ЧТО...?
ЧТО...?
Hi!
DAS VIDANYA, BORIS...
THUK
THUK
THUK
THUK
THUK
THUK
THUK

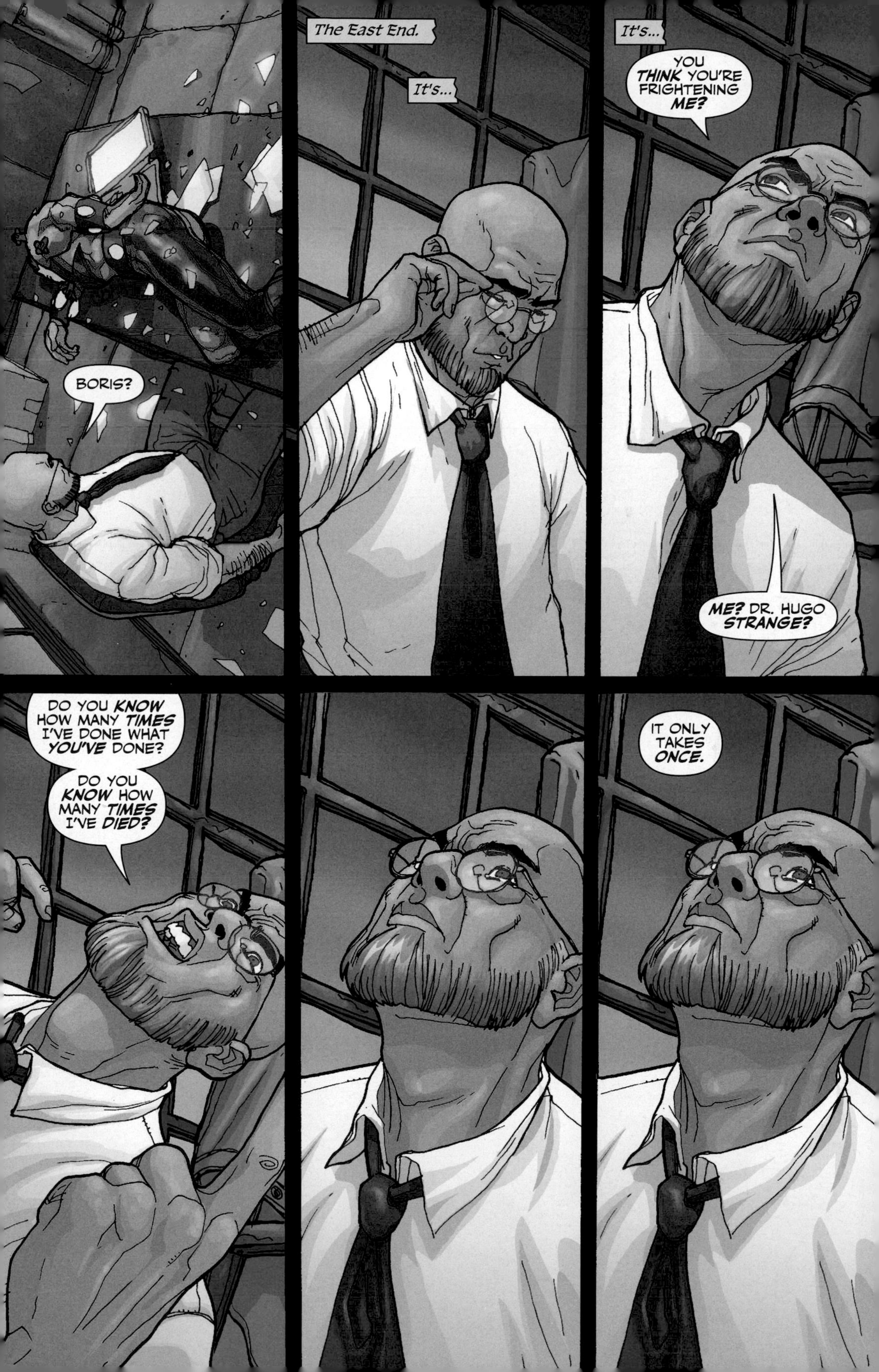
BORIS?
The East End.
It's...
It's...
YOU THINK YOU'RE FRIGHTENING ME?
ME? DR. HUGO STRANGE?
DO YOU KNOW HOW MANY TIMES I'VE DONE WHAT YOU'VE DONE?
DO YOU KNOW HOW MANY TIMES I'VE DIED?
IT ONLY TAKES ONCE.

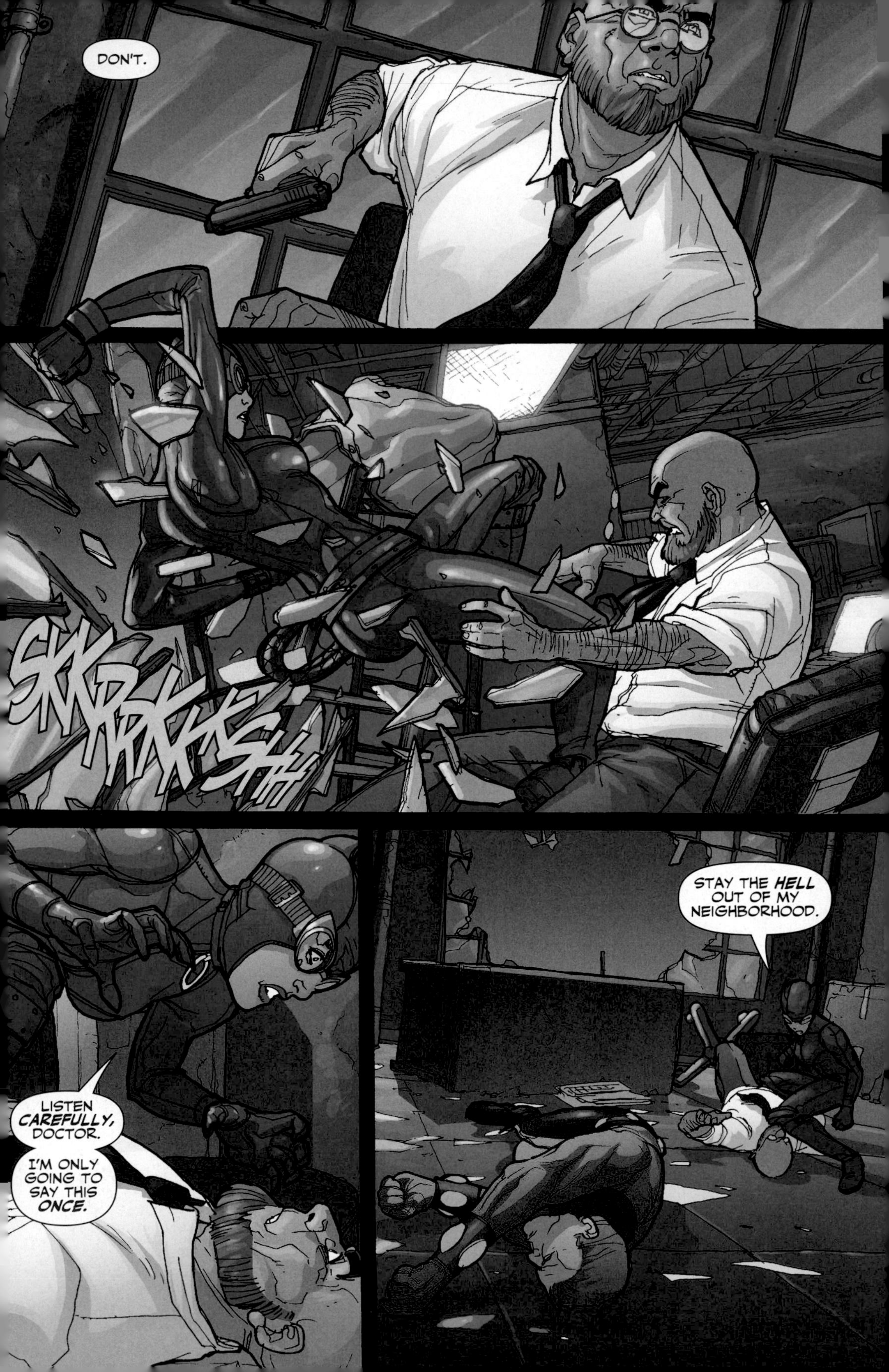
DON'T.
SKKRRKKSHH
LISTEN *CAREFULLY,* DOCTOR.
I'M ONLY GOING TO SAY THIS *ONCE.*
STAY THE *HELL* OUT OF MY NEIGHBORHOOD.

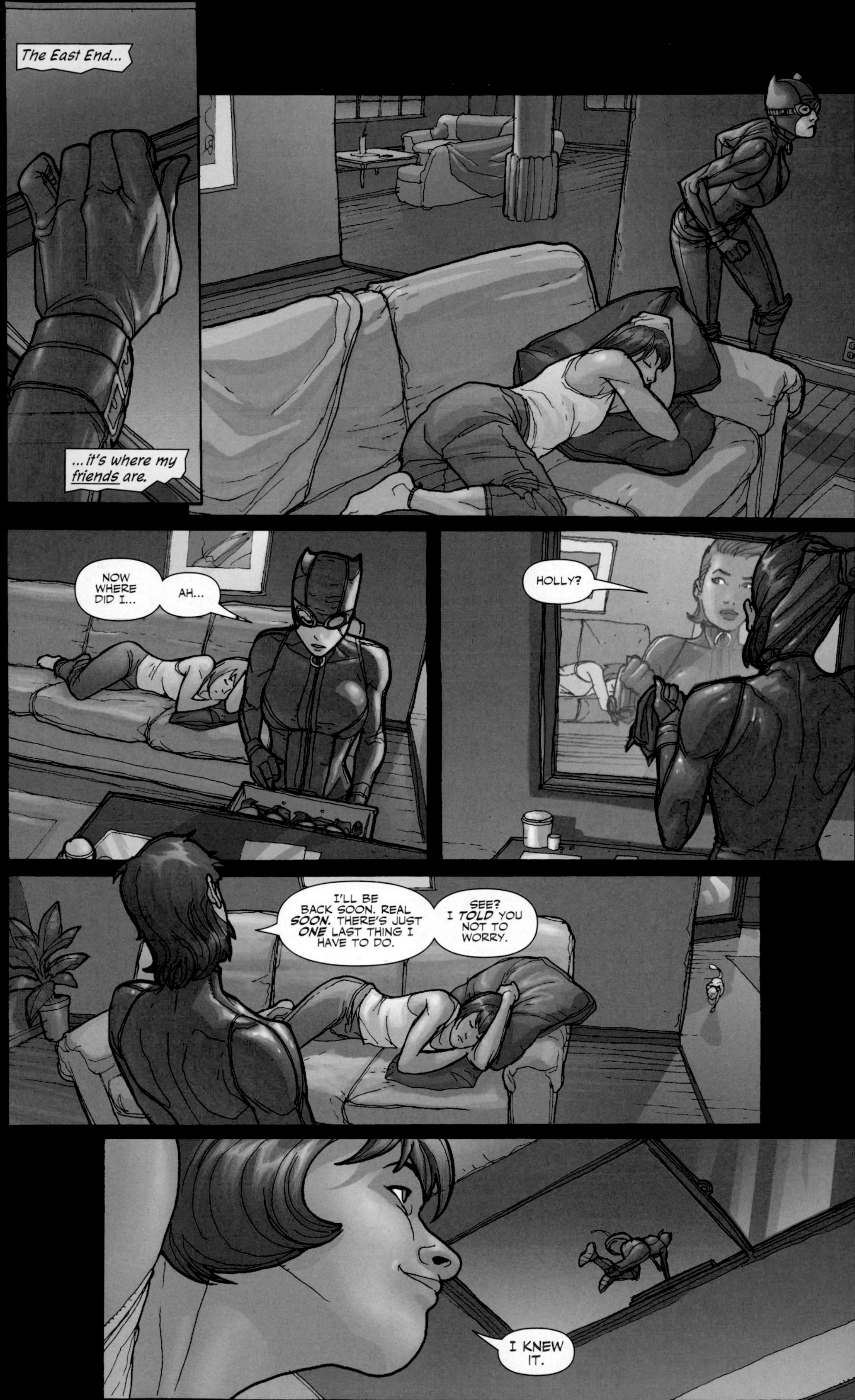
The East End...
...it's where my friends are.
NOW WHERE DID I...
AH...
HOLLY?
I'LL BE BACK SOON. REAL SOON. THERE'S JUST ONE LAST THING I HAVE TO DO.
SEE? I TOLD YOU NOT TO WORRY.
I KNEW IT.

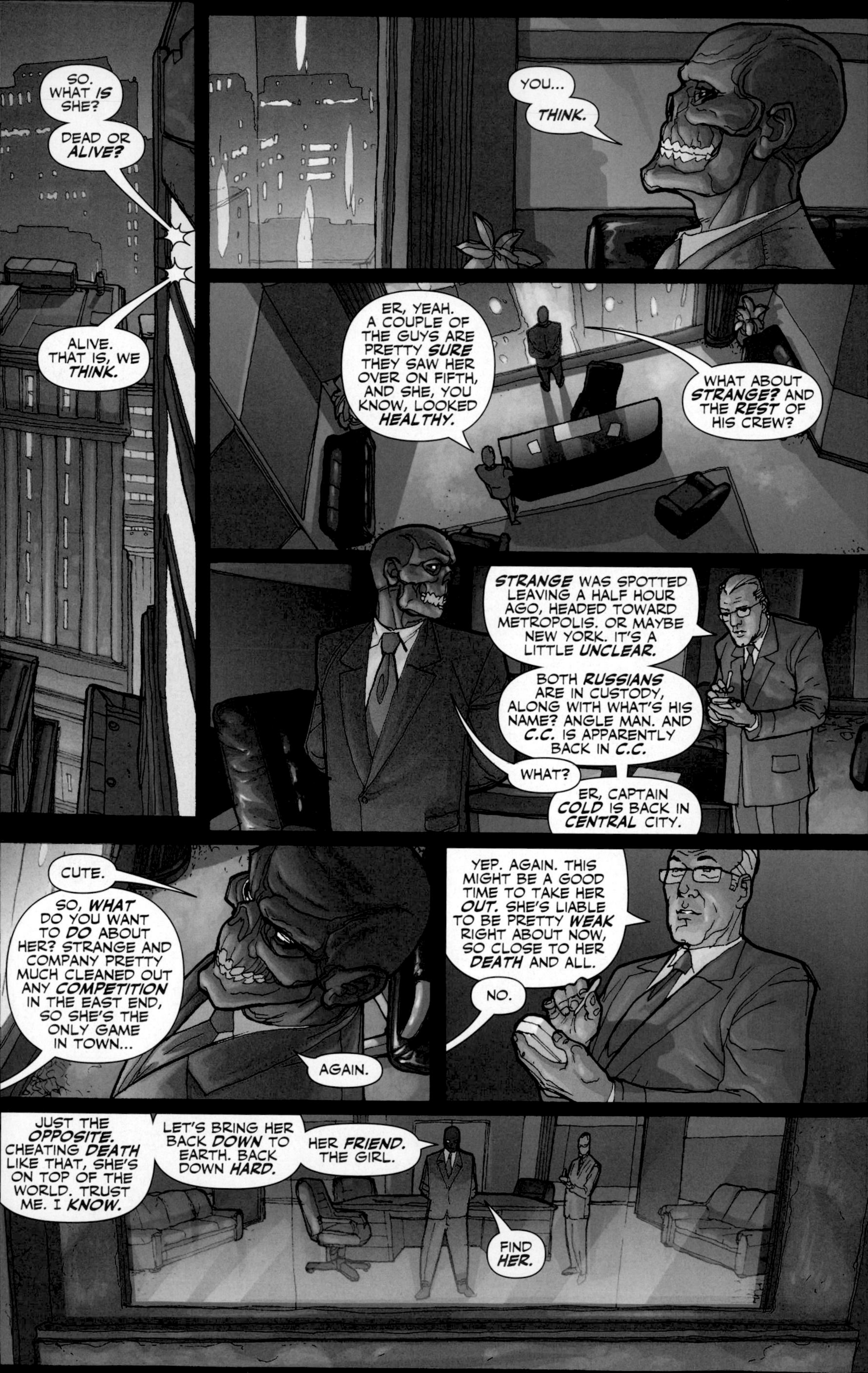
SO. WHAT *IS* SHE?
DEAD OR *ALIVE?*
YOU... *THINK.*
ALIVE. THAT IS, WE *THINK.*
ER, YEAH. A COUPLE OF THE GUYS ARE PRETTY *SURE* THEY SAW HER OVER ON FIFTH, AND SHE, YOU KNOW, LOOKED *HEALTHY.*
WHAT ABOUT *STRANGE?* AND THE *REST* OF HIS CREW?
STRANGE WAS SPOTTED LEAVING A HALF HOUR AGO, HEADED TOWARD METROPOLIS. OR MAYBE NEW YORK. IT'S A LITTLE *UNCLEAR.*
BOTH *RUSSIANS* ARE IN CUSTODY, ALONG WITH WHAT'S HIS NAME? ANGLE MAN. AND *C.C.* IS APPARENTLY BACK IN *C.C.*
WHAT?
ER, CAPTAIN *COLD* IS BACK IN *CENTRAL* CITY.
CUTE.
SO, *WHAT* DO YOU WANT TO *DO* ABOUT HER? STRANGE AND COMPANY PRETTY MUCH CLEANED OUT ANY *COMPETITION* IN THE EAST END, SO SHE'S THE ONLY GAME IN TOWN...
AGAIN.
YEP. AGAIN. THIS MIGHT BE A GOOD TIME TO TAKE HER *OUT.* SHE'S LIABLE TO BE PRETTY *WEAK* RIGHT ABOUT NOW, SO CLOSE TO HER *DEATH* AND ALL.
NO.
JUST THE *OPPOSITE.* CHEATING *DEATH* LIKE THAT, SHE'S ON TOP OF THE WORLD. TRUST ME. I *KNOW.*
LET'S BRING HER BACK *DOWN* TO EARTH. BACK DOWN *HARD.*
HER *FRIEND.* THE GIRL.
FIND *HER.*

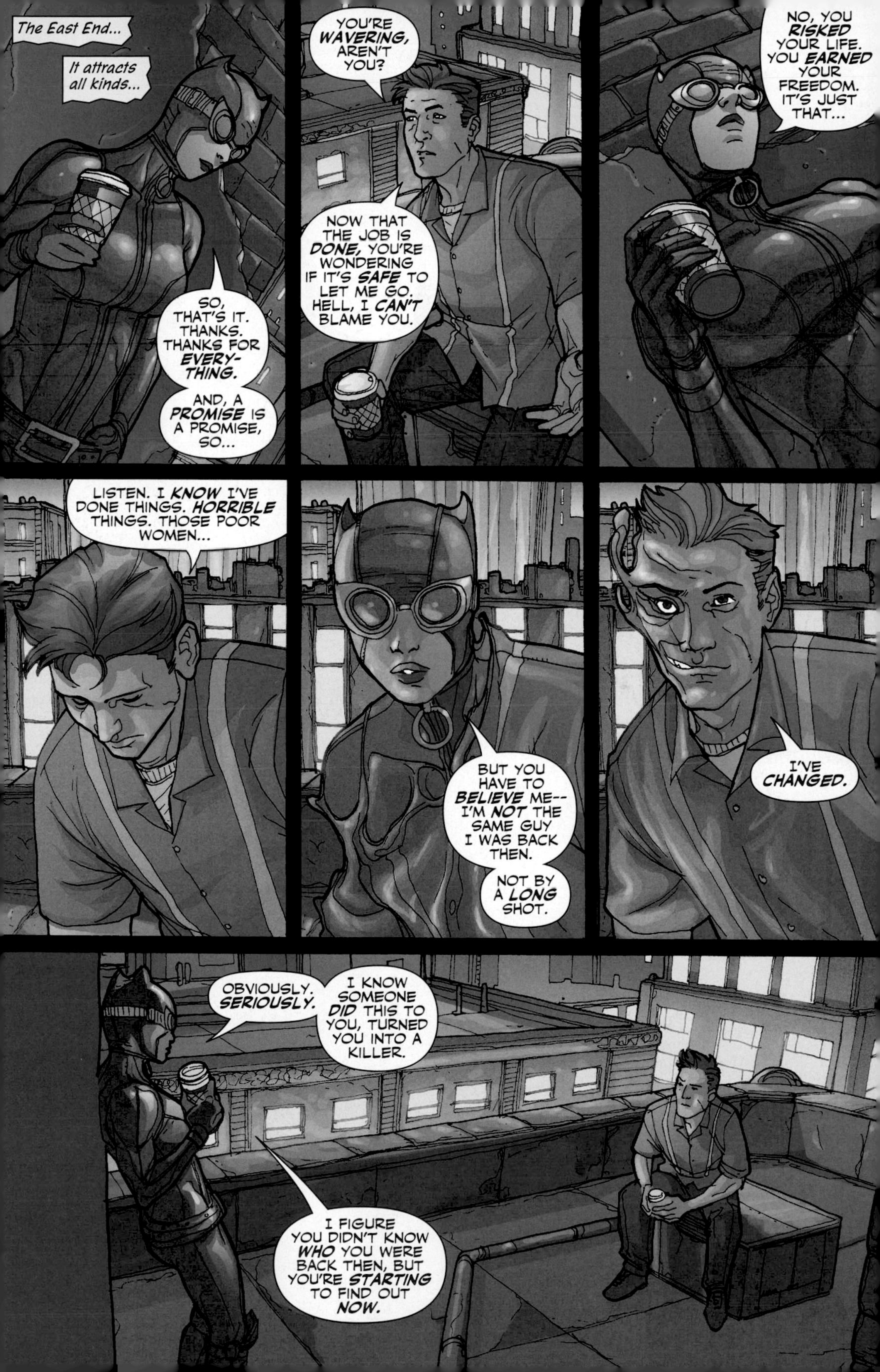
The East End...
It attracts all kinds...
SO, THAT'S IT. THANKS. THANKS FOR EVERYTHING.
AND, A PROMISE IS A PROMISE, SO...
YOU'RE WAVERING, AREN'T YOU?
NOW THAT THE JOB IS DONE, YOU'RE WONDERING IF IT'S SAFE TO LET ME GO. HELL, I CAN'T BLAME YOU.
NO, YOU RISKED YOUR LIFE. YOU EARNED YOUR FREEDOM. IT'S JUST THAT...
LISTEN. I KNOW I'VE DONE THINGS. HORRIBLE THINGS. THOSE POOR WOMEN...
BUT YOU HAVE TO BELIEVE ME-- I'M NOT THE SAME GUY I WAS BACK THEN.
NOT BY A LONG SHOT.
I'VE CHANGED.
OBVIOUSLY. SERIOUSLY.
I KNOW SOMEONE DID THIS TO YOU, TURNED YOU INTO A KILLER.
I FIGURE YOU DIDN'T KNOW WHO YOU WERE BACK THEN, BUT YOU'RE STARTING TO FIND OUT NOW.

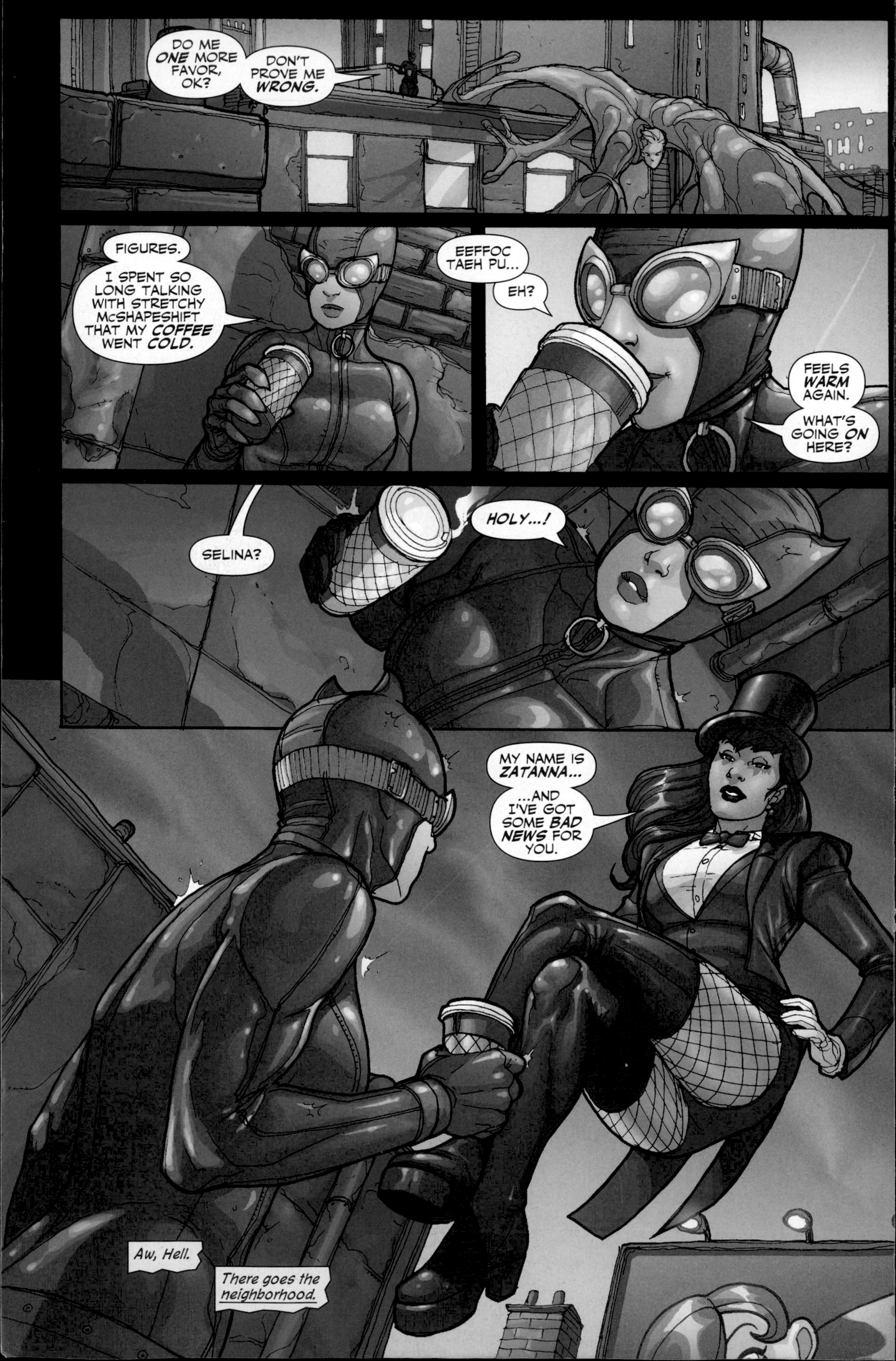
DO ME ONE MORE FAVOR, OK?
DON'T PROVE ME WRONG.
FIGURES.
I SPENT SO LONG TALKING WITH STRETCHY McSHAPESHIFT THAT MY COFFEE WENT COLD.
EEFFOC TAEH PU...
EH?
FEELS WARM AGAIN.
WHAT'S GOING ON HERE?
SELINA?
HOLY...!
MY NAME IS ZATANNA...
...AND I'VE GOT SOME BAD NEWS FOR YOU.
Aw, Hell.
There goes the neighborhood.

DC COMICS™

FROM THE PAGES OF *BATMAN*

CATWOMAN VOL. 1: TRAIL OF THE CATWOMAN

ED BRUBAKER & DARWYN COOKE

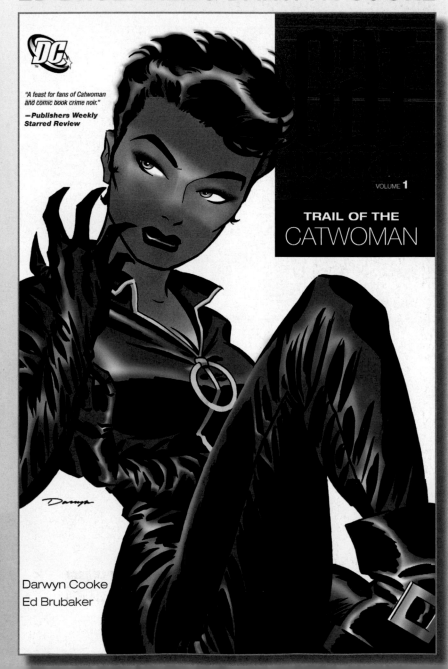

"A feast for fans of Catwoman and comic book crime noir."
—*Publishers Weekly* Starred Review

VOLUME **1**

TRAIL OF THE
CATWOMAN

Darwyn Cooke
Ed Brubaker

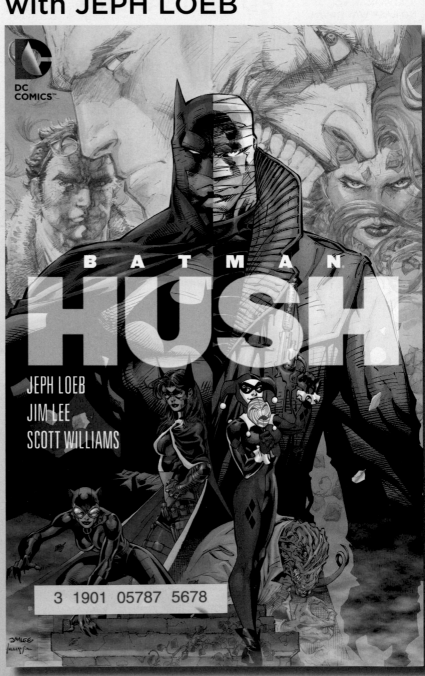